COMPUTER SIMULATION OF WATER RESOURCES SYSTEMS

IFIP Working Conference on
Computer Simulation of Water Resources Systems
Ghent, Belgium, July 30 - August 2, 1974

organized and sponsored by
IFIP Technical Committee 7, Optimization
International Federation for Information Processing

1975

NORTH-HOLLAND PUBLISHING COMPANY – AMSTERDAM • OXFORD
AMERICAN ELSEVIER PUBLISHING COMPANY, INC. – NEW YORK

COMPUTER SIMULATION OF WATER RESOURCES SYSTEMS

Proceedings of the
IFIP Working Conference on
Computer Simulation of Water Resoures Systems

edited by

G. C. VANSTEENKISTE
Professor of Engineering
Universities of Ghent and Brussels, Belgium

1975

NORTH-HOLLAND PUBLISHING COMPANY – AMSTERDAM • OXFORD
AMERICAN ELSEVIER PUBLISHING COMPANY, INC. – NEW YORK

North-Holland ISBN: 0 7204 2829 7
American Elsevier ISBN: 0 444 108378

Published by:
NORTH-HOLLAND PUBLISHING COMPANY – AMSTERDAM
NORTH-HOLLAND PUBLISHING COMPANY, LTD. – OXFORD

Distributors for the U.S.A. and Canada:
American Elsevier Publishing Company, Inc.
52 Vanderbilt Avenue
New York, N.Y. 10017

PRINTED IN THE NETHERLANDS

CONTENTS

PART THREE

Water quality models

PART FOUR

System engineering in water resources management

INTRODUCTION

THE NEED FOR AN INTERFACE

Whether viewed within the context of a developing economy or within that of a developed region, water has a unique position among the different natural resources. It is probably the major component of our every-day environment whose scarcity can effectively constrain economic advance. The study of water resources systems therefore demands equal attention to environmental and engineering considerations.

In developing countries, about two-thirds of the world's population, the unavailibility of water hampers the agricultural growth which is heavily dependent upon irrigation. All other development activities will therefore show a tendency to concentrate around water resources systems. In developed areas, on the other hand, water may become an object of competition. Quality aspects of water resources are distributing a lot of concern, and scarcity combined with maintenance of quality standards may generate unbalanced economies. Increasing population in a river basin requires more elaborate treatments of water resources to maintain the water adequate for human consumption and soil irrigation.

All this leads to the necessity of more careful planning of water resources systems. Their relationship to the natural and biological area as well as to the economical and institutional domain creates complicated and complex systems. Their analysis and understanding necessitate the construction of mathematical models. This illustrates the multi-disciplinary aspect of water resources development, utilization and conservation. Such analysis has been advanced through the growing tendency toward interfacing the environment oriented approach and the systems engineering orientation.

During the past twenty years, mathematical description of eco- and biosystems has become increasingly fashionable. Nevertheless, there is admittedly considerable unfamiliarity with the techniques. No criteria of completedness for a living system model can be stated. Many systems are too complicated for any reasonable model to include all the factors that might be important, leading to complaints of incorrectness and incompleteness. On the other hand, a model which does include most of the relevant factors may also be too complex to optimize by the existing techniques. The model does not meet the criterion of "best-fit". As every experimenter knows, systems related to nature exhibit great variability of the data, such that parameters obtained from identification techniques applied to ensemble averaged raw data may have little or no significance for the user and therefore be suspect. The simulation is further handicapped by non-uniqueness of parameter estimates and low quality experimental data. An infinite number of possible models will satisfy a specified set of excitation-response relationships.

It is most important that the heuristic insight of the environment specialist can be included in the model-building process. In this respect, hybrid computers or interactive simulation languages are almost the only tools available for the system engineer in order to use the judgments and experience of a hydrologist as they are required in the modeling process of water resources systems.

In order to cope with the highly error-prone experimental observations, optimum "masks" on the data have to be developed inductively, based on equivalent techniques as in pattern recognition, selecting a few key sampled values which generate the specific features to be matched, with the hypothetical model implemented on the computer. This crucial preprocessing allows to update the structure of the simulated model systematically before any identification technique may start.

On the other hand, a question could be stated - why bother with a model at all ? For some a model is merely a game, or a new toy. However, for those concerned with real world problems, with decisions for future investment and better use of water resources, models are becoming more valuable tools. For the planner and economist, the purpose of the model is to provide an insight as to what may happen if pumping and recharge patterns change in the future. For these answers to be meaningful, the physicist must know the weakness in his data and simulated model. He must have enough confidence in the results that he can assure their meaningfulness. Finally, the physicist must also know enough about water planning to be able to present meaningful analyses in terms which can be readily understood.

To conclude, presently-available simulation techniques are inadequate to gene-rate reasonably accurate computer models of complex eco- and biosystems, as for in-stance water resources. A large research effort is urgently required in the inter-face domain between specialists in simulation methodology and experts in environ-mental and biological systems.

This is essentially the scope of the working group on Modeling and Simulation established in the IFIP Technical Committee on Optimization. The state of the art of estimation techniques applied to water resources systems is thoroughly discussed in these Proceedings of the IFIP 1974 Working Conference held in Ghent - Belgium on July 30, 31 and August 1, 2. Participation was restricted to about seventy in-vited specialists in the identification and physical oriented area representing sixteen countries. Discussions were recorded on tape and immediately transcribed to reduce the delay of publication of the proceedings.

The organizing committee for the conference consisted of A.V. Balakrishnan (U.C.L.A - U.S.A.), M. De Boodt (University of Ghent - Belgium), W. Gardner (University of Wisconsin - U.S.A.), D. Hillel (Hebrew University - Israël), W.J. Karplus (U.C.L.A. - U.S.A.), J.R. Philip (C.S.I.R.O. - Australia), G. Vachaud (Université Scientifique et Médicale de Grenoble, France), G.C. Vansteenkiste (University of Ghent - Belgium), R. Vichnevetsky (Rutgers University - U.S.A.), S. Wajc (University of Brussels - Belgium), P.C. Young (University of Cambridge - England). The conference was essentially sponsored by Control Data Belgium and by promises of the Ministry of National Education and Culture, the National Science Research Foundation and the University of Ghent.

This international meeting illustrates different constraints dominating exact models and is a unique example that shows how only a combined team of theorists and practice-oriented researchers can stimulate any simulation effort in this do-main.

J.R. Philip, representing the physical oriented participants, accentuated this in the closing session. The first point I want to make, he said, is the following : we all have to keep repeating to ourselves that the degree of refinement and the generality of the model required of a particular system, depends quite definitely on the context and the purpose. There are many people who have said this during this meeting but I would personally suggest that Prof. Iserman's exposition of this was perhaps the most clear. The second point I will make is that I discovered that there is most prospect of having a honest and profitable dialogue with good system analysts such as those that are here, rather than with those that you sort of fall over in the streets. Thirdly, and this was a point that I think that was made most clear by Dr. Hely-Hutchinson : that systemanalysts have suffered from the hands of indifferent natural scientists from time to time and that there is a danger I think that system analysts can waste their skills trying to sell bad natural science. I must say that one kind of activity that passes as natural science is the attempt to solve purely posed inverse problems in situations where direct measurements are possible. There are situations where the inverse problem must be faced up to, but there are many cases where it is more fun than use. I think the system analyst can become the refuge of the bad scientists and I think he should not do that.

Another point that I feel is that even the good system analysts have a slight tendency to play being Prokastes. Perhaps there is a tendency for them to chop of the legs of the problem or to stretch it until it fits the scheme which they feel it poned. There is a two sort of difficulty along the following line. Natural science almost by very definition involves the search for generality and the difficulty, I think that some people have with the system analyst approach at this point, is that it seems to be so unsystematized. I would feel that perhaps if there could be some rationalisation of the approach of system analysis to the point where there can be some generalisation of methodology we are coming close to something which measures more regularly into natural science. I think that it is probably true that there is only one God system analysis, there is no enormous diversity of problems and if one asks to provide a methodology for a particular problem one would get back some different replies and sets of recommendations.

I would like to stress again on the difficult point of social contact in the modeling of large scale systems. This came again up in the papers of Dr. Elzas and Dr. Fogel. It is quite frightening to me to see technocrats who are quite happy to feed cost functions and utility functions into their models and to believe that they added to it in this way the human, the cultural other elements of their problem, especially if this is being used. In fact I am not quite so frightened for the people who don't understand what they are doing because in that case the answer that comes out of the model is at least some sort of random variable, but I am much more frightened for those who know what they are doing, for they can adjust the social inputs and the unverifiable social elements in their models say that the outputs are exactly what their masters wish. And it is that what really terrifies me !

In conclusion I speak for all of us when I say we had a splendid four days and we have learned an enormous amount and we shall all go away within our areas of ignorant refuge and our areas of tolerance will increase but I certainly hope that any increase in tolerance is not at the expense of our powers of criticism.

P.C. Young, representing the simulation group, replied : stretching the problem to fit the methods is a common criticism but I think it is one which is again obtained because of looking at the nature of the problems superficially. What we do is to tend to use different models but that does not mean that those models are necessarily any worse than the existing models, they are just different. This has been coming out several times in the week, but still best in the one diagram which showed that the input output behavior of a particular block of soil reacting to water flowing through it was a fairly simple type of response which undoubtedly could be described by ordinary differential equations in mechanistic terms. And if you are interested in that sort of behavior, then it would be a good thing to choose that particular mechanistic description rather than the one that has been choosen because it was the one that has been used at least for 15 years.

I also noted that apparently we have given the impression of not having a standardized methodology in system analysis. There is a certain truth in that but I don't think that it is quite as bad as pointed out, for what system analysis points out is that it is a systematic procedure. If we take the modeling aspect, one goes through definite stages of modeling through the physical analysis of the system : the identification phase where you try to find out what sort of model might best characterise the situation, baring in mind the nature of your problem, and finally finishing up with the parameter estimation phase where one tries to evaluate quantitatively some parameters which characterize the system within the same time you want to identify and this is very systematic indeed.

I have been told by a number of soil scientists this week, that the basic theory does not explain very well what's happening in the field. This does not surprise me and it seems to be what happens in every field, in other words you can never explain everything. That it does not succeed in all aspects could be attributed that some of the methods don't suit the nature of the problems being attacked. And this is perhaps the one message that I would like to get over in this week, namely the one that Dr. Philip started out and agreed : the nature of the model should suit the nature of the problem. And it could well be that some of the models that come out are not suited to the nature of the problem in the field and different models should come out to satisfy those particular problems. I think the one thing that the system analyst does have is the conscious feeling with open eyes that he can look at anything - not the tradition - and he can kick the tradition. This is why he gets stranded when you start criticising. You have to do this as system analyst. We should however not go into : I think we know everything, for we certainly don't. One thing that system analysts must have is modesty. He must go into a situation and ask questions and come to rational decisions based on what he hears. But he does not have to believe everything. This is the point.

Finally the cost functions in optimization. Prof. Balakrishnan and myself, we are not great supporters of optimization in the way it has been used so far in the last 15 years. It is interesting to note that even in the engineering field where things are much more easy to describe in quantitative terms where there is much more definition of the system, optimization has not been applied. Most engineering systems are of classical style and where optimization has been applied it has cost a lot of money. Cost functions in optimization we would criticize also in very much the same way as Dr. Philip would. In terms of manipulating the answers to suit the customer, this does happen ! But I am not sure that it does not happen in all fields and not just system analysis. It may happen more in system analysis because of the history of the subject and the way people came from the aerospace field into the broad area. They came out with these ideas. We are labeled by that history.

Finally I personally think we have come a little closer this week. We certainly realize how important the work of soil scientists is.

A.V. Balakrishnan as chairman of the Technical Committee on Optimization concluded : This conference brought together people with different backgrounds and it has gone in the direction of educating people in the proper use of computer systems in their particular application. And I would look at much of the discussion today as helping us towards that aim. Computer processing is available, its importance has been recognized, but it is a tool that has to be used with care. This can be done only with many working conferences of this type. It is only by keeping the view of physicists and system analysts more honest by objective criticism, that we are able to make any progress at all. From that point of view I would think that this conference has succeeded in starting a very essential dialogue in a proper atmosphere with mutual respect for each other, realizing that it takes both groups to get the very important jobs accomplished.

It is hoped that a concerted information exchange among experts in different areas will contribute efficiently to develop a useful tool for the promotion of mankind over the whole world.

August 1974   Ghislain C. Vansteenkiste
                                                     Ghent - Belgium

                                                     Vice Chairman IFIP-WG 7.1
                                                     "Modeling and Simulation"

PART ONE

MODELING AND COMPUTING TECHNIQUES IN WATER RESOURCES SYSTEMS

Modeling and Simulation of Water Resources Systems, G.C. VANSTEENKISTE, (Ed.)
North-Holland Publishing Company (1975)

MODELING AND IDENTIFICATION OF DYNAMIC PROCESSES
- AN EXTRACT -

R. Isermann
University of Stuttgart
F.R. Germany

ABTRACT

Methods for modeling and identification of dynamic processes
and their interrelationships are regarded.

In modeling processes one generally uses balance equations,
state equations and phenomenological laws. These equations
lead to definite model structures and parameters of the process
elements. Typical structures of lumped processes are specified.
Then model simplification is regarded.

For the identification of processes, measured input and output
signals are processed. A short description of some basic identification methods is given. Results of comparisons of different methods are summarized and some guidelines for the application are stated.

1. MODELING AND IDENTIFICATION OF PROCESSES

Mathematical models of dynamic processes can be obtained by two different ways: *theoretical analysis* (theoretical modeling, model building) or *experimental analysis* (identification, parameter estimation).
The general procedure for both types of analysis and their interre-
lations are shown in Fig. 1.1.

In case of *theoretical analysis* the model is calculated by using physical laws. One starts with simplifying assumptions on the process.
Then the basic equations, such as balance equations, physical-chemical
state equations, phenomenological equations and entropy balances are
stated. If the resulting system of equations can be solved explicitly,
a theoretical model with a definite structure and definite parameters
follows. Frequently, this model is complicated or extensive so that
it has to be simplified.

If *experimental analysis* is performed, the model is determined by measured input and output data of the process. One always starts with
some a-priori knowledge on the process. For example, either the model
structure is known or it is known that the model can be linearized
without the structure being known. Then input and output data are measured and the model is determined by an identification method. The resulting model can be parametric or nonparametric.

If both, the theoretical as well as the experimental analysis are carried out, the theoretical and experimental model can be compared.
Based on differences which may eventually arise, single steps of both
procedures can be corrected. So a first feedback is formed: *system
analysis in general is an iterative procedure.*

R. Isermann

PROCESS - ANALYSIS

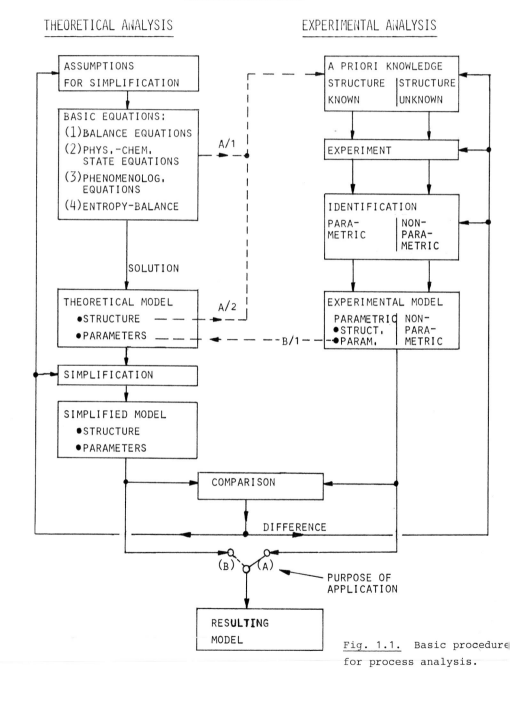

Fig. 1.1. Basic procedure for process analysis.

The selection of the type of analysis and the selection of the final, theoretical or experimental model depends on the process and the purpose of application of the model. Following advantages and disadvantages can be distinguished:

Theoretical analysis:

- The process can be modeled before it is built or is available for measurements.
- The theoretical model is valid for a whole class of processes.
- Structure and parameters of the model are analytic functions of physical process parameters.

However:

- Even for relatively simple processes the theoretical model can be complicated and extensive.
- Internal functions may not be well known in form of mathematical relationships.
- Process parameters may either not be known or only known with errors.

Experimental analysis:

- Only input and output data must be measured.
- Internal functions need not to be known. The complexity of a process does not necessarily influence the identification procedure.
- Identification methods are applicable to different kinds of processes.
- Once an identification program is established it can be used for many processes.
- An experimental model may be more accurate than a theoretical one.

However:

- The model is only valid for a special process and a special operating point.
- Analytical relationships between the model parameters and physical process parameters can not be obtained.

So it very much depends on the type of process as well as available knowledge on the process and the final goal, which way of analysis is taken. Frequently, the structure or approximate structure of a process can be gained by theoretical analysis and the parameters are then determined by exeriments. *In general process analysis is an appropriate combination of theoretical and experimental analysis.*

2. <u>MODELING OF DYNAMIC PROCESSES</u>

Theoretical analysis of dynamic processes is called (theoretical) *modeling* and can be defined as

*Process modeling is the theoretical analysis
of the time-behavior of processes.
Physical laws are used to obtain mathematical models.*

In general, four different types of basic equations are stated:

1. Balance equations for stored mass, energy or momentum (laws of conservation)
2. Physical-chemical state equations
3. Phenomenological laws for irreversible processes
4. Entropy balance equations for more than one irreversible process.

These equations are applied to the whole process or to a part of a process if the process has *lumped parameters*. For a process with *distributed parameters* the basic equations are applied to an infinitesimal small element.

In the following sections some basic equations, well known from fundamental physics, [1], [2], [3], [4], [5], [6], [7], [8], [9], [10] are stated with the goal in mind, to gain some insight in the model structures of simple process elements.

2.1 Balance equations for lumped parameter processes

For processes with lumped parameters, the balance equations are

a) Mass balance

$$\dot{M}_{in}(t) - \dot{M}_{out}(t) = \frac{dM_{st}(t)}{dt} \tag{2.1}$$

b) Energy balance

$$\dot{E}_{in}(t) - \dot{E}_{out}(t) = \frac{dE_{st}(t)}{dt} \tag{2.2}$$

c) Momentum balance

$$\vec{K}_{in}(t) - \vec{K}_{out}(t) = \frac{d\vec{I}_{st}(t)}{dt} = \frac{d}{dt}[m\,\vec{w}(t)] \tag{2.3}$$

with

$\dot{M}$, mass flow rate   I, momentum
$\dot{E}$, energy flow rate   w, velocity
$\vec{K}$, force   m, mass.

The index "st" means stored.

In case of gases and steams as a medium, a special form of the energy balance equation is used [7], after introducing two state equations

$$\begin{aligned} E_{st} &= U_{st} \\ H &= U + pV \end{aligned} \tag{2.4}$$

with

U, inner energy   p, pressure
H, enthalpy   V, volume.

Then the enthalpy balance equation follows

$$\frac{d}{dt}[\dot{M}(t)h(t)]_{in} - \frac{d}{dt}[\dot{M}(t)h(t)]_{out} - \dot{L}_{tech}(t) + \dot{Q}_{in}(t)$$

$$= \frac{d}{dt}[M(t)u(t)]_{st} \tag{2.5}$$

with

    h, specific enthalpy u, specific inner energy
    $\dot{L}_{tech}$, technical power $\dot{Q}$, heat flow rate.

For processes which can be linearized, only changes of the variables are of interest, so that

$$\dot{M}(t) = \bar{\dot{M}} + \Delta\dot{M}(t); \quad \dot{E}(t) = \bar{\dot{E}} + \Delta E(t); \quad K(t) = \bar{K} + \Delta K(t). \tag{2.6}$$

The bar means steady state. If the changes of variables are related to their steady state value

$$\Delta\dot{m}(t) = \Delta\dot{M}(t)/\bar{\dot{M}}; \quad \Delta\dot{e}(t) = \Delta\dot{E}(t)/\bar{\dot{E}}; \quad \Delta k = \Delta K(t)/\bar{K} \tag{2.7}$$

the balance equations (1), (2) and (3) are

$$\Delta\dot{m}_{in}(t) - \Delta\dot{m}_{out}(t) = T_M \frac{dm_{st}(t)}{dt} \tag{2.8}$$

$$\Delta\dot{e}_{in}(t) - \Delta\dot{e}_{out}(t) = T_e \frac{de_{st}(t)}{dt} \tag{2.9}$$

$$\Delta k_{in}(t) - \Delta k_{out}(t) = T_j \frac{dj_{st}(t)}{dt} \tag{2.10}$$

with an *integration time* [7]

$$T_M = \frac{\bar{M}_{st}}{\bar{\dot{M}}} = \frac{\text{stored mass in s.s.}}{\text{stored flow in s.s.}} \tag{2.11}$$

$$T_e = \frac{\bar{E}_{st}}{\bar{\dot{E}}} = \frac{\text{stored energy in s.s.}}{\text{energy flow in s.s.}} \tag{2.12}$$

$$T_j = \frac{\bar{J}_{st}}{\bar{K}} = \frac{\text{stored momentum in s.s.}}{\text{force in s.s.}} . \tag{2.13}$$

"s.s." means steady state.

All balance equations have the same form and result in an integral behavior of the accumulation after a change of an input or output, Fig. 2.1.

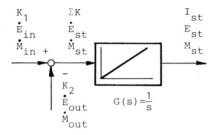

<u>Fig. 2.1.</u>   Block diagram of the balance equations.

2.2 <u>Balance equations for distributed parameter processes</u>

For processes with distributed parameters the dependence of the states on the location has to be generally regarded in three dimensions.
As an example, the balance equations are given for onedimensional
distributed parameter processes with fluid flow. The balance equations
for an infinitesimal small element with fixed boundary (tube element),
as is shown in Fig. 2.2, are [7]

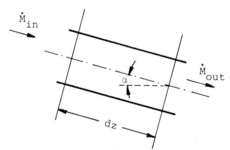

<u>Fig. 2.2.</u>   Process element with fluid flow.

a) <u>Mass balance</u>   for $A_F(z)$

$$- \frac{\partial \dot{M}(z,t)}{\partial z} = A_F(z) \frac{\partial \rho(z,t)}{\partial t} \qquad (2.14)$$

with
   A_F sectional area of fluid
   ρ density of fluid.

b) <u>Energy balance</u>   for $A_F(z) = $ const. and $\alpha = 0$

$$\frac{Dh(z,t)}{Dt} - \frac{1}{\rho(z,t)} \frac{Dp(z,t)}{Dt} = \frac{1}{A_F\rho(z,t)} \cdot \frac{\partial \dot{Q}(z,t)}{\partial z} \cdot \qquad (2.15)$$

thermal   mechanical   energy
energy   energy   supply
accumu-   accumu-   through
lation   lation   heat

Hereby

$$D(\ ) = [\frac{\partial(\ )}{\partial t}]_z dt + [\frac{\partial(\ )}{\partial z}]_t dz \qquad (2.16)$$

$$\frac{D(\ )}{DT} = \frac{\partial(\ )}{\partial t} + w(z)\frac{\partial(\ )}{\partial z}\ . \qquad (2.17)$$

Substantial local   convective
derivation deriv.   derivation

Special cases:

α) Temperature $\vartheta(z,t)$ for p = const.

$$c_p \frac{D\vartheta(z,t)}{Dt} = \frac{1}{A_F \rho} \frac{\partial \dot{Q}(z,t)}{\partial z} \qquad (2.18)$$

c_p: specific heat for p = const.

β) $\partial \dot{Q}/\partial z = 0$

$$\frac{D\vartheta(z,t)}{Dt} = \frac{\partial \vartheta(z,t)}{\partial t} + w \frac{\partial \vartheta(z,t)}{\partial z} = 0. \qquad (2.19)$$

(equation for a pure time delay)

c) <u>Momentum balance</u> for $A_F(z)$ = const.

$$\frac{D(\rho(z,t)w(z,t))}{Dt} = - \frac{\partial p(z,t)}{\partial z} + \rho(z,t) \cdot g \cdot \sin\alpha - \frac{1}{A_F} \frac{\partial R(z,t)}{\partial z} \qquad (2.20)$$

R: friction force $g = 9.81\ m/s^2$.

2.3 <u>Physical-chemical state equations</u>

In most cases not the stored mass, energy or momentum is interesting
as an output variable, but a measurable physical state variable of
the process. Then physical-chemical state equations have to be used
which express the dependence between one state variable (the accummulation) and another state variable.

<u>Examples for lumped parameter processes</u>

(a) Relation between pressure and stored mass in a gas tank:

$$M_{st}(t) = V_{st}\ \rho_{st}(t) = V_{st} \frac{1}{v_{st}(t)} = V_{st} \frac{1}{RT} p_{st}(t). \qquad (2.21)$$

Hereby: V_{st}, tank volume   R, gas constant
         ρ_{st}, gas density   T, absolute temperature.
         p_{st}, gas pressure

(b) Relation between fluid level and stored mass in a fluid tank:

$$dM_{st}(L) = A_F(L)\rho_F dL. \qquad (2.22)$$

Hereby: A_F, surface of fluid ρ_F, fluid density.
         L, fluid level

(c) Relation between enthalpy and temperature in a gas:

$$d\vartheta(t) = \frac{1}{c_p} dh.$$ (2.23)

Hereby: ϑ, temperature c_p specific heat value
h, enthalpy   for constant pressure.

Starting with the balance equation, the block diagram then changes from Fig. 2.1 to that of Fig. 2.3. As e.g. eq.(2.22) shows, the state equation can introduce a nonlinearity.

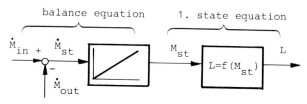

Fig. 2.3   Block diagram of a balance equation and a first state equation (shown for a fluid storing tank with fluid level L).

If the accummulation or its corresponding state variable influences the incoming mass or energy or force or the outgoing mass or energy or force, a feedback is introduced into the scheme, Fig.2.4., and the process changes from integral to proportional behavior.

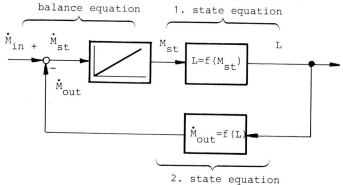

Fig. 2.4.   Block diagram of a balance equation, a first and a second state equation (fluid storing tank).

Example for a lumped parameter process

For a fluid filled tank, Fig. 2.5., the outflow depends on the fluid level by Bernoulli's law

$$\dot{M}_{out} = \rho_F A_{out} w_{out} = \rho_F A_{out} \sqrt{2gL + \frac{2}{\rho_F}(p_{in} - p_{out})}.$$ (2.24)

After linearizing one obtains

$$\Delta \dot{M}_{out} = (\frac{\partial \dot{M}_{out}}{\partial L}) \Delta L = C(L) \Delta L$$

$$C(L) = \rho_F A_{out} g \cdot [2gL + \frac{2}{\rho_F}(p_{in}-p_{out})]^{-1/2} \qquad (2.25)$$

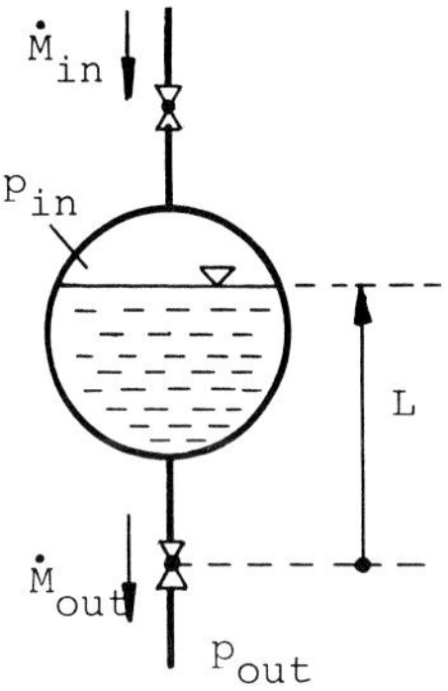

Fig. 2.5. Fluid filled tank.

So a second state equation expresses the relationship between the output variable and one input of the accummulation in the process. This state equation can also introduce nonlinear behavior.

If both, $L = f(M_{st})$ and $\dot{M}_{out} = f(L)$ can be linearized and therefore changes of $\dot{M}_{out}$ are linearly dependend on changes of M_{st}, so that

$$\Delta \dot{M}_{out}(t) = C \Delta M_{st}(t), \qquad (2.26)$$

one obtains a linear first order differential equation

$$\frac{1}{C} \frac{dM_{st}(t)}{dt} + \Delta M_{st}(t) = \frac{1}{C} \Delta \dot{M}_{in}(t) \qquad (2.27)$$

if eqs. (2.26) and (2.6) are introduced into eq.(2.1), cf. Fig. 3.6.

The time constant then is [7]

$$T = \frac{1}{C} = \frac{\Delta M_{st}(\infty)}{\Delta \dot{M}_{out}(\infty)} = \frac{\Delta M_{st}(\infty)}{\Delta \dot{M}_{in}(\infty)}$$

$$= \frac{\text{change of stored mass (energy, momentum)}}{\text{change of mass flow (energy flow, force)}} \qquad (2.28)$$

and the gain

$$K = \frac{\Delta M_{st}(\infty)}{\Delta \dot{M}_{in}(\infty)} = \frac{1}{C} . \qquad (2.29)$$

With related variables, eq.(2.7), the first order differential equation is

$$\frac{1}{C} \frac{dm_{st}(t)}{dt} + \Delta m_{st}(t) = \frac{1}{C} \frac{\overline{\dot{M}}_{in}}{\overline{M}_{st}} \Delta \dot{m}_{in}(t) . \qquad (2.30)$$

The time constant does not change. However, the gain now becomes

$$K = \frac{\Delta m_{st}(\infty)}{\Delta \dot{m}_{in}(\infty)} = \frac{1}{C} \frac{\overline{\dot{M}}_{in}}{\overline{M}_{st}}.$$ (2.31)

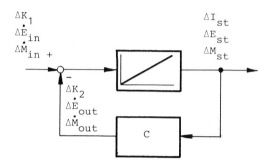

Fig. 2.6.   Block diagramm of balance equation with a linear feedback
            caused by a physical state equation.

The influence of physical-chemical state equations on the dynamics of
lumped parameter processes can be summarized as follows:

1.   Physical-chemical state equations describe the relationships
     between

     a) accummulation and the interesting (measurable) output
        variable
     b) accummulation or interesting output variable and one
        input of the storage (feedback).

2.   The feedback (case 1.b)) changes the process from integral
     to proportional behavior.

3.   If the physical-chemical state equations are nonlinear, the
     process becomes nonlinear behavior.

2.4.   Phenomenological laws

For irreversible processes the balance equations are not sufficient
to describe the process behavior, since not all processes, which fulfill the balance equations, can happen. They proceed as to increase
the entropy. Equalizing processes are such irreversible processes and
they are described by phenomenological laws, which often are linear
in relatively wide ranges [11].

A few examples are:

(a)   Fourier's law for heat conduction

$$\dot{q}_z = -\lambda \frac{\partial \vartheta}{\partial z} = -\lambda \ grad_z \vartheta$$

      $\dot{q}$, heat flow density; λ, heat conduction coefficient;
      ϑ, temperature

(b) Fick's law for diffusion

$$\dot{m}_z = -D \frac{\partial c}{\partial z} = -D \ grad_z c$$

$\dot{m}$, mass flow density; D, diffusion coefficient, c, concentration.

(c) Darcy's law

$$m_z = -k \frac{\partial \phi}{\partial z} = -k \ grad_z \phi$$

m, mass flow density, k, hydrolic conductivity, ϕ, moisture pot.

Phenomenological laws in general write as follows:

$$\text{Flow density} = - \frac{1}{\text{specific resistance}} \cdot \frac{\text{potential}}{\text{gradient}}$$

$$[\frac{\text{flow}}{m^2}] = \frac{1}{[\text{resistance} \cdot m]} \cdot [\frac{\Delta \text{ potential}}{m}]$$

or

$$\text{flow rate} = - \frac{1}{\text{resistance}} \cdot \text{potential difference.}$$

These phenomenological laws can also be regarded as equations giving relationships between state variables. However, due to the gradients they introduce locally dependent state variables. If the irreversible process occurs in a homogeneous medium, the phenomenological law has to be applied to an infinitesimal small element, and the process has to be treated as a distributed parameter process, described by partial differential equations. If more than one irreversible process takes place, entropy balance equations can be used, or phenomenological laws can be taken, which take into account the reciprocal effects [11].

2.5. Simplification of process models

In modeling processes one often obtains extensive models of high order or of complicated structure. The application of process models, however, often requires that models are of a simple form and, despite of this, that they are accurate. As both requirements are in opposition, one has to make a compromise.

The required accuracy of a model depends on the purpose of its application. If the model is used for design of a feedback controlled system, it can be shown for a frequency response [7], that permissible tolerances are very small in the middle frequency region, because of the resonance effect and therefore a strong feedback in the closed loop. With increasing frequency the tolerances increase also because the feedback is less effective the higher the frequency of a disturbance. One can also find an interesting region of the magnitude of a frequency response and it turns out, that this region is smaller the larger the order (low-pass property) of the process model. These relatively general results indicate that simplification of process models can be made especially in the region of higher frequencies and to a larger extent the larger the order of the process.

To obtain results for systematic simplification of linear process models the effects of neglection of small time constants, replacement
of small time constants by time delays and replacement of different
time constants by equal time constants on the closed loop behavior
have been investigated [7], [12]. One of the main results is that for
both, application of the model in open and closed loop, the laws of
conservation should also be fulfilled after the model is simplified.
If a model of type

$$G(s) = \frac{\prod\limits_{\beta=1}^{m} (1+T_{b\beta}s)}{(1+2DTs+s^2) \prod\limits_{\alpha=1}^{n-2} (1+T_{a\alpha}s)} e^{-T_Ds}$$

$$= \frac{1 + b_1s + b_2s^2 +\ldots+ b_ms^m}{1 + a_1s + a_2s^2 +\ldots+ a_ns^n} e^{-T_Ds}$$

is used, the stored energy (mass or momentum) is proportional to a
generalized sum of time constants

$$\Delta E_{st} = \Delta\dot{E}_{in}(0) \left[2DT + \sum_{\alpha=1}^{n} T_{a\alpha} - \sum_{\beta=1}^{m} T_{b\beta} + T_D\right]$$

$$= \Delta\dot{E}_{in}(0) \left[a_1 - b_1 + T_D\right] = \Delta\dot{E}_{in}(0) \, T_\Sigma.$$

*Simplifications of the model therefore have to be performed, so that
the generalized sum of time constants T_Σ remains constant.*

3. IDENTIFICATION OF DYNAMIC PROCESSES

It is assumed that the process to be identified is stable and has one
input and one output which can be measured. The input is assumed to
be measurable without any errors. The resulting output in general is
effected by disturbancies which enter into the process at various locations, and by measurement noise, Fig. 3.1. The task is then to find

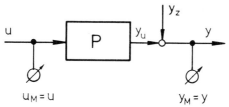

Fig. 3.1.   Process to be identified.

out the model which relates the input u(t) and the (undisturbed) output $y_u(t)$. For this reason the effect of the disturbances $y_z(t)$ must
be eliminated. Identification in general is not only an analytical
but also a stochastic problem and can be defined as follows:

*Process identification is the experimental analysis of the
time-behavior of processes.*

*Measured signals are taken and the time-behavior is
determined within a specified class of mathematical models.*

*The errors between the real process and its mathematical
model should be as small as possible.*

This definition is similar to the one given by Zadeh [13].

In general, only measured input and output signals are used and a
mathematical model is determined which fits to the measured inputs
and outputs as well as possible and which, therefore, represents a
model for the *input-output behavior*. Only if the assumed structure
of the model is identical to the (mathematical) structure of the real
process, it can be expected that the *internal behavior* of the process
is also detected by input and output measurements only.

Survey papers on identification methods can be found e.g. in [14] and
[15]. Several books on identification and parameter-estimation have
been published since 1964, [16], [17], [18], [19], [20], [21], [22],
[23], [24], [25], [26], [27], [28], [29].

3.1. Classification of identification methods

According to the definition of process identification one can classify identification methods using

· *classes of signals*
· *classes of mathematical models*
· *errors between the process and its model*.

With regard to the application additional features are

· *type of algorithms* (direct, iterative, recursive, nonrecursive)
· *operation of the process* (open or closed loop).

a) Classes of signals

Examples of *input signals* which are frequently used for process
identification are shown in Fig. 3.2. Nonperiodic and periodic
deterministic signals and stochastic or pseudostochastic signals
are distinguished. They can be artificially generated or they can
be normal operating (natural) signals.

The input and output signals are always limited

$$u_O = u(t)_{max} - u(t)_{min} \leq u_{O,max}$$
$$y_O = y(t)_{max} - y(t)_{min} \leq y_{O,max}$$

according to the assumption of linear ranges or according to operation conditions.

The *disturbance signals* $y_z(t)$ frequently consist of several components [27]

$$y_z(t) = n(t) + d(t) + h(t),$$ (3.1)

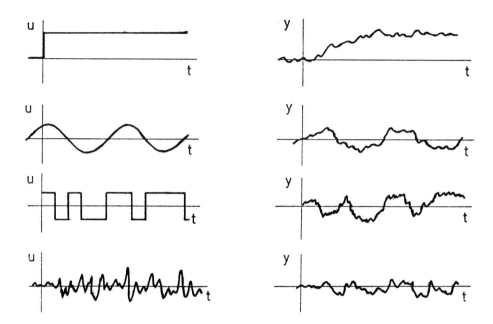

Fig. 3.2. Examples of input signals and resulting output signals.

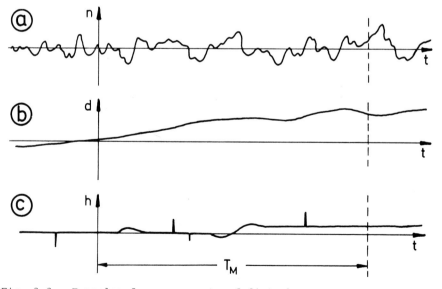

Fig. 3.3. Examples for components of disturbanc es.

compare Fig. 3.3. One distinguishes

$n(t)$: higher frequent quasistationary disturbanc es with $E\{n(t)\}=0$ or higher frequent deterministic disturbanc es with $\overline{n(t)}=0$

$d(t)$: low frequent nonstationary stochastic or deterministic dis- turbanc es like drift or seasonal trends

$h(t)$: disturbanc es of unknown character like outliers, steps etc.

For elimination of $n(t)$ averaging, correlation or regression ana- lysis is appropriate. The required measuring time T_M depends on the noise-to-signal ratio

$$\eta = \sqrt{\overline{n^2(t)}} \ / \ |K|u_O = n_{eff}/|y_O| \tag{3.2}$$

the input signal and the identification method. If σ_M is the stan- dard deviation of a model parameter then for most identification methods

$$\sigma_M \sim \eta/\sqrt{T_M} \tag{3.3}$$

is valid. The measurement time period is always limited, $T_M \leq T_{M,max}$.

The elimination of $d(t)$ in general requires special techniques which have to be adapted to the type of signal [28]. No general methods are known for the elimination of $h(t)$.

Special difficulties arise if the real input of the process cannot be measured exactly, e.g. because of measurement noise, and simul- taneously the output is also disturbed. Then the process is not identifiable.

b) Classes of mathematical models

Besides the well known classification of mathematical models ac- cording to continuous or discontinuous processes with lumped or distributed parameters, timeinvariant or timevariant behavior and linear or nonlinear behavior, following classes of mathematical models are of special interest for identification problems:

- *parametric models* (models with a definite structure, e.g. differential equations, rational broken transfer functions)

- *nonparametric models* (models without definite structure, e.g. impulse functions, frequency responses).

Parametric models are analytical functions and do contain the pa- rameters explicitly. Nonparametric models are functions in form of tables or graphs and do not indicate model parameters directly.

Furtheron models with

- *continuous signals*
- *sampled (discrete) signals*

have to be distinguished.

Parametric models are given preference if they are used for further applications which require computations. However, nonparametric models have the advantage of not requiring any model structure to be specified before identification and this is favorable for complex processes sometimes. It also depends on the final goal if continuous or discrete signals are being used. For identification of nonparametric models both types of signals are being used. However, parameter estimation of parametric models is more difficult for continuous signals than for discrete signals.

c) Errors between the process and its model

If the identification is based on the minimisation of an error between the process and its model, three types of errors are used which are shown in Fig. 3.4. Errors which are linear in the para-

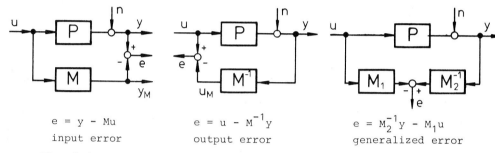

$$e = y - Mu$$
input error

$$e = u - M^{-1}y$$
output error

$$e = M_2^{-1}y - M_1 u$$
generalized error

Fig. 3.4. Type of errors between process P and model M.

meters are generally given preference. Thus, if impulse functions have to be estimated, output errors are taken, and generalised errors are used for differential (difference) equations of parametric transfer functions.

d) Type of algorithms

Especially with regard to parameter estimation methods several types of algorithms are to be differenciated

- *Algorithms for direct estimation*

    The estimates are determined in one shot. The data is processed only once.

- *Algorithms for iterative estimation*

    The estimates are searched iteratively. The data is processed several times.

- *Nonrecursive algorithms*

    The estimates are calculated after the whole data is stored.

- *Recursive algorithms*

    The estimates are calculated after each new pair of data, so that the model is updated after each measurement. Storage of data is unnecessary.

If the identification is performed with a process computer which operates on-line, and recursive algorithms are used, this is called *on-line identification*.

d) Operation of the process

The process to be identified can operate in *open loop* or *closed loop*. In the second case identification is particularly difficult, since the disturbancies are correlated with the input signal.

Using these features, it is possible to differenciate classes and subclasses of identification methods.

The *identification methods* themselves can be divided into seven classes according to the principles used, cf. table 3.1.

Table 3.1. Classes of identification methods.

Class of methods	Model parametric	non-param.	frequ. domain	time domain	Input signal	Use of computer
Step response, pulse response	x	x	–	x	steps, pulses	–
Frequency response	–	x	x	–	harmonic	–
Fourieranalysis	–	x	x	–	determ.	x
Correlationanalysis	–	x	–	x	stochast.	x
Spectralanalysis	–	x	x	–	stochast.	x
Modeladjustment	x	–	–	x	arbitr.	x
Parameterestimation	x	–	–	x	arbitr.	x

In the following sections these classes of identification methods will be shortly discussed. Some more details are given for parameter estimation methods which can be used for many classes of processes, for arbitrary input signals and for different purposes of application and which are especially attractive for the use of digital computers.

A survey of identification methods for which digital computers are used, is shown in Fig. 3.5.

3.2. Identification with nonparametric models

The first and still one of the most wide-spread identification techniques is *step response* or *pulse response measurement*. For elimination of noise several responses can be averaged. If a parametric model is required, characteristic values such as time delays and time constants are to be extracted by using tables or integration methods [22]. However, this technique is restricted to simple classes of linear models with continuous signals and to a low noise-to-signal ratio.

IDENTIFICATION METHOD		SIGNAL FLOW DIAGRAM	MODEL	A PRIORI KNOWLEDGE	INPUT SIGNAL
NONPARAMETRIC METHODS	FOURIER ANALYSIS	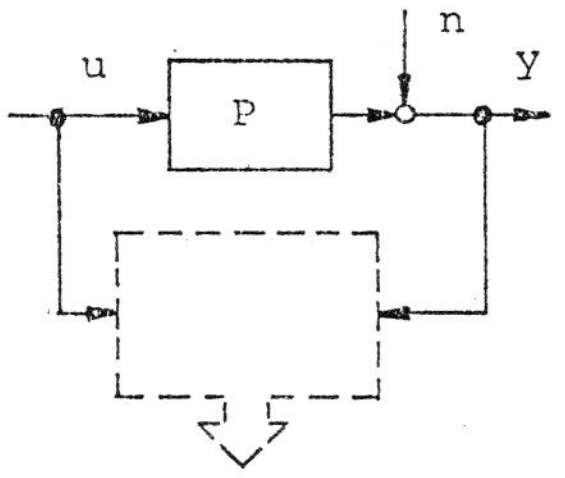 $G(i\omega)$; $g(\tau)$	$G(i\omega_\nu)$ für $0 \leq \omega_\nu \leq \omega_{max}$	PROCESS LINEAR	DETERMINISTIC NONPERIODIC PERIODIC
	SPECTRAL ANALYSIS		$\left.\begin{matrix}\Phi_{uu}(\tau)\\ \Phi_{uy}(\tau)\end{matrix}\right\}$ $g(\tau)$ für $0 \leq \tau \leq \tau_{max}$		STOCHASTIC PSEUDORANDOM PERIODIC
	CORRELATION ANALYSIS				
PARAMETRIC METHODS	MODEL ADJUSTMENT	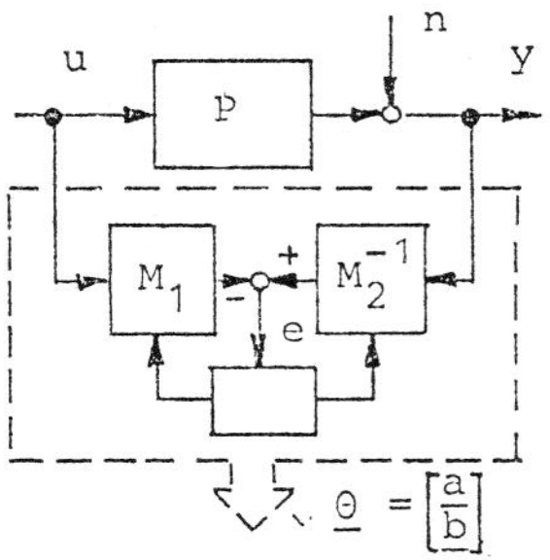 $\hat{\Theta} = \left[\dfrac{\hat{a}}{\hat{b}}\right]$	$y(t) + a_1 y'(t) + \ldots + a_m y^{(m)}(t)$ $= b_0 u(t) + b_1 u'(t) + \ldots + b_m u^{(m)}(t)$	MODEL – STRUC – TURE	STOCHASTIC PSEUDORANDOM DETERMINISTIC
	PARAMETERESTIMATION — DIRECT / ITERATIVE		$y(k) + a_1 y(k-1) + \ldots + a_m y(k-m)$ $= b_0 u(k) + b_1 u(k-1) + \ldots + b_m u(k-m)$	$p(e\,|\,\Theta)$	

<u>Fig. 3.5.</u> Characteristics of some identification methods, suitable for digital computer.

Frequency response technique is still a simple but powerful technique if a nonparametric frequency response is needed. Harmonic input signals (e.g. sinusoidal or rectangular waves) have to be used and the evaluation can be done by hand if the noise-to-signal ratio is low. However, long measurement time periods are necessary [22].

An essential decrease of this long measurement time can be gained by *Fourieranalysis*, using deterministic nonperiodic or periodic input signals as steps and pulses or multifrequency signals [18], [24]. A combination of different input signals decreases measurement time. This method, however, is restricted to linearizable processes with continuous signals.

Correlation analysis works in the time-domain and is appropriate for continuous as well as for discrete signals. The input signals can be stochastic or periodic.

According to the use of digital computers following equations are given for sampled signals. Estimates of the autocorrelation function of the input signal, and of the crosscorrelation function of both the input and output signal are obtained [17], [29], by

$$\Phi_{uu}(\tau) = \frac{1}{N} \sum_{k=0}^{N-1} u(k)u(k+\tau) \tag{3.4}$$

$$\Phi_{uy}(\tau) = \frac{1}{N} \sum_{k=0}^{N-1} u(k)y(k+\tau). \tag{3.5}$$

Both are related to each other by the convolution sum

$$\Phi_{uy}(\tau) = \sum_{\nu=0}^{\infty} g(\nu)\, \Phi_{uu}(\tau-\nu) \tag{3.6}$$

where $g(\nu)$ is the impulse response of the process. By deconvolution or by applying the method of least squares estimates of $\hat{g}(\nu)$ can be obtained e.g. [28], [29]. If the input signal is white noise $g(\nu)$ directly results

$$g(\tau) = \frac{1}{\Phi_{uu}(0)}\, \Phi_{uy}(\tau). \tag{3.7}$$

Correlation analysis can be applied to processes with high noise. Fig. 3.6 shows an impulse response identified by correlation analysis of a process with large noise-to-signal ratio.

Spectral analysis operates for the same classes of signals and processes as does correlation analysis. The evaluation, however, is performed in the frequency domain and the results are frequency responses.

All identification methods for nonparametric models do not require a priori information on the model structure. They only assume linear behavior. These methods are therefore appropriate for simple and complex linearizable processes with lumped or distributed parameters. They are preferred for comparison of theoretical with experimental models, since no assumption in the model structure is necessary and a wrong assumption therefore cannot influence the experimental result.

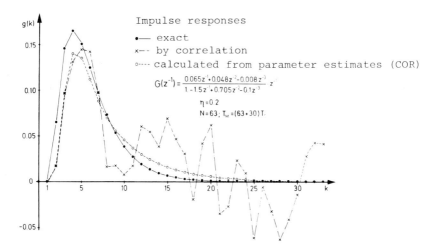

Fig. 3.6.   Identified and exact impulse responses.

3.3. Identification with parametric models

A characteristic feature of identification methods for parametric models is the assumption of a process model with definite structure and the minimisation of an error.

Model adjustment techniques have been developed for continuous signals and for models realized in hardware. An error signal e(t), compare Fig. 3.4., as well as a loss function are defined, e.g.

$$V_1 = \int_O^t e^2(\underline{\beta},t)\,dt \quad \text{or} \quad V_2 = e^2(\underline{\beta},t). \qquad (3.8)$$

   higher noise   low noise

Minimisation of loss function in regard to unknown model parameters $\underline{\beta}$ leads to

$$\frac{\partial V}{\partial \underline{\beta}} = \underline{O}. \qquad (3.9)$$

In case of V_1 the gradient is

$$\frac{\partial V}{\partial \underline{\beta}} = 2 \int_O^t e(\underline{\beta},t)\, \frac{\partial e}{\partial \underline{\beta}}\, dt \qquad (3.10)$$

and its minimum is searched by a gradient method

$$\frac{\partial \underline{\beta}}{\partial t} = -c\, \frac{\partial V}{\partial \underline{\beta}} . \qquad (3.11)$$

$\partial e/\partial \underline{\beta}$, eq.(3.10), can be obtained by using special filters, resulting from the model. Eq.(3.11) can be interpreted as to update the para-

meters as the gradient of the loss function indicates, and can therefore be regarded as a "recursive" parameter adjustment. The input signals can be arbitrary, if all interesting parameters are excited.

Parameter estimation methods have become influenced by the application of digital computers and by modern control theory which is based
on parametric models. The parameter estimation algorithms are mostly
written for discrete signals because of digital signal processing.
The estimation of parameters for models with continuous signals can
be carried out similarly to the model adjustment technique and is generally more difficult than that of discrete signals.

If the structure of the process and of the model agree sufficiently,
parametric identification can become more exact, since, in addition
to the identification of a nonparametric model, a regression analysis
takes place. Fig. 3.6. shows an example thereof. After parameter estimation has been applied, a better agreement of model and process is
obtained.

The simplest parameter estimation method is the *method of least squares.*

A linear difference equation of order m and time delay d is assumed
as a model

$$y(k) + a_1 y(k-1) + \ldots + a_m a(k-m)$$
$$- b_1 u(k-d-1) - \ldots - b_m u(k-d-m) = 0 \qquad (3.12)$$
$$k = 0, 1, 2, \ldots, N.$$

The corresponding z-transfer function is

$$G(z^{-1}) = \frac{y(z)}{u(z)} = \frac{B(z^{-1})}{A(z^{-1})} = \frac{b_1 z^{-1} + \ldots + b_m z^{-m}}{1 + a_1 z^{-1} + \ldots + a_m z^{-m}} z^{-d}. \qquad (3.13)$$

The equation error is taken because it is linearly dependent on the
parameters, and the difference equation becomes

$$y(k) + a_1 y(k-1) + \ldots + a_m y(k-m)$$
$$- b_1 u(k-d-1) - \ldots - b_m u(k-d-m) = e(k) \qquad (3.14)$$

or after z-transformation

$$A(z^{-1}) y(z) - B(z^{-1}) u(z) = e(z), \qquad (3.15)$$

which leads to the model shown in Fig. 3.7.

The lossfunction

$$V = \sum_{k=m+d}^{N+m+d} e^2(k) \qquad (3.16)$$

is minimised with regard to the parameter vector

$$\underline{\theta}^T = [a_1 \ a_2 \ \ldots \ a_m \vdots b_1 \ b_2 \ \ldots \ b_m] \qquad (3.17)$$

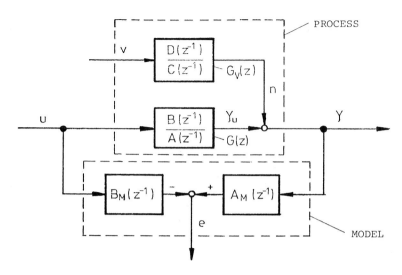

Fig. 3.7.   Structure of the model for least squares parameter
           estimation.

so that

$$\frac{dV}{d\underline{\Theta}} = \underline{0}.$$ (3.18)

This results in the least squares estimation algorithm

$$\hat{\underline{\Theta}} = [\underline{\Psi}^T \underline{\Psi}]^{-1} \underline{\Psi}^T \underline{y}$$ (3.19)

with

$$\underline{y}^T = [y(m+d)\ y(m+d+1)\ \ldots\ y(m+d+N)]$$ (3.20)

$$\underline{\Psi} = \begin{bmatrix} -y(m+d-1) & -y(m+d-2) & \ldots & -y(d) & u(m-1) & u(m-2) & \ldots & u(0) \\ -y(m+d) & -y(m+d-1) & \ldots & -y(d+1) & u(m) & u(m-1) & \ldots & u(1) \\ \vdots & \vdots & & \vdots & \vdots & \vdots & & \vdots \\ -y(m+d+N-1) & -y(m+d+N-2) & \ldots & -y(d+N) & u(m+N-1) & u(m+N-2) & \ldots & u(N) \end{bmatrix}$$
(3.21)

This is the nonrecursive direct (one shot) estimation algorithm. After
partitioning of $\underline{\Psi}$ and $\underline{y}$ one obtains the recursive direct estimation
algorithm

$$\hat{\underline{\Theta}}(k+1) = \hat{\underline{\Theta}}(k) + \underline{\gamma}(k)[y(k+1) - \underline{\Psi}^T(k+1)\hat{\underline{\Theta}}(k)]$$ (3.22)

with the corrector term

$$\underline{\gamma}(k) = \frac{1}{\underline{\Psi}^T(k+1)\underline{P}(k)\underline{\Psi}(k+1)+1} \underline{P}(k)\underline{\Psi}(k+1)$$ (3.23)

and

$$\underline{P}(k+1) = [\underline{I} - \underline{\gamma}(k)\underline{\psi}^T(k+1)]\underline{P}(k). \qquad (3.24)$$

The parameter estimates have to fulfill following requirements of convergence:

a) No bias:

$$E\{\hat{\underline{\Theta}}(N) - \underline{\Theta}_0\} = \underline{O} \qquad (N \text{ finite}) \qquad (3.25)$$

b) Consistency:

$$\lim_{N\to\infty} E\{\hat{\underline{\Theta}}(N) - \underline{\Theta}_0\} = \underline{O} \qquad (3.26)$$

c) Consistency in mean square sense: b) and

$$\lim_{N\to\infty} E\{(\hat{\underline{\Theta}}(N) - \underline{\Theta}_0)(\hat{\underline{\Theta}}(N) - \underline{\Theta}_0)^T\} = \underline{O}. \qquad (3.27)$$

Hereby, the true parameter vector is noted by $\underline{\Theta}_0$.

For to investigate the convergence of the estimates one has to know a model of the disturbanc es n(k). In general they can be described by a stochastic difference equation of form

$$G_v(z^{-1}) = \frac{n(z)}{v(z)} = \frac{D(z^{-1})}{C(z^{-1})} = \frac{d_o + d_1 z^{-1} + \ldots + d_p z^{-p}}{1 + c_1 z^{-1} + \ldots + c_p z^{-p}} \qquad (3.28)$$

where v(k) is a discrete white noise sequence.

If eq.(3.25) is applied to eq.(2.19), it follows that the error signal e(k) must be an uncorrelated sequence. With e(k) = v(k) and eq. (3.28) it follows that

$$G_v(z^{-1}) = \frac{1}{A(z^{-1})} . \qquad (3.29)$$

This means the disturbance filter must have the same dominator as the process, $C(z^{-1}) = A(z^{-1})$, and $D(z^{-1}) = 1$. Since this for real processes in general is not true, the least squares method leads to bias, and the estimates are only useful if the noise-to-signal ratio is very low.

Thus the simple least squares method cannot be applied to noisy dynamic processes. However, this method is the basis for improved parameter estimation methods. The important properties of these improved parameter estimation methods are listed in table 3.2.

The basic idea of the method of *generalized least squares* is to whiten the correlated residuals e(k) with a filter $F(z^{-1})$, Clarke [30]. A special disturbance filter $1/A(z^{-1})F(z^{-1})$, however, results from this, too, so that in many real cases no consistent estimates are to be expected.

Table 3.2. Properties of various parameter estimation methods.

Method	$G(z)$	$G_v(z)$	Assumptions on error signal $e(k)$	Estimated parameters	Computation-al expense	Kind of evaluation	Application
1. Least squares	$\dfrac{B(z^{-1})}{A(z^{-1})}$	$\dfrac{1}{A(z^{-1})}$	uncorrelated	$a_i;\ b_i$	medium	nonrecursive recursive	small disturbances
2. Generalised least squares	"	$\dfrac{1}{A(z^{-1})F(z^{-1})}$	"	$a_i;\ b_i;\ f_i$	large	nonrecursive recursive	small disturbances
3. Instrumental variables	"	$\dfrac{D(z^{-1})}{C(z^{-1})}$	—	$a_i;\ b_i$	medium	nonrecursive recursive	large disturbances; process computer
4. Stochastic approximation	"	$\dfrac{1}{A(z^{-1})}$	uncorrelated	$a_i;\ b_i$	small	recursive	small disturbances
5. Maximum-Likelihood	"	$\dfrac{D(z^{-1})}{A(z^{-1})}$	uncorrelated $p(e\|\underline{\theta})$	$a_i;\ b_i;\ d_i$	large	nonrecursive recursive	large disturbances; digital computer
6. Bayes	"	timevariant difference equation	$p(e)$ $p(\underline{\theta})$	$a_i(k);\ b_i(k)$	very large	nonrecursive	timevariant processes; digital computer
7. Correlation and least squares	"	$\dfrac{D(z^{-1})}{C(z^{-1})}$	—	$a_i;\ b_i$	small	nonrecursive recursive	large disturbances; process computer

If *maximum-likelihood estimation* is applied, Åström, Bohlin [31], a disturbance filter of form $D(z^{-1})/A(z^{-1})$ is assumed which is certainly a better approximation than that of the generalized least squares method. Even this filter, however, is not a general one. Since the residuals are nonlinear dependent on the filter parameters $D(z^{-1})$ iterative procedures for search of parameters must be used. Assuming a state space model the filter becomes even more special.

Independent of any special assumptions on the disturbance filter are the *method of intrumental variables*, Wong, Polak [32] and Young [33], and the *method of correlation and least squares*, Isermann et.al. [34]. These methods can be applied to relatively wide classes of processes. Opposite to the methods of generalized least squares and maximum likelihood they do not furnish models of disturbanc es simultaneously. However, with an additional time-series analysis these models can be estimated, too, Young [35].

The *Bayes method* is the most general method and is based on deeper theoretical argumentations. Stochastic varying process parameters are assumed. Most of the other methods can be derived from this method applying specialisations [28], [29].

Using the same simulated processes as test-cases parameter estimation methods have been compared by different authors [36], [34]. It could be shown that all consistent identification methods lead to approximately the same accuracy of the input-output model, compare Fig. 3.8. However, there are differences concerning the computational expense, the a priori known factors and the reliability of convergence for recursive methods [34], [29].

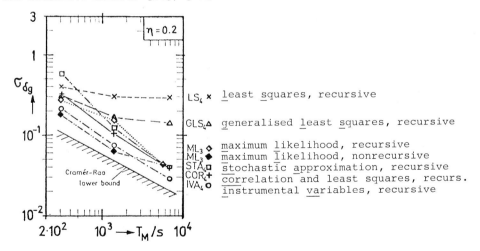

LS$_4$ × least squares, recursive

GLS$_4$ △ generalised least squares, recursive

ML$_3$ ◇ maximum likelihood, recursive
ML$_3$ ◆ maximum likelihood, nonrecursive
STA$_4$ □ stochastic approximation, recursive
COR$_4$ + correlation and least squares, recurs.
IVA$_4$ ○ instrumental variables, recursive

Fig. 3.8.   Comparison of different parameter-estimation methods, using a testcase [34], [36]. The diagram shows the measured error of the impulse response $\sigma_{\delta g}$ dependent on the measuring time T_M for a second order process (process I).

Many parameter-estimation methods are not restricted to linear processes. They can also be applied without changes to *nonlinear processes*
which are *linear in the parameters*. For estimation of *timevariant parameters* recursive algorithms should be used with time dependent
weighting of data.

If the *order of the model* is not known a priori, it can be searched
by testing methods discussed in [38].

Some special advantages show *two-step identification* methods which
give access to an intermediate nonparametric model. Correlation and
least squares parameter estimation as well as step or pulse responses
and least squares estimation are of this type [34], [29], [37]. By
means of these methods search for order is possible with only small
computational expense; a priori factors and especially starting matrices have not be known for on-line versions, divergence is not possible
and the estimated model can be easily verified.

More details and experiences on process identification and parameter
estimation methods can be found in recent books and especially in the
Proceedings of the 3rd IFAC-Symposium on Identification and Parameter-
Estimation [38].

3.4 Practical rules for process identification

Some important requirements for good identification can be summarized
as follows:

1. The *disturbanc es* are not allowed to be correlated with the input
   signal.

2. The *a priori assumptions* for a mean square consistent estimation
   have to be fulfilled. These assumptions depend on the special identification method.

3. The *input signal* has to excite persistently all modes of interest
   (persistent excitation, eg. [28], [35]). The height u_0 of the input signal has to be as large as possible, and the frequency spectrum should be large enough for all frequencies of interest. Pseudo
   random binary signals do possess these properties. Since they are
   deterministic, their autocorrelation function and frequency spectrum are known exactly, so that they easily can be adapted to the
   process. If a *normal operating signal* is used as input, one has
   to check if item 1. is not violated and if the signal is persistently exciting.

4. Regarding to continuous signals the *sampling interval* should fulfill Shannon's sampling theorem. If for discrete signals the sampl-
   ling interval is too short, numerical problems can arise. If it is
   too long, the dynamics cannot be described in full detail. Therefore ranges of appropriate sampling intervals have to be selected.
   Approximately 5 to 12 intervals per settling time t_{95} (time for
   95% transition of a transient function) seem to be a good compromise.

5. To avoid *numerical problems* (matrix inversion etc.), the sampling
   interval sould not be too short, the reference values of the signals should be small and the input signal should be persistenly
   changing.

6. *Low frequent disturbanc es* such as drift, seasonal trends, etc.,
   must be eliminated by special methods. High pass filtering can be
   applied to various types of low frequent disturbancies and are preferable to other methods like regression analysis or differencia-
   ting.

7. If the *reference values* of the input and output signal are not
   known exactly, then it depends on the single identification method,
   if they have to be estimated additionally. For some methods the
   reference value of the output has not to be known if $E\{u(k)\} = 0$.

8. After the model has been identified, a *verification* should follow.
   It depends on the identification method which checks can be applied.

9. If only a *few data* of input and output signals are available, it
   should be noticed

   a) The less usable information data have, the more   accurately
      the model structure should be known (by theoretical analysis).

   b) If there are p unknown parameters, at least N = p pairs of input
      and output data have to be used. However, the influence of noise
      cannot be eliminated then.

   c) If there are N > p pairs of input and output data, parameter esti-
      mation (a "regression technique") can be applied. The larger
      N is the better is the elimination of the effect of contimina-
      ting noise.

More details on these guidelines see e.g. [29].

LITERATURE

A. MODELING

[1] Campbell, D.P.: Process Dynamics. J. Wiley, New York, 1958

[2] Profos, P.: Die Regelung von Dampfanlagen. Springer-Verlag, Heidelberg, 1962

[3] Cermák, J.; Peterka, V. und Závorka, J.: Dynamika regulovaných soustav (dynamics of control systems for thermal and chemical processes, in czech language). Academia Prague, 1968

[4] Gould, L.A.: Chemical Process and Control. Addison-Wesley Publishing Comp., Massachusettes, 1969

[5] Mac Farlane, A.G.J.: Dynamical System Models. G.G. Harrap, London, 1970

[6] Smith, C.L.; Pike, R.W. and Murrvill, P.: Formulation and Optimization of mathematical models. International Text-book Company, Scranton, Pennsylvania, 1970

[7] Isermann, R.: Theoretische Analyse der Dynamik industrieller Prozesse. Bibliographisches Institut, Mannheim, 1971

[8] Douglas, J.M.: Process Dynamics and Control, Vol. I. Prentice-Hall, Englewood Cliffs, N.J., 1972

[9] Franks, R.G.E.: Modeling and Simulation in Chemical Engineering. Wiley-Interscience, New York, 1972

[10] Luyben, W.B.: Process Modeling, Simulation and Control for Chemical Engineers. Mc Graw-Hill, New York, 1973

[11] De Groot, S.R.: Thermodynamik irreversibler Prozesse. Biblio-graphisches Institut, Mannheim, 1960

[12] Isermann, R.: Results on the simplification of dynamic process models. Int. J. Control, 19 (1974), 149 - 159

B. IDENTIFICATION

[13] Zadeh, L.A.: From circuit theory to system theory. Proc. IRE, 50 (1962), 856 - 865

[14] Åström, K.J. and Eykhoff, P.: System identification - a survey. Automatica 7 (1971), 123 - 162

[15] Nieman, R.E.; Fisher,D.G. and Seborg, D.E.: A review of process identification and parameter estimation techniques. Int. J. Control, 13 (1971), 209 - 264

[16] Lee, R.C.K.: Optimal estimation, identification and control. Mass.: M.I.T. Press, Cambridge, 1964

[17] Jenkins, G.; Watts, D.: Spectral analysis and its application. Holden Day, San Francisco, 1969

[18] Strobel, H.: Systemanalyse mit determinierten Testsignalen. VEB Verlag Technik, Berlin, 1967

[19] Davies, W.D.T.: System Identification for self-adaptive control. Wiley-Interscience, London, 1970

[20] Box, G.E.P.; Jenkins, G.M.: Time series analysis, forecasting and control. Holden Day, San Francisco, 1970

[21] Rajbman, N.S.: What is System Identification? (in Russian) Nauka, Moscow, 1970

[22] Richalet, J.; Rault, A.; Pouliquen, R.: Identification des processus par la méthode du modèle. Gordon and Breach, Paris, London, New York, 1971

[23] Sage, A.P.; Melsa, J.L.: System identification. Academic Press, New York, 1971

[24] Isermann, R.: Experimentelle Analyse der Dynamik von Regelsystemen. Identifikation I. Bibliographisches Institut, Mannheim, HTB 515, 1971

[25] Graupe, D.: Identifications of systems. Van Norstrand-Reinhold, New York, 1972

[26] Mendel, J.M.: Discrete techniques of parameter estimations. Marcel Dekker, New York, 1973

[27] Cuénod, M.A. und Fatio, J.L.: Cours d'introduction aux méthodes d'identification. Editions Albin Michel, Paris, 1973

[28] Eykhoff, P.: System identification. J. Wiley, London, 1974

[29] Isermann, R.: Prozeßidentifikation. Springer-Verlag, Berlin, 1974

[30] Clarke, D.W.: Generalized least squares estimates of the parameters of a dynamic model. Paper 3.17, Preprints of IFAC-Symposium on Identification, Prague, 1967

[31] Åström, K.J.; Bohlin, T.: Numerical identification of linear dynamic systems from normal operating records. IFAC-Symposium Theory of selfadaptive control systems, Teddington, 1965, New York: Plenum Press

[32] Wong, K.Y.; Polak, E.: Identification of linear discrete time systems using the instrumental variable method. IEEE Trans. Aut. Control, AC-12 (1967), 707 - 718

[33] Young, P.C.: An instrumental variable method for real-time identification of a noisy process. IFAC-Automatica 6 (1970), 271 - 287

[34] Isermann, R.; Baur, U.; Bamberger, W.; Kneppo, P.; Siebert, H.: Comparison of six on-line identification and parameter estimation methods with three simulated processes. 3rd IFAC-Symposium on Identification, North Holland, Amsterdam, paper E-1 und IFAC Automatica (1974), 81 - 103, 1973

[35] Young, P.C.; Shellswell, S.H.; Neethling, C.G.: A recursive
        approach to time-series analysis. Report CUED/B-Control/TR16,
        University of Cambridge, Great Britain, 1971

[36] Isermann, R.; Baur, U.: Results of testcase A. 3rd IFAC-Symposium
        on Identification, North Holland, Amsterdam, paper E-3, 1973

[37] Isermann, R.; Baur, U.; Kurz, H.: Identifikation dynamischer
        Prozesse mittels Korrelation und Parameterschätzung. Rege-
        lungstechnik und Prozeßdatenverarbeitung 22, Heft 8, 1974

[38] Proc. of 3rd IFAC-Symposium on Identification and System Para-
        meter Estimation, The Hague, North Holland, Amsterdam, 1973

DISCUSSION

According to one of your diagrams, using a parametric approach i.e. choosing
the structure and estimating the parameter you obtain a better result. I work on cor-
relation methods with constraints and we can get as good results as yours but only
considering certain information and constraining the estimator. In your case for
instance you know à priori that all the ordinates of your function must be greater
than or equal to zero. So, you can have the same results without defining a struc-
ture. You must define a structure on your parametric curve, while in the other case
you only have to insert some physical considerations that you know they must be
satisfied. (TODINI)

O.K. that's why I said it is only possible to improve unless you know the
structure. (ISERMANN)

I was very interested in your approach. You are assuming something about
the structure of your solution and you are using this to get a better identification.
One of the basic objections to this approach is the fact that you are introducing
a certain bias by assuming à priori a certain structure. Can you elaborate on this.
To answer dr. Todini's question, when you have a small amount of data, then saying
that some function you are looking for is > 0 is not sufficient. It may be suffi-
cient when you have a very large amount of data. (NEUMAN)

But it's nonsense to identify a large number of parameters with a small num-
ber of data. (TODINI)

That's exactly the question I want to raise. In this case assuming the struc-
ture, I assume that you can use a smaller amount of data than what the statistician
would do to obtain something which is reasonably good. How does this bias with a
small amount of data affect the reliability of the solution. (NEUMAN)

What do you understand by bias ?
In the statistical sense bias mean that when the expectation for a finite time of
observation equals the exact parameter, there is no bias ; if there is a difference
then there is a bias. I cannot understand why you should introduce a bias if you
assume a structure which is in the first moment exact. (ISERMANN)

If you would assume a different structure you would obtain a different re-
sult. (NEUMAN)

No, I assume that the structure for the identification is exactly the same in this example as the simulated process that we have used in this process.(ISERMANN)

You mean that you know the structure à priori. (NEUMAN)

In this case it's only a simulation. And if we don't know the structure exactly, only approximately, the amount of improvement is not of the same extent as shown here. That's only to show what's going on if you have more information and if this more information is correct. It is very much dependent on this and to scope this problem in general, I think it is impossible. (ISERMANN)

When the physical type of equations is nonlinear, the processes become non-linear. To me this seems like putting the car before the horse. (BRUTSAERT)

We come back to one of the first slides. We start with balanced equations,they are always linear. Then we introduce a first state equation or a second one and if now the relationship between this output and this input is nonlinear this state equation introduces for the first time a nonlinear behavior to this input and this output total behavior. I think that's very simple. (ISERMANN)

Modeling and Simulation of Water Resources Systems, G.C. VANSTEENKISTE, (Ed.)
North-Holland Publishing Company (1975)

A RECURSIVE APPROACH TO TIME-SERIES ANALYSIS FOR MULTIVARIABLE SYSTEMS

P. Young and P. Whitehead
Control Division, Department of Engineering
University of Cambridge *
ENGLAND

Abstract

In this paper, the recursive Instrumental Variable – Approximate Maximum Likelihood (IVAML) method of time-series analysis for single input, single output systems is extended to the multivariable case using techniques of statistical feature selection to circumvent the problems of characterising the multivariable stochastic disturbances. A method of dynamic system identification and estimation based on the multivariable IVAML procedure is outlined and applied to the problem of characterising the dynamic relationship between Biochemical Oxygen Demand (BOD) and Dissolved Oxygen (DO) in a non-tidal river system.

1. Introduction

Of all the problems that confront the dynamic systems analyst, those connected with model identification and estimation are amongst the most challenging. A previous paper (Young, 1974) has emphasised the importance of recursive methods of time-series analysis for model identification and estimation and has also described two specific recursive methods for estimating the parameters in either conventional "black box" time-series models or the alternative and, in some senses more flexible, state-space (or internally structured) models.

From the information theoretic standpoint, the state-space model is particularly attractive since it allows for the inclusion of all *a priori* information on the internal functioning of the system under study; information which, unless the analyst is careful, can often be disregarded in the formulation of the black box or input-output representation.

The Extended Kalman Filter (EKF) technique suggested for state-space model identification and estimation in previous publications (Young, 1974; Young and Beck, 1974) is undoubtedly a flexible analytical tool. But it is just this flexibility which can be considered perhaps its biggest drawback in the parameter estimation phase: while flexibility is an enormous advantage in the identification stage of the analysis, where different model forms and structures are being assessed for their suitability against the available data, it can lead to inefficiency, both computational and statistical, when used to estimate those parameters that characterise the identified model structure.

In the present paper, an alternative approach to multivariable system parameter estimation is proposed which is both more systematic than the EKF and appears to provide a considerable improvement in statistical efficiency because of its special iterative mode of application. This new procedure, which is a particular multivariable extension of the Instrumental Variable – Approximate Maximum Likelihood (IVAML) method proposed previously for single input, single output model estimation (see e.g. Young, 1974; Young et al., 1971), is, however, considerably more restricted than the EKF: in particular it can only be applied to systems described by discrete-time, vector-matrix equations and it requires that all of the state vector is available for measurement[**]. While these are, of course, quite serious restrictions, it is felt that the procedure still has good application potential: it appears to be a rugged method, which is essential in

---

[*]Peter Young is a Fellow of Clare Hall and Paul Whitehead a Member of Wolfson College.

[**]A quite similar IV approach was suggested recently by Chan for continuous-time systems. However, this involved an increased computational load because of the need for repeated integration and there was no attempt to model the stochastic disturbances in time-series terms.

practical applications, and its assumptions about the nature of the noise
statistics are not too restrictive. In addition, it should be emphasised that,
although it is not always possible, one should always try to obtain observations
of all the state variables when attempting multivariable identification and
estimation; indeed this is implicit in much of the large body of literature on
econometric model estimation (see e.g. Johnson, 1963) which has represented
probably the most fertile area for the application of multivariable time-series
analysis in recent years (see Section 7)

2. The System Description

Consider the following discrete-time, state-space representation of a
multivariable (multi-input, multi-output), linear dynamic system,

$$\underline{x}_k = A\underline{x}_{k-1} + B\underline{u}_{k-1} \tag{1}$$

where $\underline{x}_k = [x_{1k}\ x_{2k}\ \cdots\ x_{nk}]^T$ is an n dimensional vector of state variables
that characterise the system at the kth instant of time, $\underline{u}_k = [u_{1k}\ u_{2k}\ \cdots\ u_{mk}]^T$
is an m dimensional vector of deterministic input variables, also sampled at the
kth time instant, while A and B are, respectively, $n \times n$ and $n \times m$ matrices with
elements a_{ij} (i,j = 1,2,...,n) and b_{ij} (i = 1,2,...,n; j = 1,2,...,m).

Suppose now that each element x_{ik} of the state vector $\underline{x}_k$ is available
for measurement but is contaminated by a zero mean lumped noise disturbance ξ_{ik}
which is assumed to include the effects of all stochastic inputs and other
disturbances as well as measurement noise. The vector of observations
$\underline{y}_k = [y_{1k}\ y_{2k}\ \cdots\ y_{nk}]^T$ at the kth instant is then defined by

$$\underline{y}_k = \underline{x}_k + \underline{\xi}_k \tag{2}$$

Here $\underline{\xi}_k = [\xi_{1k}\ \xi_{2k}\ \cdots\ \xi_{nk}]^T$ is the n dimensional vector of the lumped noise
disturbances which is assumed to have the following statistical properties

$$E\{\underline{\xi}_k\} = 0 \ ; \ \ E\{\underline{\xi}_k\underline{\xi}_k^T\} = Q \ ; \ \ E\{\underline{\xi}_k\underline{u}_j^T\} = 0 \ , \ \text{for all k,j} \tag{3}$$

In other words, the noise disturbances are assumed to be zero mean random
variables which may, in general, be both serially correlated in time and
correlated with each other at the same instant of time, but which are completely
uncorrelated with the deterministic input variables that compose the input
vector $\underline{u}_k$.

Substituting from equation (2) into (1) we obtain the following
relationship between the measured variables

$$\underline{y}_k = A\underline{y}_{k-1} + B\underline{u}_{k-1} + \underline{n}_k \tag{4}$$

where $\underline{n}_k$ represents the combined effects of the system stochastic disturbances
and is defined as

$$\underline{n}_k = \underline{\xi}_k - A\underline{\xi}_{k-1} \tag{5}$$

In practice a discrete time model such as (1) could be obtained either by
direct analysis of the physical system in discrete time terms, by transformation
of an equivalent continuous-time state-space model using standard methods of
transformation (Dorf, 1965), or by a combination of both. A simple but, as we
shall see, non-trivial example of this kind of system representation is the
multivariable model developed recently to explain the relationship between
Biochemical Oxygen Demand (BOD) and Dissolved Oxygen (DO) at the output of a
single reach in a non-tidal river system (Whitehead and Young, 1974). This model
takes the form of two coupled first order equations and can be written as

$$\text{BOD:} \quad x_{1k} = k_1 \frac{V_m}{Q_{k-1}} x_{1,k-1} + k_2 u_{1,k-1} + k_3 S_{k-1} \tag{6}$$

$$\text{DO:} \quad x_{2k} = k_4 x_{1,k-1} + k_5 \frac{V_m}{Q_{k-1}} x_{2,k-1} + k_6 u_{2,k-1} + k_7 S_{k-1} + k_8 C_{s,k-1} + k_9 w_{k-1} \tag{7}$$

where x_1 is the BOD at the output of the reach, which can be considered as an
aggregate or macro measure of the oxygen absorbing potential of

substances in the stream (such as decaying organic material from effluent discharges), and is defined as the oxygen absorbed in $mg\ \ell^{-1}$ over a five day period by a sample of river water in the absence of light at a constant temperature of $20^{\circ}C$;

x_2 is the DO at the output of the reach $(mg\ \ell^{-1})$;

Q is the volumetric flow rate in the stream $(ft^3\ day^{-1})$;

V_m is the mean volumetric hold-up in the reach (ft^3);

u_1 is the input BOD from the previous upstream reach in the river system $(mg\ \ell^{-1})$;

u_2 is the input DO from the previous upstream reach $(mg\ \ell^{-1})$;

S is a term dependent upon sunlight hours and chlorophyl A level to account for photosynthetic effects such as algal growth and decay;

C_s is the saturation concentration of DO $(mg\ \ell^{-1})$;

w is the input of DO due to weirs or run-off during periods of high flow $(mg\ \ell^{-1})$;

and $k_1, k_2, \ldots, k_9$ are coefficients or parameters which will be either constant or slowly time-variable depending on the period of observation[+]

Equations (6) and (7) may be easily written in the vector matrix form of equation (1) by defining the matrices (A;B) and the vectors ($\underline{x}_k$;$\underline{u}_k$) in the following manner:

$$A = \begin{bmatrix} k_1 \dfrac{V_m}{Q_{k-1}} & 0 \\[2ex] k\ k_4 & k_5 \dfrac{V_m}{Q_{k-1}} \end{bmatrix} \quad ; \quad B = \begin{bmatrix} k_2 & 0 & k_3 & 0 & 0 \\[1ex] 0 & k_6 & k_7 & k_8 & k_9 \end{bmatrix}$$

$$\tag{8}$$

$$\underline{x}_k^T = \begin{bmatrix} x_{1k} & x_{2k} \end{bmatrix} \quad ; \quad \underline{u}_k^T = \begin{bmatrix} u_{1k} & u_{2k} & S_k & C_{s,k} & w_k \end{bmatrix}$$

In this example, the sampled values for both states can be obtained from a planned experiment: DO is easily measurable by an instream probe; BOD, on the other hand, is somewhat more difficult to estimate since a sample of river water must be kept in controlled conditions for 5 days, as indicated in its definition (indeed the measurement is sometimes termed "5 day BOD"). The resulting measurement equations can be written in the vector form (2) with the elements y_{1k} and y_{2k} of the vector $\underline{y}_k$ denoting the BOD and DO observations, respectively, and with ξ_{1k} and ξ_{2k} denoting the effects of stochastic disturbances and unavoidable measurement noise.

3. The Basic Estimation Problem

The basic estimation problem posed by equations (1) and (2) is to use the noisy observations of the state variables given in (2) to obtain consistent estimates of the $n^2 + nm$ parameters that characterise the A and B matrices in (1). In order to solve this problem we first note that the ith elemental row of the composite equation (4) can be written as

$$y_{ik} = \underline{z}_k^T \underline{a}_i + \eta_{ik} \tag{9}$$

where $\underline{z}_k^T = \begin{bmatrix} y_{1,k-1}\ y_{2,k-1} \cdots y_{n,k-1}, & u_{1,k-1}, & \cdots, & u_{m,k-1} \end{bmatrix}$

[+] A large body of literature suggests that parameters such as k_1 and k_5 are temperature dependent; as a result these, and possibly some of the other parameters, may be expected to vary over long observation periods due to seasonal temperature changes.

$$\underline{a}_i = \left[a_{i1}, a_{i2} \cdots a_{in}, b_{i1}, \ldots, b_{im}\right]^T$$

and

$$\eta_{ik} = \xi_{ik} - a_{i1}\xi_{1,k-1} - , \ldots, - a_{in}\xi_{n,k-1}$$

Thus one simple approach to the problem of estimating the unknown parameters is to decompose the overall estimation problem into n separate sub-problems, each defined in terms of an estimation model such as (9) which is linear in an n + m subset of the n^2 + nm unknown parameters.

At first sight, it might appear that a consistent estimate of the parameter vector $\underline{a}_i$ in each of these elemental estimation models could be obtained by normal linear least squares regression analysis. But further examination reveals that this is not the case: because of the inherent noise on the variables associated with the unknown parameters, equation (9) is, in statistical terms, a structural rather than a regression model (Kendall and Stuart, 1961); as a result, if a simple least squares estimate of $\underline{a}_i$ is obtained in the usual manner, then the estimate will, in most cases, be asymptotically biased and thus statistically inconsistent (see Young; 1965,1968)

One of the simplest methods of obviating this problem is to use an Instrumental Variable (IV) modification to the simple least squares regression algorithm. This approach is well known in both the statistical (Kendall and Stuart, 1961) and control (Wong and Polak, 1967; Young, 1965, 1969, 1970) literature and will not be described in detail here; it will suffice merely to point out that the IV estimate $\hat{\underline{a}}_{ik}$ based on a data set of k samples is obtained by the solution of the following vector-matrix equation (which is simply a modification of the equivalent "normal equations" of linear regression analysis),

$$\hat{P}_{ik}\hat{\underline{a}}_{ik} = \hat{\underline{b}}_{ik} \tag{10}$$

Here $\hat{P}_{ik}$ is an n×n matrix and $\hat{\underline{b}}_{ik}$ is an n vector, each defined as

$$\hat{P}_{ik} = \left[\sum_{j=1}^{k} \hat{\underline{x}}_j \underline{z}_j^T\right]^{-1} \quad ; \quad \hat{\underline{b}}_{ik} = \sum_{j=1}^{k} \hat{\underline{x}}_j y_{ij} \tag{11}$$

while $\hat{\underline{x}}_j$, j = 1,2,...,k is an instrumental variable vector chosen to be as highly correlated as possible with the hypothetical "noise free" vector $\underline{x}_j = \left[x_{1,j-1}, x_{2,j-1}, \ldots, x_{n,j-1}, u_{1,j-1}, \ldots, u_{m,j-1}\right]^T$ but totally uncorrelated with the noise η_{ij} .

An alternative recursive IV solution to the problem, in which the estimate $\hat{\underline{a}}_{ik}$ after k samples is obtained as the linear sum of the previous estimate $\hat{\underline{a}}_{i,k-1}$ plus a corrective term based on the new information y_{ik}, $\underline{z}_k$ and $\hat{\underline{x}}_k$ received at the kth sampling instant, can be obtained directly from the non-recursive solution by simple matrix manipulation (Young, 1971, 1974) and takes the following form

$$\hat{\underline{a}}_{ik} = \hat{\underline{a}}_{i,k-1} - \underline{k}_k\{\underline{z}_k^T\hat{\underline{a}}_{i,k-1} - y_{ik}\} \tag{I(1)}$$

where $\underline{k}_k$ is a gain vector defined by

$$\underline{k}_k = \hat{P}_{k-1}\hat{\underline{x}}_k \left[1 + \underline{z}_k^T P_{k-1}\hat{\underline{x}}_k\right]^{-1}$$

and the matrix $\hat{P}_k$ is obtained by a second recursive algorithm

$$\hat{P}_k = \hat{P}_{k-1} - \hat{P}_{k-1}\hat{\underline{x}}_k \left[1 + \underline{z}_k^T P_{k-1}\hat{\underline{x}}_k\right]^{-1} \underline{z}_k^T P_{k-1} \tag{I(2)}$$

It can be shown (e.g. Wong and Polak, 1967; Durbin, 1954) that the estimates obtained either by the block data solution (10) or its recursive equivalent I(1) and I(2) are consistent and relatively efficient in the statistical sense (i.e. they have low variance) provided the IV vector $\hat{\underline{x}}_k$ is highly correlated with $\underline{x}_k$; indeed experimental evidence based on Monte-Carlo simulation studies indicates that with a well chosen IV vector, the IV estimation variances are near the Cramer-Rao lower bound (Neethling, 1974) and compare well with the variances of other estimators (see e.g. Iserman et al., 1973).

But how can the IV vector be selected so as to ensure that comparatively low variance estimators are obtained? Here we can be guided by experience with IV methods developed previously for single input, single output time-series models (Young et al., 1971; Young, 1974): noting the physical nature of the problem, an auxiliary model of the system is first constructed on the basis of *a priori* estimates of the unknown parameters; this model is then used to generate an output which can be considered as an initial estimate of the noise free output of the system, and which can, therefore, be used to define the IV vector. In the multivariable case considered here, the same approach can be employed, as shown diagrammatically in Fig.1. Here the auxiliary model, like the basic system model,

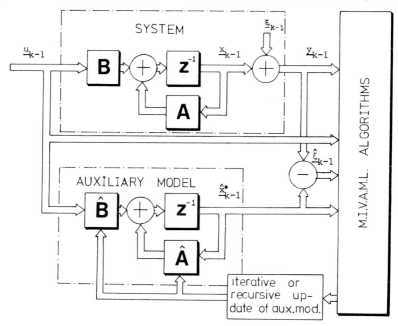

Fig. 1 Multivariable IVAML Estimation Procedure

is multivariable and is activated by the deterministic input vector $\underline{u}_k$: at each sampling instant its state vector $\hat{\underline{x}}_k^* = [\hat{x}_{1k} \, \hat{x}_{2k} \, \ldots \, \hat{x}_{nk}]^T$ provides the source for the instrumental variables needed to define the IV vector $\hat{\underline{x}}_k$ required at the next sampling instant; in particular, the IV vector is defined as follows

$$\hat{\underline{x}}_k = [\hat{x}_{1,k-1}, \hat{x}_{2,k-1}, \ldots, \hat{x}_{n,k-1}, u_{1,k-1}, \ldots, u_{m,k-1}]^T$$

where it will be noted that since the deterministic input variables are assumed to be known exactly, they can be used directly in the definition of the IV vector and need not be estimated[†].

The choice of the *a priori* estimates required by the auxiliary model can be based upon either physical knowledge of the system obtained from prior identification studies or from the biased least squares estimates obtained in an

---

[†] If the system is enclosed within a feedback loop of known structure, then it will be necessary to estimate the input variables as well since these will then be contaminated by circulatory noise in the closed loop (see Young, 1970).

initial estimation run. As the estimation improves, however, it makes sense to
update the auxiliary model in some manner in order to enhance the quality of the
IV vector and so improve the statistical efficiency of the estimates. This updating can be carried out in one of two ways: first, for on-line purposes the
recursive estimates can be used as the basis for continuous updating of the
auxiliary model parameters; alternatively, an off-line, iterative procedure can be
used in which there are repeated runs through the block of data with the auxiliary
model estimates updated only after each run is finished. This iterative procedure
is considered complete when further iteration yields negligible change in the
estimates. Both approaches are described in detail elsewhere for the single
input, single output case; the procedures are, however, identical in the multivariable situation.

Experience has shown that, not surprisingly, the iterative method is able
to "refine" the estimates and yield superior estimation performance, particularly
in applications such as macro-economic modelling where there is a relative
paucity of data. It is also interesting to observe that this iterative IV
procedure can be considered as an extension to the Two Stage Least Squares (TSLS)
methods so popular in econometrics (see, for example, Johnson, 1963); indeed we
might refer to it as Multi-Stage Least Squares (MSLS).

4. The Residual Noise Estimation Problem

Once the convergence of the basic system parameter estimates is complete,
the output state $\hat{\underline{x}}_k^*$ of the auxiliary model can be considered as a relatively
efficient estimate of the hypothetical noise free system state $\underline{x}_k$. As a result,
an estimate $\hat{\underline{\xi}}_k$ of the noise disturbance vector $\underline{\xi}_k$ can be generated by
reference to equation (2) i.e.

$$\hat{\underline{\xi}}_i = \underline{y}_i - \hat{\underline{x}}_i^* \quad ; \quad i = 1, 2, \ldots, k \tag{12}$$

This estimate of the noise vector can then be used as a basis for a time-series
characterisation of the true but unobservable noise vector $\underline{\xi}_k$.

Clearly it would be possible to follow the present state of the art and
attempt to obtain a complete multivariable model for $\underline{\xi}_k$ by first identifying a
suitable canonical (uniquely identifiable) multivariable time-series structure for
its estimate $\hat{\underline{\xi}}_k$, and then using methods of multivariable time-series analysis to
estimate the parameters defining the system within this structure (Rowe, 1970).
But this could be a lengthy and complicated procedure fraught with many problems,
not the least being the definition of a suitable canonical form.

There is, however, a simpler alternative approach: the problem of
characterising the residual noise vector $\underline{\xi}_k$ in time-series terms could be
considered as a problem of recognising statistical patterns in its estimate $\hat{\underline{\xi}}_k$.
Is it possible, therefore, to use any of the existing statistical techniques of
pattern recognition to obtain an efficient structural representation of the noise
process? Certainly it is unlikely that much would be lost by such a procedure
since, in contrast to the basic system estimation problem discussed in previous
sections, it is doubtful in practice if any *a priori* information would be
available about possible noise model structures; thus the identification of a
multivariable canonical form would itself have to be based purely on data analysis,
as are most techniques of pattern recognition. And in any case, there is nothing
particularly attractive about the existing procedures of multivariable time-series
analysis; indeed it could be argued that they have not been notably successful
when applied to practical problems.

There are, of course, many different statistical methods available in the
pattern recognition literature. But certain procedures which appear to have
particularly good practical potential are those methods of feature selection which
utilise the Karhunen-Loeve (K-L) expansion (Kittler and Young, 1973). This
expansion is based upon an eigenvector analysis of the sample covariance matrix
associated with the input representation vectors (in this case the noise vector
estimate $\hat{\underline{\xi}}_k$). The results of this analysis are used to linearly transform the

representation vector into a new coordinate system, where the transformed vector elements are mutually uncorrelated,[†] and where the information on the original representation vectors is concentrated in the first few axes.

In the present situation, the sample covariance matrix $\hat{Q}_k$ of the estimated noise vector $\hat{\xi}_i$, i = 1,2,...,k , is given by

$$\hat{Q}_k = \frac{1}{k} \sum_{i=1}^{k} \hat{\xi}_i \hat{\xi}_i^T$$

Suppose, therefore, that the vector $\hat{\xi}$ is transformed into a new coordinate system (the K-L coordinate system) by means of a linear transformation of the following form

$$\underline{\nu}^T = \hat{\xi}^T U \tag{13}$$

where U is a matrix with columns defined by the n eigenvectors $\underline{u}_j$, j = 1,2,...,n, of $\hat{Q}_k$ arranged in the descending order of their associated eigenvalues λ_j , i.e.

$$\lambda_1 \geq \lambda_2 \geq \ldots \geq \lambda_n$$

It can then be shown that $\underline{\nu}$ obtained in this manner is a vector of random variables that are mutually uncorrelated at the same time instant, i.e.,

$$E\{\underline{\nu}_i \underline{\nu}_i^T\} = \begin{bmatrix} \rho_1^2 & & & \\ & \rho_2^2 & & \\ & & \ddots & \\ & & & \rho_n^2 \end{bmatrix}$$

where the variables $\rho_j^2 = \lambda_j$, j = 1,2,...,n .

The advantage of transforming the noise estimate vector $\hat{\xi}$ into the K-L coordinate frame is that the resultant mutually uncorrelated[†] random variables that compose the transformed vector $\underline{\nu}$ can each be characterised separately in time-series terms, thus avoiding, albeit in an approximate sense, the thorny question of a suitable multivariable canonical form and, at the same time, simplifying the time-series analysis.

And there is an additional advantage: if an approximation $\underline{\xi}*$ of $\hat{\xi}$ is constructed of the form,

$$\underline{\xi}* = \sum_{j=1}^{N} \nu_j \underline{u}_j \tag{14}$$

where N < n , then it can be shown (Chien and Fu, 1967) that both the mean square error $\bar{e}^2$, where

$$\bar{e}^2 = E\{[\hat{\xi}-\underline{\xi}*]^2\} \tag{15}$$

and the entropy function H_N , where

$$H_N = - \sum_{j=N}^{n} \rho_j^2 \log \rho_j^2 \tag{16}$$

are minimised with respect to the ordering of the eigenvectors. Moreover, the total entropy $H = - \sum_{j=1}^{n} \rho_j^2 \log \rho_j^2$ associated with the coordinate system $\underline{u}_j$, j = 1,2,...,n , obtained in this manner is minimised with respect to any other coordinate system. In other words, by ordering the eigenvectors $\underline{u}_j$ in correspondence with the decreasing magnitude of their associated eigenvalues, we are able to obtain the optimal reduced K-L coordinate system, in which the first N coordinate coefficients ν_j , defined as

$$\nu_j = \hat{\xi}^T \underline{u}_j$$

† at the same time instant.

contain most of the "information" about the random noise estimate vector $\hat{\xi}$.

The significance of these results is that, in some circumstances, it may be possible to reduce the burden of the time-series analysis still further: if the approximation (13) is found to be acceptable, then only the first N ($< n$) time-series generated by the K-L transformation need to be analysed; and the resultant N single variable time-series models, together with the transformation (13) can be used to provide a computationally and structurally efficient statistical characterisation of the noise residual vector ξ .

The problem of analysing each of the N time-series associated with the vector $\underline{v}_i$, $i = 1,2,\ldots,k$, is a straightforward problem of univariate time-series analysis which can be approached in a variety of different ways, including the maximum likelihood method of Astrom-Bohlin (1965) and Box-Jenkins (1970). As emphasised previously, however, this paper is concerned with a completely recursive solution to the problem and, following the tradition of previous papers, therefore, we will consider here only the recursive Approximate Maximum Likelihood (AML) method (see e.g. Young, 1971, 1972). While this restriction should not be construed as implying that this method is necessarily the best currently available recursive approach to univariate time-series analysis, it does appear to combine relatively good computational and statistical efficiency with reasonable potential for practical application.

If it is assumed that each element of the vector $\underline{v}$ has rational spectral density, then an appropriate time-series model for each of its first N ($\leqslant n$) elements is the following autoregressive-moving average (ARMA) representation which has been discussed at length by Box and Jenkins (1970)

$$C\left[z^{-1}\right]v_{ik} = D\left[z^{-1}\right]e_{ik} \tag{17}$$

or

$$v_{ik} = \frac{D\left[z^{-1}\right]}{C\left[z^{-1}\right]} e_{ik}$$

where z^{-1} is the backward shift operator, i.e. $z^{-1}v_{ik} = v_{i,k-1}$, $C\left[z^{-1}\right]$ and $D\left[z^{-1}\right]$ are polynomials in z^{-1} of the form,

$$
\begin{aligned}
C\left[z^{-1}\right] &= 1 + c_1 z^{-1} + \ldots + c_p z^{-p} \\
D\left[z^{-1}\right] &= 1 + d_1 z^{-1} + \ldots + d_p z^{-p}
\end{aligned}
\tag{18}
$$

and e_{ik} is a serially uncorrelated sequence of random variables with variance σ_i^2 ("discrete white-noise") which is assumed independent of the deterministic input vector $\underline{u}_k$, i.e.

$$E\{e_{ik}\underline{u}_j\} = 0 \quad , \quad \text{for all } i,k,j \tag{19}$$

The order $p^\dagger$ in the ARMA model (17) will not, in general, be known *a priori* and will need to be estimated in an identification phase of the analysis using either correlation methods, such as those preferred by Box and Jenkins (1970) or alternative approaches such as those discussed by Bohlin (1970).

The ARMA model (17) can be written conveniently in the following vector form

$$v_{ik} = \underline{n}_k^T \underline{c} + e_{ik} \tag{20}$$

where $\quad \underline{n}_k^T = \left[-v_{i,k-1},\ldots,-v_{i,k-p}, e_{i,k-1},\ldots,e_{i,k-p}\right]$

and $\quad c = \left[c_1,\ldots,c_p, d_1,\ldots,d_p\right]^T$

[†] Both polynomials are assumed to be of the same order for notational convenience: in practice they may, and generally will be of different order; but this can easily be accommodated by assuming that appropriate coefficients are zero.

If we now had an estimate $\hat{e}_{ik}$ of the "white noise" input e_{ik} of the noise process, it seems reasonable to assume that we could obtain a consistent estimate of the parameter vector $\underline{c}$ using normal least squares analysis applied to the model (20) with $\hat{e}_{ik}$ replacing e_{ik} . The approximate maximum likelihood (AML) algorithm is based upon this kind of reasoning: an estimate $\hat{\underline{c}}_k$ of $\underline{c}$ is obtained from the following recursive least squares algorithm,

$$\hat{\underline{c}}_k = \hat{\underline{c}}_{k-1} - k_k^n \{\hat{n}_k^T \hat{\underline{c}}_{k-1} - v_{ik}\} \qquad \text{II}(1)$$

where

$$k_k^n = P_{k-1}^n \hat{n}_k [1 + \hat{n}_k^T P_{k-1}^n \hat{n}_k]^{-1}$$

and

$$P_k^n = P_{k-1}^n - P_{k-1}^n \hat{n}_k [1 + \hat{n}_k^T P_{k-1}^n \hat{n}_k]^{-1} \hat{n}_k^T P_{k-1}^n \qquad \text{II}(2)$$

Here $\hat{n}_k$ is defined as

$$\hat{n}_k = [-v_{i,k-1} \cdots -v_{i,k-p}, \hat{e}_{i,k-1} \cdots \hat{e}_{i,k-p}]^T$$

and $\hat{e}_{ik}$ is an estimate of e_{ik} based on the current estimate $\hat{\underline{c}}_k$, i.e., from (20)

$$\hat{e}_{ik} = v_{ik} - \hat{n}_k^T \hat{\underline{c}}_k \qquad \text{II}(3)$$

As with the IV algorithm, an off-line, iterative mode of operation can be employed in which multiple passes through the data can help to enhance the statistical efficiency of the estimates.

Each of the first N ($\leqslant$ n) serially correlated random variables that characterise the transformed vector $\underline{v}_k$ can be analysed in the above manner and the result is N separate ARMA models activated by N zero mean, "white noise" inputs e_{ik} , $i = 1,2,\ldots,N$ each of which are serially uncorrelated and have variances σ_i^2 . The complete noise model is obtained by combining these separate noise representations via the transformation (13), as shown in Fig.2.

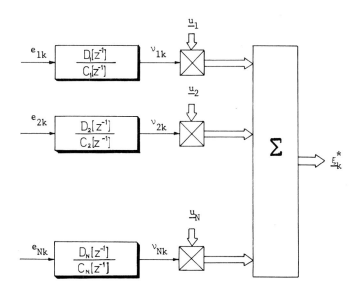

Fig. 2 Approximate Noise Model based on the K-L Expansion

5. Estimation Error Statistics

Since both the basic system and the residual noise estimation problems have been decomposed into a number of single input, single output sub-problems, it is possible to consider the estimation error statistics in terms of the results obtained in the single input, single output cases. While this may not be as theoretically satisfactory as considering the problem directly in multivariable terms, it is felt that it is acceptable for most practical purposes, especially since the recursive nature of the estimates obtained using the MIVAML approach adds an extra dimension to the estimation results by giving a visual indication of the convergence properties: for instance, collinearity problems, which occur quite often in practical estimation, become quite obvious, with certain of the recursive estimates apparently failing to converge satisfactorily, even though the residual errors may appear quite small. One can, in effect, trade the analytical niceties for a more empirical approach based on the physical properties of the recursive estimators.

Even in the single input, single output case, there are no entirely satisfactory analytical results: while both the IV and AML estimates are known to be asymptotically unbiased and consistent, it is notoriously difficult to evaluate the error covariances for both types of estimate (Young et al., 1971). In the IV case, an <u>approximation</u> to the covariance matrix $P_k(\tilde{\underline{a}}_{ik})$ of the estimation errors $\tilde{\underline{a}}_{ik} = \hat{\underline{a}}_{ik} - \underline{a}_i$ is given by

$$P_k(\tilde{\underline{a}}_{ik}) = E\{\tilde{\underline{a}}_{ik}\tilde{\underline{a}}_{ik}^T\} = q_{ii}\hat{P}_k \qquad (21)$$

where q_{ii} is the ith diagonal element of the covariance matrix Q defined in (3). Here $\hat{P}_k$ is evaluated by making an additional iterative pass through the data with the auxiliary model parameters fixed at the final estimates obtained after the iterations have converged (see Section 3). Similarly, an <u>approximation</u> to the covariance matrix of the noise parameter estimates $P_k(\tilde{\underline{c}}_{ik})$ is given by

$$P_k(\tilde{\underline{c}}_{ik}) = E\{\tilde{\underline{c}}_{ik}\tilde{\underline{c}}_{ik}^T\} = \sigma_i^2 P_k^n \qquad (22)$$

where, once again, the matrix P_k^n is obtained from a single pass through the data with the noise estimates $\hat{e}_{ik}$ generated by reference to the parameter estimates obtained after the iterations have converged. The similarity of both the results (21) and (22) with the equivalent results of linear regression analysis will be noted: this is a consequence of the similarity between the IV and AML solutions, and the regression solution.

It should be emphasised, of course, that the above results are only an approximation and should be used mainly as a guide to the relative variance of the parameter estimates. And while Monte Carlo simulation results tend to confirm that (21) and (22) often do provide a reasonable indication of the actual error variance (see e.g. Young et al., 1973), it is clear that the whole question of the statistical properties for both the IV and AML estimators needs further attention and presents an interesting and unsolved theoretical problem.

6. A Summary of the Complete MIVAML Procedure

The various stages in a multivariable dynamic system identification and estimation procedure based on the techniques described in the previous sections of this paper can be summarised as follows:
1. The form of the model (1) must first be "identified" by reference to the available data prior to parameter estimation. Although this process of identification has not been discussed in detail in the present paper, it is extremely important; there is nothing more foolhardy than attempting to obtain relatively efficient estimates of the model parameters if the form or structure of the model has not first been firmly established[†].

[†] As mentioned in the introduction, one approach to state-space model identification which appears to have good practical potential is that based on the Extended Kalman Filter methods of recursive state-parameter estimation. This approach, which is described fully by Beck (1973) and outlined by Beck and Young (1974),

/makes full use

    2. Having established a satisfactory model structure within the limitations imposed by the system representation (1), the iterative MIV method is used to estimate the basic model parameters.

    3. The recursive MIV estimates and the residual noise vector estimate $\hat{\xi}_k$ (equation (12)) are obtained from a final pass through the data with the auxiliary model parameters fixed at their final converged values.

    4. The $\hat{\xi}_k$ vector is analysed using the K-L expansion and the vector $\underline{v}_k$ of mutually uncorrelated random variables is generated by means of the K-L transformation (13).

    5. The number of significant elements of the $\underline{v}_k$ vector is assessed by reference to the quality of the $\underline{\xi}^*$ estimate in (13) for various values of N .

    6. The AML method is applied to each of the N time-series obtained in 5., yielding N separate single input, single output ARMA models.

    7. The recursive AML estimates are obtained from a final pass through the data with the $\hat{e}_{ik}$ estimates fixed at their final converged values obtained during the last iteration.

    8. The $\hat{P}_k$ and P_k^n matrices obtained in Steps 3. and 7. are used, together with estimates of q_{ii} and σ_i^2 , to evaluate the <u>approximate</u> error covariance matrices given in (21) and (22) and so determine the <u>approximate</u> standard errors on the parameter estimates.

    9. The sample covariance properties of the e_{ik} residuals are evaluated for various lags in order to assess the degree of correlation between the white noise disturbances: this provides a measure of the degree of approximation in the noise process model (see Section 7)

7. Discussion

    Before considering the application of the MIVAML procedure to a practical problem, it is worthwhile emphasising two important points about this approach to time-series analysis:

1. Although the K-L transformation ensures that the elements of the transformed vector $\underline{v}_k$ are mutually uncorrelated <u>at the same time instant</u>, it does <u>not</u> ensure that they will be uncorrelated completely: in other words, while the covariance matrix $R = E\{\underline{v}_k\underline{v}_j^T\}$ is diagonal for $k = j$, it is not necessarily diagonal for $k \neq j$. For this reason, the residual noise analysis described in Section 4 can, in general, only provide an <u>approximate</u> characterisation of the residual noise vector $\underline{\xi}$ and the analyst should always check the effectiveness of this approximation in any particular problem.

2. From the dynamic systems and control theory standpoint, the discrete-time state-space model described in Section 2 has particular significance. But the MIVAML approach is not limited to this exact type of model: it can be applied to any multivariable system which has a <u>basic</u> structure which, like the state-space model, can be broken down into the elemental row estimation sub-problems discussed in Section 3. An important example is the "reduced form" model so popular in macro-econometric modelling (see e.g. Johnson, 1963): here a vector $\underline{y}_k$ of "endogenous" or internally generated variables is related to a vector $\underline{v}_k$ of "predetermined" variables by a vector-matrix equation of the form

$$\underline{y}_k = \Pi\underline{v}_k + \underline{w}_k \tag{23}$$

where $\underline{w}_k$ is a vector of stochastic disturbances. Here the predetermined variables can consist of both "exogenous" or deterministic input variables $\underline{u}_k$ and lagged values of the endogenous variables, i.e. $\underline{y}_{k-1}, \underline{y}_{k-2}$ etc. The similarity between this model and equation (4) is obvious upon inspection: the reduced model (23) is likely to be more generally applicable, however, and can, in a certain sense, be considered as a compromise between the state-space model and the "black box" multivariable time-series models discussed, for example, by Rowe (1970).

(footnote continued from previous page)
makes full use of the recursive state and parameter estimates to assess the relative validity of various model structures.

8.   An Example: A Model for BOD-DO in a River System

The MIVAML method of time-series analysis discussed in previous sections of this paper has been tested by digital simulation and found to work satisfactorily on numerical examples. Monte Carlo assessment of the method will be carried out in due course but the results obtained so far suggest that, not surprisingly, it is quite similar in performance to the single variable IVAML method which has fairly good statistical efficiency with variances reasonably close to the Cramer-Rao minimum variance (lower) bound (see Neethling, 1974).

The first practical application of the MIVAML procedure was to the BOD-DO water quality model discussed in Section 2, using field data obtained from an 80 day experiment on a 4.7 km reach of the River Cam outside Cambridge in Eastern England. As pointed out previously, although this is only a second order model it has five inputs and, therefore, 9 unknown parameters. It will also be noted that the model is a little unusual in the sense that the A matrix parameters are time variable because of the V_m/Q_{k-1} terms. This does not cause problems in the estimation, however, since these time variable terms are merely absorbed into the definition of the terms in the structural model (9): in particular, z_k is defined differently in each elemental model; i.e. in the BOD equation case,

$$\underline{z}_k^T = \left[\frac{V_m}{Q_{k-1}} \, y_{1,k-1} \, , \, u_{1k} \, , \, S_k \right]$$
$$\underline{a}_1^T = \left[k_1 \, , \, k_2 \, , \, k_3 \right]$$

while in the DO equation case,

$$\underline{z}_k^T = \left[y_{1,k-1} \, , \, \frac{V_m}{Q_{k-1}} \, y_{2,k-1} \, , \, u_{2k} \, , \, S_k \, , \, C_{s,k} \, , \, w_k \right]$$
$$\underline{a}_2^T = \left[k_4 \, , \, k_5 \, , \, k_6 \, , \, k_7 \, , \, k_8 \, , \, k_9 \right]$$

This is yet another example of the flexibility of this approach to estimation.

Bearing in mind the suggested identification-estimation procedure described in Section 6, the model was known to be well identified because of prior analysis using the EKF. It was not surprising, therefore, that the iterative IV algorithm converged rapidly for both elemental models with no suggestion of any estimation problems such as collinearity; problems which can sometimes be encountered with multivariable models unless care is taken in the model formulation.

The final parameter estimates are given below together with their approximate standard errors (in parentheses) obtained from (21):

k_1 = 0.36 (0.1)   ; k_2 = 0.27 (0.03)   ; k_3 = 0.43 (0.07)

k_4 = -0.25 (0.07) ; k_5 = -0.26 (0.06) ; k_6 = 0.33 (0.03)

k_7 = 0.84 (0.17) ; k_8 = 0.1 (0.17)   ; k_9 (not estimated in this case due to absence of weirs in reach)

The recursive estimates obtained in the final pass through the data showed little tendency to vary over the observation interval, thus further verifying the efficacy of the model identification.

In this case, the K-L expansion technique indicated a transformation matrix U defined as

$$U = \begin{bmatrix} 0.93 & 0.36 \\ -0.36 & 0.93 \end{bmatrix}$$

and AML analysis of the resultant transformed time-series yielded the following simple autoregressive models:

$$v_{1k} = \frac{1}{1-0.47 \, z^{-1}} \, e_{1k}$$

$$\nu_{2k} = \frac{1}{1-0.43\,z^{-1}}\,e_{2k}$$

Since it was only necessary here to analyse two noise series, the K-L approximation (14) was not applied.

The final model simulation is shown in Fig.3: here the basic model output is first enhanced by residual noise forecasts using the noise models given above and then compared with the observed data. This result is a considerable improvement over earlier continuous-time models obtained by EKF analysis (see Whitehead and Young, 1974).

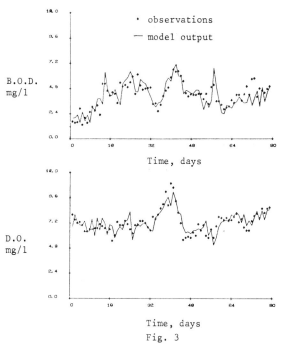

Fig. 3

Finally it should be noted that this same MIVAML procedure has since been applied to data collected from a number of reaches of the Bedford-Ouse River System in Central-Eastern England and has yielded a satisfactory model for BOD-DO in the whole of a 55 km stretch of the river between Milton Keynes and Bedford (Whitehead and Young, 1974).

9. Conclusions

This paper has described a recursive approach to multivariable time-series analysis based on an extension of the earlier single input, single output Instrumental Variable-Approximate Maximum Likelihood (IVAML) procedures that have proved so useful in practical applications. Although for convenience and clarity this new technique has been described within the context of identifying and estimating discrete-time, state-space system models, it can be applied to other discrete-time models of a similar basic structure, such as the "reduced form" equations favoured by econometricians. In addition, while the technique depends for its success on a number of largely heuristic approximations, it is felt that it still has good potential for practical application because of its overall simplicity and ruggedness combined with reasonable statistical efficiency. This potential has been demonstrated in the results of a practical example concerned with the modelling of water quality in a reach of a non-tidal river system.

References

Astrom, K.J. and Bohlin, T. (1965), IFAC Symposium Teddington, England. In Theory of Self Adaptive Control Systems (P.H. Hammond, Ed.) Plenum Press, 1966, pp.145-165

Beck, M.B. (1973), Ph.D. Thesis, Dept. of Engineering, University of Cambridge

Bohlin, T. (1970), IBM Jnl. of Res. and Dev., Vol.14, pp.41-51

Beck, M.B. and Young, P.C. (1974) in preparation

Box, G. and Jenkins, G.M. (1970), Time-series Analysis, Forecasting and Control, Holden Day: 1970

Chan, Y.T. (1973), Identification and System Parameter Estimation, Part 1 (P. Eykhoff, Ed.) North Holland/Americal Elsevier: 1973

Chien, Y.T. and Fu, K.S. (1967), IEEE Trans. on Inf. Theory, Vol.IT15, p.518

Dorf, R.C. (1965), Time Domain Analysis and Design of Control Systems, Addison-Wesley: 1965

Durbin, J. (1954), Rev.Int.Stat.Inst., Vol.22, pp.23-32

Isermann, R., Baur, U., Bamberger, W., Kneppo, P. and Siebert, H. (1973), Identification and System Parameter Estimation (P. Eykhoff, Ed.) North Holland/American Elsevier: 1973

Johnston, J. (1963), Econometric Methods, McGraw-Hill: 1963

Kendall, M.G. and Stuart, A. (1961), Advanced Theory of Statistics, Griffin: 1961

Kittler, J. and Young, P.C. (1973), Pattern Recognition, Vol.5, pp.335-352

Neethling, C.G. (1974), Ph.D. Thesis, Dept. of Engineering, University of Cambridge, to appear shortly

Rowe, I.H. (1970), Int.Jnl. of Control, Vol.12, No.5, pp.721-738

Whitehead, P.G. and Young, P.C. (1974), Proceedings of IFIP Working Conference on Modelling and Simulation of Water Resource Systems, Ghent, 1974

Wong, K.Y. and Polak, E. (1967), IEEE Trans. on Automatic Control, Vol.AC-12, p.698

Young, P.C. (1965), IFAC Symposium Teddington. In Theory of Self Adaptive Control Systems (P.H. Hammond, Ed.), Plenum Press: 1966

Young, P.C. (1968), Simulation, Vol.10, No.3

Young, P.C. (1969), Preprints 4th IFAC Congress (Warsaw), Session 26, p.121

Young, P.C. (1970), Automatica, Vol.6, No.2, p.271

Young, P.C., Shellswell, S.H., Neethling, C.G. (1971), Tech. Report, Dept. of Engineering, Univ. of Cambridge, No.CUED/B-Control/TR16

Young, P.C. (1972), IEEE Trans. on Automatic Control, Vol.AC-17, No.2, pp.269-270

Young, P.C., Naughton, J., Neethling, C.G. and Shellswell, S.H. (1973), Identification and System Parameter Estimation, Part 1 (P. Eykhoff, Ed.) North Holland/American Elsevier: 1973

Young, P.C. (1974), Bull.Inst. of Math. and its App. (IMA), Vol.10, No's.5/6, pp.209-224

Young, P.C. (1974), Automatica (in press to appear Sept. 1974)

DISCUSSION

What's the ratio between the number of parameters you have to estimate and the number of data you have ? (TODINI)

There were four parameters in the basic model and two in the noise model. That's six total parameters and 365 data. (YOUNG)

So I can understand that noise and residuals are almost Gaussian. (TODINI)

Did you have any correlation between sunlight and water temperature ?
(DAVIDSON)

Yes, there was some correlation between sunlight and water temperature.
(YOUNG)

Did you have the parameters of your BOD-model as a function of temperature ?
(DAVIDSON)

No, I didn't. Because everyday the temperature didn't vary that much ; moreover the data were pretty noisy. The BOD are not very nice measurements to do anyway. (YOUNG)

What was the temperature change ? (DAVIDSON)

I think that we worked between fifteen and twenty degrees centigrade. So, we recognize that the parameters are function of temperature, but in an actual river, you cannot start with this assumption. You have to look at data, and analyse them, you will come to a conclusion. It is very likely that this will be a function of temperature. But the evidence I have seen up to now does not make that abundantly clear. The fact that we used it over a summer period, when the temperature didn't vary much, perhaps explains why our parameters didn't give any tendance to vary very much. (YOUNG)

Well, the diameter variations are very strong when you integrate these over 365 days, the cumulative effect is enormous. (DAVIDSON)

We are using day by day data. We are looking at the essence of daily data. The diameter variations are accounted for in other ways, namely in long term assessements of the diameter effects. It's the nature of the model suiting to the nature of your problem. We did not look into the diameter effects. If we had done clearly we should have been more complete. However this is a situation where you cannot be complete. There is not only one model, there is a whole class of models, some of which more complicated than others. However, you have to make a compromise between the degree of complexity and the amount of data.
You can get to the point where you put too much detail in the model considering the amount of data. It is a fit as fitting a polynomial to a piece of data. You can always do better by taking more terms but it is extremely dangerous if you go outside the interval. You should fit the data to the degree of confidence you have in that data and no more. (YOUNG)

How well do the models take into account possible errors in the input data because, if I'm looking at these two models, it appears that u is considered to be an exactly known function. (NEUMAN)

Yes, the point of that is, if you put in u as a measured function with error, the analysis becomes very difficult. And this means that you have to find out the statistics of multivariables which is in practice very difficult. Any mathematical method has its assumptions, assumption here, is that you know these

data exactly.
Since you don't, you always have to be aware of this fact, as you go along.   (YOUNG)

May I make a brief comment on that. I think it is an important point that is raised here. It may be more than a question of errors.
It is quite true that it makes the estimation problem much more complex, and much more nonlinear, but on the other hand, very often you may have to allow to stimulate your system otherwise than what you are assuming, and in many problems assuming, and perhaps even estimating, for example the intensity of it in some alternative sense gives you somewhat more consistent estimates.   (BALAKRISHNAN)

The point is that when you are assessing the results, you take into account all the facts that you know about, some of these are not quantifiable in estimates, but are quantifiable in qualitative assessing.   (YOUNG)

For example if the estimates are negative while the number has to be positive.   (BALAKRISHNAN)

That's right. In this particular case you know that there are errors. What you are looking for, is significant output effects not due to the inputs, to see if you can account for them in various ways. We feel learning, everything in mind, we think that at the end we get a model that is reasonable, namely, which explains what we see to a degree that is acceptable. But it's always possible to somebody to come up and say, you did it wrong.   (YOUNG)

The question of this is left to the customer.   (BALAKRISHNAN)

That's right. The customer often dictates the things.
The customer can say : I don't want a model, I only want to know what this particular detail does, so the econometrician has to throw away his thinking of the rest if he wants to get the money, he must try to have the detail in it.   (YOUNG)

Did you put light and dark bottle tests before the synthesis in the string.
(DAVIDSON)

This sort of detection of algae was something we had not expected.   (YOUNG)

In a specific river in New Jersey, which is very similar in size and degree of pollution as you were talking about, we found with actual field measurement that about 30 % of the algae oxygen body B.O.D. equation is due to the fotosynthesis behaviour, so you have to take this into account and I think you have to confirm that effect with the light and dark bottle test.   (DAVIDSON)

You've always to go up against cost limitations and so on. A more sophisticated analysis now at this time is certainly worthwhile. From previous things that I have done in other areas it seems reasonable to assume that, or suspect that, there are some light effects, and take that into account.   (YOUNG)

Did you also correlate with flow rate ? Because if you increase your flow rate, you change the depth of your aquatic zone and inversely affect your balance.
(DAVIDSON)

Yes, this comes in the equation, because you remember it's a state equation, and there are inputs coming in, so that you do get the flow effects coming into the model in that way.   (YOUNG)

What was the time base of your data ?   (VAN DER BEKEN)

The measurements were daily measurements.   (YOUNG)

Did you incorporate logarithmic transformation ?   (VAN DER BEKEN)

We did not find it necessary.   (YOUNG)

Can you give some indication, Peter, of the signal to noise ratio ? Just give a quantitative feel for it of your input output measurement.

The difficulty in answering that is what do we mean by signal to noise ratio. Usually we mean the "measurement" noise over the signal-noise variance. But remember at the output here we have noise due to disturbances. Therefore, all I can say is to look at the last plot, and see that in fact we are accounting for the data in that way. The residuals are an indication of where you haven't accounted for it.:. And that may be due to the badness of our models, as well as to disturbances. So you have to be very careful. Paul Whitehead will show you some other results of the Bedford-Ouse River system where the BOD was much lower and therefore much more difficult to measure accurately, and you will see straight away this comes out if you look at the slides.   (YOUNG)

Do you need a nice variance on the estimate ?   (BALAKRISHNAN)

No, I don't think so. One thing we were starting off with the assumption that with the created instrumental variable we didn't need to use that. But we don't model the noise and therefore we do have bad information at the end and we find that in fact the match to the data is much better than if you put noise into it. For the Bedford-Ouse system I'm a little bit worried on the count that it fitted the data too well, because I know that BOD is difficult to measure. (YOUNG)

Can you mention the importance of the stochastic effects in estimating this run-off model. Can you tell us something about the sources of the stochastic effects ?   (ISERMAN)

This is a very difficult question : I think we would better ask   people in the audience, what they think the sources would be, I think they would give better answers than me, because they know a lot more about the system than I do. You can measure the flow, you can measure the rainfall, and try to account for it, and what is left over are those effects, which you haven't thought about. If you see a consistent pattern, I think you should look to where that pattern is coming from, and that is what happened to us.   (YOUNG)

In New Jersey again we found very similar plots for the BOD. We also found unrecorded sources of BOD. Contributing in part of 50 % with the BOD in the river, and I don't know how honest the people are in England versus those in the U.S.A., but there are a lot of unrecorded sources and you have to try to attempt to get a hand on the unrecorded runoff.   (DAVIDSON)

I like to comment on this, because in fact the whole time the river authorities have been working with us, they asked about this sort of thing.   (YOUNG)

Could you tell me - maybe this is off the subject, going into politics - how do you think to prevent the pollution of the river ? What contribution is your work going to make, what decisions are going to be effected by convincing people what you're doing ?
I know that we often work in a box, and satisfy each other and so forth, but when we try progress in words, there is decrepancy between disciplines, politics, engineering, mathematics. I am curious to know what role you are going to play in the over all decision makers. You know the rivers are going to be polluted, there's no question about it.   (DAVIDSON)

The first idea here is to look to the feasibility of modeling ; in fact a purely scientific goal. Secondly, the river authorities can effectively use this model to assess what will happen in the future. However there are some great dangers in doing that. By modeling the system you like to get a better understanding of the dynamics of water quality in the river, such that some more quantitative features can be calculated. This can be used in specifying the degree of treatment that the river needs. This is the sort of thing that can be done. (YOUNG)

It seems to me that biology has accidently come to this model through sunlight. You know there is a certain amount of wisdom in the good books, which should have led to the initial model taking account of such processes. It seems to me it's a very expensive way of discovering what is known. It seems to me that by the time that this particular stretch of river has the benefit of what to 1/4 million of people would really happen to know there would be quite a quantum change in the biology of the river, and it seems to me that, although it's an interesting exercise which is being performed, until studies on this fully involved biological problem have been made, we run the risk of sometimes being accused by somebody of playing games. (PHILIP)

I think, that is a very important point and the answer is not easy.
First thing is, I found a very good reference written in the early sixties. However there are many, many books. We found that reference after we had seen the effect.
Remember, we are not biologists. We take the advice of biologists. If these biologists know about this they don't tell us about it, so what do we do ?
The second point is that of course you write it in a reduced form. When you know the river in much more detail, you get this problem. Isn't doing something better than doing nothing ? And I cannot say that the detailed biological models are remarkably successful in applications, that is, actually achieving anything. There are a lot of theoretical biological models, which are naturally against very restrictive circumstances.
And I do criticize those models in these directions, as you can criticize the other models in the other direction. There is no absolute answer, there is no purity, when you're dealing with models. (YOUNG)

I'm not criticizing any particular model, I'm really making it plain that there has to be an intelligent and informed interdisciplinary effort before a model can expect the customer to take it seriously and to act on it. (PHILIP)

Well, this is relative and subjective. I don't really see the point you're making except in very general terms, namely you can never model things exactly. (YOUNG)

I just think the perturbation that seems stochastic from the point of view of one discipline, is in fact deterministic when you bring in the appropriate discipline and bridge over the crevasse that I've found here mentioned. (HILLEL)

It is better to bridge that crevasse; we know we have brought certain points out and the biologists are looking at them. You tell me where the publications are that are reasonably obtainable, but the details on these things have not been tested and validated against data in the field. That's the point. It does not exist. If they exist, it is very difficult to get them. (YOUNG)

*How many parameters did you have to identify, to get the response function ?
(NEUMAN)*

Three parameters. (YOUNG)

Now the question I would ask is : suppose that you're trying to identify this response function, say, by a method such as least squares or some other method, do you think that you would get a model which could perform in a much lower quality, than your stochastic model. I come to this question, how good is a stochastic model of this kind versus a linear or a nonlinear deterministic model ? (NEUMAN)

Will you take the flows, we can quantify this. We cannot know its quality, there are not that many studies that have been done on that subject. This was

slightly better than the comparable compartmental model, which had about 30 parameters. (YOUNG)

If you change the structure of your system just trying to obtain a response function without going into the details of how your system operates, perhaps you would be able to obtain a more general response function ; which performs better. (NEUMAN)

There is always this possibility. The reason we tried these models is, because analytically, they are in a form we can use in other studies which we might introduce using these models for, for instance control studies.
So, these models are very useful in those terms, straight away other models are not so useful, so you look at the particular model that's useful for what you take the model for. (YOUNG)

This is a very innocent question. Have you come up starting from the particular stretch of river, with anything which is very general that can be applied to any other river, under different environmental conditions, or under nearly the same conditions ? How specific is your model ? (HILLEL)

We are modeling a river system in given environmental circumstances. Now, if you want a river system in Australia, don't expect this model to apply necessarily, but there is a possibility that it will have different sources for the coefficients. (YOUNG)

Will you agree with me that its · chances to apply into Australia are proportional to how deterministic the model is. (HILLEL)

No, I would disagree with that. The fact that you can build a bigger and bigger deterministic model in more and more detail does not mean that it would necessarily apply any better than a stochastic model. (YOUNG)

I think when Peter said deterministic he meant mechanistic model, one based on first principals, based on pure science, and then I would agree. (DAVIDSON)

But it must have stochastic aspects ; if no random inputs and aspects occur I could agree with that. (YOUNG)

We made an attempt to put together the largest interdisciplinary group to study the Delaware river estuary system and it failed. It gets too big an interdisciplinary project : we had over 4 institutions, 4 states, 55 principal investigations, over 200 graduate students and multimillion dollars support. The grant lasted for 2 years and went to zero because of the energy crisis. It was failing before the energy crisis because of lack of communication : meet together to discuss things, even though we considered some of the best experts in the world on topics of biology, etc. We needed something more than just experts ! (DAVIDSON)

I was wondering about the structure of your model. I mean that P matrix which you called that variance-covariance matrix of the estimates. Are you estimating even the coefficients of this matrix ?

No, only in the sense that all estimation mechanisms which have a reasonable degree of sophistication come up with an estimate in the covariance matrix. (YOUNG)

You are speaking about peaking errors and the error of the model. I suppose that they have different statistical properties, peaking errors being always more correlated than errors in the model.

You have an estimate of covariance nature. We then look at the residuals, and we crosscorrelate the inputs to see if there is a correlation between the residuals and the inputs, which we assume there is not. (YOUNG)

Modeling and Simulation of Water Resources Systems, G.C. VANSTEENKISTE, (Ed.)
North-Holland Publishing Company (1975)

ROLE OF SUBJECTIVE VALUE JUDGEMENT IN PARAMETER IDENTIFICATION

Shlomo P. Neuman
Institute of Soils and Water
Agricultural Research Organization
P.O. Box 6,
Bet Dagan, ISRAEL

ABSTRACT

A theoretical analysis of the inverse problem associated with a continuous
model of groundwater flow indicates that, in general, the solution to this
problem is nonunique and is extremely sensitive to minor errors in the model and the data. In particular, low-amplitude random errors in the piezometric data tend to cause severe spatial oscillations in the parameters of
the model, thereby making it impossible to solve the inverse problem by
classical mathematical methods. A similar difficulty is encountered when
the flow equations are discretized in space by a numerical scheme such as
the finite difference or finite element methods. To ensure consistency
between the algebraic equations arising from the numerical method and the
data entering into the model, a solution to the discrete inverse problem
is often sought by minimizing a functional of the residual errors. It is
shown that this by no means eliminates the difficulties arising from nonuniqueness and sensitivity to errors in the data and therefore, an approach
based on the minimization of a single error-functional does not, in general
lead to satisfactory results. In order to obtain a meaningful solution it
is necessary to introduce additional criteria reflecting the modeler's subjective view point as to the most plausible shape of the solution surface.
Since these plausibility criteria are based on prior assumptions about the
spatial variation of the parameters, their use can be viewed in the context of a Bayesian philosophy. The absolute need to rely on such prior assumptions in dealing with the inverse problem means that information obtained from direct field and laboratory tests on the system to be simulated
is of vital importance to the parameter identification process. After selecting the proper plausibility criteria, a continuous or discrete set of
alternative solutions to the inverse problem is generated automatically
with the aid of mathematical programming techniques, and at this stage the
modeler is again asked to use his own value judgement in selecting a particular set of parameters from the available alternatives. The modeler
should base his decision on all available information on the flow system
as well as on the environmental conditions under which this system is expected to operate in the future. Since these considerations are difficult
to quantify, the final selection process must be performed subjectively
by the modeler and it cannot be done automatically without a risk. A post-
optimal sensitivity analysis is suggested as a means of ascertaining the
reliability of each individual parameter obtained in this manner. Examples
are given to show how the multicriterion approach can be implemented by
applying parametric linear programming to a finite element model of steady
state groundwater flow in a locally anisotropic system.

INTRODUCTION

Numerical models of subsurface flow are rapidly gaining importance in scientific investigations as well as in the control and management of the subsurface environment. However, such models are often difficult to apply under realistic field conditions due to a lack of sufficient information about the parameters entering into the model. For example, a two-dimensional model of steady state groundwater flow in an aquifer requires that the spatial distribution of the hydraulic conductivities be known with a sufficient accuracy. Usually, direct field and laboratory measurements provide only scattered and inaccurate information about the spatial distribution of these parameters. The question then arises, is there an indirect manner of supplementing our information about the parameters by analyzing the response of the flow system to certain known or partly known inputs ? For example, can the conductivities of the aquifer be determined from the steady state distribution of hydraulic heads as measured in a number of wells, given some knowledge of the boundary conditions (e.g. inflow rates) which cause this particular distribution ?

The problem of determining the parameters by analyzing the response of the system is referred to as the "calibration", "inverse", or "parameter identification" problem. The most common approach to the calibration of subsurface flow models is to rely on an ad-hoc trial and error procedure. However, there have been in recent years several attempts at developing a more rational attitude to this question. This has led to the development of various automatic calibration techniques which can be broadly classified as being either "indirect" or "direct". The indirect approach is essentially an automatic trial and error procedure that seeks to improve an existing estimate of the parameters in an iterative manner until the model response is "sufficiently close" to that of the real system. This improvement can be accomplished with the aid of empirical criteria [Kruger, 1961] or by formal mathematical procedures [Jacquard and Jain, 1965 ; Jahns, 1966 ; Vemuri and Karplus, 1969 ; Vemuri et al., 1969 ; Coats et al., 1970 ; Dupuy et al., 1971 ; Slater and Durer, 1971 ; Robinson, 1972 ; Addison et al., 1972 ; and knowles et al., 1972]. Special methods for dealing with very large systems have also been developed [Haimes et al., 1968 ; Wismer et al., 1970 ; Labidie, 1970 ; Lovell, 1971 ; Lovell et al., 1972].

The indirect approach consists of the following essential features. After an initial estimate of the parameters is obtained, a complete simulation run is performed, and the computed output is compared with that measured in the real system. If these two sets of outputs are sufficiently close so that a prescribed performance criterion is met, the procedure is terminated, and the current estimate of the parameters is adopted for the model. Otherwise, the parameters are corrected according to a predetermined policy, a new simulation run is performed, and the procedure continues iteratively in the same manner as it did before. Various indirect methods differ from each other primarily in the manner in which the parameters are adjusted during each iteration and in the criteria by which the performance of the model is measured. It is important to recognize that since each iterative cycle requires the performance of a complete simulation run, the indirect approach tends to be computationally inefficient.

The direct approach is different in that it treats the model parameters as dependent variables in a formally posed "inverse" boundary value problem. As will be discussed below, the latter problem is often improperly posed in the sense of Haddamard [Lavrentiev, 1967], but it can nevertheless be solved under certain restricted conditions. As this approach does not require repeated simulation runs, it tends to be faster than the indirect approach. The works of Stallman [1956], Nelson [1968], Nelson and McCollum [1969], Kleinecke [1971], Hefez [1972], Robinson [1972], Frind and Pinder [1973], Cole [1973], Nutbrown [1973], and Sagar et al. [1973] are examples of direct solutions to the inverse problem.

In all the methods mentioned so far an "optimal" set of parameters is obtained by minimizing a single error-criterion. However, later it will be demonstrated that this particular set of parameters does not in general optimize the predictive capabilities of the model. Moreover, there is an infinite number of near-optimal solutions to the inverse problem which differ markedly from the "optimal" solution and yet may lead to a much better predictive model. To discover these solutions, it is necessary to measure the quality of the final results in terms of additional criteria which are based on prior assumptions about the desired shape of the solution surface. Such assumptions are necessarily subjective and they reflect the modeler's personal viewpoint as to the most reasonable representation of the system to be simulated. Thus, the process of parameter identification must be viewed as a multicriterion decision process in which the subjective value judgement of the modeler plays an important role.

Emsellem and de Marsily [1971] were the first workers who recognized the need to define multiple criteria in dealing with the identification problem. Their approach is to minimize a functional of the residual errors in a direct formulation of the inverse problem while at the same time trying to maintain the solution surface as uniform (flat) as possible over the entire flow region. Here the first criterion represents a cumulative material balance error and the second criterion assumes that a uniform solution surface is physically more plausible than other shapes. Their approach is gradually to decrease the material balance error-functional by relaxing a certain measure of uniformity until a point is reached where further relaxation of this measure does not cause any substantial reduction in the value of the error-functional.

A central theme of the present paper is the recognition that, to obtain a valid solution to the inverse problem one must not avoid dealing with multiple criteria. The discussion centers around steady state groundwater flow in a locally anisotropic system but it is relevant to nonsteady flow as well. We start by examining in some detail the causes for nonuniqueness and uncertainty characterizing the inverse problem. After examining various error and plausibility criteria, we use parametric linear programming in conjunction with a finite element model of the flow system to demonstrate the need for relying on multiple criteria and hence on subjective judgement. The parametric programming procedure generates an infinite number of alternative solutions to the inverse problem, and we show that the process of selecting a particular solution can be quantified and made automatic only at a considerable risk. The final selection, just like the choice of plausibility criteria, must be done subjectively by the modeler. His choice must be based on all available information about the groundwater system as well as on the range of environmental conditions under which this system is expected to operate in the future.

NONUNIQUENESS AND UNCERTAINTY

Continuous inverse problem : The steady flow of groundwater in an anisotropic two-dimensional region, R, can be described by the following set of equations :

$$\frac{\partial}{\partial x_i} (K_{ij} \frac{\partial h}{\partial x_j}) - q = 0 \qquad \text{in R} \qquad (1)$$

$$h = H \qquad \text{on} \quad \Gamma_1 \qquad (2)$$

$$K_{ij} \frac{\partial h}{\partial x_j} n_i = - V \quad \text{on} \quad \Gamma_2 \qquad (3)$$

where Γ_1 and Γ_2 are complementary segments of the boundary, Γ, and H and V are prescribed functions of x. Equations 1 and 2 define a Dirichlet problem, (1) and (3) define a Neumann problem, and the combination of all three equations is known as a mixed boundary value problem. The reader is referred to the Notation for a definition of all symbols appearing in the text.

A classical inverse problem is one in which $\partial h/\partial x_j$ and q are known, whereas the terms K_{ij} are unknown continuous functions of x_j. Equation 1 then becomes a linear first-order (hyperbolic) partial differential equation in terms of the dependent variables K_{ij}. If there are N different variables K_{ij}, there must be a system of N independent first-order equations; otherwise, the problem does not have a unique solution [Forsythe and Wasow, 1960]. Thus, a necessary prerequisite for obtaining a unique solution to the continuous inverse problem is that there be N independent sets of data $\partial h/\partial x_j$, q, H, and V.

Another important requirement is that each dependent variable K_{ij} be associated with at least one nonzero coefficient $\partial h/\partial x_i$ at each point x_i in the flow region. Otherwise, the system of equations is insensitive to the value of K_{ij} at x_i, and therefore the solution is not unique at this particular point.

Suppose that both of the above requirements are satisfied and we have N independent sets of equations that are sensitive to K_{ij} at all points x_i. Then each solution K_{ij} of these N equations can be represented by a one-parameter family of curves, known as characteristics, and the number of characteristics passing through any given point is equal to N. If values of K_{ij} are prescribed on a given surface within the flow region, these so called "Cauchy data" uniquely determine the values of the solution at all points on the characteristics passing through that surface. The projection of these characteristics into the flow region is referred to as the range of influence of this surface; the part of this surface cut out by characteristics emanating from a specific section of the solution is known as the domain of dependence of that section [Garabedian, 1964]. It follows that the resulting Cauchy problem is properly posed (i.e., a solution exists, is unique, and depends continuously on the data) only in those parts of the flow region whose domain of dependence coincides with the available Cauchy data. On the other hand, data prescribed at more than one point along a characteristic are superfluous because their range of influence is limited to this particular characteristic.

In the special case when the system is isotropic the characteristics coincide with the flow lines. Here the Cauchy problem is properly posed only along those characteristics crossing a prescribed flux boundary Γ_2 because there the values of K are prescribed by (3). Since the Dirichlet problem does not include such boundaries, the associated Cauchy problem is nowhere properly posed. On the other hand, the Neumann problem provides more information than is necessary to solve the Cauchy problem, and the mixed boundary value problem may fall anywhere between these two extreme situations. In practice, the amount of available Cauchy data (V in equation 3 or the associated values of K_{ij}) is usually very small, and therefore the inverse problem is not everywhere properly posed.

The data entering into the inverse problem represent imprecise measurements and processed information providing a distorted picture of the system's true state. In the case where K_{ij} is known and one is solving the problem for h, the solution is not overly sensitive to errors in the data and one may therefore be justified in disregarding these errors. Unfortunately, the same does not hold true for the inverse problem, the solution of which is extremely sensitive to minor fluctuations in the accuracy of the data. We illustrate both of these points by a simple one-dimensional example.

Consider the problem where $K(x)$ is given and $\partial/\partial x\ (K\ \partial h/\partial x) = 0$ is to be solved for $h(x)$, subject to the mixed boundary conditions $h = h_o$ at $x = 0$ and $K\ \partial h/\partial x = q_L$ at $x = L$. Integrating twice and taking account of the boundary conditions we find that the solution has the form

$$h(x) = q_L \int_0^x \frac{dx}{K(x)} + h_o \tag{4}$$

Suppose now that the true function $K(x)$ is unknown and one is given instead another function, $K^*(x) = K(x) + \varepsilon(x)$, where $\varepsilon(x)$ is a random error depending on x. This leads to an inexact solution which can be expressed as

$$h^*(x) = q_L \int_0^x \frac{dx}{K(x) + \varepsilon(x)} + h_o \tag{5}$$

If $K(x) \neq 0$ and ε is sufficiently small so that $\mid K(x) \mid - \mid \varepsilon(x) \mid \geqslant \lambda$ for all x where λ is a positive constant then

$$\mid h - h^* \mid = \mid q_L \mid \int_0^x \mid \frac{\varepsilon}{K(K+\varepsilon)} \mid dx \leqslant M \max_x \mid \varepsilon \mid \tag{6}$$

where the constant M is given by

$$M = \frac{\mid q_L \mid}{\lambda} \max_x \int_0^x \frac{dx}{\mid K \mid}$$

This means that the absolute error in the value of head at any x is bounded and it can be made arbitrarily small simply by controlling $\max \mid \varepsilon \mid$. In other words, the smaller is the error in the data, $K^*(x)$, the smaller is the error in the solution, $h^*(x)$.

Consider now the inverse problem where $h(x)$ is given and $\partial/\partial x(K\ \partial h/\partial x) = 0$ is to be solved for $K(x)$, subject to the Cauchy condition $K\ \partial h/\partial x = q_L$ at $x = L$. Integrating and taking account of the Cauchy condition we find that the solution has the form

$$K(x) = \frac{q_L}{\partial h/\partial x} \tag{7}$$

Suppose that the true function $h(x)$ is unknown and one is given instead another function, $h^*(x) = h(x) + \varepsilon(x)$, where $\varepsilon(x)$ is again a random error depending on x. This leads to an inexact solution

$$K^*(x) = \frac{q_L}{\partial h/\partial x + \partial\varepsilon/\partial x} \tag{8}$$

the absolute error of which is given by

$$\mid K - K^* \mid = \mid q_L \mid \mid \frac{\partial\varepsilon}{\partial x} \mid / \mid \frac{\partial h}{\partial x} (\frac{\partial h}{\partial x} + \frac{\partial\varepsilon}{\partial x}) \mid \tag{9}$$

Here the absolute error in the value of K depends not on ε but on the derivative of ε with respect to x. Even if the errors in the data, ε, are small, their derivatives may be very large, and therefore $| \text{ K } - \text{K}^* |$ may also be very large. Furthermore, since ε is random it will tend to oscillate around h, thereby causing severe spatial oscillations in the value of K^*. In other words, low amplitude oscillations in the data, $h_*(x)$, will generate severe oscillations in the solution to the inverse problem, $\text{K}^*(x)$.

In addition to errors in the data one must also consider modeling errors due to our inability to describe accurately the true behavior of the system. Thus, equation 1 is nowhere exactly correct and it should therefore be rewritten in the form

$$\frac{\partial}{\partial x_i} \left(K_{ij} \frac{\partial h}{\partial x_j} \right) - q = \mu \qquad (10)$$

where μ is a residual error resulting from inaccuracies in the model as well as in the data. The causes for these errors in any given system are not known with certainty, and the magnitude as well as the distribution of μ are completely unknown in most cases. Thus, there are an infinite number of possible solutions to the inverse problem, each solution being associated with a different function $\mu(x_i)$. We saw in the previous paragraph that by arbitrarily setting μ equal to zero at all values of x_i, as is done for example by Frind and Pinder [1973], one may obtain meaningless results due to errors in the data even though the solution may appear to be unique. The same holds true for methods which seek a solution by minimizing some functional of the residual errors μ; these methods merely take into account inconsistencies between different sets of data entering into the inverse problem (for example, between different piezometric surfaces corresponding to various boundary conditions imposed on a given system), but they do little to eliminate the negative effect that errors in the data have on the shape of the solution surface.

We may therefore say that our uncertainty regarding the correct way of associating the residual errors with the governing partial differential equation at each point x_i, and for every set of data, is probably the single most important reason why the solution to the identification problem is inherently nonunique. Later we will show that this uncertainty can be partly overcome by making some prior assumptions regarding the desired shape of the solution surface.

Discrete Inverse Problem : When (1)-(3) are solved numerically by a grid method such as finite difference or finite element, an additional truncation or discretization error is introduced at each nodal point in the grid. Let us approximate (1)-(3) with the aid of the finite element method, and let μ_n be the total residual error at the nth node. This leads to a system of N linear algebraic equations,

$$A_{nk}(K_{xx})_m + B_{nk}(K_{xy})_m + C_{nk}(K_{yy})_m + D_{n\ell}q_\ell - Q_n = \mu_n \qquad (11)$$

$$n = 1, 2, \ldots, N \qquad \begin{array}{l} m = 1, 2, \ldots, M \\ \ell = 1, 2, \ldots, L \end{array}$$

where N is the number of nodes, M is the number of subregions (including one or more elements) having different values of K_{ij}, and L is the number of subregions having different values of q. The matrices A, B, C, D and the vector Q are defined in the appendix.

We mentioned earlier that an insufficient amount of Cauchy data may lead to nonuniqueness in the continuous inverse problem. In the discrete problem represented by (11) the parameters are assumed to remain constant within each element of the grid. Consider a particular element, e, in an isotropic system, and assume that a characteristic (i.e., a flow line) with well-defined Cauchy data passes through this particular element. This uniquely determines the value of K in e, and the latter value of K in turn plays the role of Cauchy data for all other characteristics passing through the element e. Thus, the elements (or cells if a finite difference approach is used) serve as transmitters of Cauchy information from one characteristic to another until the entire flow region may be influenced. This phenomenon of the cross-characteristic influence of Cauchy data has been previously demonstrated by Neuman [1973] and will be illustrated again later in the text. It is of enormous practical importance because it greatly reduces the amount of Cauchy data required for solving the discrete inverse problem. Sometimes it is enough to provide such data only at one node, and the problem can be solved uniquely provided that all other causes for nonuniqueness have been eliminated.

MINIMIZATION OF RESIDUAL ERRORS

When the number of unknown parameters in (11), $3M + L$, is less than the number of equations, N, the system is underdetermined. In this case one can find an infinite number of solutions to the inverse problem, all of which satisfy (11) exactly so that the residual errors, μ_n, vanish for all values of n.

When $3M+L=N$, (11) forms a system of N simultaneous algebraic equations in N unknowns. Here one can always find at least one set of parameters which satisfy (11) exactly so that $\mu = 0$ for all n. If a sufficient amount of Cauchy data has been defined by specifying the fluxes, Q_n, in a manner which guarantees that the entire flow region is influenced, then the solution may be unique (although it may exhibit severe spatial oscillations due to errors in the data, thereby being physically meaningless). However, the amount of available Cauchy data is often less than that required for uniqueness and therefore, one may obtain an infinite number of solutions, all of which correspond to zero residual errors in (11).

More interesting from a practical standpoint is the case where the number of unknown parameters exceeds the number of equations (i.e. $3M+L > N$ in (11)) so that the problem becomes overdetermined. Since the data include errors, one will almost never be able to find a set of parameters that would satisfy all of equations 11 exactly such that $\mu = 0$ for all n. Here the usual approach is to seek maximum consistency between the parameters and the error-affected governing equations by minimizing some functional of the residual errors, known also as calibration or error criterion. The choice of any particular form for this functional involves an explicit or implicit assumption regarding the distribution of the residual errors. Since this distribution is generally unknown, the choice of a calibration criterion is usually a matter of convenience and personal taste.

For calibration of our finite element model, (11) is rewritten in the form

$$\left| A_{nm}(K_{xx})_m + B_{nm}(K_{xy})_m + C_{nm}(K_{yy})_m + D_{n\ell}q_\ell - Q_n \right| \leq \varepsilon_n \qquad (12)$$

$$n = 1, 2, \ldots, N \qquad m = 1, 2, \ldots, M$$
$$\ell = 1, 2, \ldots, L$$

where $\varepsilon_n \geq 0$ represents possible ranges of the absolute residual errors $|\mu_n|$. A common approach is to use the standard least squares criterion where the functional to be minimized is

$$J_c = \sum_{n=1}^{N} (w_n \varepsilon_n)^2 \qquad (13)$$

Here the w_n are weighting factors $(0 < w_n \leqslant 1)$ that can be assigned to each node in a manner similar to that described by Lovell ['1971] and Lovell et al, [1972] or Hefez [1972]. This form gives equal weights to positive and negative values of ε_n and penalizes larger errors as the square of their size. The result is a distribution in which the number of smaller errors greatly exceeds that of the larger ones. It can be shown that a set of parameters established in this manner is a maximum likelihood estimate if and only if the residual errors μ_n are normally distributed [Jackson and Aron, 1971].

Equations (12) and (13) make it possible to calibrate the discrete model with the aid of quadratic programming [Hadley, 1964; Hefez, 1972]. Deininger [1969], Kleinecke [1971], and Hefez [1972] show how to use linear programming by minimizing a linear functional of ε_n,

$$J_c = \sum_{n=1}^{N} w_n \varepsilon_n \tag{14}$$

or by using a minimax criterion, where J_c is the maximum value of $w_n \varepsilon_n$,

$$J_c = \max_n (w_n \varepsilon_n) \tag{15}$$

The functional in (14) weights large errors less heavily and small errors more heavily than the least-square criterion does and according to Vemuri and Vemuri [1970] is more sensitive to minor changes in the parameter values. These parameters become a maximum likelihood estimate if the residual errors are exponentially distributed [Jackson and Aron, 1971]. On the other hand, the minimax criterion does not take into account the frequency with which the maximum error occurs but insures that none of the errors are too large. Other types of functionals can also be employed, but, since most of these would involve more complex mathematical procedures, there is little justification for using them unless the true error distribution is known.

The correct choice of a calibration criterion may lead to a reasonable statistical distribution of the residual errors, and thereby to a good consistency between the parameters and the noise-affected governing equations, (11). However, this by no means eliminates the problem of nonuniqueness and the strong sensitivity of the parameters to minor errors in the data, as we have previously encountered in connection with the case where μ_n is identically equal to zero. To illustrate this last point, consider a vertical cross-section through a homogeneous isotropic soil as shown in Fig. 1. The flow region has two vertical constant head boundaries near the upper corners, one horizontal constant head boundary at the bottom, one horizontal no-flow boundary at the top, and two vertical no-flow boundaries on the sides. Flow takes place from the bottom plane towards the two vertical constant head boundaries as indicated by the dashed arrows. The region is subdivided into 40 quadrilateral elements having equal values of hydraulic conductivity, K. By setting K equal to unity in all the elements, one can use the finite element method to calculate the values of h_n and Q_n at all the 55 nodes of the network. Since in the finite element method Q_n represents flow rates into or out of the system (and not flow rates within the system), its value is zero everywhere except at nodes lying on the constant head boundaries which act as sinks and sources.

Let us now use these results to set up a highly idealized inverse problem. We assume that the geometry of the finite element network is known to us, but the actual values of K_m in these elements are unknown. In solving the inverse problem we use the same network and adopt the previously calculated values of h_n and Q_n at the nodal points as input data to our problem. However, we assume that 8 of the Q_n values are unknown to us, meaning that we shall be using only a limited amount

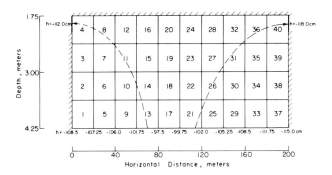

Fig.1 - Vertical two-dimensional cross-section of plot in Hula Valley, Israel, with superimposed finite element network and hypothetical h values.

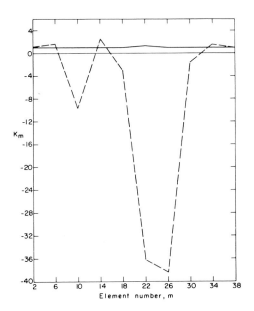

Fig.2 - Solution corresponding to minimum value of error-criterion when parameters are unconstrained, using exact (solid line) and rounded (dashed line) values of h.

of Cauchy data.

Since q is zero and the soil is known a priori to be isotropic, (12) becomes

$$\left| (A_{nm} + C_{nm})K_m - Q_n \right| \leqslant \varepsilon_n \qquad\qquad (16)$$

$$n = 1, 2, \ldots, N \; ; \; m = 1, \ldots, M$$

There are 40 unknown values of K_m, so M = 40 in (16). There is a total of 55 nodes in Fig. 1, but we can write only a number N = 47 of equations because at the remaining 8 nodes Q_n is unknown. If we adopt (14) as the error-criterion to be minimized, we can solve the problem by linear programming. With the aid of generally available linear programming routines such as IBM's MPS and MPSX or CDC's Optima one can impose arbitrary bounds on the unknown parameters. Let us see first what happens when the parameters are allowed to take on arbitrary positive or negative values such that

$$- \infty \leqslant K_m \leqslant \infty , \qquad m = 1, 2, \ldots, M. \qquad\qquad (17)$$

The solution along two horizontal layers of elements is shown by the solid lines in Figs. 2 and 3. In each layer the solution is excellent everywhere except in one element. Since only a limited number of Cauchy data, Q_n, were specified, the fact that good solutions were obtained almost everywhere can only be explained by the phenomenon of cross-characteristic influence mentioned previously in the text. However, this influence apparently did not spread equally along the entire flow region and some of the elements were only slightly affected by the available Cauchy data.

Let us now see what happens when, instead of using exact input data, one repeats the same solution process by first rounding the h_n values to their first significant figure. This introduces a maximum absolute error of $|0.05|$ cm into the data which is less than 0.25 percent of the total head difference across the flow region. The solution is represented by the dashed lines in Figs. 2 and 3 and it is seen that the parameters exhibit severe spatial oscillations around their true value. This illustrates the fact that low-amplitude random errors in the data may be amplified to a great extent in the process of solving the inverse problem, even if all other reasons for nonuniqueness have been eliminated. A theoretical explanation for this phenomenon was given earlier in the text (see equations 8 and 9).

It is thus seen that the minimization of a single error-criterion subject to the constraints in (11) does not, in general, guarantee a meaningful solution to the inverse problem. This is true when the problem is underdetermined, as well as when it is overdetermined, irrespective of the amount of data available.

IMPOSING LIMITS ON THE PARAMETERS

One way of insuring that the parameters remain physically plausible is to impose certain restrictions on the ranges within which they can vary. This leads to an additional set of constraints,

$$(K_{ij})_m^L \leqslant (K_{ij})_m \leqslant (K_{ij})_m^U \qquad\qquad (18)$$

$$m = 1, 2, \ldots, M$$

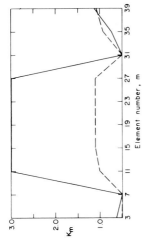

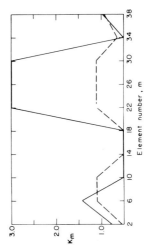

Fig.4 – Solution obtained with rounded values of h when parameters are restricted between 0.5 and 3.0 , relying on minimum value of error-criterion (solid lines) and on bicriterion approach with $J_p = 0.3$ (dashed lines).

Fig.3 – Solution corresponding to minimum value of error-criterion when parameters are unconstrained, using exact (solid line) and rounded (dashed line) values of h.

$$q_\ell^L \leqslant q_\ell \leqslant q_\ell^U \qquad \ell = 1, 2, \ldots, L \tag{19}$$

where the superscripts U and L indicate upper and lower limits, reflecting the hydrologist's subjective feeling with regard to the possible range of each parameter [Coats et al., 1970; Lovell; 1971; Lovell et al., 1972].

To establish how meaningful this method is, suppose that the hydraulic conductivity of the soil in Fig. 1 is known with certainty to be no less than 0.5 and no more than 3.0, i.e.,

$$0.5 \leqslant K_m \leqslant 3.0 \qquad m = 1, 2, \ldots, M \tag{20}$$

Let us now solve the corresponding inverse problem in the same manner as before by rounding the exact values of h_n to their first significant figure and minimizing the functional in (14) subject to the constraints in (16) and (20). The results for the same two horizontal layers of elements considered earlier are shown by the solid lines in Fig. 4. It is evident that no new information about the parameter has been gained by solving the inverse problem in this manner; the parameters exhibit random oscillations between the specified limits and one can say nothing about the solution surface except what he already knew before, i.e., that it lies somewhere between 0.5 and 3.0.

PLAUSIBILITY CRITERIA

All that has been said so far indicates that the conventional approach to parameter identification in which a solution is sought between specified limits by minimizing a single error-criterion does not, in general, lead to satisfactory results. These results are extremely sensitive to minor modifications in the distribution of the residual errors so that a slight change in the value of the error functional may lead to a drastic change in the parameters. What appears to be the optimal solution (in the sense of corresponding to the minimum value of the error-criterion) is merely an artifact of the errors, and there is an infinite number of near-optimal solutions that may differ considerably from the optimal solution and may lead to a much better predictive model. To choose between these alternatives, it is necessary to establish additional criteria of optimality which would provide a measure for the plausibility of any given set of parameters.

In essence, the purpose of introducing a plausibility criterion in addition to (18) and (19) is to provide a means for comparing various alternative solutions from the standpoint of closeness to reality. One possible continuous measure of such closeness is the functional

$$J_p = \max_{i,j,m,\ell} \{ |\alpha_k [(K_{ij})_m - (K_{ij})_m^E] | \cdot | \beta_\ell (q_\ell - q_\ell^E) | \} \tag{21}$$

$$\alpha_m = 1/(K_{ij})_m^E \qquad (K_{ij})_m^E \neq 0 \qquad m = 1, 2, \ldots, M$$

$$\alpha_m = 1 \qquad (K_{ij})_m^E = 0 \qquad m = 1, 2, \ldots, M$$

$$\beta_\ell = 1/q_\ell^E \qquad q_\ell^E \neq 0 \qquad \ell = 1, 2, \ldots, L$$

$$\beta_\ell = 1 \qquad q_\ell^E = 0 \qquad \ell = 1, 2, \ldots, L$$

where the superscript E indicates objective or subjective estimates of the expected (in a statistical sense) parameter values as obtained from field tests and other sources. The normalization factors α and β are introduced to enable calculating the relative absolute deviation of each parameter from its estimated expected value. The objective here is to minimize the maximum relative absolute deviation from the estimate as measured by the plausibility criterion J_p.

Other possibilities are to minimize the sum of the relative absolute deviations

$$J_p = \sum_{m=1}^{M} \sum_{i=x}^{y} \sum_{j=x}^{y} |\alpha_m[(K_{ij})_m - (K_{ij})_m^E]| + \sum_{\ell=1}^{L} |\beta_\ell (q_\ell - q_\ell^E)| \quad (22)$$

or the sum of the squares of the relative deviations

$$J_p = \sum_{m=1}^{M} \sum_{i=x}^{y} \sum_{j=x}^{y} \alpha_m^2 [(K_{ij})_m - (K_{ij})_m^E]^2 + \sum_{\ell=1}^{L} \beta_\ell^2 (q_\ell - q_\ell^E)^2 \quad (23)$$

where α and β are the same as they are in (21). Here again the choice of any given functional involves an assumption concerning the distribution of the parameters.

When reliable estimates of the parameters are not available, a different criterion must be used. Emsellem and de Marsily [1971] explain that it is reasonable to search for a solution resulting in the most uniform distribution of the parameters over the entire flow region thereby eliminating the tendency of the solution to exhibit random spatial oscillations about the true parameter values.

An acceptable measure of uniformity is the negative of entropy [Jackson and Aron, 1971] defined as

$$J_p = \sum_{m=1}^{M} \sum_{i=x}^{y} \sum_{j=x}^{y} \left|\frac{(K_{ij})_m}{K_{ij}^*}\right| \log \left|\frac{(K_{ij})_m}{K_{ij}^*}\right|$$

$$+ \sum_{\ell=1}^{L} \left|\frac{q_\ell}{q^*}\right| \log \left|\frac{q_\ell}{q^*}\right| \quad (24)$$

where K_{ij}^* and q^* represent average values over the entire flow region. (K_{ij}^* and q^* are treated as unknowns to be determined together with K_{ij} and q). The more uniform the solution is, the less the value of J_p is, and a completely uniform solution corresponds to $J_p = 0$.

A somewhat less efficient measure of uniformity is the functional

$$J_p = \sum_{i=x}^{y} \sum_{j=x}^{y} \max_m |(K_{ij})_m - K_{ij}^*| + \max_\ell |q_\ell - q^*| \quad (25)$$

$$m = 1, 2, \ldots, M \qquad \ell = 1, 2, \ldots, L$$

whose linear form can be considered as an advantage over (24). Other types of plausibility criteria can also be considered depending on what appears to be the most realistic structure of the particular system under study.

The choice of a particular plausibility criterion reflects the modeler's subjective feeling as to what the most plausible shape of the solution surface is. In this manner the solution will depend on prior assumptions mady by the modeler and will therefore be strongly biased in favor of the modeler's subjective conception of the flow system to be simulated. This bias, however, is an essential feature of the solution process and without it, the solution maybe completely devoid of any physical meaning.

GENERATION OF ALTERNATIVE SOLUTIONS

In principle the relationship between any calibration criterion J_c and any physical plausibility criterion J_p can be obtained with the aid of parametric mathematical programming [Hadley, 1964, p. 221]. The approach is to minimize J_c subject to constraints of the type given in (12), (16), (18), and (19) as well as the parametric constraint

$$J_p \leqslant a + b\theta \tag{26}$$

Here a is the initial upper bound on J_p, b is the rate of change of this bound, and θ is a parameter that varies continuously or stepwise between any two specified limits. For a given discrete model and a given set of data the result is a unique relationship such as that shown in Figs. 5-7. Each point on these curves represents a different set of model parameters, so that one has an infinite number of alternative solutions, each of which is characterized by different values of the ordered pair of numbers $\{J_c, J_p\}$.

Since there is always uncertainty regarding the proper choice of optimality criteria and the adequacy of data, the bicriterion function does not represent all the possible solutions to the inverse problem. Instead, the best possible solution (i.e., the one optimizing the predictive capabilities of the particular discrete model considered) lies somewhere in the neighborhood of this function within a range of uncertainty whose limits are generally unknown. To consider all the possibilities within this range, more must be known about the statistical nature of the various errors that enter into the inverse problem. Until such knowledge is available, using a bicriterion function, coupled with a post-optimal sensitivity analysis, seems to provide the nearest way of approaching the issue of uncertainty with the aid of deterministic mathematical programming techniques.

In the particular case when all the constraints as well as the objective functions are linear, a continuous bicriterion function can easily be obtained with the aid of parametric linear programming. To illustrate how this is done, consider the problem defined by (12), (14), (18), (19), and (21). In addition to the N nodal constraints (12), there are 3K constraints of the type

$$\left| \alpha_m [(K_{ij})_m - (K_{ij})_m^E] \right| \leqslant J_p \tag{27}$$

$$i = x, y \qquad\qquad j = x, y \qquad\qquad m = 1, 2, \ldots, M$$

L constraints of the type

$$\left| \beta_\ell (q_\ell - q_\ell^E) \right| \leqslant J_p \tag{28}$$

$$\ell = 1, 2, \ldots, L$$

one parametric constraint

$$J_p \leqslant \theta \tag{29}$$

and one objective function

$$\min J_c = \min \sum_{n=1}^{N} w_n \varepsilon_n \tag{30}$$

By use of standard linear programming routines one can obtain values of J_c corresponding to each value of θ within the interval $(0, \infty)$. The resulting bicriterion function is piecewise linear, consisting of straight line segments intersecting at points where changing the value of θ requires changing the components of the basis (for a definition of the term basis refer to Hadley [1962, p. 43]). Eventually, a point is reached where θ can be increased indefinitely while the same basis and the minimum value of J_c are maintained. At this point, execution of the parametric linear programming routine is automatically halted, and the bicriterion function is complete.

Fig. 5 shows a bicriterion function as obtained by parametric linear programming for the problem described previously in connection with Fig. 1, using exact values of h_n (except for the usual roundoff error), and allowing the parameters K_m to vary between $-\infty$ and $+\infty$. The plausibility criterion was chosen so as to insure maximum uniformity of the solution surface. Since in reality the parameters are indeed uniform, the correct (and exact) solution in this case corresponds to $J_p = 0$ and thereby to $J_c = 12.5$. The solution shown by the solid lines in Figs. 2 and 3 was previously obtained by relying on the minimum value of J_c, which corresponds to a J_p value of approximately 1.5. Fig. 5 clearly indicates that the maximum amplitude of the solution surface can be reduced down to $J_p = 0.9$ without practically changing the value of the error-functional, J_c. By admitting a slightly larger residual error such that $J_c = 2.0$, the maximum amplitude could be further reduced down to a value $J_p = 0.375$.

Fig. 6 shows what happens when the same solution process is repeated after the values of h_n have been rounded to their first significant figure. Here again the correct solution corresponds to $J_p = 0$, and thereby to $J_c = 56$. The oscillatory solution shown by the dashed lines in Figs. 2 and 3 was previously obtained by relying on the minimum value of J_c, which corresponds to a J_p value of approximately 38.5. Fig. 6 shows that the maximum amplitude of the oscillations can be reduced down to $J_p = 10$ without introducing any significant change into the value of J_c. In fact, by admitting a cumulative residual error of $J_c = 9$, the maximum amplitude could be reduced all the way down to $J_p = 1$, which is less than the amplitude exhibited by the solid line in Fig. 3.

When the latter problem is solved by restricting the values of K_m according to (20), one obtains the bicriterion function shown in Fig. 7. The oscillatory solution given by the solid lines in Fig. 4 was previously obtained by relying on the minimum value of J_c, which corresponds to a J_p value of 1.8. The bicriterion function indicates that the maximum amplitude of the oscillations can be reduced drastically from $J_p = 1.8$ down to $J_p = 0.3$ without significantly affecting the value of J_c. A part of the corresponding solution is indicated by the dashed lines in Fig. 4.

The geometry of the flow region depicted in Fig. 1 has been adopted from a realistic field situation encountered in the drained peat deposits of the former Hula Lake in northern Israel. Another example is given in Fig. 8 which shows actual field data measured in 18 piezometers located exactly at the same points as the nodes of the finite element network, which now includes 20 triangles. Flow takes place from the bottom horizontal boundary toward two drainage ditches represented by vertical constant head boundaries at the upper corners of the network.

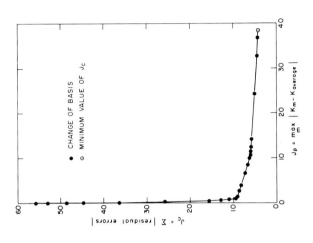

Fig.6 – Bicriterion function using rounded values of h
when parameters are unconstrained.

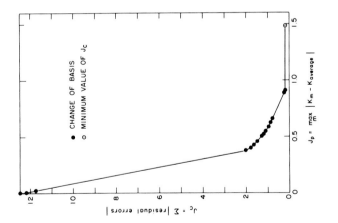

Fig.5 – Bicriterion function using exact values of h when parameters are unconstrained.

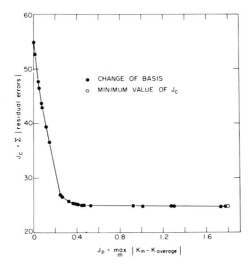

Fig.7 - Bicriterion function using rounded values of h when parameters are restricted between 0.5 and 3.0 .

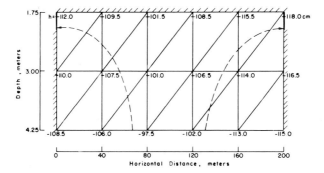

Fig.8 - Vertical two-dimensional cross-section of plot in Hula Valley, Israel, with superimposed finite element network and example of measured h values.

No flow takes place across the water table and this is represented by the horizontal no-flow boundary at the top. The two vertical no-flow boundaries are lines of symmetry between similarly shaped flow regions.

A series of recovery tests were performed in all the piezometers [Neuman and Dasberg, 1973] indicating that the soil may probably be characterized by a uniform value of hydraulic conductivity. However, these tests gave no indication as to the degree of anisotropy of the soil, and an attempt was made to obtain this value from the shape of the steady state piezometric surface. For this purpose the vertical hydraulic conductivity, K_V, was maintained uniform and constant in all the elements, and the inverse problem was solved by allowing the horizontal conductivity, K_H, to vary uniformly over the entire network between 0 and $10^4 K_H$. Fig. 9 shows the shape of the bicriterion function obtained jointly from two sets of nodal constraints, each set corresponding to a piezometric surface measured at a different date. Had one relied only on the minimum value of J_c without considering the entire bicriterion function as in Fig. 9, he would obtain the value $K_H/K_V = 68$. However, the bicriterion function clearly indicates that this result is meaningless because J_c is insensitive to the values of K_H/K_V below 200. The only conclusion that one is allowed to draw from the shape of this function is that K_H/K_V probably does not exceed three orders of magnitude.

Fig. 10 shows a bicriterion function obtained for the same problem by utilizing jointly 6 different sets of piezometric data measured at different dates. Here the minimum value of J_c corresponds to $K_H/K_V = 0$, which is obviously meaningless. On the other hand, the shape of the bicriterion function is similar to that obtained by using only two sets of data and therefore, it does not provide us with any additional information about the value of K_H/K_V.

SELECTION OF AN ACCEPTABLE SOLUTION

After having determined a range of possible alternative solutions to the inverse problem, the hydrologist is faced with the task of selecting one particular set of parameters to be introduced into his simulation model. His task is complicated by the fact that J_c and J_p represent two incommensurable attributes of the solution that cannot be brought to a common scale. In addition, J_c decreases as J_p increases, and therefore one cannot obtain an acceptable solution merely by minimizing a weighted sum of these two measures. Instead, the final selection requires a conscious and judiciuous trade off between J_c, representing the degree to which the parameters are consistent with the data, and J_p, representing the plausibility of the results. The selection process must be viewed as an art of balancing all the consequences of any given choice and making a decision on the basis of subjective value judgement and informed opinion. Since many of the factors influencing the choice are necessarily subjective, the final selection process can be quantified and made automatic only at a great risk.

The bicriterion function does not, in general, indicate which solution is best from the standpoint of optimizing the predictive capabilities of the model. It nevertheless enables the modeler to identify a narrow range of dominant solutions which, in his own judgement, appear to possess better qualities than those solutions lying outside the specified range. The width of this range reflects the modeler's uncertainty regarding the relative effects of J_c and J_p on the quality of the model. To the modeler, all the solutions within the specified range appear to have an equal likelihood of giving the best result, so that the final choice is completely arbitrary.

In trying to identify a range of dominant solutions along the bicriterion curve a decision must first be made concerning the range of environmental conditions under which the system is to be simulated by the model. If the environmental conditions will remain essentially similar to those prevailing during the calibration period, it may be reasonable to place more weight on the minimization of J_c

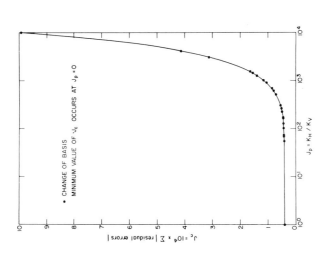

Fig.10 – Bicriterion function using six sets of measured
h values in Hula Valley plot.

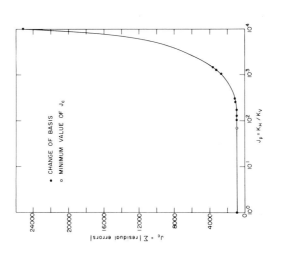

Fig.9 – Bicriterion function using two sets of measured
h values in Hula Valley plot.

(consistency between the parameters and the data) than on that of J_p (plausibility of the results). Similar considerations may hold if the modeler's confidence in the reliability of his conceptual plausibility model is less than his confidence in the accuracy of the data entering into the governing equations. On the other hand, if the operating conditions, in the future are expected to be significantly different than those prevailing during the calibration period, or if the plausibility model is considered to be reliable, more weight should be given to the minimization of J_p than to that of J_c. In this manner the simulation model becomes less of a black box and more physically based, the probability of generating a reasonably good predictive model thereby being increased.

POSTOPTIMAL SENSITIVITY ANALYSIS

If all the coefficients of a parameter in the nodal constraints (12) or (16) are very small, this parameter can vary over wide ranges without significantly affecting the value of J_c. In other words J_c is not sufficiently sensitive to this parameter and the latter cannot be reliably identified with the available amount of information. To establish the effect of changing any individual parameter as well as the ranges within which this effect is felt, the final step in each calibration process must include a postoptimal sensitivity analysis. The linear programming routines of IBM and CDC, mentioned earlier in our discussion, are especially well suited for this purpose because they can perform a sensitivity analysis on the final solution with very little extra computer effort.

By now the reader should be aware that the multicriterion approach enables one to solve the inverse problem even if the system of nodal constraints is underdetermined. However, the probability of obtaining a uniformly valid solution to the inverse problem is usually higher when this system is overdetermined. A postoptimal sensitivity analysis helps one to identify those subregions in which the parameters cannot be validly determined with the available information.

APPENDIX

Consider a two-dimensional flow region R with lateral boundaries Γ_1 and Γ_2. The steady flow of water in R is described by equations 1-3, where V represents lateral flow into the system across Γ_2. If a network of triangular elements is superimposed on R and if q is assumed to be 0 everywhere, the resulting finite element equations are [Neuman and Witherspoon, 1970]

$$G_{nm} h_m = Q_n \tag{A1}$$

where

$$G_{nm} = \sum_e \frac{1}{4S} [K_{xx} b_n b_m + K_{xy} (b_n c_m + c_n b_m) + K_{yy} c_n c_m] \tag{A2}$$

$$Q_n = - \sum_e Q^e \qquad Q^e = \frac{1}{2} \Gamma_2^e V \tag{A3}$$

and the summation is taken over all elements adjacent to node n. Here S is the area of any triangle,

$$S = \frac{1}{2}(c_2 b_1 - c_1 b_2)$$

Γ_2^e is a side of the element coinciding with the prescribed flux boundary Γ_2, and

$$a_1 = x_2 y_3 - x_3 y_2$$

$$a_2 = x_3 y_1 - x_1 y_3$$

$$a_3 = x_1 y_2 - x_2 y_1$$

$$b_1 = y_2 - y_3 \qquad c_1 = x_3 - x_2$$

$$b_2 = y_3 - y_1 \qquad c_2 = x_1 - x_3$$

$$b_3 = y_1 - y_2 \qquad c_3 = x_2 - x_1$$

where x_i and y_i are the coordinates of the i-th node in the triangle.

The above definition of Q_n corresponds only to lateral boundary sources. The effect of point sources, such as wells, is best represented with the aid of Dirac's delta function according to

$$q(x_i) = Q^e \delta(x_i - x_i^e) \tag{A4}$$

where Q^e is the flow rate from a well situated at the point x_i^e in an element R^e. For solving the inverse problem the values of Q^e are assumed to be known, and $q(x_i)$ is transferred to the right-hand side of (A1), thereby becoming part of Q_n. The contribution of point sources to Q_n is given by

$$Q_n = \sum_e \int_{R^e} Q^e \delta(x_i - x_i^e) N_n \, dR = \sum_e N_n Q^e \tag{A5}$$

where, for any triangle,

$$N_n = (1/2S)(a_n + b_n x + c_n y) \tag{A6}$$

It follows that q in (1) represents only those sources distributed over finite segments of the flow region, and its values correspond to the rate of vertical recharge and discharge per unit horizontal area of this region. In the inverse problem, q is considered to be generally unknown.

The inverse problem can now be formulated with the aid of (A1)-(A5) in the following manner :

$$\bar{A}_{ne}(K_{xx})_e + \bar{B}_{ne}(K_{xy})_e + \bar{C}_{ne}(K_{yy})_e + \bar{D}_{ne}q_e = Q_n \tag{A7}$$

where q_e is the value of q in R^e and

$$\bar{A}_{ne} = [(1/4S)b_n b_m h_m]_e$$

$$\bar{B}_{ne} = [(1/4S)(b_n c_m + c_n b_m)h_m]_e$$

$$\bar{C}_{ne} = [(1/4S)c_n c_m h_m]_e$$

$$\bar{D}_{ne} = -S/3$$

If the values of K_{ij} are to be identified only over M subregions involving one or more elements and if q is to be identified over L such subregions, (A7) becomes

$$A_{nk}(K_{xx})_m + B_{nk}(K_{xy})_m + C_{nk}(K_{yy})_m + D_{n\ell}q\ell = Q_n \qquad (A8)$$

$$m = 1, 2, \ldots, M \qquad \ell = 1, 2, \ldots, L$$

where

$$A_{nm} = \sum_e \bar{A}_{ne}$$

$$B_{nm} = \sum_e \bar{B}_{ne}$$

$$C_{nm} = \sum_e \bar{C}_{ne}$$

summation being over all elements in the mth region and

$$D_{n\ell} = \sum_e \bar{D}_{ne}$$

summation being over all elements in the ℓth region.

In the writing of finite element programs it is customary to combine four triangles into a single quadrilateral element. In so doing, Q_n for the midpoint is set equal to 0, and its original value is distributed equally among the four corner nodes. Thus the constraint corresponding to the midpoint is redundant, and the values of $\bar{D}_{ne}$ for the corner nodes become $\bar{D}_{ne} = -S^*/4$, where S^* is the area of the quadrilateral element. If the element is assumed to be locally isotropic so that $K_{xx} = K_{yy}$ and $K_{xy} = 0$, the value of h_n for the midpoint can be eliminated from the finite element equations.

NOTATIONS

Γ_1 : prescribed head boundary of R;

Γ_2 : prescribed flux boundary of R;

h   : head, L;

H   : prescribed head at Γ_1, L;

J_c : calibration criterion;

J_p : plausibility criterion;

K_{ij} : hydraulic conductivity, LT^{-1};

n_i : component of unit outer normal vector at Γ_2;

q : source term, LT^{-1};

R : flow region;

V : prescribed flux at Γ_2, $L^2 T^{-1}$;

x_i : component of Cartesian coordinate vector, L;

x : horizontal coordinate x_1, L;

y : vertical coordinate $\mathbf{x}_2$, L;

δ : Dirac's delta function;

$\varepsilon(x_i)$: maximum absolute residual error at x_i, LT^{-1};

$\mu(x_i)$: residual error at x_i, LT^{-1}.

REFERENCES

ADDISON, L.E., D.R. FRIEDRICHS, and K.L. KIPP, Transmissivity Iterative Program User's Manual, Report BNWL-1708 UC-70, Battelle Pacific Northwest Laboratories, Richland, Washington, 1972.

COATS, K.H., J.R. DEMPSEY, and H.H. HENDERSON, A new technique for determining reservoir description from field performance data, Soc. Petrol. Eng. J., 10(1), 66, 1970.

COLE, J.A., Examples of flow-balance solutions for aquifer T and S by an automatic optimisation procedure, Proceedings of the International Symposium on Development of Ground Water Resources, Madras, India, 1973.

DEINIGER, R.A., Linear programming for hydrologic analyses, Water Resour. Res., 5(5), 1105, 1969.

DUPUY, M., C. JAIN, and Ph. BESSET, Possibilités d'ajustement automatique des modèles de réservoir dans la période monophasique de production, Rev. Inst. Fr. Petrol., 26(4), 269, 1971.

EMSELLEM, Y., and G. DE MARSILY, An automatic solution for the inverse problem, Water Resour. Res., 7(5), 1264, 1971.

FORSYTHE, G.E., and W.R. WASOW, Finite-Difference Methods for Partial Differential Equations, John Wiley, New York, 1960.

FRIND, E.O., and G.F. PINDER, Galerkin solution of the inverse problem for aquifer transmissivity, Water Resour. Res., 9(5), 1397, 1973.

GARABEDIAN, P.R., Partial Differential Equations, John Wiley, New York, 1964.

HADLEY, G., Linear Programming, Addison-Wesley, Reading, Mass., 1962.

HADLEY, G., Nonlinear and Dynamic Programming, Addison-Wesley, Reading, Mass., 1964.

HAIMES, Y.Y., R.L. PERRINE, and D.A. WISMER, Identification of aquifer parameters by decomposition and multilevel optimization, Israel. J. Technol., 6(5), 322, 1968.

HEFEZ, E., The use of digital and hybrid computers for solving ground water problems (in Hebrew), Ph.D. thesis, Technion, Israel Inst. of Technol., Haifa, 1972.

JACKSON, D.R., and G. ARON, Parameter estimation in hydrology : The state of the art, Water Resour. Bull., 7(3), 457, 1971.

JACQUARD, P., and C. JAIN, Permeability distribution from field pressure data, Soc. Petrol. Eng. J., 5(4), 281, 1965.

JAHNS, H.O., A rapid method for obtaining a two-dimensional reservoir description from well response data, Soc. Petrol. Eng. J., 6(4), 315, 1966.

KLEINECKE, D., Use of linear programming for estimating geohydrologic parameters of groundwater basins, Water Resour. Res., 7(2), 367, 1971.

KNOWLES, T.R., B.J. CLABORN, and D.M. WELLS, A Computerized Procedure to Deter-
      mine Aquifer Characteristics, Rep. WRC-72-5, Water Resources Center,
      Texas Tech. University, Lubbock, Texas, 1972.
KRUGER, W.D., Determining areal permeability distribution by calculations,
      J. Petrol. Technol., 13(6), 691, 1961.
LABADIE, J., Optimal identification of groundwater reservoir parameters by non-
      linear decomposition, technical completion report on project W264,
      Water Resour. Center, Univ. of Calif., Los Angeles, 1970.
LAVRENTIEV, M.M., Some Improperly Posed Problems of Mathematical Physics,
      Springer-Verlag, New York, 1967.
LOVELL, R.E., Collective adjustment of the parameters of the mathematical model
      of a large aquifer, Rep. 4, Dep. of Hydrol. and Dep. of Syst. Eng.,
      Univ. of Ariz., Tucson, 1971.
LOVELL, R.E., L. DUCKSTEIN, and C.C. KISIEL, Use of subjective information in
      estimation of aquifer parameters, Water Resour. Res., 8(3), 680,1972.
NELSON, R.W., In place determination of permeability distribution for hetero-
      geneous porous media through analysis of energy dissipation, Soc. Petrol.
      Eng. J., 8(1), 33, 1968.
NELSON, R.W., and W.L. McCOLLUM, Transient energy dissipation methods of mea-
      suring permeability distributions in heterogeneous porous materials,
      Rep. CSC 691229, Water Resour. Div., U.S. Geol. Surv., Washington, D.C.,
      1969.
NEUMAN, S.P., and P.A. WITHERSPOON, Finite element method of analyzing steady
      seepage with a free surface, Water Resour. Res.,6(3), 889, 1970.
NEUMAN, S.P., Calibration of distributed parameter groundwater flow models
      viewed as a multiple-objective decision process under uncertainty,
      Water Resour. Res., 9(4), 1006, 1973.
NEUMAN, S.P., and S. DASBERG, Hydrology of the Hula Peat Deposits in Israel,
      Interim Report for April 1972 - July 1973, Institute of Soil and Water,
      Agricultural Research Organization, Bet Dagan, Israel, 1973.
NUTBROWN, D.A., Identification of parameters in a linear equation of groundwater
      flow, unpublished manuscript, 1973.
ROBINSON, J.S., Digital Identification of Aquifer Parameters, Report ILR No.
      1973, The Water Resources Association, Medmenham, England, 1972.
SAGAR, B., C.C. KISIEL, and L. DUCKSTEIN, Estimation of aquifer properties from
      field data, Proceedings of the International Symposium on Development
      of Ground Water Resources, Madras, India, 1973.
SLATER, G.E., and E.J. DURRER, Adjustment of reservoir simulation models to match
      field performance, Soc. Petrol. J., 11(3), 295, 1971.
STALLMAN, R.W., Numerical analysis of regional water levels to define aquifer
      hydrology, Eos Trans. AGU, 37(4), 451, 1956.
VEMURI, V., and W.J. KARPLUS, Identification of nonlinear parameters of ground-
      water basins by hybrid computation, Water Resour. Res., 5(1), 172, 1969.
VEMURI, V., and N. VEMURI, On the systems approach in hydrology, Bull. Int. Ass.
      Sci. Hydrol., 15(2), 17, 1970.
VEMURI, V., J.A. DRACUP, R.C. ERDMANN, and N. VEMURI, Sensitivity analysis method
      of system identification and its potential in hydrologic research,
      Water Resour. Res., 5(2), 341, 1969.
WISMER, D.A., R.L. PERRINE, and Y.Y. HAIMES, Modeling and identification of
      aquifer systems of high dimension, Automatika, Jan. 1970.

Current research field of author : *Identification of parameters in distributed models of subsurface flow – Finite element methods for flow in saturated-unsaturated
soils – Models of water uptake by plants (finite element) – Identification of Kernel
functions in linear models in the presence of noise – Well hydraulics in unconfined
aquifers – Field studies in the Hula peats.*

DISCUSSION

Let me correct immediately, there is no difference between direct and indirect as you used the terms. The usual criterion people use as far as I could make out, would be termed a differential equation error, the difference between the two errors squared or something like that. In either case in the so called direct method you may introduce some other constraints on the solutions. In both cases you will be simulating the response to a given assumption of the parameters. The particular method, when it is finite element or not, does not give any difference. (BALAKRISHNAN)

I mean by the difference between direct and indirect approach the following : in the indirect approach you are simulating, the model, gets a response like say that to hydraulic heads, then you can compare the calculated hydraulic head to the measured hydraulic heads after completing the computation. This is your criterion : if it is not good you go back and change the parameters and you go through. (NEUMAN)

Yes, but every time you put that set of parameters you also have to say what the boundary conditions are. (BALAKRISHNAN)

Of course, but in the direct approach you don't go through the simulated process. Your criterion no longer pursues the difference, between the calculated and measured hydraulic heads but rather the difference between the left hand side and the right hand side of your material balance equations. This is a conceptual different way of proceeding. (NEUMAN)

In the second method then, are you minimizing anything or not. Nevertheless for a choice of the parameters you do get an answer. (BALAKRISHNAN)

I don't make a prior choice of the parameters, in the direct approach ; I only make assumptions regarding the possible shape of the solution surface. Should it be smooth, should it be oscillatory, should we have a break at a certain point. Another possibility is, suppose that I am given some prior value of the parameter, then my criterion J_p would be for instance the maximum difference between values that you have from field observations K^* and the calculated values K. But in this case this would be the second criterion - basic criterion, involving the errors in the material balance. (NEUMAN)

Yes but, neither criterion has been really justified because this is after the choice of the experimentor. Given that, there is not that much difference between direct and indirect. But again the correctness is based on the fit error, fitting the material balance. (BALAKRISHNAN)

I am not so sure, because by just fitting the error, you would be looking at the minimum value of J_c. You have chosen a certain error distribution pattern. Then you would take a square error criterion and you would have to minimize this and of course the minimum value would be the best fit in the statistical sense given the assumption about the distribution. But what I am suggesting here, you should reply on this minimum value because from quite a few of these experiments, the shape of this functional is such that you have a flat minimum and you should be looking at that shape of flat minimum with respect to this additional criterion I am proposing here. (NEUMAN)

It seems to me, the value should be the predictive value, not that you have in some sense written the historical data. (BALAKRISHNAN)

I agree, this is a first step on it. It is not the final answer. (NEUMAN)

I would like to suggest an alternative possibility you said the inverse problem is very sensitive. But then you said $K_{max} = 0,523$ as an example. Now you have this future environmental condition. This, in a way, suggests the possibility if the variation of the parameters are stochastic in some sense, you might be able to design a situation where you put in stochastic variations on the parameters and design your system for this. (SHAH)

Yes, this may be the next step to use in this kind of approach. (NEUMAN)

Can I bridge to what you have said and what Prof. Balakrishnan said this morning more generally and what I have said yesterday in more specific cases. First of all, it seems to me, that your indirect method is what we would call response error, this is the difference between the responses, and what you call the direct method is what we would call the equation error. If I am right there are two things that would come out of this : a) the problem you are getting is one of identifiability which is what Prof. Balakrishnan mentioned and the bottom of your hill is not flat since you are in a valley, because you have linear dependence in the model ; b) if you are using the direct method have you used it in the case of high levels of noise on the data and did you get answers which are biased ? (YOUNG)

Yes, we used it with high levels of noise on the data. The answers are biased to all my prior assumptions. (NEUMAN)

The point is, they would be inherently biased. If you use the direct method they will be biased because of the way you formulated the problem. No matter how much data you take, they will always be biased. Now you could correct that intuitively or by statistical means. It seems to me that statistical ways would be better. (YOUNG)

First of all I think that the solution should be biased, because we do have a lot of prior knowledge of the parameters and most people who are trying to attempt this problem usually are neglecting this fact that we do have a lot of physical data on the parameters, so I think the solution should be biased. The other suggestion, that I should be using statistical criteria to choose the best solution instead of just intuition, I never have seen a statistician come up with a real realistic solution to this particular problem. (NEUMAN)

I noted in your last two slides you are attempting to evaluate K_H/K_V. You got what are essentially acceptable solutions wrapped down to $K_H/K_V \cong 0$. You just have a critical flow situation. What does it really physically mean. (PHILIP)

It does not have any physical meaning. It is absurd. (NEUMAN)

You must have solved some set of equations. (PHILIP)

I had a set of balance equations - P.D.E. - discretised by using finite element method in which K_H and K_V occurred. (NEUMAN)

So, what this really means is that the failure of continuity if you just assume that everything went straight out, is no worse than the failure of continuity with other assumptions. (PHILIP)

If you measure with these criteria, yes. (NEUMAN)

Modeling and Simulation of Water Resources Systems, G.C. VANSTEENKISTE, (Ed.)
North-Holland Publishing Company (1975)

SOIL-WATER PHYSICS AND HYDROLOGIC SYSTEMS

J.R. Philip
Division of Environmental Mechanics, CSIRO,
Canberra, Australia*

ABSTRACT

> The lecture consists mainly of a review of the physics of hydrologic
> processes involving soil-water. Some attention is given to the diff-
> icult question as to how our extensive analytical knowledge of the
> processes can be best used in a scientific approach on the scale of
> the river basin. Some problems and limitations of 'systems analysis'
> are considered.

1. INTRODUCTION

One of the major tasks of this Working Conference is 'to stimulate interdisciplinary research between simulation specialists and workers who have a major
concern with water interaction on the natural environment, coming from a pure
physical orientation'.

Let me explain at the outset that, in the vocabulary of this Conference,
I come 'from a pure physical orientation' - though my friends in particle physics
doubt that I am a physicist and my mathematical friends are all quite certain I
am not pure. Everything is relative, however; and, in the present company, I must
confess to being concerned primarily with physical phenomena, and with the task
of seeking an understanding of the phenomena which will enable us to make quantitative predictions. To my mind, that is what natural science is about. I must
admit that, personally, I have trouble in comprehending how the great new human
enterprise of simulation aims to do anything different from what natural science
has been trying to do for at least 300 years. Perhaps, after all, Newton and
Einstein were simply 'simulation specialists'. Maybe the only thing which sets
them apart is that they were especially wise and especially humble.

So much for my personal semantic problems. As I understand it, my principal
task is to provide you with a review of the present state of knowledge of the
physics of hydrologic processes involving soil water. All that is feasible is to
offer you an overall picture. The soil physicists among us will probably be bored,
or else irritated by the fact that the picture I shall present is, inevitably,
oversimplified and somewhat selective. My main concern, however, is to communicate
to the 'simulation specialists'; so the soil physicists must be patient with me.

The major part of my lecture, then, is devoted to a review of soil-water
physics. I shall go on, however, to make some remarks on the problems of scale in
hydrologic studies; and, finally, I shall presume to offer some personal comments
on the application of 'systems analysis' in hydrology and water resource
management.

2. SOIL WATER AND THE HYDROLOGIC CYCLE

In its natural state the soil is normally unsaturated: that is, it contains
both water and air. Most of the water involved in the hydrologic cycle is located

---

*Postal address: P.O. Box 821, Canberra City, A.C.T. 2601, Australia.

in unsaturated soil between the time of its arrival as rain at the soil surface
and that of its return to the atmosphere. A small fraction of precipitation does
not enter the soil, but moves overland directly into streams or lakes; and a
second small fraction percolates downward through the unsaturated 'zone of
aeration' and joins the groundwater, i.e. the water in the deep, habitually-
saturated strata of soil, alluvia, or rocks. In a dry country such as Australia,
as much as 93% of the precipitation enters the soil; and, of this, 92% returns
directly to the atmosphere, only about 1% reaching the groundwater [30,36].

The processes of water movement in unsaturated soil thus play a central
part in the scientific study of the terrestrial sector of the hydrologic cycle
and in the related problems of irrigated and dry-land agriculture, of plant ecology, and of the biology of soil flora and fauna. They are, in addition, of great
significance in connection with the transport through the soil of materials in
solution, such as natural salts, fertilizers, and urban and industrial wastes and
pollutants. Scientific phenomena of great interest and importance include infiltra-
tion(the entry into the soil of water made available at its surface); drainage and
retention of water in the soil strata; extraction of soil water by plant roots;
and evaporation of water from the soil.

The soil, the plant, and the atmosphere form a thermodynamic continuum for
water transfer [41,52], so that the proper study of natural evaporation from the
earth's surface involves not only soil physics, but also micrometeorology and (in
the case of vegetated surfaces) plant physiology.

In this review, however, I touch only peripherally on the plant and atmosphere pathways for water transfer (Section 8). My main theme is the mathematical-
physical approach to the analysis of water movement in unsaturated soils which has
been developed over the past 20 years or so, principally in North America,
England, Western Europe, and Australia.

3.   HYDRAULIC CONDUCTIVITY OF UNSATURATED NONSWELLING SOILS

We may write Darcy's law for _saturated_ media, specialized to water flow,
as

$$V = - K\nabla\Phi. \tag{1}$$

V is the vector flow velocity, Φ is the total potential, and K is the hydraulic
conductivity. The engineering device of expressing potentials per unit weight
simplifies our equations and units: K then has the dimensions [length][time]$^{-1}$.
We note that

$$\Phi = p/\rho g + \Xi,$$

where p is pressure, ρ is the density of water, g is the acceleration due to
gravity and Ξ is the potential of the external forces. V and Φ are averages
over regions with dimensions large compared with those of the individual pore
[56,57]. K is a scalar for isotropic soils and a symmetrical second-order tensor
for anisotropic soils. We limit the discussion specifically to isotropic soils,
but extension to anisotropic soils is straightforward.

The basic concepts of flow in unsaturated nonswelling soils are due
primarily to Buckingham [4]. He suggested that Darcy's law should hold for them
in a modified form with K as a function of θ, the volumetric moisture content.
Richards [70] and others [27,6] provided experimental confirmation and established
the general character of $K(\theta)$. For obvious physical reasons [36,41] K decreases
rapidly, through as much as six or more decades [16], as θ decreases from its
saturation value through the range of interest. Fig. 1 shows a typical $K(\theta)$
relationship. We therefore rewrite (1) in the form appropriate to unsaturated
nonswelling soils:

$$V = -K(\theta)\nabla\Phi. \qquad (2)$$

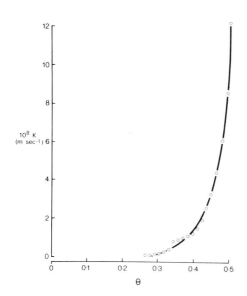

Fig. 1. Dependence of hydraulic conductivity, K, on moisture content, θ, for Yolo light clay [27].

4. TOTAL POTENTIAL AND MOISTURE POTENTIAL OF WATER IN NONSWELLING SOILS

In unsaturated soils the water is not free in the thermodynamic sense because of capillarity, adsorption, and electrical double layers [12,73]. Capillarity is dominant in wet, coarse-textured media, and adsorption assumes its greatest importance in dry media. Double-layer effects may be significant in fine-textured media exhibiting colloidal properties. Buckingham [4] was the first to appreciate that the conservative forces governing the equilibrium and movement of soil-water are amenable to treatment through their associated scalar potentials.

We define such potentials relative to the reference state of water (of composition identical to the soil solution) at atmospheric pressure and datum elevation z = 0. We then have

$$\Phi = \Psi - z. \qquad (3)$$

Ψ, the moisture potential, is the potential of the forces arising from local interactions between soil and water [58]. It is not essential either to know or to specify these forces in detail: it suffices that Ψ can be measured by well-established techniques [71,9,20]. In water-wet nonswelling soils $\Psi = 0$ at saturation and decreases with θ to very large negative values (typically -10^4m) at the dry end of the moisture range of interest. Fig. 2 depicts the $\Psi(\theta)$ relation for the soil for which $K(\theta)$ is given in Fig. 1.

The partial volumetric Gibbs free energy associated with the local soil-water interaction is $\rho g\Psi$ and it follows that (in the absence of solutes) the liquid and vapour systems are connected at equilibrium by the relation

$$H = \exp g\Psi/RT, \tag{4}$$

where H is relative humidity, R is the gas constant for water vapour, and T is the absolute temperature.

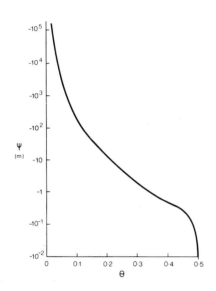

Fig. 2. Dependence of moisture potential, Ψ, on moisture content, θ, for Yolo light clay [27].

5.   GENERAL PARTIAL DIFFERENTIAL EQUATION OF FLOW IN UNSATURATED NONSWELLING SOILS

Combining (2) and (3) with the continuity requirement yields

$$\partial\theta/\partial t = \nabla\cdot(K\nabla\Psi) - \partial K/\partial z. \tag{5}$$

When the relations between K, Ψ, and θ are single-valued, (5) may be rewritten in terms of a single dependent variable. In terms of θ, the equation is

$$\frac{\partial\theta}{\partial t} = \nabla\cdot(D\nabla\theta) - \frac{dK}{d\theta}\cdot\frac{\partial\theta}{\partial z} . \tag{6}$$

Both the _moisture diffusivity_ D, defined by

$$D = Kd\Psi/d\theta,$$

and the coefficient $dK/d\theta$ are, in general, strongly-varying functions of θ. $D(\theta)$ for the soil of Figs. 1 and 2 is shown in Fig 3. In terms of Ψ, (5) becomes

$$\frac{d\theta}{d\Psi} \cdot \frac{\partial\Psi}{\partial t} = \nabla\cdot(K\nabla\Psi) - \frac{dK}{d\Psi} \cdot \frac{\partial\Psi}{\partial z} , \tag{7}$$

with the various coefficients of Ψ.

Richards [70] developed (5) and (7). Childs and George [7] recognized the diffusion character of (6) for a horizontal one-dimensional system. Klute [3] explicitly derived (6). The approach was extended [36,37,42] to include water transfer in vapour and adsorbed phases in the same formalism.

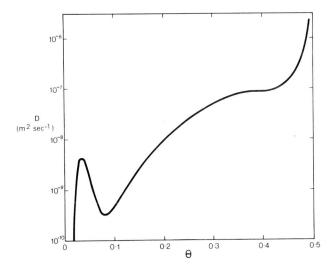

Fig. 3. Relation between moisture diffusivity, D, and moisture content, θ, for Yolo light clay [37]. For $\theta \leqslant 0.06$, D includes dominant contribution in vapour phase.

The strong nonlinearity of Fokker–Planck equations (6) and (7) cannot be ignored, and progress in unsaturated flow studies has depended centrally on their solution. We return to a discussion of nonlinear Fokker–Planck and diffusion equations in Section 7 below.

6. APPLICATIONS AND EXTENSIONS

Appropriate solutions of (6) and (7) accord with experiment and offer insight into the physics of such diverse phenomena as infiltration [36,56,42,48], capillary rise [53], evaporation from soil [36,40], drainage and retention of soil-water [41,77,10,84], and extraction of soil-water by plant roots [41,16,8].

Limitations to this approach have been reviewed elsewhere [56]. The analysis has been extended to nonisothermal systems by Philip and de Vries [66,82,83]. Jury [22] has provided a useful and incisive commentary on this work by reinterpreting it in terms of the formulation of the thermodynamics of irreversible processes.

Some progress has been made with the extension to hysteretic systems [primarily those with hysteresis in the $\Psi(\theta)$ relation]. One fundamental problem is that of the mathematical representation of hysteretic properties. Miller and Miller [26] gave a penetrating but qualitative discussion. Poulovassilis [67] gave the first account in terms of the independent domain model. Childs [5] extended the flow equation to hysteretic systems. Similarity hypotheses [51,29] simplify the problem, though there remains some question as to the adequacy of the independent domain model [80,79,68].

Extensions to take account of the complication of aggregation (or cracking) [54,55] and the effects of soil air [85,34,35,28] and of hydrodynamic stability [19,61,69] are also under way.

The foregoing developments have provided a fruitful framework for study of the hydrology of nonswelling soils, but they take no specific account of the effects of volume change, which can be important in soils of high colloid content. Some steps towards the required generalization have been made: they are reviewed more fully elsewhere [59,62]. A sufficient hydrologic characterization of swelling soils involves not only the K- and Ψ-functions (which, as we have seen, form a sufficient characterization of nonswelling soils in nonhysteretic situations), but also a 'void-ratio function' (describing volume-change characteristics), together with the soil particle density.

The resulting equations for the flow and volume-change in one-dimensional swelling systems are similar to the flow equations for nonswelling soils. In some simple, but important, cases, they are identical in form and the same methods of solution apply; but, in general, they are more complicated and more difficult. The theory of equilibrium and flow phenomena in <u>vertical</u> swelling systems is fundamentally different from that for vertical nonswelling ones. The differences have practical consequences for groundwater hydrology [59] and irrigation technology [60].

7.   SOLUTION OF NONLINEAR DIFFUSION AND FOKKER-PLANCK EQUATIONS: EXAMPLE OF INFILTRATION

Equations (6) and (7) may be solved by the brute-force use of high-speed computers, so long as the problem is well-posed and the computation scheme stable. Many computations of this type have, in fact, been made in the last 15 years or so. My own work, however, has been concerned more with quasi-analytical and analytical methods - from the viewpoint that they tell us more about the fundamental structure of the solutions and, hence, about the general character of the phenomena which they describe. 'Quasi-analytical' solutions depend on the methods of mathematical analysis for the establishment of their basic form, even though some 'coefficients' require to be determined numerically. When the solution may be found completely by mathematical analysis, we call it 'analytical'. Both analytical and quasi-analytical solutions are 'exact' in the (somewhat optimistic) usage of fluid mechanics [81].

The principal exact solutions and the relevant techniques have been reviewed at length in [56], [3], and [64], so I shall not go into details here. It will suffice to discuss the example of one-dimensional infiltration for the case when water is suddenly supplied in excess at the surface of a homogeneous soil with uniform initial water content.

A fundamental related solution is that of the analogous problem for a <u>horizontal</u> system. This is a similarity solution of the one-dimensional nonlinear diffusion equation [2], namely

$$x(\theta,t) = \phi_1(\theta) \cdot t^{\frac{1}{2}} . \tag{8}$$

Here x is the horizontal coordinate. The function ϕ_1 is the solution of a non-linear ordinary equation which may be found by a simple and accurate numerical technique [42,38]. ϕ_1 may be obtained analytically for an indefinitely large class of functional forms of $D(\theta)$ [49]. The importance of this solution is that it provides the leading term of the perturbation solution of related problems involving the complication of (arbitrary) two- and three-dimensional geometry and/or gravity. The latter is embodied in the first-order term on the right of (6).

For our example of one-dimensional infiltration, the solution is of the form [36,42,39]

$$z(\theta,t) = \phi_1(\theta)t^{\frac{1}{2}} + \phi_2(\theta)t + \phi_3(\theta)t^{3/2} + \ldots \quad . \qquad (9)$$

Here ϕ_2, ϕ_3, etc. are the easily-obtained solutions of linear ordinary equations. For the example depicted in Fig. 4, the first four terms of (9) suffice to yield an accurate solution (error $\leqslant 0.5\%$) for t as large as 10^6 sec. The same solution applies for capillary rise (vertical upward flow) [53] with the sign of the odd terms on the right on (9) reversed. The radius of practical convergence is, however, less; and the solution is supplemented by the exact solution in the limit as $t \to \infty$.

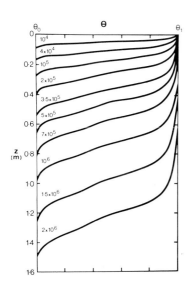

Fig. 4. Computed moisture profiles for one-dimensional infiltration in Yolo light clay [36,42,43]. Numerals on each profile represent value of t (sec) at which profile is realised. Profiles for $t \leqslant 10^6$ sec calculated from the first four terms of series (9); those for $t > 10^6$ sec based on (10).

Solution (9) is supplemented by <u>asymptotic solution</u>, valid for large t,

$$z(\theta,t) = (t - t_0)v + \zeta(\theta) \quad . \qquad (10)$$

The velocity of the moisture profile, v, is given by

$$v = [K(\theta_1) - K(\theta_0)]/(\theta_1 - \theta_0) \quad .$$

ζ follows from a simple quadrature and t_0 from a matching procedure [43].

One consequence of (9) is the physically-based, two-parameter infiltration equation [36]

$$i = St^{\frac{1}{2}} + At \quad ,$$

with the differential form

$$v = \tfrac{1}{2} St^{-\frac{1}{2}} + A$$

describing the time-dependence of infiltration capacity. i is the cumulative infiltration at time t from the beginning of the process; and v is here the infiltration capacity.

Where similarity methods apply, they have the great virtue of reducing the number of independent variables by one. Integral methods, on the other hand, offer the prospect of effectively achieving the same simplification for many real-world problems which stubbornly refuse to fit the Procrustean bed of similarity. Green and Ampt [18] unconsciously used a primitive integral method by simply supposing the advancing moisture profiles to be step functions. This assumption is exact for D proportional to a Dirac delta-function at the wet end of the moisture range [45, 63]. Green and Ampt's work has recently excited the interest of some hydrologists. It must not be overlooked, however, that the Green-Ampt approximation fails for two- and three-dimensional systems [cf. 56]. Parlange proposed a more sophisticated integral method [31-33]: see [24,65] for subsequent developments.

8. WATER TRANSPORT IN THE SOIL-PLANT-ATMOSPHERE CONTINUUM

In this section we turn our attention briefly to the processes of water transfer in plants, in the air layer occupied by vegetation, and in the lower atmosphere.

A full discussion of the processes of water movement in plants would lead into areas of plant, cell, and membrane physiology where we shall not venture. Treatments in the literature include [41], [52], [8] and [72,74-76]. Slatyer [75] gives a useful discussion of the anatomy of the water pathways through the plant.

Water is taken up by the plant roots and is transferred through the root tissues to the conducting vessels of the plant, and in these vessels to the mesophyll tissues of the leaves; it moves through these tissues to the evaporation sites, which are primarily the walls of the substomatal cavities. These various flows are in the liquid phase down a gradient of potential which is thermodynamically of the same character as Φ, introduced in Section 4. I use this symbol here also, though it will be understood that Ψ, which I again write for $(\Phi - z)$, is now made up primarily of hydrostatic and osmotic components. For a given plant cell Ψ is a function of the turgor (or water content) of the cell. The final transfer of water from the substomatal cavities through the stomata of the leaves is a process of molecular diffusion of water vapour.

Schematically (Fig. 5) one can look on the passage of water through the system as a flow through a sequence of resistances in series down a gradient of Φ. This concept gives a useful first picture, but it must be emphasized that for real plants the three-dimensional disposition of roots, leaves and other plant parts makes for a more complicated hydraulic problem. Attempts to use the one-dimensional model for predictive purposes in the field are, in consequence, somewhat unsatisfactory [52].

We next consider processes in the lower atmosphere. Evaporation involves not only the transport of liquid water to, and of water vapour from, the evaporation site, but also the supply of energy (latent heat) needed for the phase change. A proper consideration of water transfer in the lower atmosphere thus requires that we take cognizance not only of the transfer processes for water, but also for heat.

In regions in which air is either still or in laminar motion (these include the stomatal cavities and stomata of plants), both heat and water vapour are transferred by molecular diffusion, and we describe the process by an equation of the form

$$q = - D_m \nabla\theta, \tag{11}$$

where q is the flux density of the particular entity, θ its concentration, and D_m the appropriate molecular diffusivity.

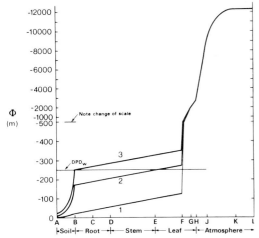

Fig. 5. The soil-plant-atmosphere continuum showing profiles of total potential Φ: (1) during normal transpiration; (2) during temporary wilting; (3) at permanent wilting. Points of the transpiration path: A, soil (a definite distance from plant root); B, surface of root hairs and of absorbing epidermal cells; C, cortex; D, endodermis; DE, vessels and tracheids in xylem; E, leaf veins; F, mesophyll cells; FG, intercellular space and substomatal cavity; GH, stomatal pore; HJ, laminar sublayer if present (see text); JK, turbulent boundary layer; KL, free atmosphere; DPD_w denotes Φ-value at incipient plasmolysis of root cells (after [41]).

Laminar motions occur only exceptionally in the lower atmosphere. They may be realized in calm, stable, conditions, in the laminar sub-layers developed on aerodynamically smooth rigid surfaces such as smooth ice-sheets, and in the lowest layers of very dense vegetation.

The normal state of affairs is a turbulent one; and the dominant transfer process is then turbulent diffusion, which may be described by the equation

$$q = -D_t \nabla \theta. \tag{12}$$

Eq. (12) is the same as Eq. (11) except that D_m is replaced by the turbulent diffusivity, D_t. D_t varies spatially. Above many natural surfaces D_t is roughly proportional to height above ground.

D_t is typically of the order of 0.1 m^2 sec^{-1} at a height of 1 m above ground level, whereas D_m is about 2×10^{-5} m^2 sec^{-1}. The dominance of the turbulent process will be evident.

Below the top of the vegetation the study of transfer process is complicated by the fact that the foliage operates as a source or sink for various entities such as water, heat, and momentum. The flux densities within the canopy vary with height above the ground, and may vary quite differently for each entity (see, for example, Denmead [11]). A one-dimensional model cannot represent this complicated behaviour, though a two-parameter model appears useful in elucidating these processes [52,50].

Finally, we note that thermodynamics provides a basis for treating the processes in these various domains in a unified way. We have in Eq.(4) the connexion between moisture potential and relative humidity. This, together with the identification of soil moisture potential and plant water potential, enables us to consider both liquid-phase transport processes in the soil and the plant, and vapour-phase processes in soil, plant, and atmosphere as occurring down gradients of total potential.* Gradmann [17] was the first to recognize the thermodynamic continuum through the plant and the atmosphere, but it seems to have been neglected until van den Honert [21] discussed it. Later work included the soil domain in the continuum and treated the atmospheric domain more realistically [36,41]. The one-dimensional model of the soil-plant-atmosphere continuum is illustrated in Fig. 5. As I mention above, this model is schematic in the sense that it evades the complications of the three-dimensional geometry of the real system (which should be faced in any model designed for quantitative predictive purposes).

9.   SOIL-WATER PHYSICS AND THE PROBLEM OF SCALE

Soil-water physicists are called on, increasingly, to contribute to large-scale hydrological and ecological studies. The present Working Conference is one such occasion. We are not, however, always ready (or, indeed, able) to contribute all that the customers hope for. This is, I think, understandable. The soil-water physicist is (more or less) a natural scientist, and tends to be, by nature and talent, an analyst. On the other hand, the customers are naturally synthesists.

Soil-water physicists have concentrated their attention on the small scale: their greatest successes have been in the study of local processes taking place on and under a single small area of ground surface. This has made good scientific sense, and has enabled us, with relatively modest resources, to arrive at a fairly satisfactory understanding of many soil-water phenomena.

But this has left unanswered the question as to how we may best use our understanding of small-scale local processes on the large scale of the river basin or ecological unit. In general, it is true that the larger the scale, the greater the heterogeneities in the system. The problem itself may become elusive and nebulous; and, in any case, the labour of sampling and of integration becomes formidable. The beautiful economy of analytical scientific methods is soon lost in the sheer magnitude, complexity, and imprecision of the task of synthesis.

In my opinion, there is a deep methodological difficulty here. One hears sometimes that 'systems analysis', modelling', 'simulation' - call it what you will - is the panacea[†]. It seems to me, however, that there is no magic passage through the impasse: we must bring to the problem not only space-age hardware and software, but also all the continuing respect for the real-world phenomenon, and

---

*The matter is more complicated when temperature gradients are important; but we limit ourselves here to the isothermal conditions often approximately realized in practice.

†The role of systems analysis as panacea is very understandable. Persons possessing great responsibility, authority, and power remain, nevertheless, human beings; and, like the rest of us, they love to hear good news. And the good news which the messengers have been bringing over the last decade or so is that systems analysis is alive and well and is ready and able to solve their problems.

all the intellectual honesty, we can muster.

10.   SYSTEMS ANALYSIS: SOME PROBLEMS AND LIMITATIONS

Perhaps you will allow me, in conclusion, to offer a personal perspective on systems analysis. As you will all know very well, systems analysis originated as an engineering technique for analyzing complicated electromechanical systems; and it has a very proper and successful role in handling systems in which all the individual components are well understood and can be represented reliably and accurately in the analysis. Application of systems analysis has tended to expand, however, into ever-widening fields: and the significance of such essays has not always been clear.

A notable example is the Club of Rome 'Limits to Growth' study [25], based on the techniques of Forrester [13-15]. I'm afraid that the picture I get from a careful reading of Forrester's books on methodology is most worrying: the major effort is devoted to making elementary mathematics seem terribly difficult and abstruse, and in this way attention is diverted from the really profound diffi- culties, such as the questions of the accuracy and stability of the sub-models and of the reliability of inputs of empirical data.

There seems to be a danger that, when systems analysis is applied in very broad fields, it is prone to the forms of intellectual dishonesty noted by Andreski [1]: the disguising of simplistic and/or old ideas, and of slip-shod work, in space-age jargon and in a spurious mathematization.

Beyond this, there are further problems connected with the economic, poli- tical, and sociological elements in very large systems. These involve the general philosophical and methodological difficulties of the social sciences, particularly those concerned with values [e.g. 78]. A value-free social study is all too prone to home in happily on trivia, but to be impotent vis à vis the basic human issues.

In regard to the application of systems analysis to purely hydrologic systems (by which I mean water systems free of sociological content), my appeal, then, is that the systems analysts should never lose touch with the real-world natural phenomena which their sub-models and models purport to represent. The great virtue and power of natural science has derived from its willingness to defer to the phenomenon: that is why natural science is a solid human achievement, not an exercise in fantasy. As for the application of systems analysis to wider water resource systems with significant sociological content, my hope is that enthusiasm will be tempered by responsible sensitivity to the limitations of the tool and to the dimensions of the task.

It may well be that these worries of mine are groundless. Perhaps they will be dispelled in the course of this Working Conference. I hope so.

11.   REFERENCES

[1]   Andreski, S. (1972). "Social Sciences as Sorcery". (Deutch: London.)
[2]   Boltzmann, L. (1894). Ann. Phys. (Lpz.) 53, 959-964.
[3]   Braester, C., Dagan, G., Neuman, S., and Zaslavsky, D. (1971). Rep. Hydro-
       dynamics Hydr. Eng. Lab., Technion.
[4]   Buckingham, E. (1907). U.S.D.A. Bur. Soil Bull. 38.
[5]   Childs, E.C. (1964). Soil Sci. 97, 173-178.
[6]   Childs, E.C., and Collis-George, N. (1951). Proc. R. Soc. A201, 392-405.
[7]   Childs, E.C., and George, N.C. (1948). Disc. Faraday Soc. 3, 78-85.
[8]   Cowan, I.R. (1965). J. Appl. Ecol. 2, 221-239.
[9]   Croney, D., Coleman, J.D., and Bridge, P.M. (1952). Road Res. Tech. Pap. 24.
[10] Day, P.R., and Luthin, J.N. (1956). Soil Sci. Soc. Amer. Proc. 20, 443-447.
[11] Denmead, O.T. (1964). J. Appl. Meteorol. 3, 383-389.
[12] Edlefsen, N.E., and Anderson, A.B.C. (1943). Hilgardia 16, 31-299.
[13] Forrester, J.W. (1968). "Principles of Systems: Text and Workbook". 2nd
       Prelim. Ed. (Wright-Allen: Cambridge, Mass.)
[14] Forrester, J.W. (1969). "Urban Dynamics". (M.I.T. Press: Cambridge, Mass.)
[15] Forrester, J.W. (1971). "World Dynamics". (Wright-Allen: Cambridge, Mass.)
[16] Gardner, W.R. (1960). Soil Sci. 89, 63-73.
[17] Gradmann, H. (1928). Jahr. Wiss. Bot. 69, 1-100.
[18] Green, W.H., and Ampt, G.A. (1911). J. Agric. Sci. 4, 1-24.
[19] Hill, D.E., and Parlange, J.-Y. (1972). Soil Sci. Soc. Amer. Proc. 36, 697-
       702.
[20] Holmes, J.W., Taylor, S.A., and Richards, S.J. (1967). In "Irrigation of
       Agricultural Lands". (Eds. R.M. Hagen, H.R. Haise, and T.W. Edminster.)
       pp. 257-303. (Amer. Soc. Agronomy: Madison, Wisc.)
[21] Honert, T.H. van den (1948). Disc. Faraday Soc. 3, 146-153.
[22] Jury, W.A. (1973). "Simultaneous Transport of Heat and Moisture through a
       Medium Sand." Ph.D. Thesis, Univ. of Wisconsin.
[23] Klute, A. (1952). Soil Sci. 73, 105-116.
[24] Knight, J.H., and Philip, J.R. (1973). Soil Sci. 116, 407-416.
[25] Meadows, D.H., Meadows, D.L., and Behrens III, W.W. (1972). "The Limits to
       Growth." (Universe Books: New York.)
[26] Miller, E.E., and Miller, R.D. (1956). J. Appl. Phys. 27, 324-332.
[27] Moore, R.E. (1939). Hilgardia 12, 383-426.
[28] Morel-Seytoux, H.J. (1973). Adv. Hydrosci. 9, 119-202.
[29] Mualem, Y. (1973). Water Resourc. Res. 9, 1324-1331.
[30] Nimmo, W.H.R. (1949). J. Inst. Eng. Aust. 21, 29-34.
[31] Parlange, J.-Y. (1971). Soil Sci. 111, 134-137.
[32] Parlange, J.-Y. (1971). Soil Sci. 111, 170-174.
[33] Parlange, J.-Y. (1971). Soil Sci. 112, 313-317.
[34] Peck, A.J. (1965). Soil Sci. 99, 327-334.
[35] Peck, A.J. (1965). Soil Sci. 100, 44-51.
[36] Philip, J.R. (1954). J. Inst. Eng. Aust. 26, 255-259.
[37] Philip, J.R. (1955). Proc. Nat. Acad. Sci. India (Allahabad) 24A, 93-104.
[38] Philip, J.R. (1955). Trans. Faraday Soc. 51, 885-892.
[39] Philip, J.R. (1957). Aust. J. Phys. 10, 43-53.
[40] Philip, J.R. (1957). J. Meteorol. 14, 354-366.
[41] Philip, J.R. (1957). Proc. 3rd Congr. Irrig. Drain. 8.125-8.154.
[42] Philip, J.R. (1957). Soil Sci. 83, 345-357.
[43] Philip, J.R. (1957). Soil Sci. 83, 435-448.
[44] Philip, J.R. (1957). Soil Sci. 84, 163-178.
[45] Philip, J.R. (1957). Soil Sci. 84, 257-264.
[46] Philip, J.R. (1957). Soil Sci. 84, 329-339.
[47] Philip, J.R. (1958). Soil Sci. 85, 278-286.
[48] Philip, J.R. (1958). Soil Sci. 85, 333-337.
[49] Philip, J.R. (1960). Aust. J. Phys. 13, 1-12.
[50] Philip, J.R. (1964). J. Appl. Meteorol. 3, 390-395.
[51] Philip, J.R. (1964). J. Geophys. Res. 69, 1553-1562.

[52] Philip, J.R. (1966). Ann. Rev. Plant Physiol. 17, 245-268.
[53] Philip, J.R. (1966). In "Water in the Unsaturated Zone". Symp. Wageningen
       UNESCO 1, 471-478.
[54] Philip, J.R. (1968). Aust. J. Soil Res. 6, 1-19.
[55] Philip, J.R. (1968). Aust. J. Soil Res. 6, 21-30.
[56] Philip, J.R. (1969). Adv. Hydrosci. 5, 214-296.
[57] Philip, J.R. (1970). Ann. Rev. Fluid Mech. 2, 177-204.
[58] Philip, J.R. (1970). Soil Sci. 109, 294-298.
[59] Philip, J.R. (1971). In "Salinity and Water Use". (Eds. T. Talsma and J.R.
       Philip.) pp. 95-107. (Macmillan: London.)
[60] Philip, J.R. (1972). Proc. 8th Int. Congr. Irrig. Drain. C.13-C.28.
[61] Philip, J.R. (1972). Soil Sci. 113, 294-300.
[62] Philip, J.R. (1973). Proc. 3rd Int. Congr. Theor. Appl. Mech. pp. 279-294.
       (Springer: Berlin.)
[63] Philip, J.R. (1973). Soil Sci. 116, 328-335.
[64] Philip, J.R. (1974). Soil Sci. 117, 257-264.
[65] Philip, J.R., and Knight, J.H. (1974). Soil Sci. 117, 1-13.
[66] Philip, J.R., and Vries, D.A. de (1957). Trans. Amer. Geophys. Union 38,
       222-232.
[67] Poulovassilis, A. (1962). Soil Sci. 93, 405-412.
[68] Poulovassilis, A., and Childs, E.C. (1971). Soil Sci. 112, 301-312.
[69] Raats, P.A.C. (1973). Soil Sci. Soc. Amer. Proc. 37, 681-685.
[70] Richards, L.A. (1931). Physics 1, 318-333.
[71] Richards, L.A. (1949). Soil Sci. 68, 95-112.
[72] Richards, L.A., and Wadleigh, C.H. (1952). In "Soil Physical Conditions and
       Plant Growth". (Ed. B.T. Shaw.) pp. 73-251. (Academic Press: New York.)
[73] Schofield, R.K. (1935). Trans. 3rd Int. Congr. Soil Sci. 1, 30-33.
[74] Slatyer, R.O. (1960). Bot. Rev. 26, 331-392.
[75] Slatyer, R.O. (1967). "Plant-Water Relationships." (Academic Press: New
       York.)
[76] Slatyer, R.O., and Denmead, O.T. (1964). In "Water Resources, Use, and
       Management". (Melbourne Univ. Press: Melbourne.)
[77] Staple, W.J., and Lehane, J.J. (1954). Can. J. Agric. Sci. 34, 329-342.
[78] Stretton, H. (1969). "The Political Sciences: General Principles of
       Selection in Social Sciences and History." (Routledge & Kegan Paul: London.)
[79] Topp, G.C. (1971). Soil Sci. Soc. Amer. Proc. 35, 219-225.
[80] Topp, G.C., and Miller, E.E. (1966). Soil Sci. Soc. Amer. Proc. 30, 156-162.
[81] Van Dyke, M. (1954). "Perturbation Methods in Fluid Mechanics." (Academic
       Press: New York.)
[82] Vries, D.A. de (1958). Trans. Amer. Geophys. Union 39, 909-916.
[83] Vries, D.A. de, and Philip, J.R. (1957). J. Geophys. Res. 64, 386-388.
[84] Whisler, F.D., and Watson, K.K. (1968). J. Hydrol. 6, 277-296.
[85] Youngs, E.G., and Peck, A.J. (1964). Soil Sci. 98, 290-294.

Current research field of author : *Application of physics and mathematics to research problems of flow and transfer processes in soils and porous media, plants and the lower atmosphere.*

DISCUSSION

I will not agree with everything that has been said , but I do agree with a lot of what was said in the second half. Indeed, I am against modeling à la Forrester, and I think it to be an example of nonsense. There is nothing wrong in looking at things in those ways as long as you don't try any press on people because it came out of a computer model and that computer model came out of MIT ; since it fit in two points you should extrapolate it to the next century telling that we go to a catastrophe. Indeed the system analyst would look at the model and linearize it for instance about the 1970 conditions and so he will come to a nice conclusion : that the essential part of the Forrester Model is the capital investment natural resources loop and everything follows from that loop. Forrester could come out with the same conclusion by just looking at those two factors, because it is evident that you have a growth followed by a decay. I disagree that the very good work that has been done in a particular area should not constrain us to not opening our eyes and looking at other types of representation, because if we are so constrained, we can be blind. I am convinced of that, from looking at various processes mostly not electromechanical : Chemical processes for instance are notoriously difficult to model. But in the large agregate sense there is definitely a simplicity of behaviour in dynamic terms. We must look why that is. It is true to say that no one has come up with a law of large systems. Many people have come to it into one form or another. In linear systems it is self evident that there is such a law because we know that any large system, 150 differ. equ., are dominated by one or two modes of dynamic behaviour. And to know what has happened to the one or two modes we know what will happen in aggregate terms about that system. We should not forget that the other modes are there because if we happen to close the loop for instance, for a feedback control, we can excite those modes, they become troublesome and they change the nature of the system behaviour, but we bear all these things in mind. (YOUNG)

I would like to ask a crucial question and that is the question of scale. The soil physicists have a nicely behaved mechanistic model of transport phenomena of natural and transformation energy in the micro system which has a scale of about a meter or several meters, one or two or three dimensionally. The problem is that hydrology deals with such larger systems. The question is whether soil physics has anything to offer to hydrology not only in terms of describing the soil which is a small link in the continuous chain of relevance or processes comprising the hydrologic cycle but also in terms of the methodology for the treatment of larger systems. It seems that there are two possibilities, one would be to continue operating on a small scale and that means going to the system-analyst of the larger and better computers and constructing the larger system out of small elements of the size or concept that soil physicists have developed in the way that dr. Philip has helped soil physicists since several years. The other possibility is to go directly into the larger scale and try to treat the larger scale by lumping its heterogeneities into an effective larger whole and characterizing on a much larger natural scale some of the concepts that have proved to be so useful on a micro scale, for instance the concept of hydraulic conductivity. When soil physicists speak about hydraulic conductivity they imply a scale : so many cm^3. Is it possible to go to m^3 and 100 m^3 and include in a continuous whole the heterogeneity that is present in small scale, but can be ironed out statistically into an effective parameter for the acquifer. What is the promise on this respect ? Or is there a third approach ? (HILLEL)

There is one point to state straight off, and that is when it comes to the heterogeneities on the large scale, phenomena with scales of 100 m or more, I think it is probably true as what dr. Neuman pointed out, that one does not need to foresee much about the unsaturated zone and your question still is valid as far as the saturated regime is concerned and I think the answer is you have heterogeneities on a certain scale but you have in some sense heterogeneities in the large to elaborate problems about enlarging your volume element over which you define your coefficient such as conductivity. That's fine for steady situations. But in unsteady situations you can quite obviously involve yourself in some troubles and you might have to go through a two parameter description more or less along the lines of the way you have worked out. In the unsaturated situation one has to be rather careful about the averaging proces in the cracking soil and clearly in that case, this type of analysis, or the generalisation of it, applies to systems subject of volume change in cracking. The averaging volumes have to be large compared with the crack-ing situation. (PHILIP)

Perhaps substituting for the concept of hydraulic conductivity the concept of hydraulic resistance which allows one to go serially from one zone to another through the continuous domain of the flow process. Presumably resistance is the ratio of the effective distance of trouble to the hydraulic conductivity. One can possibly use this concept increasingly in the description of the soil in the unsaturated zone and derive some effective hydraulic conductivity. (HILLEL)

From the physicist's side your attitude towards the problem has been exactly the same as ours from the data processing side. Our problems have been to try to justify our own approach in the face of tremendous enthusiasm from the part of the physicists with whom we have been dealing. The result is that at every stage we have insisted on very careful analysis of our own techniques. This has extended the pro-ject to probably three times what was thought reasonable by the physicists with whom we were dealing. We have found that there are two aspects of simulation which seem to be difficult to substitute by any other method. The first is cross checks between various types of reading. This includes magnetic-meter readings to detect different types of rocks and level readings in boreholes, etc. All types of different techno-logies come in. It seems that simulation is the only technique that can correlate these readings. Secondly there are many quantities in real systems which seem to be very difficult to measure, seepage through dikes for instance, unless you can examine every part of the dike and take unnumerable samples, it is very difficult to know exactly what is coming through. The same applies to acquifers, pump tests. We have developed some source philosophy doing this project with regard to mechani-stic and empirical models. We used the mechanistic way if possible and we go into very great detail, the approximations we have to make in regard, particularly to discrete space and discrete time. We use empirical models when we cannot use mecha-nistic and here a very clear statement is made as to what we don't know. We try very hard to take mechanistic approach in areas where it is possible to take a cross check by means of measurements. In this case one can split the model into small modules and one can to a greater extent use that part of the model to express the validity in the areas where it is not possible to measure. Again we have gone to manual rather than automatic refinement. The reason is that the main value in the model is the clarification of the structure and the understanding. I am not sure if it is possible to prove anything positive by means of a model, although it seems to be possible to prove negatively if the various correlated readings don't fit. We were quite surprised in the beginning that two of our first predictions to the physicists came through. That is the existence of a certain dike and also the exi-stence of various items in the particular region. This is much the same approach as yours. (HELY-HUTCHINSON)

I can sympathise with you on suffering from enthusiasm from the other side. A very interesting paper in that respect was that of dr. Neuman in which he gave us an example of an inverse attempt of evaluating characteristics. And he showed just how purely posed the problem was. The moral from that exercise is that it would be so much better towards scientific problems to spend say a 1000 % on boring some holes and say 2000 % on computing. It is an unfortunate fact that the system-ana-lyst is often called in, to patch out a lousy scientific job and we can't really blame the system-analyst in any sense for that, except that he ought to be "stuner" with his customers. (PHILIP)

I was happy to hear the question raised by dr. Hillel and dr. Philip but we did not quite take it up. What to do with the relatively small measurements of hy-draulic conductivity that might be used for the area that they represent, in terms

*of the possibility of using them for predicting say fluxes of water over larger areas
and I wondered if not the system-analysts could not tell us something about the use
of hydraulic conductivity measured in rather small plots at different places over
the surface of the earth. How these could be used with some degree of certainty in
predicting the flux of water that might arrive at some points, at least in terms of
giving some ideas of what might happen or not happen. I feel like we still have not
quite come to grips with bringing together these two methods of approach. (BIGGAR)*

The question of the unsaturated conductivities are not really a problem because all you are really concerned about is transport over distances rather small
compared with the total scale of your large basin problem. If you are talking about
the problems of heterogeneity in the saturated zone, then there is no easy answer,
the more that you can do in the way of observing and characterising what you've got,
the better chance you have of doing something accurate. (PHILIP)

*I would like to answer the question in relation to what I told earlier.
With the field measurement we achieve using Zaslavsky approach. It seems that we
can get to the point where hydraulic conductivity can be taken as a regional average
of what you call effective conductivity for large scale. The measurements that we
made, have shown that it covered really well within the range of measurements that
have been made by other methods, and not only laboratory methods but two or three
field methods. And it shows not only with the approach that dr. Neuman got the other
day on the broke down of the water table on the effect of delay supplied from the
covering material. It seems there could be some kind of approach where you could
get to hydraulic conductivity which I would present regionally, towards even saturated soil. (DE BACKER)*

*I would like to comment on that sentence of the written text of dr. Philip
saying that you didn't see the difference between the simulation people and what
those in natural science have been trying to do for the last 300 years. As a man
using a computer very often in trying to solve such problems I feel that in this
sentence you are posing a contradiction which does not exist. I feel I am still belonging to people doing the natural science. The only difference that I could possibly detect is that the models that we are using could not be solved by hand or
by a simple calculator but by high speed computers. In doing so we extent our possibilities in the assumptions that have to be made in order to solve differential
equation of the form that you have written on the blackboard. The applicability of
certain solutions can be extended to other fields. It may be true what you said you
always met the wrong system-analysts. I am not quite sure what the difference is
between me and the system-analyst. I feel I am using simply the same basic physical
laws that you are using, only I use a different tool to solve the equations and to
apply the laws. (VAN KEULEN)*

This is precisely the point I wanted to make. I find it difficult to understand why we have to have a new vocabulary of modeling, system-analyst, it's all
doing natural science. I do think there is something which is very useful and I am
going to learn this during this meeting in systems analysis and that is, it is also
a disguised label for the whole business of the combination of observations and the
statistical processing of data in sophisticated ways. This has always been one of
the essential handmakings of natural science and nothing is changed except the labels. (PHILIP)

*Every model is approximate and there is nothing "holy" in a particular type
of model. There are certain basic scientific laws. If you obey them, you come to
different types of models. One particular model would be good in one particular set
of circumstances and another set of circumstances. From what I have been hearing
I am not surprised the model at a small level may not be particularly good at the
large level. The point is that the system-analysts perhaps looks at a wider variety
of systems in many particular areas, and he perhaps therefore sees a certain generality of things which is not seen being enforced by nature. We like it, to look at
different systems, particularly dynamic systems. We see similarities in different*

areas and we think we can learn from this, and that really is why the system-analyst is called "system-analyst" which is not a very good term. In England if you look for a job announced as advertisment you will find it is a computer programmer. If the term is used well it describes a particular profession. However it is often used badly. I think it is a profession. (YOUNG)

I accept that completely but I would draw the analogue with the mathematical statistician who equally is   concerned with seeing in all sorts of phenomena, in all sorts of fields of science, the central relationships. But the mathematical statistician has tended to recognize his role perhaps more clearly and not seem to elbow the natural scientist out of what the natural scientist might think is something that he thinks he knows, something about namely the phenomena. There is perhaps a greater resource of humility in the convential mathematical statistician than is yet been discovered by the system-analyst. (PHILIP)

There is one point, the statistician does not deal and does not know about under much evidence, dynamic systems. It is an important difference. The understanding of dynamic systems is not easy, it comes after a long process of learning and the statistician in general does not understand him. He uses transfer models, I am not so sure that he understands what he has got in his hands. (YOUNG)

Modeling and Simulation of Water Resources Systems, G.C. VANSTEENKISTE, (Ed.)
North-Holland Publishing Company (1975)

TOWARDS A COMPREHENSIVE SIMULATION OF TRANSIENT WATER TABLE FLOW PROBLEMS

G. Vachaud, M. Vauclin and R. Haverkamp
Institut de Mécanique
(Laboratoire associé n°6 au C.N.R.S.)
Université Scientifique et Médicale de Grenoble
B.P. 53 - F. 38041 - Grenoble-Cedex, FRANCE

SUMMARY

Following a brief review of the meaning of simplifying assumptions traditionally used for treating transient water table flow problems, a critique
of this approach is presented in view of discrepancies found between experimental results an analog simulation. It is then shown that a model
based on the physics of water flow between the soil surface and the saturated zone can adequately be used for describing this problem. The rest
of this paper deals with the study of feasability and adequacy of numerical techniques for solving the flow equation, and on the need to obtain
reliable hydraulic characteristics of the porous medium.

As a general assumption we will consider isothermal flow in an isotropic
and rigid soil.

THE TRADITIONAL APPROACH - SIMULATION AND MODELING

For a long period of time, simulation and modeling of transient water table
aquifer problems have been based upon a series of assumptions which we shall not
describe in detail. The most important are :

1.a. The flow is restricted within a domain $\mathcal{D}$ which is limited below by an impervious, or semi-pervious boundary, and above by an unknown moving boundary defined
as the water table. This boundary is also a piezometric level, corresponding to
h = 0, where h is the water pressure, relative to atmosphere, expressed in term
of hydrostatic head (fig. 1).

1.b. When the flow is steady, the water table is also a flow-line. When the flow
is transient, two cases should be considered :
. firstly, in the case of a lowering water table, one assumes usually that the
   soil drains instantaneously. If Δz is the change of level of the water table
   during a time interval Δt, the drained volume of water, per unit surface area,
   is estimated to the value

$$\Delta V_w = S.\Delta z$$

S defined as the storage coefficient, is identical to the effective porosity ε.
. secondly, in the case of a rising water table by infiltration, one assumes
   an instantaneous and conservative transfer of the water flux from the soil
   surface to the aquifer. The storage coefficient has usually the same meaning
   as in the previous case.

It is known that in the most general case (i.e. without further assumptions) the flow will be described by simultaneous solution of two independent
equations :

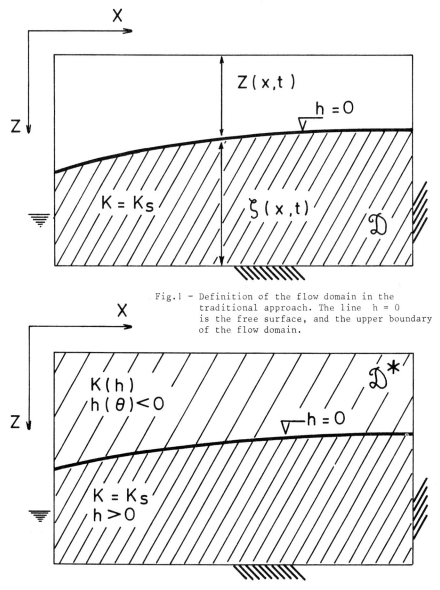

Fig.1 - Definition of the flow domain in the
traditional approach. The line h = 0
is the free surface, and the upper boundary
of the flow domain.

Fig.4 - Definition of the flow domain in the
saturated-unsaturated flow approach.
The line h = 0 is a characteristic piezometric surface, but not a boundary of the
flow domain.

i) Laplace's equation in $\mathcal{D}$, i.e. $\nabla^2 H = 0$ $\hspace{4em}$ (1)

ii) the moving free surface equation :

$$S \frac{\delta z}{\delta t} = K_s \left[\frac{\delta z}{\delta x} \frac{\delta H}{\delta x} - \frac{\delta H}{\delta z} \right] \hspace{4em} (2)$$

which represents the upper boundary condition.

Both equations (1) and (2), with proper boundary conditions at the fixed frontiers, should be solved in order to obtain the potential field in $\mathcal{D}$, and the depth of the water table (moving boundary) at any time t. Besides the symbol defined in fig. 1, the following are used :

> z is the depth of the water table, Oz being oriented positively downward ;
> K_s is the saturated hydraulic conductivity ;

and

> H is the total hydraulic potential, expressed as a water head, and given by : H = h - z.

Analog models such as viscous flow models or transient electric models will simulate exactly the system of equations 1 + 2. It is well known that viscous flow models are most suited to the case of transient flow, and can be used either for 2 - dimensional flow in the vertical plane XOZ or in the horizontal plane XOY. R-C type electric model or hybrid models for the transient case, are mostly restricted to the simulation of horizontal plane flow, but there exist some applications to transient three dimensional flow.

l.c. Very often, for numerical or analytical solution, a set of supplementary assumptions are used :
i. the Dupuit-Forchheimer assumption that the radius of curvature of the water table is large enough for considering the water head to be constant on any vertical line (i.e. H = - z). This assumption, applied to the system of eq. 1 and 2, leads to the well-known Boussinesq equation

$$\frac{S}{K_s} \cdot \frac{\delta \zeta}{\delta t} = \frac{\delta}{\delta x} \left[\zeta \cdot \frac{\delta \zeta}{\delta x} \right] \hspace{4em} (3)$$

where ζ (x, t) is the thickness of the aquifer.

Note that at the same time the solution of eq. 3 provides the position of the free surface at any t > 0, as well as the potential field throughout $\mathcal{D}$.

ii. the linearization assumption, that the change of head is small enough in $\mathcal{D}$ to permit writing :

$$\frac{S}{T} \cdot \frac{\delta \zeta}{\delta t} = \frac{\delta^2 \zeta}{\delta x^2} \hspace{4em} (4)$$

where T is the transmissivity of the aquifer (T = K $\cdot$ $\bar{\zeta}$ where $\bar{\zeta}$ is the mean thickness).

Therefore simulation techniques based on equations 1 and 2 are more rigorous than numerical or analytical solutions obtained from eq. 3 or 4. The set of supplementary assumptions l.c was mainly introduced in order to facilitate numerical modeling techniques which are quite difficult for the case of equation 1 and 2, where the unknown upper boundary has to be estimated explicitly in order to produce the needed boundary condition.

So far however, the main problem from our point of view is not to compare
the relative merit of each type of modelization technique (i.e. analog, hybrid or
numeric) for solving our problem, but rather to assess the validity of the basic
assumptions (i.e. 1.a and 1.b) with the aid of which the flow equations are established.

THE FLAWS OF THE "TRADITIONAL" APPROACH

Experimental evidence can be found in the literature showing that usually
assumption 1.a and 1.b are not valid. It is now well established, since the work
of Richards, 1931, that there exists above the water table an important zone of
soil, which is partially saturated, and which controls the transfer of water from
the soil surface to the aquifer and vice versa. It is also known that the drainage
of that slab of soil is not instantaneous, as implied in eq. 1.b. It should be
noted that some models were presented 20 years ago, still assuming 1.a to be valid,
but using instead of 1.b an assumption of an exponentially delayed yield (Boulton,
1964).

We will discuss in the next chapter the proper way of describing the physics of flow taking into account the role of the unsaturated zone, but we want
first to show experimental evidence of the quantitative values of the errors introduced by the use of assumptions 1.a and 1.b.

Drainage and recharge experiments were done in our laboratory on a two
dimensional slab of soil (3m in length, 2 m in height, 0.05 m in thickness) with
continuous monitoring of inflow-outflow volume of water and of changes of water
content and water pressures in the entire flow domain. Details have been published
elsewhere (Vachaud et al, 1972) and some data will be presented at this working
group in the paper of M. Vauclin et al.

The same experiments were also simulated using a Hele Shaw viscous flow
analog (basically eq. 1 and 2).

Let us first consider the results obtained during a transient drainage
experiment, which are presented in fig. 2. The boundary conditions are summarized
in fig. 2.a. The water table was initially in hydrostatic equilibrium at depth H_o;
at time $t \geqslant 0$, the piezometric level was suddenly set at depth H_1 for $x = 0$, without allowing inflow through the vertical right side of the model. The saturated
hydraulic conductivity of the soil was found to be $K_s = 40$ cm/hr, and the effective porosity $\varepsilon = 0.29$ (ε is defined as the difference between "saturated" and
"residual" water content and is assumed to be identical to S (Prill et al, 1963)).

In fig. 2.b are given the total outflow of water measured directly from
the soil and obtained by viscous flow analog (in that case, series of pictures
were taken each 0.5 sec and the outflow volume was directly obtained from water
table drawdown by the use of assumption 1.b, using the classical scaling variables
for determining the time).

In fig. 2.c the changes of depth of the water table with time are given
for two positions. The experimental curves were directly obtained from the water
pressure field in the soil slab, whereas the analog curves were directly inferred
from pictures of the viscous flow.

Finally fig. 2.d presents the theoretical value of the effective porosity
used in eq. 1 as well as the values of the storage coefficient S obtained during
the drainage experiment by the ratio between changes of water content profiles at
different values of x, and different time, and measured drawdowns of the water
table for the same sets of values (x, t) (see Vachaud et al, 1973, for further details).

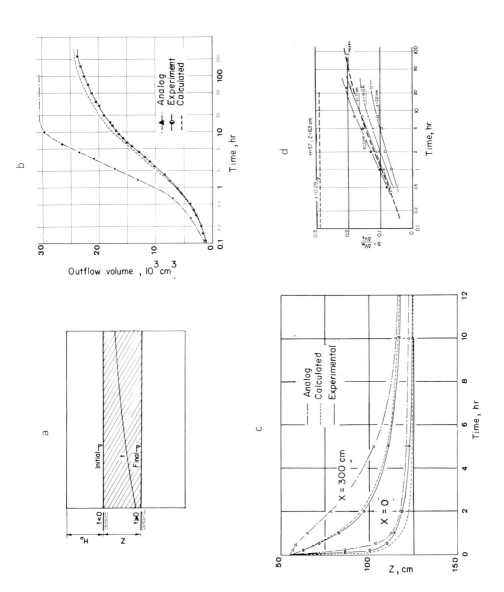

Fig.2 – Comparison between experimental, analog and numerical results relative to a two dimensional transient drainage problem. The analog results were obtained on a Hele-Shaw viscous flow model; the calculated values were given by numerical solution of the complete saturated-unsaturated flow problem (chapter 3).

It is clear from this series of data that during a drainage case :
1. the traditional assumptions, or the use of eq. 1, overestimate the total outflow (since they include the volume of water which actually remains stored in
   the unsaturated zone by capillarity) and grossly underestimate the duration of
   the flow (since it assumes the hydraulic conductivity in the total flow domain
   to be a constant, which is completely wrong).
2. the use of assumption 1.b underestimates the drawdown of the water table. This
   is apparently in contradiction with the previous findings. But we should remember that in the traditional approach there is a direct, and linear relationship between ΔV_w and Δz. In the real case we will see that the water table is
   nothing but a piezometric line and that there can exist a great change of pressure without (or with a negligible) outflow.
3. it is impossible to assume S to be a constant. Therefore eq. 3 and 4, if used,
   should be corrected for this remark. (Note that the concept of delayed yield
   suggested by Boulton is not suitable, since it assumes only $S = S(t)$ instead
   of $S = S(x, t)$).

We now look at some results obtained in the same way during a recharge experiment done on the same soil with the boundary condition given by fig. 3.a.
Initially, the piezometric level was set at depth H_o ; at time $t \geqslant 0$ a constant
flux infiltration was imposed at the soil surface on a width L_o ; there was no
flow through the vertical left side and the piezometric level was maintained at
H_o on the vertical right side ; at the same time the outflow was recorded. The
following points should be noted :

Fig. 3.b gives the cumulative volume outflow of water measured directly
and determined from analog experiments. Fig. 3.c shows the rise of the water table
at position $X=0$, one curve being determined from the water pressure field in the
slab of soil, the other being obtained by photography of the analog model. Finally,
fig. 3.d presents the value of an equivalent recharge coefficient, given by the
ratio between the volume input at the level of the water table, and the imposed
volume of inflow at the soil surface.

From these results , we note that during the recharge experiment :

1. it is not possible to obtain information on the duration of the transfer of
   water from the soil surface to the water table by the use of equation 1. 2.
   This very important parameter is completely neglected by the traditional approach.
2. There exists no agreement, because of the previous finding, between the simulated and real rise of the water table for a given time t.
3. It is impossible to assume that the water flux is conservative during the transfer from the soil surface to the water table, since in that case the curve in
   fig. 3.d would have been a horizontal line of ordinate 1.

Therefore, the traditional approach seems to be quite incorrect with regard to the simulation of a transient drainage or of a transient recharge experiment. This is mainly due to the fact that the basic assumptions on which this approach was based, are not physically sound. For this reason we now wish to propose
and discuss one other approach, based on the physics of flow in the saturated and
unsaturated zones of soil.

THE SATURATED - UNSATURATED FLOW APPROACH

As it is not our purpose to describe in detail the physics of water transfer in the unsaturated domain (basic informations can be found in classical books
such as those of Childs, 1969 ; Nielsen et al, 1972 ; Hillel, 1971 ; and others),
we will confine ourself herein to the presentation of a physical model, and of
some methods of numerical solutions, with the aid of previous works of J. Rubin
(1968), R.A. Freeze (1969) and I. Remson et al (1971). The validity of this approach is discussed in detail by M. Vauclin et al (1974) in another paper presented
at this conference.

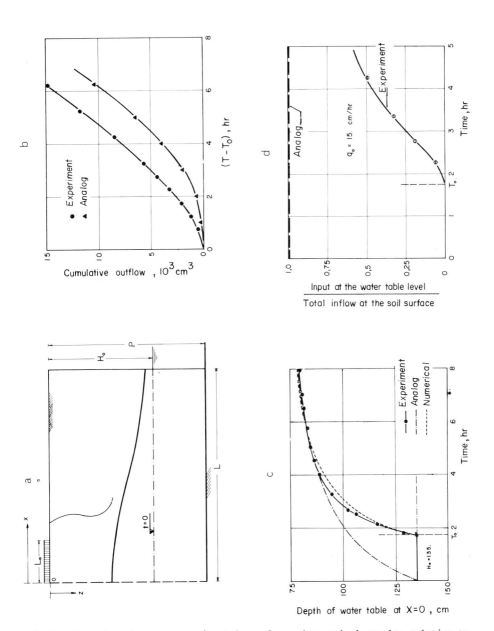

Fig.3 – Comparison between experimental, analog and numerical results relative to a two-dimensional transient recharge problem. T_o is the duration of the transfer of water from the soil surface to the water table in its initial position.

Basically, this approach rests on the following points :

3.a. Considering a continuity in the liquid phase from the saturated zone to the soil surface through the partially saturated zone, or "unsaturated zone", we now impose r the domain of flow to be $\mathcal{D}^*$, defined in fig. 4, limited below by the impervious layer, and above by the soil surface. With respect to traditional assumption 1.a, it is noted that now the upper boundary of the flow domain is fixed, and its condition is known at all times.

3.b. The water content θ (volume of water/volume of soil) varies continuously from the soil surface to the bottom of the aquifer. The fundamental variable will be the hydraulic potential H, defined at any point of the domain $\mathcal{D}^*$ by :

$$H = h - z \tag{5}$$

where h is the water pressure, relative to the atmosphere, expressed in term of water height.

Unlike the definition in chapter 1, h is a function of θ in the unsaturated zone. The curve h - θ is the soil water characteristic, or suction curve, generally subject to hysteresis. In the domain $\mathcal{D}^*$, h will generally vary continuously, with the following characteristic values :

> h > 0 in the aquifer below the water table
> h = 0 at the water table
> h < 0 in the **unsaturated** zone above the water table.

It must be noted that the saturated zone in fact is not limited on the upper side by the water table but by the capillary fringe (see Childs, 1969 for a through discussion of this phenomenon).

3.c. Equation 1 was obtained from Darcy's law and the mass conservation equation in the saturated domain.

In the unsaturated domain, it is known that :

(1) Darcy's law is still generally valid, but in the form :

$$\overline{q} = - K \overline{\text{grad}} (h-z) \tag{6.a}$$

where K, hydraulic conductivity, is now a function of θ, or h (since h = h(θ)).

(2) The mass conservation law is :

$$\text{div } q = - \frac{\delta\theta}{\delta t} \tag{6.b}$$

Combining 6.a and 6.b yields :

$$c \cdot \frac{\delta h}{\delta t} = \text{div } [\ K(h) \ \overline{\text{grad}} \ H \ ] \tag{6}$$

where c, the capillary capacity, is defined as :

$$c = \frac{\delta\theta}{\delta t} \quad \text{(Richards 1931)}$$

The physical meaning of 6.b implies that it is impossible to have a transient flow in the unsaturated domain without change of water content (until the domain becomes saturated).

A remarkable property of eq. 6 is that it represents the flow in the unsaturated domain as well as in the saturated domain. In that last case indeed, one obtains $\theta = \theta_s$ (saturated water content)
$$K = K_s$$
$$c = 0$$
Therefore eq. 6 reduces to :

$$K_s \text{ div } [\overline{\text{grad H}}] = 0 \Rightarrow \nabla^2 H = 0$$

which is eq. 1.

If we express the boundary conditions at the soil surface, and on the sides, in term of hydraulic head H (DIRICHLET's conditions) or in terms of water flux i.e. ~~grad~~ H (NEUMANN's conditions), we are able to describe the transfer of water in the entire domain $\mathcal{D}^*$ by an unique equation, written in our 2-dimensional plane flow case as :

$$c \frac{\delta H}{\delta t} = \frac{\delta}{\delta x} [K \frac{\delta H}{\delta x}] + \frac{\delta}{\delta z} [K \frac{\delta H}{\delta z}] \qquad (7)$$

with :

$$c = c(h) \quad , \quad \theta = \theta(h)$$
$$K = K(h) \qquad \text{for } h < 0$$

and :

$$c = 0$$
$$K = K_s \qquad \text{for } h \geqslant 0$$

Before discussing the use of numerical techniques for solving eq. 7, let us now elucidate some ideas on the contrast existing between the use of the deterministic approach for simulating the water flow (i.e. to solve eq. 7 knowing the boundary conditions and the phenomenological variables) and the application of a "black-box" system.

TO BE BLIND OR CLEAR - SIGHTED ?

For many users of techniques of simulation for solving problems of transient water table aquifers, there is some repulsion to use eq. 7. Most of them are indeed afraid of the strongly non-linear character of this equation, and of the fact that the k(h) and θ(h) relationships are generally unknown and difficult to obtain. Moreover, it is to be said that few experimental results have been published to this date on the real influence of the unsaturated zone on a large scale problem, e.g. a pumping test. We know that it should not be neglected, but we cannot give in such a case an order of magnitude of the errors introduced by neglecting the unsaturated domain.

It is therefore of common practice, in many cases dealing with hydrogeology or management of aquifers, to use the traditional approach (and most generally the Boussinesq linearized equation), and to infer the transfer in the unsaturated zone by the use of a "black-box" system = knowing the entry at the soil surface (for example the effective rain) and the input at the water table (as determined by the rise of the piezometric level after a rain event) a "characteristic" function of transfer is obtained by the classical use of a Laplace's transform. But is appears quickly that for a given site this function of transfer must be

continuously changed, since its values depend mainly of the unknown depth of the
piezometric level (in our language, we will say : of the initial water content
profile), and of the effective rain. This is a very limiting result, since the
method cannot be safely used for the purpose of prediction ; consequently it is
advisable to abandon this "black-box" system.

This failure can be easily explained by an understanding of the flow process in the unsaturated zone : it is obvious that a unique function of transfer
cannot be used in lieu of a strongly non-linear equation.

Instead of remaining blind, we prefer to attack the problem using a deterministic approach. This judgment is still strengthened by the fact that the time
spent to obtain proper representative data on K(h) and θ(h), and to develop an
algorithm to solve equation 7 is in fact shorter, and more effectively used, than
the time wasted in trying to adapt, for each event, a function of transfer to a
given set of boundary conditions. The main advantage of a deterministic approach
is however that once a method of solution is developed   it is not only possible
to model, but also to predict safely the water flow.

The choice being made we should say that only numerical techniques can
actually be used. It is indeed not possible to solve equation 7 with the use of
an analog model, since in each node in the unsaturated domain the water content
θ(x,z) varies continuously. Consequently the analog conductivity and pressure
head terms should vary simultaneously with time, with corresponding non linear
relationships. A simulation model, if ever possible, will be extremely expensive
and time consuming, and could be achieved only on huge electrical networks, no
less elaborate than those of small computers.

Some numerical hybrid method have been developped, mainly the Continuous
Systems Modeling Program (C.S.M.P.), and will be presented here by our colleague
Van Keulen. Let us say simply that for being efficient, the CSMP must be used on
a big computer (series IBM 360 or equivalent) ; furthermore this technique is limited to simulation of flow in the unsaturated zone, and cannot describe inter-
ferences between saturated and unsaturated zone (i.e. : drainage, or recharge of
an aquifer).

This is a serious obstacle which can only be overcome by pure numerical
techniques. As we will see later, the problem is simply due to the fact that when
the equation is elliptical in certain parts of the flow domain (as it is in the
saturated zone) iterations are necessary.

To what concerns now the numerical techniques, we will finally have the
choice between the use of finite element, or finite difference methods.
Dr. S. Neuman is to present here the use of finite element methods based on the
Galerkin's approach. Hence we will limit ourselves to the presentation of our experience with finite difference methods, discussing the advantages, and also some
objections to the use of particular schemes of finite differences.

THE CHOICE OF A PROPER FINITE DIFFERENCE SCHEME

Returning to eq. 7, some additional remarks are called for :

i) for $h < 0$, the equation is parabolic while it becomes elliptical for $h \geqslant 0$.
ii) the boundary between both domains (elliptic and parabolic) varies with time
and is unknown at any $t > 0$;

These two remarks give the guidelines for the possible choice of a proper
scheme to be utilised. As the method envisaged must be applicable for a mixed pa-
rabolic-elliptical problem an explicit system seems to be obvious. However such a
system is subject to stringent stability conditions creating a limiting value for
the time step in relation to the distance step. Although this would not pose too

great a difficulty on an investigation of the early stages of flow, it becomes cumbersome and inefficient for long term flow (especially for simulation on small computers).

In order to obtain the stable and fast character of a classical implicit difference method, coupled with over-relaxation techniques, we rather suggest the use of an iterative method corresponding to a semi-implicit solution. The A.D.I. Iterative Procedure (ADIPIT), developed by D.W. Peaceman and H.H. Rachford (1955) provides a highly efficient numerical method for solving equation 7. One of the main advantages of this method is its economy in computer time arising from the solution of the simultaneous equations in alternating directions with the aid of Gaussian elimination. As tridiagonal algorithms are used for the solution, no memory problems exist for small computer, like the IBM 1130 - 16 K, even when a large number of nodes is involved (we have used it for 396 nodes). Since in the iteration process used for generating new sets of improved values the dominant eigenvalue of the iteration matrix is decisive for convergence, this accelerator is chosen, as recommended by Wachspress (1966), with the result that usually 3 to 4 iterations are enough.

Consequently, the ADIPIT algorithm seems to be particularly adaptable to simulation of eq. 7, as it has the unconditional stability of an implicit method, with a second order accuracy in both space and time provided that the time increment is kept constant during one complete iteration cycle in both directions.

Restrictions to the use of this method can be found in the case where singularities exist in the flow domain, as analyzed by Rushton (1974). But more seriously, the use of this method is limited to simulation of flow in homogeneous systems, with rather regular geometric boundaries (note that this remark applies generally to any finite difference scheme). If heterogeneities exist in the soil profile (for example superposed slabs of soil) the use of finite element techniques is recommended.

CONCLUSION - WHAT ABOUT THE HYDRAULIC CHARACTERISTICS OF THE SOIL ?

Finally, whatever good the simulation technique is, its ability to simulate the real phenomenon rests on the physical representativity of the K(h) and θ(h) relationships. A particular stress should be put on that point.

If we start in considering the example summarized in fig. 2 and 3 wherein these two relations were obtained carefully (fig. 5) i.e. in the laboratory using the transient analysis of changes of water content and water pressure (Vachaud et al, 1973), we can then judge of the representativity of the numerical solution of eq. 7 with the ADIPIT scheme. In fig. 2.b and 2.c are plotted the numerical values for the outflow and the water table position during the drainage experiment, while in fig. 3.b and 3.c are given the corresponding values for the recharge experiment. Details on the method are given by M. Vauclin in his paper to this conference, but clearly a good agreement is obtained between numerical and experimental values, and in any case much better than solutions given by viscous flow analogs.

In practice however these two functions are generally unknown, and are often determined by an "inverse technique", which to our feeling is as dangerous as the "black-box" system. This technique rests mainly on the following flow chart :

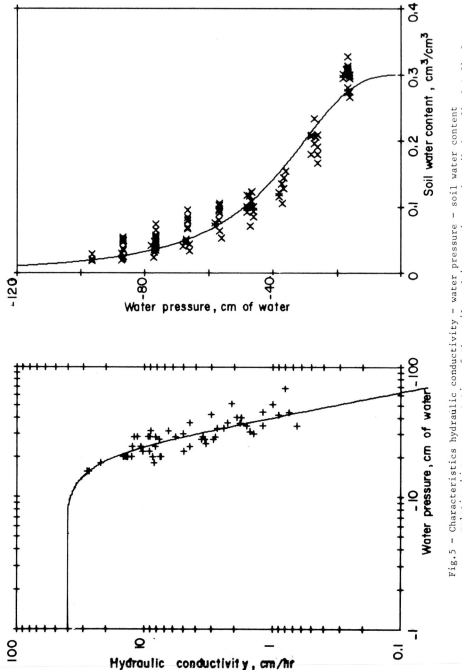

Fig.5 – Characteristics hydraulic conductivity – water pressure – water content relationships representative of the soil used in experiments described on fig.2 & fig.3.

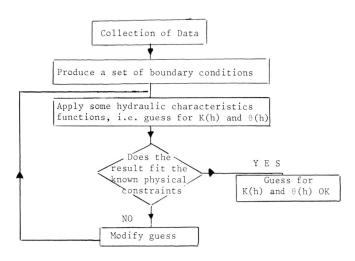

Assuming the shape of guess for $K(h)$ or $\theta(h)$ being physically sound (and we know that functional forms of the type $K = K_s \cdot \dfrac{\alpha}{\alpha + h^\beta}$ and $\theta = \theta_s \dfrac{A}{A + h^B}$ are fairly representative of the nature of the curves), an important problem is that the "best" determination of $K(h)$ and $\theta(n)$, say K^* and θ^*, obtained by a systematic iterative way, are not only function of h, but also function of truncation errors in the numerical scheme, of the goodness of the fit criteria, of the choice of the parameters (and their number) that characterized the curve, etc... But the most crucial point still concerns the problem of uniqueness of the solution. Since the $K(h)$ and $\theta(h)$ relationships are non linear, and not directly connected, it is not impossible that there exists several combinations of variables α, β, A and B, say a multiplicity of at least two sets of $K(h)$ - $\theta(h)$ relationships satisfying the same set of physical constraints. In the light of our actual knowledge at present no final answer can be given to that question.

Before advancing further in simulation techniques, we would like to conclude by looking at the past, and towards the future.

We would first like to state that despite its inability to describe the physical phenomenon for many years the "traditional" flow approach was positive in the fact that it gave us orders of magnitude and some understanding of the flow process. This approach has however reached now a milestone, and we should now force ourselves to use a more deterministic way of considering the description of water transfer in the soil.

This has not been possible until few years ago, since on one hand the physics of flow in the partially saturated domain is a fairly young science, and on the other hand development of experimental techniques and use of high speed computers to solve the flow equations were restricted.

We have now come to a point of opening new opportunities in the development of scientific hydrology by understanding the flow process, and by use of large scale computer facilities. But problems still remain to solve before going further, and among them the most important deals with determination of the soil hydraulic properties on a macro-scale. We would thus like to urge researchers in soil physics to systematize methods of field determination of $K(h)$ and $\theta(h)$ by independent measurement of changes of θ and h (many examples are described in the "IAEA Symposium on the use of radio isotopes in Soils Physics", Vienna,

October 1973), and also to determine, by a statistical approach, representative values of these function (as done by Nielsen et al, 1973 or by Brooks and Corey, 1964).

REFERENCES

BOULTON N.S., Analysis of data from non-equilibrium pumping tests allowing for delayed yield from storage, Proc. Inst. Civil Engnrg. 28 : 603-610, 1964.
BROOKS R.H. and A.T. COREY, Hydraulic properties of porous media, Hydrology paper n°3 - Colorado State University, Fort-Collins, 1964.
CHILDS E.C., An introduction to the physical basis of soil water phenomena, Wiley Intersciences, Wiley ed. 493 pp., 1969.
FREEZE R.A., The mechanism of natural groundwater recharge and discharge, 1. Water Resources Research, 5 : 153-171, 1969.
HILLEL D., Soil and water - Physical Principles and Processes, Physiological Ecology - Academic Press, 288 pp., 1971.
NIELSEN D.R., JACKSON R.D., CARY D.W. and D.D. EVANS, Soil water, American Society of Agronomy, 175 pp., 1972.
NIELSEN D.R., BIGGAR J.W. and K.T. ERH, Spatial variability of field-measured soil-water properties, Hilgardia, 42 : 215-260, 1973.
PEACEMAN D.W. and H.H. RACHFORD, Numerical solution of parabolic and elliptical differential equations, J. Soc. Ind. Appl. Math. 3 : 28-41, 1955.
PRILL R.C., JOHNSON A.I. and D.A. MORRIS, Specific yield laboratory experiments showing the effect of time on columns drainage, U.S. Geol. Survey, Water Supply paper 1662-B, 1965.
REMSON I., HORNBERGER G.M. and F.J. MOLZ, Numerical methods in subsurface hydrology, Wiley Interscience, J. Wiley ed., 1971.
RICHARDS L.A., Capillary conduction of liquids through porous medium, Physics - 1: 318-333, 1931.
RUBIN J., Theoretical analysis of two dimensional transient flow of water in unsaturated and partly unsaturated soils, Soil Sci. Soc. Am. Proc, 32 : 607-615, 1968.
RUSHTON K.R., Critical analysis of the alternating direction implicit method of aquifer analysis, J. of Hydrology, 21 : 153-172, 1974.
VACHAUD G., M. VAUCLIN and J. KHANJI, Etude expérimentale des transferts bidimensionnels dans la zone non saturée, Application à l'étude du drainage d'une nappe à surface libre, La Houille Blanche, 1 : 65-74, 1973.
VAUCLIN M., G. VACHAUD and J. KHANJI, Two dimensional numerical analysis of transient water transfer in saturated-unsaturated soils, IFIP Working conference on modeling and simulation of water resources systems, Univ. of Ghent, July 1974, 1974.
WACHPRESS E.L., Iterative solution of elliptic system, Prentice Hall Inc. N.J. 298 pp., 1966.

DISCUSSION

It is an interesting paper. The point which is interesting to me is, it can perhaps be a bridge between the two sides that obviously came up in my talk. It is my opinion that we have to understand each other which we will not do by starting in one camp and remaining there. In that sense, could I just make some comments from the system-analyst point of view on what you just said. System-analysts would look at the data as we call it, would come to certain conclusions straight away. If we look at the top right hand of the diagram in figure 2, it is quite likely that anyone who has been concerned with dynamic systems would look at that and say : the experiment is making a step change in the input conditions and we are looking at the output of that system. The response that we see there unless I am very much mistaken is the response of a second or more likely a third order linear dynamic system. Or it could be so described. That does not mean that it is necessarily such a system, but that would come into the mind of a system-analyst and he would say : if I am interested in the input output behavior, can I circumvent the problem of solving the Laplace equations and other things like this ; can I come up with a simpler representation which takes into account the physics of the situation and yields a differential equation which is much simpler to estimate. There is no disagreement between us, it is a different way of looking at it. It's as valuable as the alternative. If you look at the next figure you see that we have a system with pure transportation delay followed by a first order response. The system-analyst would look and say, could I explain that in physical terms and could it be useful in the modeling, whereas the classical approach starts from an analysis of the physics without looking at the data too much.
The final point that I would make : I have learned a new term which is : the inverse problem and what we would call parameter estimation. It seems to me that there is a large body of parameter estimation theory which can attack those problems and if they hadn't been used, we should look if they can not be used. So could we try to come to the meeting point. (YOUNG)

You can define a black box model and use a transfer function. But on the other hand from the physics we know that the system is very strongly nonlinear. So one black box to fit the system is not sufficient. You should use and define many black boxes. Therefore we think that it is easier to attack directly the problem as we have done. (VACHAUD)

I agree with you, except that you don't use necessarily a series of black boxes, by learning the relationship in these special circumstances you could have come up with a differential equation model which would saved you a lot of calculation, which may have nonlinear terms in, you see it is the opening of mind that says : try to look at simpler models that can include the physics, but not necessarily in a traditional way. It may not work ! I just mean, you have to look ! (YOUNG)

It is difficult to predict which model is the most appropriate. I have been working with geophysicists for some time, trying to adapt the best system. The black box approach was difficult to use. (VACHAUD)

I don't necessarily mean a black box when I say a different type of model. You can take a mechanistic model, but it could be simpler, that's the point. In the rainfall flow, for instance, the idea there was, it was not a linear model, it was linear in the parameters but it had to do with an effective rainfall flow, it is in fact a nonlinear model because the rainfall has been processed by nonlinear techniques. It is half way house that works sometimes, not all of the time. (YOUNG)

I can see what dr. Young is heading at, but I don't think he perhaps appreciates that in the soils context, the scale functions can be of very different character for different soils. In the sense that he might come up with a third order differential equation or whatever, which happen to fit a situation of sandy loam. This would work fine if the whole area was so and you had no physical curiosity in what was going on.
From the other hand if you are also interested in a soil of clay and any smooth sand and you wish to discuss all of it within the same area of this course, I do not think you can turn your back on what we know about the physics which lead us to equations which are sufficiently general. (PHILIP)

There is no disagreement because in different cases you are using different functions anyway. (YOUNG)

The point is they are the same functionals for the different soils. (PHILIP)

We have different parameters depending on the different situations. (YOUNG)

If in fact the representation for one soil would be third order and for another soil a second order system or what you will. This implies a sort of discretisation of how to treat three different cases and it means a different set of parameters with different, presumably, relations to the physics. I would like to agree with dr. Young but I find some intellectual "Hurtles". (PHILIP)

You have different functions for different soils, we have different systems which may have the same structure but different parameters. (YOUNG)

My mind of the problem here is, the model is based on a supposition of what the physical mechanism is ; the physical mechanism is formulated into equations, the equations are placed into the model and the solution requires knowledge of the parameters. Now the difference between a situation where these models can be determined experimentally, independently of the solution of the model, or where for one reason or another, it is impossible or undesirable, to do so, is important. It is indeed often impossible to measure the parameters independently. So you try to get at the parameters by implying the model at its best and if possible by putting the parameter into the equation, come up with the results and try to match them with the data. Moving free surface is provided by this heatflow perfectly.
I would like to say something of the parameters which are the functional dependence in this case of the hydraulic conductivity and the suction on the water content. These two factors are entirely empirical, they are not universal, they can describe only the concave part of the curve, the curve has an inflection, so there is a convex part, that's the crucial part, that's the part where the transition occurs from saturation to unsaturation.
Probably important in this particular case is having a method of measuring these functionals in the real world independently of the model. (HILLEL)

*With respect to the functionals handled in the paper; when it comes to the simulation man, we feel the real necessity to **characterize** any of these parameters ; because by simply having the data obtained from the soil profile we have all the information we need to make our modeling. But with all this trying to curve fitting these data with meaningless parameters we are spinning our wheels, I am not trying to put a lot of soil physicists out of business. (BRUTSAERT)*

This is precisely where the simulation people should come to the soil physicists and say these are the parameters we need, please help us to devise methods of measuring them and so this is the way to collaborate. (HILLEL)

Relating to the second diagram : the analogue, is that the heatflow ? Do you think it is fair to make a comparison of two physical systems ? Because the analogue is compared with another analogue, which is again a physical model namely the experimental, and you say that for modeling, this particular system is out of line.

I am just thinking on the fairness of comparison. (BRUTSAERT)

I must take very strong exceptions from your conclusions from what I consider to be very beautiful results. I think that your interpretation of these results in extension to what you probably consider as field conditions is basically wrong and I think it is wrong because you forgot to consider the effect of scale. You are looking at laboratory model of 3 by 5 m ? If you take the same curve that you take from laboratory data and don't change the scale from 3 m to 10 m, the characteristics of the soil would change accordingly toward a soil which is more sandy in its character so that the effect of the unsaturated zone would go sharply down and therefore whatever conclusions you may draw from your laboratory results would have no applications whatsoever to large field scale.

Among the problems we have to solve and you can read this in my last paragraph are the determinations of the hydraulic properties of the soil in a macroscale. (VACHAUD)

I felt à priori a little sceptic, when we try to sell our models to the water resource people when they are based on laboratory experiment, I think they are not interested in laboratory experiments, they are interested in what they observe in the real world system and that information is provided by analyzing the observed data in the field. The parameters which you use may not have any direct physical significance. (WHITEHEAD)

I try to expand the theory of the field by using laboratory experiments.
(VACHAUD)

You cannot forget the attorney, you should keep an eye on how you can convey the validity of what we are doing to the attorney. What is he more likely to believe and sell, and what is a jury more likely to believe and of course when you make a decision on whether a nuclear power plant is or is not violating the stream temperature or dissolved oxygen. So I think mechanistic models will sell and I am glad that some people shared this view in the room. (DAVIDSON)

Modeling and Simulation of Water Resources Systems, G.C. VANSTEENKISTE, (Ed.)
North-Holland Publishing Company (1975)

SOME CRITERIA FOR COMPREHENSIVE MODELING OF TRANSPORT PHENOMENA IN THE SOIL - PLANT - ATMOSPHERE CONTINUUM

D. Hillel
Dept. Soil & Water Science
The Hebrew University Faculty of Agriculture
Rehovot, ISRAEL

INTRODUCTION

This conference brings together specialists in the mathematical sciences of computer modeling and specialists in the natural (or environmental) sciences of hydrology and soil physics. The former are expert in the techniques of analog and numerical simulation and systems analysis, but may not necessarily know just where their techniques can be, or ought to be, applied to best advantage. The latter specialists, in contrast, are only lately becoming aware of the full possibilities inherent in the simulation approach toward the solution of problems which seem to defy solution by the traditional methods of analysis.

We are, on the one hand, like the stereotypical professional actor, constantly in search of a good plot to play; and, on the other hand, the undiscovered playwright who yearns for the elusive performer to redeem and enliven his plot. It is only when, by an act of good fortune, the twain meet and join forces, that we can expect a really good show.

I belong in the group of soil physicists, and particularly in that outdated subgroup among them who received their basic training in the primitive prehistoric times before computers became so ubiquitous and inescapable. So, I suffer from insufficient expertise in making full use of the computer, as the powerful tool that we all know it can be in our research. What I bring to this meeting, therefore, is some practical experience with the problems encountered in the environmental and agricultural management of soil and water, and some fundamental familiarity with the physical laws governing observable phenomena in this area.

My purpose in this paper is to set out a few notions gleaned out of the soil-water system, the problems it presents, and the potentialities of the simulation approach to the solution of such problems.

Now, a truism : the soil is a highly complex system. It consists of solid components, mineral and organic, irregularly fragmented and variously associated or structured in an intricate geometric pattern. The solid matrix is not rigid or inert, but interacts with the fluids which permeate the inter-particle voids. These fluids are air of varying composition and water with various solutes. This complex is practically never in a state of static equilibrium, as the soil heats and cools, wets and dries, swells and shrinks, disperses and flocculates, cracks and disintegrates, and undergoes chemical changes. Finally, the soil serves as the habitat for a great variety of microscopic and macroscopic organisms which multiply and decay and interact in ways almost too complex to describe.

I mention all this merely to place our theories and models in their proper perspective. No theory can encompass the soil-water-plant system in its entirety, but only an idealized, simplified and consistently well-behaved model which resembles the real system in some respects but not in others. Any theory, therefore, is but a partial description of the real system's possible behavior.

In applying to the complex natural system oversimplified concepts and theories borrowed from "pure" or hypothetical systems, we must be careful not to take our models too seriously. Because of our limited understanding, we have no other way but to simplify our system in order to deal with specific phenomena apart from the total complex of things. Yet we must repeatedly remind ourselves that nature does not separate phenomena but on the contrary links them together inextricably.

Our tendency to isolate phenomena and study them separately in a particularistic way has lately brought us to an impasse. Specialization has made us myopic. For too long, we have disregarded the continuity of natural phenomena. For instance, agricultural scientists, in their single-minded pursuit of greater crop yields (in itself a very worthy objective) have been unaware or unconcerned that some of their fertilizers and pesticides may contaminate the environment outside their particular field.

Now it is no longer enough to devise isolated models in order to characterize particular phenomena. Now we must reassemble the components of the system into a unified whole, allowing for their mutual interactions. To do so, we must overcome self-imposed artificial boundaries between seemingly distinct disciplines, the adherents of which have become strangers to one another through the development of separate jargons and habits of thought.

The simulation approach seems to offer us a way to re-integrate our fragmented knowledge. The computer in the service of a team of scientists may be able in some cases to fuse inter-related phenomena more effectively than individual human minds relying only on the tools of classical analysis. Numerous processes in nature are essentially non-linear, and the analytical solution of many of these is either impossible without excessive simplication or at least extremely cumbersome. Fortunately, the newer languages of computer modeling require less rigorous initiation so that they enable even environmental and natural scientists who are relatively unsophisticated mathematicians to concentrate on the real phenomena of interest rather than on the intricacies of the numerical analysis. The systematic results of computer simulation of increasingly complex systems will never obviate experimentation, which is needed for supplying parameters, calibrating, and testing the simulation (if for nothing else !), but such results can help us to economize experimentation and increase its efficiency by guiding it to where it is needed most. To put it more simply, simulation may help us to decide what ought to be studied or measured next, - a crucial question which is all-too-often left entirely to the unconscious intuition of individuals. (Intuition, of course, will always be an indispensable fountainhead of innovation, but it ought to be tested against a systematic and comprehensive description of the natural world).

The simulation approach has its pitfalls. A simulation model is not an end in itself. Its value is proportional to the degree to which it helps us to understand and manage reality. A model which is too simplistic will probably be too unrealistic. One which is too complex may also be unwieldly or incomprehensible. Yet the optimal order of complexity is difficult to establish, as our developing knowledge and techniques make feasible gradually increasing orders of complexity.

One seemingly obvious fallacy of simulation is to construct a model to fit a specific set of data, and then to claim as a surprising achievement the good agreement of the model with the very data which it was forced to fit. This fallacy of circular thinking is still too common among simulationists. To my mind, a simulation model can only be tested convincingly against an independent set of data and with independently obtained parameters. Even then the fit may be fortuitous, unless it is based on sound knowledge of the cause and effect mechanisms involved. Finally, we need some objective criterion for what constitutes "goodness of fit" of data to a model. The subjective desire of a simultanionist to succeed may lead him to claim "good-agreement" without sufficient justification. The very ease with which simulation models can be manipulated beyond the realm of sound knowledge and data constitutes a danger in itself. For these and other reasons, it is still a moot question as to whether the art and science of simulation is already ripe to serve as a guide in the actual practice of soil and water management. If the great promise of simulation is to be fulfilled, it must not be left to the simulationists alone. It needs the naturalists.

PHYSICAL PROCESSES IN THE SOIL

We shall now briefly summarize the main theories of soil physics which may need to be considered along with related phenomena in the context of any mechanistic simulation of the soil-water system.

Water movement

The flow of an incompressible flind in a rigid, homogeneous, isotropic, and isothermal porous medium can be described by a combination of two equations :
(1) Darcy's law which states that the flux of water (q) is proportional to, and in the direction of, the driving force which is the effective potential gradient.

$$q = -K\nabla\phi \tag{1}$$

where ϕ, the hydraulic potential, is the algebraic sum of the matric potential (ψ) and the gravitational potential. Expressed in head units (free energy per unit weight), the hydraulic potential can be written as

$$\phi = \psi - z \tag{2}$$

where z is the gravitational level expressed as depth below the soil surface. K is the hydraulic conductivity which in an unsaturated soil is a function of the water content, θ.
(2) The continuity equation, which states that the time rate of change of water content in a volume element of soil must equal the divergence of the flux

$$\frac{\partial\theta}{\partial t} = -\nabla.q \tag{3}$$

These two relations are combined to give

$$\frac{\partial\theta}{\partial t} = \nabla.(K\nabla q) \tag{4}$$

which, in one-dimensional form, becomes

$$\frac{\partial\theta}{\partial t} = \frac{\partial}{\partial x}\left(K\frac{\partial\phi}{\partial x}\right) \tag{5}$$

If the system considered is vertical, and the z direction is taken as positive from the soil surface downward, we obtain

$$\frac{\partial\theta}{\partial t} = \frac{\partial}{\partial z}\left[K\frac{\partial(\psi-z)}{\partial z}\right] = \frac{\partial}{\partial z}\left(K\frac{\partial\psi}{\partial z}\right) - \frac{\partial K}{\partial z} \tag{6}$$

If the soil system has a sink in it (i.e., if water is removed at some rate S_w in a manner not accounted for the flux divergence), we can write

$$\frac{\partial \theta}{\partial t} = \frac{\partial}{\partial z} \left(K \frac{\partial \psi}{\partial z} \right) - \frac{\partial K}{\partial z} - S_w \tag{7}$$

For cylindrical flow to a line sink the equation is

$$\frac{\partial \theta}{\partial t} = - \frac{1}{r} \frac{\partial}{\partial r} \left(r K \frac{\partial \phi}{\partial r} \right) \tag{8}$$

where r is the radial distance from the center of the cylinder.

The relation of K to θ in an unsaturated soil has been expressed by various empirical equations, but is best measured in situ on a realistic scale without prior assumptions.

Solute Movement

The rate and direction of solute movement in a soil system depends in principle on the pattern of water movement, but is also affected by diffusion and hydrodynamic dispersion.

If the latter effects are negligible, solute flow by convection can be formulated as

$$J_c = q \, c = \bar{v} \, \theta \, c \tag{9}$$

where J_c is the flux of solute, q as before is the flux of water, c the concentration of solute in the flowing water, $\bar{v}$ the average velocity of flow, and θ as before is the volumetric fraction of water in the soil.

The rate of diffusion of a solute (J_d) in bulk water at rest is related by Fick's law to the concentration gradient

$$J_d = - D_o \cdot \frac{\partial c}{\partial x} \tag{10}$$

in which D_o is the diffusion coefficient.

In the soil the effective diffusion coefficient D_s is decreased owing to the fact that the liquid phase occupies only a fraction of the soil volume, and also owing to the tortuous geometry of the path

$$D_s = D_o \, \theta \, \xi \tag{11}$$

in which ξ, the tortuosity, is an empirical factor smaller than unity and which can be expected to decrease with decreasing θ.

In addition to molecular diffusion, convective flow generally causes hydrodynamic dispersion, an effect which results from the microscopic non-uniformity of the flow velocity in the various pores. Thus, a sharp boundary between two miscible solutions becomes increasingly diffuse about the mean position of the front. The magnitude of the dispersion coefficient, D_h, has been found to depend linearly on the average flow velocity, v

$$D_h = \alpha \, v \tag{12}$$

where α is an empirical coefficient.

The diffusion and dispersion effects can be combined with the convective transport equation to give the overall flux of solute, J

$$J = - (D_h + D_s) \frac{\partial c}{\partial x} + \bar{v} \, \theta \, c \tag{13}$$

With continuity brought into consideration, the one-dimensional transient movement of a non-interacting solute in soil becomes

$$\frac{\partial(\theta c)}{\partial t} = \frac{\partial}{\partial x} (D_{hs} \frac{\partial c}{\partial x}) - \frac{\partial(qc)}{\partial x} + S_s \tag{14}$$

where S_s is a source or sink term representing the rate of addition or subtraction of the solute due to uptake by plants or microbes, volatilization, precipitation, or dissolution; and D_{hs} is the combined coefficient of dispersion and diffusion.

Additional Transport Phenomena

Limitations of space preclude an elucidation of heat conductance and of the simultaneous and interactive flow of heat and water in non-isothermal system, though these phenomena can be very important indeed in many cases.

WATER EXTRACTION BY PLANTS

Plants growing in the field, particularly in arid regions, are required by their climatic environment to extract from the soil and transpire to the atmosphere huge quantities of water. To grow successfully, each plant must achieve a water economy such that the demand made upon it is balanced by the supply available to it. The problem is that the climate-induced evaporative demand is practically continuous, whereas rainfall occurs only occasionally and irregularly. To survive during dry spells between rains, the plant must rely upon the reserves of water contained in the soil.

A fundamental problem encountered in any attempt at an exact physical description of soil-water uptake by plants is the inherently complicated space-time relationships involved in this process. Roots grow in different directions and spacings, and at different rates. Also, they exhibit sectional differences in absorptive activity depending upon age and location. Furthermore, old root die while new ones proliferate, depending not only on age but also upon the physical and chemical environment (e.g. temperature, moisture, nutrients, salinity, aeration, etc.). Hence, it is extremely difficult to measure or define the microscopic gradients and fluxes of water and solutes in the immediate vicinity of roots.

Soil moisture content and potential are seldom uniform throughout the root zone. How the root system of a plant senses the root zone as a whole and integrates its response so as to utilize soil moisture to best advantage is a phenomenon still imperfectly understood. One classifical view (Wadleigh, 1946) which has since been disproven is that the plant root system adjusts its water withdrawal pattern in a way which maintains the soil moisture potential constant throughout the root zone. In fact, the usual pattern of water withdrawal after a rain or irrigation is such that the toplayer is depleted first and the zone of maximal extraction moves gradually into the deeper layers. In the course of this action, considerable differences in potential, amounting to several bars, can develop within the root zone as well as between the root zone and the untapped subsoil. Hence, the measurement of soil water content or potential at some arbitrary depths, as well as the gross averaging of conditions prevailing in different parts of the root zone, can hardly characterize the root zone as a whole or correlate with root activity at any par-

ticular phase of the extraction-replenishment cycle. Nor is the root system itself
static in nature, as new roots branch out, older ones suberize and eventually die,
and the whole systems grows deeper into the soil.

Since the soil often extends in depth considerably below the zone of root
activity and is in the nature of a bottomless barrel, it is of interest to establish how the pattern of soil water utilization by plants relates to the pattern
of water flow within and through the soil profile. Some drainage through the root
zone is needed to prevent deleterious accumulation of salts, yet excessive drainage
might involve unnecessary loss of water and nutrients. If groundwater is present
at a shallow depth it can contribute to the supply of crop water requirements by
upward capillary flow, but it might also infuse the root zone with harmful salts.

To properly manage the water economy of a crop, these dynamic processes
must be integrated quantitatively. Given the complexity of the system, it now
seems that only the methods of dynamic simulation can offer us any real hope for
comprehensive treatment.

The current approach to plant water uptake is based on recognition that
the field environment forms a unified system which Philip (1966) has called the
"SPAC" (for "soil-plant-atmosphere continuum"). In this system, water flows in a
"transpiration stream" down a gradient of potential energy from soil to root to
stem to leaf, whence it evaporates and diffuses out to the atmosphere. Employing
the analogy of Ohm's law for an electric current through a series of resistors
(van den Honert, 1948), the transpiration stream can be represented as a catenary
process through successive segments, in each of which the flux is proportional to
a resistance

$$q = -\frac{\Delta\phi}{R} \tag{15}$$

For steady-state flow, we can write

$$q = -\frac{\Delta\phi \text{ soil to root}}{R_{soil}} = -\frac{\Delta\phi \text{ roots to stem}}{R_{roots}} =$$

$$= -\frac{\Delta\phi \text{ stem to leaf}}{R_{stem}} \tag{16}$$

As shown by D'Hollander in this conference, the resistance of the soil
segment, which is proportional to the average length of the flow path and to the
inverse of the hydraulic conductivity, is in the nature of a variable resistor
attached to a capacitor. This is so because the hydraulic conductivity varies with
soil water content and potential.

The effective flow path obviously depends on root density. Gardner (1964)
expressed the soil resistance term as inversely proportional to the conductivity
of the soil and to the density of the root system. Thus

$$R_s = 1/B \, K \, L \tag{17}$$

where L is the length of roots per unit volume of soil and B is a constant which
must be determined empirically. One difficulty in this formulation is that root
activity may not be simply proportional to root length.

Methods of estimating root length and distribution in the soil profile were developed by Newman (1965), Melhuish (1967), and Melhuish and Lang (1968). The entire subject of water extraction by plants has been analyzed by Philip (1957), Gardner (1960), Cowan (1965), Slatyer (1967), and Klute and Peters (1969). Experimental studies of root extraction patterns have been reported by Ogata et al. (1959), Rose and Stern (1967), van Bavel et al. (1968), and others.

MODELS OF WATER EXTRACTION BY PLANT ROOTS

The Macroscopic Approach

In principle, there are two ways to approach the problem of modeling the uptake of soil water by roots. The first is to regard the root system in its entirety as a diffuse sink, which permeates the soil continuously, though not necessarily at a uniform intensity or strength throughout the rooting zone. The local strength of the sink term is related to the effective density of the roots in each layer. This approach, which is termed "macroscopic", disregards the flow patterns toward individual roots and thus avoids the geometric complication involved in analyzing the distribution of fluxes and potential gradients on a micro scale.

The macroscopic approach was taken by Ogata et al. (1959), Whisler et al. (1968) and more recently by Molz and Lemson (1970, 1971), and by Nimah and Hanks (1973).

The numerical model of Whisler et al. (1968) was based on the rather unrealistic assumption of steady state flow from a water table at a constant depth, for which the following equation applies

$$0 = \frac{\partial}{\partial z} [K(\theta) \ \frac{\partial \psi}{\partial z}] + \frac{\partial K(\theta)}{\partial z} + S_w \tag{18}$$

subject to the following boundary conditions

$$\psi \Big|_{z=L} = 0 \tag{19}$$

$$q = - \Big| K(\theta) \ (\frac{\partial \psi}{\partial z} + 1) \ \Big|_{z=0}$$

wherein L is the depth of the water table. They stated that under these conditions the extraction of water in each zone should be proportional to the surface area of absorbing root and to soil wetness. They further assumed that the flow of water within the roots occurs against negligible resistance (so that the entire root system is at uniform potential) and that the transpiration rate is constant. They used an arbitrary function to approximate the K vs. ψ function and provided no real test of their model against actual data.

Molz and Remson (1970, 1971) developed a model based on transient-state flow and allowing water movement through the soil profile as well as extraction by the root sink. Their numerical model was based on the Douglas-Jones predictor-corrector method, and the solutions obtained were compared with published experimental results. While acknowledging that the macroscopic approach can be applied best to root systems dense enough so that water is extracted in a homogeneous manner throughout the root zone (at a rate depending on depth, wetness, transpiration rate, etc.), they hold that water extraction is sufficiently uniform even at "moderate to low" root densities. Their model takes no account of hysteresis or of the osmotic potential of the soil solution. The major shortcoming of their model, however, is that it does not yield the pattern of water extraction in a mechanistic way, but imposes empirically-fitted equations relating the extraction rate to depth, wetness, and transpiration rate.

Nimah and Hanks (1973) developed a numerical model designed to predict water content profiles, evapotranspiration, water flow from or to the water table,
root extraction and root water potential under transient conditions approximating
those of a field. Their model indicates a strong dependence on soil hydraulic properties and rooting depth, but only a weak dependence on the magnitude of the so-
called "limiting root water potential". The latter is an arbitrary level of root
water potential at which they presume that the plant wilts. (Actually, wilting is
more likely determined by the leaf water potential, which may be appreically lower
than that of the roots). Their arbitrary root resistance term was set equal to
$(1 + R_c)$, where R_c is a flow coefficient in the plant root system assumed to remain constant. Their potential term did include an osmotic component, but in a manner which would not take into account the increasing concentration of salts in the
immediate periphery of the absorbing roots. In this model, which made no provision
for hysteresis or soil layering, the root water potential was calculated to make
the plant root extraction over the whole profile equal the constant potential transpiration as long as the value of ψ_{root} remained higher than the "limiting" value
defined above. The model was compared with field determinations of water extraction
by a crop of oats.

Most of the models published so far do not take into account the diurnal
fluctuation and daily variation of potential evapotranspiration, or the possible
effect of temperature gradients in the soil on root water uptake and soil water
flow in the profile.

The Microscopic Approach

This approach analyzes the radial flow of water to a single root, which is
taken to be a line sink. The soil water flow equation is cast in cylindrical coordinates and solved for the distribution of potentials, water contents, and fluxes
from the root surface outward to some distance r from the root axis. On the assumption that a typical root can be represented by an infinitely long, narrow cylinder
of constant radius and absorbing characteristics, so that the water movement toward the root is radial, an appropriate form of the flow equation is

$$\frac{\partial \theta}{\partial t} = \frac{1}{r} \frac{\partial}{\partial r}(r D_w \frac{\partial \theta}{\partial r}) \tag{20}$$

where θ, t, r are the soil wetness, time, and radial distance from the root axis,
respectively, and D_w is the hydraulic diffusivity $(= K \frac{d\psi}{d\phi})$. Assuming constant flux
at the root surface, Gardner (1960) solved this equation subject to the following
initial and boundary conditions

$$\theta = \theta_o , \qquad \psi = \psi_o , \ t = 0 \tag{21}$$

$$q = 2\pi \ aK \frac{\partial \psi}{\partial r} = 2\pi \ a \ D_w \frac{\partial \theta}{\partial r} , \quad r = a, \ t > 0$$

wherein a is the root radius; K, D_w, θ, r, t are as before, and g is the rate of
water uptake per unit of root length.

With K and D assumed constant, the following solution is obtained

$$\psi_{soil} - \psi_{root} = \frac{q}{4\pi K} (\ln \frac{4Dt}{r^2} - \gamma) \tag{22}$$

where γ is Euler's constant. From this equation, it is possible to calculate the gradient $\Delta\psi$ that will develop at any time between the soil at a distance from the root and the suction at the root surface. This gradient is proportional directly to the rate of water uptake and hence to the climatic evaporational demand, and inversely to the hydraulic conductivity.

Although this analysis has provided a valuable semi-quantitative understanding of water movement to roots, the restrictive assumptions regarding constant flux to each unit length of root, and constant hydraulic conductivity, preclude a realistic description of the pattern of water uptake by the root system as a whole, in which q and K, as well as matric and osmotic potentials, change in time and space as successive soil layers are depleted and as new roots grow into deeper layers.

Several investigators have since used the cylindrical model (e.g., Molz et al., 1968; Lambert and Penning de Vries, 1973). It has the advantage of yielding more detailed information on conditions prevailing in the close proximity of the roots rather than being restricted to consideration of grossly averaged conditions as in the case of the macroscopic approach. However, the difficulty here is in determining the proper boundary condition for the root surface. Most authors used a constant flux conditions or a constant hydraulic head conditions, neither of which is realistic. Another problem is how to integrate the uptake by a whole root system distributed in a heterogeneous profile. Obviously, the results for a single root cannot simply be multiplied to obtain a realistic appraisal of an entire root-zone.

Modeling the Total Plant Environment

The plant lives in two realms. It senses conditions prevailing in both the atmosphere and the soil and responds in some internally integrated fashion which is still to be understood and simulated properly. An effort in this direction has lately been made by Lambert and Penning de Vries (1973). This approach permits consideration of the diurnal fluctuation of evaporativity and inclusion of other interrelated plant functions such as photosynthesis and respiration. The degree of complexity, however, and the number of parameters and simplifying assumptions needed for the model, increase greatly. It is still questionable whether, at the present state of our collective knowledge, a realistic model of plant response to its total changeable environment can already be attained. It is a challenge which requires the collective endeavors of plant physiologists, microclimatologists, and soil physicists, all of whose contributions should perhaps be orchestrated by those special modern wizards variously called systems analysts or simulation specialists.

REFERENCES

COWAN, I.R., J. Appl. Ecology 2, 221, 1965.
GARDNER, W.R., Soil Sci. 86, 63, 1960.
GARDNER, W.R., Agron. J. 56, 41, 1964.
KLUTE, A. and PETERS, D.B., In : "Root Growth", Butterworth, London, p. 105, 1969.
LAMBERT, S.R. and PENNING DE VRIES, F.W.T., Theoretical Prod. Ecology, Agr. Univ.
    Wageningen, Internal Rept. 3, 1973.
MELHUISH, F.M., Am. Bot. 32, 15, 1967.
MELHUISH, F.M. and LANG, A.R.G., Soil Sci. 106, 16, 1968.
MOLZ, F.J., Agron. J. 63, 608, 1968.
MOLZ, F.J. and REMSON, I., Water Resour. Res. 6, 1346, 1970.
MOLZ. F.J. and REMSON, I., Agron. J. 63, 72, 1971.
NEWMAN, E.I., J. Appl. Ecol. 6, 261, 1969.
NIMAH, M.N. and HANKS, R.J., Proc. Soil Sci. Soc. Am. 37, 522, 1973.
OGATA, G., RICHARDS, L.A. and GARDNER, W.R., Soil Sci. 89, 179, 1960.
PHILIP, J.R., 3rd Int. Congr. Irr. Drainage 8, 125-8, 154, 1957.
PHILIP, J.R., A. Rev. Pl. Physiol. 17, 245, 1966.
ROSE, C.W. and STERN, W.R., Aust. J. Soil Res. 5, 11, 1967.
SLATYER, R.O., "Plant-Water Relationships", Academic Press, N.Y., 1967.
VAN BAVEL, C.H.M., BRUST, K.S. and STIRK, G.B., Proc. Soil Sci. Soc.Am.23, 317,
    1968.

VAN DEN HONERT, T.H., Disc. Faraday Soc. 3, 146, 1948.
WADLEIGH, C.H., Soil Sci. 61, 225, 1946.
WHISLER, F.D., KLUTE, A. and MILLINGTON, R.J., Proc. Soil Sci. Soc. Am. 32, 167, 1968.

DISCUSSION

I have several comments to make : first of all, I am a little disappointed in some statements in Prof. Hillel's speech, because yesterday he suggested to describe the water flow through the soil plant system, that Ohm's law was a rather simple description of this flow and I was really wondering if he would come up with some other better suggestions. Secondly, Prof. Hillel suggested that there is a certain pattern in root extraction if you analyze the sink curve in the depth, but I would say it depends completely on what the preconditions were in soil moisture content with depth and of the root pattern, so that you cannot speak of a general pattern of the roots in the soil.
The approach Molz and Remson is in fact only for steady state conditions and they use a very unrealistic approach by not taking into account the gradient the water has between the soil and the roots.
Moreover, the daily fluctuation of transpiration has been described by Gardner already in 1968 I think. (ABENDT)

I have no particular answer to these. As regards the statement I made yesterday, I made a different statement, I didn't say I was against the use of Ohm's law, in general. I said that I was against this law for the particular problem involved. (HILLEL)

If you are willing to assume a linear relationship between some potential in the soil and some potential in the plant such as Ohm's law, then you need to introduce some resistivity. We have two ways of determining this, one rather independent of the other, dr. Feddes has gone out to the field of evaluating these by different methods, than the ones we have used. Can you suggest any different way of determining these coefficients. (NEUMAN)

Yes ! What dr. Feddes said, he calculated on the effective structure pattern a value of the roots resistance. I did not criticize the attempt of using the analogy of Ohm's law. I was looking at the independent tests of the models which means testing it against independently obtained data such as data of root length like the group of Hopkin in Wageningen obtained. (HILLEL)

Prof. Hillel made some very good remarks on the area of system-analysts. He said the system is very complex, we don't know which measurements to take and if system dynamic simulation can offer us a comprehensive approach. I would welcome some comments and questions from the simulation group. (SHAH)

I have a question about your remarks about circular reasoning and independent measurements for building and verifying the model. I completely agree with the basic ideas but I think one must be very careful in describing the thing you mean in that case exactly. I understand that if you built the model by taking measurements under certain circumstances on a certain item, give the parameters, do some **computation and come back to look if this is the same ; I think it's clear to most** *of us to say that's not what we wish. On the other hand you could establish parameters on an item by measuring and getting an almost exactly similar item to control the obtained computational data later. Do you object against that too ? How general do you want to go to avoid circular reasoning. Does it mean if I had a model* *working in a moderate climate, should it also work in an arid climate ?   (ELZAS)*

No, I accept that a model can be of limited use provided that you are aware of this limitation and use it not beyond the confines of the model's validity. But even then, to find these confines, the proof is on you that there is a model based on fundamental principles such that you can adapt to fit the situation. (HILLEL)

I think you should do both, but I fear it is almost unfeasible at this stage of time, with the very limited amount of experience that we have to make any model of any generality of any subject. It will always apply to a small restricted part of the situation and the duty of the systems people is to define clearly these are the boundaries and outside I don't know. (ELZAS)

I imagine there is a whole world of quantitative physical science in which what you are saying is not true, where in fact there is an area of discussion where quantitative prediction is possible and where there is a good and acceptable relationship between the model and reality. This is what natural science is all about and there are areas where natural science really does work believe it or not. (PHILIP)

The nature of the model should match the nature of the problem and if you are talking about planning purposes and operational things like this, it seems to me that none of the models that have been mentioned here for any of the systems we talk about are any good in the long term anyway. The large conceptional physical model cannot be validated very well at all, there just are no methods of doing this. You get a lot of extra content in the model that could explain the sort of thing that could happen when adjusted changes occur in the environment of the system. It could do that. But if it has not been evaluated and you don't have the parameters very well, then there is not much use for doing that. Similarly the systems model has not got that surface content. It tries to model what is here now and in the near future. But for planning purpose, do we plan 50 years ahead or using control ideas do we plan for the immediate future and update our plans as we go along what the urban modelers call a "rolling plan". It seems to me this is what we should do. So we want a simple model which can be updated. The conceptional physical model has its validity but in different areas. (YOUNG)

In the movement of water through the system are there no places where there are chemical reactions involving water. Where is the sink term in your transport equation ? (DAVIDSON)

In all the models this is negligible in a first approximation. I can interest you in an innovation in our research. We have come up what we consider to be a new method of conserving water in the soil. The idea is to break the soil surface into clamps and treat the clamps with materials surface activities, chemicals, which make the soil hydrofobic rather than hydrophilic. When irrigation is applied water runs off the clamps in the large cavities between the clamps directly in the deeper layers. The surface remaining dry doesn't slake and form a bottle neck for further entering of water into the soil. Another advantage when the soil dries out, we are usually accustomed to finding a saturated soil surface and to extracting large quantities of water from the soils. In that case the treated surface yields no water and we very dramaticaly reduce evaporation by this means. The third is that weed germination is prevented since the seed of weeds resides in the soil and waits for wetness condition to be optimal. The total effect is we maintain a field open to water and air stable, we prevent evaporation without the need of potentially harmful herbicides with environmental side effects. We are now in the process of testing this. There are problems we do not exactly know how to solve for instance there is on optimal size of aggregates and depth of the aggregated layer from the point of view of the combined depth in infiltration and evaporation. If the clamps are too small infiltration is reduced because the clamp cavities assume the size of capillaries and water entry is inhibited if they are too large one observes the entry

of air columns coming into the soil and as a consequence enhanced increase of evaporation. There is an optimization problem. Of course, here the depth of aggregated
layer has influences on the cost of the treatment. We perhaps need a modeling specialist in the modeling of this subsystem in the larger soil water plant continuum.
(HILLEL)

Current research field of author : *Soil-plant-atmosphere water relations - Field
water balance and water use efficiency in dryland and irrigated agriculture - Water
conservation - Rainfall-runoff relations - Soil structure management - Flow of water
and solutes to groundwater - Environmental problems related to soil and water pollution.*

Modeling and Simulation of Water Resources Systems, G.C. VANSTEENKISTE, (Ed.)
North-Holland Publishing Company (1975)

MODELING OF ENVIRONMENTAL SYSTEMS

J.C.J. Nihoul
Institut d'Astronomie et de Géophysique
Université Catholique de Louvain, BELGIUM

Foreword

This chapter is a synopsis of the mathematical model which has been the framework of the theoretical and experimental research conducted in the last three years in the scope of the Belgian National Program on the Environment. Sea Project[*].

The successive steps in the construction of the Model have been described in several progress reports and published papers and the details are not reproduced here. A list of references is attached.

A detailed description of the modern concepts and techniques of marine modelling can be found in Modelling of Marine Systems
Edited by Jacques C.J. Nihoul
Elsevier Publ. Amsterdam 1974.

The ordering of this chapter closely follows that of the book, and the same notations are used.

1. DEMARCATION OF THE SYSTEM

SUPPORT

The support of the model is the Southern Bight of the North Sea and the Scheldt Estuary.

The hydrodynamical part of the model is extended to the whole North Sea whenever necessary to provide appropriate Nothern boundary conditions for the Southern Bight.

SCOPE

The primary objective of the model is the study of the space and time characteristics of water motion, surface elevation, temperature, salinity, turbidity, oxygen, nutrients, trace metals, chlorinated hydrocarbons and living species[**].

REDUCTION OF SCOPE. COMPARTMENTS

Attention is restricted to the most important compartments :

(i)	dissolved substances	
(ii)	suspensions	
(iii)	plankton	phytoplankton
		zooplankton
(iv)	fish	pelagic
		benthic
(v)	schellfish and molluscs	

[*] Sponsored by the Ministry for Science Policy, Belgium.

[**] Petroleum products are examined in a separate program.

(vi)   bottom sediments
(vii)   macro- and meio-benthos
(viii) bacteria   faecal
                    marine heterotrophic
                    benthic

The state variables include the specific mass [*] of each compartment and the aggregate concentrations of the selected chemicals in compartments (i) to (vi).

REDUCTION OF SUPPORT. SPACE AVERAGING

All over the support except in the Scheldt estuary the turbulent mixing ensures a uniform density.

While separate three-dimensional and combined depth-averaged and width averaged two-dimensional models are being developed for the Scheldt estuary, the model for the Southern Bight is further simplified by assuming constant mass density and considering only average properties over the total depth.

The mechanical variables are then reduced to the two horizontal components of the depth-averaged velocity vector and the surface elevation.

For the study of specific chemical and ecological interactions, the support may be divided in a limited number of *niches* where similar conditions prevail. In a first approach, one may study the dynamics of the aggregate properties of the niche, obtained by further integrating (averaging) over the horizontal dimensions of the niche. Niche (or box) models of this sort have been developed and tested against the experimental observations made in the Ostend "Bassin de chasse", a closed sea basin at the coast which has been extensively studied in the past.

2. STATE VARIABLES AND CONTROL PARAMETERS

The state variables are defined by the scope of the system as stated above. As a result of turbulence and other erratic or rapidly oscillating motions of the sea, each variable shows fluctuations around a mean value. Only these mean values are significant for the model. The evolution equations are written for the mean variables and only the general effect of the fluctuations (through non-linear terms in the basic equations) is taken into account.

3. EVOLUTION EQUATIONS

The assumption of uniform sea water density which is justified by experiment (apart from the Scheldt estuary where slightly different models are being developed) allows a decoupling between the mechanical variables and the others. The hydrodynamic equations can be solved independently of the other evolution equations and the values of the flow velocity determined by the former substituted in the latter which in turn can be solved knowing the interactions between the constituents.

---

[*] mass per unit volume.

The *hydrodynamic models* which one can develop in this way differ whether one is interested in unsteady sea motions produced by tides and storm surges or in the residual - "steady" - circulation which results from the average of the actual flow over a time sufficiently long to cancel out tidal oscillations and transitory wind currents.

The evolution equations for the concentration variables are coupled through the terms expressing the interactions of the constituent α with other constituents β, γ, ... They also depend on the water motion determined by the hydrodynamic models.

In a first approach, it is rewarding to separate the two effects and study first the dispersion (by currents, sedimentation and turbulence) of a "passive" constituent, i.e. one which does not have significant interactions with others. Then, to investigate the interactions (e.g. the path of a pollutant in the food chain), one can develop *niche models* concerned with mean concentrations over some reasonably homogeneous regions of space. Niche models are not affected by the detailed hydrodynamics of the sea ; only its effects on imputs and outputs at the niche's frontiers remain to be known.

Although *passive dispersion models* can only give conservative estimates of the distribution of chemicals and species in the sea and *niche models* can only give an average knowledge of the interactions, they provide nevertheless a first valuable insight into the mechanisms of the marine system.

Of course, the model can combine dispersion and interactions and provide the detailed prediction of the state of the system at all points and time.

However the gigantic amount of computer work which is required to solve large systems of coupled partial differential equations commends that the full scale simulation be restricted to dramatic cases where estimates are insufficient or to special problems (like the dumpings) where, in the area of interest, only a limited number of constituents are involved in a significant way.

The general dispersion-interaction model is described in (Nihoul (1973a)) and subsequent papers. Different simplified forms of this model, pertinent to special studies, are given in the following and illustrated by examples of application.

4. TIDES AND STORM SURGES MODEL

(i)   State variables

Mean depth-averaged horizontal velocity vector $\bar{u}$
Water height   H

(The surface elevation ζ is given by H = h + ζ where h is the water depth).

(ii)   External forces per unit mass of sea water

Tide generating force $\underline{\xi}$
Gradient of atmospheric pressure $\nabla(p_a/\rho)$
Wind stress (divided by ρ) $\underline{\tau}_s$
Relation of wind stress to wind velocity $\underline{v}$ at reference height

$$\underline{\tau}_s = \frac{C}{H} \underline{v} \|\underline{v}\|$$

(iii)   Evolution equations

$$\frac{\partial H}{\partial t} + \nabla \cdot (H \overline{\underline{u}}) = 0$$

$$\frac{\partial \overline{\underline{u}}}{\partial t} + \overline{\underline{u}} \cdot \nabla \overline{\underline{u}} + f \underline{e}_3 \wedge \overline{\underline{u}} = \underline{\xi} - \nabla \left(\frac{p_a}{\rho} + g \zeta \right)$$

$$+ a \nabla^2 \overline{\underline{u}} - \frac{D}{H} \overline{\underline{u}} \|\overline{\underline{u}}\| + \frac{C}{H} \underline{v} \|\underline{v}\|$$

where the $\underline{e}_1$ and $\underline{e}_2$ axes are horizontal, the $\underline{e}_3$-axis vertical and where

$$\underline{\nabla} = \underline{e}_1 \frac{\partial}{\partial x_1} + \underline{e}_2 \frac{\partial}{\partial x_2}$$

(iv)   Control parameters

  f : Coriolis parameter (twice the vertical component of the angular velocity of the earth).

  ρ : specific mass of the sea water.

  a : horizontal effective viscosity.

  D : bottom friction coefficient.

  C : atmospheric drag coefficient.

  h : depth.

5. MODEL OF RESIDUAL CIRCULATION

(i)   State variables

  Stream function ψ

  The two components of the residual flow rate vector $\underline{U}_o$ are given by :

$$U_{o,1} = - \frac{\partial \psi}{\partial x_2}$$

$$U_{o,2} = \frac{\partial \psi}{\partial x_1}$$

(ii)   External forces per unit mass of sea water

  Residual stress $\underline{\theta}$

$$\underline{\theta} = (\underline{\tau}_s)_o + (\underline{\tau}_t)_o$$

where $(\underline{\tau}_s)_o$ is the residual wind stress and $(\underline{\tau}_t)_o$ the residual tidal stress   (Nihoul 1974)

$$(\underline{\tau}_t)_o = - \left(g \zeta_1 \nabla \zeta_1 + \nabla \cdot (H^{-1} \underline{U}\, \underline{U}) \right)_o$$

where ζ_1 denotes the surface elevation produced by tides and transitory wind forces.

(iii)   Steady state residual equation

$$K \nabla^2 \Psi - \frac{\partial \Psi}{\partial x_1} \left(f \frac{\partial h}{\partial x_2} + \frac{2K}{h} \frac{\partial h}{\partial x_1} \right) + \frac{\partial \Psi}{\partial x_2} \left(f \frac{\partial h}{\partial x_1} - \frac{2K}{h} \frac{\partial h}{\partial x_2} \right)$$

$$= h w_3 + \frac{\partial h}{\partial x_2} \theta_1 - \frac{\partial h}{\partial x_1} \theta_2$$

where θ_1 and θ_2 are the two horizontal components of $\underline{\theta}$ and where w_3 is the vertical component of $\underline{\nabla} \wedge \underline{\theta}$.

(iv)   Control parameters

K : Bottom friction coefficient for residual flow
f : Coriolis parameter
h : depth.

6. PASSIVE DISPERSION MODELS

(i)   State variables

Depth-averaged concentration of any passive constituent α or depth-averaged temperature $\overline{c}$

$$\left(\overline{c} = \overline{r}_\alpha \quad \text{or} \quad \overline{c} = \overline{\theta} \right)$$

Depth-averaged horizontal velocity vector $\overline{\underline{u}}$
(given by separate hydrodynamic model).

Water height H
(given by separate hydrodynamic model).

(ii)   Imputs - Outputs

Total imput in a water column of unit base $H\Lambda$
(including volume sources, surface and bottom fluxes.
If these result in a net output. Λ is negative)

(iii)   Evolution equation (Nihoul 1973b)

$$\frac{\partial \overline{c}}{\partial t} + \overline{\underline{u}} \cdot \nabla \overline{c} + H^{-1} \nabla \cdot \left(\gamma_2 \frac{H \sigma_3}{\overline{u}} \overline{c} \, \overline{\underline{u}} \right)$$

$$= \Lambda + H^{-1} \nabla \cdot \left(\gamma_1 \frac{H^2}{\overline{u}} \overline{\underline{u}} (\overline{\underline{u}} \cdot \nabla \overline{c}) \right) + \nabla \cdot \widetilde{\kappa} \nabla \overline{c}$$

(iv)   Control parameters

σ_3 migration (sedimentation or ascension) velocity
    $\sigma_3 = 0$ for temperature and neutrally buoyant constituents

$\widetilde{\kappa}$ horizontal eddy diffusivity

γ_1, γ_2 shear effects coefficients (Nihoul 1971, 1972, 1973b, 1974).

7. NICHE INTERACTIONS MODEL

(i)   State variables

Averages over the whole niche's space of all interacting chemical and ecological state variables r_α or θ $\qquad\qquad s_\alpha$

(ii)   Imputs - Outputs

Total imput (output if negative) in the niche (including volume sources and fluxes or flows in and out the niche at the boundaries) $\qquad\qquad S_\alpha$

(iii)   Evolution equations

$$\frac{ds_\alpha}{dt} = S_\alpha + I_\alpha \quad (t \ , \ s_1 \ , \ s_2 \ , \ \ldots \ s_n)$$

I_α represents the rate of production (or destruction of s_α by chemical, biochemical or ecological interactions. In general, I_α is a function of time and all interacting variables s_β. I_α depends on the particular interactions involved. In many cases, it can be simply approximated by combinations (in sums and products) of simple laws such that

a	k_α	(constant)
b	$k_{\alpha\beta} \, s_\beta$	(linear)
c	$k_{\alpha\beta\gamma} \, s_\beta \, s_\gamma$	(bilinear)
d	$k_1 s_\alpha - k_2 \, s_\alpha^2$	(logistic)
e	$k_1 \dfrac{s_\beta}{k_2 + s_\beta}$	(Michaelis-Mentem-Monov)

where the k_α , $k_{\alpha\beta}$ and $k_{\alpha\beta\gamma}$ are functions of time and control parameters.

(iv)   Control parameters

Several control parameters influence the interaction laws and appear in particular in the expressions of the coefficients k_α , $k_{\alpha\beta}$ ... In some cases, it is simpler to consider these coefficients as resulting control parameters to be determined experimentally.

8. EXAMPLES OF APPLICATIONS

8. 1. Tides and Storm Surges Model

The model has been applied with success by Ronday (1973) to the calculation of tides in the North Sea and in the Southern Bight.

8. 2. Residual circulation model

The model has been applied with success by Ronday (1972), Runfola and Adam (1972), Nihoul and Ronday (1974) to the calculation of the residual circulation in the North Sea and in the Southern Bight.

8. 3. Passive dispersion model

The model has been applied with success by Nihoul (1972) and by Adam and Runfola (1972) to the determination of the dispersion pattern subsequent to a dye release or a dumping.

8. 4. Niche Interactions Model

The model has been applied with success by Pichot and Adam to the study of chemical, biochemical and ecological interactions in the Ostend "Bassin de Chasse" [Nihoul (1974)].

REFERENCES

ADAM, Y. & Y. RUNFOLA (1972). Numerical Methods for the computation of Shear Effect Diffusion, *Prog. Nat. sur l'Env. Phys. et Biol.-Poll.Eaux-Projet Mer*, Report N14.

NIHOUL, J.C.J. (1971). Proc.North Sea Science Conf., Aviemore, Scotland, 1, 89.
(1972). Bull. Soc. Sc. Lg., 10, 521.
(1973a).Mem. Soc. Sc. Lg., 4, 115.
(1973b).Proc. Second IUTAM-IUGG Symposium on Turbulent Diffusion in Environmental Pollution, Charlottesville, U.S.A., 1973.
(1974). Modelling of Marine Systems, Elsevier Publ. Amsterdam.

NIHOUL, J.C.J. & F.C. RONDAY (1974). The influence of the "tidal stress" on the residual circulation, *Prog. Nat. sur l'Env. Phys. et Biol.-Poll.Eaux-Projet Mer*, Report N32.

NIHOUL, J.C.J. & F.C. RONDAY (1974). Coherent Structures and Negative Viscosity in Marine Turbulence, *Prog. Nat. sur l'Env. Phys. et Biol.-Poll.Eaux-Projet Mer*, Report N 34.

RONDAY, F.C. (1972). Modèle Mathématique pour l'étude de la circulation résiduelle dans la Mer du Nord, *Marine Science Branch., Manuscript Report Series*, N° 27, Ottawa.

(1973). Modèle Mathématique pour l'étude de la circulation due à la marée en Mer du Nord, *Marine Science Branch., Manuscript Report Series*, N° 29, Ottawa.

RUNFOLA, Y. & Y. ADAM (1972). Residual and wind-driven circulation in the Southern Bight, *Prog. Nat. sur l'Env. Phys. et Biol. Poll.Eaux-Projet Mer*, Report N15.

Modeling and Simulation of Water Resources Systems, G.C. VANSTEENKISTE, (Ed.)
North-Holland Publishing Company (1975)

METHODS OF ANALYSIS IN WATER QUALITY SIMULATION MODELS

Ch. Hirsch
Department of Fluid Mechanics
Vrije Universiteit Brussel, BELGIUM

ABSTRACT

The basic equations occuring in the mathematical modeling of various water quality problems are reviewed and discussed from the standpoint of numerical resolution. These equations can be classified according to their structure as well as to the number of dimensions used in the analysis of practical problems.

Two main numerical methods of general application are applied in practice ; finite differences and finite elements. Accuracy and stability problems occur as well as the important question of numerical diffusion and dispersion.
Some comparative elements between these two main numerical methods are discussed.

1. BASIC FORMULATION OF WATER QUALITY MODELS.

The basic physical phenomenon in water quality problems is the convective and dispersive transport of interacting physical entities, like mass, momentum, heat concentration of dissolved suspended constitutes, etc...
The general transport equation of a substance C in a turbulent flow can be written

$$\frac{\partial C}{\partial t} + \vec{\nabla} (\vec{u} \, C) = \vec{\nabla} (\bar{\bar{D}} \, \vec{\nabla} \, C) + S \tag{1}$$

$\vec{u}$ is the velocity vector, $\bar{\bar{D}}$ the diffusion matrix and S is the generalized source term describing the external influences of the system.
This equation is coupled to the flow equations

$$\frac{\partial \rho}{\partial t} + \vec{\nabla} (\rho \, \vec{u}) = 0 \tag{2}$$

where ρ is the specific mass of the fluid, and

$$\rho \frac{\partial \vec{u}}{\partial t} + \rho (\vec{u} \, \vec{\nabla}) \, \vec{u} = - \vec{\nabla} p + \vec{\nabla} \bar{\bar{\tau}} + \vec{F} \tag{3}$$

where p is the hydrodynamic pressure, $\bar{\bar{\tau}}$ is the general shear stress tensor including viscous and turbulent stresses and $\vec{F}$ are the external forces such as gravity, Coriolis forces, etc...

With an eddy viscosity assumption for the turbulent stresses, equation (3) can be written under the general form of equation (1).

In following systems, seas, estuaries, lakes, groundwater flows, etc..., the physical conditions are generally of a three-dimensional nature and variations of the basic physical parameters in all of the three space directions can become important. However the complete resolution of the basic equations in three dimensions is beyond the present capacity of computers so that a reduction to two-dimensional formulation is necessary.
Fortunately, in many situations, variations in one direction are less important than in the two others, as often is the case in groundwater flows or their influence can be taken into account by an averaging of the equations over that direction as is the case in many tidal problems, shallow water situation, etc...

141

Even in the three-dimensional model of estuaries and coastal seas of Leendertse (1973), the third direction is cut into slices and the averaged (over a slice) two-dimensional equations are solved slice per slice. Therefore we will limit ourselves to a discussion of one or two-dimensional problems.

Calling u_1, u_2 the two velocity components of $\vec{u}$; x_1, x_2 the two considered physical dimensions and H the length of the third averaged direction in each point $H = H(x_1, x_2)$, the averaged equation can be written in most cases

$$\frac{\partial}{\partial t} (H\ C) + \frac{\partial}{\partial x_i} (H\ C\ u_i) = \frac{\partial}{\partial x_i} (D_{ij}\ H\ \frac{\partial C}{\partial x_j}) + S \tag{4}$$

A general form of the diffusion matrix D_{ij} can be written, neglecting molecular diffusion

$$D_{ij} = \alpha_{ijk\ell} \frac{u_k u_\ell}{|u|} \tag{5}$$

and when reduced to its principal axes, only the longitudinal and transverse coefficients D_1 and D_2 will remain.
The integrated flow equations can be cast into the same form as equation (4) by the introduction of an eddy viscosity concept

$$\tau_{ij} = \varepsilon^{(ij)} \frac{\partial u_i}{\partial x_j} \qquad\qquad \text{no summation on i, j} \tag{6}$$

The general convective-dispersive equation in two dimensions (4) is of the parabolic type if all terms are important. However situations occur when some mechanism is more important than another and a classification can be made according to the relative importance of diffusion versus convection.

Defining some characteristic diffusion coefficient D, characteristic velocity U and length L, the relative importance of diffusion versus convection is measured by the ratio of HCU and DHC/L. This enables to define a generalized Reynolds or Peclet number UL/D as the ratio of convective to diffusive transport.

If $\dfrac{UL}{D} \gg 1$ diffusion can be neglected

          $\dfrac{UL}{D} \ll 1$ convection can be neglected

and in all other cases, both terms are significant in the overall mass transport.

When diffusion effects are negligible, that means for UL/D → ∞, equation (4) [or equation (1)] becomes of hyperbolic nature, while for other cases the transport equation is of the parabolic type. However, in absence of convective effects, the steady state equation (1) or (4) are steady field equations of elliptic type.

The presence of the convective terms in a general unsteady problem does not change the parabolic nature of the equations, but if D_{ij} is symmetric, writing equation (4) in the form

$$\frac{\partial}{\partial t} (H\ C) = \frac{\partial}{\partial x_i} [D_{ij}\ H\ \frac{\partial C}{\partial x_j} - H\ C\ u_i] + S \tag{7}$$

the non-symmetrical character of equation (7) appears. This is one of the main problem in the numerical resolution of these convective-diffusive equation, especially for high values of UL/D.

One-dimensional forms of equation (4) occur in various problems and are also often used for stability analysis of numerical elements.

Some physical examples are :

a. Unsteady_unconfined_groundwater_flow.

$$S \frac{\partial h}{\partial t} = \frac{\partial}{\partial x} (h K \frac{\partial h}{\partial x}) \tag{8}$$

where h is the height of the free water table and S the storage coefficient.
Equations of this form correspond to UL/D = 0 since convection terms do not
occur. Unsaturated groundwater flow equations also have the same structure
[Giesel, Reuger, Strebel (1973)].

b. Dispersion_in_homogeneous_porous_media.

$$\frac{\partial C}{\partial t} + u \frac{\partial C}{\partial x} = D \frac{\partial^2 C}{\partial x^2} \tag{9}$$

Typical values of UL/D are between 15 - 150, Gupta (1973).
A system of 2 coupled equations (9) is discussed in Rubin & James (1973).

c. Open_channels_(surges),_tidal_flows.

In these cases influence of dispersion (turbulent eddy viscosity) is neglected,
and the system is governed by a pair of first order partial differential equations of hyperbolic type. This corresponds to infinite values for UL/D.

$$b \frac{\partial h}{\partial t} + \frac{\partial Au}{\partial x} = Q \tag{10.a}$$

$$\frac{\partial u}{\partial t} + u \frac{\partial u}{\partial x} + g \frac{\partial h}{\partial x} + F_x = 0 \tag{10.b}$$

see for instance Prandle, Crookshank (1974).

Two-dimensional equations occur in following simulation models.

a. Groundwater_field_equations.

$$\frac{\partial}{\partial x} (K_1 b \frac{\partial h}{\partial x}) + \frac{\partial}{\partial y} (K_2 b \frac{\partial h}{\partial y}) - q = S \frac{\partial h}{\partial t} \tag{11}$$

where h is the head (b=1 in a confined aquifer).
Since no convective terms appear, the parameter UL/D is zero. This equation
is still parabolic, but becomes elliptic in steady flows. Another elliptic
equation occurs in steady lake circulations, where the unknown is the stream-
function, Gallagher (1973).
Equation (11) describes also a pure diffusion process (pollutant, heat, ...)

b. Convective-dispersive_equation.

This equation under the form (4) or (7) with i=1,2 describes transport of a
mass constituent in seas, estuaries, porous media when integrated vertically,
or heat transfer in lakes and rivers.
Vertically integrated equations describe for example salinity profiles. Depending on the particular problem, values of UL/D range from the order of magnitude 10 to 1000, lower values occuring in groundwater problems, higher values
in estuaries.

c. Tidal flows.

Here again, neglecting the longitudinal shear stresses in the vertically integrated equations, an hyperbolic system of equations is obtained, Dronkers (1964),
of the form

$$\frac{\partial u}{\partial t} + u \frac{\partial u}{\partial x} + v \frac{\partial u}{\partial y} = q_1 \tag{12.a}$$

$$\frac{\partial v}{\partial t} + u \frac{\partial v}{\partial x} + v \frac{\partial v}{\partial y} = q_2 \tag{12.b}$$

where q_1 and q_2 contain the external influences like Coriolis forces, bottom-
stresses, wind stresses and gravity.

Numerical resolution of these various simulation models can be obtained mainly by
the use of finite difference methods and more recently also by finite element
methods. These two numerical techniques are of general application and will be
discussed in the following. The method of characteristics, of more restricted
use, will not be discussed.

One can formulate general requirements for a confident numerical scheme, see
Potter (1973) for an introduction.

a. Stability : errors may not oscillate with increasing or constant amplitudes, nor
                grow exponentially when the number of iterations increases. A dis-
                cussion of this question for finite difference methods can be found
                in Richtmeyer & Morton (1967) with a proof of the equivalence of
                stability and convergence under certain conditions (Lax's equivalence
                theorem).

b. Absence of numerical diffusion : numerical diffusion is a phenomenon occuring in
                all digital methods which causes the damping of high wave-numbers
                (or short wave-lengths). This is a consequence of the introduction
                of calculation meshes of finite dimension, say Δx, since the scheme
                will not be able to describe wave-lengths shorter than 2 Δx.

c. Absence of numerical dispersion : numerical dispersion is connected to numerical
                diffusion and is the phenomenon by which different wave-number com-
                ponents travel with different velocities. Numerical diffusion and
                dispersion can be estimated by the complex ratio of a computed wave
                to a physical wave after the physical wave has propagated one wave-
                length.

d. Conservation properties : the numerical method should not destroy the physical
                conservation of such entities like mass, momentum, energy, etc...
                From the point of view of transport of a given mass constituent,
                eventually influenced by chemical or biological reactions, it is
                particularly important that mass shouldn't be destroyed through nu-
                merical spurious non-conservation.

These effects are generally dependent on the order of accuracy of the numerical
scheme. Lower order finite difference schemes, for instance, have strong numerical diffusion and dispersion, even when they are stable.
This explains why nearly all used schemes found in the literature are of higher
order.

2. FINITE DIFFERENCE METHODS.

It is not our intention to discuss here the properties of a particular scheme, but rather to stress some general aspects which have come out from the experience in simulation models in the latest years.

Even with stable and convergent finite difference schemes one obtains a numerical solution which is not, due to the finite dimensions of the step sizes, an exact replica of the solution of the differential equation.
This is best seen through a Fourier decomposition of the solution, considering one wave mode and looking for the dispersion relation between the frequency and the wave-number on the mesh. Comparing with the dispersion relation of the corresponding differential equation, the ratio of the real parts is a measure of the numerical diffusion, and the difference in phases (or the ratio of the imaginary parts) is a measure of the numerical dispersion. In other words, through the finite difference scheme the amplitude of a wave is reduced by numerical diffusion and the numerical dispersion leads to variations in the propagation velocities. An interesting representation is used by Leendertse (1967) in the form of a complex propagation factor, defined as the ratio of the computed wave to the physical wave after the latter has propagated over one wave-length. The modulus of this factor is different from one when numerical diffusion exists, and the argument is different from zero when numerical dispersion exists.

It is well known that these effects can generally be neglected for small wave-numbers, that is large waves, but become important for waves of small wave-lengths. This is easy to understand since the finite difference grid is not able to "see" wave-lengths shorter than the grid spacing Δx.

2.1. Numerical diffusion and dispersion.

Consider the one-dimensional convective-diffusive equation with constant coefficients.

$$\frac{\partial C}{\partial t} + u \frac{\partial C}{\partial x} = D \frac{\partial^2 C}{\partial x^2} \tag{13}$$

With $t = n \Delta t$ and $x = i \Delta x$, an explicit space centered scheme is

$$(C_{i,n+1} - C_{i,n}) + \frac{u \Delta t}{\Delta x} (C_{i+1,n} - C_{i-1,n}) = \frac{D \Delta t}{(\Delta x)^2} (C_{i+1,n} - 2C_{i,n} + C_{i-1,n}) \tag{14}$$

while a space-centered implicit scheme can be written as

$$(C_{i,n+1} - C_{i,n}) + \frac{u \Delta t}{\Delta x} (C_{i+1,n+1} - C_{i-1,n+1}) = \frac{D \Delta t}{(\Delta x)^2} (C_{i+1,n+1} - 2C_{i,n+1} + C_{i-1,n+1}) \tag{15}$$

The propagation factors, as calculated by Leendertse (1970) are shown in figures 1 and 2 for the modulus (diffusion) and the phase (dispersion).
The abscissa $L/\Delta x$ is equal to

$$L/ \Delta x = 2\pi/(k \Delta x)$$

where k is the wave-number and L is the wave-length.
According to the wave-number range which is needed for the description of the physical phenomenon, suitable values for $u \Delta t/\Delta x$ and $U \Delta x/D$ can be chosen.
For smooth physical variations, with a smaller number of harmonics (k large) the figures 1 and 2 show that high values of $u \Delta t/\Delta x$ may be chosen. Note that each curve corresponds to a fixed value of the mesh number $U \Delta x/D$.

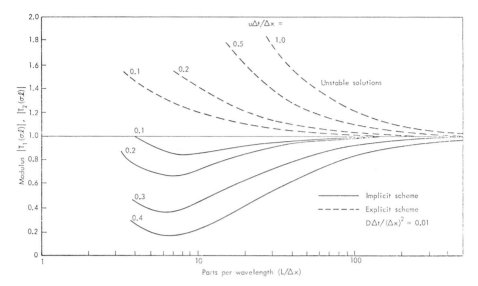

Fig.1 — Modulus of the propagation factor of the explicit and implicit schemes

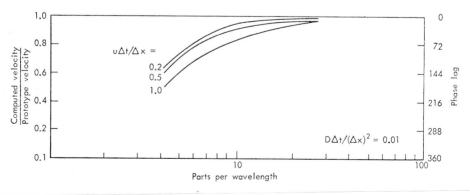

Fig.2 — Phase angle of the propagation factor

From theoretical and empirical results, Leendertse (1967), Stone & Brian (1963), Vichnevetsky (1974), a value of k $\Delta x \leq 1$ may be adopted and from figures 1 and 2 it is seen that values of U $\Delta x/D < 10$ have to be chosen with implicit schemes, in order to avoid numerical diffusion and dispersion.

This is important also when values of the physical diffusion coefficient are to be found by adjusting the numerical results to observation data. It is obvious from figures 1 and 2 that the obtained values will depend on Δx, Δt and on the difference scheme adopted. In order to avoid this, higher order or more elaborate schemes have to be used.

For instance, the alternating direction implicit scheme equation (15) + equation (14) at t = (n+2) Δt has a diffusion factor given by figure 3, which is indeed much more favorable than the former schemes. Much higher values of U $\Delta x/D$ can be chosen in this case.

An interesting method for the estimation of the step size Δx and the time step Δt is proposed by Dailey & Harleman (1973), based on a reduction criterion of numerical dispersion and which applied as well to finite element methods.

Since high wave-numbers dissipate and disperse as a consequence of the numerical approximation, the time and distance steps Δt and Δx should be fixed by the value of the smallest wave which is to be satisfactory represented in the simulation. A way of estimating the maximum wave-number is based on the observation that equation (13) can be considered as a linear system which will give an output concentration distribution when subjected to an instantaneous mass injection for instance, represented by an unit impulse. In this case the input spectral density will contain all the wave-numbers and the output spectral density can be calculated as a function of kD/U.

Figure 4 [from Dailey & Harleman (1973)] represents the normalized spectral density $^\circ S$ (k,x) in function of the distance from the injection point for various values of the generalized Reynolds-Peclet number Ux/D.

One clearly observes that for increasing values of Ux/D more high wave-numbers are damped. The maximum wave-number k_{max} can be estimated on basis of the value of 4 kD/U at which the spectral density falls below a given cut-off level, say 5 %. Figure 5 is obtained in this way in function of the parameter Ux/D.

With the conditions

$$k_{max} \, \Delta x \; \leq \; 1 \tag{16}$$

and $\quad$ U $\Delta t/\Delta x \; < \; 1$ $\tag{17}$

one obtains for each value of distance x from the injection point the maximum mesh Reynolds-Peclet number U $\Delta x/D$.

as $\quad$ U $\Delta x/D \; \leq \; \dfrac{1}{k_{max} \, D/U}$ $\tag{18}$

Since a physical dissipation and dispersion occurs, k_{max} decreases in function of distance, allowing larger space steps at higher distances with the same amount of reduction of numerical diffusion and dispersion. It is to be noted that the numerical dispersion is reduced when conditions (16) and (17) apply with the condition

$$D \, \Delta t/(\Delta x)^2 \; \leq \; 1/2 \tag{19}$$

although it never will be completely absent.

The situation becomes more complicated in two dimensions where longitudinal and transverse dispersion coefficients are different, and also when non-linear terms are taken into account.

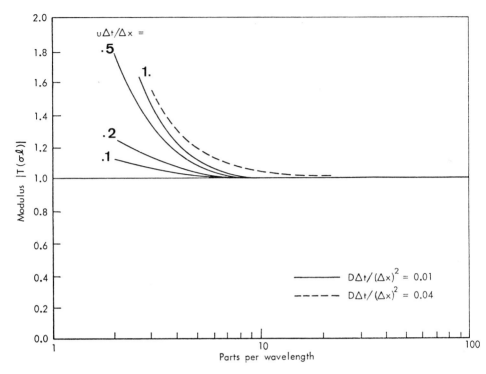

Fig.3 — Modulus of the propagation factor for the multioperation method

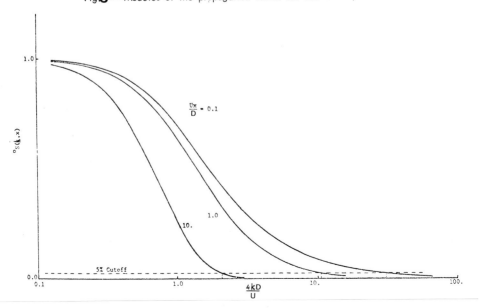

Figure 4 Normalized Spectral Density $^{o}S(k,x)$

For instance, in the resolution of the Burgers equation

$$\frac{\partial u}{\partial t} + u \frac{\partial u}{\partial x} = \nu \frac{\partial^2 u}{\partial x^2} \tag{20}$$

at a Reynolds number UL/ν of 100, Domingos & Filipe (1972) compared various difference schemes and found that none of them remained stable for mesh Reynolds numbers $U \Delta x/\nu$ of 10 or higher.

Summarizing, it appears that all finite difference schemes suffer from numerical diffusion and dispersion. Reduction of these effects is possible through higher order schemes [(Roberts & Weiss (1966)] or optimization schemes [(Stone & Brian (1963)], [Shamir & Harleman (1967)].
Some general guide-lines can be stated such as time and space centering of the difference schemes, use of a staggered mesh in two dimensions, reduction of $U \Delta x/D$, small values of $u \Delta t/\Delta x$ and higher order schemes. For instance, a Cranck-Nicholson scheme of equation (13) will oscillate for $U \Delta x/D > 2$, Price (1968). These difficulties have led many investigators to look after other methods, see Bredehoeft (1971).

2.2. Conservation properties and non-linear instabilities.

In the simulation of a transport phenomenon of a given substance, like mass of a constituent, the physical requirement of mass conservation should be satisfied by the numerical scheme. This is an important condition which is not fulfiled by all numerical difference schemes, see Potter (1973) for an introduction. Numerical non conservation of mass leads to spurious creation or destruction and it is obvious that this has to be avoided in every simulation model.
This is therefore an absolute requirement for every transport model. When considering the flow equations in tidal flow problems, other conservation laws like conservation of momentum, energy are physical requirements. Equation (4) for $D = u_i$ is the momentum equation written under conservation form, whereas with the use of the continuity equation, the equivalent forms (12.a) and (12.b) are not written under conservation form.
In order that the difference scheme should conserve momentum, it should therefore be applied to the equation (4) instead of equation (12).
However, there are sometimes practical reasons which render the momentum conservative difference equations less accurate, through the occurrence of large truncation errors in the reccurrence relations of an implicit scheme, Leendertse (1972), for instance.
The non-conservative momentum equations of the form (12) become therefore more accurate. Although this could lead to wave decay during computation, numerical experience showed no generation of instabilities for this reason.

This is in fact connected to an important aspect of the convective flow equations, namely the occurence of non-linear instabilities first observed by investigators working in the field of weather forecasting, Phillips (1959). The origin of these non-linear instabilities can be traced back to the misrepresentation of the short waves due to the finite grid size. It is well known that non-linear terms generate high and fractional harmonics leading to a transfer of energy from long to short waves. But since the grid cannot represent wave-lengths shorter than 2 Δx, energy is accumulated leading to instabilities, if the short waves are not damped. This could occur through an artificial viscosity external or build-in like in the Lax-Wendroff schemes for hyperbolic equations, or in implicit methods by numerical diffusion of these waves.
Generally, this will be insufficient since the non-linear terms are continuously feeding back the short wave into the system causing the non-linear instabilities. This effect cannot be reduced by reduction of the time step and must be avoided especially with long term simulations.

It has been shown by Arakawa (1966) that non-linear instabilities can be avoided if the numerical scheme conserves quadratic quantities like kinetic energy, square vorticity, and Arakawa proposed finite difference expressions which satisfy these requirements. In this way an interaction is introduced between the grid points such that the advection terms finite difference analog put bounds on a quadratic quantity in each grid point and avoids the formation of wave-lengths equal to 2 Δx.
It has been shown by Leendertse (1972) that his model conserves the square of the water height or the potential energy in constant depth systems, and that this quadratic conservation property could not have been obtained in a momentum conservation form of the equations. However in variable depths situations non-linear instabilities could occur and have indeed been observed. Arakawa pointed out that only one conserved quadratic property is sufficient in order to avoid non-linear instabilities, but that as many quadratic physical properties as possible should be conserved in order to simulate the frequency spectrum of the system.
Of course, in practice only a limited number of quantities can be conserved in the finite difference scheme, since each quantity implies different limitations on the possible expressions. A detailed discussion of various conservative schemes can be found in Grammeltvedt (1969).

Summarizing, at least two quantities should be conserved in any simulation model which includes the calculation of the velocity field, namely mass of all the constituents and one quadratic property.

3. FINITE ELEMENTS METHODS.

The difficulties in obtaining accurate simulations with finite difference methods have led investigators to search other methods. The method of characteristics has occasionally been used by Gardner & al (1964), Pinder & Cooper (1970), Reddell & Sunada (1970), Bredehoeft & Pinder (1973), since it does not present problems of numerical dispersion. However, this method is difficult to program and is not of general application.
Another method was proposed by Price & al (1968) based on Galerkin's procedure. This method used piecewice continuous polynomials and showed up to be of high-order accuracy for a wide range of values of the parameter UL/D, in a one-dimensional problem. With the advent of the method of finite elements and particularly with the method of weighted residuals which detached the finite element method from the requirement of variational principles, Zienkiewicz (1971), a general method was in this way provided which could be applied to two or three-dimensional problems and benefit from the advantages of Galerkin's method.
The method of wheighted residuals can be described as follows for a general differential equation $L\phi = 0$.
Dividing the domain into finite elements of n nodes, each unkown function ϕ is represented in an element by a linear combination of its nodal values ϕ_i (which will be the unknowns of the problem) through

$$\phi_e = \sum_{i=1}^{n} \phi_i N_i (x,y) \tag{21}$$

where N_i are the known shape functions.
The method of wheighted residuals sets the following expression to zero

$$\int W_j (x,y) L \phi_e \, dS = 0 \tag{22}$$

The method of Galerkin consists in the choice of the wheight functions $W_j = N_j$, hence equation (22) becomes

$$\int N_j (x,y) L \sum_{i=1}^{n} N_i (x,y) \phi_i \, dS = 0 \tag{23}$$

The system of equation (23) is a system of ordinary differential equations in ϕ_i, of the first order in the time (or an algebraic system for steady problems).

The method of finite elements has been applied in the last few years to nearly all water quality simulation problems, see Oden & al (1974), Adey & Brebbia (1973), Pinder (1973), and others.
No general method for error estimation of finite element techniques exists at present time and it is therefore not possible to present a general comparison between this method and finite differences. However some indications appear from recent works, in particular Dailey & Harleman (1973), Smith & al (1973), Taylor & Davis (1972). It appears that finite element solutions with simple linear elements have about the same accuracy as higher order finite difference methods with respect to numerical diffusion and dispersion. They possess good stability and conservation properties and are very well adapted to implement arbitrary boundaries.
A large room for improvement is still open, in particular with the formulation of the time, or the various finite differences expressions for ordinary differential equations. Following Taylor & Davis (1972), a trapezoidal integration scheme in time applied to the tidal flow equation shows no numerical diffusion nor dispersion while a finite element in time does, both being unconditionally stable.

On the other hand no analysis of quadratic conservation properties in connection with non-linear instabilities with finite elements has yet been done.

CONCLUSIONS.

All numerical methods introduce spurious elements in the computed solutions. Finite difference methods have been and still are thoroughly analyzed and this has led to elaborate higher order schemes in order to try to reduce numerical diffusion, dispersion and non-linear instabilities. Finite element methods perhaps present an alternative to finite differences with the hope they should show up less errors. Considerable analysis in this aspect is still necessary and the way for improvement in both methods is still open.

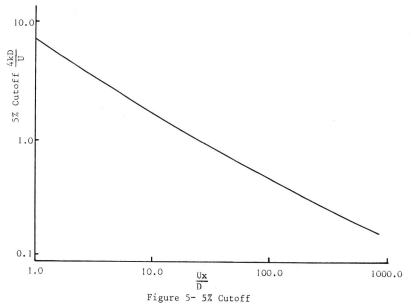

Figure 5- 5% Cutoff

REFERENCES.

ADEY, Z.A. & BREBBIA, C.A. (1973)
Finite Element Solution for Effluent Dispersion.
International Conference on Numerical Methods in Fluid Dynamics, University
of Southampton, U.K.

ARAKAWA, A. (1966)
Computational Design for long-Term Numerical Integration of the Equations
of Fluid Motion.
Two-Dimensional Incompressible Flow, pt. I.
J.Comp.Phys. 1, 119.

BREDEHOEFT, J.D. (1971)
Comment ...
Water Resources Res. 7, 755.

BREDEHOEFT, J.D. & PINDER, G.F. (1973)
Mass Transport in Flowing Groundwater.
Water Resources Res. 9, 194.

DAILEY, J.E. & HARLEMAN, D.R.F. (1973)
A Numerical Model of Transient Water Quality in a One-Dimensional Estuary
based on the Finite Element Method.
Int. Conf. on Num. Methods in Fluid Dynamics, Southampton, september 1973.

DOMINGOS, J.J.D. & FILIPE, J.M.C. (1972)
A Comparative Study of Difference Schemes.
Proc. of the 3rd Int. Conf. on Num. Methods in Fluid Dynamics, Lecture
Notes in Physics 18, Springer.

DRONKERS, J.J. (1964)
Tidal Computations in Rivers and Coastal Waters.
North-Holland Publ. Co., Amsterdam.

GARDNER, A.O. & PEACEMANN, D.W. & POZZI, A.L. (1964)
Numerical Calculation of Multi-dimensional miscible Displacement by the Method
of Characteristics.
Soc. Petrol. Eng. J. 4, 26.

GALLAGHER, R.H. & LIGGETT, J.A. & CHAN, S.T.K. (1973)
Finite Element Shallow Lake Circulations Analysis.
Journal of the Hydraulics Division, A.S.C.E., 99, 1083.

GIESEL, W. & REUGER, M. & STREBEL, O. (1973)
Numerical Treatment of Unsaturated Water Flow Equations.
Water Resour. Res. 9, 174.

GRAMMELTVEDT, A. (1969)
A Survey of Finite-Difference Schemes for the Primitive Equations for a
Barotropic Fluid.
Monthly Weather Review, 97, 384.

GUPTA, S.P. & GREENBORN, R.A. (1973)
Dispersion during Flow in Porous Media with Bilinear Absorption.
Water Resour. Res. 9, 1357.

LEENDERTSE, J.J. (1967)
Aspects of a Computational Model for Long-Period Water Wave Propagation.
RM-5294-PR, Rand Corporation, Santa Monica, California.

LEENDERTSE, J.J. (1970)
A Water Quality Simulation Model for Well-Mixed Estuaries and Coastal Seas :
Vol I, Principles of Computation.
RM-6230-RC, Rand Corporation, Santa Monica, California.

LEENDERTSE, J.J. (1972)
The Behaviour of the Water Quality Simulation Model.
P-4810, Rand Corporation, Santa Monica, California.

LEENDERTSE, J.J. & ALEXANDER, R.C., LIN, S.K. (1973)
A Three-Dimensional Model for Estuaries and Coastal Seas :
Vol I, Principles of Computation.
4-1417-OW.RR, Rand Corporation.

ODEN, J.T. & al (1974)
Int. Symposium on Finite Element Methods in Flow Problems.
University of Wales, Swansea.

PINDER, G.F. & COOPER, H.H. (1970)
A Numerical Technique for Calculating the Transient Position of the Saltwater
Front.
Water Resour. Res. 6, 875.

PINDER, G.F. (1973)
A Galerkin Finite Element Simulation of Groundwater Contamination on Long
Island, New York.
Water Resour. Res. 9, 1657.

PHILLIPS, N.A. (1959)
An Example of Non-Linear Computational Instability. The Atmosphere and Sea in
Motion, Rockefeller Institute Press, New York, p. 501.

POTTER, D. (1973)
Computational Physics.
J. Wiley & Sons, New York.

PRANDLE, P. & CROOKSHANK, L. (1974)
Numerical Model of St. Lawrence river Estuary.
Journal of Hydraulics Division, HY4, Proc. ASCE, 100, 517.

PRICE, H.S. & CAVENDISH, J.C. & VARGA, R.S. (1968)
Numerical Methods of Higher-Order Accuracy for Diffusion Convection Equations.
Soc. Petrol. Eng. J. 8, 293.

REDDEL, P.L. & SUNADA, S.K. (1970)
Numerical Simulation of Dispersion in Groundwater Aquifers.
Hydrol. Pap. 41, Colo. State Univ., Fort Collings.

RICHTMEYER, R.D. & MORTON, K.W. (1967)
Difference Methods for Initial Value Problems.
Interscience, New York.

ROBERTS, K.V. & WEISS, N.O. (1966)
Convective Difference Schemes.
Math. Of Computation, 20, 272.

RUBIN, J. & JAMES, R.V. (1973)
Dispersion-affected Transport of Reacting Solutes in Saturated Porous Media.
Water Resour. Res. 9, 1332.

SHAMIR, U.Y. & HARLEMAN, D.R.F. (1967)
Numerical Solutions for Dispersion in Porous Mediums.
Water Resour. Res. 3, 557.

SMITH, I.M. & FARADAY, R.V. & O'CONNOR, B.A. (1973)
Rayleigh-Ritz and Galerkin Finite Elements for Diffusion-Convection Problems.
Water Resour. Res. 9, 593.

STONE, H.L. & BRIAN, L.T. (1963)
Numerical Solution of Convective Transport Problems.
A.I.Ch.E. Journal 9, 681.

TAYLOR, C. & DAVIS, J. (1972)
Tidal and long-Wave Propagation. A Finite Element Approach.
Dept. of Civil Engineering, University of Wales, Swansea, Rep O/R/189/72.

VICHNEVETSKY, R. (1974)
Physical Criteria in Computer Methods for Partial Differential Equations.
Annales A.I.C.A., 1, 3.

ZIENKIEWICZ, O.C. (1971)
The Finite Element Method in Engineering Science.
Mc Graw-Hill, New York.

DISCUSSION

A general point : I don't see a model like this is any more mechanistic than the one that we were talking about, in fact the water quality models that we were talking about seemed to be referred as black box and they are not black box at all, we went through exactly that particular equation. The point about the models that we used is, they are based upon a different way of looking at the mechanistic behaviour of the system. In fact the model that we finished up with is a continuous type of reactor mechanization of what is happening, now this is a mechanistic way of looking at it, it is not a black box approach. It just does not happen to correspond with the normal mechanistic way of looking at it. So I think it is necessary to get the terms right. When it happens to be a mathematical model which has been treated using estimation techniques does not mean it is black box, it can be a mechanistic model. (YOUNG)

I think when one speaks of mechanistic models in this sense that one first uses a physical conservation law. (HIRSCH)

But the water quality models of this morning were based on that. I never got, because of the question, to the point to show you that it was a continuous type reactor which of course had the same laws. (YOUNG)

In your equation, how do you calculate this value of μ, is it a constant on a function of time and space ?

For the graphs I have shown, it was constant, just to show the numerical method. (HIRSCH)

Little criticism has been given to the method of characteristics as being particularly suitable to avoid numerical dispersion.(BRUTSAERT)

I agree, but I did not consider it because it is not of general application. It is more restricted application than finite elements for instance. (HIRSCH)

In the framework of mass transport equation : it is applicable, is it not ?
(BRUTSAERT)

Yes, but the proper mean effort is much stronger, more difficult to program. (HIRSCH)

Can you give any remarks about stability of this system ?

I mentioned it only as an example of a system which has an artificial dispositive which dampens the short waves, so which is less sensible to nonlinear stabilities, but the drawback of it is that it affects also the normal waves, so that is the reason why we considered it as a less sufficient method in this case. (HIRSCH)

Modeling and Simulation of Water Resources Systems, G.C. VANSTEENKISTE, (Ed.)
North-Holland Publishing Company (1975)

NUMERICAL EXPERIMENTS ON FREE SURFACE WATER MOTION WITH BORES

Maurizio Pandolfi
Istituto di Macchine e Centro Studi Dinamica Fluidi
Politecnico di Torino, ITALY

INTRODUCTION

The analogy between the equations describing the one or two dimensional unstea
dy flow or the two dimensional steady supersonic compressible flow and the water
motion with a free surface according to the "shallow water theory" is well known
(Ref. 1,2). In both problems the equations are non linear and hyperbolic. Until
no discontinuities appear in the flows, the integration of such equations is easy.
Difficulties are always associated with discontinuities, viz. shock waves in gasdynamics or bores or hydraulic jumps in water motion.

In gasdynamics two different approaches have been commonly used to compute
flows with shocks.

According to the first approach, shocks are explicity computed during their
evolution on the basis of the Rankine-Hugoniot equations (Ref. 3, 4, 5, 6). In the
second one, the Euler equations are rearranged in what is known as the divergence
or conservation form and the integration is carried out in such a way that the
shocks should appear as sharp transitions, spread over few mesh intervals.

Features of the shock explicit treatment approach are few computational points,
fast computations, accurate results and, often, more complicated codes due to the
additional logic for the shock calculations.

On the contrary, quite more points are needed when shocks are ignored, computer times are longer, spurious oscillations (numerical wiggles) appear near   the
shocks and may evolve and propagate through the flow field; the program codes are,
of course, simpler. This paper intends to show how numerical methods of the first
type mentioned above, which have been used in gasdynamics successfully, can be applied to problems in the category of shallow water motion.

In my opinion, there are two interesting points in this paper. One is the pre
sentation of some numerical examples supporting the philosophy of treating discontinuities explicitly.

The other is a demonstration of how techniques traditionally confined to problems related to aerospace sciences can be easily applied to the solution of environmental problems.

The numerical examples I present in this paper belong to three classes of phy
sical phenomena:
- unsteady one-dimensional flow in channels
- steady supercritical two-dimensional flow in channels
- steady two-dimensional flow around a blunted obstacle in a supercritical stream.
These examples involve the formation and the evolution of discontinuities such as
bores or hydraulic jumps.

THE EQUATIONS OF MOTION

The equations of motion according to the shallow water theory are very similar, even simpler, of those for compressible flow in gasdynamics. For example,the
Euler equations for unsteady quasi one-dimensional flow in gasdynamics are:

$$
\begin{array}{ll}
P_t + u P_x + \gamma u_x + \gamma u \alpha = 0 & \text{(continuity)} \\
u_t + u u_x + T P_x = 0 & \text{(momentum)} \\
S_t + u S_x = 0 & \text{(energy)}
\end{array}
$$

(1)

where $P = \ln p$, $T = \exp(\frac{\gamma-1}{\gamma} P + \frac{S}{\gamma})$ and $\alpha = (dA/dx)/A$ (A is the cross area of the duct).

All the quantities have been here normalized with respect to reference values: reference lenght l_∞, reference pressure p_∞ and temperature T_∞, reference velocity $V_\infty = \sqrt{p_\infty/\rho_\infty}$ and reference time $t_\infty = l_\infty/V_\infty$.

The corresponding equations for the unsteady flow in a channel with constant depth and variable width are:

$$
\begin{array}{ll}
H_t + u H_x + 2 u_x + 2\alpha u = 0 & \text{(continuity)} \\
u_t + u u_x + h H_x = 0 & \text{(momentum)}
\end{array}
$$

(2)

where h is the water level, $H = 2\ln h$ the reference velocity is defined as $V_\infty = \sqrt{g\, l_\infty/2}$, $\alpha = (dA/dx)/A$ (A is the width of the channel).
Only two variables (H, u) describe the flow in hydraulics, instead of three (P, u, S) as in gasdynamics.
The same analogy, shown by Eq. (1) and Eq. (2), holds also for two-dimensional steady or unsteady flows.
If shock waves develop in gasdynamics, they have to be computed during their evolution with an explicit treatment (Ref. 3 and 4), by taking into account the Rankine-Hugoniot equations:

$$
\frac{P_1 w_1}{T_1} = \frac{P_2 w_2}{T_2} \qquad \text{(continuity)}
$$

(3)

$$
p_1(1 + \frac{w_1^2}{T_1}) = p_2 (1 + \frac{w_2^2}{T_2}) \qquad \text{(momentum)}
$$

$$
T_1(1 + \frac{\gamma-1}{2\gamma} \frac{w_1^2}{T_1}) = T_2(1 + \frac{\gamma-1}{2\gamma} \frac{w_2^2}{T_2}) \qquad \text{(energy)}
$$

where $w_i = u_i - U_s$ (i = 1,2).
The labels 1 and 2 refer to the two sides of the shock wave which propagates with the speed U_s. The corresponding equations for the bore, the hydraulic shock, are the following:

$$
h_1 w_1 = h_2 w_2 \qquad \text{(continuity)}
$$

(4)

$$
h_1^2(1 + \frac{w_1^2}{h_1}) = h_2^2(1 + \frac{w_2^2}{h_2}) \qquad \text{(momentum)}
$$

where $w_i = u_i - U_s$ and U_s indicates the propagation speed of the bore.
Eq. (3) and (4) are very similar also in the case of two-dimensional steady or unsteady shocks.

The close analogy between the two physical phenomena suggests to solve the hydraulic problems with the same numerical procedure used in gasdynamics. If programs for numerical computations in gasdynamics are available, only minor changes and corrections in the codes are needed to solve the corresponding problems in hydraulics.

The general numerical procedure to integrate the partial differential equations in gasdynamics and the methods to compute explicitly the evolution of shock waves are reported in (Ref. 3, 4, 5, 6) and have been tested in a large variety of problems.
The integration is carried out by a finite difference method according to the two levels (predictor – corrector) scheme suggested in (Ref. 7). The explicit computation of shocks in based on the general philosophy indicated by G. Moretti; the shocks are treated as discontinuities and their evolution is computed by means of the compatibility equations along characteristic lines.
Hereafter I present some numerical examples of hydraulic problems involving the development of bores and hydraulic jumps. The results have been represented in the sequence from Fig. 1 to Fig. 7 by plotting the water isolevel lines.

UNSTEADY ONE DIMENSIONAL FLOW IN CHANNELS

Example n.1 (Fig. 1)

A semi-infinite channel with constant width and depth is filled with water initially at rest. The channel is bounded at left by a wall. This wall begins to move at the time $t = 0$ from left to right according the law $b \equiv t^2$. According to the theoretical analysis, an imbedded bore is expected to form on the first characteristic at the point denoted by a circle in Fig. 1. However the bore has been numerically fitted earlier, but it doesn't grow up and propagates as a very weak shock till a time near to the theoretical one for its formation.
Then it begins to pick up strength.

Example n.2 (Fig. 2)

In this example the wall is moving with a law $b \equiv t^3$. Theoretical analysis predicts the formation of an imbedded bore at the point indicated by a circle in Fig. 2 which is located between the moving wall and the first characteristic.
The shock is numerically fitted very early and, as before, does not pick up strength until the theoretical point for its formation. In fact it propagates at the beginning as a characteristic as it can be observed in Fig. 2.
These first two examples have been presented to proof the reliability of the explicit treatment of imbedded bores in very classical problems.

Example n.3 (Fig. 3)

This example deals with a time dependent technique to compute steady flows.
A constant depth channel is placed between two infinite capacity reservoirs with different water levels. The channel width is shaped in a convergent-divergent fashion along the abscissa x.
  The steady flow through the channel is subcritical in the convergent portion of the channel till the throat; thereafter, it becomes supercritical, if the level in the downstream reservoir is low enough. However for a particular range of values of this level, a hydraulic jump is expected to take place in the divergent portion of the channel; thereafter, the stream becomes subcritical till it matches, at the end of the channel, the water level in the discharge reservoir.
I can obtain this steady flow as asymptotic result of the following transient (time-dependent technique).
I assume that at the time $t = 0$ the channel is closed by a wall at $x = 1$ and open at $x = 0$, so that the level is every-where equal to the one of the left reservoir and the water is at rest. Suddenly the end wall is removed and a depression wave propagates upstream. During this transient a shock is generated by the coalescence of characteristics going from right to left. First it moves upstream and then downstream, till it gets stabilized in the equilibrium location tipical of the steady state flow. Some numerical oscillations develop after the bore during the transient and reflect some numerical problems. However these perturbations disappear in a short time.

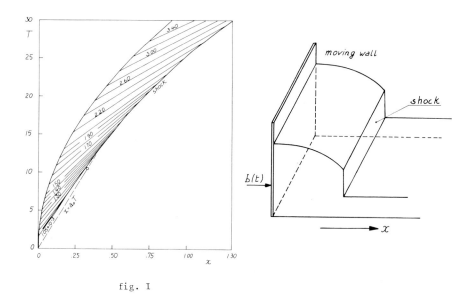

fig. I

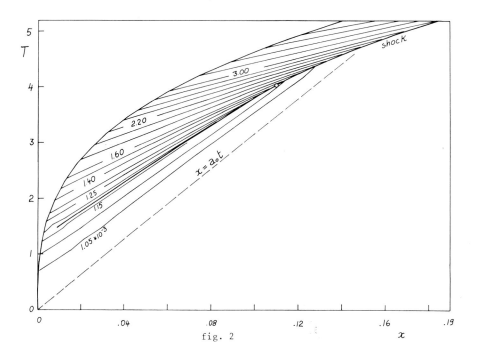

fig. 2

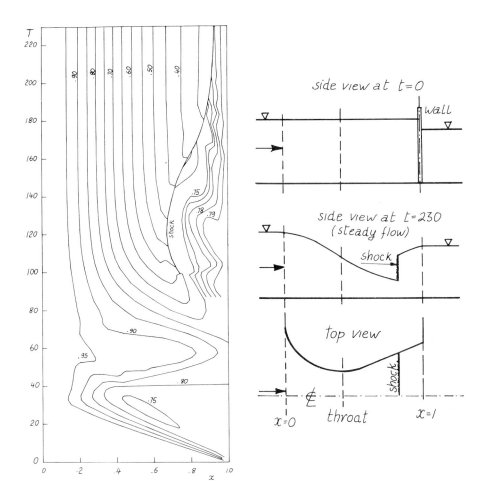

fig. 3

Example n.4 (Fig. 4)

The rising tide of the ocean can generate bores of remarkable intensity in channels
or rivers open to the sea. A beatiful picture of these effects is reportes at pag.
368 of (Ref. 1).   This numerical example describes this phenomenon; for the sake
of simplicity only one tidal cycle and only the first harmonic of the tide are con‑
sidered.
The smooth tidal wave entering the river tends to generate an imbedded bore; the
circle reported in Fig. 4 indicates the theoretical point of the bore formation.
The imbedded bore is, numerically fitted earlier but begins to pick up strength
only at the proper location. The depression wave of the second half of the   tide
cycle will decrease then its intensity. More details on these examples are repor ‑
ted in (Ref. 8).

TWO-DIMENSIONAL SUPERCRITICAL FLOW IN CHANNELS

The examples, I give here, deal with supercritical streams in channels with con ‑
stant depth. According to the geometry which describes the channel shape along the
abscissa Z, compression or depression waves are generated at the walls. The analo‑
gy in these flow between gasdynamics and hydraulics is very often used to interpret
the experimental results on water table facilities for simulation of gasdynamical
problems.

Example n.5 (Fig. 5)

A supercritical stream (Froude = 3) is flowing in a channel with uniform transver‑
sal distribution of level and velocity at Z = 0.   The upper wall is shaped so that
the channel width is increased gradually to a new value. The bottom wall remains
straight. Depression waves are initially generated at the upper wall and are re   ‑
flected at the bottom one. In the second portion of the channel enlargement com ‑
pression waves move down from the upper wall: they coalesce till an oblique hydrau‑
lic jump is formed. At Z = 10 the hydraulic jump is reflected at the bottom wall‑
and moves towards the upper wall.

Example n.6 (Fig. 6)

In this example the width of the channel is constant with Z and both the walls are
shaped in the same fashion so that the channel axis is displaced and straight after
the abscissa Z = 5.   The oblique hydraulic jump is now generated from the compres‑
sion waves starting at the bottom wall. A second oblique hydraulic jump tends to
be formed by the compression waves given by the upper wall; however these waves are
absorbed by the first shock, now reflected on the upper wall, before they can gene‑
rate the second hydraulic jump.

TWO-DIMENSIONAL SUPERCRITICAL FLOW OVER A BLUNTED OBSTACLE (Fig. 7)

Gasdynamicists easily recognize in Fig. 7 a typical example of supersonic compressi‑
ble flow over a blunt body followed by a slender after-body. The bow shock is pla‑
ced ahead of the nose ; a pocket of subsonic flow in the front of the shock layer
is followed by a supersonic flow with smooth transition through a sonic line.
The computations which allow to obtain these numerical results are done in two
steps. First the sub and super-sonic flow region is computed in front of the body
by means of a time dependent technique (Ref. 5); the equations of the steady two
dimensional flow are elliptic and hyperbolic in this region; however they are tran‑
sformed in hyperbolic equations by introducing the unsteady terms according the
well known time dependent technique philosophy and are then integrated with a fini‑
te difference method by marching in time.

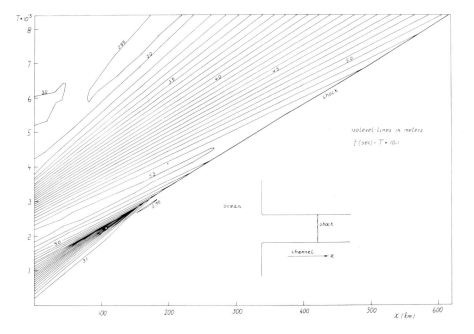

fig. 4

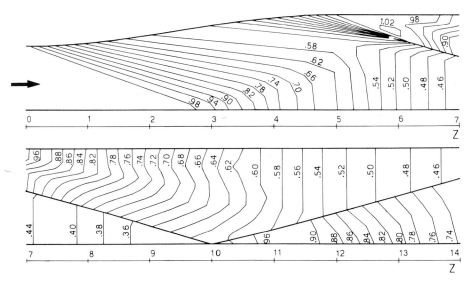

fig. 5

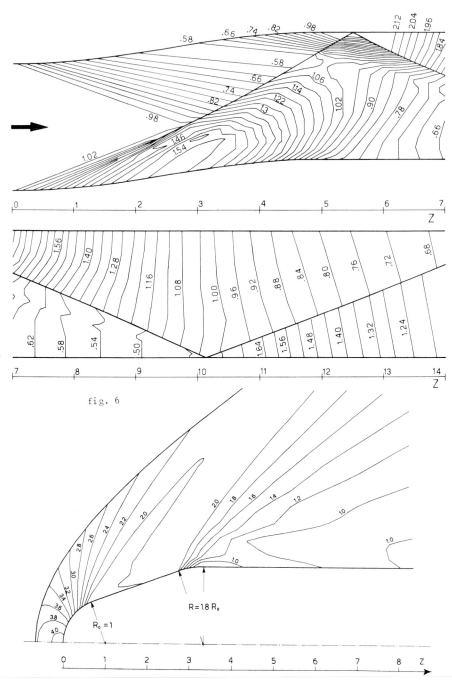

fig. 6

fig. 7

Once the flow is supersonic, the steady hyperbolic equations of motion are inte -
grated along the abscissa Z (Ref. 6). However the results plotted in Fig. 7 refer
to the computations of a hydraulic example: the supercritical uniform water stream
(Froude = 3.0) over the blunted pile of a bridge. Instead of the bow shock wave we
have here the hydraulic jump which wraps the bridge pile. The computational methods
are the same I used in the equivalent problem in gasdynamics: the two-dimensional
unsteady flow computation in the front according to the time-dipendent technique,
and the steady supercritical two-dimensional flow computation on the side of the
bridge pile.

REFERENCES

1. J.J. Stoker, Water waves, Interscience Publishers, 1965.
2. R. Courant, K.O. Friedrichs, Supersonic Flow and Shock Waves, Interscience
   Publ. 1967.
3. G. Moretti, Complicated One-Dimensional Flows, Polytechnic Institute of Brooklyn, PIBAL, Report n. 71-25, September 1971.
4. G. Moretti, Thoughts and After Thoughts About Shock Computations, Polytechnic
   Institute of Brooklyn, PIBAL Report n. 72-37, December 1972.
5. G. Moretti, M. Abbett, A Time Dependent Computational Methods for Blunt Body
   Flows, .A.I.A.A. Journal, vol. 4, n. 12, December 1966.
6. G. Moretti, M. Pandolfi, Entropy Layers, Computer and Fluids, vol. 1, 1973
7. R.W. Mac Cormack, The Effects of Viscosity in Hypervelocity Impact Cratering,
   A.I.A.A. 7th Aerospace Sciences Meeting, Paper n. 69-354, 1969
8. M. Pandolfi, Numerical Computations of One-dimensional Unsteady Flow in Channels,
   Meccanica, AIMETA, December 1973.

Current research field of author : *Numerical Integration of Partial Differential
Equations in supersonic aerodynamics (external and internal flow), unsteady compressible flow in ducts or turbomachinery, unsteady free surface water motion in
channel, steady supercritical free surface water motion in channels and over bridge
piles - Main feature is the explicit treatment of discontinuities as shock waves
or bores and hydraulic jumps.*

Modeling and Simulation of Water Resources Systems, G.C. VANSTEENKISTE, (Ed.)
North-Holland Publishing Company (1975)

DESIGNING SIMULATION MODELS FOR
OPTIMISATION STUDIES

J. C. Wilkinson & D. K. Smith
Department of Operational Research
University of Lancaster
Lancaster, England

ABSTRACT

The performance and total cost of a complex water resource system can frequently be measured only by means of a computer simulation model. The expense of obtaining such measures for each of a virtually infinite number of possible configurations which may be contemplated at the design stage of a system to serve any large area, together with the nature of some internal characteristics of such systems, precludes the use of classical search procedures to find the best configuration. A purpose-designed search procedure is required which recognises the limitations imposed by the simulation model. But just as the way in which function evaluations are obtained (by simulation) has implications for the search procedure, so the method of search may have implications for the design of the simulation model. And the total process of designing an optimal water resource system will be more efficient if the simulation model and optimising routine are seen not as distinct and independent phases, but as complementary and inter-active parts of an integrated procedure.

INTRODUCTION

The complexity of water resource systems today is such that their properties and characteristics cannot be adequately studied by mathematical analysis. Instead, simulation models are constructed and used, in conjunction with sequences of (usually synthetic) data of rainfall and/or streamflow, to study vicariously how systems do or will behave. The idea is extended to the study of systems' behaviour when modifications are made or proposed, and it is but a short conceptual step to the study of completely hypothetical systems. The development of simulation modelling techniques, and the computer technology which has made such techniques feasible, thus affords the water engineer an invaluable aid to the solution of his problems, which he may profitably use as early as the design stage of his work, since he may then evaluate the consequences of any proposal he is considering before he commits expenditure to the construction of any dam, pumping station or other component of the water resource system. With such a tool at his disposal, the engineer will of course advance many alternative design proposals, and compare the evaluations of these with a view to selecting the best. In assessing the long-term requirements of a large geographical area, however, with for example several possible sites for the establishment of new reservoirs, and many possible different sizes of reservoir at each, together with aquifers and potential sites for pumping stations, the number of alternatives that confront the engineer is vast, and he cannot be sure that those he chooses to evaluate by use of the simulation model will include the best possible configuration, or even one that is close to the best.

What is needed is a procedure, which by preference will be automatic, to examine the total set of alternatives in a systematic manner, and present the design engineer with a ranking of the "top ten" of these. Twenty years ago this proposal would have been unthinkable, but the rapid development of systems analysis and O.R. in this time, and the corresponding development of computers, have provided the engineer and hydrologist with the necessary technical skills and machinery for analysing complex models of water resource systems. Unhappily, despite this development, there has grown up a divergence of outlook as regards the construction and scope of simulation models of river systems. Either the model has been designed by a mathematician, with a particular type of mathematical technique in mind, and the model is biassed towards the use of this particular search method; or, it has been designed to be as accurate a representation of the system as is possible, and any optimisation is a secondary consideration. In the first case, the model is a poor representation of the real world, and only a limited number of features may be studied with confidence; in the latter case the model is often too complex for analysis by the optimiser, and those features in which the planner is particularly interested cannot be compared with ease.

With continued interest in systems analysis applied to water resource systems, it is essential that this gap between hydrologists and planners on one hand, and operational researchers and analysts on the other, be bridged. This paper puts forward a middle way, where the model of the water system is as accurate as is desired, and contains those features that the user is interested in, while retaining the facility for an optimisation routine to be incorporated, and the system automatically improved. To do this requires understanding of the modeller's viewpoint by the analyst, and vice versa, so that the model supplies enough information for the search routine to be efficient, and the search routine is structured to use this information fully and efficiently.

Shanno & Weil (1972) identify the four processes that must be linked in any O.R. project, in order to produce useful results. These are:

1)   Defining a sensible problem from the underlying reality
2)   Building a mathematical model
3a)   Devising new techniques or
 b)   implementing existing ones to perform the desired analysis of the model
4)   Performing this analysis to get numerical results.

Very little interest has been shown by water resources planners in stage (3a), and existing methods have been used. However, by combining (3a) with (2), and viewing these stages together, it is possible to implement new techniques, with consequent benefit to the planner.

THE SIMULATION MODEL

For most water resource systems, the problem facing the designer is the choice of a set of sites and design sizes to supply specified demands and to maintain reliability. The planning objective is to choose that set (out of those available and feasible) that meets both the design criteria and is 'best' in some sense (e.g. minimum cost, maximum profit or return on investment, or maximal for environmental objectives).

For the river systems we have considered, the objective is minimum cost, while maintaining a very high reliability, but in the following discussion, this objective is not essential. The models in use are based on a short time interval for input data on river flows: at present the period is one day. Flow sequences are produced from synthetic data, cross-correlated logarithmicly in order to maintain accuracy at low flows. The daily figures are deduced from monthly observations by means of a method described by Bloomer and Sexton (1972). This time interval is necessary to yield data on the reliability of the system to meet demands, which are measured daily, since a longer interval will obscure (by cumulative effects) the rare events that mark failures to supply.

The systems being modelled are represented by several major rivers, with inter-basin transfers, pumped storage reservoirs and pumping from rechargeable aquifers; thus the component mix comprises these elements, together with the sizes of pump and pipeline that connect them. Once the components have been selected, the capital cost of installing them may be calculated, from economic data. The simulation run provides the cost of operating the system, and also the reliability data described earlier.

This type of model is familiar to many planners, and may be extended to incorporate development plans and changes in demand patterns, as well as constraints on amenity, flood control etc.

OPTIMISATION OF SUCH MODELS

In conventional terms, any simulation model being studied for optimisation yields the problem

$$\text{minimise (or maximise)} \quad f(x) = f_1(x) + f_2(x)$$

$$\text{subject to} \quad g_i(x) \geq 0 \text{ and } x \in \{x_1, \ldots, x_N\} = S$$

where x is the vector of component sizes, which are restricted in two ways: firstly by the set of constraints $\{g_i\}$, and secondly, by being forced to take one of a range of possible values from the set S, of size N. (Here N may be very large, so that direct enumeration of all possibilities is not a realistic possibility). In most cases of interest, either components must be limited to a discrete set of values, or changes in components are fixed by manufacturing limits.

The function f (which may be a vector valued function) is made up to two parts: one, f_1, is derived from x and is an analytic expression, such as the capital cost described above, and f_2 is a function calculated by the simulation run, and is one that may not be expressed analytically. The f and $\{g_i\}$ are likely to be non-linear, and probably not easily approximated by polynomials, or other mathematical functions.

In some cases, it would be possible to apply a conventional optimisation technique to solving this problem, using penalty functions for eliminating the constraints and choosing the 'nearest' member of S from an optimisation over a continuous space. Such a procedure would prove, except in small problems, very unsatisfactory, because of the significant time required to calculate one function value. Other difficulties with the use of classical optimisation techniques arise from the discrete space S and the likelihood of multi-modal response functions. The former problem - of nonlinear optimisation over a constrained discrete space - is the subject of much research (Geoffrion & Marston (1972) is a recent survey paper), but up to the present, success has been limited. The multi-modal nature of the response surface arises from the non-linearity of the function and its interactions with non-linear constraints; search techniques for such surfaces are also the subject of current research (e.g. Opacic (1973), Hill (1969), Bekey & Ung (1974)). Those methods that have proved reasonably useful need a large number of function evaluations, and, of course, cannot ever guarantee to locate the optimum of several local optima, unless the number of these is known in advance.

Any optimisation method faces two decisions at each point in the search: in which direction to make the next exploration, and what distance to move in that direction. Most classical methods make use only of values of the function (and, where applicable, first and second derivatives) in order to make these decisions, and so for success rely on a large number of function evaluations, made one after another.

This type of approach is not suitable for a function derived from a simulation model. Two major differences between this and an analytic function are identifiable: 1) the time taken to run a simulation is very significant, several orders of magnitude greater than a function evaluation and 2) the model itself

possesses an underlying structure which may be utilised in guiding and aiding the
search. This relates to individual components, and to groups of components which
form subsystems in the model. As a consequence of these two properties, it is
clearly beneficial to design a search method that studies not just the most recent
function value, but also the progress of the search to date, together with information collected during the simulation run that can be used in making the necessary
search decisions.

AN OPTIMISATION STRATEGY

The simulation run provides a large amount of information relevant to the
properties of the system with a given set of component sizes. The aim of any
analyst or any analytical method is to condense this into usable quantities, and
then to use these to propose changes that will either improve the performance
objective or that will provide further information which will be used in such
improvement.

For the automatic optimiser, the identification of relevant sets of output
data must be performed in advance; and rules for using these sets must be incorporated in the search methods. Thus the analyst must have some knowledge of
the policies used by the hydrologist in extracting usable information from this
data.

An example, based on our studies of the rivers Welland and Nene in the U.K.
will illustrate some of the data sets and methods of analysis. This system
embraces a pumped storage reservoir (Fig. 1), an artificially recharged aquifer
(Fig. 2), and several demand centres, met both from these sources and from direct
extraction from the two main river channels in the system (Fig. 3). (See also
Jamieson (1974)). The model has been constructed to use daily flow sequences in
order that 'rare events' may be more easily observed. Following a run of the
model, information sets are available:

a)   for storage sites, both annual summaries and cumulative histograms of the
        water contents,

b)   for pipelines, usage data, including the volumes of water pumped and the
        frequency of use, again summarised annually.

These sets are available even when the particular combination of components is
infeasible for one or another reason.

When the point in the component space is feasible, then the first priority
is to reduce cost. Since capital costs dominate operating costs, a reduction in
component size will, in general, achieve this. Each component is studied, together with the data sets that correspond to it. For reservoirs, the frequency
of very low levels is used to judge whether making the storage capacity less would
cause the system to become infeasible. For pipelines, the several records are used
to check whether the same volume of water could be pumped were the pipe size to be
reduced. Each separate study yields a recommended change in the size of a component, and so a search step may be made with several alterations at once. This is
an immediate improvement over the conventional 'one-at-a-time' search.

For a point in component space which is not a feasible solution, it is
necessary to move to a point that is a permitted solution. The data records are
thus examined first to identify the reasons for the infeasibility - usually a
failure to meet one demand or other, and then to find that component which seems
most likely to improve the feasibility measure at minimal increase in the total
cost. Associated with each possible point of infeasibility is a set of components
that have direct effects on this - thus the size of a storage site and the size
of the pipes that supply it are likely to have a direct effect on any demands met
by that site. And with each of these components a cost curve is available, based

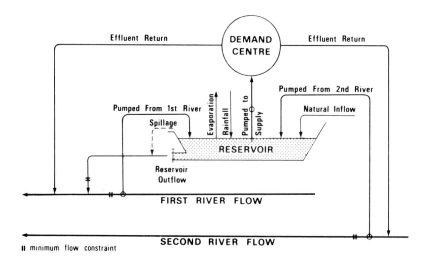

FIG. 1   COMPONENT MODEL OF PUMPED-STORAGE RESERVOIR

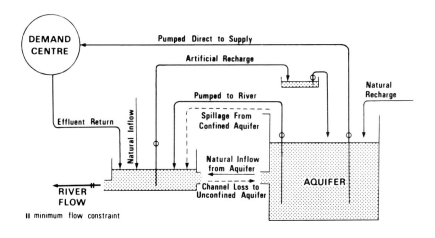

FIG. 2   COMPONENT MODEL OF A PUMPED AQUIFER

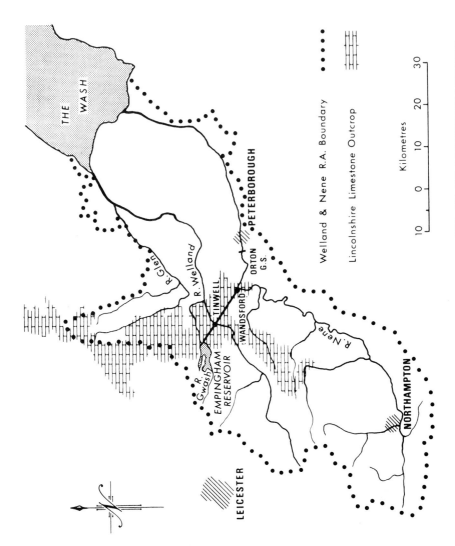

Fig. 3   CONJUNCTIVE USE OF EMPINGHAM RESERVOIR AND THE LINCOLNSHIRE LIMESTONE

on past runs and capital cost data. Thus a series of steps may be made which have the aim of removing the infeasibility. Again, several steps may be combined into one, in order that the search be accelerated.

These two basic modules can be combined with others that do not make such explicit use of the information from a simulation run, and a complete search algorithm has been implemented successfully. In comparison with a conventional search technique, the reduction in function evaluations is very considerable. A diagram shows the effect in two dimensions (Fig. 4). Typical results give a local optimum after about 30 runs of the simulation model, for a model comprising seven components. A classical technique, such as Powell's or Rosenbrock's method, would frequently still be on the first or second iteration after this number of function evaluations.

In a more general case, the optimiser will have analytical routines programmed to perform any desired analysis; the same underlying methods may be used, and the search should prove efficient.

CONSEQUENCES

For the model-builder, the intention of using an optimisation technique coupled with the simulation imposes some structure on the simulation model itself. Immediately, the planner is concerned with information and statistics that are of value to his work - and these will be determined by the interests and objectives of the planning process under study. Additionally, he will be required to view the problems faced by the search routines, and to include in his model the information that is needed to overcome these problems and yield an efficient optimiser. Certain principles will apply to any model designed in conjunction with an optimisation routine, including the following:

1)   It will be necessary to incorporate routines that produce and handle information that can be accessed by both the model and the search mechanism, so that some of the consequences of steps in search space may be estimated. These should use such information as the searcher deems valuable, in view of the specific needs of the optimiser: at least summaries of the usage of components being studied and information pertinent to changing the sizes of these.

2)   The model should be designed so that any assumptions about the size of components are avoided, or made explicitly so that they may be used as constraints. (In our experience this is one of the more stringent conditions: the modeller often designs the model with a preconceived notion of the system, and does not consider the consequences on the model of vastly different component sizes. These consequences may be directly observed, in which case they may be easily eliminated; or indirectly, as when, for example, an analysis of a run assumes that an event that is seen to occur often with one set of components will always occur). Operating rules too should be written without any previously fixed ideas about the size of the system, and all checks that the rules imply must be made explicitly.

3)   The model-builder can learn from the designer of networks in other fields of study. Water in rivers, pipes and channels can be represented as flows in arcs of networks: the nodes of such a network represent sources and sinks, confluences and storage points. The advantage of this kind of representation is that the properties of individual components are emphasised, and data sets may be easily linked with parts of a network. However, unless the connections between components are clearly noted, then this format will not be the panacea it appears. For any water resource system is not just a set of components, but made up of subsystems which themselves have characteristic properties and data sets. Thus (Fig. 1) a pumped storage scheme comprises links to one or more rivers, demands and

inflows, as well as the basic reservoir - all of these may be components
with which the planner is concerned.

CONCLUSIONS

As water resources development becomes more important, the need will
increase for well planned reliable supplies. We have attempted to show how a
link may be made between those who develop models and those who use and study them,
in order that each may contribute to the better use of scarce water, and each may
learn from the other's knowledge and expertise.

ACKNOWLEDGEMENTS

The authors wish to thank the Water Resources Board, Reading (now Water
Research Centre) for financial support and technical advice.

REFERENCES

Bekey, G.A. & Ung, M.T. (1974). A comparative evaluation of two global search
        algorithms, IEEE transactions on systems, man and cybernetics, V.SMC4
        p.112-116.
Bloomer, R.J.G. & Sexton, J.R.(1972). The generation of synthetic river flow
        data, Water Resources Board Paper no. 15.
Geoffrion, A.M. & Marston, R.F. (1972). Integer programming algorithms: a frame-
        work and state-of-the-art survey, Management Science V18 p.465-491.
Hill, J.D. (1969). A search technique for multimodal surfaces, IEEE transactions
        on systems, science and cybernetics, V.SSC5 p.2-8.
Jamieson, D.G. et al (1974). The hydrological design of water-resource systems,
        Water Resources Board.
Opacic, J. (1973). A heuristic strategy for multimodal search, International
        Journal of Systems Science, V4 p.485-500.
Shanno, D.F. & Weil, R.L. (1972). Management Science - a view from nonlinear
        programming, Communications of the Association for Computing Machinery,
        V15 p.542-549.

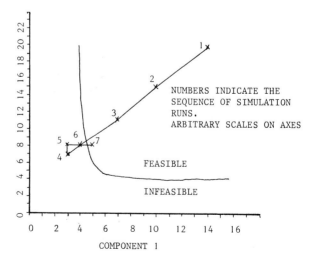

Fig. 4. A 2-Dimensional search, showing the two
        regions that are explored

DISCUSSION

In your study on designing simulation models for optimization studies, did you come out with any results about the indication of the optimization on the structure of the model. How do we best formulate the model for optimization rather than change the optimization to suit the model.

A lot of people have been working on using specific mathematical models that are easier to optimize. We try to use the models as a direct tool, to provide some direct information of interest for its work. So we did not want to modify the simulation techniques to go beyond. (WILKINSON)

Are the simulation techniques entirely subjective or can we only say it is the modelist conception of what the situation is. They could be guided by the question how you want to model it, to get a better performance on the optimization, such as discrepancies of threshold parameter which are called model redundancies lowering down the system.

The model was built for optimizing this, assuming that certain situations are never going to arrive. One recommendation came from this, that you don't estimate any assumption when you go to model. (WILKINSON)

Would you consider into the future the optimization with the uncertainty built in or are you considering it entirely deterministic ? (YOUNG)

The uncertainties are **there** through some flows. There is uncertainty in the function evaluation that you cannot precisely define the cost over a long period of time. (WILKINSON)

I could not follow the first question and remark made about adapting a model for easier optimization. As far as I know, a model is designed to represent something as closely as possible and in all my experience I have never succeeded in building two different models of the same subject, one being easier to optimize than the other. Could you comment on this ? (ELZAS)

What I was suggesting is a change in the way a simulation model is normally used. Traditionally is as you say. What I was suggesting is the following, because the simulation model generates   principally so much information as it goes, we have to record this information and just use this itself in addition to just a function evaluation, in order to guide the way in which the model is used. So we are not really just altering the representation of the situation, but rather the information that's collected there. By how much the constraint is violated is itself very valuable in guiding us, in the size of the step we want to take next.

By that I understand that the subject you model is not deterministic on its own. The thing that you are modeling knows his variances. For example you could change flow rates, measures of reservoirs, etc. You still have that freedom. (ELZAS)

Yes. (WILKINSON)

Are you taking into consideration the uncertainty in demand and what is the time base in the optimization studies ? (SIKKA)

Variation demands can be built in. We have been asked to optimize the simulation model, we did not built it ourselves. The demand has been assumed constant. (WILKINSON)

PART TWO

SURFACE-AND GROUNDWATER
HYDROLOGY SIMULATION

Modeling and Simulation of Water Resources Systems, G.C. VANSTEENKISTE, (Ed.)
North-Holland Publishing Company (1975)

WATERSHED RUNOFF SIMULATION: A COMPARATIVE
STUDY ON MAIN METHODS' EFFICIENCY

L. Valadares Tavares [*]
Technical University of Lisbon
I.S.T., Av. Rovisco Pais, Lisbon

ABSTRACT

Many watershed runoff simulation models have been presented. However, few comparative and critical studies have been carried out to examine their efficiencies in order to solve specific hydrologic problems.

Simulation of daily river discharges from given rainfall depths making use of scarce data and small computing facilities is an important class of hydrologic problems because it often occurs in developing and undeveloped regions.

Therefore, this paper presents a comparative study of the efficiency of the main models to solve this group of hydrologic problems. Data from a portuguese river (river PAIVA) are used.

The potentialities of main methods are identified and their complementarity is discussed.

A multi-disciplinary model is developed to integrate these different approaches and numerical conclusions are herein presented.

1. INTRODUCTION

Many models have been proposed to simulate the watersheds behaviour. Watershed behaviour simulation is understood as building a process to obtain runoff features (such as river flows and water quality parameters), from the given correspondent rainfall depths, assuming that some watershed features are known.

Often, the methodology and the techniques which are used to build up each model are based on one single branch of Science. The strong diversity of model features can be explained, by the possibility of adopting several distinct scientific disciplines, with the same purpose.

Many reports have been published to emphasize the main advantages of each model, but few studies have been presented with the following aims:

-   To compare model abilities and shortcomings, in order to solve specific practical problems.
-   To combine the main possibilities of different scientific disciplines in order to build up more efficient models.

---

[*] Professor of the Civil Eng. Dept.

In this paper, these two mentioned topics are studied and discussed using real data coming from a portuguese watershed, the basin of the river PAIVA at CASTRO DAIRE.

Firstly, the specific class of hydrologic problems studied in this paper is described and well defined.

Secondly, the application of the selected models to the class of problems is analysed. The results obtained are compared and the main potentialities of each methodology are discussed.

Finally, an integrated model of these approaches is developed and presented herein.

2. WATERSHED RUNOFF SIMULATION PROBLEMS TO BE STUDIED

The aim is to generate the daily river discharge for a certain section of the river from the daily rainfall given for the basin.

The basin lag time is not higher than one day. The historical data available is limited, namely, daily river discharge has been recorded for a short time (e.g. 5 years), and daily rainfall average depth for a reasonable number of years (e.g. 15 years) which included the runoff period.

Some general information about the watershed geophysics and geology are known.

To carry out this study only small size computing facilities are available (central memory area not higher than 30k reals).

The class of hydrologic problems to be studied in this paper was defined this way because it is a common and important situation in non-developed countries:

    a) Organized hydrological data are referred to units of time usually not smaller than one day.

    b) Making the unit/time of generated river discharge one day, is sufficiently detailed for practical application.

    c) Runoff data periods are shorter than, and included within, rainfall depth data periods.

If the studied watershed has a basin lag time higher than one day, it may be divided into several parts with lag time inferior to this limit and thus this paper analyses can still be used.

                                     *

The watershed of river PAIVA at CASTRO DAIRE was studied as a relevant example of this class of simulation problem.

The PAIVA drains into the DOURO a main river in the North of Portugal (Fig. 1).

This basin is underlain by granite and about 85% of this is covered by soils presenting medium or high infiltration capacity, even when wet. The basin area is 286km2.

Mean daily rainfall depths and daily river discharges are known for periods of 15 and 5 years, respectively. The means and the variation coefficients of monthly, semestral and yearly rainfall depths are presented in Table 1.

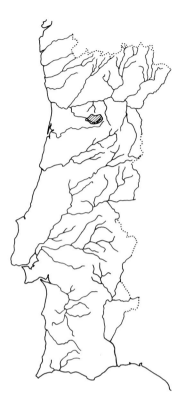

Fig. 1   River PAIVA Basin at CASTRO DAIRE

The mean monthly potential evaporo-transpirations are also known (8).

In Portugal, the water year starts on the first of October.

3.   MAIN HYDROLOGIC MODELS

Due to the high number of proposed models the selection of the main ones is inevitably a very controversial issue. However, applying all of them to the problem is impossible. Therefore, before making that selection, a classification of the scientific disciplines on which these models are based was carried out. Afterwards, from each group, a representative one was selected.

These are the main branches of Science which are used to build up hydrological models:

a)   Physical Description (Class A models)

To generate runoff from rainfall the watershed is considered as a set of elementary units and the real physical process of transforming rainfall into runoff is subdivided into a high number of successive elementary operations. The degree of detail of this analysis is as high as possible. Building up a model based on this attitude includes the description of these elementary units and operations as well as to estimate the correspondent parameters.

b) Statistical Analysis (Class B models)

The aim of this methodology is to search for statistically significant relations between the studied magnitudes. The adopted criteria to evaluate the significance degree of these relations are based on the fractions of those magnitude variations which are explained by them. Physical causality concepts are not used by these methods.

c) Systems Theory (Class C models)

In the present, the General Systems Theory is precisely described by several authors (for example, (5)). The watershed is studied as a system and input as well as output magnitudes are defined. Generally, rainfall is considered as an input and runoff as the output. The system is not studied as a set of elementary parts and the input/output relations are modelled using Systems Theory theorems and techniques. These relations are estimated by studying the recorded real pairs of input-output. Elementary relations are initially assumed, and successively transformed in order to maximize the closeness between real and simulated output for the same, recorded, real input.

From these three classes the following models were selected:

1) STANFORD MODEL: Stanford Watershed Model Mk.4.

This model is described in (4) and it is representative of class A.

2) STATISTICAL MODEL: Regression Analysis.

It is the application of the regression theory and it may represent class B.

3) VEN TE CHOW MODEL: General Hydrologic System Model.

It is representative of class C and it is described in (2).

4) NASH MODEL: Conceptual Model for River Flow Forecasting.

It is described in (6) and it includes classes A and C methods.

4. THE APPLICATION OF MAIN MODELS TO THE PROBLEM

4.1. Stanford Model

This model is not applicable to this problem because:

a) It implies using quite powerfull computing facilities (not less than IBM 370).
b) It implies knowing hourly rainfall and runoff. If 6 hour values are known perhaps it can still be applied using a generation technique to determine hourly values.

4.2. Statistical Model

Daily river discharge has to be related to daily rainfall depth by using regression methods.

4.2.1. Rainfall Statistical Analysis

For some regions (namely, Portugal) several authors have noticed (8) that hydrological features such as the time distribution of annual river discharge depends on the year dryness. Thus, the 15 years period was studied to identify wet, dry and average water years. This criterium was assumed:

Wet year: annual rainfall higher than the 85% quantil of the annual rainfall statistical distribution (1 772mm)

Dry year: annual rainfall lower than the 15% quantil of the annual rainfall statistical distribution (978mm).

Then, these examples can be given:

Dry year   : 1956/57 (H =   975mm)
Average year: 1958/59 (H = 1 596mm)
Wet year   : 1959/60 (H = 2 559mm)

4.2.2. Regression Analyses

a) Regression of daily river discharge (Q_t) on daily rainfall depth (H_t).

This analysis was applied to wet and dry years as well as wet and dry semestres. For these four cases there was no significant statistical improvement by considering rainfall occurred during days previous to (t-1). These results are presented in Table 2.

b) Regression of daily river discharge on daily rainfall depth and on previous daily river discharge.

Again there was no significant statistical improvement by considering days previous to (t-1). These results are presented in Table 3.

4.2.3. Comments

a) Generally, the fraction of the daily river discharge variability which is explained by these statistical models is small.

b) The regressions of runoff on rainfall and on previous runoff have smaller residual variance than the regressions of runoff on rainfall.

c) The dryer the studied period, the smaller the variance explained by these regression models.

d) As an example, the daily river discharges were generated for the first 6 months of 1959/60 using the model on Table 3 (Fig. 2).

e) The regression parameter estimations are quite sensitive functions of the dryness of the analysed period.

f) The computing facilities and the execution times which are required for these statistical analyses are well known and quite reduced.

4.3. Ven Te Chow General Hydrologic System Model

The direct effective rainfall graph and the direct runoff hydrograph have to be known for each storm. Obtaining these fractions from the total rainfall and runoff recorded graphs is a subjective and controversial operation (3). Besides that, the following statistical relations have to be estimated using the recorded rainstorms:

a) Regression of $\dfrac{P_e}{M_{P_e}}$ on $\dfrac{Q_p}{M_{Q_p}}$

b) Regression of $\dfrac{Q_p}{M_{Q_p}}$ on $\dfrac{\overline{Q}}{M_{\overline{Q}}}$

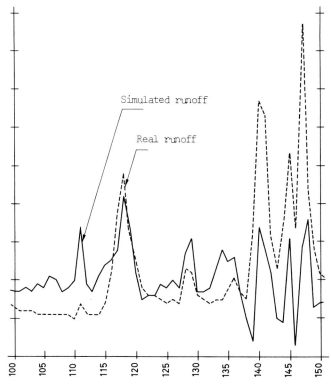

Days (starting on the 1st Oct.)

Fig. 2   Simulated and Real Runoff for the First
6 Months of 1959/60 Using Table 3 Model

P_e, Q_p and $\overline{Q}$ are the direct effective rainfall, the peak and the mean values of the direct runoff and M_{P_e}, M_{Q_p} and $M_{\overline{Q}}$ are the respective maximum values for the collection of recorded rainstorms.

This model is not applicable to the problem because:

- Only the superficial behaviour of the analysed watershed is simulated by this model. That is, the direct runoff is obtained from the direct effective rainfall. To solve the problem the surface runoff, subsurface flow and the base flow have to be calculated from the total rainfall.

- Estimating the mentioned regressions implies analysing the rainfall and runoff graphs using units of time smaller than one day. The hour is the recommended time unit.

4.4.   Nash Model

4.4.1.   Model Application

This model is based on some physical and systems analyses. The infiltration, evaporo-transpiration and surface runoff generation processes are simulated by physical description. The process of transforming the generated runoff components into river discharges at a specific section is based on Systems Theory. These methods are also adopted to optimize model parameter estimations.

Field capacity, maximum infiltration capacity and potential evaporo-transpiration have to be estimated.

In this model, and to determine volumes of runoff due to individual rainfall events, the basin is analogous to a vertical stack of M horizontal soil layers, each containing a certain amount of water at field capacity (6) and for each layer the hydric balance is computed. Evaporation from the top layer occurs at potential rate and from the nth one only after exhaustion of the $(n-1)$th and at the potential rate multiplied by R^{n-1} being R a parameter ($R < 1$).

If U is the surface runoff which is generated by this model during time unit t_1, then the correspondent river discharge during unit t ($Q(t)$) is given by:

$$Q(t) = \frac{1}{K \, \Gamma(N)} \; e^{-\frac{(t-t_1)}{K}} \cdot \left(\frac{t-t_1}{K}\right)^{N-1} \cdot U \quad \text{for } t > t_1 \qquad (4.1.)$$

This model is generally used with hourly data.

K, N, M and R estimates are optimized by numerical methods.

Using the daily available data this model was applied assuming N = 1 and M = 1. K was estimated by computing the slopes of the recorded discharge recession curves. The resulting K estimate was: $K = 25 \text{ day}^{-1}$.

4.4.2. Comments

1) In Fig. 3 an example of real and simulated hydrographs is presented. About 70% of the initial daily river discharge variance is explained by this model.

2) During flow or medium discharge periods the model behaviour is satisfactory but for high flows periods the simulated discharges are quite lower than the real ones. It may be noticed that a similar conclusion can be drawn from a figure presented in Nash paper (6) which resulted from use of hourly data and not having assumed N = 1 and M = 1.

3) In that paper the authors show in a quantified way how useful the numerical optimization of parameter estimates can be in order to improve the developed models.

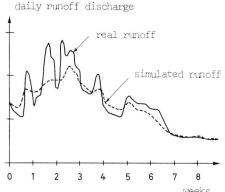

Fig. 3 Simulated and Real Runoff Using the Simplified Nash Model

5.   COMPARATIVE COMMENTS TO THE OBTAINED RESULTS

Considering the defined class of hydrologic problem studied in this paper and comparing the presented results these main methodologies potentialities can be detected:

1) Physical Description

These methods are useful to simulate the infiltration and surface runoff generation processes. The Stanford model is inapplicable to this problem and a simplified version of the Nash model is easily applied. The main shortcoming of this model is, that it is unable to simulate, the non-linearities of the watershed. The model generated hydrographs have bigger errors for high discharge periods than for dry periods.

Using physical methods first estimates of model parameters can also be determined.

2) Statistical Methods

The generated results using the regression methods have important errors.

Using these models the simulation errors are higher for dry periods than for high discharge periods as it was pointed out in 4.2.3.b). The contrary was said about the physical methodology.

These two conclusions show how these two methods have complementary potentialities.

3) Systems Theory

This methodology is successful when transforming generated runoff components into river discharges at a certain section. It is also useful to improve the physical initial estimates of model parameters through numerical optimization techniques.

6.   A MULTI-DISCIPLINARY MODEL (DHIM 73)

6.1. Basic Principles

According to comments on chapter 5 these principles were settled:

1) The infiltration and the direct surface runoff generating process can be built up using Nash model.

2) To improve this model the simulation of watershed non-linearities is essential. This is not achieved by detailing the adopted physical model of the basin.

3) Physical and traditional techniques are useful to get initial values for the model parameter estimates.

4) These first estimates can be improved by numerical optimization.

5) Finally, Statistical techniques can be efficiently used to reduce the residual errors of generated hydrographs.

6.2. DHIM 73 General Description

The physical process of generating direct surface runoff from rainfall depends on the soil moisture state. Therefore two distinct processes were considered.

The process A is applicable if the basin soil does not behave as if it was saturated and otherwise process B is used. This saturated behaviour can be caused by two reasons: the field capacity being reached by the soil moisture or the infiltration capacity being exceeded by the rainfall intensity.

a) Process A

The day t rainfall, $H(t)$, generates a total runoff, $CH(t)$. C is the runoff coefficient and it is a function of $H(t)$ and also of the time of the year which is given by t (or simply given by the month in which includes t). $CH(t)$ includes the direct surface runoff, the subsurface flow and the baseflow. The time distribution of CH_t is assumed to be given by formula (4.1.) with $N = 1$. To compute the daily variation of soil moisture this relation can be used:

$$H(t) - CH(t) = E(t) + (V(t) - V(t-1)) \qquad (6.1.)$$

being $E(t)$ the day t evaporo-transpiration and being $V(t)$ the soil moisture at the end of day t. $V(t)$ has to be positive and lower than M (field capacity).Therefore if when using (6.1.) $V(t)$ becomes negative or higher than M, it is made equal to zero or to M, respectively.

b) Process B

If the soil behaves as if it was saturated, the fraction of rainfall which generates direct surface runoff is higher than that which unsaturated behaviour situations imply. Then, the direct surface runoff is given by $C^*[H(t) - E(t)]$ if $H(t) \geq E(t)$. If $H(t) < E(t)$, it is equal to zero. C^* is an appropriate parameter. A fraction of $C^*[H(t) - E(t)]$ expressed by $\alpha\, C^*[H(t) - E(t)]$ is included in day t river discharge and $(1 - \alpha)\, C^*[H(t) - E(t)]$ is distributed by the following days, using formula (4.1.).

Now, the quantitative criteria to distinguish the saturated situations from the unsaturated ones have to be discussed.

Several criteria were used and the most successful one is:

If $[H(t) + V(t)] \geq M$ = saturated behaviour

If $[H(t) + V(t)] < M$ = unsaturated behaviour

Up to this point this model parameters are: K, C, C^*, α and M. Their physical meaning is clear and well defined:

K - Considering (4.1.), $(\frac{-1}{K})$ is the logarithm of the daily decreasing rate of river discharge generated by a rainstorm with effective duration smaller than one day.

C - Runoff coefficient for unsaturated behaviour.

C^*- Fraction of $[H(t) - E(t)]$ which is transformed into surface runoff for unsaturated behaviour.

α - Fraction of $C^*[H(t) - E(t)]$ which is included in day t river discharge.

M - Field capacity.

To estimate these parameters, physical methods are used. After that, some numerical optimization techniques are adopted. K, M and the means of monthly C values, $\overline{C}_i$ (with $i = 1,...,12$), were initially estimated by using traditional hydrological techniques.

The monthly average values of $E(t)$, $\overline{E}_i$ (with $i = 1,...,12$), are known (8). Within each month i, $E(t)$ was assumed equal to $\overline{E}_i$.

With this initial K estimate daily decreasing rates of river discharge produced by the simplified Nash model are very close to the real ones.

Using the initial M estimate all the hydrograph peaks were detected by the model.

Therefore, these two estimates were considered sufficiently precise and no further improvement was searched.

In order to make C a function of the season and of the rainfall this expression was adopted:

$$C_i = \overline{C}_i \ (1 + 0,4 \ . \ P_1 \ arctg \ u_i)$$

being:

C_i -   month i runoff coefficient

$\overline{C}_i$ -   mean of month i runoff coefficient

and:

$$u_i = \frac{H_i + H_{i-1}}{2} - \frac{\overline{H}_i + \overline{H}_{i-1}}{2}$$

with:

H_i -   month i rainfall

$\overline{H}_i$ -   mean of month i rainfall

For some generic day, t, C^* and α are only functions of $H(t)$.

Then:

$$C_t^* = C_0^* \ (1 + P_2 \ 0,4 \ arctg \ v_t)$$

$$\alpha_t = \alpha_0 \ (1 + P_3 \ 0,4 \ arctg \ v_t)$$

with $v_t = H(t) - E(t)$

Analysing the real hydrographs C_0^* and α_0 estimates were determined.

In Table 4 the values of aforementioned parameters are presented (10).

To optimize P_1, P_2 and P_3 values implies discussing model efficiency criteria as well as selecting the most convenient numerical methods to be used.

After optimizing P_1, P_2 and P_3 estimates, purely statistical methods are used to reduce the residual variability. Being $Q_S(t)$ and $Q_R(t)$ the simulated and real daily river discharges, respectively, this time-series is defined:

$$W(t) = Q_R(t) - Q_S(t)$$

To study $W(t)$ the statistical methodology presented by Box & Jenkins (1) is adopted. Then, to use this model and after calculating $Q_S(t)$ values, $W(t)$ time-series have to be generated and added to $Q_S(t)$.

6.3.   Numerical Optimization of Model Parameters

6.3.1.   Model Efficiency Criteria

This is a very controversial issue.

To quantify model inefficiency several functions have been proposed:

$$F_1 = \sum_{t=1}^{N} \left[Q_S(t) - Q_R(t) \right]^2$$

$$F_2 = \sum_{t=1}^{N} \left[\frac{Q_S(t) - Q_R(t)}{Q_R(t)} \right]^2 \qquad \text{only summing up terms with } Q_R(t) > 0.$$

$$F_3 = \sum_{t=1}^{N} |Q_S(t) - Q_R(t)|$$

$$F_4 = \sum_{t=1}^{N} \{ \ln \left[\max Q_S(t), Q_R(t) \right] - \ln \left[\min Q_S(t), Q_R(t) \right] \}$$

6.3.2. Numerical Optimization Methods

In hydrologic simulation problems, these four functions are not well behaved and usually they present several local minima and maxima. Considering that the analytical expressions of F_1, F_2, F_3 and F_4 as functions of P_1, P_2 and P_3 are unknown, two numerical methods were selected:

a)   Rosenbrock method (9)
b)   Powell method (7).

6.3.3. Optimization Results

The four mentioned objective-functions were used. F_3 and F_4 minima are the most and the least stable ones, respectively. F_3 is very unsensitive to parameter variations. Using the parameter values which are associated to F_3 or F_4 minima the simulated runoff is not closer to the real hydrographs than if F_1 or F_2 minima are considered. Therefore, further studies were made using only F_1 and F_2 as well as eventual combinations of these two functions.

To minimize F_1 or F_2, the optimum P_1, P_2 and P_3 values which are computed using Rosenbrock or Powell methods are very similar. The computing times for the last one are lower than for the first method. Therefore, from now on Powell procedure was adopted.

6.4. DHIM 73 Application to the Simulation of the River PAIVA Basin at CASTRO DAIRE

The physical parameter estimates have already been presented (Table 4).

P_1, P_2 and P_3 optimization was carried out for these three periods of three water years:

Period I   (wet period):
        1958/59; 1959/60; 1960/61

Period II   (medium period):
        1957/58; 1958/59; 1959/60

Period III   (dry period):
        1956/57; 1957/58; 1958/59

Powell method was used to minimize:

$$F_1 = \sum_{t=1}^{N} \left[Q_S(t) - Q_R(t) \right]^2$$

$$F_2 = \sum_{t=1}^{N} \left[\frac{Q_S(t) - Q_R(t)}{Q_R(t)} \right]^2$$

The days for which $Q_R(t)=0$ are not included in this sum.

$$F^* = F_1 + F_2 \cdot \left[\frac{\sum_{t=1}^{N} Q_R(t)}{N} \right]$$

The computed results are given on Table 5.

As an example, real and simulated hydrographs are presented on Fig. 4.

These conclusions can be drawn:

a) The simulated hydrographs are very close to the real ones.

b) The peak daily river discharges are detected and well simulated by this model.

c) Using F_1 the residual variances are lower than those resulting from the use of F_2.

d) Using F_1, the P_1, P_2 and P_3 optimum values are much more dependent upon the annual amount of rainfall than F_2 parameter optimum estimates.

e) About c) and d) topics, F^* has intermediate features between those of F_1 and F_2.

f) P_1, P_2 and P_3 convergence for their optimum values is stable using F_1, F_2 or F^* as objective functions (Fig. 5).

g) Therefore, to simulate a runoff hydrograph F_1 is recommended if the annual rainfall depth is known. If this amount is unknown F_2 is preferable to F_1. For intermediate situations F^* is useful.

Finally, the Box & Jenkins statistical methodology was applied to the residual time-series:

$$W(t) = Q_R(t) - Q_S(t)$$

On Table 6, determined results are presented.

Therefore, applying the DHIM 73 model to this problem the unexplained residual variance is equal to 5% of the initial variance.

7. CONCLUSIONS

A) Main hydrologic simulation models are based on one single branch of science. For watersheds simulation the most useful scientific subjects are the Physical Description, the Systems Theory and the Statistical Methods.

B) From the presented analyses and to solve the problem main potentialities methodologies were identified:

- Statistical Analysis cannot be used in the first stage of the modeling process. It is a quite useful technique to be introduced into the model as a last refinement.

- Physical Description is useful to simulate the infiltration and the runoff components generation processes but a high degree of detail is not necessary. Watershed non-linearities have to be considered by this model.

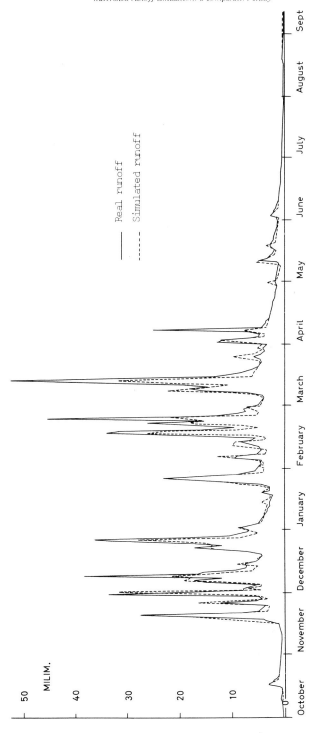

Fig. 4 Real and Simulated Hydrographs Using DHIM 73
(River PAIVA at CASTRO DAIRE)

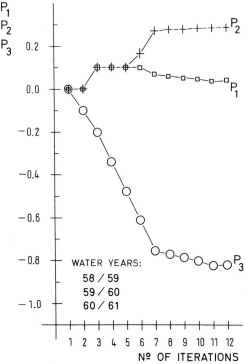

Fig. 5 P_1, P_2 and P_3 Convergence to their Optimum Values

- The Systems Theory is particularly useful to obtain the daily river discharge at a specified section from the runoff components which were generated by physical methods. Numerical optimization techniques can be successively used to improve model parameter estimation.

C)   These described potentialities are obviously complementary. As a clear proof (5.2)) conclusion can be quoted. That is, unexplained variance by regression analysis is higher for wet years than for dry ones. For the physical model the contrary result was obtained. Therefore, the successive use of these methodologies is advisable.

D)   With the purpose of integrating these different approaches a model was developed (DHIM 73). The DHIM 73 simulated runoff is very close to the real one (the unexplained variance is about 5% of the initial variance). This model can be easily estimated and applied to solve practical problems. The reason of this efficiency is the integration of the three mentioned scientific methodologies.

For each class of hydrologic problems and to improve simulation model efficiency the optimum way of combining these scientific subjects has to be studied. The analyses which were described in this paper are an example of research for a specific type of problem.

Other similar studies for other objectives should be carried out. This attitude is incompatible with assuming that the best hydrologic model for all seasons, for all regions and for all situations can be selected once for all.

8. ACKNOWLEDGEMENT

This research was sponsored by CALOUSTE GULBENKIAN FOUNDATION.

9. REFERENCES

(1) - BOX and JENKINS, "Time-series Analyses. Forecasting and Control", Holden-Day, San Francisco (1971).

(2) - CHOW, V.T. and V.C. KULANDAISWAMY, "General hydrologic system model", A.S.C.E., 6, 791-803 (1971).

(3) - CHOW, V.T., "Stochastic hydrologic systems", U.S.-Japan Bi-Lateral Seminar in Hydrology, 1-15, Water Res. Publ., Fort Collins (1971).

(4) - HYDROCOMP INT., "Simulation programming operations manual", H. Int., Palo Alto, U.S.A. (1970).

(5) - KLIR, G.F., (ed.) "Trends in General Systems Theory", Wiley Inter-science, N.Y. (1972).

(6) - NASH, I.E., P.E. O'CONNELL and I.P. FARRELL, "River flow forecast-ing through conceptual models. Part II - The Brosna catchment at Ferbane", Journal of Hydrology, 10, 317-329 (1970).

(7) - POWELL, M.I.D., "An efficient method for finding the minimum of a function of several variables without calculating derivatives", The Computer Journal, 7, 155-161 (1964).

(8) - QUINTELA, A., "Recursos de águas superficiais em Portugal Continen-tal", author edition, Lisbon (1966).

(9) - ROSENBROCK, H.H., "An automatic method for finding the greatest or least value of a function", The Computer Journal, 3, 175-180 (1960).

(10) - VALADARES TAVARES, L., "Métodos de simulação hidrológica", author edition, Lisbon (1973).

ANNEX 1

TABLE 1

Means (μ) and Variation Coefficients (C.V.)

of PAIVA Basin Rainfall Depths

(1944/45 - 1959/60)

	O	N	D	J	F	M	A	M	J	J	A	S	First 6 months	Last 6 months	Year
μ (mm)	91	167	209	180	161	208	88	123	53	14	25	54	1 016	359	1 375
CV (-)	0.44	0.67	0.62	0.95	1.02	0.63	0.63	0.51	0.58	1.03	0.89	0.87	0.35	0.36	0.28

TABLE 2

Linear Regression of $Q(t)$ on $H(t)$ and $H(t-1)$

for river PAIVA at CASTRO DAIRE

$$Q(t) = a + b H(t) + c H(t-1) + \varepsilon_t$$

Period	a (mm)	b (-)	c (-)	σ_Q^2 (mm2)	V (mm2)	F (-)
Wet year (1959/60)	4.66	-0.36	0.12	56.43	20.70	0.63
Dry year (1956/57)	1.16	-0.15	0.12	3.20	2.09	0.35
First 6 months (1959/60)	7.93	-0.38	0.11	85.25	30.46	0.64
Last 6 months (1956/57)	0.66	-0.05	0.02	0.45	0.41	0.09

being: σ_Q^2 - Variance of $Q(t)$

ε_t - Normal random variable with zero mean and variance V

F - Fraction of σ_Q^2 which is explained by this model

TABLE 3

Linear Regression of Q(t) on Q(t-1), H(t)

and H(t-1) for river PAIVA at CASTRO DAIRE

$$Q(t) = a + b\,H(t) + c\,H(t-1) + d\,Q(t-1) + \varepsilon_t$$

Period	a (mm)	b (-)	c (-)	d (-)	σ_Q^2 (mm2)	V (mm2)	F (-)
Wet year (1959/60)	4.66	-0.16	0.29	0.23	56.43	14.06	0.75
Dry year (1956/57)	1.16	-0.19	0.10	0.14	3.20	1.32	0.59
First 6 months (1959/60)	7.93	-0.14	0.33	0.25	85.25	23.67	0.72
Last 6 months (1956/57)	0.66	-0.27	0.07	0.20	0.45	0.39	0.13

being:

σ_Q^2 - variance of Q(t)

ε_t - normal random variable with zero mean and variance V

F - fraction of σ_Q^2 which is explained by this model.

TABLE 4

Physical Estimates of DHIM 73 Model

(River PAIVA Basin at CASTRO DAIRE)

$\overline{C}_i$ (-)												K (day^{-1})	α_0 (-)	C_0^* (-)	M (mm)
O	N	D	J	F	M	A	M	J	J	A	S				
0.21	0.51	0.62	0.16	0.10	0.71	0.55	0.35	0.41	0.32	0.21	0.11	25	0.395	0.58	200

TABLE 5

P_1, P_2 and P_3 Optimization Results for River
PAIVA at CASTRO DAIRE

Three years Period	Real runoff Variance (mm2)	Objective Function											
		F_1				F_2				F^*			
		Estimated Parameters			Residual runoff variance (mm2)	Estimated Parameters			Residual runoff variance (mm2)	Estimated Parameters			Residual runoff variance (mm2)
		P_1	P_2	P_3		P_1	P_2	P_3		P_1	P_2	P_3	
Wet	31.6	0.04	0.28	-0.82	7.3	-0.68	-0.55	-0.49	11.1	-0.51	0.42	-0.84	8.1
Medium	15.9	0.06	0.29	-0.23	3.0	-0.68	-0.55	-0.49	4.7	-0.56	0.10	-0.25	3.6
Dry	8.8	-0.26	0.76	0.19	1.6	-0.68	-0.55	-0.49	2.5	-0.52	0.15	0.03	1.7

TABLE 6

Statistical Model for the Residual
Runoff Time-Series (W (t))

Most adequate model:

$$W(t) = a\, W(t-1) + b\, W(t-2) + \varepsilon_t$$

with: $W(t) = Q_R(t) - Q_S(t)$

a, b - estimated parameters

ε_t - normal random variable with zero mean
and variance V (mm2)

Three years Periods	a	b	Real Runoff Variance (mm2)	W(t) Variance (mm2)	Residual Variance V (mm2)	% of explained variance by DHIM73
Wet Period	0.52	0.24	31.6	7.3	2.4	95.5
Dry Period	0.52	0.20	8.8	1.6	0.7	94.2

DISCUSSION

At the very beginning of July, a competition of conceptional models was held in Geneva. The competition was the comparison of the results of ten different models including a sort of Stanford watershed model, which was too expensive. The competition was done with 6 river basins all over the world using 6 years of data rainfall runoff and temperature and 2 more years of only rainfall to produce the runoff. I think you should look at the conclusions and recommendations of this. Even statistics on the results has been done and proposed to evaluate the differences of the models. (TODINI)

Current research field of author : *Watershed runoff simulation – Water resources management.*

Modeling and Simulation of Water Resources Systems, G.C. VANSTEENKISTE, (Ed.)
North-Holland Publishing Company (1975)

THE ARNO RIVER MODEL
PROBLEMS, METHODOLOGIES
AND TECHNIQUES

E. Todini
IBM Scientific Centre
Pisa, Italy

ABSTRACT

The main aspects of the problems that arise when an entire
river basin behaviour has to be simulated with mathematical
models are presented, together with some of the original
algorithms and techniques used to set up a flood simulation
mathematical model of the Arno river.

INTRODUCTION

Since 1970 the IBM Scientific Centre and the Hydraulics Institute of
Pavia University have been setting up a mathematical model of the Arno river in
order to simulate floods.

The aim of the joint research is to obtain a tool in order to predict
water levels and discharges at certain sections of the main channel, given the
amount of rainfall on the upstream catchment area.

All the models described in the following paper were developed by the
joint research group, namely by M. Gallati, F. Greco, U. Maione, L. Natale,
L. Panattoni, J. Wallis and the writer himself.

1. A SURFACE RUNOFF MODEL

The water that falls over the catchment area gives rise to a certain
number of different phenomena: evaporation, seepage, transpiration, surface
runoff, etc. depending on such factors as the initial status of the basin (dry or
wet), rain intensity, geology, vegetation etc. [6] .

During flood events the surface runoff constitutes the main contribution to the discharge that is measured at the outlet of the basin. But other phenomena, such as the infiltration, must be taken into account because of the great
reduction of the "effective" rainfall that gives rise to the surface runoff depending on the initial conditions of the catchment area.

When a certain level of water is reached in the basin the water flows
into the drainage network and gives rise to a flood wave which propagates along
the main channel.

Furthermore during its flow towards the sea the wave will be increased by the flood waves coming from the tributarys.

To solve the problem of the mathematical simulation of the surface
runoff during flood events two main phenomena have been sketched out and for

each of those a different mathematical model has been set up.

The first phenomenon, i. e. the rainfall-runoff process, models the generation of a flood wave at the outlet of a catchment area for a given rainfall, while the second phenomenon, i. e. the flood routing process, regards the propagation and the subsidense of a flood wave which flows in a reach, given the incoming waves from the main channel and from the tributarys. Hence the Arno river basin (approximately 8200 km^2) has been divided into a number of subbasins where the rainfall-runoff model is being set up, and the outflow of each subbasin is then routed along the main channel towards the sea with a flood routing model.

In the following sections, problems that arise when mathematical models of the above mentioned phenomena have to be specified will be presented, together with the techniques that have been adopted in order to solve their mathematical formulation.

2. RAINFALL-RUNOFF MODEL

As previously stated the rainfall runoff process is one of the two phenomena we deal with.

The interaction of all the factors that influence this process is at present time extremely difficult to specify in terms of a concise mathematical notation. Moreover the data, required to set up a detailed mathematical model, are few or non existing for most of the river basins of the Arno or for that matter elsewhere in the world, and the available ones are affected by errors which is in the best cases around 10%.

Hence a linear approximation which allows the identification of the behaviour of the basin as an impulse response function (the Instant Unit Hydrograph) based only on the input (rainfall) and the output (runoff) functions of the system was regarded as the most convenient.

The basin is sketched as a lumped parameter linear system where only the rainfall function i(t) and the runoff function q(t) are known, and where

$$\xrightarrow{\quad i(t) \quad} \boxed{\quad u(t) \quad} \xrightarrow{\quad q(t) \quad} \qquad (2.1)$$

u(t) is the impulse responce function of the system that must be determined.

The rainfall is introduced in the model as a lumped input function averaging the raingages records by means of Thiessen poligons, while the output discharges are measured at the outlet of the basin by a gaging station.

If the input and the output functions are sampled at Δt time intervals, the linear mathematical model which represents the phenomenon can be written with matricial notation as :

$$q = Hu + \epsilon \qquad (2.2)$$

where :

$$q = \begin{vmatrix} q(1.\Delta t) \\ q(2.\Delta t) \\ . \\ . \\ q(n.\Delta t) \end{vmatrix} \qquad (2.3)$$

represents the n length vector of the output discharges and n t is the length of the record;

$$u = \begin{vmatrix} u(1.\Delta t) \\ u(2.\Delta t) \\ . \\ . \\ u(m.\Delta t) \end{vmatrix} \qquad (2.4)$$

represents the m ordinates of the unknown impulse response function with $m\Delta t$ the finite memory of the system and, omitting to write Δt from now on :

$$H = \begin{vmatrix} i(1) & & \mathbf{0} \\ i(2) & i(1) \\ . & . \\ . & . \\ . & . \\ i(n-1) & i(n-2) & \dots\dots\dots & i(n-m+2) \\ i(n) & i(n-1) & \dots\dots\dots & i(n-m+1) \end{vmatrix} \qquad (2.5)$$

represents the (n, m) matrix of the input, while

$$\epsilon = \begin{vmatrix} \epsilon(1) \\ \epsilon(2) \\ . \\ . \\ \epsilon(n) \end{vmatrix} \qquad (2.6)$$

represents the n length error vector which takes into account the errors in the data measurements and the modeling error.

On the usual assumptions of zero mean Gaussian independent noise the ordinates of function u (which will be called parameters) can be identified by means of the least square estimator as the solution of the following unconstrained problem :

$$\min \Phi(u) = \frac{1}{2} \epsilon^T \epsilon = \frac{1}{2} (q-Hu)^T (q-Hu) \qquad (2.7)$$

It can be easily shown that the estimates of u, owing to the high level of noise which is embedded in the system, will have a great variance [5] .

When only a few flood waves are available (as it is usual in hydrology) the mean value of the estimates of u can be far from the true value, while in the limit (that is with an infinite number of samples) it should converge to the true value.

The variance of the estimates can be dramatically reduced if we are able to introduce into the estimator a certain set of physical constraints that, being satisfied by the true values of the parameters should also be satisfied by their estimates.

In the rainfall runoff model an equality constraint and a set of inequality constraints can be specified. In fact the impulse response function represents the percentage of an impulse rainfall measured at subsequent time lags at the outlet of the system. Therefore we can impose the following constraints on our parameter :

$$u \geqslant 0 \tag{2.8}$$

$$c^T u = 1 \tag{2.9}$$

The (2.9), in which

$$c_j = \frac{\sum_{k=1}^{n-j} i_k}{\sum_{k=1}^{n} q_k}$$

represents the losses of water between the input and the output of the system.

The constrained least squares estimator becomes, after expansion of (2.7) and elimination of the constant terms :

$$\begin{cases} \min \quad \Theta(u) = \dfrac{1}{2} u^T H^T Hu - u^T H^T q \\[2ex] \text{s.t.} \qquad u \geqslant 0 \\[2ex] \qquad\quad c^T u = 1 \end{cases} \tag{2.10}$$

which can be solved as a quadratic programming problem, $H^T H$ being a symmetric positive definite matrix which ensures the existence and the uniqueness of the solution.

While the problem of a stable estimate of the parameters, with a small number of flood waves can be achieved by means of the constrained estimator [5], another problem arises when the effective rainfall, actually relevant to the surface runoff process, has to be determined.

Actually the rainfall runoff problem is not linear when the total amount of water that falls over the catchment area is considered, so that a great deal of effort is often spent to determine the "effective" rainfall. At present time only heuristic and unsatisfactory approaches have been used such as the separation of hyetographs with some empirical function which should take into account the infiltration and the evaporation losses.

We have been experimenting with a different approach to the classical one described above. We are splitting the total rainfall into two or more precipitation inputs on the basis of antecedent precipitation indexes, obtaining simultaneously different impulse responses for each input of the system. These indexes can be thoutht of as thresholds separating watershed conditions that lead to different effects of the precipitation on the outflow discharges.

The model of the rainfall-runoff process becomes

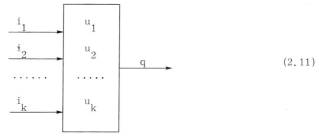

$$(2.11)$$

and its analytical formulation remains (2.2) provided that :

$$H = \left| \ \ H_1 \ \vdots \ H_2 \ \vdots \ \ \ldots \ \ \vdots \ H_k \ \right| \qquad (2.12)$$

is the partitioning matrix of (n, km) dimension of the input functions where H_j is defined by (2.5) for the jth input, and

$$u = \left| \begin{matrix} u_1 \\ \ldots \\ u_2 \\ \ldots \\ \vdots \\ \ldots \\ u_k \end{matrix} \right| \qquad (2.13)$$

is the (km) length vector of unknowns.

The expression of the constrained estimator is still (2.10) provided that :

$$c = \left| \begin{matrix} c_1 \\ \ldots \\ c_2 \\ \ldots \\ \vdots \\ \ldots \\ c_k \end{matrix} \right| \qquad (2.14)$$

is the (km)length vector of the coefficients of the equality constraint.

This technique gives very good result even for basins where long drought periods are present provided that a long continuous record of input and output functions is available.

3. FLOOD ROUTING PROCESS

The flood routing process in a channel reach depends mainly on the geometrical characteristics of the reach and on the physical nature of the river bed which will produce different friction losses.

This phenomenon can be studied with the De Saint Venant equations whose validity for unidimentional flows is widely recognized and applications of their integration for the Arno can be seen in [1] .

In this paper I would like to stress the problem that arises when the integration of D. S. V. equations to a natural channel has to be performed.

First of all a great number of cross sections must be provided (in the case of the Arno river we found that we had to describe the geometry with approximately one section each 400 m) to compute the geometrical quantities that appear in the D. S. V. equations, such as the wetted area, the wetted perimeter, the hydraulic radius, the superficial width and the bottom slope.

Furthermore an implicit finite differences scheme was adopted to solve the equations because of the Courant relation which ensures the stability of an explicit scheme only if

$$\Delta t \; \leqslant \; \frac{\Delta x}{V + \sqrt{g \dfrac{A}{B}}} \qquad\qquad (3.1)$$

where Δt is the integration time step, Δx the distance between two successive cross sections, while g is the gravity acceleration, A the wetted area, B the superficial width and V the mean velocity.

Therefore to perform a stable integration with an explicit scheme we should have had to adopt a $\Delta t \cong 10'' \div 20''$ which would have meant a very large number of time steps as the duration of the flood event for the Arno is two or more days.

Fortunately the implicit scheme can easily be solved [2] . In fact the phenomenon has a small variation in time, which means the previous time step solution will constitute a very good initial guess solution of the successive step.

The non linear model which uses D. S. V. equations is set up minimizing the sum of the squares of the residuals of the observed and the computed flood waves at a downstream section, given the flood wave at an upstream section.

The parameter that must be adjusted for a given reach is the roughness coefficient which will take into account not only the distributed friction losses, but also the losses of energy due to eddies, bridges and the inaccuracies in the determination of the river bed geometry.

Once the roughness coefficient has been determined with historical data, an incoming flood can be routed along the reach and levels and discharges can be determined at each cross section at different times.

A simpler approach to the flood routing problem is the linear system approach.

The flood routing phenomenon can be regarded as linear if the variation in time of the discharges is not very fast [3] . And hence as shown for the rainfall-runoff model, it is possible for a given reach to determine, by means of historical data of input and output discharges, an impulse response function which will take into account the geometrical and physical characteristics of the reach.

Applications to the Arno river of the linear model showed that were statistically indistinguishable from those of the D. S. V. non linear approach although the linear model computational and data requirement was much smaller.

In addition a confluence problem was treated with the linear model with two inputs and the results were extremely accurate as it can be seen from a split sample test in [5] . But for the purposes of the Arno river model the non-linear flood routing model was chosen because of its capability of giving the discharges and the levels at any cross section, and hence allow to simulate the possible benefits that hydraulic works can produce in order to prevent flood effects.

CONCLUSIONS

I would like to emphasize that all the models are implemented in conversational mode using facilities, such as a graphic feature, to allow a fast set up of the models. In fact the graphic display of a feature of the results gives an immediate answer to what happens when a parameter,such as the roughness coefficient for D. S. V. flood routing model or the antecedent precipitation index for the rainfall runoff model, is being varied.

All these facilities should allow the trasferability and a quick set up of the Arno river model to other rivers providing the data relevant to the newly considered basins available.

REFERENCES

1. Greco, F. , and Panattoni, L. (1973). Interactive simulation program for water flood routing systems. Proc. of 5th I. F. I. P. Conference on Optimization Techniques,Rome, Vol. 4, 231-240.
2. Greco, F. , and Panattoni, L. An implicit method to solve De Saint Venant equations. (to be published on Journal of Hydrology).
3. Hayami, S. (1951). On the propagation of flood waves. Disaster Prevention Research Institute, Kyoto University.
4. Natale, L. , and Todini, E. (1973). Black-box identification of a flood wave propagation linear model. Proc. of the XV I. A. H. R. Congress, Istanbul, Vol. 5, 165-168.
5. Natale, L. , and Todini, E. (1974). A stable physically constrained parameter estimation technique for linear models using quadratic programming. Hydraulics Institute of the University of Pavia.
6. Tennessee Valley Authority. (1965). Design of a hydrologic condition survey using factor analysis. Research paper N. 5, Knoxville, Tennessee.

DISCUSSION

Could you comment on your second constraint you are using in the water ba-
lance ?   (VAN DER BEKEN)

Those constraints are not necessarily in the limit, with an infinite number of samples, and even this is not necessary. (TODINI)

The input are precipitations on days ; you don't take into account infil-
tration.   (VAN DER BEKEN)

No, this equation in the case of multiple inputs would produce that the area
of the impulse response for the first input would be,suppose,0,3 and the impulse
response for the second input would be 0,7. So you would have a greater loss in the
first input and a smaller loss in the second input. It takes into account the losses,
not looking what the water that you lose is doing. I am only interested in flood
prediction. (TODINI)

I think it is interesting to draw comparisons with two different approaches
to the same problem which come up with what looks very similar sorts of accuracies
on the sort of basis that dr. Todini has been mentioning. I disagree with him on
one point when he says that the effective rainfall approach is not very good. I
think it is a useful approach because it can account for adjusting nonlinearities
in the long term as against hourly data which is not effective very much in this
way. It seems terminate à priori information like you are terminating à priori in-
formation in the constraints. You can include other à priori information. (YOUNG)

Yes, but for the modeling of the long term, we take into account for example for certain types 20 days before to set up the threshold, so I take into account the à priori information. (TODINI)

But in a different sort of way I think. For instance temperature could be
brought in as well. (YOUNG)

We wanted a very simple model that worked - and it worked as well as other
very complicated models as the Stanford watershed model is. (TODINI)

The model assumed here takes account of the basic regression structure where
I think it gets its statistical efficiencies from the constraints. An alternative
approach is to not assume that structure, to build a different type of model which
takes into account the full nature of the noise. (YOUNG)

In what season did you study the floods for the application of this model ?
(VAN DER BEKEN)

We had daily data for 6 years of precipitation and runoff measures. We had
three sample tests on 2 years more where we had only the precipitation. It included
the whole year. (TODINI)

These results are only results of precipitation or also of snow melt.
(VAN DER BEKEN)

We were not working on snow melt. (TODINI)

Could you give more details on the implicit method you were using ?

The method is a recognition of the linearity of the continuity equation.
It will appear in one of the next publications of the journal of hydrology. (TODINI)

I think your very simple model is working very well because you are mainly simulating something which is linear. (VACHAUD)

Between total rainfall and total runoff, it is not linear. (TODINI)

If you try to make some correlation between the piëzometric level, the rise of the waterflow and the influx, the degree of nonlinearity is much higher. (VACHAUD)

I can use any number of inputs. I am not restricted. I showed two, but I can use as much as I want. (TODINI)

The important point raised here is that model can be linear in the parameters but does not have to be a linear model. (YOUNG)

It is a highly nonlinear problem here from the fact of the threshold. We tried with only one input to model a continuous thing and what dr. Gorez told us, happened : you overestimate the low flow all the time and you underestimate the higher flows. (TODINI)

But furthermore you can extend very well the behavior if you look at the soil. (VACHAUD)

You have the precipitation that occurs and sets a threshold. Divide the input into two vectors, one with some sort of data and zeros and the other, zeros and some other data. And then use the deconvolution in this way and you obtain immediately the total impulse response. (TODINI)

Yes, but you can also write the continuity equation when your soil is dry. After filling, you start your model. (VACHAUD)

Current research field of author : *Since 1970 I'm working within a group which aim is the study of methodologies related to flood mathematical models. The Arno river basin has been chosen to set up and test those methodologies. We are studying the rainfall-runoff problem in the sub-basins of the Arno and the flood-routing problem in the main stream of the river. A certain number of computer programs and graphic techniques have been set up for this purpose.*

Modeling and Simulation of Water Resources Systems, G.C. VANSTEENKISTE, (Ed.)
North-Holland Publishing Company (1975)

A CATCHMENT SIMULATION MODEL DEVELOPED FOR URBAN AND URBANISING CATCHMENTS WITH PARTICULAR REFERENCE TO THE USE OF AUTOMATIC OPTIMISATION TECHNIQUES

S.R. Wood M.Sc.
Anglian Water Authority
ENGLAND

INTRODUCTION.

Hydrological design techniques for use in an urban environment have developed relatively little since the introduction of the "rational" method nearly a century ago (Kuichling 1889, Lloyd-Davies 1906). There are fundamentally two problems facing the drainage design engineer in urban catchments, firstly, the design of storm sewer systems, and secondly, the design of works on the river system. The latter design requires an understanding of how the artificial drainage network interacts with the existing hydrological regime in changing water yields, low flow sequences, flood frequencies and flood magnitudes. Increasingly a third, interrelated problem needs to be solved, that of establishing the effects of urbanisation on water quality, a topic not included in the study undertaken.

Two major developments affecting design practice have been, with regard to sewer design, the Road Research Laboratory method (Watkins 1962), and with regard to the impact of changes in land use on river flow regime, Crawford and Linsleys development of catchment simulation models (1966). Whilst the former method has been widely adopted and variously modified in the United Kingdom, the adaptation of the latter technique for use in predominantly urban catchments has been little investigated, notable exceptions being the work undertaken by James (1965) and Hydrocomp (1971,1973).

This paper describes part of the study undertaken at Birmingham University, England into developing a readily usable design method for modelling the changes in streamflow regime produced by urbanisation. It was hoped that the method would yield more accurate and reliable results than techniques currently adopted, yet require a minimum of input data, and a maximum interaction with the user to enable knowledge of the physical system to be fully utilised. To remove absolute subjectivity in the selection of model parameter values, enabling results to be far more transferrable, and to ensure that the solutions were as close to the defined optimum as possible, it was considered desirable to link the model developed to an automatic optimisation technique.

REQUIREMENTS OF THE MODEL

Before consideration of the types of model best suited to the aims of the study, the following requirements of a model for use in an urban environment were identified;

(1) The ability to predict flood peaks, volumes and frequencies from historic rainfall traces to facilitate the design of flood relief works and flood reservoirs, and to assist in the formulation of flood plain management policies.

(2) The ability to predict low flow sequences, particularly for consideration of effluent discharge control and other water quality matters.

(3) To evaluate the water balance of a catchment for water resource analysis.

(4) To enable estimates to be made of changes in any of the above, brought about by changes in the extent of catchment development.

(5) The general lack of data from urban catchments required that any model be transferable, that is, as many parameters as possible which control the operation of the model must relate to some physically measurable variable.

On consideration of the types of model that would most satisfy the specified requirements, the following were quickly dismissed;

(a) Physical models, because of the difficulties of relating the reality of catchment properties and rainfall events to a physical model.

(b) Analytical models, because of the many unknowns and the general lack of analytical techniques for any solution of the urban hydraulic and hydrologic system.

(c) Stochastic models, because of the lack of records which would allow the satisfactory definition of statistical parameters.

With the removal of these techniques two types of deterministic model remained, firstly the catchment simulation model (also known as the conceptual or component model), and secondly, the empirical model.

Empirical models, such as that described by Nash (1960), or relative to urbanised catchments, those described by Hall (1973) and Rao, Delleur and Sarma (1972), rely upon the correlation of physically measurable variables to statistics of some distribution which approxiamates to the instantaneous unit hydrograph of the storm runoff component of the flood hydrograph.

The storm runoff component is found by seperating out the baseflow component of the flood hydrograph. The volume of storm runoff thus derived is equated to the rainfall input, and by making assumptions about the distribution of rainfall losses, an "effective rainfall" can be obtained. From this effective rainfall and the storm runoff distribution a unit hydrograph may be obtained, which can be defined by relating measures of its shape to physical measures of the developed catchment. To regenerate storm runoff for a flood event a design rainfall curve, or effective rainfall pattern is applied to the unit hydrograph.

Relative to the aims of the study and the requirements of the model it was decided to adopt the catchment simulation approach rather than use empirical models. Simulation models directly utilise unmodified rainfall and runoff traces and reproduce all states of flow, enabling probability levels to be assigned to various flow states. It was further considered that such techniques give tremendous insight into the relationship of the various components in the physical system, and their reaction to meteorological conditions imposed upon them, albeit in a simplified and analytically imprecise manner. In such a way the use of simulation models is very much an interactive process helping both to provide solutions to the problem set, and to show the users representation of the physical system at work, which by inference might lead to a better understanding of the system, and further refinement of the model.

THE MODEL STRUCTURE

The primary area identifier within any catchment was taken to be surface cover i.e. developed areas for the "urban zone", and areas of different vegetation cover for the "rural zone". After making this general division of the catchment the simulation consisted primarily of two parts, that which yielded the runoff from the urban zone, and that which yielded the runoff from the rural zones, the runoffs being routed to the control section combined or seperately, depending upon the particular form of the model utilised.

The need to provide model operation on sub-catcments depended upon the nature and size of the catchment, the time base being employed, and the number of control sections in the system. Typically for daily operation on a small catchment (below 100 sq. km.), where the system response was short relative to the data input timebase, a single catchment model proved adequate. On an hourly basis, however, satisfactory modelling in terms of spatial and temporal distribution of rainfall and runoff required the division of the catchment into several sub-catchments.

Impermeable area was determined to be the principle parameter governing the definition of the level of urbanisation in terms of model input and much work was done in determining how this could best be assessed, attempting to balance the accuracy of the assessment with the speed with which that assessment could be performed. Whilst realising that a measure of impermeability in itself seemed hardly sufficient to define such a complex phenomenon as catchment development, it was hoped to include other measures in the analysis of the results by correlating them with optimised model parameter values at different levels of urbanisation.

It was found that the established definition of impermeable area as used in sewer design was sufficiently accurate i.e. all those developed areas which drained to a sewer could be considered totally impermeable. The problem existed however of determining the impermeable portion, as defined, given any area containing development.

An analysis of eight different types of development, and where relevant, housing density, enabled average proportion of impermeable area to be predicted. Thus, an urban area containing any mixture of the types of development classified could be split into impermeable and permeable portions, the permeable portion being modelled as for a short root crop area in the rural zone, except that the surface runoff from such areas was input to the urban runoff storages rather than passed directly to the channel. The method allowed a fairly rapid determination of impermeable area for design purposes, which gave very good agreement with detailed estimation from large scale plans, performed for comparison.

(i) Urban runoff simulation

In any time period precipitation was directed to fill spare capacity in the "interception" storage, which storage was depleted by evaporation, any excess becoming available for routing through an overland flow storage. In the context of the urban zone, interception storage was taken to mean that amount of water retained on the surface when flow into the sewers ceased, and was in reality both surface retention and depression storage capacity. The overland flow storage had a lower limit of zero and no upper limit, and existed to delay and attenuate excess precipitation before reaching the sewer system.

Dependent upon the required complexity of the model, the amount of information available regarding the sewer system, and its physical complexity, that is , whether it was a combined or seperate system, and how many overflows existed, the incoming water (including any from permeable areas in the urban zone where overland flow was occuring) was routed through either a single sewer storage or by the R.R.L. method to the point of discharge into the river system. If the R.R.L. method was specified the stormwater discharges to the stream were routed to the downstream control section by the Muskingum method. If the simple single storage was specified the outflow from the storage was simply added to the runoff from the rural zone and routed through a common channel storage to obtain the total outflow hydrograph at the control section being considered.

If the capacity of the sewer system in a particular sub area being analysed was known then any water in excess of this capacity was kept in a delay storage, surcharge not being allowed, and was released as spare capacity became available in the system.

(ii) Rural runoff simulation

The method of estimation of runoff from rural areas centred around the use of the Meteorological Offices method of estimating soil moisture defecit (s.m.d., the cumulative balance of inflow and outflow from the soil moisture storage). This method, developed by Penman (1950) and Grindley (1967), divides a natural catchment into several zones identified primarily by their crop cover.

Catchments are generally divided into three zones; a long root zone representative of woodland areas, a short root zone representative of grass and several crop types, and a riparian zone representative of areas near to the watercourse where the water table is so close to the surface that an unlimited supply of water for any crop cover may be assumed.

The method is based upon the definition of a "root constant", being that value of s.m.d. below which evapotranspiration may take place at the potential rate, but above which evapotranspiration is limited to an extent defined empirically by Penman (1963).

At each time interval a balance is made of s.m.d., actual evapotranspiration, surface runoff (which may take place when s.m.d. is zero, that is,

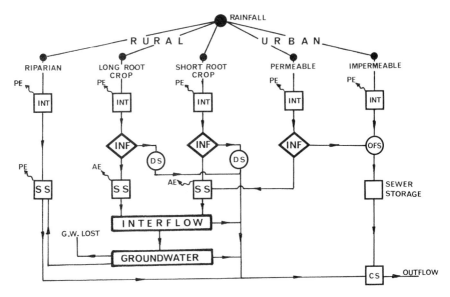

Fig.1   The model structure in flow chart form

PE = potential evapotranspiration, AE = actual evapotranspiration, INT =
interception storage, INF = infiltration function, DS = detention storage,
OFS = overland flow storage, SS = soil storage, CS = channel storage.

the soil is at "field capacity"), and seepage to other subsurface stores for
each crop area defined by its root constant. The rate at which water is allowed to seep to the unsaturated zones below was set as a function of the amount
in soil moisture storage after evapotranspiration demands had been met.

        This simple soil moisture model has the advantage that it is widely
accepted and the necessary data for its operation is generally readily available for most British catchments.

        The riparian area could be regarded as having an infinite root cons-
tant as evaporation always took place at the potential rate, any excess precipitation over this amount and the amount of any capacity in the interception
storage contributed directly to channel storage.

        The storage immediately below the soil moisture storage was defined
as the interflow storage which was depleted by both lateral flow to the channel and deep percolation to the groundwater storage.

        Groundwater storage was depleted by providing baseflow to the river
channel, and where applicable, allocating an amount to compensate for any water lost through the aquifer system to adjacent areas.

(iii) Model flexibility

        Unless otherwise stated the outflow from all storages took the gene-
ral conceptual form,

$$Q_t = KS_t^a \qquad\qquad (1)$$

        Q_t = Outflow from the storage in time interval t
        S_t = Storage at the start of time interval t
        K = Storage coefficient
        a = Storage exponent

        Obviously with "a" set to unity a simple linear storage was obtained,
and it was in this mode that the storages were defined by default. The flexibility was included in case the linear approxiamation, say in the modelling of

the baseflow component, proved inadequate.

In addition to the ability to operate the storages on a non linear basis, general flexibility was built into the model in the following ways. Firstly, several storages were optional, being included by default, but ignored should the model user consider them unimportant in the physical system being modelled, or as representing a greater degree of refinement than was required. These optional storages were the interception, detention and inter- **flow storages for the** rural zone, and the overland flow storage for the urban zone. This left as compulsory the soil moisture and groundwater storage for the rural zone, the interception and sewer storages in the urban zone, and the channel storage for the runoff from both zones. Secondly, the ability to change time base at predetermined points enabled the model to keep in balance during periods of little interest, usually on a daily basis, but switch to, say, an hourly basis for a storm event. This facility greatly reduced the amounts of input data, without making the model significantly less reliable.

Flexibility in the ability to model areas of different crop cover, and the types of sewer model available have previously been mentioned.

MODEL OPTIMISATION TRIALS

There is a perpetual conflict in model building between model comp- leteness and model simplicity, but this conflict is particularly acute when constructing a model which is to be automatically optimised. The model is required in as simple a form as possible not only because of the ease of use and comprehension, but because of the many function iterations required, and this implies more approxiamation in the modelling of the physical system. However, the ultimate accuracy and generality of the model depends upon its completeness. In effect, a tradeoff is required between a comprehensive model "optimised" by trial and error methods, which perhaps never operates in its truly optimum role, and a simpler model which may be optimised automatically, thus operating in its optimum state, for the catchment under consideration. The strategy adopted in the model development as far as complexity was conc- erned was to develop the model in stages, incorporating in the structure only those stages which gave an arbitrarily defined increase in the measure of fit per unit of increased computer time.

The automatic optimisation trials on the model were carried out not to evaluate the techniques they implicitly used, but simply, given the model structure and operation defined, to discover which optimisation technique was most satisfactory in obtaining optimum sets of model parameter values.

The three optimisation methods used in the trials were those propos- ed by Beard (1967), Powell (1964) and Rosenbrock (1960) respectively. A much more detailed comparison of these methods and several others, both as techni- ques in their own right, and as applied to the Dawdy and O'Donnell model (1965) is given elsewhere by Ibbitt (1970).

Whilst seeking objectively defined parameter values, the need to uti- lise knowledge of the physical system determined that constrained optimisation should be used, a step which would also prevent physically incorrect parameter values being determined, either by bad initial parameter selection or by inco- mplete model structure.

All parameters were initially scaled to unity in order to produce a better response surface, and the constrained parameter values were transformed by the method of Box (1966), allowing the optimisation to search notionally in an unconstrained space.

In order to meet the requirements of the automatic optimisation, the model was developed so as to contain a minimum of control parameters and be as efficient as possible in terms of computer time per function evaluation. Conceptual storages within the model were used exclusively in the linear mode, both halving the number of control parameters and reducing the problem of parameter independence which so often leads to inefficient optimisation.

A further aid to overcoming the problems set by the automatic optim- isation was to keep the number of "threshold" parameters to a minimum.

Threshold parameters have the effect of causing components in the model to become redundant when the limits set by those parameters are not exceeded during
a model run. The three possible threshold parameters in the model were interception, soil storage and sewer storage capacities, and it was ensured that
the data set used in calibration included the typical range of meteorological
conditions experienced, in order that proper weighting could be given to the
influence of components whose operation was affected by these threshold parameter values.

The objective function has great significance in defining the response
surface and thus the efficiency of the search technique, for a given model and
data set. All the objective functions examined were of the general form,

$$F = \sum_{i=1}^{m} \left(\frac{O_i - P_i}{O_i^n} \right)^k \tag{2}$$

F = Value of objective function
O_i = Observed runoff in time period i
P_i = Predicted runoff in time period i
m = Number of time periods

Because of the options in the model the number of variables to be
optimised was not a constant. In general, the two extremes of 6 and 13 variables were tested.

Initial trials showed that the Beard method was unsuitable in that it
was very inefficient in computer time even with the fewer number of variables,
and that its rate of progress relative to the other two methods, for a similar
number of function evaluations, was poor. Some results of the initial trials
are shown in Table 1. The Beard method, therefore, was not considered further.

The remaining tests with the Powell and Rosenbrock methods showed that
with larger numbers of parameters progress towards the optimum became slow,
exhibiting a superlinear relationship between the number of variables to be
optimised and the rapidity with which convergence was achieved. Indeed it was
occasionally not possible to obtain satisfactory convergence with the larger
number of parameters as the number of iterations involved required an inhib-
itive amount of computer time.

The non-linear relationship between the number of parameters and the
rapidity of convergence prompted an investigation into splitting the parameters into two groups and attempting sequential optimisation. The constants
governing routing throughout the model were set at their initial estimated
values and the model optimised for water balance (n=0, k=1 eqn. 2), the
optimised parameters were then fixed and the routing parameters optimised to
define the temporal distribution of the output, weight being given to the
higher flows (n=0, k=2). Results of this split testing, and also of trials
carried out by first optimising with regard to low flows (n=2, k=2), then
high flows as before are shown in Table 2. Tests carried out for the latter
method, when optimisation was performed on all parameters, for both the high
and low flow weighted objective function in order to determine into which
part of the optimisation each parameter should be placed, highlighted the
sensitivity of both objective functions to the value of each of the model
parameters. Some parameters, in particular those governing infiltration and
seepage from the soil storage, were almost equally as important in determining
the volume and temporal distribution of runoff i.e. such parameters should
have appeares in both halves of the sequential optimisation.

It can be seen from Table 2 that the sequential optimisation method,
despite the inherent problems created by parameter interdependence gave better
results that the model tested on a single large optimisation of all 13 parameters. A test of a repeated sequential optimisation on low flows and high flows
showed that whilst one sequential run explained 85.0% variance, two runs explained 87.6% variance, and three runs 88.1%.

The success of all trials was found to be sensitive to the selected
values of the control parameters governing the optimisation strategy. These

No. of function evaluations	Value of objective function (n=0, k=2)		
	1	2	3
Initial	74.5	74.5	74.5
5	56.6	50.1	54.3
10	52.7	40.7	41.5
50	44.4	25.2	20.8
100	38.3	19.7	14.2
200	36.6	15.1	11.4
500	35.7*	13.6	10.5

Table 1. Initial comparison of optimisation techniques.

Method: 1 Beard 2 Powell 3 Rosenbrock. Using 6 parameter model on 100 days of River Rea daily data 1968.
* Optimisation declared after 354 function evaluations.

Method	Optimisation Stages	Value of objective function		
		n=0, k=1 42.3	n=2, k=2 0.32	n=0, k=2 146
1	(i) Water balance 6 parameters (ii) Routing 7 parameters	10.7 12.8	0.06 0.14	102 27.4
2	(i) Low flows 7 parameters (ii) High flows 6 parameters	13.2 16.7	0.02 0.07	86.4 21.9
3	High flows 13 parameters	22.4	0.18	28.7

Table 2. Comparison between single and sequential optimisation.
Using Powell method with 13 parameters on River Rea hourly data 1968.
Values underlined indicate the objective function optimised in each stage.

control parameters determined the permissable size and number of step lengths taken along each search direction and also the criteria against which final convergence was declared. Little guidance was available for the selection of these parameters and "trial and error" changes in their values had to be adopted in order to ensure that the most satisfactory search strategy was used.

The trials indicated that the techniques were capable of producing optima in the constrained areas in which the search was permitted. These optimal sets of model parameters had been objectively defined, and could probably have only been achieved by chance using trial and error methods. However, both methods were increasingly slow and inconsistent with larger numbers of parameters and were, in some cases requiring thousands of function evaluations before a convergence was declared. There is obviously great scope in the field of hydrological modelling for the development of techniques which require significantly fewer function evaluations, and operate by collecting more information than is necessary for the calculation of the single objective function in each call upon the model, and use this information to "think" more between iterations. A saving in this direction would enable more complete models of the physical system to be used with automatic optimisation. If models are developed so as to minimise parameter interdependence, it would appear that sequential optimisation or multiple objective functions might be useful methods.

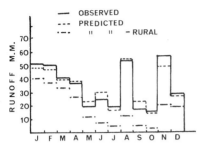

Fig.2 Monthly yield sim-
ulation. River Rea 1970.

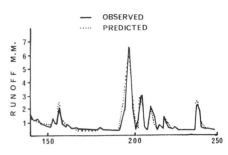

Fig.3 Daily flow simulation
River Rea 1969 (part)

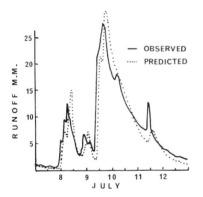

Fig.4 Hourly flow simulation
River Rea July 1968

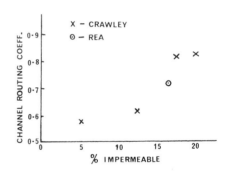

Fig.5 Relationship of model
parameter to level of urbanisation

MODEL TESTS

  The model was developed and tested on two catchments in England. The
first was that of the River Rea in the south-west suburbs of Birmingham and the
second was the Crawters Brook catchment in Crawley, Sussex.

  The Rea catchment has a primarily combined sewer system, is traversed
by some 40 km. of canals, and contains two large flow balancing and storage
reservoirs for a water treatment works in the catchment along with other
numerous artificial ponds and lakes. The development within the catchment
covers the full range of industrial, commercial and housing types. Whilst the
catchment was fully instrumented the records were short and thus represented
the catchment at only one stage of development.

  The Crawters Brook catchment possesses a seperate sewer system and the
development was that associated with Crawley New Town, mainly housing but with
some commercial development. The catchment flow records covered the whole period of urbanisation but their time base was such that detailed flood analysis
was not possible.

  The model was initially developed on the River Rea using daily data,
then on the Crawters Brook using daily data, at four discrete stages of development, to enable relationships between model parameters and degree of urbanisation to be obtained. The model was subsequently developed on an hourly

basis using the River Rea records again. The model has worked successfully on both catchments and work is in progress on testing it on the Crawters Brook catchment using a 3hr. timebase, the smallest that can reliably be abstracted, and on a completely rural catchment to test the models'generality, and to provide another point for the model parameter - level of urbanisation relation. Examples of the results obtained are given in Figs 2-5.

CONCLUSIONS

The structure and development of a simulation model for use in an urban environment has been described, with particular reference to the use of automatic techniques for the optimisation of the model parameters. Several of the shortcomings of the optimisation methods have been outlined, and ways of overcoming them tried. Results of the use of the optimised model on two British catchments have been briefly shown.

REFERENCES

Beard L. R. (1967) Optimisation techniques for hydrologic engineering. Water Resources Res. 3, No. 3; 307-321

Crawford N. H. and Linsley R. K. (1966) Digital simulation in hydrology: Stanford watershed model IV. Technical Report 39, Department of Civil Engineering, Stanford University, California.

Dawdy D. R. and O'Donnell T. (1965) Mathematical models of catchment behaviour. Proc. of the ASCE 91 (HY 4): 123-137

Grindley J. (1967) The estimation of soil moisture defecit. Meteorological Mag. 96: 97-108

Hall M. J. (1973) The hydrological consequences of urbanisation: An introductory note. Paper 10. CIRIA Research Colloqium on Rainfall,Runoff and Surface Water Drainage of Urban Catchments. University of Bristol 2-4 April 1973

Hydrocomp (1971) Studies in the application of digital simulation to urban hydrology. Report prepared for the Office of Water Resources Research Department of the Interior. OWRR 14-31-0001-3375

Hydrocomp (1973) Computer simulation for design criteria for urban flow storage systems. Report prepared for the Office of Water Resources Research. Department of the Interior. OWWR 14-31-0001-3704

Ibbitt R. P. (1970) Systematic parameter fitting for conceptual models of catchment hydrology. Ph.D. Thesis, Univ. of London, London: 400 pp

James L. D. (1965) Using a digital computer to estimate the effect of urban development on flood peaks. Water Resources Res. 1(2): 223-233

Kuichling E. (1889) The relation between the rainfall and the discharge of sewers in populous districts. Trans. ASCE 20 (Jan): 1-56

Lloyd-Davies D. E. (1906) The elimination of storm-water from sewerage systems. Proc. ICE 164(2): 41-67

Nash J. E. (1960) A unit hydrograph study, with particular reference to British catchments. Proc. ICE Vol 17: p249

Penman H. L. (1950) The water balance of the Stour catchment area. Jour. IWE 4: 457-469

Penman H. L. (1963) Vegetation and hydrology. Commonwealth Bureau of Soils. Technical Communication No. 53

Powell M. J. D. (1964) An efficient method for finding the minimum of a function without calculating derivatives. The Computer Jour. Vol 7: p155

Rao R. A. Delleur J. W. and Sarma B. S. P. (1972) Conceptual hydrologic models for urbanising basins. Jour. ASCE Vol.98 (HY 7): 1205-1220

Rosenbrock H. H. (1960) An automatic method of finding the greatest or least value of a function. The Computer Jour. Vol.3:303-307

Watkins L. H. (1962) The design of urban sewer systems. Road Research Lab. Technical Paper No. 55. HMSO. 96pp

DISCUSSION

Did you do any experiments with predicting ?

Not in an operational way, it does not try to use the next step from what it knows today. (WOOD)

Is it intended that it will be operational ?

Yes, the parameter will be measured directly from the catchment given the rainfall trace, and evaporation records. (WOOD)

I would like to contribute a few words to the excellent paper of dr. Wood. We tried something similar to compute the urbanization effect in the New York Metropolitan area, because we felt also that the urbanization definitely is in connection with the surface conditions. On the other hand by this type of long range record we came to a very interesting conclusion. Most of the operations in the runoff conditions are caused either by very sophisticated water supply systems where from one watershed to the other is transferred the water perspective by regional sewage systems, on the other hand we were able to compare the different urbanization phases with the geological formations based on the percent of impermeabilus areas. Single familial residential areas, which is a suburban type residential area practically has the surface characteristic of clay-sand. The multiple family residential area, practically appartment house, is compared to the basalt type geologic formation in surface flow. I am always talking about the peak surface flow. We have also large commercial, industrial or public areas, only to 50 % have the same characteristic as dolomite. On this basis you could tell if you built for instance a whole city like N.Y. city and sandy area, you create such surface geologic formations. The other hand surprising phenomena is that by creating artificial lakes or by making extensive drainages you far more alter the surface runoff conditions. A good example is in the Carpation basin in Rumenia. They have now constant readings for 160 years. The drainage area is 2,5x bigger than the area of the Zuiderzee. The result is that the flood conditions were increased by 15 % (peak flood). In the same time the drained areas which were used as farm land represent about 12 % of the area. On the other hand in New Jersey where the lake area was increased by 5 % the peak flow decreased by 4 %. So our conclusion was that the urbanization effect is not so great as we contribute to the urbanization. Of course like in Hong Kong or Hamburg, where the area is too big and you have a constant uniform pattern, definitely if you properly analyze, it must have a great effect on the peaks of its flows. But in smaller urbanized areas (300 km²) if there is no artificial exchange in water supply and sewage systems, the effect is almost negligible. (HALASI-KUN)

I think the above catchments are very small particular to the rain. Some dramatic changements to completely developed catchments took place. The water supply system partly flow back into the river. (WOOD)

Current research field of author : *Completing work on doctoral thesis investigating the consequences of urbanisation on catchment hydrology and water resources using a digital simulation model. The model has worked successfully on all time bases used (monthly, daily, hourly) and uses the Rosenbrock method to automatically optimize model parameters. The model internally monitors interception and detention storages, soil moisture levels, groundwater storage, actual evaporation, surface runoff, interflow and base flow for both non-urban and urban zones, and, where relevant, sewer flows from urban zones. Flexibility in the internal structure of the model and its development as a software package for practical use has been a vital part of the study.*

Modeling and Simulation of Water Resources Systems, G.C. VANSTEENKISTE, (Ed.)
North-Holland Publishing Company (1975)

MODELING THE CONJUNCTIVE AVAILABILITY OF SURFACE- AND GROUNDWATER OF A GRABEN IN THE ARID SOUTHWEST OF THE UNITED STATES

Willem F. Brutsaert
Department of Civil Engineering, Aubert Hall
University of Maine
Orono, Maine, 04473, USA

ABSTRACT

This study is part of an interdisciplinary analysis of the economic evaluation of the Water Resources of the Rio Grande Region of New Mexico. It was elemental in obtaining dynamic water availabilities in time and space.

The relationship of dynamic groundwater availability and aquifer behaviour under projected stresses was modeled by a groundwater system simulator based on a mass balance of the hydrologic basin. Conditions from extreme dry to extreme wet were modeled, combined with a range of different water demands. A vast amount of information was thus obtained in the form of aquifer responses for different conditions. An analogous relationship was constructed from these data by stepwise multiple regression analysis and was of the following form

$$\Delta d = f(d_n, L)$$

where Δd = change in water-table elevation for the time period considered, d_n = water table elevation at the end of the previous time period, and L = a lump factor combining surface water inflow and outflow, precipitation, and beneficial and nonbeneficial water uses.

Other results readily obtainable from the simulation runs are river accretion or depletion curves as a function of time. These curves show the diversion effects of groundwater pumping upon the river.

INTRODUCTION

The complexity of today's water resource systems makes it almost mandatory that their management be achieved through the application of the technology of a variety of disciplines, and the legal and institutional structures of water use make their understanding and application a further requisite to good management. Although economic justification should be the foundation of decisions on alternative uses of water, the social and cultural implications must be fully considered since the optimal use of water usually implies a maximization of the benefits returned to society through a broad range of beneficial uses. In order to formulate plans and policies for future water resources development, the assessment of future water supplies and requirements necessitates a major consideration of future rates and patterns of economic development. The results of this paper deal with the assessment of future water supplies.

Before an economic evaluation of water use can be made, the availability of surface water and groundwater must be determined. If there is a continual

exchange between the surface water of the river and the groundwater of the surrounding alluvium, groundwater availabilities are not simply related to pumping
but are also controlled by precipitation, amount and frequency of runoff in
streams, return of irrigation water, and evapotranspiration. The management of
such a system should consequently be based on a conjunctive operation of surface
and groundwater.

For a comprehensive alternative water use analysis it is necessary to know
both the groundwater availability and the behavior of the aquifer under projected
stresses, in other words, the dynamic groundwater availability. Since historical
records of hydrologic systems, in most instances, are inadequate to permit direct
analysis of basin behavior under projected stresses, a systems simulator was designed for the purpose of this study. The most efficient and practical simulator
appeared to be a mathematical analogue of the hydrologic basin, solved by digital
computer.

AREA DESCRIPTION

The arid southwestern region referred to in this study is the Albuquerque
region. It is defined as a heavily populated area along the Rio Grande in Sandoval, Bernalillo, and eastern Valencia Counties. The principal irrigated areas
are along the Rio Grande in southern Sandoval, Bernalillo, and Valencia Counties.
The major population center is Albuquerque, with smaller population centers at
Bernalillo, Los Lunas, and Belen (Figure 1).

Topography and Climate. The topography of the Albuquerque Region varies widely
from mountains to broad, relatively featureless plains. The eastern subregion is
bounded on the east by the Sandia and Manzano Mountains and on the west, from north
to south, by the Jemez Mountains which decrease to a sandy ridge that separates
the eastern from the western subregion; on the north it is bounded by White Rock
Canyon, a narrow tortuous gorge, and on the south by the Socorro Region.

The climate of the Albuquerque Region is predominantly semi-arid in the
lower elevations and semi-humid in the mountainous regions. The mean average temperatures range from 46 degrees Fahrenheit (7.8°C) at Cuba to 54 degrees (12.2°C)
in the Albuquerque area, with a regional average of about 52 degrees Fahrenheit
(11.1°C). Annual precipitation ranges from over 20 inches (510 mm) in the mountains to about 8 inches (203 mm) at Los Lunas, with an average of about 11 inches
(279 mm). Precipitation averages about 8.5 inches (216 mm) in the eastern portion
of the Albuquerque Region. The average frost-free period is from May 13 to October 8, 150 days, but ranges from 113 days at Cuba to 160 days in the Bernalillo-
Belen area.

Drainage Area. The drainage area of the Rio Grande Basin from the headwaters to
San Bernardo, the southern limit of the Albuquerque Region, is approximately
19,230 square miles (49,805 km²) including 2,940 square miles (7614 km²) of the
San Luis closed basin in Colorado. The only perennial stream is the Rio Grande
River. Its flow averages 776,100 acre-feet per year (31 m³/sec), and consists of
spring snowmelt in Colorado and Northern New Mexico, and runoff from summer rainfall. All its tributaries are ephemeral and flow only during torrential summer
rains. The Jemez is the largest tributary and flows southeastward into the Rio
Grande near Algodones.

Many arroyos drain the east and west mesas along the Rio Grande river.
Those on the west side discharge directly into the river north of Arroyo de la
Barranca. The arroyos south of Arroyo de la Barranca, as well as the ones on the
east side, are mostly intercepted by canals or drains or simply filtrate into
alluvial fans (Bjorklund and Maxwell, 1961).

Hydrogeology. The Albuquerque Region is located within the Albuquerque basin

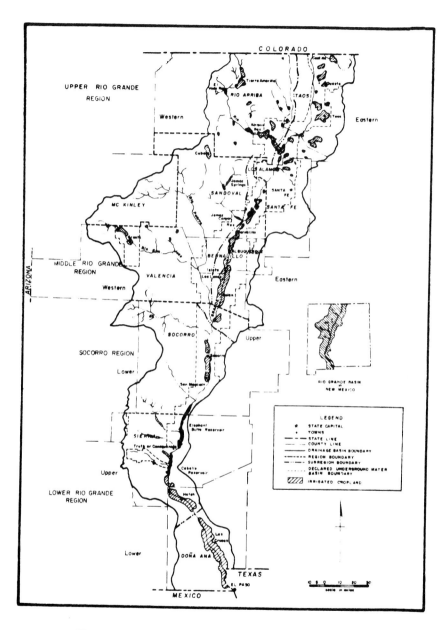

Figure 1. Rio Grande drainage basin in New Mexico

which is the largest of a series of basins that make up the Rio Grande Graben or
rift. The Albuquerque basin extends for 90 miles (144 km) from La Bajada escarp-
ment and the Jemez uplift on the north to the San Acadia constriction on the
south. The basin is roughly 30 miles (148 km) wide; it is bounded to the east by
the Sandia-Manzano uplift and to the west by the Puerco Platform, Lucero uplift,
and Ladron uplift (Kelley, 1952). The eastern uplifts (Sandias, Manzanos) are
generally higher than the western bounding structures which consist mainly of the
Puerco Platform. The Puerco Platform is low and considerably faulted. Small vol-
canoes and fissure flows mark the boundaries at several localities.

The basin-fill sediments are generally classed together as the Santa Fe
formation or Santa Fe group, of middle Miocene to Pleistocene age (Bjorklund and
Maxwell, 1961). The thickness of the underlying sedimentary rocks is unknown, but
Precambrian rocks may be 10,000 feet (3048 m) below sea level in parts of the
basin whereas they are about 9,000 feet (2743 m) above sea level in the Sandia
uplift and about sea level in the Puerco Platform (Joesting, et al., 1961).

Based on estimated rock densities obtained from gravity anomaly maps across
the Rio Grande trough north of Albuquerque (Joesting, et al., 1961), the total
thickness of sedimentary rocks (Santa Fe group) in the trough is about 15,000 feet
(4572 m). The total relief of the Precambrian basement along the Sandia front is
about 20,000 feet (6096 m). These results are in general agreement with the aero-
magnetic profiles across the trough. Magnetic anomalies are related to variations
in both the magnetization and uplift of the Precambrian rocks.

The sediments of primary concern are the Santa Fe group, alluvial fans, and
valley alluvium. The Santa Fe group consists of beds of unconsolidated to loosely
consolidated sediments and interbedded volcanic rocks. The deposits range from
boulders to clay and from well-sorted stream channel deposits to poorly sorted
slopewash deposits (Reeder, et al., 1967). The permeability of the Santa Fe group
is generally high: properly constructed wells easily yield several hundred
gallons per minute .

Alluvial fans cover the Santa Fe deposits and extend westward from the base
of the Sandia and Manzano Mountains. They are usually above the water table, so
they are not aquifers; however, in places they consist of well-sorted stream
gravel and permit the infiltration and downward percolation of flood flows.

Valley alluvium of Recent age overlies the Santa Fe group in the Rio Grande
flood plain. It is approximately 80 to 120 feet (24 to 37 m) thick, but in
general is hard to differentiate from the underlying Santa Fe group. Most of the
irrigation wells along the Rio Grande are developed within this alluvium and yield
up to 3000 gpm (0.19 m^3/sec).

The Santa Fe group combined with the valley alluvium make up the aquifer
system of the eastern Albuquerque Region. This aquifer is unconfined and is hydro-
logically connected with the Rio Grande river. Locally, "artesian" pressures have
been observed (Reeder, et al., 1967). These artesian pressures are to be understood as strong upward movement of groundwater from deeper layers in the central
portion of the basin due to natural recharge in the higher areas along the Valley.
The eastern boundary of the aquifer is spectacularly defined by the Sandia and
Manzano uplifts. The less spectacular upfaulted blocks near the Rio Puerco form
the western boundary. The lower boundary of the reservoir is not so clearly defined: saturated thickness may be as much as 12,000 to 16,000 feet (3657 to 4876
m).

WATER MANAGEMENT

Surface Water. Since the early 1900's, surface-water irrigation in the Rio Grande
basin in New Mexico has been under the jurisdiction of irrigation districts,

conservancy districts, and community ditch systems. The principal organized district in the Albuquerque Region is the Middle Rio Grande Conservancy District (MRGCD), formed in 1925 and serving 81,610 acres (33027 ha). In addition to the above, there are numerous community and private ditch systems on the tributaries of the Rio Grande. The acreages served by these individual ditch systems vary in size from a few acres to over 200 acres (81 ha).

Ground Water. The management of the ground-water resources in the Rio Grande drainage basin is primarily a private entity function. However, the New Mexico State Engineer can control the use of ground water in an area by defining and declaring a ground-water basin. Nearly all of the irrigated cropland in the Albuquerque Region is in a declared groundwater basin with only isolated tributary units outside of these basins (Figure 1). Therefore, the development of groundwater is under the jurisdiction of the New Mexico State Engineer.

It has long been recognized that the Rio Grande river and the underlying ground water reservoir are hydraulically connected. New Mexico, therefore, initiated a method of administration of conjunctive ground and surface waters which was probably unique in the United States; i.e., new appropriations of Ground water in the Rio Grande Basin are permitted under the conditions that the appropriator (1) acquire and retire from usage surface water rights in amounts sufficient at each point in time to compensate for the increasing effects of his pumping on the stream, or (2) provide for replacement water such as under the San Juan-Chama project. This project refers to interbasin transfer of water.

HYDROLOGIC DATA

Nearly all surface water of the Albuquerque Region is supplied by the run-off from the Upper Rio Grande Region. The Albuquerque Region is an area of water consumption and not of water generation.

Surface Water. Most of the Region's water supply and use is along the main stem of the Rio Grande (i.e., the eastern subregion as shown in Figure 1 which includes most of the Middle Rio Grande Conservancy District). The water supply of the MRGCD comes primarily from the flow of the Rio Grande as measured at Otowi. The western subregion includes the drainage areas of the Jemez River, and the Rio Puerco and its tributary, the Rio San Jose. Much of the water generated by these tributaries is used within the tributary basin.

The historical flows of the Rio Grande are presented in Figures 2 and 3 for the Rio Grande at Otowi and the Rio Grande near Bernardo. The gaging stations at Otowi and Bernardo correspond respectively with the northern and the southern boundaries of the study area. The decrease of flow in time at Otowi is demonstrated in Figure 2. The consumption of water within the reach is apparent from Figure 3.

Groundwater. The Albuquerque Region groundwater system is, to a large extent, affected by the urban development of the city of Albuquerque. Groundwater use is expected to increase rapidly and affect groundwater levels (Reeder, et al., 1967).

Due to differences in permeability, saturated thickness, and recharge or discharge of groundwater, the water table slopes irregularly at a low gradient, diagonally down-valley (Reeder, et al., 1967). The water table slopes from the bases of the Sandia and Manzano Mountains on the east and from the Rio Puerco on the west toward a generally southward-trending zone about eight miles west of the Rio Grande.

Precipitation, and seepage from the river and from drainage and irrigation canals are the main sources of recharge. Discharge is mainly due to pumping; evapotranspiration is of little significance except to the north and south of the

W.F. Brutsaert

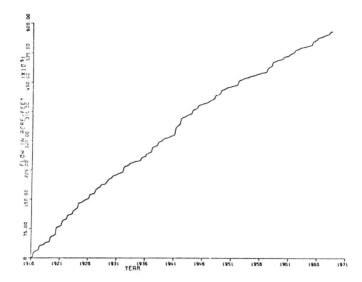

Figure 2. Mass flow curve for the Rio Grande at Otowi Bridge
near San Ildefonso, New Mexico, 1916-1968 (1 acre-
foot = 1234 m^3).

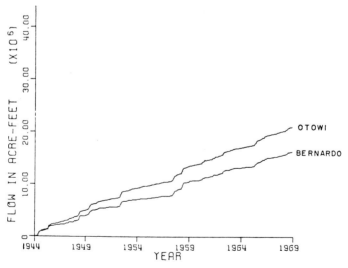

Figure 3. Mass flow curve for the Rio Grande at Otowi Bridge near San
Ildefonso, New Mexico and for the Rio Grande at Bernardo,
New Mexico, including Floodway, Conveyance Channel, Bernardo
Interior Drain, and San Juan Riverside Drain 1944-1968 (1 acre-
foot = 1234 m^3).

city of Albuquerque in the agricultural and phreatophyte areas.

The Rio Grande river channel in most of its reach throughout the Albuquerque Region is not entrenched into the Valley floor (Reeder, et al., 1967).
There has been some aggradation in some places which has raised the river channel
slightly above the Valley floor. Moreover, pumping of groundwater and low irrigation drains keep the water table substantially below the average river level.
As a consequence, the river loses water to the groundwater system in most of the
Albuquerque area. This trend of increasing induced recharge from the river is
expected to continue.

Transmissivities range from 6000 gallons/day/foot (74.5 m^2/day) in the
alluvial fans along the mountains to 600,000 gallons/day/foot (7453 m^2/day) near
the Rio Grande river (Reeder, et al., 1967). From estimates saturated thick-
nesses (Joesting, et al., 1961), hydraulic conductivities were calculated and
ranged from 11.7 to 112 ft/day (from 3.56 m/day to 34.13 m/day). The estimated
specific yield (storage coefficient) is 0.2 for both sides of the river (Bjorklund
and Maxwell, 1961).

SYSTEMS SIMULATOR

The hydrologic system with which this study is concerned, can be schematically represented as in Figure 4:

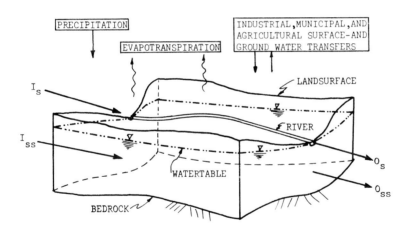

Figure 4. Schematic representation of hydrologic system.

In this Figure, I = inflow, 0 = outflow, and the subscripts s and ss, respectively,
stand for surface and subsurface. Figure 4 is simply a representation of the
statement of continuity: i.e., the conservation of mass which is the basis for
developing the fundamental flow equation or mathematical analogue, written as:

$$\frac{\partial}{\partial x} \left(K_{xx} h \, \delta y \, \frac{\partial H}{\partial x} \right) \delta x + \frac{\partial}{\partial y} \left(K_{yy} h \, \delta x \, \frac{\partial H}{\partial y} \right) \delta y = Q + \delta x \, \delta y \, S \, \frac{\partial H}{\partial t} \qquad (1)$$

where K_{xx} = principal component of hydraulic conductivity tensor, coinciding
with x-direction, [L/T]; K_{yy} = principal component of hydraulic conductivity tensor, coinciding with y-direction, [L/T]; h = saturated thickness of quifer, [L];
S = storage coefficient, dimensionless; Q = net rate of withdrawal, [L³/T];
δx,δy = dimensions of differential element; x,y = space dimensions, [L]; t =
time dimension, [T]; H = water table elevation above a datum (potentiometric
head), [L].

The above equation is a nonlinear partial differential equation obtained by
combining Darcy's law with the continuity principle and is applicable to transient,
two-dimensional flow in heterogeneous, anisotropic, incompressible, unconfined,
saturated, porous media, but is subject to the Dupuit-Forchheimer assumptions and
should be used with these limitations in mind. The most important limitations are
flow in the horizontal x,y-plane, and fully penetrating constant head (river, lake)
boundary conditions.

Equation 1 has no general analytical solution; therefore, a finite difference approximation is utilized to obtain a numerical solution with the aid of a
digital computer. Application of the finite difference approach requires subdivision of the study area into a system of finite grid blocks. For each of these
blocks a discretized form of equation 1 is written. The resulting system of simultaneous equations is either solved directly by Gauss-Elimination or by Line Successive Over Relaxation, depending upon the size of the problem: i.e. number of
equations. For a detailed description of the model the reader is referred to a
report by Brutsaert et al. (1973), which includes the mathematical analysis as
well as a program listing and user's guide.

The first step when applying the model to a particular study area is to
verify or calibrate its behavior. This verification consists of simulating a
historical period, for which both groundwater levels and stream records are available, until model and prototype match. Checking and updating should be continued
as more data become available.

The next step is the simulation (or extrapolation) of future possible conditions. Conditions can be altered to give different responses. Conditions from
extreme dry to extreme wet combined with a set of water demands ranging from large
to small may be included.

A vast amount of data is thus obtained in the form of aquifer responses for
given conditions. Realizing that these data are the result of the solution of a
continuity equation of the form

$$I - 0 = \Delta S/\Delta t \qquad (2)$$

it is possible to construct an analogous relationship from the data obtained. In
equation 2, I = inflow, 0 = outflow, and ΔS = change in storage during a time
period Δt. The relationship postulated was of the following form

$$\Delta d = f(d_n, L) \qquad (3)$$

where Δd = change in water-table elevation for the time period (year) considered,
d_n = water table elevation (with reference to river level) at the end of previous
time period (year), and L = a lump factor combining surface water inflow and outflow, precipitation, and beneficial and nonbeneficial water uses.

Results of the simulation runs can be tabulated with averaged spatial responses: i.e., results would not reflect a variation in water-table elevation
along lines perpendicular to the river bed. It is assumed that average conditions
would suffice since lateral aquifer response would average out.

A stepwise multiple regression analysis, combining linear and nonlinear
(exponential and logarithmic) terms of the different factors obtained from the

simulation runs, can be performed to obtain a surface-groundwater interrelation-ship equation.

RESULTS AND DISCUSSION

The area modeled by the conjunctive use surface water-groundwater simulator is shown on Figure 5. A total of 160 grid blocks covered the study area of 20 x 64 miles (32 x 102.4 kilometers).

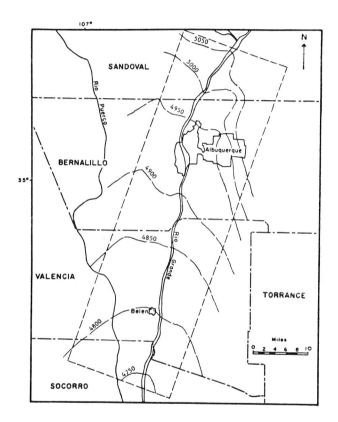

Figure 5. The Albuquerque study area with 1968 water-table contours.

Historical conditions from 1962 to 1968 were simulated to verify and ad-just model parameters. Major outputs (or inputs) are industrial and municipal water demands for the Albuquerque area. Agricultural groundwater usage, mainly to the north and to the south of the city, was estimated from consumptive-use data and from irrigated acreage patterns (Lansford et al., 1973).

Groundwater velocities are characteristically slow in the Albuquerque area, ranging from 0.2 to 0.3 ft/day (6.1 to 9.1 cm/day). Aquifer response due to pumping should, therefore, be quite pronounced on a short-term basis. On the other hand, groundwater withdrawal in the Albuquerque area will increase induced recharge from the river and will also increase the gradient to the north, thereby increasing flow into the area from the north.

Analysis of the Albuquerque groundwater basin behavior is based on fifteen simulation runs (20 years each) with the computer model. Pumping patterns, precipitation, and river stages were combined to represent varying hydrologic conditions. The following surface- groundwater interrelationship was obtained by stepwise multiple regression analysis of the Albuquerque simulation data:

$$\Delta d = -113.1 - 28.4 \ EXP(d_n/200) + 21.4 \ \log_{10}(L + 3 \times 10^6) \qquad (4)$$

where Δd = decline (-) or rise (+) of the water table in any time period (feet), d_n = depth (feet) to the water table in antecedent year with respect to river level considered as zero, and L = a lump factor in acre-feet per year. The lump factor consists of the following: river inflow (+), river outflow (-), 5% of annual average precipitation (+), nonbeneficial evapotranspiration losses (-), and the agricultural, minicipal, and industrial water needs supplied by the groundwater system (-). The average L value for the Albuquerque Region is -148,450.

The application of the above relationship can be demonstrated in different ways. For this analysis a present water-table elevation at river level and a normal projected growth for the Albuquerque area is assumed. As seen on Figure 6, water levels are expected to drop about 50 feet during the next 30 to 40 years, at

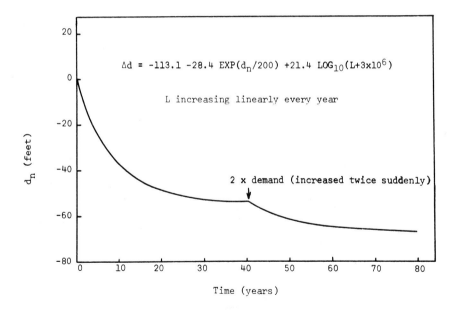

Figure 6. Depth (feet) to the water table $[d_n]$ with respect to time for the Albuquerque area, New Mexico.

which time virtual equilibrium conditions are reached: i.e., hydrology in balance with Albuquerque water demands. The equation gives only average water levels (no spatial variation); however, it is easily understood that the largest water-table drop is expected in the vicinity of the city of Albuquerque; this could be on the order of 80 feet tapering off to the north and south to about 30 feet, as well as to the east and west. Figure 6 also demonstrates the effects of a sudden doubling of the water demand.

A summary of these results is probably best accomplished by Figure 7.

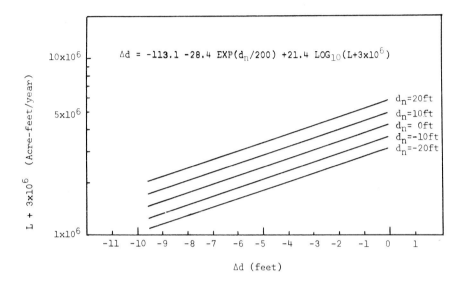

Figure 7. Expected declines in the water-table level in the Albuquerque area utilizing varying depths to water table (1 Acre-foot/year = 3.989 x 10^{-5} m^3/sec; 1 foot = 30.48 cm).

Entering this graph from the ordinate with a particular value of L, different values for Δ d (+ or -) are obtained, depending upon the water-table elevation of a previous year (d_n) with reference to the river level.

The surface-groundwater interrelationship of a certain region is most clearly demonstrated by calculations of river accretion and depletion as affected by pumping. Figure 8 is an attempt to summarize the results in this manner. The Rio Grande in the Albuquerque Region is seen to lose water. More specifically the accretion or depletion per mile can be estimated for any future time: for example, 10 years from the present about 4.4 cfs/mile (0.078 m^3/sec/km) or 3,185.6 acre-feet/year/mile will be depleted from the Rio Grande.

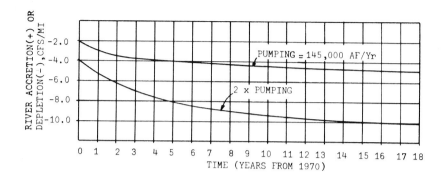

Figure 8. Average pumping effects as a function of time, Albuquerque region, New Mexico (1 cfs/mi = 0.0177 m³/sec/km ; 1AF/Yr = 1,227. m³/year).

CONCLUSION

The Albuquerque Region groundwater system is related to the surface water regime. Pumping the aquifer at projected rates has and will have an increasingly distinct diversion effect upon the Rio Grande River as demonstrated by Figure 9. The management of such a system should consequently be based on a conjunctive operation of surface water and groundwater.

REFERENCES CITED

Bjorklund, L.J., and B.W. Maxwell. 1961. Availability of Ground Water in the Albuquerque Area, Bernalillo and Sandoval Counties, New Mexico, N. Mex. State Engineer Tech. Rept. 21, 117 pp.

Brutsaert, W.F., and C.C. Way. 1973. A conjunctive Use Surface Water-Ground Water simulator. New Mexico Water Resources Research Institute Report No. 033, 56 pp.

Joesting, H.R., J.E. Case, and L.E. Cordell. 1961. The Rio Grande Trough Near Albuquerque, New Mexico. N. Mex. Geol. Soc. Guidebook, Twelfth field Conference, pp. 148-150.

Kelly, T.E., B.N. Myers, and L.A. Hershey. 1970. Saline Ground Water Resources of the Rio Grande Drainage Basin - A Pilot Study. U.S. Office of Saline Water, Research and Development Progress Rept. 560, 71 pp.

Lansford, R.R., S. Ben-David, T. Gebhard, Jr., W.F. Brutsaert, and B.J. Creel. 1973. An Analytical Interdisciplinary Evaluation of the Utilization of the Water Resources of the Rio Grande in New Mexico, New Mexico Water Resources Research Institute Report 020, 152 pp.

Reeder, H.O., L.J. Bjorklund, and G.A. Dinwiddie. 1967. Quantitative Analysis of Water Resources in the Albuquerque Area, New Mexico. N. Mex. State Engineer Tech. Rept. 33, 34 pp.

Current research field of author : *Numerical modeling of groundwater systems - both in saturated and partially saturated media - modeling of immiscible multiphase flow in porous media. Most recently : (1) Exploring the applicability of Monte Carlo simulation to water quality modeling (River BOD-DO model) (2) Modeling of water and nutrient transport from septic tanks to surface water bodies considering dispersion, and adsorption in both the partially saturated and fully saturated zone.*

DISCUSSION

Did you determine what kind of accuracy you were getting or did you compare against an explicit method or finite element method ?   (DAVIDSON)

This was not a study to try to find the best numerical procedure, we used a comfortable procedure that gives good results and the strength of the model came from a calibration versus historical data. (BRUTSAERT)

I was surprised to see from the slide that the corrected NSOR was performing less good than the original NSOR.   (NEUMAN)

No, the steeper the curve the better, the smaller the number of iterations ; so the corrected NSOR is better. (BRUTSAERT)

The K values have no physical significance.   (VAN DER BEKEN)

You are right they are to some extent curve fitting parameters. One does have of course, a feeling of the permeability, of the field, but that is insufficient to feel confident. (BRUTSAERT)

You have to calibrate your Q values of the equation, or did you assume them known ?   (NEUMAN)

We did know the pumping quite well : $\pm$ 5 %. (BRUTSAERT)

No direct recharge included ?   (NEUMAN)

Return from irrigation is included. (BRUTSAERT)

Can you comment on the variability of the historical data ?   (SHAH)

We simulated 10 years of data, 1960 - 70 roughly. Due to the lack of physical data you have to build in some confidence in your model, it is a necessity. (BRUTSAERT)

What I was wondering : you extrapolate from 10 to 80 years. Can you turn it backwards from 80 to 10 ?   (SHAH)

The information was not used backwards. We hope the best for the extrapolation. (BRUTSAERT)

Did the data over 10 years have large variations, or were they consistent ?   (SIKKA)

There are variations. Pumping will be a factor. For the rainfall we had an average precipitation of 200 mm. A lot of snowfall gives river divergence rather than regular pumping. Therefore, the year was divided in 4 seasons, taking into account irrigation. (BRUTSAERT)

Modeling and Simulation of Water Resources Systems, G.C. VANSTEENKISTE, (Ed.)
North-Holland Publishing Company (1975)

TESTS OF DIFFERENT RIVER FLOW PREDICTORS

B. Lorent
Fondation Universitaire Luxembourgeoise
Arlon, BELGIUM

ABSTRACT: this paper is concerned with some different rainfall-river flow models applied to the SEMOIS River for giving one-day ahead predictors. All these models use daily river flow, rainfall and potential evapotranspiration data. In the first part of this paper, linear models are examined and the advantage of building seasonal models is discussed. In the second part, a method is developed to compute the assumed daily fraction of running water, while taking into account the interception and infiltration phenomena. A surface runoff is hereby obtained, and we will use this as input for our river flow models. Again we will present seasonal models.

I - INTRODUCTION.

I A - We present in this paper some results of a research of which the main purpose is to predict the river flow of the Semois River (Belgium) at the output of its belgian drainage basin (Membre) from mesurements of the rainfalls. To build this predictor, we have available a six year record of daily data for the river flow in Membre, the rainfalls in different stations and the potential evapotranspiration (which is computed using a method based on an energy balance [1]).

All these data, river flow Q, rainfall PB, potential evapotranspiration ETP are expressed in 0.1 mm. per day. Therefore, in order to obtain the river flow in m^3/sec. (daily mean value), we have to divide its value in 0.1 mm./day by the factor 0.703, taking into account a drainage basin of 1229 km^2.

I B - The models used are entirely or partially "black boxes". The physical characteristics of the basin are not explicitly introduced. However, it is clear that these intervene through the dynamics of the river flow which depends both on the meteorological past and the physical characteristics.

I C - This paper presents one-day ahead predictors for the river flow. This problem is particularly interesting if we want to know the evolution of a swelling. These models can also be used to simulate the river flow for different possible meteorological futures and to simulate swellings related to exceptional rainfalls.

I D - For a more detailed description of the hydrometeorological characteristics of the basin of the Semois River, we advise the reader to read [2]. However, in the following table, we present some information about the data.

```
    a) Characteristics of the river flow Q:
              -Standard deviation:   16.5
              -Mean value:           15.3
              -Maximum value:        164.
              -Minimum value:          1.3

    b) Characteristics of the rainfall PB:
              -Standard deviation:   53.6
              -Mean value:           29.6
              -Maximum value:        492.
```

c) Monthly mean values (0.1 mm./day) – 1967 to 1972.

		River flow Q	Rainfall PB	Evapotranspiration ETP
January	:	27.2	31.4	0.7
February	:	33.6	38.2	2.7
March	:	21.0	27.9	7.9
April	:	18.8	26.7	19.0
May	:	13.8	31.2	25.9
June	:	8.5	26.3	31.3
July	:	6.0	28.7	36.2
August	:	5.6	30.9	27.4
September	:	5.9	26.0	16.8
October	:	8.1	20.1	7.5
November	:	17.0	44.1	1.9
December	:	19.1	24.1	0.5

The diagrams joined to this paper give a good idea of these data.

II – THE IDENTIFICATION METHOD.

II A – All the models we present have the form:

$$Q(k) = \underline{a}^T . \underline{Z}(k) + e(k)$$

with: $Qp(k) = \underline{a}^T . \underline{Z}(k)$, the predicted value of $Q(k)$,

$e(k) = Q(k) - Qp(k)$, the error of prediction.

$\underline{a}^T = (a_1, \ldots , a_N)$, a vector of optimized parameters,

$\underline{Z}(k)$, a vector function of the past observations, for instance:
$$\underline{Z}(k) = (Q(k-1), Q(k-2), \ldots , PB(k-1), \ldots)$$

II B – The optimal vector $\underline{a}$ is the vector that minimizes the cost function:

$$J_K = \sum_{k=1}^{K} (Q(k) - \underline{a}^T . \underline{Z}(k))^2$$

The identification is made recursively so that it is possible to work in real time and to improve the quality of the model each day, by adding new data (see [6] and [7]).

The algorithm is the following:

$$\underline{S}(k+1) = \underline{S}(k) - \underline{S}(k) . \underline{Z}(k+1) . \underline{Z}^T(k+1) . \underline{S}(k)/F$$

where : $F = 1 + \underline{Z}(k+1) . \underline{S}(k) . \underline{Z}(k+1)$, a scalar.

$$\underline{a}(k+1) = \underline{a}(k) + \underline{S}(k+1) . \underline{Z}(k+1) . (Q(k+1) - \underline{a}^T(k) . \underline{Z}(k+1))$$

$\underline{S}(k)$ is a square matrix (NxN) decreasing with k increasing.
$\bar{Q}p(k) = \underline{a}^T(k-1) . \underline{Z}(k)$ is the optimal predictor at time k.

II C – To compare the quality of two different models we will use the mean square error (MSE), namely the mean value of $e^2(k)$, where the $e(k)$'s are obtained by computing all the predicted values of $Q(k)$ by means of the last values of the parameters. We will also use the RME, the relative mean error computed as follows:

$$RME = \sqrt{\frac{MSE}{MSQ}}$$

where the MSQ is the mean value of $Q^2(k)$ computed over the considered period.

III - SOME LINEAR PREDICTORS. [8],[9]

We will first study some linear models between either the river flow Q and a mean value PB of the rainfall (computed over all the drainage basin) or the river flow Q and both the mean value PB of the rainfall and the potential evapotranspiration ETP.

All these models are identified through the least-square method just described.

III A - A difference equation model with one or two inputs.

We have successively found:

1) For the relation between Q and PB:

$$Qp(k) = 1.40 \ Q(k-1) - 0.71 \ Q(k-2) + 0.22 \ Q(k-3)$$
$$+ \ 0.028 \ PB \ (k-1) + 0.034 \ PB(k-2) - 0.012 \ PB(k-3)$$
$$- \ 0.335$$

The mean square error of prediction MSE is 12.7 and the RME is 0.162

2) For the relation between Q and both PB and ETP:

$$Qp(k) = 1.40 \ Q(k-1) - 0.70 \ Q(k-2) + 0.22 \ Q(k-3)$$
$$+ \ 0.028 \ PB(k-1) + 0.035 \ PB(k-2) - 0.013 \ PB(k-3)$$
$$+ \ 0.035 \ ETP(k-1) - 0.018 \ ETP(k-2) - 0.042 \ ETP(k-3)$$
$$+ \ 0.169$$

The MSE is 12.3 and the RME is 0.159

III B - Two seasonal models.

We know that the effect of a rainfall is different in the summer and in the winter. Indeed, in the summer, a high amount of water is intercepted by the vegetation and the dry soil. On the other hand, during the winter, the soil is satured and most of the rainfalls produce a high surface runoff. It is then interesting to use two different models, one for each season. We have found:

1) For the summer (May till October) :

$$Qp(k) = 1.20 \ Q(k-1) - 0.56 \ Q(k-2) + 0.25 \ Q(k-3)$$
$$+ \ 0.011 \ PB(k-1) + 0.023 \ PB(k-2) + 0.007 \ PB(k-3)$$
$$- \ 0.395$$

The MSE is 4.5 and the RME 0.187. Using the single model, we have found: MSE = 5.5 and   RME = 0.207

2) For the winter (November till April) :

$$Qp(k) = 1.40 \ Q(k-1) - 0.67 \ Q(k-2) + 0.18 \ Q(k-3)$$
$$+ \ 0.041 \ PB(k-1) + 0.047 \ PB(k-2) - 0.027 \ PB(k-3)$$
$$- \ 0.134$$

The MSE is 17.2 and the RME is 0.14. Using the single model, we have found:
MSE = 21.8 and   RME = 0.16

Using the two seasonal models, we find that the MSE averaged over the whole
year is 10.8 and the RME 0.149. Recall that with the single model we had obtained
a MSE of 12.7 and a RME of 0.162

The difference between the parameters of the summer and the winter proceeds
essentially from the saturation of the soil which plays an important role in
determining the fraction of the global rainfall that affects the river flow in the
next few days. In the following chapter, we will study a non linear model that
transforms the global rainfall PB into an assumed surface runoff PN, that will then
be used as the input of a difference equation model similar to those studied above.
By using this non linear transformation, we will take into account the seasonal
variations of the rainfall-river flow laws we have just observed.

IV - DETERMINATION OF AN ASSUMED SURFACE RUNOFF. [3],[4],[5]

IV A - The physical phenomena.

1) The amount of water PB of a rainfall can be decomposed as follows:

$$PB = PN + S + E \quad (a)$$

where:
- PN is the surface runoff, namely the fraction of running water,
- S is the amount of water that stays on the soil or that is intercepted by the
vegetation. Later on, this water will evaporate or infiltrate.
- E is the amount of water that evaporates during the rainfall.(E is usually low)

Let's call PN/PB the "running coefficient". It is an important characterist-
tic of a rainfall.

2) The physical laws that govern the value of the different terms in the water
balance (a), are complicated and it is difficult to determine them. We will note
the influence of the physical characteristics of the drainage basin such as the
slope, the vegetation, the soil composition, ... We also observe the influence of
the meteorological past: indeed, the rainfalls and the evapotranspiration of the
preceding days determine the soil moisture and therefore the laws of infiltration,
interception, running,... The characteristics of each rainfall are important and
snow or a frozen soil are also essential factors.

3) Beside the difficulty of the problem itself, the study is conducted on a drainage basin of 1229 km^2 where the physical characteristics are very diversified.
Secondly, we are working with daily data and therefore we have to express all the
terms of relation (a) on a daily basis (0.1 mm./day)
We will consequently search for a model that allows one to verify each day
the equilibrium relation (a) while at the same time taking into account the meteorological past. With this model, we will then compute an estimated surface runoff PN
which will be introduced as input in our river flow model.

IV B - The model for the computation of PN.

Each day, the following equilibrium relation has to be verified:

$$PB(k) = PN(k) + S(k) + ET(k)$$

where:
- PB(k) is the total amount of water precipitated on day k.(PB(k) is a mean value
computed for all the drainage basin but we can also build the same model with

localized data).
- PN(k) is the computed surface runoff on day k.
- S(k) is the part of the total rainfall PB(k) that is stored on the surface of
the soil.
- ET(k) is the part of the total rainfall PB(k) that is supposed to evaporate on
day k.

We will use in or model a soil reservoir that will be filled up by the rainfalls and emptied by the infiltration and the evapotranspiration.

Let us call:
- I(k), the amount of water that infiltrates on day k.
- ST(k), the total amount of water that is stored in the soil reservoir at the
end of the day k.
- STmax, the maximum storage capacity of the reservoir.

We now make the following assumptions:

1) When PB(k) is greater than ETP(k), the potential evapotranspiration on day k,
we put:
$$ET(k) = ETP(k)$$

and: $\quad\quad\quad S(k) = D(k-1).(1-e^{-P(k)/b})$

$$= B(k).D(k-1) \quad\quad \text{with:} \quad B(k) = 1-e^{-P(k)/b} \quad , \quad b \geqslant D(k-1)$$
$$D(k-1) = STmax - ST(k-1)$$
$$P(k) = PB(k) - ET(k)$$

Then: $\quad\quad\quad PN(k) = PB(k) - ET(k) - S(k)$

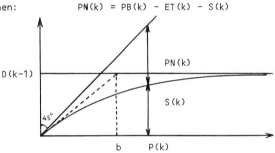

2) When PB(k) is less than ETP(k), we put:

$$ET(k) = PB(k)$$

and: $\quad\quad\quad S(k) = 0$

Then: $\quad\quad\quad PN(k) = 0$

3) Finally, we need a recursive relation for the computation of the daily storage
ST(k) that is needed to compute D(k).
Let us call:
$$DE(k) = ETP(k) - ET(k)$$

We can then propose the following recurrence relation for the amount of
storage:
$$ST(k) = ST(k-1) + S(k) - DE(k) - I(k)$$

With the following assumption for the infiltration:

$$I(k) = A.(ST(k-1) + S(k)) \quad \text{where} \quad A = Imax/STmax \; < \; 1$$

we can write: $ST(k) = (1-A).(ST(k-1) + S(k)) - DE(k)$

or: $ST(k) = (1-A).(ST(k-1) + B(k).D(k-1)) - DE(k)$ $(\star)$

IV C - Remarks.

1) This model is purely hypothetical and not physically proved although an expression similar to that given for S(k), has been obtained before for the interception by the vegetation.(see [4])

        Later on this paper we will appreciate the effectiveness of its prediction capabilities.

2) Three parameters have to be found: STmax, Imax, b .
For b, we can take different kinds of values such as:
        b = c (constant) $>$ STmax
        b = c.D(k-1) with c $>$ 1
We will chooze the value of these parameters such as to minimize the MSE.

3) It is important to observe that, when the weather is dry, S(k) is equal to zero, and ST(k) decreases quickly because of I(k) and the high value of DE(k). Thus the amount of stored water goes to zero. When it rains again, a high amount of water will be stored in the soil reservoir and at first the surface runoff will be low.
        On the other hand, with heavy rainfalls for a number of days, B(k) is close to one, ST(k) goes to (1-A).STmax, which means that the soil becomes satured, and hence the running coefficient PN/PB of our model becomes high.

4) It is interesting to note that on a given day, the running coefficient increases with the amount of precipitated water.

5) This model supposes that the evapotranspiration takes place at a potential rate, first from the rainfalls on day k, and later, from the stored water, when the potential evapotranspiration exeeds the amount of precipitated water.

6) When it rains on a frozen soil, we will take as initial conditions at day k:

$$D(k-1) = DN \; , \; \text{where DN has the value of a low storage capacity.}$$

This will lead to a high value of surface runoff.

IV D - Applications.

        The joined diagrams show for the year 1970 the set of data used and a computed surface runoff using b=D(k-1) and the optimal values STmax=1050 (0.1 mm.) and Imax=15 (0.1 mm./day). We see clearly that this computed surface runoff is very well related with the river flow. A model using PN as input, has been identified:

$$Qp(k) = 1.21 \; Q(k-1) - 0.48 \; Q(k-2) + 0.14 \; Q(k-3)$$

$$+ 0.075 \; PN(k-1) + 0.092 \; PN(k-2) - 0.034 \; PN(k-3)$$

$$+ 0.907$$

The MSE is now reduced to 7.8 and the RME to 0.127

$(\star)$ When DE(k) is greater than (1-A).(ST(k-1) + S(k)), we put:
                              $ST(k) = 0$

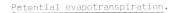

Potential evapotranspiration.

Precipited water.

20 mm./day

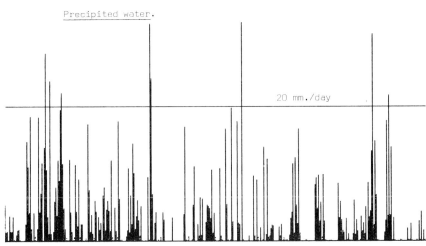

Supposed surface runoff.

20 mm./day

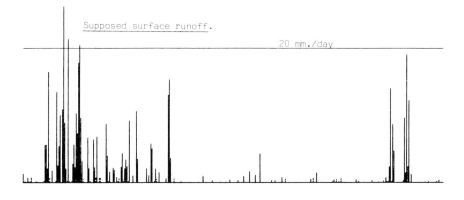

River flow.

SEMOIS RIVER-1970.

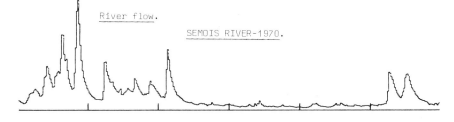

Because the dynamics of the studied process can change with the season, we will again consider seasonal models. We have:

- For the summer:

$$Qp(k) = 0.91 \ Q(k-1) - 0.28 \ Q(k-2) + 0.19 \ Q(k-3)$$

$$+ \ 0.065 \ PN(k-1) + 0.185 \ PN(k-2) + 0.048 \ PN(k-3)$$

$$+ \ 0.69$$

The MSE obtained is 2.4 and the RME 0.136. The single model give us: MSE = 3.4   and   RME = 0.162

- For the winter:

$$Qp(k) = 1.24 \ Q(k-1) - 0.49 \ Q(k-2) + 0.11 \ Q(k-3)$$

$$+ \ 0.080 \ PN(k-1) + 0.084 \ PN(k-2) - 0.040 \ PN(k-3)$$

$$+ \ 1.38$$

The MSE obtained is 12.1 and the RME is 0.119. The single model give us: MSE = 12.3 and   RME = 0.120

Using these two models together, the MSE averaged over the whole year, is 7.2 and the RME 0.122

V - EFFECT OF THE MEAN RAINFALL OF DAY k ON THE RIVER FLOW Q(k).

In the previous models, we have assumed that there was no instantaneous effect of PB or PN on the flow Q, since our models contain no term in PB(k) or PN(k). To examine what the effect of the surface runoff at day k would be on the river flow at the same day, we have identified a model that contains PN(k). This model is:

$$Qp(k) = 1.20 \ Q(k-1) - 0.47 \ Q(k-2) + 0.13 \ Q(k-3)$$

$$+ \ 0.006 \ PN(k)$$

$$+ \ 0.079 \ PN(k-1) + 0.090 \ PN(k-2) - 0.032 \ PN(k-3)$$

$$+ \ 0.93$$

The MSE is 7.6 . we see that the difference with the previous model is very small. Indeed the coefficient of PN(k) has a low value. (We must recall that the highest values of PN(k) are around 200 (0.1 mm.:day)). It means that PN(k) has a low effect. This fact would be different if we had used a set of localized values of PN .

CONCLUSION: as we have shown   , we have improved the quality of our models by computing a rainfall runoff while taking into account the meteorological past. As we can observe   on the diagrams, this method essentially removes from PB that part of the rainfall that does not contribute to an increase in the river flow. We have thus obtained a new input for the river flow prediction model, whereby the MSE has been substantially reduced. A further research will try to improve the quality of the models by using difference equations where the parameters are functions of the level of the surface runoff, the level of the flow,... We will also identify models with localized rainfalls as inputs.

[1] BULTOT, F. et DUPRIEZ, G.L. - Estimation des valeurs journalières de l'évapo-
    transpiration potentielle d'un bassin hydrographique. JL of Hydrology
    vol 21, Amsterdam, 1974.

[2] BULTOT, F. et DUPRIEZ, G.L. - Etude hydrométéorologique des précipitations
    sur les bassins hydrographiques belges.- I. Bassin de la Semois.
    Institut Royal Météorologique de Belgique, Publications, série A n°64.

[3] LARRAS, J. -Prévision et prédétermination des étiages et des crues. Eyrolles
    Paris (1972)

[4] BULTOT, F., DUPRIEZ, G.L., BODEUX, A. - Interception de la pluie par la
    végétation forestière. Estimation de l'interception journalière à l'
    aide d'un modèle mathématique. JL of Hydrology 17 (1972) 193-223.

[5] de MARSILY, G. - La relation pluie - débit dans le bassin versant de l'Hallue.
    Ecole nationale des mines de Paris, Centre d'informatique géolo-
    gique (77-Fontainebleau, 35 rue St Honoré) (1971).

[6] KASHYAP, R.L. et RAO, A.R. - Real time recursive prediction of river flows.
    Automatica 9 (1973) 175 - 183.

[7] YOUNG, P.C. - Applying parameter estimation to dynamic systems. Part 1
    Control engineering, oct 1969, 119 - 125.

[8] JENKINS, G.M. et BOX, G.E.P. - Time series analysis forecasting and control.
    Holden day 1970.

[9] CORLIER, F. - Modèle mathématique des débits journaliers de la Sambre.
    Faculté des sciences agronomiques de Gembloux. Belgique.

Current research field of author : *I am developing algorithms for river flow prediction. I am particularly interested in : real time recursive prediction methods of
river flows - algorithms for simultaneous estimation and classification in order to
represent the rainfall-runoff process by means of piecewise linear models - use
of adaptative methods to show off possible modifications in the rainfall-runoff process. I am presently testing one-day-ahead forecasts of the Semois river by using
the daily riverflow, rainfall and potential evapotranspiration data.*

Modeling and Simulation of Water Resources Systems, G.C. VANSTEENKISTE, (Ed.)
North-Holland Publishing Company (1975)

CONCEPT AND OPTIMIZATION OF A
DAILY STREAMFLOW MODEL

R. Bosman, F. De Smedt, G. Vandewiele and A. Van der Beken
Center of Statistics and Operational Research and
Institute of Environmental Sciences - Hydrology Section
Vrije Universiteit Brussel

ABSTRACT

Planning a water-reservoir in a catchment area should
be based upon a long time-series of discharge measurements. Unfortunately, these data are often only available for a short period.

A conceptual model was elaborated using daily precipitation, temperature and discharge measurements in order
to extend the discharge time-series.

Parameter optimization of eight parameters was made by
the "Pattern-search" method. The method was applied
to the data of a period of 6 years for the catchment
area of 115 km^2 of the river Zwalm, an affluent of the
Upper-Scheldt. The results are satisfactory as shown
in Table 1 and Fig. 5.

INTRODUCTION

For the planning of a water-reservoir it is necessary to dis-
pose of a long time-series of discharge measurements in order to make
valuable predictions.

Generally these data are not available or only for a relatively short period. This was the case for the preliminary study of a
project in the catchment-area of the river Zwalm, an affluent of the
Upper-Scheldt (Van der Beken and De Troch, 1973). At the mouth of
this river, gage-observations are made only since 1967. So we tried
to simulate discharge data in the past by correlating, by means of a
conceptual model, daily precipitation and temperature to daily discharge.

AVAILABLE DATA

Precipitation P(t)

Since 1951 daily precipitation observations are available from
five stations around the Zwalm-catchment-area. These data are used to
calculate, by means of the Thiessen-method, the total precipitation
over the catchment-area which has an area of 115,5 km^2. One will remark that no intensity observations are available and that consequently only total daily precipitation data are at our disposal.

Temperature T(t)

Also since 1951 we have the disposal of daily minimum and
maximum temperatures, observed in a station in the catchment-area.
For daily temperature we take the arithmetic mean of minimum and maximum.

Discharge Q(t)

In 1967 a limnimeter was installed near the mouth of the Zwalm. These measurements allow us to calculate, by means of a discharge-curve, the total discharge of the catchment area.

All three observations (precipitation, temperature and discharge) are made daily at 8 a.m. But, whereas the precipitation and temperature observations cover the 24 hours preceding the measurement, this clearly is not the case for the discharge observations. To avoid this incongruity the total discharge of a period of 24 hours is taken as the arithmetic mean of the discharges at the beginning and at the end of this period (see below).

THE MODEL

A conceptual model was developed in its first stage by De Smedt (1973). The output of the model is the total daily discharge, the input consists of precipitation and temperature data of the day in question and of all the previous days.

The elaboration of the model is based on several hydrological hypotheses about net-precipitation, losses and distribution of direct runoff and groundwater. This is illustrated by the flowchart in Fig. 1. The percentages which are mentioned are only tentative estimates.

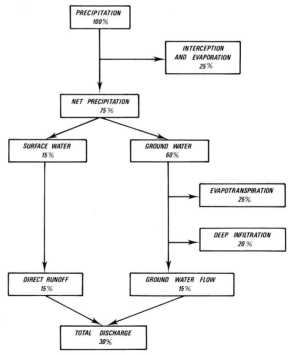

Fig. 1.   Flowchart of the conceptual model V.U.B.

Except for a stochastic part, the total discharge $A(t)$ is the sum of the groundwater base flow $A_G(t)$ and the direct runoff $A_D(t)$.

$A_G(t)$ is given by the following formula :

$$A_G(t) = \sum_{i=1}^{\infty} P(t-i)a_1^{T(t-i)}a_3^{\sum_{j=1}^{\infty} P(t-i-j)a_1^{T(t-i-j)}a_2^j} a_6 a_5^{i-1} a_7^{\sum_{j=1}^{i} T(t-j)} \tag{1}$$

$A_D(t)$ is given by :

$$A_D(t) = \sum_{i=1}^{\infty} P(t-i)a_1^{T(t-i)} \left(1 - a_3^{\sum_{j=1}^{\infty} P(t-i-j)a_1^{T(t-i-j)}a_2^j} \right) a_8 a_4^{i-1} \tag{2}$$

$0 < a_1, a_2, a_3, a_4, a_5, a_7 < 1 \qquad a_6, a_8 > 0$

a_1 is a parameter which describes the loss by interception and evaporation

a_2 is an anteprecipitation coefficient

a_3 regulates the splitting up into groundwater and surface water

a_4 and a_5 describe the recession part of the hydrograph

a_6 describes the loss by deep infiltration

a_7 describes the loss by evapotranspiration

a_8 describes the loss by evaporation of surface water

The fundamental hypotheses and corresponding derivations can be found in the unpublished thesis by De Smedt (1973). They will be published elsewhere in the near future.

In order to simulate daily discharge data it is necessary to assign values to the unknown parameters a_i (i = 1,8). Rough approximations of these parameter values can be derived from the percentages in Fig. 1 and from the study of the observed hydrographs. The optimal parameter values are calculated by means of an optimization technique, using the available discharge data : one tries to choose the parameter values so that the difference between calculated and observed discharge data becomes minimal. It is clear that this difference can be measured by several criteria.

PARAMETER OPTIMIZATION

For the determination of the optimal values of the parameters and of the criterion-function we use the Pattern-Search, a technique developed by Hooke and Jeaves (Wilde, 1964, p.145).

This choice can be justified as follows :
- no derivations are used;
- as we had no good idea of the shape of the criterion-surface we preferred a search-method which makes no special demands in connection with the shape;
- the calculations are easy;

- the method has a good reputation for minimization of a sum of squares criterion function.

The basic principle of the Pattern-Search is that one tries to follow the "valleys" of the criterion-surface as close as possible. Meanwhile the length of the steps increases as long as the direction followed seems to be successful.

We begin at a given starting point $\bar{b}_o$. In our case this will be the rough approximation of the eight parameter values. All the parameters are now perturbed one by one, i.e. the value of the first parameter is increased with a given amount δ_1. Using the new parameter values the value of the criterion function is calculated; if this value is smaller than in $\bar{b}_o$ we will continue from the new point; in the other case we go to the symmetrical point (parameter value minus δ_1) where we calculate the value of the criterion function again; if it is smaller than in $\bar{b}_o$ we continue from the new point, otherwise we return to the original point $\bar{b}_o$. This procedure is repeated successively for all the parameters. At the end of this "local search" we are in a new "base" point $\bar{b}_1$.

The direction from $\bar{b}_o$ to $\bar{b}_1$ seems to be successful. Therefore we will double the step from $\bar{b}_o$ to $\bar{b}_1$ so that we arrive in a new so-called "temporary" point $\bar{t}_1$. $\bar{t}_1$ is determined by

$$\bar{t}_1 = \bar{b}_1 + (\bar{b}_1 - \bar{b}_o) = 2\bar{b}_1 - \bar{b}_o \tag{3}$$

In $\bar{t}_1$ we start a new local search which brings us to a new base-point $\bar{b}_2$. Here we jump to a new temporary point $\bar{t}_2 = 2\bar{b}_2 - \bar{b}_1$, etc...

It is clear that, when reaching a minimum or crossing a valley, we might jump too far. This means that we cannot find a new base-point which is better than the last one. In that case we return to the last base-point, reduce the exploratory steps δ_1 and start again the whole procedure.

The iterations will end when the increment of the value of the criterion function becomes insignificant. The flowchart of the computer-program, given in Fig. 2 will make it all clear.

The criterion function which was optimized is the sum of squares of the deviations

$$SSQ = \Sigma \left[\ln Q(t) - \ln A(t) \right]^2 \tag{4}$$

By taking the logarithms we diminish the variation on a measurement of a peak-discharge relatively to the variation on a measurement of a low-discharge. One then can argue on the assumption that the variances are all the same. This is useful when the conceptual model is considered as a regression model (see next paragraph).

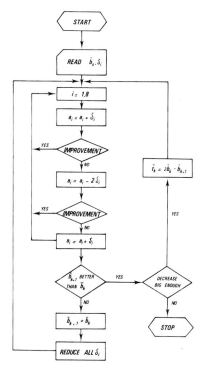

Fig. 2. Flowchart of the pattern-search method

RESULTS

The optimization by Pattern-Search was done by a computer program on the Brussels Free University CDC 6500. The whole optimization was accomplished in 3072 sec. For administrative reasons this was done in two runs of 1536 sec. each. It takes 160 iterations to reach the optimum. Remark that this means that the increment of the criterion function value falls below a given limit. At that moment all parameter values were not yet stabilized. This is illustrated in the graphs of Fig. 3.

The SSQ-value, however, is stabilized very soon as can be seen in Fig. 4. The E-value is a measure of efficiency, proposed by Nash (Watt and Hsu, 1970), and defined as follows :

$$E = \frac{U^o - U}{U^o} \qquad (5)$$

where

$$U^o = \sum_t \left[\frac{Q(t) - \bar{Q}}{Q(t)} \right]^2 \text{ is the so-called no-model error}$$

and

$$U = \sum_t \left[\frac{A(t) - Q(t)}{Q(t)} \right]^2 \text{ is the model error.}$$

Q is the arithmetic mean of all Q(t).

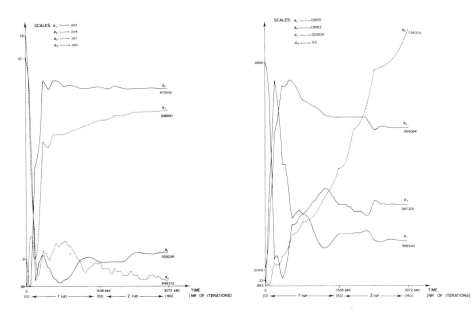

Fig. 3.   Evolution of the parameters a_i

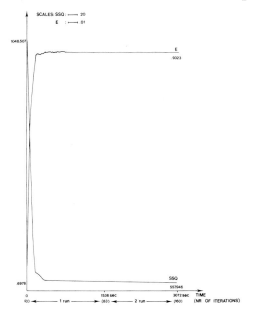

Fig. 4.   Evolution of the criterion function SSQ
and the efficiency E

The starting and end values of the eight parameters of the criterion function and of E is given in Table 1.

Table 1. Starting and end values of parameters a_i, SSQ and E

	a_1	a_2	a_3	a_4	a_5
Starting values	.971	.9	.98	.78	.983
End values	.929206	.972938	.998881	.648313	.987325
	a_6	a_7	a_8	SSQ	E
Starting values	.0045	.9995	.22	1048.507	.6978
End values	.009094	.998540	1.56325	557.946	.9323

Note that, when the discharge data are not modified by averaging as mentioned in the second paragraph, the results are inferior. The SSQ value becomes 668 while the E-value drops to .9182.

An example of the simulated daily discharges in comparison to the observed daily discharges is shown in Fig. 5.

CONCLUSION

Although the results presented in this paper cannot be accepted as fully satisfactory, they are well comparable to many other published results in the realm of discharge simulation. Useless to say that the model should be developed further in its conceptual aspects. The main advantage, however, is that only daily precipitation and temperature data are used as input to the model. Therefore, the model can be applied very easily to all drainage basins where discharge measurements are available only for a short period.

We already mentioned that the model can be considered as a non-linear regression model. It is our intention to use the end values of the Pattern-Search as starting point for the application of an iterative linear regression method. An important advantage of this procedure will be that it allows to determine confidence intervals for the parameter values. At the present time results of this method are not yet available.

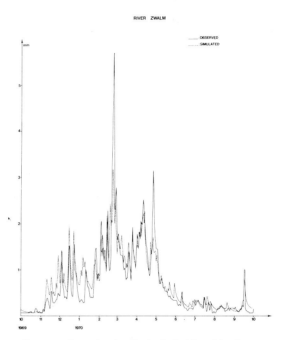

Fig. 5.   Observed and simulated daily discharges
           for the hydrological year 1970

REFERENCES

De Smedt, F. (1973). Statistische studie van de relatie neerslag-
    afvoer toegepast op het waterbekken van de Zwalm (A statisti-
    cal study of the rainfall-runoff relationship, applied to the
    drainage basin of the Zwalm). Unpublished thesis, Faculty of
    Applied Sciences, Vrije Universiteit Brussel, 145 pp.

Van der Beken, A. and De Troch, F. (1973). De simulatie van de af-
    voer in het waterbekken van de Zwalm volgens verschillende me-
    thodes (The simulation of the discharge in the drainage basin
    of the Zwalm according to different methods). Revue-C-Tijd-
    schrift, Brussel, vol. VI, N° 6/7 : 161-174.

Watt, W.E. and Hsu, C.T. (1970). Continuous basin snowmelt runoff
    simulation. Hydrology Symposium N°8, vol. 2. National Re-
    search Council of Canada. Subcommittee on Hydrology.

Wilde, D.J. (1964). Optimum seeking methods. Prentice Hall, Inc.
    N.J. 202 pp.

DISCUSSION

I would like to stress that this model has an advantage of using only daily measurements. This is usual for Belgium : we have only daily measurements and discharges. Other comment : there is an essential difference between this model and the classical models of the Stanford type. The functions are continuous functions. The classical models use reservoir type equations, so they are not continuous. If you would like linear regression methods, you need derivatives and the Stanford model types cannot be used. Other comment : we use logarithmic transformation for the discharge. I think from the hydrological point of view it is necessary to use logarithmic transformation because the standard deviations of the measurements are certainly not equal in the whole range of discharge measurements. Last comment : the calibration has been done for 6 years. We have seen other calibrations done for one year, so I think we could come up with a much better result if we should calibrate the model on 1 year, but I think it's useless to do this for hydrological reasons. You certainly have to take into account longer periods. Moreover, we were in a very bad position. We started in 1967 which was influenced by the bad years 1965, and 1966, but we did not have any data on these years as far as discharge measurements are concerned. (VAN DER BEKEN)

I did not quite follow your point that you were identifying 8 parameters from a set of 2 000 observations. Yes, the last curve you had, the fit was only good in some points, not in others. Had this to do with the errors in your data ? (SHAH)

The ordinates are logarithmic, so the fitting might be not so bad. (BOSMAN)

I think the log-transformation is a very good point, but in my country we would like to know the flood first of all. Therefore you could argue that it might be better not to do it. (PHILIP)

The purpose of the model is not a flood model ; it is only a water yield model, applicable for water reservoir design. (VAN DER BEKEN)

Speaking from the operational research side I am interested in the way the criterion functions change very rapidly over the first few iterations ; and then they seem very intensive to a change in parameters except for this one parameter where it really shocked off. Would you like to comment on this. Is it a fault in the model, which would raise the question : is this realistic ?

We hoped it was realistic. But the physical meaning showed us that there must be some errors in the model. We shall try to study the model further on. (BOSMAN)

Specifically, could you say why you choose to stop at some 3 000 instead of let's say 500 sec, when the criterion function seems to be going on to the end. And indeed, conversely why stop now when your parameter a_8 is still going up.

a_3 and a_8 don't stabilise due to the structure of the phauna. We are not satisfied with this. I think we should use instead of antiprecipitation index, the net precipitation, we should use antiprecipitation index with the groundwater. This can be done with pattern search methods. We started with linear regression method initially however. We should adapt our model so that a_3 and a_8 are balancing each other. (VAN DER BEKEN)

You say it is a water yield model. Looking at that hydrograph form, the input of the reservoir would not be very happy from the water yield point of view. It seems from the water balance over the year, that quite a bit more water is simulated than what actually would have flown into the reservoir. The initial recharge period is overestimated quite substantially but even at the recession period it is still overestimated. So there is a net overestimation over the whole year.

If there is an error it is certainly an underestimation.

Modeling and Simulation of Water Resources Systems, G.C. VANSTEENKISTE, (Ed.)
North-Holland Publishing Company (1975)

COMPARISON OF METHODS OF SIMULATING A DOLOMITIC AQUIFER

J. R. Hely-Hutchinson*, J. M. Schutte** and P. C. J. L. de Lange*

ABSTRACT

The hydraulic action of a dolomitic aquifer was represented on four media.

Empirical and physical functions were included in the models, whose basic purpose was to indicate the reaction of borehole water levels to rainfall, drainage and pumpage. One method of solution consisted only of calculation, while the other three also involved interactive refinement. In view of the geological complexity of the aquifer, the output curves were considered to fit the data satisfactorily.

The models served firstly to cross-check field readings derived from many types of instrument and method; secondly to estimate hard-to-measure quantities, and thirdly to predict responses to unusual conditions of rain= fall and pumpage. Clues were incidentally provided to the existence of unforeseen geological features, and pointers arose to errors in data.

The properties of the individual methods were compared, and an improved medium was proposed.

INTRODUCTION

Dolomitic limestone aquifers constitute valuable sources of water in many parts of the world. In some semi-arid regions of Southern Africa, they form the main water supplies for rural towns with growing populations (2). In the area under investigation, the Grootfontein compartment serves a farming district and a municipality of some 32 000 inhabitants.

Until recently, no limits were set to the quantity of groundwater abstracted by farmers. It has however been estimated that nearly half the average annual recharge is at present used for irrigation. Future development of pumpage has therefore been restricted while an assessment is made of the water potential. The large storage capacity of the aquifer, and broad variability in annual recharge, led the responsible scientists to analyse the hydraulic processes with the aid of dynamic models, whose main objects were as follows:

1. to cross-check readings taken by several types of instrument and method,
2. to estimate quantities, such as seepage, which are hard to measure directly,
3. to predict responses to unusual events and conditions.

The maximum dimensions of the aquifer are roughly 12 and 25 km (Fig 1), and the material consists of both soil and rock. The soil areas on the surface are covered by vegetation, mostly the result of arable farming. The boundaries of the groundwater compartment below consist of diabase dykes, and the slope of the

* of the National Electrical Engineering Research Institute, Council for Scientific and Industrial Research, Pretoria, Republic of South Africa.
** of the Hydrological Research Institute, Department of Water Affairs, Pretoria, Republic of South Africa.

phreatic surface is about one in a thousand.   The permeability of the underlying
dolomite is in the region of 0,2 mm/s, which is of the same order as that of sand,
while the effective porosity, at approximately 3%, is much lower.   Diffusion
coefficients are thus large.

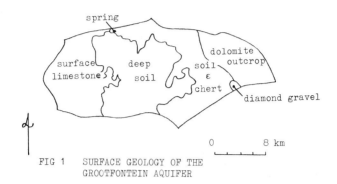

FIG 1   SURFACE GEOLOGY OF THE
         GROOTFONTEIN AQUIFER

    Complications arose in creating models, because the textures of both rock
and soil vary greatly.   Furthermore, the dolomite outcrops in some places,
while in others, the overburden runs deep.   Such complexity made it hard to
simulate the aquifer in terms of a model based entirely on physical principles,
and lack of detailed information indicated the advantages of interactive refine=
ment.

FORMULATION OF THE PROCESSES

    The physical processes were represented as follows.

    Interception was deduced, for specific types of vegetation, from
monthly figures of rainfall and rainfall-days.   Evapotranspiration was derived
from similar figures, and also from pan-evaporation tests.   Run-off was restrict=
ed to very wet years, and was subtracted, together with interception, from gross
precipitation.   Evapotranspiration served to reduce topsoil moisture (Fig 2).

    The zone of aeration embraces the soilwater, pellicular and capillary regions
Its response was observed over a period of ten days after a heavy rainfall event.
It was found that a saturated layer sank from the soil-surface to a depth which
varied from two to seven meters, depending on location.   Such variations in downward
flowrate were believed to arise from the presence of semi-permeable strata within
the overburden.   These serve to delay the transmission of water in a manner which
it is hard to predict, due to difficulties in pinpointing their locations and
extents.

    The chosen representation of seepage through topsoil involved rapid infill
to a given level of saturation.   Thereafter, water enters the pellicular region,
the assumed mechanism of which took the form of a delay, whose distribution in
time was weighted, during refinement, to fit observed recharge characteristics.
In the second model, the delay consisted of independently set monthly coefficients,
and in the fourth, a first order decay (Fig 2).

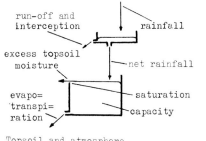

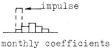

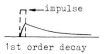

Topsoil and atmosphere   Pellicular region

FIG 2   REPRESENTATIONS OF UPPER LEVELS

Water seeps thence to the capillary region, which is often ignored in a dolomitic aquifer.   In the following models, it was regarded as part of the zone of saturation.

There is no known general analytical solution to the equation of the phreatic surface, which forms the upper boundary of the zone.   Practical solutions are realised on solid media, and by numerical methods.   In the simulations de= scribed below, it was modelled in discrete space, the action of each discrete segment obeying the following law:

$$\dot{Z}_i = \sum_j \left[\frac{pdb_{ij}}{SC_i} \cdot \frac{(Z_j - Z_i)}{L_{ij}} \right] - I_i$$

where

Z_i represents the water level in segment i

Z_j represents the level in adjacent segments j

L_{ij} represents the effective distance between i and j

d is the effective depth of the aquifer

b_{ij} is the length of the intersegment boundary

C_i is the geographical area of the segment

S is the effective porosity

I_i is the net rate of change of head due to recharge and pumpage

p is permeability

This equation may be represented in either analog (Fig 3) or digital form (see page 7).

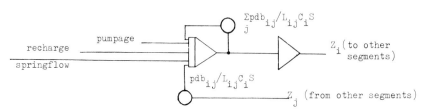

FIG 3   ·ANALOG MODEL OF GROUNDWATER SEGMENT   (unscaled)

INFORMATION RELEVANT TO THE MODELS

The information on which the hydrological models were based may be classi=
fied as follows:

1.   Directly measured data, comprising rainfall, pumpage, springflow and
     waterlevels.
2.   Inferred quantities, relating to recharge, interception, evapo=
     transpiration, seepage, run-off and recharge delay.
3.   Material investigations, leading to the estimation of permeability,
     transmissivity, effective porosity, topsoil depth, topsoil saturation
     and dyke locations.

As sometimes occurs in investigations of this type, deductions were re=
quired from the models before a systematic data-gathering facility could be
organised (6).   With regard to the authority of the available information, it is
noteworthy that the raingauges, observation boreholes and pumpage points are
distributed irregularly over the area (Fig 4).

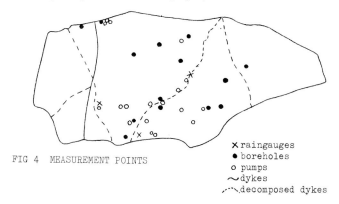

FIG 4   MEASUREMENT POINTS

✗ raingauges
● boreholes
○ pumps
∼ dykes
⁓ decomposed dykes

Full records of rainfall and springflow have been compiled over a period
of eight years.   Some variations have been noted between readings from different
raingauges, but this was not considered serious enough to invalidate the use of
values averaged over the whole compartment.   Pumpage records are complete for
three quarters of the period, but there are many gaps in figures relating to
water levels, gaps which occur at random intervals.   Computation problems were
however alleviated by the fact that such levels were used as boundary
values.

Data were edited and corrected where they could not be explained in terms of normally accepted hydraulic processes, and where, in addition, non-hydraulic explanations could be advanced. Examples included boreholes in which readings were influenced by windpumps, the local effect of which might render the measure= ments unrepresentative of the segments to which they were meant to apply. Other suspected sources of error included false recordings, due to say transposition of numerals or substitution or misalignment of charts. About 10% of the data were eventually rejected on these grounds. Such omissions are continually re= examined as fresh evidence becomes available from instruments and models.

Inferred quantities were regarded as of lower fidelity, and altered more freely during refinement. Interception and evapotranspiration were estimated, as explained above, from rainfall-days and other data. Seepage into and out of the compartment was assessed partly from the models, partly from changes in groundwater level on either side of a boundary, and partly by observing the re= action time of a nearby sinkhole.

The nature of the material was analysed at spot points by means of core samples, but the spatial relevance of these samples was difficult to assess in a fragmented composition. Pump tests and magnetometer readings provided informa= tion on permeability, porosity and soil depth averaged over a wider area.

ORGANISATION OF THE SIMULATIONS

In order to render a model derived from such information relevant to as many types of climate as possible, the simulation period was selected to include a broad range of weather conditions. This provision was considered important in view of the empirical nature of some of the included functions. The span from 1965 to 1972 embraces two heavy recharge events and an intervening series of drier years. The first of the major recharges occurred long enough after the start for the impact of significant errors in estimating soilwater initial condi= tions to have greatly diminished. The span was not broad enough to encompass more than one of the six-year climatic cycles indicated in the time series analysis (page 7), or any of the eleven year cycles indicated in long-term records of waterlevel (2).

The action of the aquifer, which is partly serial, can be conveniently split into two stages, representing the conversion of rainfall to recharge, and the conversion of recharge and pumpage to waterlevels respectively. While it was an advantage to refine the models as single units, this was not considered essen= tial, as many of the responses to recharge events could in practice be differentiated from those due mainly to pumpage or drainage.

The ground plans of the three interactive models were subdivided into some 16 segments. The sizes, shapes and locations of these were selected according to a compromise between regularity of grid, influence of observation and abstraction boreholes, and boundaries of areas of like geological material. Changes in ground= water slope gave possible indications of changes in influence and composition.

FAST HYBRID MODEL

The first constructed model was confined to the zone of saturation, and programmed on a compact hybrid machine. The ground plan was divided into lozenges of equal size, with two sides parallel to the groundwater contours. Forcing functions, which at this stage covered a period of only four years, were stored in the digital section of the computer in respect of recharge, which was estima= ted by observing changes in waterlevel in a nearby sinkhole. The phreatic sur= face was simulated on the analog section.

Hybrid models possess the main advantages of rapid solution of differential equations and also, in the case of compact machines, ease of interaction. Problems may arise, in analog programming, in respect of scaling, but not so markedly in connection with simulands such as the present one, in which interrelationships between the main values (waterlevels) were of direct interest to the client. These values thus needed to be simultaneously displayed to the same scale.

The digital section was programmed in ASSEMBLER. Due to the speed of this low level language, responses could be portrayed in quasi-static form, and levels simulated at each instant in time were thus matched simultaneously to the data. Refinement was completed quickly, and some of the generated curves were found to fit closely. It was however deduced that parameters over and above transmissivity and effective porosity could be added to the model to improve the fit. The need for extra parameters threw additional light on the structure of the aquifer it= self. In brief, it was inferred that:

1.   the transfer function between rainfall and recharge varied greatly in time and volume over the area (Fig 5),

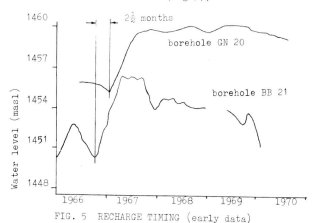

FIG. 5   RECHARGE TIMING (early data)

2.   an extra dyke was probably present near the centre of the area,
3.   the previously assumed value of the diffusion coefficient should be greatly reduced,
4.   several streams and occlusions were present.

INTERACTIVE HYBRID MODEL

In order to provide easier manipulation of the parameters, the upper stage of the model was then programmed in BASIC (4). The object of this second simu= lation was to establish analogues of as many hydraulic functions as possible. A digital algorithm was added to the previous groundwater simulation, to repre- sent the transfer function from net rainfall to recharge. This addition enabled the response of the zone of aeration to be more closely investigated, and several non-linear effects were added to the analog program. Digital to analog conversion was slowed down by a factor of 50 to 1, and thus solution of the groundwater equations was completed in a matter of seconds, so the display was not quasi- static; but owing to the ease of programming in BASIC, refinement was again rapid. A closer fit was achieved to the data, but this was partly due to the inclusion of seepage effects defined empirically with regard to both level and time, which could not be used for predictive purposes.

The main deduction, in respect of hydraulics, was the possible presence of semi-permeable strata in the overburden. Some changes were also made to the seep= age pattern, and tentative predictions were advanced as to the effect of great= ly increasing pumpage. Certain inexplicable curve-shapes pointed to errors in data-gathering procedures. It was in fact found that portions of one response had been substituted from a different borehole.

TIME SERIES ANALYSIS

In view of the fact that parts of both the above simulations were derived from performance figures rather than physical principles, it was decided to in= vestigate the properties of a purely empirical method, namely time series analysis. In the ensuing exploratory study, characteristic frequencies and relationships were determined in respect of rainfall, pumpage and springflow.

The autocorrelation of pumpage exhibited a marked periodicity of 12 months, which was probably determined mainly by the planting season.   Rainfall and springflow are not so strongly cyclic.   Rainfall data tend to repeat at intervals of both 11 and 13 months, and thus to generate interference once every 6 years.

Cross-correlation highlights time-lags of roughly 4 months between rain= fall and springflow, 5 months between pumpage and springflow, and 9 months be= tween rainfall and pumpage.   The last of these relationships may merely confirm that the planting season usually occurs three months before maximum rainfall.

The response of springflow to an impulse of rain was checked (Fig 6) against the reaction of the fourth model to a similar stimulus.

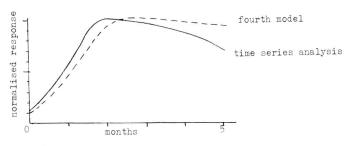

FIG 6   IMPULSE RESPONSE

DIGITAL MODEL

By the time that the fourth model was programmed, the authority of the data had been more clearly established, and its volume expanded.   Interception was added to the representation of the upper levels, and the mechanism of recharge, stretching as far down as the lower edge of the soilwater region, was programmed in BASIC.   The long-term correctness of this program is supported by analyses of tritium profiles (1).   Seepage effects were no longer represented empirically in time.

The mechanisms of the pellicular and groundwater regions were modelled in SIM, a digital language suitable for compiling on a minicomputer (5).   Inter= action with the dedicated machine was found to be good; programming was easy and repeatability was, as expected in a digital program, absolute.   A further advantage concerned diffusion, a function which often,on an analog com= puter, is defined by means of both an input and a feedback potentiometer (Fig 3). On a digital computer, it can be modified by means of a single instruction. However, execution was slow, each run of the zone of saturation consuming between one and four minutes.   The model was thus not as simple as the first two to tune.

The deviation between the simulated points $(\hat{y})$ and the 489 approved measure= ments of waterlevel (y) in all boreholes, may be expressed as follows:

$$\sqrt{\frac{\Sigma(y-\hat{y})^2}{489}} \;=\; 403 \text{ mm, or } 6.7\% \text{ of maximum range } (6\text{ m}).$$

The standard error of the approved borehole measurements was assessed from engineering considerations at 50 mm, and those of other measurements at from 5 to 50% of reading.   Examples of measured and simulated curves are shown in Fig 7.

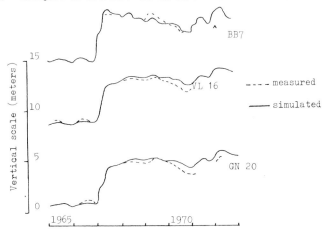

FIG 7   BOREHOLE RESPONSES

FULFILMENT OF PURPOSE

The functions for which the models were originally intended, namely:

1.   cross-checks on field-readings,
2.   estimates of hard-to-measure quantitites,
3.   prediction of responses to unusual stimuli,

were thus realised in practice.   Readings from raingauges, radiation counters, magnetometers, flowmeters and wattmeters (on electric pumps) were cross-checked.   Indications were obtained in respect of quantities such as seep= age, which are difficult to assess from direct measurements.   The final model has been used for predicting responses to normal and excessive pumpage during a series of particularly dry seasons, and to several other types of condition.

With regard to the validity of such predictions, the most markedly empirical functions in the described models are in the upper levels, yet the simulated rises in waterlevel seem to have fitted reasonably well· Thus this part of the structure may be considered reliable.

The zone of saturation was modelled according to physical principles, which appear intrinsically more dependable than empirical formulae.   During the drier years, when recharge did not predominate, fair correspondence with the data was also obtained.   Smallest deviations occurred for the Western half of the aquifer, where the main farms lie.   Thus, for practical purposes, the action of the zone seems to be usefully represented.

Therefore the total model might provide useful indications of flow and waterlevels over periods similar climatically to the above, if such forecasts commence at least one simulated year after the initial conditions for invisible functions are set.

With regard to information, it appeared that the most significant types of data concerned rainfall, pumpage, waterlevels and springflow.   It was helpful that these were available over a period during which precipitation varied greatly, but the uneven distribution of observation boreholes was a dis= advantage.   Other information was generally used only in support of findings, but became crucial in the case of the external seepage pattern, for which two equally promising models were proposed. A choice was eventually made between them on the basis of evidence from core samples and magnetometer tests.

MERITS OF METHODS

It emerged that, in spite of the relative paucity and unreliability of the early data, the main qualitative results were learned from the first two simu= lations. Hence it may be deduced that none of the individual methods is subject to fundamental problems. As is usual in computer based analyses, pointers arose at the start as to what to emphasise in succeeding data-logging and -processing. However, it must be borne in mind that exact figures derived from initial models are in many cases misleading, and this underlines the need for a more exhaustive study, after such results have been scrutinised.

The apparent properties of the media themselves are summarised in the following table:

	ASSEMBLER/ ANALOG (1)	BASIC/ ANALOG (2)	TIME SERIES (3)	BASIC/SIM (4)
Advantages	very rapid solution	fair speed, easy refine= ment, easy programming	determines periodicities	potential accuracy, repeatability, easy programming, easy expansion
Disadvantages	tough pro= gramming, coarse model, two-pot problems, limited size	limited size, two-pot problems	not inter= active as used	slow execution, slow refinement

It seems to the authors that the least significant of these properties is accuracy. Only rough indications are required for the problem under investiga= tion. Flexibility, as provided by models 1, 2 and 4, helped to counter the initial lack of knowledge of the simuland. Repeatability bridged gaps in discontinuous work. A dynamic simulation seemed essential in view of the rele= vance of response time. Interactive refinement had a strong educational value. Ease of programming and modification spurred progress, as did speed of solution.

Thus a stored record of structure is important. It would be an advantage to vary parameters defined by more than one machine coefficient during inter= active refinement, a function which could be carried out through a background/ foreground system. A quasi-static display aids modification, and might profit from added symbology.

It is felt that a technologically advanced hybrid, with a complement of digital coefficient units, digitally set non-linear elements and hand potentio= meters, and a background/foreground system, would possess sufficient speed and accuracy to enable the whole of this sort of simulation to be interactively analysed. As less than 20 integrators are required to obtain a close fit, set= ting-up time should not prove excessive. Scaling of a model whose main outputs are of similar type, simultaneously displayed, should be straightforward.

By the use of such a system, it is believed that the above type of problem could be simply programmed, and rapidly refined to a conclusion.

ACKNOWLEDGEMENTS

The authors are specially indebted to Mr D. Bredenkamp of the Hydrological Research Institute, who provided data, suggestions and interpretations through= out the investigation; to Mr M. Mulder of the same organisation, who submitted

records of rain and waterlevel; to Mr J. Filter of the National Electrical
Engineering Research Institute, who carried out the time series analysis; and
to Mr C. Neethling, formerly of the same organisation and now a Doctoral student
at the University of Cambridge, who programmed and refined the first model.

REFERENCES

1.   Bredenkamp, D.B., Schutte, J.M. ε Du Toit, G.J.   Recharge of a dolomitic
      aquifer as determined from Tritium profiles, IAEA conference, Vienna,
      1974.

2.   Bredenkamp, D.B. ε Vogel, J.C. Study of a dolomitic aquifer with Carbon
      14 and Tritium, IAEA conference, Vienna, 1970

3.   Claborn, E.J. ε Moore, W.L. Numerical simulation of watershed hydrology,
      Texas University, 1970

4.   Hely-Hutchinson, J.R. Design and performance of a hybrid computing system
      based on a minicomputer, SACAC symposium on minicomputers, 1973

5.   Rubin, O. ε Dehning, R. The use of a minicomputer for simulating con=
      tinuous systems, SACAC symposium on minicomputer, 1973

6.   Weber, J.E., Kisiel, C.C. ε Duckstein, L. On the mismatch between data
      and models of hydrologic and water resource systems, Water Resources
      Bulletin, December 1973

DISCUSSION

*Could you elaborate in some more detail on your choice of digital versus
analog workload of the computation scheme ? (VANSTEENKISTE)*

Rainfall is extremely seasonal - you get periods of very heavy recharge and
periods when recharge is not significant so it is very convenient to refine the two
regions separately, you can refine this region during a period of recession, and this
during heavy recharge. The other thing is that the functions here, appear to be inferior it is possible to simplify quite a lot, which is more naturally suited to
the digital computer. (HELY-HUTCHINSON)

Which time scale have you used ? (D'HOLLANDER)

About ten milliseconds in the first simulation (simple analog) for 5 to 6
years, and this enabled us to use a quasi static display which means you display
the whole of the characteristics at once and when you alter one part you could see
the effect on the other part. For the others, we used a slow moving display because
the program is so slow on the digital. So when you want to alter manually, you have
to repeat the program to see what the effect was. (HELY-HUTCHINSON)

Current research field of author : *The work of the Division includes small to medium sized simulations on Analog, Digital, Hybrid and semi-automatic Laplace media,
in close co-operation with customers in the medical, hydrological, electrical, mechanical and other fields.*

Modeling and Simulation of Water Resources Systems, G.C. VANSTEENKISTE, (Ed.)
North-Holland Publishing Company (1975)

STABILITY OF THE SOLUTION OF WATER FLOW IN AN HETEROGENEOUS AQUIFER

Salvatore Troisi
Water Research Institute
C.N.R. Laboratory of Bari - ITALY

ABSTRACT

One of the most important problems in the evaluation of the peculiarities of a non-homogeneous aquifer concerns the distribution of the transmissivity. Such a term is indeed necessary primarily for the application of some appropriate techniques in the management of underground water resources.

This is a global approach that may be converted into a problem of parameter identification, in which the structure of the differential equation, describing the phenomenon under investigation, is known, as well as the behaviour of the independent variable, while the coefficients of the same differential equation are the unknowns to be determined.

This kind of equation refers to a fictitious representation of physical phenomena and, in order to avoid errors or misinterpretation it must comply with some specific and fundamental requests.

INTRODUCTION

In dealing with the underground water resources, some scientists have focused their attention on the problem of water flowing through fissured rocks. This field of research has not been sufficiently considered in the past, either be cause of the intrinsic difficulties to refer in quantitative terms complicated natural phenomena, or because appropriate methodological instruments were not available for the evaluation of the characteristic parameters.

Due to the increasing demand of water, two main ways have been developed : the former enables us to develop new "in loco" experimental techniques for the fissured aquifers, especially in limestone soils, the latter consists of the formulation of new methodologies and new calculation techniques.

This latter topic will be treated in this report.

By the way, we like to mention that in the field of underground waters management, the effort to carry out in mathematical terms real complex situations is not often followed by practical applications of the results as it appears in many other technological fields.

BASIC EQUATIONS

When in a fissured aquifer the identification of a triorthogonal system of fissures is possible and the main coordinating axes belong to the fracture planes (and the step and the fissure width are constant in all directions) as it is well known, the equations for the isotopic homogeneous and porous systems can be applied.

In confined aquifer of constant thickness, E, after combining the continuity equation with the equation of motion we obtain

$$\frac{\partial^2 \phi}{\partial x^2} + \frac{\partial^2 \phi}{\partial y^2} + \frac{\partial^2 \phi}{\partial z^2} = \frac{S}{T} \frac{\partial \phi}{\partial t} \tag{1}$$

where, $S = m\gamma(\beta + \frac{\alpha}{m})$ E, JACOB (1949), is the nondimensional coefficient of storage and $T = K E$, is transmissivity of the aquifer. Similarly, in the case of homogeneous and anisotropic aquifer of constant thickness E we can obtain :

$$T_{xx} \frac{\partial^2 \phi}{\partial x^2} + T_{yy} \frac{\partial^2 \phi}{\partial y^2} + T_{zz} \frac{\partial^2 \phi}{\partial z^2} = S \frac{\partial \phi}{\partial t} \tag{2}$$

where T_{xx}, T_{yy}, T_{zz} are the components of the tensor of transmissiving along the main coordinating axes. All the previous equations can properly apply also so confined aquifers.

When the variations of the water table are neglegible as compared to the aquifer thickness, for an homogeneous and isotropic unconfined aquifer we have :

$$\frac{\partial^2 \phi}{\partial x^2} + \frac{\partial^2 \phi}{\partial y^2} + \frac{\partial^2 \phi}{\partial z^2} = \frac{m_e}{T} \frac{\partial \phi}{\partial t} \tag{1'}$$

and for an anisotropic unconfined aquifer

$$T_{xx} \frac{\partial^2 \phi}{\partial x^2} + T_{yy} \frac{\partial^2 \phi}{\partial y^2} + T_{zz} \frac{\partial^2 \phi}{\partial z^2} = m_e \frac{\partial h}{\partial t} \tag{2'}$$

where m_e is the effective nondimensional porosity.

These equations may have many solutions, rigorous or approximate, a following the different initial and boundary conditions.

To be more precise, in the case of an unconfined aquifer we should also consider the vertical flow motivated by the downward displacement of the water table as well as the partial leak of the aquifer. To treat similar aspects some attempts have been made, but up today, there are not yet available equation for the simultaneous treatement. Recent studies have been carried out about the accuracy of the solutions with simplified hypothesis, but the results, cannot be yet immediately utilized.

HOMOGENEITY

The study of the hydrodynamic aspects contained in the quoted equation has been already performed (1) and we want now to treat briefly the concept of the hydrogeological homogeneity. This is indeed one of the basic hypothesis, by means of which the formulation of the analytical equations valids either for porous or fissured aquifers has been possible.

As it is known, the hydrodynamic behaviour of an hydrogeological system depends both on the physical characteristics, tied to the concepts of isotropy, and on the homogeneity. The formed is an intrinsic characteristic of the medium, the latter applies only to a definite volume of the aquifer.

In fact, it is possible to assume a mean value of the physical characteristics, only if the sizes of the rock masses are sufficiently great.

The first cause of a non-homogeneity lies on the real porous medium, due to the simultaneous presence of full and empty spaces (interior structure of the medium). The second cause is due to the different lithological characteristics or chaotic order of the fractures. The last cause is due to the geological structure of the aquifer.

It appears therefore very helpful to recall the concept of "homogeneity scale".

This can be defined as the smalles elementary volume of the aquifer in which it is possible to prove the homogeneity.

The "homogeneity scale" expresses the practical possibility for the application of the fundamental equations of the underground flow since they can be applied only for rock masses greates than aquifer's characteristic homogeneity scale.

It could happen that some soil anomalies, even analytically descrivable, must be disregarded, if the phenomenon is in a smaller size than the homogeneity scale : this is one of the most important limits of the mathematical treatment of the underground water. In such a case we only be able to give a general idea of the real movement. As general consideration, we might say that each porous or fissured medium can have one an own homogeneity scale, which only obviously can be useful if it is far smaller than the total aquifer volume.

HETEROGENEOUS AQUIFERS

In reality we have always non-homogeneous media and only when a homogeneity scale is correctly chosen the problem can be driven to a situation in which the equations for homogeneous aquifers are still valid. Therefore in complicated geological formations it may happen that so excessively large homogeneity scale must be considered as to exceed the total volume of the same aquifer.

In these cases the concept of the homogeneity scale is not longer applicable and we are therefore obliged to tackle directly the study of a non homogeneous system. This is generally the case of the fissured aquifers, BENEDINI, GIULIANO and TROISI (1972), LOUIS (1968), LOUIS and MAINI (1970).

THE INVERSE PROBLEM

Following the previous statements we may remember that many studies have been already made on the fissured aquifer by means of mathematical models, MICHE (1960), BAREMBLATT, ZHECTON and KOCHINA (1960), but generally limited to the problems of oil field exploitation.

These studies are very interesting from a theoretical viewpoint, but there are many difficulties in practical application. Therefore, especially in the management of the underground water resources, our attention may only be focused on the possibility of representing the aquifer's behaviour by means of realistic models, keeping in mind the necessity of an easy and effective application.

In this framework we can explain why an interest to "the inverse problem" is always growing up, and have tried a methodological example applied to coastal aquifer in the vicinity of Brindisi, MAIONE and TROISI (1972).

FORMULATION OF THE PROBLEM

In order to set the possibility and the rules of the management it is imperative that the aquifer be characterized by some essential parameters, such as

the Transmissivity and the Storage Coefficient. In more general terms, the structural and topological configuration of the model, the parameters of which must be
determined or at least properly estimated, should be considered known a priori.

If we assume now laminar flow in an uncompressible liquid, which does not
interact with the solid boundary the hypothesis of non-homogeneity brings to the
assumptions that the transmissivity T is a function of all the three coordinates
x, y and z. For the sake of semplicity we can suppose that the medium is isotopic
and therefore $T = T(x,y,z)$ is a scalar function, moreover we can say that the flow
is bidimensional. As known, in these hypothesis the flow can be described by the
"diffusion equation".

$$\frac{\partial}{\partial x} \left(T \frac{\partial \phi}{\partial x} \right) + \frac{\partial}{y} \left(T \frac{\partial \phi}{\partial y} \right) = S \frac{\partial \phi}{\partial t} \qquad (3)$$

where :

ϕ = piezometric level $[L]$
T = transmissivity $[L^2 \ T^{-1}]$
S = storage coefficient $[0]$
t = time $[T]$

In the inverse problem, ϕ is known while $T(x,y)$ and $S(x,y)$ are the unknown parameters the spatial distribution of which must be determined. Equation (3)
must be associated with the boundary conditions.

In steady state flow, the equation (3) becomes

$$\frac{\partial}{\partial x} T \frac{\partial \phi}{\partial x} + \frac{\partial}{\partial y} T \frac{\partial \phi}{\partial y} = 0 \qquad (4)$$

In the forthcoming, we shall refer to equation (4), although the same
considerations can be applied also to equation (3).

METHODS OF PARAMETRIC IDENTIFICATION

Strictly speaking, the problem of the parametric determination can be reduced to the solution of equation (4) or (3).

This problem, considering unknown $T(x,y)$, is like the integration of a
partial derivative equation of first order. More accurately the problem can be
as follows formulated.

We consider a line F in the space (x,y,z) with the following parametric
equations :

$x = x(\tau)$
$y = y(\tau)$
$z = z(\tau)$ \qquad with $a \leqslant \tau \leqslant b$

We determine now the integral surface $T = z(x,y)$ of the equation (4)
which intersects the curve F of equation :

$z = z(x(\tau),y(\tau)) = z(\tau)$

As known, the integral surfaces of equation (4) can be considered as made up by the "characteristic lines" having parametric formulations $x = x(\sigma,\tau)$; $y = y(\sigma,\tau)$ $z = z(\sigma,\tau)$ and can be derived, solving the system ("characteristic system")

$$\frac{\partial x}{\partial \sigma}(\sigma,\tau) = \frac{\partial \Phi}{\partial x}(x,y)$$

$$\frac{\partial x}{\partial \sigma}(\sigma,\tau) = \frac{\partial \Phi}{\partial y}(x,y)$$

$$\frac{\partial z}{\partial \sigma}(\sigma,\tau) = T(\frac{\partial^2 \Phi}{\partial x^2} + \frac{\partial^2 \Phi}{\partial y^2})$$

with the boundary conditions

$$x = x(0,\tau); \quad y = y(0,\tau) \qquad (6)$$

where the variable σ is equal to zero on the line F.

From equation (5) we obtain the coordinates (2)

$$x = x(\sigma,\tau)$$
$$y = y(\sigma,\tau) \qquad (7)$$
$$z = z(\sigma,\tau)$$

which define a characteristic line for each τ value and represent the integral surface with the variation of τ.

Taking σ and τ from the first two equations (7) as x and y functions and substituting them in the third equation, the parametric equation can be represented in an cartesian system.

The streamlines are therefore identified by the parameters and τ.

For example, if a value of τ is fixed, we establish by (5) the point of the line F through which only a characteristic line passes, described by the variable σ.

From an analytical point of view, therefore, the problem seems to be not very difficult and at any rate it might be considered completely solved.

However other difficulties of a different type and weight intervene in the practical solution of the problem.

The first one lies in the fast that the analytical solution and therefore the integration of the equation, require the knowledge of the mathematical law which represents the behaviour of the piezometric level on the aquifer , $\Phi(x,y)$.

It is well know that this behaviour, on the contrary, is established starting from a distribution or interpolated by means of more or less sophisticated procedures in order to obtain a continuous distribution of the isopiezic lines.

Undoubtly it is not advisable to attempt a "curve fitting" of the procedure in the field of the piezometric level as this would prove highly difficult since we have two independent variables.

To oversome these difficulties a modified procedure has been tried.

In fact, besides the isopiezic lines we can also have the streamlines, which meet one each other perpendicularly consider that the streamlines are the projection on the σ,τ plane of the characteristic curves.

If we refer the ground water flow to the system streamlines and isopiezic lines (coordinates σ,τ,z), we obtain :

$$\frac{dT}{d\sigma} \cdot \frac{d\phi}{d\sigma} + T\,\frac{d^2\phi}{d\sigma^2} = 0 \qquad\qquad (8)$$

We could reach the same results of equation (8) by considering the ground water flow referred directly to the streamlines.

This equation (8) is a simple differential equation with variable coefficients in the unknown parameter $T(\sigma)$, and it can be easily explained from a physical viewpoint. From this equation it follows that along, every streamline, the transmissivity T is univocally determined by the potential gradient along the variable abscissa σ.

That is the value of T along one of the flow tubes in which the aquifer can be subdivided is independent upon of any adjacent tube.

The relationship among the distributions of T along two continuous lines is established by the fact that the integral surface $T(\sigma)$ is constituted by the characteristic lines crossing the curve F. From a point of the curve F one characteristic line starts and the point itself corresponds to the value of the integration constant of equation (8). Finally the behaviour of T along the variable σ is univocally determined from the τ value, which locates the point of F where it crosses the characteristic line.

This enables to determine the distribution of T in the aquifer by means of a numerical integration of the equation (8), line by line separately.

The subdivision of the aquifer in independent elementary tubes simplifies the system, which results now constituded by independent subsystems. Even if we disregard the difficulty connected with the drawing of the streamlines, (which it is feasible by the experience and proper technical means), the characteristic method has in this case some opinable aspects.

Equations such as (3) and (4) represent a physical idealization of the phenomenon HADANARD (1902), LAVRENTIEV (1967), and must comply with fundamental requisites, which are related to the existence of a unique solution. Furthermore it must be considered that the solution stability as affected by small variations for the presence of errors in the problem's inputs.

In the determination of transmissivity distribution, besides the uncertainity of the isopiezic level and the imprecision of the streamlines, we must take into account that the boundary conditions are assigned starting only from some scattered points.

Also in this case we have some analytical equations for the interpolation of the experimental data and the problem itself could have a unique solution.

The last condition states whether the way by which the inverse problem has been formulated is wrong or not and therefore whether the variability of the solution is based on the input uncertainty.

These kind of considerations obliged many scientists to treat in an other way the problem of the aquifer identification, some of them have hied to adopt not an analytical solution but a "quasi solution", coming from a proceeding of a parametric optimisation.

The solution must be unique not only for a single and isolated value or the parameters referring to the boundary conditions, but even for any other value not far from the expected solution.

This explains the law of variation of T and S for small differences of the boundary values caused by the experimental data.

In other words we choose an initial transmissivity distribution $(T_1, T_2 \cdots T_n)$ which must be close to the real one.

Arranging for more convenience the n parameter in a vector T and being T^o the vector relative to this first trial, we simulate the aquifer solving the equations with a proper algorithm.

A difference between the real and calculated piezometric levels will result, which must be minimized by assuming different values of some parameters within predetermined limits. Such an operation can now be performed by means of mathematical procedure. We define in fact an objective function J(T) that is an analytical function of the difference existing between the calculated and the measured value.

The procedure of automatic research consists of building up systematically a vector array T^o, T^1, ... T^k, so that :

$$J(T^o) > J(T^1) > \ldots\ldots\ldots\ldots > J(T^k) \ldots\ldots\ldots\ldots$$

which is convergant to a minimum with a finite number of steps.

As far as the T^o choise is concerned, we will make use of all available information on the behaviour of J, so that the first trial results are not far from the true solution.

For the value of next trial we need to establish two fundamental points, that is : a) the direction (in the n dimension space where T is defined) along which we must choose the next point, b) the amplitude of the step along the chosen direction.

As far as point a) is concerned not all the directions must be taken in account but just those for which the following relation is valid. :

$$J(T^{k-1}) > J(T^k)$$

In other words, stopping the Taylor function to the first term

$$J(T^k) \cong J(T^{k-1}) + < \nabla \; J(T^{k-1}), \; \Delta T > \qquad (9)$$

it must follow that

$$< \nabla \; J(T^{k-1}), \; \Delta T > \; < 0$$

Many methods generate the K term by the (k-1) term by means of such a relationship :

$$T^k = T^{k-1} - m_{k-1} A_{k-1} \nabla J(T^{k-1})$$

where A_{k-1} is a matrix and m_{k-1} a proportional factor which can be considered as constant during the proceeding, or can depend by the k-1 step, previously considered.

Equation (9) can be definitely written :

$$J(T^k) \cong J(T^{k-1}) - m_{k-1} < \nabla J(T^{k-1}), A_{k-1} \nabla J(T^{k-1}) >$$

For example A_{k-1} can coincide with the unit matrix I (steepest descent method). The main difficulties with these proceedings consist in the limited determinable transmissivity number n, as regards to the number which could scarcely describe the aquifer.

In fact the complexity of the proceeding and the time of calculation impose some limits to the number of operational parameters. Many authors solved this difficulty decomposing the aquifer in homogeneous areas, to which mean values of the considered parameters can be attributed although in this way we lose many informations regarding the trend of piezometric levels. We are now trying to reduce the dimension of the problem, that is to make a parametric optimization with the usual calculation means, without loosing the contact with the hydrogeological reality.

REFERENCES

BAREMBLATT G.I., ZHELTON IN.P., KOCHINA I.N., Basic concepts in the theory of
    seepage of homogeneous liquids in fissured rocks. Jour. Appl. Math. and
    Mech. (PMM) vol. XXIV, n.5, 1960.
BENEDINI M., GIULIANO G., TROISI S., Alcune considerazioni sulla trattazione mate-
    matica sul problema del moto in acuiferi fessurati. Geol. Appl. e Idrogeol.
    vol. VII, Bari 1972.
HADAMARD, Sur les problèmes aux derivée partialles et leur significations physiques-
    Bil. Univ. Princeton, 13, 1902.
JACOB C.E., Engineering hydraulics. Proceedings of the Fourth Hydraulics Confer-
    ence Iowa Institute of Hydraulic Research, Juwe 12-12.
LAVRENTIEV M.M., Some Improperly Posed Problems of Mathematical Physics-Springer-
    Verlag 1967.
LOUIS C., Etude des écoulements d'eau dans les roches fissurées et de leurs in-
    fluences sur la stabilité des massif rocheux. EDF. Bull. Div. Etudes et
    Recherches, Ser. A n°3, 1968.
LOUIS C., and MAINI Y.N., Determination of in situ hydraulic parameters in jointed
    rocks. Int. Soc. Rock. Mechanics, 2nd Congress Belgrad 1970.
MICHE R., Recherches théotiques sur les écoulements de filtration non permanents.
    Application aux fluctuations périodiques. Soc. Hydrot. France, Journées
    de l'Hydraulique. Nancy 1960.
MAIONE B., TROISI S., Metodi per la risoluzione del problema inverso in una falda
    sotterranea. XIII Convegno di Idraulica e Costruzioni Idrauliche, Milano
    1972.

Current research field of author : *Underground Water Management.*

Modeling and Simulation of Water Resources Systems, G.C. VANSTEENKISTE, (Ed.)
North-Holland Publishing Company (1975)

DETERMINATION OF THE PERMEABILITY AND STORAGE COEFFICIENT
OF AN AQUIFER IN LOUVAIN-LA-NEUVE THROUGH ANALOG SIMULATION

R. Gorez and D. Johnson
Laboratoire d'Automatique
Université Catholique de Louvain
Louvain-La-Neuve, BELGIUM

ABSTRACT

The object of this study is the determination of the local
values of the hydraulic parameters of an aquifer, by means
of experimental data resulting from an artificial recharge. The chosen mathematical model is outlined and commen-
ted. The results of the simulation of this model on a
general purpose electronic analog computer are compared to
the experimental results.

INTRODUCTION

A number of wells have been bored on the new University
campus of Louvain-La-Neuve, in order to ensure the water supply of
the University and the new city. An optimal management of the water
resources requires an adequate mathematical model of the aquifer.
This led to a data-collecting campaign whose main objective is the
establishment of this model and the determination of its parameters:
transmissivity, permeability and storage coefficient. A study was
initiated in order to determine the local values of these parameters
from the results of an artificial recharge.

The preliminary study which follows has the following objectives : 1) to check, by means of simulation, the validity of the
model used to describe a local artificial recharge, with a view to
using it in a pollutant diffusion model;

2) to roughly identify the values of the parameters appearing in this model.

At the present stage of this study, the simulation was carried out on an analog computer, by means of the CTDS method. The
values of the parameters were determined by trial and error by choosing, amongst the curves depicting the time variations of the pie-

zometric heads in the model, those which were nearest to the experimental curves. In the future, we intend to carry out the simulation
on a hybrid computer, using the CTDS method and to implement more
sophisticated parameter identification algorithms. (least-squares methods, EKF...).

OUTLINE OF THE EXPERIMENT

The experimental rig (fig 1) consists of a well and two further measurement points at 5 and 15 meters respectively from the
well. The piezometric heads of the aquifer can be measured at these
three points.

The well itself consists of a 22 cm diameter tube in a 40 cm
diameter hole. The annular region around the tube is filled with gravel, sand, etc... - the average porosity of this media is 30 %.

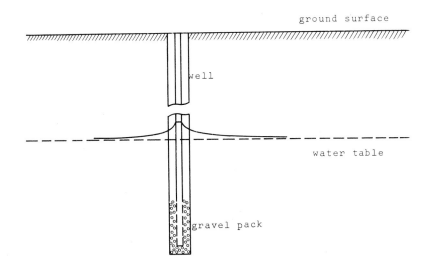

Fig. 1

The experiment is an artificial recharge, i.e. a constant flow is injected into the well until a pseudo-equilibrium is obtained. The recharge flow is then cut off and during the recovery period, the heads at the measurement points are plotted versus time up to the moment where the aquifer has reached its steady reference level.

MATHEMATICAL MODEL OF THE AQUIFER

We assume a perfectly radial flow from a completely penetrating well in an isotropic homogeneous unconfined aquifer of infinite radial extent, whence the equation :

$$\frac{1}{r} \frac{\partial}{\partial r}(rH \frac{\partial H}{\partial r}) = \frac{S}{K} \frac{\partial H}{\partial t} , \qquad (1)$$

$H(r,t)$ = piezometric head

S = storage coefficient (specific yield)

K = permeability of the aquifer

r = distance from the well axis

t = time.

The variations of H are relatively small and if we write

$$H(r,t) = \overline{H} + h(r,t) , \qquad (2)$$

we may linearize equation (1) and obtain the classical equation for a confined aquifer :

$$\frac{1}{r} \frac{\partial}{\partial r}\left[r \frac{\partial h}{\partial r} \right] = \frac{S}{T} \frac{\partial h}{\partial t} , \qquad (3)$$

where $T = K\overline{H}$ is the transmissivity of the aquifer and is supposed constant.

With the simulation in mind, we discretized partial differential equation (3) using finite differences :

$$r_i = i \, \Delta r , \qquad i = 0,1,2\ldots$$

$$h_i = h(r_i,t) ,$$

$$\frac{dh_i}{dt} = \frac{T}{Sr_i} \frac{\psi_{i+\frac{1}{2}} - \psi_{i-\frac{1}{2}}}{\Delta r} \, ,$$

$$\psi_{i+\frac{1}{2}} = \left(r \frac{\partial h}{\partial r} \right)_{r_i + \frac{\Delta r}{2}} = \frac{\left(r_i + \frac{\Delta r}{2} \right) \left(h_{i+1} - h_i \right)}{\Delta r} \, ,$$

$$\psi_{i-\frac{1}{2}} = \left(r \frac{\partial h}{\partial r} \right)_{r_i - \frac{\Delta r}{2}} = \frac{\left(r_i - \frac{\Delta r}{2} \right) \left(h_i - h_{i-1} \right)}{\Delta r} \, .$$

The simulation of these equations on an analog computer is quite straightforward, and requires 2 summers, 1 integrator and 1 inverter per node. It is possible to use only one operational amplifier per node, by eliminating the intermediate variables $\psi_{i\pm\frac{1}{2}}$; this yields :

$$\frac{dh_i}{dt} = \frac{T}{S(\Delta r)^2} \left\{ \left(1 + \frac{\Delta r}{2r_i} \right) h_{i+1} - 2h_i + \left(1 - \frac{\Delta r}{2r_i} \right) h_{i-1} \right\} \, . \qquad (5)$$

Introducing a time scale factor $\dfrac{T}{S(\Delta r)^2}$, we obtain :

$$\frac{dh_i}{dt} = \left(1 + \frac{\Delta r}{2r_i} \right) h_{i+1} - 2h_i + \left(1 - \frac{\Delta r}{2r_i} \right) h_{i-1} \, . \qquad (5')$$

The initial values $h_i(0)$ can be determined from the initial pseudo-equilibrium curve :

$$h(r) = C_1 - C_2 \ln r \, , \qquad (6)$$

where C_1 and C_2 are constants whose values are easily obtained by means of the initial heads at the two measurement points.

It would also be possible to carry out a change of variables before discretizing, i.e. :

$$r = Re^u \, , \qquad (7)$$

which transforms (3) into :

$$\frac{1}{r^2} \frac{\partial^2 h}{\partial u^2} = \frac{S}{T} \frac{\partial h}{\partial t} \, , \qquad (8)$$

and equations (5) then become :

$$\frac{dhi}{dt} = \frac{T}{S(\Delta u)^2} \frac{1}{u^2} (h_{i+1} - 2h_i + h_{i-1}) . \qquad (9)$$

We considered equations (5') with Δr = 2.5m : the measurement points therefore correspond to i = 0,2 and 6 respectively. It would be possible to implement equations (5) (for i = 1 to 5) in order to simulate the portion of the aquifer between the well and the last measurement point, by considering the measurements at both ends as forcing functions $h_0(t)$ and $h_6(t)$ for the first and last equations respectively.

The only unknown parameter is then the time scale factor which will be adjusted in order to obtain the best possible fit between $h_2(t)$ and the curve plotted at the 5 m measurement point.

This procedure has two major drawbacks :
1) it allows the identification of the ratio T/S only
2) the model does not allow for the rapid decrease of the water level in the well during the first half-hour of the experiment; it should be noted the initial measured head in the well is largely in excess of that calculated from equation (6).

Concerning the first drawback mentioned, T could be determined from the values obtained during the recharge, if the flow rate Q of the latter is measured; indeed, equation (6) also reads :

$$h(r) = C - \frac{Q}{2\pi T} \ln r .$$

As for the second drawback, either the first half-hour of the experiment can be reglected and the initial value of h_0 corrected accordingly (the heads at the two measurements points do not vary appreciably before 30'), or else the local changes in transmissibility and specific storage which occur in the vicinity of the well can be introduced into the mathematical model.

Moreover, the flow in the neighborhood of the well is certainly not purely radial and has therefore a vertical component due to the fact that the actual well cannot be considered as a completely penetrating well.

We shall take these different points into account by considering a simplified discrete model of the well, and its surroundings,

consisting of two "capacitors" joined by a "resistor" - one of the
capacitors corresponds to the water contained in the well tubing, the
other to the water stocked in the annular region around the tube. We
assume the external flow to be purely radial.

SIMPLIFIED MODEL FOR THE WELL

From Fig.1, and using a conservation equation of the form

$$\frac{d(\text{quantity of water})}{dt} = \text{input flow rate - output flow rate} \quad (10)$$

we obtain, for the well itself and for the annular region respectively :

$$\pi r_w^2 \frac{dh_w}{dt} = T_o(h_w - h_o) , \quad (11)$$

$$S_o \pi(r_o^2 - r_w^2) \frac{dh_o}{dt} = T_o(h_w - h_o) + 2\pi r_o T \left(\frac{\partial h}{\partial r}\right)_o , \quad (12)$$

where index w is relative to the well itself (tube), and o to the
border between the annular region and the aquifer; T_o and S_o are,
respectively, the transmissivity and yield coefficient of the annular region.

Due to the discretization of equation (3), the partial deri-
vative $\left(\frac{\partial h}{\partial r}\right)_o$ in (12) must be expressed as a lateral finite difference :

$$\left(\frac{\partial h}{\partial r}\right)_o = \frac{-h_2 + 4h_1 - 3h_o}{2\Delta r} . \quad (13)$$

The experimental curve $h_w(t)$ may then be put to use in two
ways, either by discarding equation (11) and introducing $h_w(t)$ as
a forcing function in (12), the only data involved in the identification procedure then being those collected at the 5m measurement
point, or by keeping equation (11) and carrying out the identification by means of a comparison between the experimental and simulated
curves for $h_w(t)$.

It should be noted that, if one decides to ignore the rapid

decrease of $h_w(t)$ during the first half-hour of the experiment, and, if it is assumed that after this brief transitory period, the levels h_w and h_o are identical, then (11) and (12) may be replaced by a single equation :

$$\pi\{r_w^2 + S_o(r_o^2-r_w^2)\} \frac{dh_o}{dt} = 2\pi r_o T \left(\frac{\partial h}{\partial r}\right)_o . \qquad (14)$$

Equation (14) may then be used to determine T (supposing that r_o, r_w and S_o are known) by comparing the experimental and simulated curves for $h_o(t)$. In practice, the simulation is carried out using a time scale factor equal to $T/S(\Delta r)^2$, which entails that the parameter to be determined in (12) or (14) will be the storage coefficient S.

RESULTS

The simulation of the above model on a general-purpose electronic analog computer is quite straightforward.

Equations (5') and (14) yield curves expressing the time variations of the piezometric heads and which fit the experimental curves quite closely, except for the level in the well during an initial period of a half-hour. The value of S/K or S/T may therefore be estimated with a good degree of accuracy. As for the separate identification of the parameters, the sensitivity of the procedure is not very high, 50 % variations of S having but little influence on the behaviour of $h_o(t)$.

Further tests are currently being performed using (11) and (12) instead of (14). The model then accounts for the rapid decrease of $h_w(t)$ at the beginning of the experiment. It appears however that the three coefficients which will appear in the r.h.s. of equations (11) and (12) when the latter are normalized, should be made to vary independently from one another. Multi-parameter identification techniques of a more sophisticated nature than a simple curve-fitting should then be implemented.

REFERENCES

The Use of Analog and Digital Computers in Hydrology, Proc. of the Tucson Symposium, IASH/AIHS, 1969.

Ferris, J.G., Knowles, D.B., Brown, R.H., and Stallman, R.W., Theory of Aquifer Tests, U.S. Government Printing Office, Washington, 1962.

Kruseman, G.P., and De Ridder, N.A., Analysis and Evaluation of Pumping Tests Data, Int. Inst. for Land Reclamation and Improvement, Washington, 1970.

DISCUSSION

Would you not consider that the linearization of your equation might have accounted for the change in the shape of your curve ? (NEUMAN)

This anamolie has been observed when we have simulated both the nonlinear and the linear. So it is not a matter of linearization. (GOREZ)

Is it possible that you had a small decompression of the acquifer so that you don't have as rapid a decrease in the water table decline as predicted theoretically, because obviously there is nothing that accounts for compressibility of the medium in the set of equations. I am sure that dr. Neuman may have something to say on this. (BRUTSAERT)

I think that this may be a possible explanation for this effect. Decompression that you get some water first from storage by elastic compaction of the tail, possibly expansion of the water itself. (NEUMAN)

Was the purpose of linearization to determine the parameters in a simple way ? (DAVIDSON)

We intend to insert this model into a more complicated model for pollutant diffusion. There are some limitations of analog equipment. It would be difficult for us to simulate the nonlinear equations. The purpose of linearization is to simplify the hardware. (GOREZ)

Did you look at any gradient search techniques for effeciently finding the parameter. (DAVIDSON)

We didn't choose any gradient technique at this time, but we intend to do so using a hybrid computer. (GOREZ)

How many pressure measurements were made in each depth ?

Three : one at the well, a second at 5 meters, a third 15 meters from the well; but only one at each point. (GOREZ)

Were the pressure meters tensiometers or piezometers ? (VACHAUD)

Piezometers. (GOREZ)

Modeling and Simulation of Water Resources Systems, G.C. VANSTEENKISTE, (Ed.)
North-Holland Publishing Company (1975)

EXPERIMENTAL ARTIFICIAL RECHARGE

L. De Backer
Département de Génie Rural
Université Catholique de Louvain
Heverlee, BELGIUM

ABSTRACT

This paper presents a particular phenomenon which occurs during artificial
recharge under ponded water bassin above a deep groundwater table. It
consists of a developing unsaturation front moving upward close to the
bottom of the bassin as the water level in the bassin decreases. Unsaturation starts at the interface of a soil layer of lower hydraulic conductivity than the one underneath it. The infiltration rate decrease is proportional to the fall of the water depth due to the fact that the decrease
of the hydraulic conductivity of the top layer is inversely proportional
to the increase in the thickness of the unsaturation front. It is shown
that the slight modification of Darcy law involves the introduction of the
bubbling pressure of the soil top layer into Darcy's equation. Field saturated hydraulic conductivity and the thickness of the control top layer of
soil are necessary to calculate the flux as a function of the water depth
in the bassin. Part of the reduction of the recharge rate considered
usually to be due to clogging can be attributed to the development of such
an unsaturation front which comes very close to the muddy bottom of the recharge bassin. The simple relationship presented might be of a great help
in model and simulation of water resources system involving groundwater
recharge bassin.

INTRODUCTION

Artificial groundwater recharge comes up whenever and whereever man dis-
turbs the natural hydrological cycle. Thus, it leads to an accelerated cycle in
which man must take into account its own disturbance parameters and render them
compatible to natural parameters. Urbanization, therefore, becomes a hydrological
headache (G. Lindh, 1972) when man decides the undertaking of water resources management in a hurry such that both types of parameters remain poorly defined.

The speed with which the University of Louvain (U.C.L.) is building the
new University town scheduled to count 50.000 people by the year 1980, has lead
the Hydrogeological Committee of U.C.L. to tackle simultaneously the hydrological
problems both on the scientific as well as on the technical points of view. Pros
and cons are competing on the fact that the technicians are usually forcing hands
to the scientists.

Fortunately, an available model (SAMMIR) has been used to apply the yet
scarce data available for rough identification of the aquifer parameters and some
groundwater as well as river flow discharges simulation in the region studied
(Lapania, 1974). Rainfall run-off water quantities (Lorent, 1974) require the

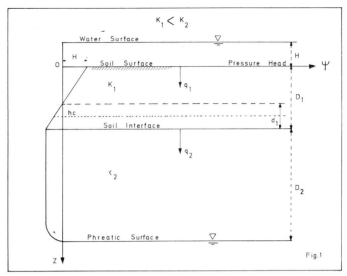

Figure 1. Theoritical pressure head distribution in unsaturated flow
through a layered soil profile where hydraulic conductivities
increase with depth, $K_1 > K_2 > K_3$

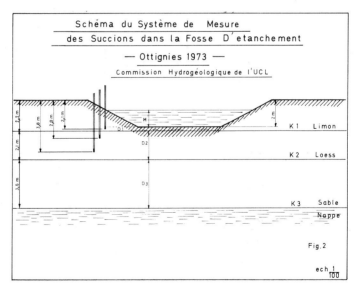

Figure 2. Field experimental recharge bassin and tensiometer positions with
respect to the indicated soil layers and groundwater table.

establishment of a storm bassin which, for topographical and land ownership reasons, reaches the center of town. To render the aspect and the environment of the
storm bassin esthetical and sane implies the maintaining of a constant water level
in the bassin. Knowledge of the infiltration rate, hence soil physical characteristics, is necessary due to the presence of a deep groundwater table in a sandy
aquifer. Parameter identification and pump-in recharge simulation of this aquifer
are presented elsewhere in this symposium (Gorez, 1974).

This paper presents the behavior of the satured as well as unsaturated
physical characteristics of the soil profile underneath an experimental bassin as
the water level in the bassin decreases. Generally, in a case like this, only saturated flow conditions are taken into account in numerical models. Futhermore,
the unsaturation phenomenon taking place might well be partly responsable for the
decrease in infiltration rate which is usually considered as mainly due to clogging of the bassin bottom.

THEORITICAL BASIS

The theory of flow which describes the transition from saturation to unsaturation is based upon the unequality of flows through a stratified soil profile
which has a top layer whose physical characteristics allows for a flux, q_1, smaller than that, q_2, of the second layer. It has been shown (Bear and al., 1965)
(fig. 1) that, when $q_1 < q_2$, the condition for saturation to unsaturation transition is realized when :

$$H < D_1 \left(\frac{K_2}{K_1} - 1\right) - h_c \left(\frac{D_1}{D_2} \frac{K_2}{K_1} + 1\right) \tag{1}$$

where H is the ponded water depth, D_1, D_2 and K_1, K_2 are respectively the thicknes-
ses and the hydraulic conductivities of layers 1 and 2, and h_c is the bubbling
pressure of the soil in layer 1. Since H is never negative, it follows that unsaturation will always take place as long as :

$$h_c < \frac{D_1 (K_2/K_1 - 1)}{(1 + \frac{D_1}{D_2} \frac{K_2}{K_1})} \tag{2}$$

Indeed, an unsaturated zone will develop as soon as the capillary pressure or suc-
cion becomes greater than the bubbling pressure.

According to Darcy's law, the flux going through layer 1 can be written
as :

$$q = K_1 \left[\frac{H}{D_1} \left(\frac{1}{1 - d_1/D_1}\right) + 1\right] \tag{3}$$

when the capillary fringe (h_c) is negligeable as compared with the hydraulic head
H; d_1 is the thickness of the unsaturation zone in layer 1. When h_c is not negligeable as compared to the hydraulic head H, equation (3) becomes :

$$q = K_1 \left[\frac{H + (h_c)}{D_1} \left(\frac{1}{1 - d_1/D_1}\right) + 1\right] \tag{4}$$

from which the unsaturation zone thickness, d_1, can be derived provided all other
parameters are known. For water, h_c is always negative.

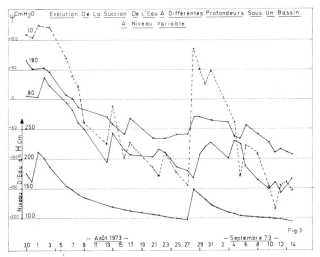

Figure 3.   Daily pressure heads ψ at 10, 80, 180 cm under the bassin bottom
and water depths H in the recharge bassin during the August and
September 1973 drawdowns.

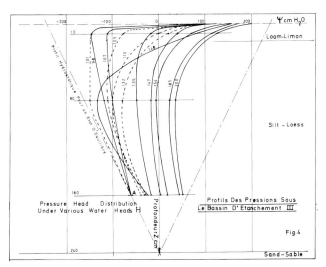

Figure 4.   Pressure head distribution profiles at the indicated water depths
during the August (solid lines) and September (broken lines) 1973
drawdowns.   The refill profile between drawdowns is for H = 148.
Pressure head equilibrium profile (dashed line on the left) goes
through point A and reaches a nul value at the silt-sand interface, origin of the gravitational pressure profile (dashed line on
the right).

TABLE I.

Comparison between calculated and measured fluxes.

H cm	K_{10} × 10^5 cm/sec	K_{80} × 10^5	K_{180} × 10^5	$\bar{K}$ × 10^5	$\bar{\psi}$ cm H_2O	q calc. cm/sec × 10^5	q meas. cm/sec × 10^5
200	1,12	4,04	10,7	5,1	72	9,13	9,25
185	1,10	3,74	10,7	4,84	61	8,35	8,38
154	0,7	3,16	8,77	3,76	27,5	6,58	6,58
147	0,44	2,91	6,56	2,9	7,1	5,25	5,25
135	0,188	2,28	4,72	1,72	– 30	3,16	3,16
107	0,089	2,65	3,06	1,06	– 91	2,06	2,05
98	0,030	1,29	1,94	0,41	– 108	0,766	0,777
148	1,097	1,94	129,2	3,91	– 26	7,73	8,01
132	0,226	2,65	12,43	2,28	– 29	4,35	6,59
110	0,212	1,08	6,61	1,41	– 45	2,56	2,58
105	0,06	0,76	4,00	0,634	– 76	1,14	1,16
101	0,021	0,55	2,92	0,282	– 122	0,55	0,585

EXPERIMENTAL SET UP

The field experimental recharge bassin is shown in figure 2. Underneath
the 2 meter deep bassin whose bottom represents the reference level, there is a
20 cm layer of loam (D_1) which has a bubbling pressure (h_c) of about - 80 cm of
water. D_2 is a fine silt layer of 220 cm thickness $(h_c \simeq - 120$ cm $H_2O)$. The water table is located 6 meters below the reference level in a sand called Bruxel-
lien.

Four tensiometers were installed through the bottom of the bassin respectively at 10 cm, 80 cm, 180 cm and 260 cm from it. Unfortunately, the deeper tensiometer in the sand broke in the gravel bed forming the top of the sand layer.

The bassin was filled up with water several times before the tensiometer
measurements were made. These started in July 1973 but as long as the water depth
fluctuated above 150 cm, the pressure head ψ remainded positive. During the August
4 week dry spell, (fig. 3), the water depth decreased from 200 cm to 98 cm and the
pressure head ψ became negative as soon as the water head H dropped below 150 cm.
Bubbling occured on August 13 at the 10 cm and 80 cm levels according to the respective bubbling pressures. After the August 27 storm, the bassin was refilled up
to 148 cm and the pressure heads underwent fluctuations due to entrapped gas redistribution.

RESULSTS AND DISCUSSION

Pressure head distributions (ψ vs Z) at the indicated water heads H are
presented in figure 4. Continuous lines are for the August dry spell. The storm
event is indicated for H = 148 cm. The broken lines represent the readjustement
of the pressure heads up to close to the supposed capillary pressure head equilibrium profile which is drawn through point A and goes to the silt-sand interface.
It was drawn in this manner because the small scatter of pressure head values
around point A seems to indicate that a shallow phreatic surface probably exists
at the silt-sand interface. Indeed, the gravitational head profile (dashed line
on the right) drawn from that interface corresponds perfectly to that capillary
pressure head equilibrium profile for nul flow.

From the slopes of the water level drawdown versus time giving the measured fluxes and the corresponding hydraulic gradients between tensiometers, the hydraulic conductivities K_{10}, K_{80}, K_{180} of each layer (0 to 10, 10 to 80 and 80 to
180 cm) were calculated as well as the harmonic mean hydraulic conductivity $\overline{K}$ and
the mean pressure head $\overline{\psi}$. Using $\overline{K}$ and the sum of the hydraulic gradients, we back
calculated the fluxes. Table 1 shows the comparison between the calculated flux
$q_{calc.}$ and the measured flux $q_{meas.}$. To obtain a hydraulic conductivity-pressure
head relationship, $\overline{K}$ versus $\overline{\psi}$ was plotted as shown in figure 5. A disturbing fact
appears, it is that the hydraulic conductivity decreases even under positive mean
pressure head. This would mean that an uncontrollable phenomenon as clogging did
occur at least during the first drawdown. On the second drawdown, mean pressure
heads were all negative. Therefore, the question is raised : is unsaturation effectively involved, as commonly expected, in the decrease of hydraulic conductivity ? In other words, is the clogging due to solid particles or to gas ?

Looking at the K_{10} and K_{80} values in Table I, it appears that unsaturation
always takes place according to condition (2). Equation (4) is hence used to calculate the thickness of unsaturation d_1 with h_c = - 80 cm. Figure 6 shows the comparison of our results (broken line) as compared to those of Fisch (1959) reported by
Zaslavsky (1969). The shapes of the two relationships are very different. Although our data curve presents also an asymptote toward higher water heads, it approaches the value d_1/D_1 = 1 very smothly and not as if the unsaturation front

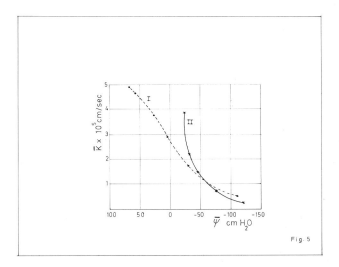

Figure 5. Harmonic mean hydraulic conductivity $\overline{K}$ and mean pressure head $\overline{\psi}$ relationships during the first I and second II drawdowns.

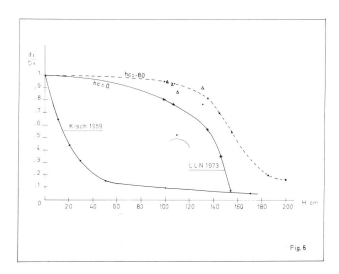

Figure 6. Unsaturation thickness ratio d_1/D_1 as a function of water depth H (D_1 = 20 cm). Kisch (1959) data are compared with our data using equation (4) for h_c = − 80 cm of water (broken line) and equation (3) assuming h_c = 0 (solid line).

would poke through the bassin bottom and bubble out into the water. Using equation (3) (i.e., $h_c = 0$) does not yield any other comment than that a few data points, not presented, turned out to be negative at high H values as shown in figure 7.

The K_1 and d_1 versus ψ_{10} inverse relationaships illustrated in figure 7 answer the question raised above. K decreases of more than one order of magnitude when the water depth H decreases of one half even at pressure head positive values of ψ_{10}. Indeed we see that the layer D_1 is always partially unsaturated (broken line). This means that for water depth H smaller than 200 cm, the hydraulic conductivity of layer D_1 is always smaller than the saturated hydraulic conductivity of the loam. The unsaturation thickness d_1 is almost as important as the layer thickness D_1 but seems to never reach this value. It is interesting to notice that when d_1 is calculated with the help of equation (3) assuming $h_c = 0$, the d_1 curve intercepts the abscissa at a positive pressure head $\psi_{10} = 80$ cm of water at which K_1 starts only to decrease sharply.

Figure 8 shows the K_1, d_1 linear relationship which intercepts the ordinate at $K_{1S} = 1,35 \times 10^{-5}$ cm/sec. The value of $K_1 = K_{1S}$ is called "field satured" hydraulic conductivity because it represents a saturated conductivity integrated throughout the loam soil profile and even over a wide area covered by the same loam. Indeed, this value falls in the range of values found in field by Lacroix and Vreuls (1973) using the bore hole method (K = 1,82 x 10^{-5} cm/sec) and by Lapania (1974) calculating the hydraulic conductivity of surface material in the pumping test method of Walton (1962) (K = 1,23 x 10^{-5} cm/sec).

Hence, the knowledge of the K_1 vs d_1 relationship in the control top layer seems essential in establishing groundwater recharge bassin models in water resources systems.

Zaslavsky (1969) gives equations allowing for the calculation of the unsaturated thickness d_1 but these require the knowledge of the infiltration rate which is precisely what we want to calculate and too many experimental constants.

Figure 8 indicates, however that the K_1 vs d_1 relationship is of the form :

$$K_1 = K_{1S} - b \ d_1/D_1 \tag{5}$$

Since $K_1 = 0$ for $d_1/D_1 = 1$, this condition gives the value of the slope $b = K_{1S}$, thus equation (5) becomes :

$$K_1 = K_{1S} (1 - d_1/D_1) \tag{6}$$

Combining equations (4) and (6) yields :

$$q = K_{1S} \ \frac{H + (h_c)}{D_1} + (1 - d_1/D_1) \tag{7}$$

Equation (7) is verified in the case of complete unsaturation of the control top layer D_1, i.e. when $d_1 = D_1$, $H = h_c$ and $q = 0$, as well as in the case of full saturation of D_1, i.e. when $d_1 = 0$, $H > |h_c|$ and :

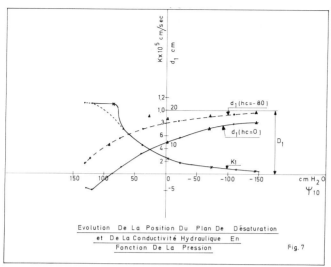

Figure 7. Experimental relationships between the hydraulic conductivity K_1 as well as the unsaturation thickness d_1 and the pressure head ψ_{10} of the first layer D_1 (loam), using equation (4) (broken line) and equation (3) (solid line).

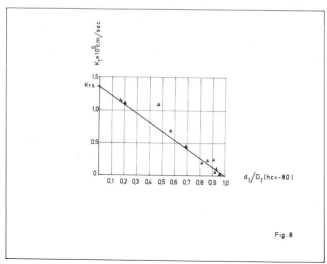

Figure 8. Experimental relationship between the hydraulic conductivity K_1 and the unsaturation thickness ratio d_1/D_1 (K_{1S} value is extrapolated).

$$q = K_{1S} \left[\frac{H + (h_c)}{D_1} + 1 \right]$$ (8)

Equation (8) is nothing else but Darcy law in saturated condition. Zaslavsky has also shown that the plot of the measured infiltration rate versus the water depth on the soil surface allows for determining the ratio K_{1S}/D_1 as for steady saturated flow. Our field measured data of q and H taken from table I are presented in figure 9 and compared with the theoretical relationships given by Zaslavsky without taking the bubbling pressure, h_c, into account and by equation (8) in which the air entry pressure is considered after translating the theoretical line with slope K_{1S}/D_1 from the origin along the abscissa at $H = |h_c|$. The fit of the experimental points might not look to good but it should not be forgotten as seen in figure 3 that the flow was not really steady during the field experiments.

In addition, the K_1 versus d_1/D_1 relationships given by equation (6) can be obtained from :

$$\tan \alpha = \frac{K_{1S}}{D_1} = \frac{K_1}{D_1 - d_1}$$

by imposing values of d_1/D_1 from 0 to 1 in the relation :

$$K_1 = D_1 (1 - d_1/D_1) \tan \alpha$$ (9)

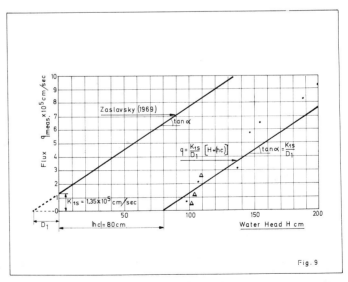

Figure 9.   Experimental and theoretical infiltration rates as a function of water depth in the bassin.

CONCLUSION

In the case of steady flow through unsaturated stratified soil with hydraulic conductivity increasing with depth, artificial groundwater recharge rate of infiltration bassin can be calculated as a function of water head on the bassin bottom provided that the field saturated hydraulic conductivity, the thickness and the bubbling pressure h_c of the soil control top layer are known.

More work is needed toward unsteady flow calculation in order to provide programmers with simple reliable relationships in models and simulation in the field of groundwater resources systems.

ACKNOWLEDGMENT

This research was sponsored by the Hydrogeological Committee of the University of Louvain.

REFERENCES

BEAR J., D. ZASLAVSKY and S. IRMAY, 1965 : Physical Principles of Water Percolation and Seepage. Arid Zone Research, UNESCO.

GOREZ R., 1974 : Determination of the Permeability and Specific Storage of an Aquifer in Louvain-la-Neuve through Analog Simulation. IFIP, Modeling and Simulation of Water Resources Systems, Gand, July-August, 1974.

LACROIX A. et M. VREULS, 1973 : La Mesure de la Perméabilité des Sols Fins. Travail de fin d'études. Faculté des Sciences Appliquées, Université de Louvain (U.C.L.).

LAPANIA E., 1974 : La Nappe Aquifère du Plateau de Lauzelle (Belgique). Thèse de doctorat, Faculté des Sciences, U.C.L.

LINDH G., 1972 : Urbanization : a Hydrological Headache. Ambio. December, 1972, p. 185-201.

LORENT B., 1974 : Tests of Different River Flow Predictors. IFIP, Modeling Simulation of Water Resources Systems, Gand, July-August, 1974.

SAMMIR : Centre d'Informatique Géologique. Ecole Nationale Supérieure des Mines de Paris. 35, rue St. Honoré. Fontainebleau.

WALTON W.C., 1962 : Selected analytical Method for Well and Aquifer Evaluation. Ill. State Water Survey, Bull. n° 49.

ZASLAVSKY, 1969 : Saturation Unsaturation Transition in Infiltration to a Non-Uniform Soil Profile. Soil Sc. 107, 160-165.

Current research field of author : *soil moisture balance - groundwater hydrology - natural and artificial groundwater recharge - Field Data Gathering by Telemeasurement System using the public Telephone network.*

Modeling and Simulation of Water Resources Systems, G.C. VANSTEENKISTE, (Ed.)
North-Holland Publishing Company (1975)

THE USE OF SIMULATION MODELS IN THE STUDY OF SOIL
MOISTURE TRANSPORT PROCESSES

H. van Keulen
Department of Theoretical Production Ecology
Agricultural University
Wageningen, The Netherlands

ABSTRACT

The development of high speed computers in recent years, along with the
availability of sophisticated simulation languages facilitate the use of
computer models in the study of transport processes in soils.

It is shown that a model of evaporation from the soil surface yields
satisfactory results and special difficulties encountered during its
development and operation are discussed.

Special attention is paid to the hierarchical approach in model building
as a means of overcoming problems of multilevel models as well as those
of very costly and time consuming execution of detailed models.

It is concluded that simulation models are a strong tool in the study of
transport processes in the soil, not only in solving specific problems but
also in pinpointing to weak areas in our knowledge and hence to the
design of new experiments.

INTRODUCTION

Transport processes in the rather complicated porous soil system play an
important role in many disciplines. Agronomists are dealing with them because they
govern processes of plant growth by supplying the necessary water and minerals to
the plant root. In more recent years, specially water management engineers,
responsible for the continuous supply of good quality water for human consumption
and agricultural purposes are interested in the behaviour of the soil water, and
those concerned with problems of pollution are forced to predict the fate of
solutes landed in the soil on purpose or accidentally.

The transport processes are characterized by a simultaneous change in the
amount of material with time and place. In mathematics such distributive systems
are described by partial differential equations. Analytical solutions for these
equations can in general only be found for problems that are so simple, that they
are only of academic interest, or under greatly simplifying assumptions making
the conclusions arrived at of little practical value. Where the analytical solutions
fail to provide an answer, the brute force of the computer may help to solve the
problem.

The development of sophisticated simulation languages containing features
to overcome the main disadvantages of digital calculation machines, which contrary
to natural systems operate discontinuously and sequentially, has facilitated the
use of these machines. Moreover these languages easily handle problems of numerical
integration, providing a number of methods each with its own advantages in specific
situations.

The application of one of these languages, the Continuous System Modeling
Program (CSMP), developed by IBM for its 360 and 370 series of machines for the

development of simulation models for transport processes in the soil has been
demonstrated by De Wit & Van Keulen (1972). In this paper a model for soil
evaporation is described and a technique to use such models in plant productivity
studies is proposed.

THE EVAPORATION MODEL

Evaporation from the soil surface is one of the main causes of non-
productive water loss under conditions where the atmospheric demand is high (arid
and semi-arid regions) and the soil is not or only sparsely covered for prolonged
periods of time. To estimate the amount of water available for plant growth, it
is of primary importance to be able to predict the evaporative losses. For this
purpose a simulation model was developed that calculates the evaporative flux from
a bare soil surface from meteorological data and from physical properties of the
soil. A detailed description of this model is presented elsewhere (Van Keulen, 1974).

Based on the principles of the finite difference method, as pointed out by
De Wit & van Keulen (1972), the simultaneous flow of heat and water in a soil column
is calculated.

Moisture is transported either in liquid form under a potential gradient or
in the vapor phase under a gradient of vapor pressure, taking into account the
appropriate transport coefficients.

Heat is transported by diffusion along a temperature gradient and by mass
transport along with the flow of water.

The surface temperature is calculated from the energy balance at the soil
surface: absorbed short wave radiation, sensible heat loss, outgoing long wave
radiation, heat flow into or out of the soil and evaporative heat loss.

The evaporative heat loss is obtained from the difference in vapor pressure
between the soil surface and the atmosphere and the aerodynamic resistance for
vapor transport above the soil surface. The aerodynamic resistance is calculated
from the wind speed, taking into account the roughness height of the surface
elements, according to a semi-empirical formula developed by Chamberlain (1968).
The vapor pressure at the soil surface is obtained from the surface temperature,
taking into account the vapor pressure depression due to increasing soil moisture
potential.

Sensible heat loss is calculated from the temperature difference between
the soil surface and the atmosphere and the resistance for heat exchange, the latter
being proportional to the vapor exchange coefficient. Outgoing long wave radiation
is estimated with an empirical formula given by Brunt (1932). Soil heat flux is
calculated from the difference in temperature between the soil surface and the
middle of the first, 1 cm thick, compartment, and the moisture content dependent
heat conductivity of the soil.

In figure 1 the measured and calculated cumulative evaporation of a uniform
löss column under laboratory conditions is given, while in fig. 2, the measured
(γ-ray attenuation) and calculated soil moisture profiles are compared. The agreement
in the cumulative evaporation is excellent, the moisture profiles however show
deviations. This may be attributed to disturbances in the soil column, as the
drying of the soil caused shrinkage, leading to cracks at the soil surface and
to the development of air spaces at some points along the perspex walls. These
disturbances presumably caused changes in the hydraulic properties of the soil,
while in the simulation program constant K-Θ and Ψ-Θ relations are used. Moreover
these relations were determined in duplicate columns, which may not have been
completely identical, thus causing different hydraulic properties too.

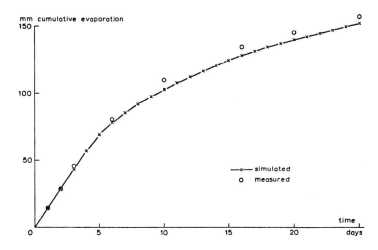

Fig. 1. Comparison between measured and simulated cumulative evaporation from a uniform column of löss.

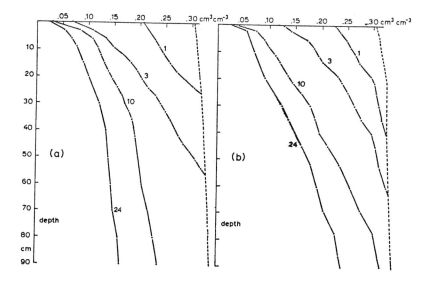

Fig. 2. Measured (a) and simulated (b) soil moisture profiles in a uniform löss column under constant evaporative conditions. Numbers along the graph indicate days after the start of the experiment.

It may be concluded however that the present model gives satisfactory results in predicting the evaporative water loss from a bare soil surface. This is supported by the results shown in figure 3, where the same model has been applied to a field situation.

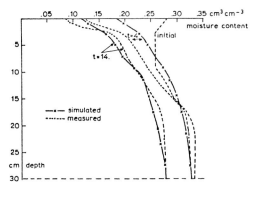

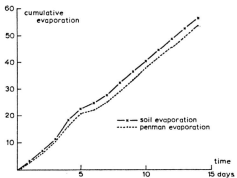

Fig. 3. Comparison between measured and simulated soil moisture profiles and cumulative evaporation from a field experiment in Avdat, Israel.

The determination of the physical parameters of the soil, specially under field conditions, is still one of the biggest problems in the modeling approach. Although it is possible to test the validity of a model under laboratory conditions and to estimate the physical properties from a given field by successive trial and error through comparison with actual field data, this procedure remains unsatisfactory as one is never sure that not a difference in response of the system between field and laboratory occurs. It seems to me therefore of the greatest importance, that the methods to determine the physical properties of soils in situ are improved.

THE APPLICATION OF SOIL MOISTURE TRANSPORT MODELS

Apart from gaining more insight into the relevant processes, which is one of the purposes for the development of simulation models, in our case the main aim is the application of such models to predict the availability of water for plant growth.

It turns out however, that, while the periods of interest for plant production are in the order of a hundred days, the time constant of the soil water

system is in the order of minutes or even seconds due to the explicit method of
integration. To simulate such systems, one has to proceed in time with intervals
that are in the same order as the time constant of the system. It is obvious, that
computer time and budget will soon become the limiting factors for the application
of such models. It is therefore necessary to introduce a different approach in
the description of soil moisture flow in models that are mainly aimed at the
calculation of crop production.

For the process of infiltration a simplification is introduced in which the
water entering the soil is divided over the soil compartments from the top one,
each one successively filling up to field capacity till all the water is dissipated
or till the remainder has drained below the maximum rooted depth.

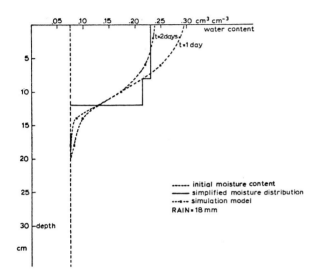

Fig. 4. Comparison of the moisture distribution after ilfiltration
calculated with the simulation model and with the "simplified"
method.

In figure 4 a comparison is shown of the moisture distribution in an initially dry
soil profile after a rain of 18 mm, calculated with the simplified model and with
the simulation model (Van Keulen & Van Beek, 1971; Stroosnijder et al., 1972). It
shows that after one day about 95% of the water is in the same soil zone in both
cases, while the differences in actual moisture content at various depths will
hardly influence the availability to the roots. Under various conditions, the
results may deviate somewhat, leading to differences of about 25% in storage in
the same soil zone. It is emphasized however that a different situation exists
when so much irrigation water is applied that the storage capacity of the soil,
i.e. the amount that can be stored in the potential root zone, is highly exceeded.
Under perma-dry conditions which exist in most of the arid and semi-arid zones, this
schematisation gives satisfactory results. Such simplifications should however
always be compared with the results of models based on physical laws.

To describe the process of evaporation from the soil surface in a simple
way, a "mimicking" procedure has been developed. The term "mimicking" is used here
to define a procedure in which the response of the system to a given set of external
conditions is obtained by a special programming or calculation scheme, which in

itself has no physical or physiological meaning. Such a "black box" may also be constructed in situations where the causal relations are not known (Jansen, 1974).

To obtain the evaporation, first the potential evaporation is calculated with the formula of Penman (1956), which gives good agreement with the calculated soil evaporation as shown in figure 3. The actual rate of evaporation is then determined by the moisture potential at the soil surface. Because redistribution of the water between soil compartments as a result of developing potential gradients is omitted in the crop growth model, the total evaporative water loss must be divided over the various compartments. For each compartment the rate of water extraction is written as:

$$E_x = F * AEVAP$$

with $F = (\theta - \theta_1) * e^{(-P*d)}$

in which θ = actual water content in compartment
θ_1 = water content at air dryness
P = proportionality factor
d = depth of centre of compartment below soil surface

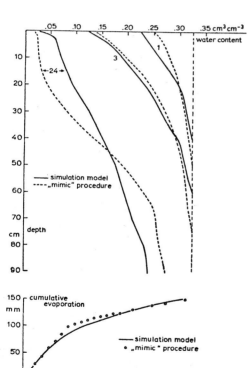

Fig. 5. Comparison of the moisture distribution and the cumulative evaporation, calculated with the simulation model and with the "mimicking" procedure.

In figure 5 a comparison is shown between the results of the simulation model and the "mimicking" procedure, in which for P the value 15 was used. It is obvious that this value depends on the moisture transmission properties of the soil under consideration. As the relation between the two depends both on the actual value of the conductivity and on the shape of the K-Θ relationship no attempt is made to give a general formula, but it is proposed to calculate the value of P by comparison of the simulation model with the "mimicking" procedure for each soil.

CONCLUSION

From the foregoing it is concluded that simulation models are a strong tool in the prediction of the behaviour of soil moisture under varying conditions. A serious disadvantage is however the very small time constant of the soil moisture system, which limits their use in general to short term processes, although simplifications may be introduced on basis of the results obtained with the simulation models.

The determination of the soil physical parameters in situ should get proper attention to improve the applicability of the simulation models.

REFERENCES

Brunt, D. (1932). Notes on radiation in the atmosphere. Q.J. Roy. Met. Soc. 58: 389.
Chamberlain, A.C. (1968). Transport of gases to and from surfaces with bluff and wave-like roughness elements. Q.J. Roy. Met. Soc. 94: 318.
Janssen, J.G.M. (1974). Simulation of germination of winter annuals in relation to microclimate and microdistribution. Oecologia (Berlin) 14: 197.
Keulen, H. van and G.C.E.M. van Beek (1971). Water movement in layered soils - A simulation model. Neth. J. agric. Sci. 19: 138.   .
Keulen, H. van (1974). Simulation of soil and plant water relations in arid regions. Simulation Monographs, Pudoc, Wageningen (in prep.).
Penman, H.L. (1956). Evaporation: An introductory survey. Neth. J. agric. Sci. 4: 9.
Stroosnijder, L., H. van Keulen and G. Vachaud (1972). Water movement in layered soils. 2. Experimental confirmation of a simulation model. Neth. J. agric. Sci. 20: 67.
Wit, C.T. de and H. van Keulen (1972). Simulation of transport processes in soils. Simulation Monographs, Pudoc, Wageningen.

Current research field of author : *Investigation and modeling of crop growth in arid regions, with special emphasis on water use - Modeling of evaporation - Crop growth modeling in general.*

DISCUSSION

*It seems to me that you take great pride in being as precise as possible
in doing the modeling and you then are extremely loose when you start using words
as better, best, good. You never tell us what you mean by these statements. Another
point is, you made a statement which I think is extremely dangerous, you said, if
you did not get an agreement you went back and you put in more detail. That's not
necessarily a good way of getting a better agreement. (YOUNG)*

I did not specify good, better, best due to lack of time. The second one,
I think you probably misunderstood : the point is not that putting in more detail
should give you any better result à priori but the point is that, when you have
described a process with a number of equations which you think are representing the
process and you don't get agreement between the observed and the calculated results
you should go back to your set of mathematical equations, study them again and see
if you did not leave anything out.   (VAN KEULEN)

*I might say there is a very close analogy between your material energy ba-
lance use and the one that we did on the rivers where we look at the evaporative
enthalpy loss of heated water to the atmosphere. Do you have an evaporative enthalpy
loss term ? (DAVIDSON)*

No. (VAN KEULEN)

*We found that in the river the evaporative enthalpy loss term is roughly
50 % of the heat loss when you look at the long way, the short way, the force conduction and then look at the evaporative enthalpy loss term itself, which is a large
quantity. I suspect you have to look at it. The second question has to do with the
time base for input data in your heat exchange formulas. We found that using daily
average versus data based say on hourly readings, you can pick up another 30 to
40 % deviation between the cumutative effects and those which are actually accumu-
lating on your integral or shorter time history. The heat exchange factors change
enormously over a cycle of 24 hours. (DAVIDSON)*

Yes, when possible we use weather data on the smallest base that is available, that means on the base of the calculation. In many cases you don't have
them. We have developed some procedures which convert daily averages back into
daily courses. (VAN KEULEN)

*You mentioned that you have very small timesteps like minutes, I was won-
dering whether this would not be a direct consequence of using CSMP which I understand is quite an explicit procedure. Using evaporation data like we did, we could
use timesteps of a day or more. (NEUMAN)*

In the runoff model where we use evaporation, I use timesteps of a day with
this limiting procedure, I got satisfactory results. (VAN KEULEN)

What kind of integrator do you use ? (TODINI)

Either Runge Kutta or Milne with variable timesteps. (VAN KEULEN)

You can have larger timesteps. (TODINI)

I agree with that. (VAN KEULEN)

Modeling and Simulation of Water Resources Systems, G.C. VANSTEENKISTE, (Ed.)
North-Holland Publishing Company (1975)

TWO DIMENSIONAL NUMERICAL ANALYSIS OF TRANSIENT WATER TRANSFER
IN SATURATED-UNSATURATED SOILS

M. Vauclin, G. Vachaud and J. Khanji
Institut de Mécanique
Université Scièntifique et Médicale de Grenoble
B.P. 53 - F. 38041 - Grenoble-Cedex, FRANCE

SUMMARY

In a previous paper presented at this conference (Vachaud et al, 1974), which will be referred from now on as paper n°1, it has been stated that water transfer from the soil surface to the lower boundary of a water table aquifer can be correctly described by one equation, based on the physics of flow in the saturated and unsaturated zones. It is our purpose to present here a numerical solution of this equation, which will be applied to two processes : firstly transient drainage of an aquifer ; and secondly recharge by infiltration from the soil surface. In both cases, we will describe two dimensional vertical plane-flow problems. The validity of the numerical simulation is tested by comparison with experimental measurements previously obtained on a slab of soil.

NUMERICAL ANALYSIS

The flow equation

We use the flow equation, described in paper n°1, which is based on Darcy's law and mass conservation of water. This equation is given by :

$$c(h) \; \frac{\delta H}{\delta t} = \frac{\delta}{\delta x} [\, K(h) \; \frac{\delta H}{\delta x}] + \frac{\delta}{\delta z} [\, K(h) \; \frac{\delta H}{\delta z}] \qquad (1)$$

wherein :
.H is the hydraulic potential (cm of water) given by $H = h-z$;
.h is the water pressure head (cm of water) ;
.z is the vertical distance from the soil surface, oriented positively downward;
.x is the horizontal distance, Ox oriented positively from left to the right ;
.K is the hydraulic conductivity (cm/hr).

It is known from paper 1 that h varies continuously, in the flow domain bounded by the soil surface, a lower boundary and vertical sides, from positive values in the saturated zone to negative values in the unsaturated zone. The characteristic value $h = 0$ defines the position of the free surface at time $t > 0$.

In the unsaturated zone (between the soil surface and the free surface of the water table), the flow parameters are :

$$h < 0 \quad ; \quad K = K(h) \quad ; \quad \theta = \theta(h) \quad \text{and} \quad c(h) = \frac{\delta \theta}{\delta h}$$

where θ is the volumetric water content and $c(h)$ the capillary capacity.

299

While in the saturated zone

$$h \geqslant 0 \quad ; \quad K = K_s \quad ; \quad \theta = \theta_s \quad ; \quad c = 0$$

where index s refers to natural saturation.

Example of boundary condition - Analysis of a drainage

Consider the drainage problem analyzed previously on a smaller scale by
J. Rubin, 1968, and defined as falling water table ditch drainage case.

The flow medium consists of a slab of homogeneous soil underlain by a horizontal barrier at depth P and divided by equally spaced trenches at distance 2L.
The trenches penetrate fully the soil, and a horizontal water table in static equilibrium exists initially at depth H_o. At time t = 0, the water level in the trenches is instantaneously lowered to depth H_1, and is then maintained at this value
during the experiment.

Because of symmetry we will consider only the half-flow domain defined in
fig. 1, with the origin O at the upper left hand corner of the slab. The free surface FGH is represented at an arbitrary time t, where FG is the seepage zone. It
is assumed that the flow is plane.

The initial and boundary conditions corresponding to this case are
1. $H = -H_o$ ∀x,   ∀z   t < 0   (hydrostatic equilibrium)

2. $H = -H_1$ x=0,   at ŒF t $\geqslant$ 0   (in the ditch)

3. $H = -z$ x=0,   at FG t $\geqslant$ 0   (seepage face)

4. $\dfrac{\delta H}{\delta x} = 0$ x=0,   at OG t $\geqslant$ 0   (no horizontal outflow from above water table)

5. $\dfrac{\delta H}{\delta z} = 0$ z=0,   at OA ∀t   (no flux through the soil surface)

6. $\dfrac{\delta H}{\delta x} = 0$ x=L,   at AB t $\geqslant$ 0   (by symmetry)

7. $\dfrac{\delta H}{\delta z} = 0$ z=P,   at BC ∀t   (impervious boundary)

The boundary condition corresponding to the recharge experiment are defined later on.

The simulation method

Equation (1), submitted to this set of initial and boundary conditions,
was solved numerically by the use of the "Alternating Directions Implicit and Iterative" (ADIPIT) finite difference scheme, described in detail by Douglas et al,
1959 and J.Rubin, 1968. The reasons conducting to this choice were developped in
paper n°1.

The discretization scheme based on the physical description of the mass
conservation equation in a volume element Δx.Δz.1 centered on a node (i, j) is

$$\text{div } \bar{q} = - c \frac{\delta H}{\delta t} \tag{2}$$

where $\bar{q}$ is the Darcian flow velocity, and space indexes i, j are defined by

$$x = (j-2) \Delta x, \qquad z = (i - 1,5) \Delta z$$

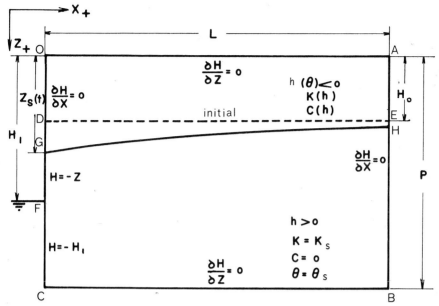

Fig.1 - Definition of initial and boundary conditions for a two-dimensional problem of falling water table

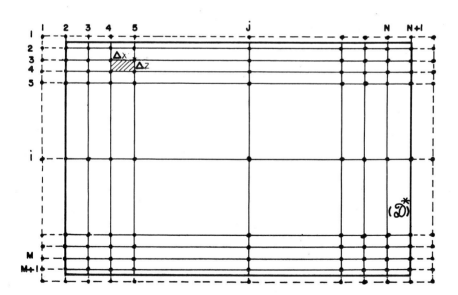

Fig.2 - Definition of the network of points used in the discretisation scheme.

the time index k, is defined by :

    t = k.Δt

the spatial grid (Δx.Δz) is a rectangular grid covering the rectangular flow domain; at the sides where a flux condition is imposed the grid is extended one-grid
point (fig. 2).

$H_i^{k,r}$ is the value of the main variable H, at a grid point (i,j), at time
k, in a cycle of iteration r.

The discretization of the two simultaneous systems of flow equations involved by the use of the ADIPIT method is given in appendix 1.

Finally the flow chart, given in appendix 2, was built for being used by
small computers such as an IBM 1130-16 K used in our simulation tests.

EXPERIMENTAL MEASUREMENTS

The flow domain and its simulation - Falling water table problem

The experiments were run in the laboratory on a slab of soil 3 m long,
2 m high and 5 cm in thickness. The soil was packed as homogeneously as possible
(with an average dry density of 1,57 g/cm³) between two perspex walls supported by
a frame and resting on an impervious horizontal boundary. For this experiment, the
left vertical end side of the slab was connected to a constant head reservoir used
to set the height of the external piezometric level and to measure directly the
total outflow volume from the slab ; no flow was allowed through the right vertical end side.

The soil used as porous medium was a fine river sand of fairly regular
grain size distribution with 50% in weight passing through a mesh of size 0.3 mm.
Characteristics of the soil, of the experimental settings and of the measuring
methods have already been published (Vachaud et al, 1973) and are given in detail
in a research report available upon request.

Initially the water table was set at a depth H_o = 55 cm, and the experiments were started after a hydrostatic equilibrium (H $\overset{o}{=}$ -H$_o$) was attained in the
entire slab. Then for t ⩾ 0, the boundary conditions corresponding to the ones
described in fig. 1 were applied with the particular following values

    H_1 = 125 cm   ,   L = 300 cm   ,   P = 200 cm.

During the falling water table experiment, cumulative outflow volume was
controlled continuously ; measurements of changes of water content θ and of pressure water head h were conducted in order to obtain direct evaluation of the hydraulic conductivity - water content - water pressure head relations as well as
water content and water pressure distribution. Since our final purpose was to obtain a proper simulation of the experiments, it was necessary to determine directly the phenomenological relationships entering into the flow equation, and also
to obtain spatial distribution of the variables needed to test the validity of the
modeling technique.

The measuring techniques

The experimental method concerning the measurement of θ(x, z, t) and of
h (x, z, t) have been already described in detail (Vachaud et al, 1973). Let us
summarize briefly that the water contents θ were obtained by attenuation of gamma-
ray emitted by sources of 241 Am. Two measuring platforms were used, one for the

sources, the other for the detectors. Each platform was equipped with 3 sensors, two on the same horizontal line, 30 cm apart, two on the same vertical line 20 cm apart. Each detector being connected to its own scaler, it was thus possible, for a given position of the platform in the x, z plane, to measure simultaneously and independently changes of water content in 3 points. Automatic displacement of the platforms in the horizontal or the vertical direction was commanded, at the end of a counting sequence, by two independent motors. The displacement of the platforms was managed in such a way that one could come back regularly to the same positions.

The water pressure heads were directly measured by the use of 20 tensiometers, each one connected to its own transducer (STATHAM PM 131 TC), which were mounted on one of the perspex walls. A transducer was also used to measure the accumulated outflow volume flowing from the left hand side reservoir.

Acquisition and treatment of the data

The acquisition of the data was based on a cycling procedure defined by a series of two sequences :
- the counting period of the gamma equipment, which was usually set on 60 sec. During this period the measuring platforms were fixed in a given position.
- the scanning period, which was set on 40 sec. During this period, all the scales and transducers were scanned, and the platforms were moved in order to reach their final position before the initiation of the next counting period.

Each 100 seconds, the following series of data were obtained and punched on a teletype :
- time from the beginning of the test
- localization of the platform
- water content at 3 points (x_1, z_1) (x_2, z_1), (x_2, z_2) each coordinate being determined by the localization of the platform
- total outflow volume
- water pressure head and hydraulic head for the 20 tensiometers.

The data were treated by an IBM 1130 computer. Treatment included the systematic use of a plotter in order to follow rapidly the changes of θ or h at given points, and also to obtain at a given time a map of iso-values of water content, or of hydraulic potential using the Numerical Surface Techniques (NST)program.

An example of listing of data obtained from the computer at the end of a sequence is given fig. 3.

Determination of the soil hydraulic characteristics

The soil water pressure - water content characteristic ("the suction curve") was directly obtained by correlation between measurement of water content and of water pressure at given points and given time. Due to natural heterogeneity, some fairly important dispersion was obtained. An average representative curve for the domain has been plotted in fig. 4.

The hydraulic conductivity - water content relationship was obtained by transient analysis of the changes of water content. With regard to the two-dimensional aspect of the flow, integration of eq. 2 is not as simple as in the case of a mono dimensional flow (Watson, 1966). At given time values, water flux q(x,z) was determined by integration of eq. 2 using the boundary conditions and the flow direction (obtained from the mapping of potential field). This mapping was also used for determining the water potential gradient $\overline{\text{grad}}$ H and then, by the use of Darcy's law, the K(θ) or K(h) relationship. Further details on this determination are given by Vachaud et al, 1973.

Under the water table, the average values of water content and hydraulic conductivity are

M. Vauclin, G. Vachaud and J. Khanji

T= 0.223 H. Z= 21.84 CM. X= 56.44 CM. X= 86.44 CM.

Z= 41.84 CM. TETA3=0.1090 TETA1=0.1830 PX=1010. PZ=2479.

TETA2=0.2926

TV= 0.242 H. VA= 0.00 CM3. VB=2928.48 CM3. TH= 0.231 H.

		X= 19.0	X= 49.0	X= 79.0	X=109.0	X=139.0	X=169.0	X=199.0	X=229.0	X=259.0
Z= 1.60	PSI		-50.33							
	PHI		-51.93							
Z= 21.60	PSI			-36.52			-35.56		-35.30	
	PHI			-58.02			-56.96		-56.20	
Z= 41.60	PSI		-30.62	-14.35		-24.43				-24.65
	PHI		-72.22	-75.75		-65.83				-65.65
Z= 61.60	PSI	-20.79			-10.45					
	PHI	-82.79			-71.85					
Z= 81.60	PSI		-4.10					5.05		14.22
	PHI		-85.60					-76.34		-66.77
Z=101.60	PSI						26.87		31.55	
	PHI						-74.52		-69.34	
Z=121.60	PSI		24.10	32.30		40.16				
	PHI		-97.39	-89.09		-81.23				
Z=141.60	PSI	30.30			55.48					
	PHI	-111.69			-85.91					
Z=161.60										

Fig.3 - Example of measurements obtained at the end of a measuring cycle (each 100 sec) PSI and PHI are respectively the water pressure head h, and the hydraulic potential H measured with a transducer at point (X, Z), at time t. V_B is the cumulative outflow ; TETA 1, TETA 2, TETA 3 represent values of the water content at each measuring point.

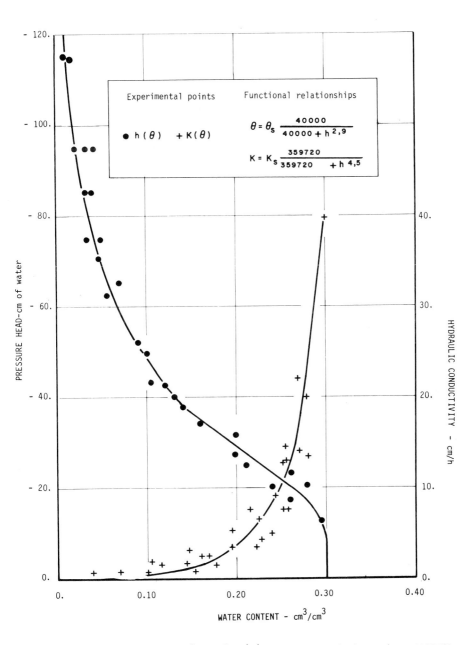

Fig.4 – Characteristics: hydraulic conductivity – water content – water pressure head relationships obtained during the drainage experiment.

$$\theta_s = 0.30 \pm 0.05 \text{ cm}^3/\text{cm}^3$$

and $K_s = 40 \pm 5$ cm/hr.

THE DRAINAGE EXPERIMENT - NUMERICAL AND EXPERIMENTAL RESULTS

In order to solve eq. 1, the sole variables to be known are K(h) and θ(h). The experimental curves given by fig. 4, are plotted with h as variable ; from a least square regression analysis of the data points, the following functional form is obtained

$$K = K_s \frac{A}{A + |h|^B} \quad , \quad \theta = \theta_s \frac{\alpha}{\alpha + |h|^\beta} \tag{3}$$

with A = 359 720.49 , B = 4.5
      K_s = 40 cm/hr   , K in cm/hr , h in cm of water
      α = 40 000   , β = 2.9
      θ_s = 0.3 cm^3/cm^3 , θ in cm^3/cm^3 , h in cm of water.

The dimensions of the spatial grid are fixed on Δx = 20 cm, Δz = 10 cm. The time step varies from 1 sec to 5 hr. The computer time requires for each time step is 4 min, using a 396 nodes grid.

Study of local variables

Firstly we will consider simulated and observed changes of local variables such as water content, water head and water flux.

In fig. 5 the observed and simulated water content profiles at X = 40, 100, 160 and 220 cm for t = 1 hr and 100 hr are given. Local discrepancies can be easily explained by the fact that relations 3 used for the simulation were smoothed ; a general good agreement is obtained at any time between experimental and numerical profiles.

In fig. 6 the map of the hydraulic potential computed at time t = 1 hr, is plotted together with experimental values obtained at the same time, from transducer readings. The agreement here is excellent, and it is clear that the hydraulic potential field is continuous within the entire flow domain to the soil surface.

Distribution of water flux at t = 0.1 hr and 1 hr is shown in fig. 7 under a vectorial form : at each node the flux, obtained by discretization of Darcy's law using a central difference scheme, is represented by a vector oriented orthogonaly to the potential field, and with a length proportional to the modulus of the flux ($\sqrt{q_x^2 + q_z^2}$ where q_i is flux component on axis i). If we define arbitrary the capillary fringe by the thickness of the domain above the water table where $(\theta_s - \theta) < 0.01$, which means in our case a domain of 15 cm above the water table, it is obvious from fig. 7 that the water table cannot be considered as the upper limit of the flow. The fluxes in this capillary fringe, even after 10 h, are of the same order of magnitude as under the water table (Childs, 1969).

Of particular interest is the repartition of flux on the boundary x = 0. For any t > 0, this boundary can be divided in three domains :
- in the upper part, above the water table, the pressure head of water is negative, and therefore no horizontal flow can occur through the vertical side ;
- in the lower part, under the water level in the ditch, the vertical side is an equipotential line, which impose no vertical component of the flow in this domain ;

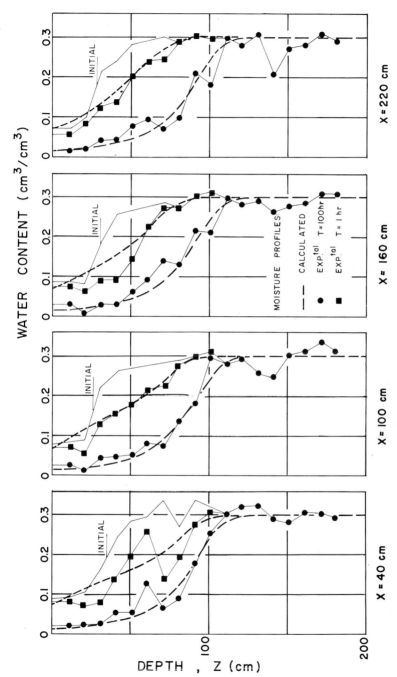

Fig.5 - Observed and calculated water content profiles at x = 40, 100, 160, 220 cm
for t = 1hr and 100hr for the drainage case.

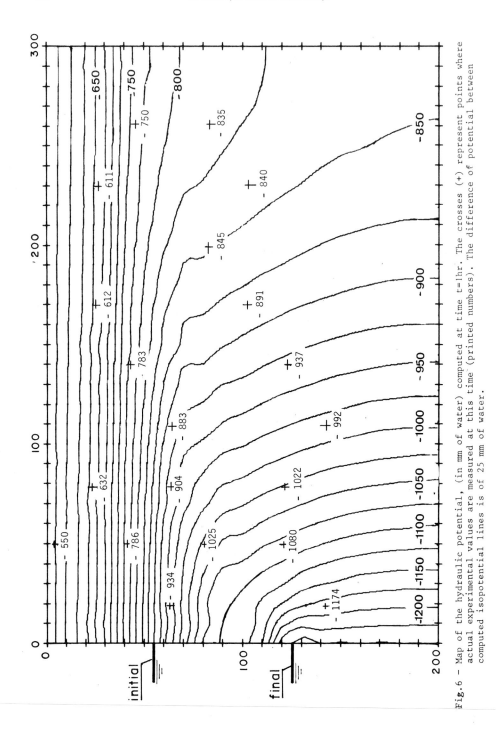

Fig. 6 - Map of the hydraulic potential, (in mm of water) computed at time t=1hr. The crosses (+) represent points where actual experimental values are measured at this time (printed numbers). The difference of potential between computed isopotential lines is of 25 mm of water.

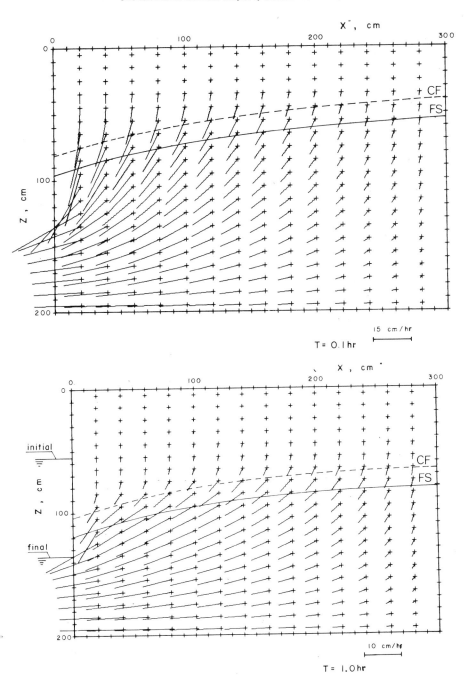

Fig.7 – Distribution of water flux at t = 0.1 hr and 1.0 hr for the drainage case. The lines indicated by C.F. and F.S. are respectively the Capillary Fringe and the Free Surface.

- in the middle part, between the water table in the soil and the water level in the ditch, there is a face of seepage, where the water pressure head is $h = 0$, and with vertical and horizontal component of the flux.

Repartition of q_x and q_z, obtained by numerical simulation, on that limit at 0.1 hr and 1 hr are given in fig. 8. Note that the vertical component q_z is maximum in the seepage face. Furthermore at the depth $z = H_1$ there is a singularity with brutal discontinuity in q_z, and maximum in q_x. The integral $\int_{z_s}^{p} q_x \, dz$ corresponds to the instantaneous discharge per unit thickness of soil.

Large_scale_variables

Our interest will now be focused on the determination of changes of water table position and cumulative outflow volumes. We have shown previously (see pa-per n°1) at this conference that the traditional approach of simulation of tran-sient water-table problems was completely inadequate for obtaining those two terms.

In fig. 9 a comparison is given between experimental and simulated water-table positions for different values of time. Experimentally the water table at a time $t > 0$ was obtained by two-dimensional interpolation, with the use of the NST program applied to water pressure head instantaneous measurements. Numerically it is obtained also by vertical interpolation between two successive nodes where h changes from a negative to a positive value.

A fair agreement is generally obtained but always much better than with the use of the Hele-Shaw analog (Vachaud, 1973). We should note that small discre-pancies near the outflow face are mainly due to the incremental prediction of the depth z_s, upper limit of the seepage face. Better agreement will be obtained with the choice of a smaller size of spatial increment Δz, but this will of course yields to a large increase of computational time, and to a need for larger storage capacity.

Finally the estimated cumulative outflow obtained with the model can be compared with success with experimental values. The curve has been given in pa-per 1. The full-scale error on the estimation of total outflow is 3 % instead of 28 % obtained by viscous flow analog ; furthermore there is no time-lag (remember that with a viscous analog, the outflow ceased after approximately 15 hr, instead of an approximated duration of 200 hr in the physical case).

We can now conclude that if proper parametric representation of the $k(h) - \theta(h)$ functions is used, this numerical technique leads to a good simula-tion of the experiment, which is so far much more reliable and representative of the physics of flow than the traditional approach.

We will now briefly test the same numerical model on very different boun-dary conditions representative of a recharge experiment.

THE RECHARGE EXPERIMENT - NUMERICAL AND EXPERIMENTAL RESULTS

Definition_of_the_problem

Fig.10 shows a schematic diagram of the flow medium which is now consi-dered. By symmetry it represents a plane flow problems of infiltration of water, supplied at constant rate q_o at the soil surface on an infinite line of width $2L$ centered between two ditches, penetrating completely the soil, with a spacing $2L'$. A horizontal water table exists initially, in hydrostatic equilibrium, at a depth H_o ; this level is maintained constant in the ditches.

All the other variables and parameters are the same as used before. In the experiment that we will describe :

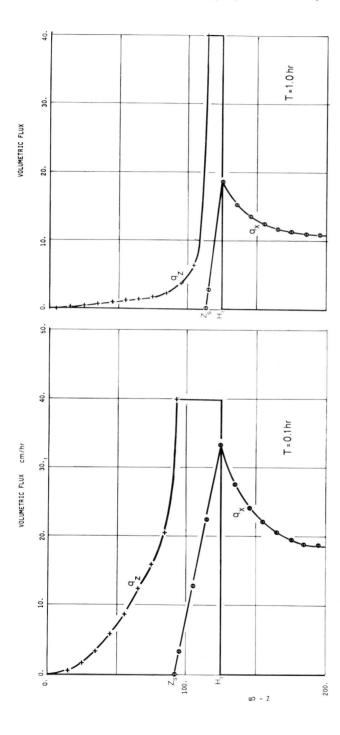

Fig.8 – Repartition of the components of flux q_x, q_z for t = 0.1 hr and t = 1 hr at the outflow face x = 0 .

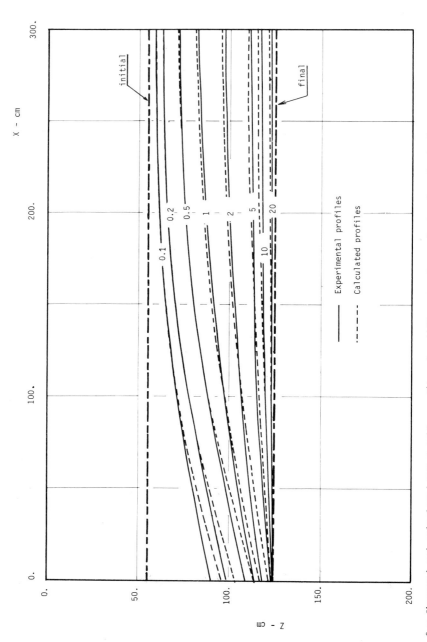

Fig.9 - Observed and calculated water table profiles for different values of time for the drainage case. Parameter: time in hour from the initiation of the drainage.

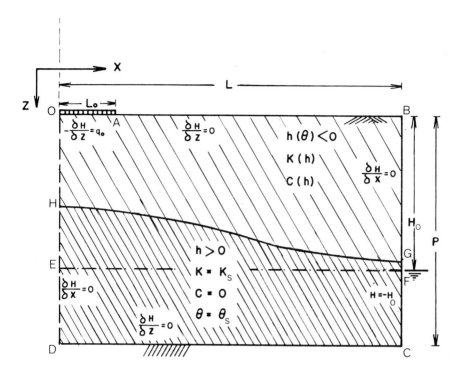

Fig. 10 — Definition of initial and boundary conditions for a two-dimensional problem of recharge of the water table.

H_o = 135 cm , L_o = 50 cm and q_o = 14 cm/hr.

The water table is schematized on fig. 10 at an arbitrary time after formation of the mound. The initial and boundary conditions corresponding to this case are :

1. $H = -H_o$ $\forall x$, $\forall z$ $t < 0$ (hydrostatic equilibrium)

2. $-K.\dfrac{\delta H}{\delta Z} = q_o$, z = 0 , $x \leqslant L_o$ $t \geqslant 0$ (constant flux infiltration at OA)

3. $\dfrac{\delta H}{\delta Z} = 0$ z = 0 $x > L_o$ $\forall t$ (no evaporation on AB)

4. $\dfrac{\delta H}{\delta x} = 0$ x = L $z < z_s$ $t \geqslant 0$ (no horizontal flux at BG)

5. $H = -z$ x = L $z_s \leqslant z < H_o$ $t \geqslant 0$ (seepage face if any at FG)

6. $H = -H_s$ x = L $z \geqslant H_o$ $\forall t$ (in the ditch)

7. $\dfrac{\delta H}{\delta z} = 0$ z = P $\forall x$ $\forall t$ (DC in an impervious bottom)

8. $\dfrac{\delta H}{\delta x} = 0$ x = 0 $\forall z$ $\forall t$ (no horizontal flux at OD by symmetry)

As in the case of the falling water table, the same problem was treated experimentally and numerically. Direct determination of the $\theta(h)$ and $K(h)$ relationships was also done during the infiltration, but hysteresis was not found significant for this type of soil as compared to the magnitude of local heterogeneities. Consequently the functional relationships defined by eq. 3 were also used for this problem.

Finally it has to be noted that for the earlier stage the physical problem of infiltration is that of a very sharp moving boundary (wetting front). This numerical difficulty can be eliminated by the use of the KIRCHOFF's transformation (Rubin, 1968)

$$U = \int_{H_0}^{h} K \, dh.$$

Consequently the numerical analysis of this problem is done in two stages:

i - for $t < T_o$, where T_o is arbitrarily defined as the time of transfer from the soil surface to the water table, the KIRCHOFF's transform is applied to eq. 1, yielding to

$$F(U) \frac{\delta U}{\delta t} = \frac{\delta^2 U}{\delta x^2} + \frac{\delta^2 U}{\delta z^2} - G(U) \frac{\delta U}{\delta z} \qquad (4)$$

with proper boundary conditions expressed in U. In equation 4 F(U) and G(U) are functions of K and h (Remson et al, 1971). Eq. 4 being of parabolic nature is solved by the simple use of the A.D.I. scheme, (without iteration) (see Khanji et al, 1974).

ii - for $t \geqslant T_o$, eq. 1 is solved directly using the ADIPIT scheme, since in this case the problem is described by an elliptic equation (the saturated zone). If $h^*(T_o, x, z)$ and $\theta^*(T_o, x, z)$ are the solutions of equation 4 at time T_o, then they are used as the initial values for the step ii).

The transfer time T_o is determined by testing changes of water content in the capillary fringe above the water table in its initial resting position. In the case of this experiment T_o = 1.75 hr.

Study of local variables

In fig. 11 the observed and simulated water content profiles are given for x = 20, 60, 80, 140 and 200 cm at time t = 1 hr and 8 hr. Note that the flow is typically bidimensional, as the infiltration is oriented essentially downwards for x = 20 cm (under the zone of infiltration), essentially upwards for x = 200cm, and influenced strongly by a horizontal component in the mid-range.

Agreement between simulated water content (obtained by procedure i) (T = 1 hr) and ii) (T = 8 hr) and experimental profile is very satisfactory, without taking into account the local heterogeneities.

As an example a map of potential field computed at T = 3 hr is given in fig. 12. Distribution of water flux obtained at t = 3 hr is also shown, under a vectorial form, in fig. 13. It is clear that at this time the raise of the water table mound induces, in the right hand side of the slab, upward oriented fluxes.

Large scale variables

We have shown in paper n°1 (fig. 3.c) that the traditional approach fails completely to describe the changes of level of the water table with time since the transfer time for water to flow from the soil surface to the groundwater cannot be taken into account in this approach. On the other hand this numerical approach is rather performant for simulating the physical problem, as it can be shown in fig. 14 by comparison between experimental and computed water table profiles at given time values. Computed values are also reported in fig. 3.c in paper n°1 together with the proper parameters.

This is also valuable for the computation of the outflow volume of water in the ditch. Computed values of the outflow are compared to experimental values as demonstrated in fig. 3.b of paper n°1.

CONCLUSION

We have shown in paper n°1 that any approach which neglects the contribution of the flow in the unsaturated zone as well as in the capillary fringe fails largely to predict transient water-table aquifer problems, inducting generally large overestimation of total volume outflow, and underestimation of the duration of the transfer. It is now possible to overcome those points and to obtain a fair simulation of the physical process by numerical integration of the flow equation taking into account the transfer of water simultaneously in the saturated and the unsaturated domain.

It is worth noting that although apparently more difficult (taking into account strong non linearities), the problem is also in fact practically easier to solve in that case than in the previous approach : since the upper boundary condition is known at any time (it is in this case the soil surface) the discretization scheme is much more easier to handle than when this boundary condition is moving and unknown (the "moving free surface" in the traditionnal approach).

Consequently a great advantage of the simulation technique presented is that the model can be adapted to different flow cases, such as recharge, evaporation, etc..., by a simple change of initial and boundary condition at the soil surface, and of the acceleration parameter applied.

Moreover, the technique of simulation is applicable on a computer with a rather small storage capacity (in our case a 16 K-bits IBM 1130). In the examples that we have presented, the time performance is rather mediocre but the initial conditions imposed to the water table were extremely drastic (drawdown of 70 cm on a length of 300 cm). They were applied to obtain a comparison between the numerical solution and the experimental data, but the faster and the bigger the chan-

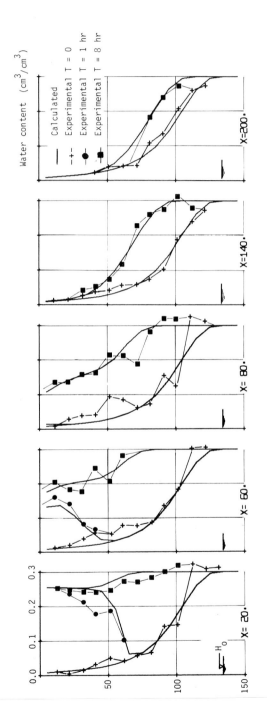

Fig.11 – Observed and calculated water content profiles at x = 20, 60, 80, 140, 200 cm for t = 1 hr and 8 hr for the recharge case.

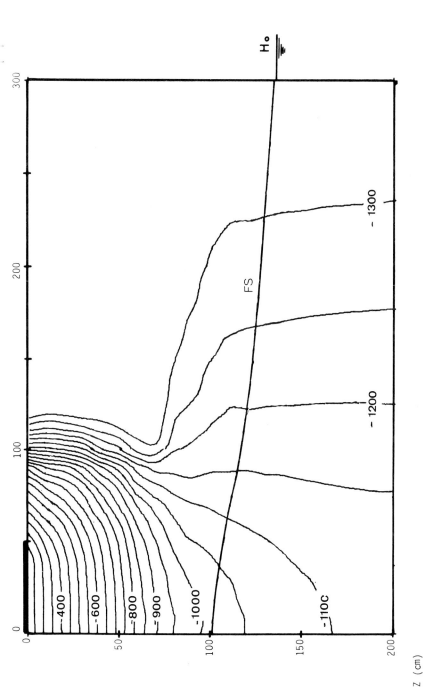

Z (cm)

Fig.12 — Map of the hydraulic potential (in mm of water). Computed at t = 3 hours for the recharge case. The difference of potential between isopotential lines is of 50 mm of water. The line FS indicates the positioning of the water table.

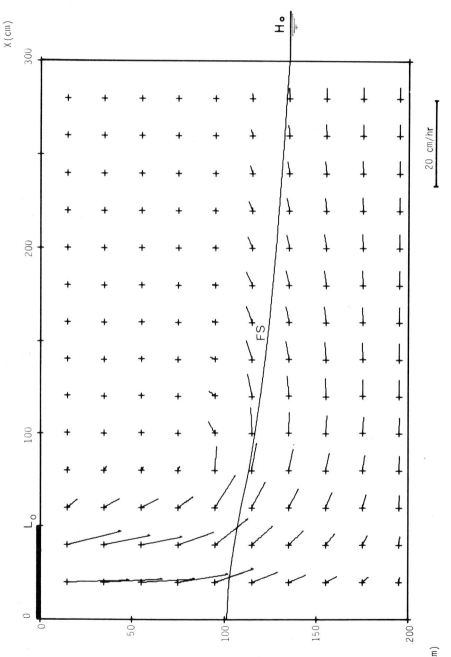

Fig. 13 – Distribution of water flux computed at t = 3 hr for the recharge experiment (q_o = 14 cm/hr).

ges of water pressure in the saturated zone at the earlier stages of the drainage the larger the number of iterations, and consequently the computer time required for simulation : in that case 3 to 4 min. for each time step with 396 nodes). The procedure is much faster for the recharge experiment, described in sequence i) where flow is only restricted to the unsaturated zone : the use of an activation process of nodes permits to obtain an estimation of an average time step of 10-20 sec.

APPENDIX I

If the hydraulic potential value at node (i, j) at time k, and iteration r, is denoted by $H_{i,j}^{k,r}$, then the two systems of difference equations approximating the equation 1 are given by :

i) "Vertical sweeping"

$$C_{i,j}^{k+\frac{1}{2},\ 2m} \cdot \frac{H_{i,j}^{k+1,\ 2m+1} - H_{i,j}^{k}}{\Delta t} + I_m \bar{K}_k (H_{i,j}^{k+1,\ 2m+1} - H_{i,j}^{k+1,\ 2m}) = \Delta_x (K^k \Delta_x$$

$$H^{k+1,\ 2m})_{i,j} + \Delta_z (K^k \Delta_z H^{k+1,\ 2m+1})_{i,j} \quad (1)$$

ii) "Horizontal sweeping"

$$C_{i,j}^{k+\frac{1}{2},\ 2m} \cdot \frac{H_{i,j}^{k+1,\ 2m+2} - H_{i,j}^{k}}{\Delta t} + I_m \bar{K}_k (H_{i,j}^{k+1,\ 2m+2} - H_{i,j}^{k+1,\ 2m+1}) = \Delta_x (K^k \Delta_x$$

$$H^{k+1,\ 2m+2}) + \Delta_z (K^k \Delta_z H^{k+1,\ 2m+1})_{i,j} \quad (2)$$

The different terms used in the equations 1) and 2) are defined as follows :

$$\Delta_x (K^k \Delta_x H^{k+1,r})_{i,j} = \frac{1}{(\Delta x)^2} [K_{i,j+\frac{1}{2}}^{k} (H_{i,j+1}^{k+1,r} - H_{i,j}^{k+1,r}) - K_{i,j-\frac{1}{2}}^{k} (H_{i,j}^{k+1,r} - H_{i,j-1}^{k+1,r})]$$

$$\Delta_z (K^k \Delta_z H^{k+1,r})_{i,j} = \frac{1}{(\Delta z)^2} [K_{i+\frac{1}{2}\ j}^{k} (H_{i+1,j}^{k+1,r} - H_{i,j}^{k+1,r}) - K_{i-\frac{1}{2},\ j}^{k} (H_{i-j}^{k+1,r} - H_{i-j}^{k+1,r})]$$

$$C_{i,j}^{k+\frac{1}{2},\ 2m} = (\frac{d\theta}{dH})_{i,j}^{k+\frac{1}{2},\ 2m}$$

$$K_{i\pm\frac{1}{2},j}^{k} = \frac{1}{2} (K_{i,j}^{k} + K_{i\pm1,j}^{k}) \ ; \ K_{i,j\pm\frac{1}{2}}^{k} = (K_{i,j}^{k} + K_{i,j\pm1}^{k}) \frac{1}{2}$$

$$\bar{K}_k = K_{i+\frac{1}{2},\ j}^{k} + K_{i-\frac{1}{2},\ j}^{k} + K_{i,j+\frac{1}{2}}^{k} + K_{i,j-\frac{1}{2}}^{k}$$

Wherein r is the advanced iteration number = (2m), (2m + 1), (2m + 2) with m as number of iteration step (4 in our case).

$I_m = R^m$ - with R = 0.15 for our case - is the iteration parameter which varies cyclically for each iteration. For each time step the cycles are repeated until the maximum variation of the hydraulic head-values obtained in two consecutive iterations, is smaller than $\varepsilon = 10^{-2}$cm

$$\max_{\forall i, \forall j} \left| H_{i,j} - H_{i,j} \right| < 10^{-2}$$

The I_m terms are added to increase the speed of convergence of the iterative procedure.

The position of the upper limit of the seepage face is obtained by testing the distribution of the hydraulic potential at the frontier X = 0. The H-values are correct if there is no upward and sideways flow away from the seepage face. On the other hand, if the hydraulic potential values are incorrect, the iterative procedure is repeated with an other position of the seepage face $Z'_s = Z_s + \Delta Z$.

APPENDIX II

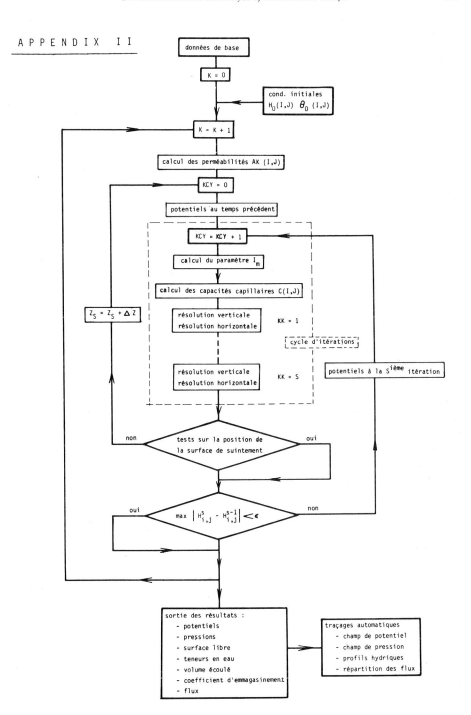

REFERENCES

CHILDS E.C., An introduction to the physical basis of soil water phenomena, Edited by Wiley-Interscience, John Wiley & Sons Ltd., 1969.

DOUGLAS J., D.W. PEACEMAN, H.H. RACHFORD, A method for calculating multidimensional immiscible displacement, AIME Trans. 216 (297-308), 1959.

KHANJI D., M. VAUCLIN, G. VACHAUD, Compte-rendu à l'Académie des Sciences de Paris, Série B (381-384), 1974.

REMSON I., G.M. HORNBERGER, F.J. MOLZ, Numerical Methods in subsurface hydrology, Edited by Wiley - Interscience, John Wiley Sons Inc., 1971.

RUBIN J., Theoretical analysis of two dimensional transient flow of water in unsaturated and partly unsaturated soils, Soil Science Society of Am. Proc. Vol. 32, n°5 (607-615), 1968.

VACHAUD G., M. VAUCLIN, D. KHANJI, Etude expérimentale des transferts bidimensionnels dans la zone non saturée, Application à l'étude du drainage d'une nappe à surface libre, Houille Blanche n°1 (65-74), 1973.

VACHAUD G., M. VAUCLIN, R. HAVERKAMP, Towards a physically based analysis of transient water table flow problems, Paper presented at the IFIP Working conference on modeling and simulation of water resources Systems (GENT - July-August 1974), 1974.

WATSON K.K., An instantaneous profile method for determining the hydraulic conductivity of unsaturated porous materials, Water Res. Res, 2 : 709-715, 1966.

DISCUSSION

It is possible to simulate very easily with a small computer recharge. Dr. Hillel was asking me about hysteresis, I would like to say that with the size of model that we have, with 6 parameters, it was extremely difficult to obtain a homogeneous sample that you obtain with a soil column. So we did have some very large discrepancies between profile at different distances. And if you consider the water suction, water content curves I would like to say that the zone of its attitude along the curve coming from heterogeneity was about 1 % order of magnitude of hysteresis. So we neglected hysteresis. Neglecting hysteresis we did have some problems, because flow was a little faster when simulated than we had, but only 1 or 2 %. (VACHAUD)

If you would have taken hysteresis into account, would there be a better fit qualitatively ? (HILLEL)

Maybe, but it would take a much longer time. In that case I think it is not worth doing it. If you take the paper by Nielsen and Biggar, it can be shown that hysteresis can be smaller than heterogeneity. (VACHAUD)

I am just asking of the direction of discrepancy between the computed and the measured results. Is it so that hysteresis would have improved ? (HILLEL)

It would ! But only 1 % if you have to pay 10 times more ! (VACHAUD)

If your interest was in the outflow based upon the changing conditions, then you could formulate I think, a mechanistic model relating those sort of variances which, given a set of conditions, it would be useful in saying what would happen at the outflow. And that model would not do what your model does, it would not tell you what is happening inside ; but there are some applications, where that sort of model would be satisfactory. And there is no reason at all why that should be any worse, doing that particular job than a much more complex model doing a different job. (YOUNG)

The way the model is constructed is completely governed by the purpose for which you built the model. By having a model like this, and by calculating outflow, there is a possibility to relate the outflow to some physical parameter and when you are interested in a bigger problem entering a relation like this, which is again another model, you get a hierarchical approach in models, the one at the lowest level describes the proces in detail but they can give you certain relations which you can enter in a higher level or less detailed model and use it for greater distances. (VAN KEULEN)

I come back to the aircraft. You can describe it in a complicated way as you want. But in terms of for instance the control problem it would be ridiculous to do so because you would never be able to design a controller. So you come down to a linearized model at different operating points and you design on the basis of that. That's not a perfect model but it suites the nature of your problem. (YOUNG)

May I come back to the comment on CSMP. This approach is more convenient for this problem terms of computer time or computer size ; but there is in principal no difficulty in using a simulation language like CSMP for this model. (VAN KEULEN)

With CSMP, once you are in the saturated zone, which is undefined, you have to change your variables ! The variable is not water pressure anymore but water content. (VACHAUD)

Why should CSMP not allow to bring your term to zero ? (VAN KEULEN)

You cannot iterate. (VACHAUD)

Yes, you can ! (VAN KEULEN)

This approach should be abandoned all together for infiltration problems, in favour for the two plane flow approach. In the way of these results, would you care to comment on the statement in literature ? (BRUTSAERT)

If it is true, you have to be careful, though. If you have some infiltrations and if air cannot flow, you cannot choose that equation. But if you have airflow, then the equation can be used. In our system of very small area, air was flowing, but if you would have a total soil surface then a two phase flow should be used. (VACHAUD)

Modeling and Simulation of Water Resources Systems, G.C. VANSTEENKISTE, (Ed.)
North-Holland Publishing Company (1975)

GALERKIN METHOD OF SIMULATING WATER UPTAKE BY PLANTS

Shlomo P. Neuman
Institute of Soils and Water,
Agricultural Research Organization,
The Volcani Center, P.O. Box 6
Bet Dagan, ISRAEL

Reinder A. Feddes and Eshel Bresler
Institute of Land and Water Management Research
Wageningen, THE NETHERLANDS

ABSTRACT

A Galerkin-type finite element method is used to simulate the nonsteady
flow of water in a multidimensional soil-plant environment. The finite
element approach can handle nonuniform soils having irregularly shaped
boundaries and arbitrary degrees of local anisotropy. The soil can be
unsaturated, saturated, or partly saturated. It can be slightly compressible and this is taken into account indirectly within the saturated zone
through the hydrologists' concept of specific storage. Flow can take place
in a two-dimensional region or in a three-dimensional region having a
radial symmetry. Particular emphasis is placed upon the simulation of atmospheric boundaries and water uptake by plant roots. The atmospheric
boundaries include seepage faces at which the pressure head must be uniformly equal to that of the surrounding air, evaporation surfaces at which
the maximum possible rate of flux is prescribed by atmospheric conditions,
whereas the actual flux may depend upon the moisture conditions prevailing
underground, and infiltration surfaces at which the maximum possible flux
is prescribed by external conditions such as rainfall and irrigation,
whereas the actual flux may again depend upon the soil moisture content.
These nonlinear atmospheric boundary conditions are handled by a unique
iterative procedure relying on the ease with which fluxes normal to the
boundary are assigned in the finite element approach. The rate of water
uptake by plants is controlled by the atmospheric demand for transpiration
as well as by the conditions prevailing in the root-soil system, and is
determined automatically by the computer program. An example is included
describing two-dimensional flow in a complex field situation encountered
in The Netherlands. In this example flow takes place under cropped field
conditions through five anisotropic layers. Water is supplied to the
system by infiltration from two unlined ditches and is withdrawn from the
system by evaporation, transpiration, and leakage to an underlying pumped
aquifer.

INTRODUCTION

Problems of seepage in unsaturated and partly saturated porous media lead
to quasilinear partial differential equations that are extremely difficult to
solve by analytical methods. Many attempts to solve these equations by finite difference techniques have been reported in the literature. The fundamental idea here
is to replace all derivatives by finite differences and thus reduce the original
continuous initial-boundary-value problem to a discrete set of simultaneous algebraic equations. For a review of this approach and a survey of pertinent literature the reader is referred to Braester et al. [1971].

In dealing with nonuniform soils of complex geometry and arbitrary anisotropy, the finite difference approach is often difficult to apply. The treatment
of irregularly shaped atmospheric boundaries, such as seepage faces and evaporation or infiltration surfaces, is difficult with this approach because prescribed
flux boundary conditions often lead to complex expressions and nonsymmetric matrices [Forsythe and Wasow, 1960, p. 202]. The finite element method, on the other
hand, does not recognize any of these difficulties and can easily handle irregularly shaped flow regions composed of nonuniform soils which can have arbitrary degrees
of anisotropy. The method is based on the Galerkin method which leads to an integral representation of the problem, rather than to the more familiar differential
form.

The finite element method was first applied to problems involving saturated-unsaturated flow in porous media by Neuman [1972, 1973, 1974]. In this report
the method is extended to account for evaporation and infiltration boundaries,
water uptake by plant roots, and axisymmetric flow to a well. A two-dimensional
example is included to demonstrate the power and versatility of the finite element
method.

GOVERNING EQUATIONS

The following discussion is written in an indicial notation whereby quantities with a single subscript (or index) represent components of vectors, and
quantities with two subscripts are components of second rank matrices or tensors.
When an index appears twice in any given term of an algebraic expression, this
term must be summed over all admissible values of that particular index (e.g., i
and j in eq. 1 below).

The flow of water in a slightly compressible unsaturated or partly-satu-
rated soil can be described by [Neuman, 1973]

$$L(\psi) = \frac{\partial}{\partial x_i} [K^r(\psi)K^s_{ij} \frac{\partial \psi}{\partial x_j} + K^r(\psi)K^s_{i3}] - [C(\psi) + \beta S_s]\frac{\partial \psi}{\partial t} + S = 0 \qquad (1)$$

where L is a quasilinear differential operator defined in the flow region,
x_i (i = 1,2,3) are spatial coordinates (x_3 the vertical), K^r is relative hydraulic
conductivity (0 $\leqslant K^r \leqslant$ 1), K^s_{ij} is conductivity tensor at saturation, ψ is pressure
head, C is specific moisture capacity (defined as $\partial\theta/\partial\psi$), β is 1 in the saturated
zone and 0 in the unsaturated zone, S_s is specific storage (defined as the volume
of water instantaneously released from storage per unit bulk volume of saturated
soil when ψ is lowered by one unit), t is time, and S is a positive sink term
(or, equivalently, a negative source term). In our case, S represents the volume
of water taken up by the roots per unit bulk volume of the soil in unit time.

The quantities K^s_{ij} and S_s are functions of position only. The term S_s
reflects the combined elastic properties of the medium and the water when one is
willing to assume that lateral strains are negligible and that the total stress
at each point remaine fixed in time. The exact definition of S_s for fully saturated media can be found in the recent work of Gambolati [1973a] who shows [1973b]
that its use as a constant is justified as long as vertical strains do not exceed
5 percent. The applicability of this concept to unsaturated conditions requires
further investigation. In the present work it is assumed that S_s can be disregarded in the unsaturated zone because the effect of compressibility on the storage
of water is negligibly small in comparison to the effect of changes in the moisture content.

The pressure head, ψ, is taken to be positive in the saturated zone and
negative in the unsaturated zone. In the absence of hysteresis, K_r and ψ are
monotonically increasing single-valued functions of θ, and C is the derivative of
θ with respect to ψ.

According to Feddes et al. [1974] the sink term is often expressed as

$$S = K^r K^s_{11} (\psi - \psi_r) \, b'$$ (2)

where ψ_r is pressure head in the roots and K^s_{11} is principal conductivity parallel to the horizontal (x_1) axis (all diagonal components of K^s_{ij} are implicitly assumed to be zero in the root zone). The term b' is an empirical quantity referred to herein as root effectiveness function. Assuming that the rate of uptake by roots is proportional to the pressure head gradient across the soilroot interface, as well as to the cross-sectional area of the flux, it is then evident that b' must be related to the ratio between the specific surface area of the roots and the impedance (thickness divided by conductivity) of the soilroot interface. In the absence of any proven physically-based model for water uptake, Eq. 2 is adopted in the present study as a working hypothesis.

Eq. 1 must be supplemented by appropriate initial and boundary conditions. As hysteresis is not considered in the present work, ψ is a single-valued function of θ and therefore, the initial conditions are simply

$$\psi(x_i, 0) = \Psi_o(x_i)$$ (3)

where Ψ_o is a prescribed function of x_i. In addition to this, one must specify either the pressure head or the normal flux at each point along the boundary. If Γ_1 is the segment of the boundary, Γ, along which pressure heads are prescribed and Γ_2 is the complementary segment of Γ along which normal fluxes are prescribed (such that $\Gamma = \Gamma_1 \cup \Gamma_2$), then the boundary conditions become :

$$\psi(x_i, t) = \Psi(x_i, t) \qquad \qquad \text{on } \Gamma_1$$ (4)

$$K^r (K^s_{ij} \frac{\partial \psi}{\partial x_j} + K^s_{i3}) n_i = -V(x_i, t) \qquad \text{on } \Gamma_2$$ (5)

Here Ψ and V are prescribed functions of x_i and t, and n_i is the unit outer normal vector on Γ.

ATMOSPHERIC BOUNDARY CONDITIONS

Along soil-air interfaces, in the absence of ponding, the soil can loose water to the atmosphere by evaporation or gain water by infiltration. While the potential (i.e., maximum possible) rate of evaporation from a given soil depends only on atmospheric conditions, the actual flux across the soil surface is limited by the ability of the porous medium to transmit water from below. Similarly, if the potential rate of infiltration (e.g., the rain intensity) exceeds the infiltration capacity of the soil, part of the water may be lost by runoff. Here, again, the potential rate of infiltration is controlled by atmospheric or other external conditions, whereas the actual flux depends on antecedent moisture conditions in the soil.

Thus, the exact boundary conditions to be assigned at the soil surface cannot be predicted a priori, and a solution must be sought by maximizing the absolute value of the flux (while maintaining the appropriate sign) subject to the requirements [see Hanks et al., 1969] .

$$\left| K^r (K^s_{ij} \frac{\partial \psi}{\partial x_j} + K_{i3}) n_i \right| \leq \left| E^*_s \right|$$ (6)

$$\psi_L \leqslant \psi \leqslant 0 \tag{7}$$

where E_s^* is the prescribed potential surface flux (positive when directed into the system as in infiltration, and negative when directed out of the system as in evaporation) and ψ_L is the minimum allowed pressure head at the soil surface. Both E_s^* and ψ_L may vary with time.

Methods for calculating E_s^* and ψ_L on the basis of atmospheric data are presented by Feddes et al. [1974]. They suggest that the total potential evapotranspiration from both soil and crop, E^*, be calculated by the combination equation

$$E^* = \frac{\delta (R_n - G) + \rho_a c_p (e_z^* - e_z) / r_a}{(\delta + \gamma)LH} \tag{8}$$

where δ is slope of saturation vapor pressure curve, R_n is net radiation flux, G is heat flux into soil, ρ_a is density of moist air, c_p is specific heat of air at constant pressure, e_z^* is saturated vapor pressure and e_z is unsaturated vapor pressure at elevation z and ambient temperature, r_a is resistance to vapor diffusion through air layer around leaves [for table of values see Feddes, 1971], γ is psychrometric constant, and LH is latent heat of water vaporization. The potential evaporation, E_s^*, is calculated from a simplified form of (8) by neglecting the aerodynamic term and taking into account only that fraction of R which reaches the soil surface [see Ritchie, 1973]

$$E_s^* = \frac{\delta}{(\delta + \gamma)LH} R_n \, e^{-0.39(LAI)} \tag{9}$$

where LAI is the leaf-area index.

The value of ψ_L in (7) can be determined from equilibrium conditions between soil water and atmospheric vapor. Feddes et al. [1974] suggest using the formula

$$\psi_L = \frac{RT}{Mg} \ln (f) \tag{10}$$

where R is universal gas constant, T is absolute temperature, M is molecular weight of water, g is acceleration due to gravity, and f is relative humidity of air.

The potential rate of transpiration by plants, $E_{p\ell}^*$, which we assume is equal to the maximum possible rate of water extraction by roots per unit horizontal area of the soil, is also dependent on atmospheric conditions. This quantity can be calculated directly from (8) and (9) according to

$$E_{p\ell}^* = E^* - E_s^* \tag{11}$$

This quantity will be required later in the text.

A seepage face is another kind of atmospheric boundary at which water seeps out from the saturated portion of a porous medium. The length of the seepage face varies with time in a manner that can never be predicted a priori. On the other hand, pressure head along the seepage face must be uniformly zero (if atmospheric pressure is also taken to be zero).

The numerical treatment of these atmospheric boundary conditions is made quite simple by the finite element method, as will be demonstrated below.

APPLICATION OF GALERKIN METHOD

Eqs. 1-7 are solved by the Galerkin method in conjunction with a finite element discretization scheme. According to the Galerkin method, an approximate solution to this problem at any given instant of time, t, is obtained in the form of a finite sequence.

$$\psi^N(x_i, t) = \psi_n(t) \, \xi_n(x_i); \qquad n = 1, 2, \ldots, N \qquad (12)$$

where $\{\xi_n(x_i)\}_{n=1}^N$ is a set of N linearly independent coordinate functions, and $\psi_n(t)$ are time-dependent coefficients yet to be determined. In choosing the coordinate functions, $\psi(x_i, t)$ is assumed to be a square-integrable function (in the Lebesque sense) belonging to a Hilbert space, H. The approximate solution, $\psi^N(x_i, t)$, must belong to an N-dimensional subspace of H, H^N, whose elements satisfy all continuity criteria as well as boundary conditions of the problem. Eq. 12 implies that each element of H^N can be expressed uniquely as a linear combination of all the ξ_n-s. Thus, the functions $\{\xi_n\}_{n=1}^N$ must be chosen so as to constitute a complete set spanning the subspace H^N, thereby forming a basis for H^N [see Oden, 1972].

If Ω denotes the interior of the flow region over which $\psi(x_i, t)$ is defined, then the norm of ψ, $|| \psi ||$, is obtained from

$$|| \psi ||^2 = \int_\Omega \psi^2 \, d\Omega \qquad (13)$$

It is said that ψ^N converges in the norm to ψ whenever

$$\lim_{N \to \infty} || \psi - \psi^N || = 0 \qquad (14)$$

The aim of the variational approach is to determine the coefficient ψ_n of ψ^N in such a manner as to insure convergence in the norm to the true solution. In the finite difference approach one usually requires that his solution converge uniformly over the closure of the entire flow region, $\bar{\Omega}$, where $\bar{\Omega} = \Omega \cup \Gamma$. Although uniform convergence always implies convergence in the norm while the converse is not necessarily true, convergence in the norm is faster [Mikhlin, 1964] and this is an advantage of the variational method.

The Galerkin method stipulates that in order to determine the coefficients of ψ^N so as to minimize $|| \psi - \psi^N ||$, $L(\psi^N)$ in eq. 1 must be orthogonal to each of the N coordinate functions, ξ_n :

$$\Omega_n(\psi^N) = \int_\Omega L(\psi^N) \, \xi_n \, d\Omega = 0 \quad ; \quad n = 1, 2, \ldots, N \qquad (15)$$

In other words, the functional $\Omega_n(\psi^N)$ must vanish for each value of n.

FINITE ELEMENT DISCRETIZATION

In using the finite element discretization scheme, the flow region $\bar{\Omega}$ is subdivided into a network of elements. It is convenient to adopt a network composed of triangular elements for plane flow and a network composed of concentric rings of constant triangular cross section for axisymmetric problems. Let the corners of these elements be designated as nodal points and let x_i^n be the space coordinates of the n-th node. Each node, n, is associated with a unique subregion of $\bar{\Omega}$ $\bar{\Omega}^n$, containing all elements in the immediate vicinity of n (see shaded area in Fig. 1). In addition, each node is associated with a global coordinate function $\xi_n(x_i)$, which is linear in x_i inside each element and piecewise linear over $\bar{\Omega}$, such that

$$\xi_n(x_i^m) = \delta_{nm} \qquad \text{for all } x_i^m \text{ in } \bar{\Omega} \tag{16a}$$

$$\xi_n(x_i) = 0 \qquad \text{for all } x_i \text{ not in } \Omega^n \tag{16b}$$

where δ_{nm} is Kronecker delta (i.e., $\delta_{nm} = 1$ if $n = m$ and $\delta_{nm} = 0$ if $n \neq m$) and Ω^n is the interior of $\bar{\Omega}^n$.

Owing to their unique shape, ξ_n are sometimes referred to as pyramidal, roof, or chapeau functions. By introducing them into eq. 12, the latter equation becomes a piecewise linear two-dimensional Lagrange interpolation formula for ψ^N in $\bar{\Omega}$. In other words, the value of ψ^N at any node in $\bar{\Omega}$ is equal to the coefficient, ψ_n, corresponding to that node.

In order to express ξ_n explicitly in terms of the space variables, x_i, it is convenient to consider a single element, $\bar{\Omega}^e$, as shown in Fig. 2. Let $\{\xi_n^e(x_i)\}$ be a set of local coordinate functions that are linear in x_i and satisfy the requirements.

$$\xi_n^e(x_i^m) = \delta_{nm} \qquad \text{for all } x_i^m \text{ in } \bar{\Omega}^e \tag{17a}$$

$$\xi_n^e(x_i) = 0 \qquad \text{for all } x_i \text{ not in } \bar{\Omega}^e \tag{17b}$$

This together with eq. 16 implies that the global coordinate functions, ξ_n, are the union of the local coordinate functions, ξ_n^e,

$$\xi_n^e(x_i) = \bigcup_e \xi_n^e(x_i) \tag{18}$$

where the union sign is taken over all elements, e. The relationship between ξ_n^e and x_i is given elsewhere [Neuman, 1973].

By virtue of eq. 18 it is now possible to rewrite the global functional from eq. 15, $\Omega_n(\psi^N)$, in terms of equivalent local functionals over individual triangles, $\Omega_n^e(\psi^N)$, so that

$$\Omega_n(\psi^N) = \Omega_n(\psi_m \xi_m) = \Omega_n[\psi_m(\bigcup_e \xi_m^e] = \sum_e \Omega_n^e(\psi_m \xi_m^e) = 0 \tag{19}$$

where the summation is taken over all elements and

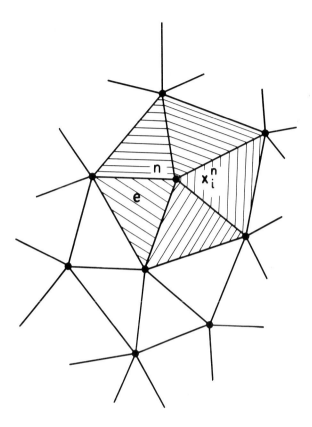

Fig.1 - Network of triangular elements.

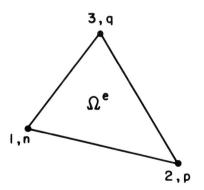

Fig.2 - Single triangular element.

$$\Omega_n^e \ (\psi_m \xi_m^e) = \int_{\Omega^e} L(\psi_m \xi_m^e) \ \xi_n^e \ d\Omega \tag{20}$$

Since the Galerkin method applies only at a given instant of time, the time derivative $\partial\psi/\partial t$ appearing in $L(\psi)$ must be determined independently of the orthogonalization process. Experience indicates that for the numerical method to converge in the case of unsaturated flow, $\partial\psi/\partial t$ must not be replaced by $\partial\psi^N/\partial t$ as it is usually done in the finite element approach. A much more stable solution is obtained by defining the nodal values of the time derivatives, $\partial\psi_n/\partial t$, as weighted averages of $\partial\psi/\partial t$ over the entire flow region, R :

$$\frac{\partial\psi_n}{\partial t} \equiv \frac{\int_\Omega (C + \beta \ S_s) \ \frac{\partial\psi}{\partial t} \ \xi_n \ d\Omega}{\int_\Omega (C + \beta \ S_s) \ \xi_n \ d\Omega} \tag{21}$$

The physical meaning of this definition will be explained later. In addition to this, it is assumed that K_{ij}^s and S_s are constant in each element while K^r and C vary linearly according to

$$K^r = K_\ell^r \ \xi_\ell^e \tag{22a}$$

$$C = C_\ell \ \xi_\ell^e \tag{22b}$$

where ℓ stands for the corners of the triangle.

By combining eqs. 19-22 and using Green's first identity, one obtains a set of quasilinear first-order differential equations

$$A_{nm} \ \psi_m + F_{nm} \ \frac{d\psi_m}{dt} = Q_n - B_n - D_n \qquad n, \ m = 1, \ 2, \ \dots, \ N \tag{23}$$

where, for a vertical cross-section described by the coordinates x_1 and x_3,

$$A_{nm} = \sum_e K_\ell^r K_{ij}^s \ \int_{\Omega^e} \xi_\ell^e \ \frac{\partial\xi_n^e}{\partial x_i} \ \frac{\partial\xi_m^e}{\partial x_j} \ d\Omega$$

$$= \sum_e \frac{\alpha}{4\Delta} \ \bar{K}^r \ [\ K_{11}^s b_n b_m + K_{13}^s (b_n c_m + b_m c_n) + K_{33}^s c_n c_m \ ] \tag{24a}$$

$$F_{nm} = \sum_e \int_{\Omega^e} (C_\ell \xi_\ell^e \xi_n^e + \beta S_s) d$$

$$= \sum_e \frac{\alpha\Delta}{12} \ [\ (2C_n + C_p + C_q) + 4\beta S_s \ ] \qquad \text{if } n = m \tag{24b}$$

$$F_{nm} = 0 \qquad\qquad \text{if } n \ne m \tag{24c}$$

$$Q_n = - \sum_e \int_{\Gamma^e} V \xi_n^e \ d\Gamma = -\sum_e \frac{(LV)_n}{2} \tag{24d}$$

$$B_n = \sum_e K_\ell^r K_{13}^s \int_{\Omega_e} \xi_\ell^e \frac{\partial \xi_n^e}{\partial x_i} \, d\Omega = \sum_\varepsilon \frac{\alpha}{2} \bar{K}^r (K_{13}^s b_n + K_{33} c_n) \qquad (24e)$$

$$D_n = \sum_e \int_{\Omega_e} S \xi_n^e \, d\Omega \qquad (24f)$$

The subscripts n, p, q refer to the three corners of each triangle as shown in Fig. 2, Δ is the area of the triangle, $\alpha = 1$ for plane flow and $\alpha = 2\pi\bar{x}_1$ for axi-symmetric flow, $\bar{x}_1$ is the average horizontal (or radial) coordinate given by $\bar{x}_1 = (x_1^n + x_1^p + x_1^q)/3$, $\bar{K}^r$ is the average relative conductivity given by $\bar{K}^r = (K_n^r + K_p^r + K_q^r)/3$, and b and c are geometric coefficients defined in the appendix. The term $(LV)_n$ represents the flow rate across any side of the triangle, of length L, which includes nodal point n. V is assumed to be uniform along L.

In the case of horizontal plane flow, B_n must be set equal to zero for all values of n. It is important to recognize that the matrix A_{nm} is sparse and symmetric, whereas Q_n is zero at all internal nodal points which do not act as sinks or sources. In addition, one notes that F_{nm} is a diagonal matrix (i.e., all its terms outside the main diagonal are zero), this being a direct consequence of the averaging process implied by (21). The physical meaning of this averaging process is now evident : F_{nm} is the amount of water stored in the entire flow system when the value of ψ at node n changes by one unit in unit time. Thus, F_{nn} is global coefficient of storage corresponding to nodal point n. The vector D_n will be treated later in connection with water extraction by plant roots.

INTEGRATION OVER TIME

To integrate (23), the time domain is discretized into a sequence of finite intervals, Δt, and the time derivatives of ψ_n are replaced by finite differences. If the entire flow system remains unsaturated at all times, good results can be obtained by employing the time-centered scheme

$$(A_{nm}^{k+1/2} + \frac{2}{\Delta t^k} F_{nm}^{k+1/2}) \psi_m^{k+1} = 2Q_n^{k+1/2} - 2B_n^{k+1/2} - 2D_n^{k+1/2}$$

$$- (A_{nm}^{k+1/2} - \frac{2}{\Delta t^k} F_{nm}^{k+1/2}) \psi_m^k$$

$$n, m = 1, 2, \ldots, N \qquad (25)$$

where k represents the time $t = t^k$ and $\Delta t^k = t^{k+1} - t^k$. In order to evaluate the coefficients in (25), one must know the values of $\psi_n^{k+1/2}$ at $t^{k+1/2} = t^k + \Delta t^k/2$. At the beginning of each time step, these are predicted by linear extrapolation from previously calculated values according to

$$\psi_n^{k+1/2} = \psi_n^k + \frac{\Delta t^k}{2\Delta t^{k-1}} (\psi_n^k - \psi_n^{k-1}) \qquad (26)$$

The resulting set of simultaneous linear algebraic equations is then solved by a highly efficient Gauss elimination algorithm (which takes account of the sparse and symmetric nature of A_{nm} and F_{nm}) for the values of ψ_n^{k+1} at all nodes.

Due to the nonlinear nature of (25), these results must be improved by an iterative process. At each iteration, the most recent values of ψ_n^{k+1} are used to obtain an improved estimate of $\psi_n^{k+1/2}$ from

$$\psi_n^{k+1/2} = 1/2 \ (\psi_n^k + \psi_n^{k+1}) \tag{27}$$

After having reevaluated the coefficients, the equations are again solved by Gauss elimination for improved values of ψ_n^{k+1}. The iterative procedure continues as long as it is necessary to achieve a satisfactory degree of convergence.

Since this iterative procedure is fully implicit, it is usually very fast. Experiments with a fully implicit quasi-linearization (Newton-Raphson) scheme have failed to produce comparable results. This may probably be due to the high sensitivity of the Newton-Raphson method to the initial estimate of $\psi_n^{k+1/2}$, and due to the increased amount of computational effort required for each iteration.

If part of the system is saturated and S_s in this part is zero, the values of F_{nn} corresponding to nodal points in the saturated zone vanish because C is zero, and the governing equations there become elliptic. This means that sudden changes in boundary conditions around the saturated zone have an instantaneous effect on the values of ψ everywhere in this zone, and ψ is no longer a continuous function of time. For example, by imposing a certain boundary condition at time $t = t^k$, all values of ψ in the saturated zone change instantaneously and the values of ψ_p^k at the start of the time step, Δt^k, become unknown. Thus, the right-hand side of (25) is unknown, and the equations cannot be solved.

To overcome this problem, one must adopt a fully implicit backward difference scheme in terms of ψ,

$$(A_{nm}^{k+1/2} + \frac{1}{\Delta t_k} \ F_{nm}^{k+1/2})\psi_m^{k+1} = Q_n^{k+1/2} - B_n^{k+1/2} - D_n^{k+1/2} + \frac{1}{\Delta t^k} \ F_{nm}^{k+1/2}\psi_m^k \tag{28}$$

Here the coefficients are still evaluated at half the time step, k+1/2, and this is done in order to dampen the tendency of ψ to oscillate around its limit. Such oscillations are frequently encountered in highly nonlinear systems such as the one dealt with herein and a well-known method of overcoming this problem is to employ under-relaxation techniques. The effect of evaluating the coefficients at half the time step is to under-relax the system.

With this scheme one can obtain a solution without knowing the values of ψ_n^k at the start of the time step in the saturated zone. The only exception to this rule occurs at nodes that pass from a state of saturation to a state of incomplete saturation during a time step. The values of $F_{nn}^{k+1/2}$ corresponding to such nodes may differ from zero and (28) can no longer be solved without knowing the values of ψ^k. However, as $S_s = 0$, $F_{nn}^{k+1/2}$ represents only storage due to changes in the moisture content, θ. Such changes occur only within the negative range of ψ values whereas when ψ is positive, $C = \partial\theta/\partial\psi$ is zero. Thus, whenever a value of ψ_n^k in the saturated zone becomes unknown due to a sudden change in the boundary conditions, one is justified in replacing this value by zero in (28).

PRESCRIBED BOUNDARY CONDITIONS

At nodal points lying on Γ_1 type boundaries of the flow region, the values of ψ_n are prescribed by (4) whereas the values of V (and therefore Q_n) are unknown. In the present work the values of ψ_n are assumed to vary linearly on Γ_1 during any given time interval.

Suppose that the value of ψ_p at some node p must be equal to a prescribed value Ψ_p, at the end of Δt^k. This is accomplished by replacing the p-th equation by a dummy expression of the form

$$A_{pp} \ \psi_p^{k+1} = \Psi_p \tag{29}$$

where $A_{pp} = 1$ (no summation is implied in eq. 29) and, at the same time, replacing the values of ψ_p^{k+1} in all the remaining equations by ψ_p and transfering the corresponding terms to the right hand side. This method is especially well suited for the Gauss elimination algorithm because the size of the left-hand side matrix remains unchanged, all terms along the main diagonal remain non-zero, and the matrix remains symmetric.

After having determined the values of ψ^{k+1} at all nodes, the value of the nodal flux, $Q_p^{k+1/2}$, can be calculated explicitly from the p-th equation.

At nodal points lying on Γ_2 type boundaries of the flow region, the values of $Q_n^{k+1/2}$ are prescribed by (5) and (24d). At nodes that lie inside the flow region and do not act as sources or sinks, $Q_n^{k+1/2}$ must be set equal to zero. At internal sources or sinks whose strength is known, $Q_n^{k+1/2}$ is simply the known amount of water generated at node n in unit time during Δt^k.

EVAPORATION AND INFILTRATION BOUNDARY CONDITIONS

The finite element method is exceptionally well suited for the treatment of (6) and (7) because the type of boundary condition can be easily changed at each node from one iteration to another. During the first iteration in each time step, the surface nodes are treated as a prescribed flux boundary and are assigned an arbitrary fraction of the potential flux, usually 0.1. If the computed values of ψ satisfy (7) the absolute value of the flux at each node, n, is increased by $|\psi_L|/|\psi_n|$ in the case of evaporation, or by $|\psi_L|/|\psi_L-\psi_n|$ in the case of infiltration, subject to (6). If some value of ψ_n lies outside the limits specified by (7) then, during the subsequent iteration, n is treated as a prescribed pressure head node with $\psi = \psi_L$ for evaporation or $\psi = 0$ for infiltration. This situation is maintained as long as (6) is satisfied. If, at any stage of the computation, the calculated flux exceeds the potential flux so that (6) is not satisfied, n is assigned the potential flux and is again treated as a prescribed flux boundary. The iterative procedure continues until convergence is achieved at all nodes in the finite element network.

SEEPAGE FACES

A seepage face is an external boundary of the saturated zone where water leaves the system and ψ is uniformly zero. Under transient conditions, the length of the seepage face varies with time in a manner that cannot be predicted a priori. If one treats the seepage face as a prescribed pressure head boundary with $\psi = 0$, the length of this face remains fixed, and this is contrary to the physics of transient flow. On the other hand, the seepage face cannot be treated as a prescribed flux boundary because the values of Q_n there are generally unknown. How, then, should a seepage face be treated ?

Let us consider all nodes which, at any stage of the calculation, can belong to a given seepage face by having zero values of ψ and negative values of Q_n (recall that Q_n is negative when the flow at node n is directed out of the system). Suppose that, knowing the position of the seepage face at time t^k, it is desired to predict its position at time t^{k+1}. During the first iteration, ψ is set equal to zero along the initial length of the seepage face and the latter is treated as a prescribed ψ boundary. At the same time, Q is set equal to zero at all nodes with $\psi < 0$ and this segment is treated as a prescribed flux boundary. The solution is expected to yield negative values of Q at nodes where ψ is prescribed to be zero, and negative values of ψ at nodes where Q is prescribed to be zero. If, instead, a positive value of Q is encountered at a node where $\psi = 0$, the value of Q there is set equal to zero and, in the next iteration, this node is treated as a prescribed flux boundary. On the other hand, if a positive value of ψ is encountered at a node where Q = 0, the value of ψ there is set equal to zero and, in the next iteration, this node is treated as a prescribed pressure head boundary.

Experience has shown that in order for the solution to converge, this modification of the boundary conditions should always proceed sequentially from node to node, starting at the saturated end of the seepage face. In addition, after having set Q equal to zero at any node during a given iteration, Q at all the subsequent nodes must also be set equal to zero. The iterative process continues in the manner described earlier until a sufficient degree of convergence is achieved at each node in the network.

It should be noted that owing to the ease with which prescribed flux boundary conditions are treated in the finite element method, the handling of seepage faces is considerably more simple than in the finite difference approach.

WATER UPTAKE BY PLANT ROOTS

The rate of water uptake by plant roots depends upon atmospheric conditions (potential rate of transpiration, $E_{p_0}^*$) as well as upon conditions prevailing underground. Since this rate cannot be predicted _a priori_, we set the values of Q_n at all nodal points in the root zone equal to zero (indicating that we are not dealing with sources or sinks of known strength), and instead use D_n to express the rate of extraction by plants (see eqs. 23 and 24). In order to simplify the analysis, we restrict ourselves to rectangular nodal patterns in the root zone as shown below.

Let us suppose that the root zone is represented by a rectangular nodal pattern such as the one shown in Fig. 3. Next, let us number all vertical columns of nodes and all vertical columns of elements in the root zone sequentially from left to right and confine our attention to a single nodal column, i. The bottom node in this column is designated NB_i, and the top node is designated NT_i. The node at the soil surface immediately above NT_i is assumed to be contributing only to direct evaporation and not to root extraction, so that it is not considered to be part of the root zone. Each column of elements is divided into two identical segments, as is indicated by the broken vertical lines in Fig. 3. The extraction rate in any two segments neighbouring on the same nodal column is assumed to remain uniform in the horizontal direction. This, of course, does not prevent the extraction rate from varying horizontally between any two adjacent nodal columns, so that the two-dimensional nature of the analysis is by no means violated in this manner.

Let us calculate the rate of extraction from the area centered around nodal column i and lying between the two nearest vertical broken lines. Since S varies only in the vertical direction, we can express D_n in (24f) as

$$D_n = \frac{1}{2} (W_{i-1} + W_i) \sum_L \int_L S \zeta_n^L \, dx_3 \tag{30}$$

where ζ_n^L is the one-dimensional equivalent of ξ_n^e along the vertical direction (i.e. $\zeta_N^{L_n}$ is a linear function of the vertical coordinate, x_3, which takes on the value unity at node n and the value zero at all other nodes : e.g.

$$\xi_n^{L_n} = \frac{x_3 - x_3^n}{L_n} \quad ; \quad \zeta_{n+1}^{L_n} = \frac{L_n - (x_3 - x_3^n)}{L_n} \quad ,(\text{see Fig. 3}),$$

and the summation is taken over all one-dimensional elements, L, in the immediate neighbourhood of node n. If one further assumes that S varies linearly in the vertical direction between any two adjacent nodes according to

$$S = S_m \zeta_m^L \tag{31}$$

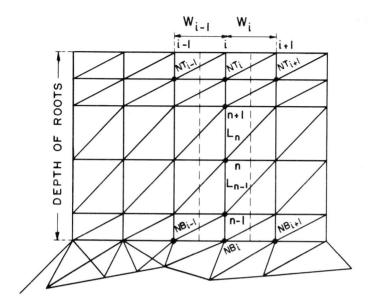

Fig.3 - Rectangular nodal pattern in root zone.

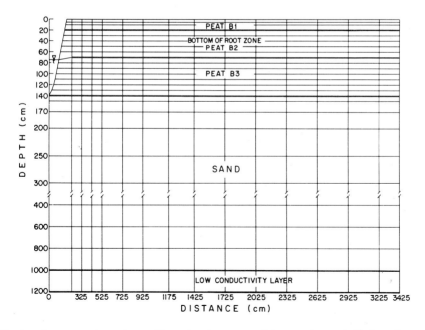

Fig.4 - Cross-section of two-dimensional system with superimposed finite element
network.

then (30) takes the form

$$D_n = \frac{1}{2} (W_{i-1} + W_i) \sum_L \int_L S_m \zeta_m^L \zeta_n^L dx_3$$

$$= \frac{1}{2} (W_{i-1} + W_i) \sum_L L \left(\frac{S_n}{3} + \frac{S_{n \pm 1}}{6}\right) \tag{32}$$

Substituting (2) into (32) yields

$$D_n = \frac{1}{2} (W_{i-1} + W_i) \sum_L L K_{11}^S \left\{ \frac{[K^r b'(\psi-\psi_r)]_n}{3} + \frac{[K^r b'(\psi-\psi_r)]_{n \pm 1}}{6} \right\} \tag{33}$$

where ψ_r is assumed to remain constant with depth.

The total rate of transpiration per unit surface area, $E_{p\ell}$, is given by

$$E_{p\ell} = \frac{2}{W_{i-1} + W_i} \sum_{n=NB_i}^{NT_i} D_n ; \qquad\qquad D_n < 0 \tag{34}$$

Since we do not allow flow to occur from the roots into the soil, only negative values of D_n are considered in (34). Thus, our purpose is to maximize the value of $E_{p\ell}$ subject to the requirement that it does not exceed the potential rate of transpiration (see eq. 11), i.e.,

$$|E_{p\ell}| \leq |E_{p\ell}^*| \tag{35}$$

In addition, the pressure head in the roots should not be allowed to get below the wilting point, ψ_w (which is usually taken as -15000 cm of water), i.e.,

$$\psi_r \geq \psi_w \tag{36}$$

This constrained maximization process is accomplished by the following iterative procedure. At the beginning of each iteration, ψ_r is set equal to the prescribed value of ψ_w. Then, using prior values of $\psi^{k+1/2}$ and $(K^r)^{k+1/2}$, the value of $D_n^{k+1/2}$ is determined for each node in the column by means of eq. 33. Considering only negative values of D_n (positive values are set equal to zero), the magnitude of $E_{p\ell}$ is calculated with the aid of (34). If $|E_{p\ell}|$ is less than $|E_{p\ell}^*|$ or equal to it, the current values of D_n are adopted for the solution of (25) or (28). If, on the other hand, $|E_{p\ell}|$ is greater than $|E_{p\ell}^*|$, all the values of D_n are multiplied by $|E_{p\ell}^*| / |E_{p\ell}|$ so as to make their sum equal to $E_{p\ell}^*$. By combining (33) and (34), one then obtains

$$E_{p\ell}^* = \sum_{n=NB_i}^{NT_i} \sum_L L K_{11}^S \left\{ \frac{[K^r b'(\psi-\psi_r)]_n}{3} + \frac{[K^r b'(\psi-\psi_r)]_{n \pm 1}}{6} \right\} \tag{37}$$

where the summation over n is taken only for those nodes at which D_n is negative. Eq. 37 enables one to calculate explicitly the value of ψ_r corresponding to $E_{p\ell}^*$.

A similar procedure is performed for each nodal column in the root zone, until all the components of D_n are known. One can then solve (25) or (28) for new values of ψ at all nodes in the finite element network, and then proceed to the next iteration in the same manner as before. The iterative procedure continues until convergence in the values of ψ is achieved at all nodes in the network.

The reader will note that in this manner, different species of plants with unequal rooting depths can be treated simultaneously. In addition, the rooting depth may vary with time simply by assigning new values to the function b' at any given time step. In other words, one can actually follow changes in root development during the growing period provided that b' as a function of plant and time is known to each depth. Methods for determining b' have been discussed by Feddes et al. [1974].

EXAMPLE

The present example is taken from the subirrigation experimental field "De Groeve" in the Netherlands [Feddes and Van Steenbergen, 1973] . The field spreads over 16 hectares of peaty soil having an average thickness of 1.40 meter. The peat is underlain by sandy soils down to a depth of about 10 meters. The bottom of the sand is separated from an underlying aquifer by 2 meters of sediments having a relatively low hydraulic conductivity. Outside the experimental field, the aquifer is penetrated by wells which intermittently extract water from it for domestic supply. The field is traversed by several unlined ditches in which the water level is controlled by man.

Proper management of the field requires estimating water losses which occur in the upper layers due to leakage into the pumped aquifer, plant transpiration, and soil evaporation when the water level in the ditches is maintained at a predetermined elevation. Ultimately, the local research project will consider the effect of subirrigation and water management on agricultural crop production and the effect of controlling the height of water in the ditches so as to minimize water losses from the root zone while at the same time recharging the underlying aquifer.

Saturated hydraulic conductivities of the various soil layers were measured in the field by the auger hole method and in the laboratory with the aid of constant head and falling head permeameters [Wit, 1967] . The variation of hydraulic conductivity with water content was determined in the laboratory together with the retention curves.

Only one half of a vertical cross section between two ditches is considered due to the symmetry of the field. A scheme of this cross section together with the superimposed finite element network are illustrated in Fig. 4. The vertical dimensions of the elements were made small in the root zone where large hydraulic gradients are expected to occur, and larger at the bottom of the saturated zone where these gradients are expected to be relatively small. The horizontal dimensions of the elements in the vicinity of the ditch were made smaller than in the central portion of the field due to the relatively large horizontal hydraulic gradients expected to occur near the inflow face. According to laboratory water retention data, the peat soil has been divided into three layers having distinct material properties. The retention curves for these three layers as well as for the underlying sand are shown in Fig. 5. The vertical hydraulic conductivities in these layers are shown in Fig. 6 as functions of the soil water content. The peat and sand layers are assumed to be anisotropic, having horizontal conductivities ten times as large as the vertical ones. The bottom low-conductivity layer is isotropic with a saturated conductivity value of 0.044 cm.hr^{-1}.

The only crop grown in the field is potatoes. Initially the depth of the root zone is taken to be 40 cm. The root effectiveness function, b', is assumed to vary with depth and time in a manner similar to that previously adopted for red cabbage by Feddes et al. [1974] (see Fig. 7). During the first 168 hours curve 4 in Fig. 7 is adopted to represent b', whereas curve 5 is adopted for later times.

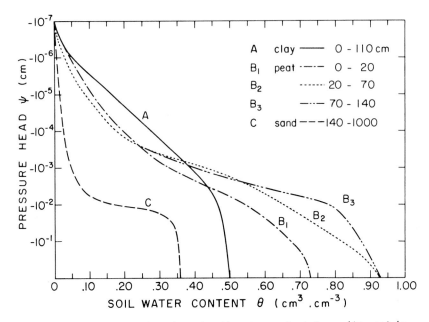

Fig.5 - Pressure head as a function of soil water content for soils used in
experiments.

    In the ditches the water level is maintained at a constant depth of 74 cm
below the soil surface, and this is also the initial depth of the water table. At
the start of the calculations, the water is under static conditions and hydraulic
heads are equal in the entire system. At later times, no flow is allowed to take
place across the vertical boundaries of the system depicted in Fig. 4. The hydraulic head in the pumped aquifer, at the bottom of the system in Fig. 4 varies with
time in a continuous manner, as shown in Fig. 8, which is similar to what has been
observed in the field. No flow is allowed to take place across the unsaturated face
of the ditch. The maximum allowable rates of plant transpiration and soil evaporation vary with time in the manner illustrated in Fig. 8.

    The magnitude of the first time step, Δt^1, was one hour. During the first
48 hours, the magnitude of Δt gradually increased from 1 to 12 hours. A time step
of 24 hours was adopted for all later computations. Convergence was assumed whenever the maximum change in ψ at all nodes in the finite element network between
two consecutive iterations in a time step did not exceed 1 cm.

    Fig. 9 shows the cumulative volume of water leaving the soil surface via
evapotranspiration, the volume of water leaking out of the system into the underlying aquifer, and the volume of water infiltrating into the system from the ditch.
It is noted that the loss of water due to evapotranspiration and leakage exceeds
the inflow from the ditch, a fact which is reflected in the lowering of the water
table by as much as 27 centimeters, as is indicated in Fig. 10.

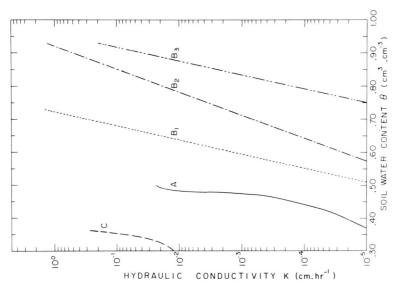

Fig. 6:   Hydraulic conductivity versus soil water content for soils used
in experiments.

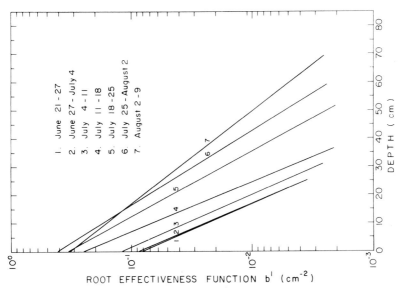

Fig. 7:   Variation of root effectiveness function with depth and time for
red cabbage on clay (see Feddes et al. [1974]).

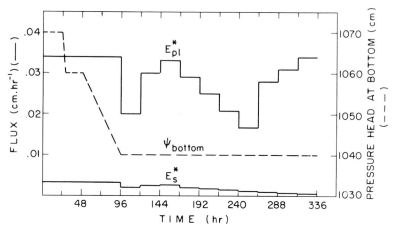

Fig. 8:   Variation with time of hydraulic head in underlying aquifer and
            maximum possible rates of soil evaporation and plant transpiration
            in two-dimensional systems.

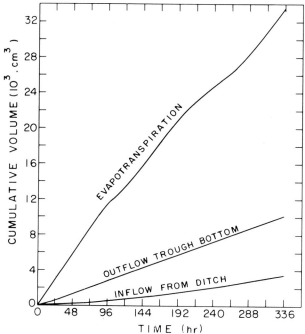

Fig. 9:   Cumulative evapotranspiration from ditch, and leakage into underlying
            aquifer in two-dimensional system.

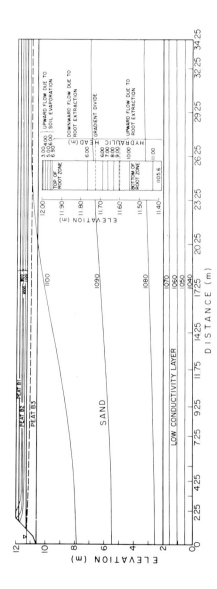

Fig.10 – Contours of equal hydraulic head at t = 336 hours in two-dimensional system.

Fig. 10 shows contours of equal hydraulic head as well as the water table (defined as the locus of all points where $\psi = 0$) at $t = 336$ hours. The hydraulic head is measured in meters above the bottom of the low conductivity layer. In trying to visualize the directions of flow in various parts of the system, the reader must recall that due to the assumed local anisotropy in the peat and sand layers, the flow lines in these layers are not necessarily perpendicular to the contours of head. On the other hand, the low conductivity layer is isotropic and therefore, the flow lines are perpendicular to the hydraulic head contours. Due to the large vertical head gradients occuring in the vicinity of the root zone, a blowup of this zone has been included in Fig. 10 to enable examination of the details.

Fig. 10 shows that, except in the vicinity of the ditch, near-vertical flow takes place in most parts of the system. In the sand and the low conductivity layer the flow is directed downward toward the underlying aquifer. The hydraulic gradients are relatively large in the low conductivity layer and considerably smaller in the highly conductive sand.

In the peat one can distinguish between four different zones of flow. Near the soil surface the flow is directed upward in response to the atmospheric evaporation demand. In the upper part of the root zone the flow is directed downward and, in the lower part, the flow is directed upward. This flow is due to root extraction and it converges toward a particular soil level at which the rate of water uptake by roots happens to be maximum. Most of the flow below the water table is directed downward.

This example clearly demonstrates the flexibility of the finite element approach and its capability in treating complex situations which one often encounters in the field.

NOTATIONS

b'	: root effectiveness function;
$C = \partial\theta/\partial\psi$	: specific moisture capacity;
C_p	: specific heat of air at constant pressure;
e_z	: unsaturated vapor pressure at elevation z and ambient temperature;
e_z^*	: saturated vapor pressure at elevation z and ambient temperature;
E^*	: maximum possible rate of evapotranspiration;
E_s	: actual rate of soil evaporation;
E_s^*	: maximum possible rate of soil evaporation;
$E_{p\ell}$	: actual rate of plant transpiration;
$E_{p\ell}^*$	: maximum possible rate of plant transpiration;
f	: relative humidity of air;
g	: acceleration due to gravity;
G	: heat flux from atmosphere into soils;

k	: time step number;
K^r	: relative hydraulic conductivity;
$K^s_{ij} = K^s_{ji}$	: saturated hydraulic conductivity tensor;
LAI	: leaf area index;
LH	: latent heat of water vaporization;
M	: molecular weight of water;
n_i	: unit outer normal on Γ;
N	: number of nodes in finite element mesh;
Q	: flux of water;
r_a	: resistance to vapor diffusion through air layer around leaves;
R	: universal gas constant;
R_n	: net radiation flux at soil surface;
S	: positive sink term corresponding to rate of water uptake by plants per unit bulk volume of soil;
SF	: seepage face;
S_s	: specific storage;
t	: time;
T	: absolute temperature;
V	: prescribed rate of water flux across Γ_2;
W_i	: width of i-th column of elements in root zone;
x_i	: vector of Cartesian coordinates;
x_3	: vertical coordinate;
β	: unity in saturated zone; zero in unsaturated zone;
γ	: psychrometric constant;
$\Gamma = \Gamma_1 \cup \Gamma_2$	: boundary of flow region;
$\bar{\Gamma}$	: closure of Γ;
Γ_1	: prescribed pressure head boundary;
Γ_2	: prescribed flux boundary;
δ	: slope of saturation vapor pressure curve;
δ_{nm}	: Kronecker delta;
Δ	: area of triangular cross-section of element;
$\Delta t^k = t^{k+1} - t^k$	: size of (k+1)th time step;
ζ^L_n	: local linear coordinate function associated with node n in element L;
θ	: volumetric water content;
θ_s	: porosity;
Ω	: interior of flow region;
$\bar{\Omega}$	: closure of flow region;
ψ	: pressure head;
ψ_L	: minimum pressure head allowed at soil surface;
ψ_r	: pressure head in roots;

ψ_w : wilting pressure head;

ψ : prescribed pressure head on Γ_1;

ψ_o : initial pressure head in Ω;

ρ_a : density of moist air;

$\xi_n = U_e \, \xi_n^e$: global coordinate function associated with node n;

ξ_n^e : local coordinate function associated with node n in element e.

REFERENCES

BRAESTER, C., DAGAN, G., NEUMAN, S.P., and ZASLAVSKY, D., "A Survey of the Equa-
    tions and Solutions of Unsaturated Flow in Porous Media," First Annual Re-
    port, Project No. A10-SWC-77, Hydraulic Engineering Laboratory, Technion,
    Haifa, Israel, pp. 176, 1971.
FEDDES, R.A., "Water, heat and crop growth," Thesis.Comm.Agric.Univ. Wageningen
    71-12, pp. 184, 1971.
FEDDES, R.A. and VAN STEENBERGEN, M.G., "Sub-irrigation field 'De Groeve'", Nota
    735, Inst. for Land and Water Management Res., Wageningen, pp. 184, 1973
    (in Dutch).
FEDDES, R.A., BRESLER, E. and NEUMAN, S.P., "Field test of a modified numerical
    model for water uptake by root systems," Unpublished manuscript, 1974.
FORSYTHE, G.E., and WASOW, W.R., "Finite-Difference Methods for Partial Differen-
    tial Equations," John Wiley and Sons, New York, pp. 444, 1960.
GAMBOLATI, G., "Equation for One-Dimensional Vertical Flow of Groundwater : 1.
    The Rigorous Theory, "Water Resources Research, Vol. 9, No.4, pp. 1022-
    1028, 1973a.
GAMBOLATI, G., "Equation for One-Dimensional Vertical Flow of Groundwater : 2.
    Validity Range of the Diffusion Equation," Water Resources Research, Vol.9,
    No. 5, pp. 1385-1396, 1973b.
HANKS, R.J., KLUTE, A. and BRESLER, E., "A numeric method for estimating infiltra-
    tion, redistribution, drainage, and evaporation of water from soil,"
    Water Resources Research, Vol. 5, No. 5, pp. 1064-1069, 1969.
MIKHLIN, S.G., "Variational Methods in Mathematical Physics," Pergamon Press,
    Oxford, pp. 584, 1964.
NEUMAN, S.P., "Finite Element Computer Programs for Flow in Saturated-Unsaturated
    Porous Media," Second Annual Report, Project No. A10-SWC-77, Hydraulic
    Engineering Laboratory, Technion, Haifa, Israel, pp. 87, 1972b.
NEUMAN, S.P., "Saturated-unsaturated seepage by finite elements," Proc. ASCE,
    J. Hydraul. Division, Vol. 99, No. HY12, pp. 2233-2250, 1973.
NEUMAN, S.P., "Galerkin method of analyzing non-steady flow in saturated-unsatura-
    ted porous media", Chap. 10 in Finite Element Method in Flow Problems,
    Taylor-Zienkiewicz-Gallagher ed., John Wiley & Sons (in press), 1974.
ODEN, J.T., "Finite Elements of Nonlinear Continua," McGraw-Hill Book Company,
    New York, pp.432, 1972.
RITCHIE, J.T., "A model for predicting evaporation from a row crop with incomplete
    cover," Water Resources Research, Vol. 8, No. 5, pp. 1204-1213,1972.

DISCUSSION

Did you calculate the root or did you measure it ?   (BIGGAR)

Yes, we calculated it assuming a law from a linear flow assumptions through the soil plant root system and by measuring at various places in the system, we could arrive at some expression for the b-factors. What these b-factors especially physically mean is not so clear you can consider that it is something related to the effective root surface area and dr. Philip has developed a cylindrical root flow model together with dr. Gardner and in fact we are using this model. (FEDDES)

Do you think it is more correct to describe the atmospheric conditions, maybe seepage, with finite elements, you can do it also very well with finite difference. (VACHAUD)

Yes, but I think there are several advantages with finite elements in this respect at least. One great advantage, it is very easy to change the type of boundary condition from a Neuman to a Dirichlet during the same time step Δt. So this leads to a very efficient way of iterating. What you can do is you are assuming a certain flux you get a certain pressure, you compare it with what you expect, you change the type of boundary condition : now you impose a certain pressure, etc. This is especially true when you have irregular boundaries but it is also true when you have regular boundaries. (NEUMAN)

On your last picture, what you called gradient device form of a known flux, you got three directions of a flux of water up- and down. (VACHAUD)

Yes, in the upper zone you apparently get an upper flux if you consider the direction of the hydraulic gradient due to soil evaporation, but through the n factor and sort of root activity, you can see that you have water flowing from a certain zone to a certain depth zone from above and from underneath. If you analyse the sine profiles you often get forms like shown in the figure. This pointed to the same idea that was actually measured that we have circle zones on maximum root activity. (FEDDES)

Did you add tensiometers ? What is the profile in the root zone ? (VACHAUD)

We had to move the tensiometers in these clay soils. (FEDDES)

I am troubled by the black-box-finite element. I wonder if it is sound in principal to calculate the effective root resistance, which in what this b is, from the very data from which the model is constructed. (HILLEL)

This b-factor was derived from linear flow assumptions through the soil plant root system. So we considered a certain resistance in the plant in one of the models. If you have flux under steady state conditions $\frac{\psi - \psi \text{ soil}}{r \text{ soil}}$ and this r is some b/k hydraulic conductivity. b is not known but we can get some idea from other data where b is considered to be some factor from the root depth, which is well known. b was particularly difficult to obtain and it took years of experiments to select some theories because with very non steady state conditions I could not do this type of thing. I hope somebody will come up with a good definition of b or what determines the active root surface area, but for the moment we tend to think about that. (FEDDES)

What we really tried to do here is to see if we can use this very simple model for the root uptake, and to get something that is close to what we and dr. Philip observed in the field and the conclusion was that you indeed can at least calibrate such a model and obtain good results. From a physical standpoint I know

that dr. Molz is working on physically based ideas along this line. But these physical models are complicated and I am not sure that we have enough physical background to cope with them. The basic weakness of this kind of approach is, you can
calibrate them to one set of conditions and you have no sureness whatsoever that
you will get a good prediction. (NEUMAN)

*Dr. Feddes replied in terms of qualitative relationships on what this b is.
It includes the root resistance and some other factor related to the effective density. My question was since b is measured independently, b is calculated from the
same set of data which is used to calibrate the model, and you end up with a model
which fits the data for which it was constructed. Is this circular thinking ?
Should not the model be based in principal on parameters which can be measured independently ? (HILLEL)*

*I tend to disagree for when you accept this reasoning, you come to the state
where you say : I don't know the laws or factors that are governing the process, so
let's build the model. (VAN KEULEN)*

There are two possibilities : let us not build any model because we don't
understand the physics. The other possibility is : we have done laboratory or field
experiments, we do have a linear law which gives insight in the experiments that,
for instance, dr. Feddes has performed. We are suggesting here : don't use this
model for prediction at this present stage of knowledge. We just suggest this as
a possibility which should be checked in the future. People can definitely come up
with better physical understanding of water uptake by plants definitely incorporating into the model. (NEUMAN)

*There is a priori guessing against trying to describe an observed phenomena
with how to use a mathematical formulation in terms of classic differential equations, or using a finite element or finite difference method to do so. We should
state explicitly that you have not built a general model but what you have done is
describe an experiment. (VAN KEULEN)*

To summarize : we have done one experiment - and we have shown that with
this type of model, we can calibrate the parameters so that the model behaves like
our experiment. Nothing more than that. (NEUMAN)

We are not intending to use the model or any kind of problem which we cannot measure. A way of working in this kind of problem is that we have some type of
project, we measure a lot, and we try to calibrate by using b like is shown. Once
calibrated and we did the experiment, we try to evaluate something like if the water table was this high or that low, etc. (FEDDES)

Modeling and Simulation of Water Resources Systems, G.C. VANSTEENKISTE, (Ed.)
North-Holland Publishing Company (1975)

HYBRID SIMULATION OF A DYNAMIC MODEL
FOR WATER MOVEMENT IN A SOIL - PLANT - ATMOSPHERE CONTINUUM

E. D'Hollander
Department of Soil Physics
State University of Ghent, BELGIUM

I.Impens
Department of Biology
Universitaire Instelling Antwerpen, BELGIUM

ABSTRACT

Water use effeciency of a crop was for a long time the subject of many experiments in a broad area such as plant characteristics, soil conditioners and atmospherical influences.
The lack of a general model has often caused serious controverses on the contradictory results.

In this paper the water movement through the soil - plant - atmosphere continuum is considered as an energetic process as well as a transport phenomenon. From the energy balance an electrical analogon is developed which takes into account the atmospheric heat budget and the potential gradients describing the waterflow through soil and plant.

This model is adapted for a hybrid simulation which permits a flexible identification with field experiments.

Some results illustrate the use of the model ; in particular the strong influence of root distribution on plant water use is demonstrated.

I. INTRODUCTION

For many years the research on the watermetabolism in the soil - plant - atmosphere continuum led to relatively poor results. Mainly the 'steady-state' approach, which neglects the time lags between cause and effect, and the insufficient field experiments, disregarding the inter-relationships of important systemvariables may explain this.

The complete water houskeeping has to be studied by a dynamic model which represents the dynamic characteristics of the water movement, and which takes into account the fundamental principles of evaporation.

The main purpose of this paper is to demonstrate how hybrid simulation can aid to realise a suitable model to meet this requirements.

From engineering point of view we can see the soil - plant - atmosphere continuum as a multivariable control system with the evapotranspiration as the variable to be controlled. This parameter depends merely on a series of meteorological factors and on the water status of the crop.

The stomatal resistance acts as the principal controlling variable.
This 'pilot valve' is governed directly by the net radiation and the crop
water content. Whereas the radiation can be seen as an external disturbance,
the crop water content is determined by the dynamic soil - plant system
behaviour.

The mathematical formulation of the crop evapotranspiration esta-
blishes the most effective parameters. These are rearranged as functions
of ordinary measurements.

Special attention is paid to the flow of water through soil and plant.
While the transpiration is calculated by the digital machine, the soil-plant
system is simulated by an hybrid controlled analogue network.

II. FUNDAMENTALS

1. Evapotranspiration formula

For stationary conditions and disregarding some minor effects the
heat budget for a crop can be written as :

$$Rn + LE + H = 0 \tag{1}$$

with Rn = net radiation plus heat flow to the soil
LE = transpiration heat flux
H = sensible heat flux

For the sensible heat flux we can write the relation :

$$H = Cp.\rho . \frac{Ts - Ta}{Ra} \tag{2}$$

with Ts = the surface temperature of the crop
Ta = the ambient air temperature
Ra = the crop boundary layer resistance

On the other hand the crop evapotranspiration is related to the
absolute humidity of the air as follows :

$$LE = L \frac{\chi^{\circ}(Ts) - \chi a}{Rc + Ra} \tag{3}$$

with $\chi^{\circ}(Ts)$ = density of pure water vapour at crop surface temperature
χa = absolute humidity of the air at a reference height
Rc   = the stomatal crop resistance
L   = the latent heat of vaporization of water

Goff and Gratch have set up a formula for $\chi^{\circ}(Ts) = f(Ts)$, so that
formulas (1), (2) and (3) can be resumed in a general transcendental equation :

$$LE = L \left\{ \frac{f \left| Rn + LE.Ra/(Cp.\rho) + Ta \right| - \chi a}{Ra + Rc} \right\} \tag{4}$$

By this equation the net radiation, air temperature, air humidity as
atmospherical parameters and the diffusion resistances in the laminar crop
layer and in the stomates, are related in a complex fashion, illustrating
the interrelation and the impact of the various parameters on evapotranspiration.

The evapotranspiration, conceived as an energetic process, is determined by two factors :

- micrometeorological : Ta, χa, Rn and Ra

- crop parameters   - structural   : Ra
                     - physiological : Rc

The transport process is regulated by the stomatal resistance Rc,
which over the water potential of the crop takes account of the water
status of plant and soil.

2. Adaptation to field measurements

Using Montheith's formula for the diffusion resistance, Ra is found
to be inversely proportional to wind speed :

$$Ra = A/U \qquad (5)$$

with A = a constant depending on the structure, the height and the
        roughness of the crop
     U = the wind speed

The stomatal resistance, Rc, is composed of two resistances in series :
one depending on the radiation, the other related to the crop water content.
Hyperbolic function approximations give a representation of the following form :

$$Rc = A + \frac{B}{Rn} + \frac{C}{\psi_c + \psi_w} \qquad (6)$$

A, B and C are crop constants ; ψ_w is the permanent wilting point, taken at -20 bar.

ψ_c represents the crop water potential which is achieved by the simulation
network of crop and soil.

III. THE ANALOGUE NETWORK

In view of an electrical analogue for the waterflow network, the terms
'potential','flow' and 'water content' may be considered as electrical quantities.

1. Representation of the crop

According to equation (6), the state of the crop is uniquely defined by
its water potential, which is assumed to be linearly in proportion to the crop
water content θ_c.
This relation is equivalent to the capacity formula :

$$\psi_c - \psi_w = \frac{\theta_c}{Cc} \qquad (7)$$

The capillar potential gradient exists over a stem resistance (Rst),
leading to an expression for the waterflow to the crop :

$$\frac{d\theta_c}{dt} = \frac{\psi_c - \psi_r}{Rst} \qquad (8)$$

where ψ_r stays for the root water potential.

The crop capacity Cc can be expressed as function of the initial crop water content :

$$Cc = - \frac{\Theta_c^\circ}{\psi_w} \tag{9}$$

Equations (7), (8) and (9) result in the following scheme :

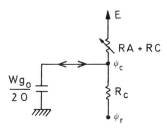

2. Soil aspects

We consider the soil as a homogeneous environment characterised by its diffusivity-water content relationship, resulting from laboratory measurements. The roots are supposed to be cilindrical and of the same size Z and radius r_w. They are uniformely distributed in the soil on a average distance 2 R.

In this way, disregarding the influence of gravity, we get radial symmetry and the waterdiffusion from the bulk soil to the roots can be given by the diffusion equation :

$$\frac{\partial \Theta}{\partial t} = \frac{1}{r} \frac{\partial}{\partial r} r D(\Theta) \frac{\partial \Theta}{\partial r} \tag{10}$$

The boundary conditions are summarized as follows :

1. in the middle between two roots, there is no waterflow :

$$\frac{\partial \Theta}{\partial r} = 0 \qquad\qquad \text{for } r = R \tag{11}$$

2. at root surface the net waterflow equals the crop needs :

$$\frac{\partial \Theta}{\partial r} = \frac{\psi_r - \psi_c}{A.Z.Rc} \cdot \frac{1}{2\pi r_w D(\Theta)} \qquad \text{for } r = r_w \tag{12}$$

3. Electrical analogon for the soil

For the hybrid simulation, the continuous time discrete space method (CTDS) is used, so the soil is divided into n layers with size Δr.
In this way the diffusion equation is reduced to n-2 differential equations :

$$\frac{d\Theta_i}{dt} = \delta_{i+\frac{1}{2}} (\Theta_{i+1} - \Theta_i) - \delta_{i-\frac{1}{2}} (\Theta_i - \Theta_{i-1}) \tag{13}$$

with $\quad \delta_{i\pm\frac{1}{2}} = \dfrac{r_{i\pm\frac{1}{2}}}{r_i} \dfrac{D(\Theta_{i\pm\frac{1}{2}})}{\Delta r^2} \tag{14}$

The distance between the layers, Δr, is calculated from the root density, $A (cm/cm^3)$:

$$\Delta r = \frac{1}{n} (\frac{1}{\sqrt{\pi \ A}} - r_w) \tag{15}$$

The boundary conditions are transformed in two supplementary differential equations :

$$\frac{d\Theta_n}{dt} = -\delta_{n-\frac{1}{2}} (\Theta_n - \Theta_{n-1}) \tag{16}$$

$$\frac{d\Theta_1}{dt} = \delta_{1+\frac{1}{2}} (\Theta_2 - \Theta_1) - \frac{\psi_r - \psi_c}{2\pi \ \Delta r \ r_1 \ A \ Z \ Rc} \tag{17}$$

The complete electrical analogon to be simulated is shown in figure 2 on the next page.

IV. HYBRID SIMULATION

The hybrid simulation is achieved on a PDP-15-AD4 hybrid combination of the State University of Ghent. In general the digital part of the computer is used to solve continuously the transcendental crop equation (4) by iteration, while the dynamic part simulates the water relations of plant and soil.

1. Data input

All data are read in digitally. The meteorological data, Rn, χa (proportional to the relative humidity of the air), U and Ta are values registrated on every thirty minutes and are interpolated linearly.
The diffusivity characteristics are stored in vector form, in a way suited for table look-up.
The analog-digital interaction is clearly illustrated by the schematic representation of the equations we want to simulate.

2. Implementation of the differential equations

The mathematical model to be simulated is :

$$\frac{d\psi_c}{dt} = \frac{\psi_w}{\Theta_c^\delta} (\frac{\psi_c - \psi_r}{Rst} - E) \tag{18}$$

$$\frac{d\Theta_1}{dt} = \delta_{1+\frac{1}{2}} (\Theta_2 - \Theta_1) - \frac{1}{2\pi \ r_1 \ \Delta r} \frac{\psi_r - \psi_c}{A \ Z \ Rc} \tag{19}$$

$$\frac{d\Theta_i}{dt} = \delta_{i+\frac{1}{2}} (\Theta_{i+1} - \Theta_i) - \delta_{i-\frac{1}{2}} (\Theta_i - \Theta_{i-1}) \qquad (20)$$

$$i = 2, \ldots\ldots, n-1$$

$$\frac{d\Theta_n}{dt} = -\delta_{n-\frac{1}{2}} (\Theta_n - \Theta_{n-1}) \qquad (21)$$

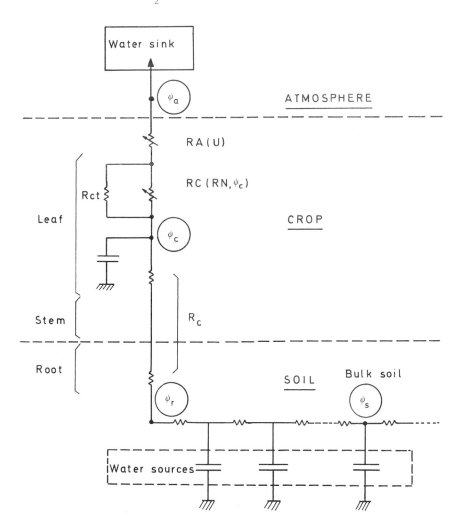

The patchboard and hybrid connections of this system are illustrated by the following figures :

a) equation (18) :

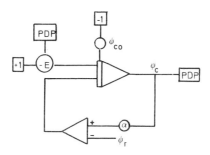

The evapotranspiration is continuously calculated and adjusted by the digital machine, from the meteorological data and the ψ_c readout from the analog computer. Since the analog machine synchronises the whole system, linear interpolation is achieved by means of a patched saw tooth function. The time scale equals one second of computing time to one hour of real time. This gives an adjustment of all system parameters on every two minutes of real time.

b) equation (19) :

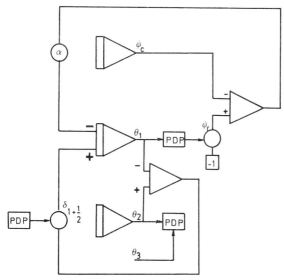

Θ_1 and Θ_2 are read by the PDP-15, which calculates therefrom the corresponding root potential, and adjusts it for each calculation cycle.

c) equation (20) :

These equations lead to a chain network.

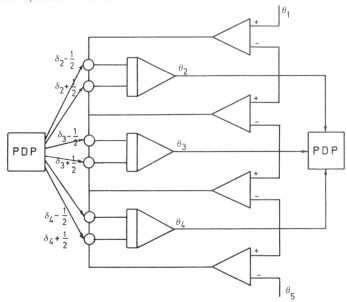

The δ - coefficients depend on the local diffusivities, which are function of the layer water contents. After reading the water contents of each layer, the diffusivities are determined according to the characteristic tables of the soil, whereafter the digital coefficient units, representing the δ - coefficients, are adapted to the observed waterstatus.

d) equation (21) :

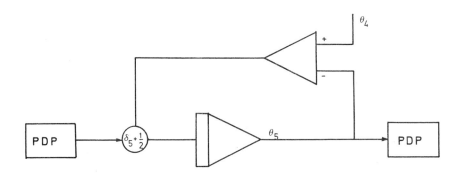

This scheme terminates the analogue patching. Practically n is taken 5, to divide the soil between two adjacent roots into ten layers.

V. RESULTS AND DISCUSSION

Since the primary object of this research was to understand the consumption of water by the plant, we retained five crop parameters : the initial crop water content Θ_c°, the crop resistance (stem plus root), Rst, the root radius r_w, the root length par volume unity, A, and the rooting depth Z.

The diffusivity characteristics of clay and sandy loam were taken as soil parameters, demonstrating the influences of structure on a wilting period.

As source for meteorological data a repeating type day was choosen. Since practical experiments were not available, the model was submitted to a series of theoretical tests, in view of a factorial analysis of the crop parameters with regard to a wilting period. In this way each parameter was designed a maximum and a minimum value and the difference in average wilting time for all combinations with a selected parameter high and those with the same parameter low, was taken as its impact on the crop evapotranspiration.

The results demonstrated the dominant influence of the root factors A (51 %), Z (34 %) and r_w (12 %), whereas Θ_c° and Rst seemed to have a minor influence (only a few percents).

These quantitative issues are generally in accordance to the qualitative expectations. The rooting depth, Z, is very important, because of its determining effect on the available water resources. The major influence of the root distribution, A, is explained by its relation to the average root distance (see eq. (15)). The small effect of the initial water content of the crop, Θ_c°, is also comprehensible since this causes only a transient response, which is negligible on the long term. The stem resistance, Rst, had practically no influence on the wilting period because of its small range. On the other hand it is directly in proportion to the recharging time constant of the crop water capacity, as can be derived from equation (18).
In general the wilting period for a sandy loam soil is about 30 % smaller than the corresponding combination for a clay soil ; this is mainly due to the greater water reserve of clay. For specific parameter combinations however, there are significant differences.

As an example, a typical simulation run output is given :

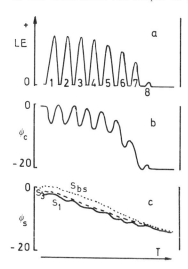

These figures give the crop evapotranspiration (a) ; the crop water potential (b) and the soil potentials from bulk soil to root layer (c), for a wilting crop during a drying period of almost eight days.

VI. CONCLUSION

The study of the soil - plant - atmosphere continuum by a hybrid simulation model illustrates the flexibility and the power of this tool in the simulation of complex dynamic systems. It indicates a new way of arranging practical experiments, and although the basic equations are only approximative, they are quite satisfactory. This shows that many minor variables and their interrelationships have an antagonistic influence on the system.

Finally we conclude that the use of a hybrid computer for solving nonlinear dynamic models may contribute a lot in studiing and identifying hydro - ecological systems.

ACKNOWLEDGEMENT

We are grateful to Prof. Dr. Ir. M. De Boodt and Prof. Ir.G.C.Vansteenkiste for encouraging our research in this domain.

REFERENCES

1. Goff, J.A. and Gratch, S., 1946, Trans. Amer. Soc. and Vent. Eng.,
      Vol. 52, p. 95

2. Montheith, J.L., 1963, Gass exchange in plant communities. Environmental
      control of plant growth, Acad. Press, N.Y., p. 95-110

DISCUSSION

One equation of your model was very familiar to me : the water uptake by the roots was represented by the same formula, only you defined $\dfrac{\psi_1 - \psi_2}{R}$ *as* $\dfrac{b}{k}$.
(FEDDES)

Indeed. Only your 'b-factors' are given a physical representation in our model. In fact we tried the Ohm's law for describing the waterflow into the plant. This agrees with our insight in the electrical analogue, and even if the resistances are not linear, it gives a good approximation.   (D'HOLLANDER)

What was the reason for the demarcation to model the atmospheric conditions in a digital manner and leave the quantity itself under the soil as analogue ? (SHAH)

The main reason was the following : the evapotranspiration formula is a transcendental one, which must be calculated by iteration. The digital machine is excellently suited for this task. The set of differential equations however,

representing the dynamic part of the system, are not simple to handle. Having an analogue machine coupled to the digital one, it is obvious to integrate those equations on the analogue part.
A second reason is that you can easily change some parameters by hand on the analogue computer. Studying a system you often have to do this. (D'HOLLANDER)

Was the analogue part a continuous or a discrete network ? (BRUTSAERT)

As we used the continuous time discrete space method, the soil was divided into discrete layers, where the moisture state was solved continuously in time. (D'HOLLANDER)

You consider the aerodynamic resistance as a function of wind speed. Do you also incorporate the properties of the crop ? (FEDDES)

Yes, but these are deterministic parameters, which are calculated before the dynamic simulation starts. Therefore we used the Montheith's formula. (D'HOLLANDER)

Could you explain us what are the parameters that you do not know and try to get from field experiments ? (NEUMAN)

The purpose of this model was to understand which are the significant crop parameters involved during a drying period, namely : - 3 root parameters
- the crop water capacity
- the stem resistance.
(D'HOLLANDER)

What are your root parameters ? (NEUMAN)

These are : - root length per volume unit
- rooting depth
- root radius. (D'HOLLANDER)

Are these fixed in time ? (NEUMAN)

These are fixed for a typical simulation run, being at most about 20 days. (D'HOLLANDER)

Is it right that we did practically the same thing in different ways ? (NEUMAN)

You can say so, the subject was quite similar. But I think that you worked with other diffusing characteristics in the succesive layers of the soil. (D'HOLLANDER)

I think this is a beautiful demonstration of a physical model. It was maybe only unfortunate that you didn't have any field data to compare with. I just think on one result that seems inconsistent with the model. Last slide : that shows the difference between the potential of water in the soil and at the root. To my openion, the difference in potential should be increasing in the drying phase because the conductivity in the soil is decreasing. This is puzzling me. (HILLEL)

To answer this on a soilphysical base, is difficult, because I am only a system-analyst for this purpose, but from electrical point of view it is not strange to me : when the crop is drying, the stomatal resistance acts as a controlling variable, so this limits the water stream from the soil in function of time. At the end of the wilting period, the waterflow will be very small, and this allows for the bulk soil potential to come near the root potential, even if the capillary conductivity decreases. (D'HOLLANDER)

Can I give just one comment. Hydrologists were trying to calculate the amount of water reaching from the surface through the unsaturated zone, down to the groundwater table and are using models just like we saw during the first day, where one represent the unsaturated zone including the root zone by reservoirs. This gives certain reservoir laws for the whroughting of the water through the unsaturated zone and these models are used on a day to day basis; the so called "Mirrow" model, developed by Mirrow, Israël, and many of these models give good results. I think that this kind of approach leads to at least one positive result : it can give a little bit more physical insight into the process than these reservoir type models and as we will get more and more information and knowledge about the actual physical laws governing the movement of water from the soil into the plant, these models will improve. (NEUMAN)

Modeling and Simulation of Water Resources Systems, G.C. VANSTEENKISTE, (Ed.)
North-Holland Publishing Company (1975)

MODELING OF SOLUTE INTERACTIONS WITH SOILS

H.Laudelout, R.Frankart, R.Lambert, F.Mougenot, Pham Manh Le
University of Louvain, Belgium

ABSTRACT

Two simulation modules are presented on the transformation
of mineral nitrogen compounds in nitrifying reaction and
on the ion exchange reactions between Ca and Na in which
use is made of the known physiological relationships between
substrate concentration and growth and oxidation rates on
the one hand and of the full information represented by the
exchange isotherm on the other hand.

x x x

Considerable progress has been made during the last few
years with respect to the simulation of convective transport of
unreacting solute through porous media. The modeling of the interaction of cations with soil colloids or of mineral nitrogen compounds with the microflora and organic colloids has also been attempted many times. In order to make the rate equations or equilibrium
relationships amenable to integration into an analytical or numerical formulation describing solute movement, fairly drastic simplifications of these relationships were made. These simplifications
have consisted in admitting first order kinetics in the case of
biological oxidation instead of the largely prevailing hyperbolic
relationship. In ion exchange reactions, empirical selectivity
coefficients were used due to their approximate constancy in a
fairly wide range of exchangeable cations composition.
    The purpose of this communication is to present two simula-
tion modules, the one referring to nitrification, the other to ion
exchange. They have in common that they make full use of the information available on the process they purport to describe, they may
nevertheless be fit in a numerical scheme describing convective
solute transport.
    The model describing the oxidation of ammonium by mixed
populations of Nitrosomonas and Nitrobacter involves four simultaneous differential equations describing growth and rate of substrate
oxidation by the two bacteria which derive the free energy necessary
for the synthesis of their cell substance from the two reactions :

$$NH_4^+ + 1.5 \; O_2 \quad \rightarrow \quad NO_2^- + 2H^+ + H_2O$$

$$NO_2^- + 0.5 \; O_2 \quad \rightarrow \quad NO_3^-$$

with molar growth yields of 6.2 and 3.5 x 10^9 cells per mM of substrate respectively.
    If S is the substrate concentration the kinetics of growth
follows the Monod equation :

$$\frac{dn}{dt} = \frac{k_o \; n \; S}{C_1 + S} \tag{1}$$

where k_o and C_1 are constants characteristic of the organism.
The rate at which substrate is oxidized is given by :

$$- \frac{dS}{dt} = \frac{V_m \, S}{K_m + S} \qquad (2)$$

which is the well-known Michaelis equation.

The four differential equations are simultaneous since the
substrate of Nitrobacter is produced in the first step of the
process. Furthermore, the rate of substrate oxidation is dependent
of the cell number n. If it is true that molar growth yield Y and
specific growth rate k_o are constant, then we have for the specific
oxidation rate :

$$V_m = - \frac{dS}{dt} = \frac{k_o n}{Y} \qquad (3)$$

The eight parameters pertaining to the growth and oxidation rates
of both bacteria may be found in the literature as well as data
concerning their molar growth yields. Furthermore, the temperature
characteristics of these parameters have also been the subject of
experimental determination, which makes it possible that time curves
for the evolution of ammonium, nitrite and nitrate concentrations
may be calculated for temperatures ranging between 0 and near optimal temperatures.

The result of such a calculation made after translation of
the 4 equations in CSMP and integrating is shown in Fig.1. It is
obvious that the intermediary product may or may not appear according to the temperature at which oxidation occurs. Since nitrite
reacts with soil in a chemical denitrification process according
to first order kinetics it can easily be shown that in tropical
soils this type of kinetics may lead to sizable losses of nitrogen
immediately after ammonium fertilizers application.

The calculation presented by the curves of fig.1 may supply
an explanation of an observation of Braune and Uhlemann (1968) on
the seasonal variations of nitrite content of river water or on the
greater amount of nitrite found in river water incubated at higher
temperatures.

The simulation model described above can easily be completed
with respect to the effect of oxygen concentration and pH since the
relevant kinetics are well-known and their parameters have been
determined (Laudelout et al., 1974). The model could further be
improved by using the actual relationship between growth constant
or yield and generation numbers rather than constant values as done
here.

The actual problem is whether modular simulation models
involving the actual kinetic relationships and the high number of
relevant parameters are better suited for general modeling than
simplified systems where relationships and parameters are lumped
together in a way that is justified by the fit with actual experiments and ad hoc adjustment of some parameters. How far these simplifications are obtained at the expense of generality will only be
known when the actual use of simulation models became more wide-
spread.

The same question may also be raised with respect to the
second example of simulation module that is presented below for
ion exchange reactions.

Full use of all the information expressed in an ion exchange
isotherm may be necessary if the proportion of one cation in the top
layer of the experimental column varies from zero at the beginning

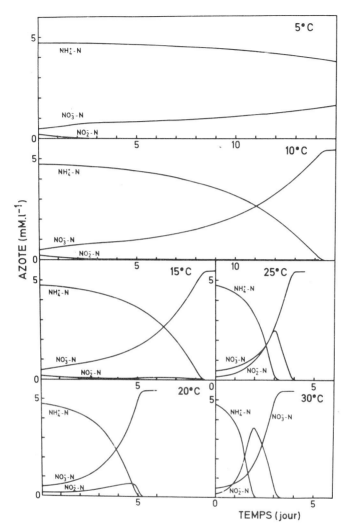

Figure 1: Time course of ammonium, nitrite and nitrate concentrations
calculated with the following values of the parameters, μ
being the Arrhenius temperature characteristic. Nitrosomonas k = 1.97 day^{-1} (μ = 14.1 k cal.mole^{-1}),
C_1 = 0.17 mM(μ = 17.4), K_m = 0.52 mM(μ = 17.4),
R = 6.24 x 10^9 cell.mM^{-1}.
Nitrobacter k = 1.30 day^{-1}(μ = 8.7), C_1 = 0.39 mM(μ =21.5)
K_m = 0.56 mM(μ = 19.5).

of the experimental to one at the end, a not uncommon situation.
The principle of the numerical method used for the simulation
of an exchange isotherm is as follows : the selectivity coefficient
K_c in the Na-Ca exchange at a total normality C_o may be expressed by:

$$K_c = f(Y) = 2C_o \frac{Y(1-Y)^2}{X(1-X)^2} \cdot \frac{\gamma_{Na^+}^2}{\gamma_{Ca^{++}}} \qquad (4)$$

where X and Y are the equivalent fractions of Ca in the solution and
on the clay surface respectively, the γ refer to the activity coefficients in solution.
The thermodynamic equilibrium constant K is given by :

$$K = K_c \cdot f_{Ca}/f_{Na}^2 \qquad (5)$$

where the f refer to the activity coefficients of the adsorbed ions.
The value of an activity coefficient may be expressed in
terms of a power series of the equivalent fraction of the other ion.
If in these power series the terms of the third degree and higher
are neglected, by application of the Gibbs-Duhem rule, Margules
approximation is obtained, i.e. a parabolic relationship is found,
the parameters of which are related to the intrinsic properties of
the ions involved in the exchange (Laudelout and Van Bladel, 1966).
This fact has been used for calculating the exchange isotherm
by Lai and Jurinak (1971). Unfortunately this is only found to be
valid for the case of uni-univalent exchange.
When heterovalent exchange is studied, it is found that at
least a third degree polynomial is required for expressing the
relationship between the selectivity coefficient K_c and the equivalent fraction of one of the adsorbed ions. The relationship will thus
be as follows :

$$f(X,Y,C_o) = 2C_o \frac{Y(1-X)^2\gamma_+^2}{(1-Y)^2 X\gamma_{++}} - (a + bY + cY^2 + dY^3) = 0 \qquad (6)$$

If X and Y are not equilibrium values, the equation above is not
satisfied and the equivalent ionic fraction must increased by an
algebraic quantity Z such that :

$$f\left((X - Z.R), (Y + Z), C_o\right) = 0 \qquad (7)$$

where R is the number :

$$R = \frac{CEC.\alpha}{C_o} \qquad (8)$$

in which CEC is the cation exchange capacity of the soil studied
and α the soil/water ratio.
The roots of this equation are not easily found by the usual numerical procedures and for this reason the value of Z was determined
by a numerical method akin to the half interval search. Given the
new value of X after mixing the soil solution in a given layer with
that of the layer above it, and the Y value existing before mixing
a test was first made to see whether the point (X,Y) was below or
above the exchange isotherm by examining the sign of the products
$f(\epsilon,1-\epsilon,C_o) \times f(X,Y,C_o)$ and $f(1-\epsilon,\epsilon,C_o) \times f(X,Y,C_o)$, where ϵ is a

small value. A positive or negative increment Z is then applied to Y and X is decreased correspondingly by Z.R , this process of incre- menting Z is continued until it is found that the isotherm has been crossed, the incrementation is then decreased by one step and the process is repeated again using steps ten times smaller, the itera- tion process being stopped after three or four such approximations.

Logical controls have to be provided in the programme so that X and Y remain larger than O and smaller than 1.

The exchange isotherms obtained at 5, 10 and 25 mE. at 25° are presented in Fig.2 where the full lines have been recalculated by using the numerical method outlined above, entering arbitrary values of the divalent fraction in solution and calculating the corresponding value of the adsorbed fraction at each of the total normalities studied. The agreement between the theoretical curve and the experimental values is well within the experimental error.

The values of the coefficients of the polynomial regressions of the selectivity coefficient on the adsorbed divalent at 25°C were as follows :

$$K_c(25°C) = 2.96 + 18.10Y - 57.87Y^2 + 53.05Y^3 \qquad (9)$$

These coefficients are not likely to vary greatly from one soil to another since the standard free energy of exchange given by averaging the polynomials over the whole exchange composition do not vary greatly.

Whatever the merit of this procedure, it has the advantage of substituting a procedure which is valid even approximately so over the whole composition range to an expression valid over only limited portions of that range.

REFERENCES

Braune,W., and Uhlemann,R.(1968). Int.Rev.Ges.Hydrobiol., 53, 453.
Lai,S.H., and Jurinak,J.J.(1971). Soil Sci.Soc.Amer.Proc., 35, 894.
Laudelout, H., Lambert,R., and Fripiat,J.L.(1974). Arch.Mikrobiol. (in press).
Laudelout,H., and Van Bladel,R.(1966). I.A.E.A. Technical Report Series, 65, 8.

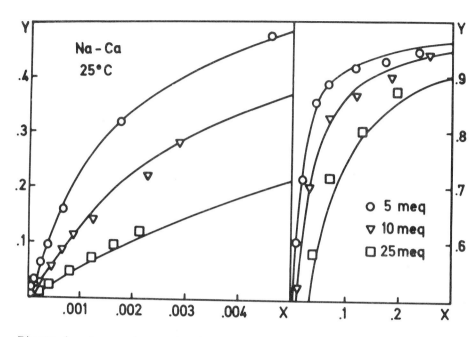

<u>Figure 2</u> : Ion exchange isotherm simulated with the polynomial relationship (9) at three total normalities in two ranges of composition of equilibrium solution.

Modeling and Simulation of Water Resources Systems, G.C. VANSTEENKISTE, (Ed.)
North-Holland Publishing Company (1975)

SOME FUNDAMENTAL ASPECTS OF LIQUID DISTRIBUTION IN POROUS SOLIDS RELATED TO INTERFACIAL CHARACTERISTICS

F. De Bisschop and F. De Wulf
Laboratory Soil Physics and Laboratory Agricultural Pedology
State University of Ghent, BELGIUM

ABSTRACT

Static as well as dynamic liquid distributions in porous solids of constant pore geometry, depend upon interfacial parameters, i.e the wetting characteristics of the solid-liquid system.

The signification of so called hydrophillic and hydrophobic surface substances has been studied both theoretically and practically. A discussion about the fundamentals of the wetting proces leads to conclusions about the exactitude of Youngs law in it's original formulation.

Practical methods for accurate determinations of the wetting characteristics of solids and PF-characteristics are proposed.

INTRODUCTION

The liquid distribution in porous media is mainly governed by parameters as pore size, surface tension of the liquid, contact angle between the liquid and the solid surface, interfacial tension and liquid volume.

For a given porous material, some of these parameters remain almost independent of the wetting agent, although the final liquid distribution, as well as the total liquid uptake may depend largely upon the actual physicochemical properties of the wetting liquid.

Besides pertinent negative aspects resulting from the abundant use of surfactants in the synthesis of insecticides, pesticides a.o., tensio activa may contribute to a control of soil water distribution as what is merely the aim of "Soil Conditioning".
Small amounts of surfactants are indeed known to cause tremendous changes in what is called "The available water for plant growth".

In the actual scope of soil water control, both water attractive (hydrophyllic) and water repellent (hydrophobic) soil conditioners are said to be obtainable, although the real significance of this terminology is often not respected.
This contribution is therefore intended to clear up the physicochemical meaning and the mode of action of surfactants, related to the water holding capacity of soils as well as other porous materials. Data resulting from theoretical and practical observations appear to be of direct importance in the formulation of physical models for static and dynamic liquid distributions in porous solids.

THE RELATION BETWEEN THE WETTING CHARACTERISTICS OF SOLIDS AND THEIR WATER

HOLDING CAPACITY

Both static and dynamic liquid distributions in porous solids are
functions of a force, resulting from molecular interactions at the interfaces :
solid-liquid ; liquid-vapour and solid-vapour.

These interactions have been defined thermodynamically as free energies
per unit surface and are commonly accepted to be in agreement with Young's law :

$$y_{s.v} - y_{s.1} = y_{1.v} \quad \cos \theta \tag{1}$$

where : $y_{s.v}$; $y_{s.1}$ and $y_{1.v}$: interfacial free energies at the solid-vapour,
the solid-liquid and the liquid-vapour inter-
face.
θ : contact angle between the liquid and the solid surface.

The original concept, leading to equation (1), based upon mechanical
equilibrium considerations, was often criticised, although it is still accepted
as a practical approximation, eventually taking into account a term π_e, called
"Film Pressure" according to ZISMAN (1964).

$$y_{s.v} - y_{s.1} - \pi_e = y_{1.v} \quad \cos \theta \tag{2}$$

This extension is of little practical significance, since its use
necessitates the determination of a quantity Γ, called "Surface Excess", i.e the
number of moles per unit surface, quantity which can hardly be measured upon
adsorption.

$$\pi_e = \int_o^p \Gamma(p) \, d \, \ln p \tag{3}$$

where p : vapour pressure

Attempts have been made (Gregg and Sing (1967)) to derive equations (1) and (2)
on a thermodynamic basis.

For the equilibrium illustrated in fig.1, the total free energy should be minimum.
Considering the variations in the system, that take place, upon displacing the
contact angle a distance dx, and taking into account the definition of interfacial free energy :

$$y_i = \left[\frac{\delta F}{\delta O_i} \right]_{T,V,m...} \tag{4}$$

where : F : free energy
O$_i$: interfacial surface
T : absolute temp
V : total volume of the phase in consideration
m : total mass of the phase in consideration
and where the subscripts outside the parentheses indicate that these parameters
are kept constant, one might state (fig.1).

$$dF = -y_{s.v} \, dx + y_{s.1} \, dx + y_{1.v} \quad \cos \theta . \, dx = o \tag{5}$$

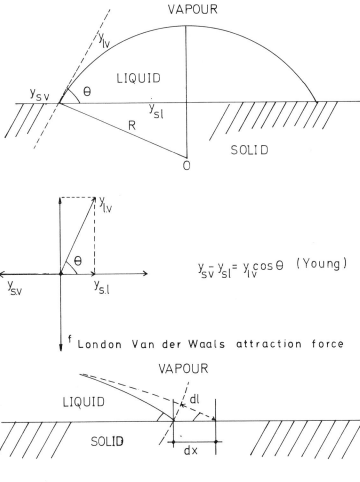

Fig. 1

Equation, from which obviously equation (2) results. However, it is not clear in this reasoning what happens to the total liquid volume upon displacing the wetting angle. Indeed, it has to be considered if one would not have to take into account an additional work term in this process :

$$dF' = d(P.V) \qquad (6)$$

where : P : external (vapour) pressure
        V : liquid volume

This observation leads to the following statements, resulting in a more accurate formulation for a thermodynamic equilibrium condition, and proving that the introduction of the film pressure term in equation (3) is redundant :
For the model, illustrated in fig.1, the minimum interfacial energy condition leads to :

$$\frac{d}{d\Theta} \left[y_{s.l} \; \pi R^2 \sin^2 \Theta \; + 2\pi \; R^2 (1-\cos\Theta) \; y_{l.v} \; + (A - \pi R^2 . \sin^2 \Theta \;) \; y_{s.v} \right] = o \qquad (7)$$

where : A : total surface of the solid-vapour interface
        R : radius of curvature of the liquid drop

Equation (7) may be simplified to :

$$\frac{d}{d\Theta} \left[R^2 \; (y_{s.l} - y_{s.v}) \; \sin^2 \Theta + 2 \; (1-\cos\Theta) \; y_{l.v} \right] = o \qquad (8)$$

from which results :

$$y_{s.v} - y_{s.l} = y_{l.v} \; \frac{2R.\dfrac{dR}{d\Theta} \; (1-\cos\Theta) + R^2 \sin\Theta}{R.\dfrac{dR}{d\Theta} .\sin^2 \Theta + R^2 \sin\Theta.\cos\Theta} \qquad (9)$$

The liquid volume can be calculated from

$$I = \pi R^3 \left[1 - \cos\Theta \; - \frac{1}{3} (1 - \cos^3\Theta \;) \right] \qquad (10)$$

from which follows, for the second equilibrium condition, i.e the independence of the liquid volume of Θ :

$$\frac{dI}{d\Theta} = 3 \; \pi R^2 . \frac{dR}{d\Theta} \left[1 - \cos \; \Theta - \frac{1}{3} (1 - \cos^3\Theta \;) \right] + \pi \; R^3 \left(\sin\Theta - \cos^2\Theta.\sin\Theta \right) = o \qquad (11)$$

leading to : $\dfrac{dR}{d\Theta} = \dfrac{R.\sin^3\Theta}{\cos^3\Theta - 3 \cos\Theta + 2}$

$$(12)$$

Substituting in equation (9) $\frac{dR}{d\Theta}$, by its value found in equation (12), one obtains, assuming $\Theta \neq o$:

$$y_{s.v} - y_{s.1} = y_{1.v} \frac{1 + \dfrac{2\sin^2\Theta}{\cos^2\Theta + \cos\Theta - 2}}{\cos\Theta - \dfrac{\sin^4\Theta}{\cos^3\Theta - 3\cos\Theta + 2}} \tag{13}$$

which may be rearanged subsequently to :

$$y_{s.v} - y_{s.1} = y_{1.v} \frac{2\sin^2\Theta + (\cos\Theta - 1)(\cos\Theta + 2)}{\cos\Theta(\cos\Theta - 1)(\cos\Theta + 2) - \dfrac{\sin^4\Theta}{\cos\Theta - 1}} \tag{14}$$

and :

$$y_{s.v} - y_{s.1} = y_{1.v} \frac{\cos\Theta(\cos\Theta - 1)^2}{\cos\Theta(\cos\Theta - 1)^2(\cos\Theta + 2) - \sin^4\Theta} \tag{15}$$

and so on :

$$y_{s.v} - y_{s.1} = -y_{1.v} \frac{\cos\Theta(\cos\Theta - 1)^2}{\cos^4\Theta - \sin^4\Theta - 3\cos^2\Theta + 2\cos\Theta} \tag{16}$$

and finally to :

$$y_{s.v} - y_{s.1} = y_{1.v} \cos\Theta \tag{17}$$

Hence, the Young equation is to be considered as mathematically exact and may be of fundamental interest for the physical description of liquid distributions in solid-liquid systems.

Indeed, with abstraction of the geometrical factor, which is to be considered in most cases as an unknown constant, the force F, acting at the liquid-vapour interface in porous systems, is known as :

$$F \simeq A. \, y_{1.v} \cdot \cos\Theta$$

where : A : constant factor, dependent on geometrical characteristics of the pores.

Laboratory techniques have been developped (Rigole and De Bisschop 1972) to determine the relation between the contact angle and the liquid-vapour interfacial tension, not only for clean solid surfaces, but also for solids, partially covered with impurities, e.g. organic adhesives (fig. 2).

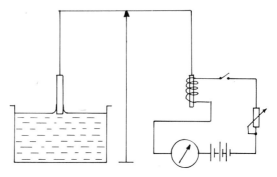

Fig. 2$_a$ Basic scheme of the Wilhelmy plate method

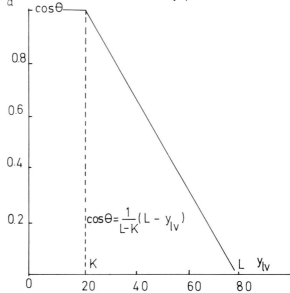

$$\cos\theta = \frac{1}{L-K}(L - y_{lv})$$

Fig. 2$_b$ Wetting characteristic of an organic adhesive

For practical purposes, these wetting characteristics may be considered as linear relations :

$$\cos \Theta = \frac{1}{L-K} (L - y_{1.v}) \tag{19}$$

For a given solid surface, one might again consider equation (18), substituting $\cos \Theta$ by its value defined in equation (19), resulting in :

$$F \approx \frac{y_{1.v}}{L - K} (L - y_{1.v}) \tag{20}$$

or alternatively, substituting $y_{1.v}$:

$$F \approx (K-L) \cos^2 \Theta - L \cos\Theta \tag{21}$$

In a way, equations like equation (20) and (21), illustrate the response of a solid-liquid system to a wetting tendency (fig. 3). Indeed, relative changes in water holding capacity of porous solids, as a function of interfacial tension or contact angle, appear to be in agreement with the equations given above. Their use is of pertinent practical significance, in the treatment of soil surface layers with organic soil conditioners. Among these substances, the emulsified adhesivers are most frequently used. Dependent upon their chemical constitution, and based upon preliminary laboratory investigation, the application of soil conditioners has resulted in a wide variety of possibillities. Extremely hydrophobic as well as rather moderate or even hydrophillic soil characteristics have been obtained.

The best illustration of these effects is given by the water adsorption isotherm, better known as PF-curve.

DETERMINATION OF WETTING CHARACTERISTICS

Both surface tension and wetting characteristics may be most accurately determined by the so called "Wilhelmy Plate method", where the force, acting on a platelet, vertically in contact with the liquid surface is measured, preferably by means of an electronicaly compensated balance.
The force given then by : (fig. 2)

$$F' = 2 (1 + t) y_{1.v} \cos \Theta \tag{22}$$

where : 1 : length of the platelet
t : thickness of the platelet

The platelet is made of Platinum so that adsorbed films may be prepared by evaporation as well as electrolysis or comparable effects e.g : the deposit of organic adhesives from emulsion by the action of a D.C. current. Estimations of surface coverage are obtained from (Nutt and Andes 1960).

$$\cos \Theta = \varepsilon_s \cos\Theta_1 + (1 - \varepsilon_s) \cos\Theta_2 \tag{23}$$

where : Θ : contact angle on partially occupied surface
ε_s : "degree of occupation" when $0<\varepsilon<1$.
Θ_1 : contact angle on complete covered solid surface
Θ_2 : contact angle on the clean solid.

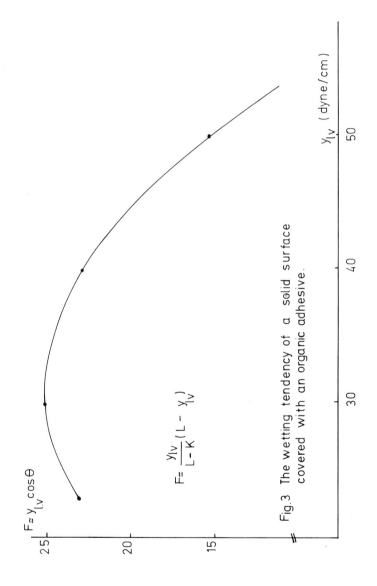

Fig.3 The wetting tendency of a solid surface covered with an organic adhesive.

$$F \approx \gamma_{l.v} \cos \Theta$$

$$F \approx \frac{\gamma_{lv}}{L-K}(L - \gamma_{lv})$$

The technique for measurements of wetting characteristics makes use of a series of calibration liquids, i.e of known $y_{1.v}$ values.

DETERMINATION OF PF-CURVES

The basic scheme of a PF-measurement apparatus and mode of operation is illustrated in fig. 4. It corresponds partly to the classical soil physical methods as proposed earlier by De Wiest (1969) a.o.
Some technical refinements are elaborated to meet more accurately the physical working conditions, i.e temperature and pressure regulation, measurement of in- and outflow by means of a recording balance system, and damping of residual pressure variations by means of a precisely adapted capillary tubing. This resulted in a quite more complicated apparatus than the classical one, as illustrated schematically in fig. 5. The most interesting features of this apparatus are related to the pressure regulation system, as the temperature control and the recording balance system are adapted commercial devices.

The pressure is measured by means of a transducer, giving a linear output voltage as a function of pressure at constant temperature. Variations of the latter are kept smaller than 0,01 °C.

The floating output signal is applied to a first amplifier stage, to reduce noise and to obtain a single ended output, which is fed to a comparator circuit, as illustrated in fig. 6. The comparator circuit contains a temperature compensated zener reference and a linear ten turn potentiometer.
The performance of this circuit is to be resumed as giving an over-all pressure regulation and resettability better than 1 % within the whole range of the transducer.

Due to its own noise level, the pressure transducer introduces a saw-tooth pressure variations of about 1.5 mm H_2O. As this figure might be significant at low pressure values one might take advantage of the damping action of a capillary tube, connected between the pressure transducer and the measuring cell. The damping action of this capillary tube is to be understood as follows : According to Taylor (1931), the gas flow through the capillary is given by :

$$\frac{dn}{dt} = \frac{\pi r^4}{16 \, \eta l R t} (P'^2 - P^2) \qquad (24)$$

where : r : capillary radius
  η : viscosity
  T : absolute temperature
  l : length of the capillary
  P' - P : pressure drop across the capillary.

Assuming the gas meeting the ideal gas law, one obtains :

$$\frac{dP}{dt} = \frac{\pi r^4}{16\eta \, lV} (P'^2 - P^2) \qquad (25)$$

where : V : volume of the measuring cell.

In equation (25), η, r, l and V are constants, while P' and P are time dependent in a way like illustrated in fig. 7. Mathematical considerations lead to the following expression for P'(t).

$$P'(t) = b + \sin (j + | \cos (j . \frac{\pi}{2}) |) \frac{\pi}{2} \times (a.t - \frac{j - | \sin(j.\frac{\pi}{2}) |}{2}).d$$

$$(26)$$

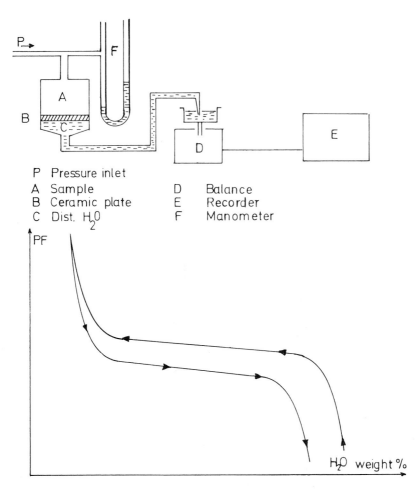

P   Pressure inlet
A   Sample   D   Balance
B   Ceramic plate   E   Recorder
C   Dist. H_2O F   Manometer

Fig 4 : Basic scheme and mode of operation of PF-measurement.

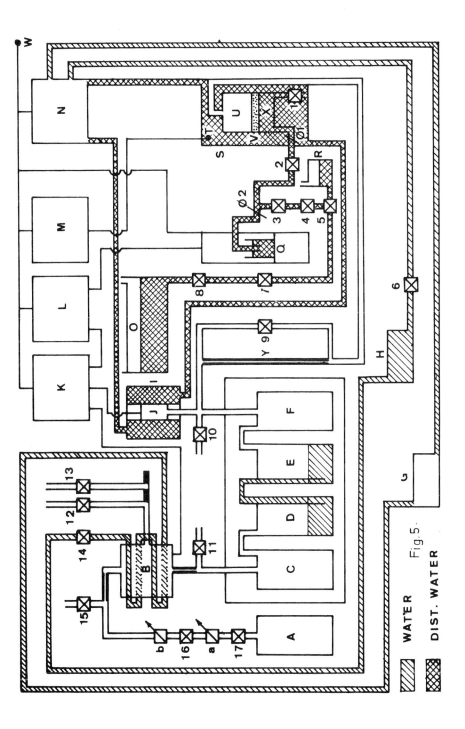

Fig.5.

Fig. 5   SYMBOLS

A: Compressed   air.

B: Electric   control   valve.

C, D, E, F: Flow through system (air saturated with H_2O)

G, H: Cooling H_2O suply.

I: Container with pressure transducer.

J: Pressure transducer.

K: Pressure control and regulator.

L: Recorder.

M, N Temp. control and thermostatic bath

O, R: Dist. H_2O suply.

P: Electronic balance

Q: Receptacle

S: Container with pressure cell.

T: Temperature sensor

U: Sample holder

V: Porous plate

$Ø_1$ $Ø_2$: Security valves

⊠   Valves

⬚   Manometers

▬▬   Capillary

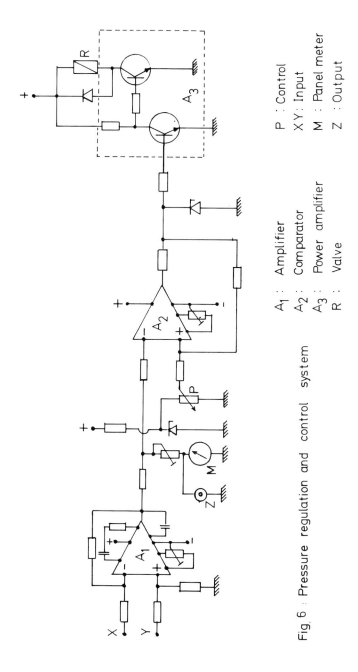

Fig. 6 : Pressure regulation and control system

A₁ : Amplifier
A₂ : Comparator
A₃ : Power amplifier
R : Valve

P : Control
X Y : Input
M : Panel meter
Z : Output

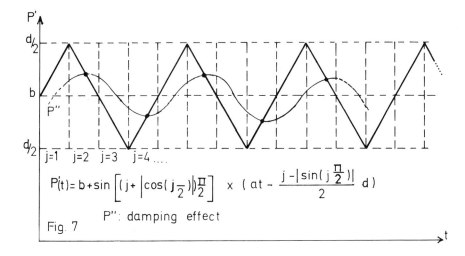

$$P'(t) = b + \sin\left[\left(j + \left|\cos\left(j\frac{\pi}{2}\right)\right|\right)\frac{\pi}{2}\right] \times \left(at - \frac{j - \left|\sin\left(j\frac{\pi}{2}\right)\right|}{2}\,d\right)$$

P″: damping effect

Fig. 7

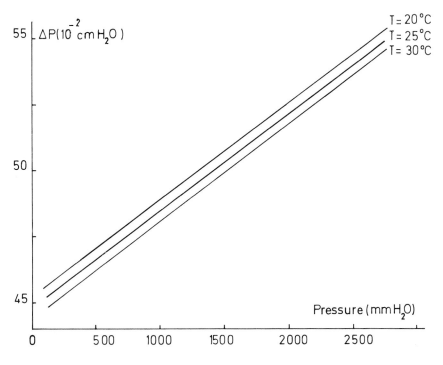

Fig.8 : Calculation of the damping characteristics of a capillary

where : b : mean pressure value

$$a : \left[\frac{dP'}{dt}\right] t = o$$

d : amplitude

Substituting in equation (25) P'(t) by its value obtained in equation (26) leads to an equation, which is to be integrated numerically. As a result, a suitable capillary may be proposed, giving the desired attenuation of pressure variations in the measuring cell. A practical situation is illustrated in fig. 8 for the following experimental data :

$$\left[\frac{dP'}{dt}\right]_{t=o} = 0,1 \text{ mm } H_2O \text{ sec}^{-1}$$

$$d = 1,5 \text{ mm } H_2O$$

capillary length : 10 cm
capillary radius : 0,17 mm

General information and data about sample manipulation have been given by De Wulf (1972).

CONCLUSION

The water holding capacity of porous solids of constant pore geometry is to be calculated on comparative basis as a function of interfacial parameters.

Practical methods have been proposed to determine the wetting characteristics of solids or substances, adsorbed on solid surfaces. Extensive information is given about the construction of a PF-measurement apparatus.

AKNOWLEDGMENTS

The authors whish to thank Prof. Dr. Ir. De Boodt and Prof. Dr. De Leenheer of the Faculty of Agricultural Sciences State Univ. Ghent, for their encouragement of this contribution as well as Prof. Dr. Rigole, Faculty of Sciences, for very helpfull discussions. Mr Maes, Department of Applied Mathematics, has given appreciable thechnical support.
REFERENCES

De Wiest : Flow through porous Media, 255
          Academic Press. New York. (1969)
De Wulf : Pedologie, 22,3, 318-327, Ghent, Belgium. (1972)
Gregg and Sing : Adsorption, Surface Area and Porosity,151
          Academic Press. London & New York. (1967)
Nutt and Andes : J. of Polym. Sc. 45, 255. (1960)
Rigole and De Bisschop : The formation of Adhesive Links by means
          of Emulsions.
          Mededelingen Fak. Landbouwwetenschappen, 37, 3 Ghent,
          Belgium (1972).
Taylor : A treatise on physical chemistry vol. 1, 175,
          Second edition. Mac. Millen Cie. (1931)
Zisman : Contact Angle, Wettability and Adhesion Am. Chem. Soc. Series : Advances
          in Chemistry 43, 2 (1964).

Modeling and Simulation of Water Resources Systems, G.C. VANSTEENKISTE, (Ed.)
North-Holland Publishing Company (1975)

WATER RESOURCES AND PLANT LIFE IN THE EGYPTIAN DESERT

K.H. Batanouny
Department of Botany, Faculty of Science
University of Cairo, EGYPT

INTRODUCTION

Like all the other lands lying within the great desert belt, Egypt is
characterised by a warm and almost rainless climate. The country embraces an area
of 1002 thousand sq.km, and the population of nearly 36 millions is mainly concentrated in an area of 35500 sq.km. Only 1.1% of the population inhabit the desert
area. The cultivated area amounts to about 2500 sq.km.

If the scanty rainfall that falls within the borders of Egypt were the
sole source from which the country derives water supplies, the whole country would
be one of the harshest deserts all over the world. But, fortunately, the Nile, tra-
versing the entire country from south to north for a distance of 1530 km, brings
down into Egypt large volumes of water. The flow of the Nile was a matter of crucial importance to the Egyptians since remote times. Records by Arab scholars have
been kept for many centuries giving the high and low stages of the Nile as indicated by the Nilometre at Cairo in the period 640-1517 A.D. (Tussun, 1922).

Apart from the Nile water, the water resources in the rest of the country
are limited and variable. This paper presents the conditions in the desert.

CLIMATIC ARIDITY

Application of several formulae and systems suggested for the classification of the climate shows the intensive aridity of the climate in the Egyptian desert, with the exception of some parts of the narrow Mediterranean coastal strip.
Low rainfall and intensive evaporation as shown in Table 1 are aspects of climatic
aridity. The mean evaporation rate is very high compared with the scanty rainfall.
Low evaporation values in the delta are due to the effect of irrigation. High values as much as 16.4 mm/day are recorded in the inland desert. It is obviously
clear that the scanty rainfall can not balance this high evaporating power.

The potential evapotranspiration values, according to the formula of
Thornthwaite, computed for representative stations in Egypt are : Alexandria,
1095 mm; Cairo,1170 mm; Asyut,1248mm; Qena,1415 mm; and Aswan,1505 mm (Thornthwaite
et al.,1956); Almaza,1136 and Giza,1042 mm (Kassas and Imam,1957) and Burg El Arab
along the Mediterranean coast,994.6 mm (Ayyad,1973). Such high values compared
with low rainfall indicate severe aridity.

Table 1 gives some data on rainfall at 23 stations located at various la-
titudes and distributed among different geographical terrains of the country, namely : the Mediterranean coastal zone, lower Egypt (Nile delta), upper Egypt (Nile
valley south of Cairo), Red Sea coastal zone and the oases in the Western Desert
(Fig. 1). The data presented show that the rainfall does not exceed 10 mm per year
in most parts of the country, particularly south of Cairo latitude, where the annual rainfall is far below the generally accepted limit of the desert boundary.
The highest average annual rainfall is 192.1 mm at Alexandria, while the other
coastal stations have rainfall less than 150 mm. The rainfall decreases rapidly
as one proceeds inland from the coast till it reaches values of 26.1 mm/year at
Cairo, some hundred and seventy kilometres inland. Asyut, which lies some three

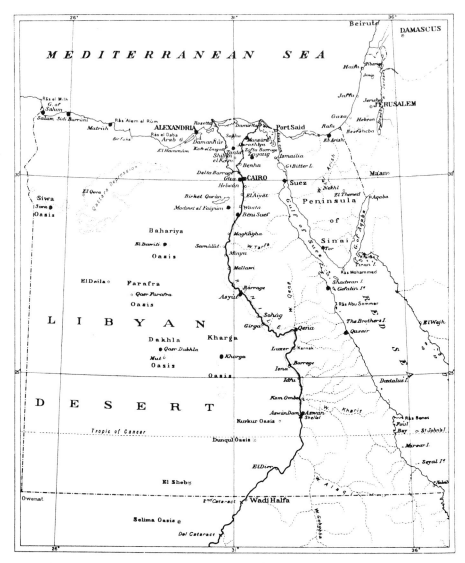

Fig.1 - A map of Egypt, indicating meteorological stations and localities
referred to in the text.

hundred kilometres south of Cairo, has but 0.4 mm rainfall per year, which is the lowest record in Egypt.

In many parts of the country, there is a prolonged dry season extending for 8 or 9 months every year. The number of rainy days with at least i mm/day a-mounts to 12.9 to 31.3 in the Mediterranean zone, 5 to 13 in lower Egypt and less than 5 in the other parts of the country.

Rainfall in Egypt is characterised by its high variability and irregulari-ty. The variability is not only temporal, but also spatial. Fig. 2 shows the in-consistency of rainfall from year to year in Almaza (inland station near Cairo) and Mersa Matruh (along the Mediterranean coast), taken as representative stations. In Mersa Matruh, the rainfall amounts to 275 mm in 1948, while it is only 67.4 mm in 1946. At Almaza station, a high value of 63.5 mm is recorded in 1951, whereas in 1946 the rainfall record is only 9.0 mm. There is a great deviation from the means which amount to 144.1 mm at Mersa Matruh and 23.5 mm at Almaza.

Apart from the variation of rainfall from year to year, there is a marked variation in the amount of rainfall in the corresponding winter months of the dif-ferent years. Fig. 3 shows the monthly rainfall records at Sidi Barrani along the Mediterranean coast for the period 1956-1965. The data reveal that in January 1956, the rainfall amounts to 24.2 mm, while it reached 173.9 mm in January 1964. In December 1958, only 2.8 mm fell, while in the corresponding month in 1964, it a-mounted to 115.3 mm. Also in October 1963, 20.5 mm fell, while not a single drop fell in October 1964. The wide variation in the annual rainfall is evident; 92.7mm fell in 1963 and 342.7 mm in 1964.

Rainfall records indicate that, for Sidi Barrani : 50% of the annual pre-cipitation falls at rates of less than 10 mm/day, 25% falls at rates of 10-20 mm/day, and the rest 25% falls at rates over 20 mm/day.

Heavy, but sporadic storms, may occur at wide intervals. They are usually of the thunderstorm type and may cause abundant precipitation within limited areas leading to great floods. As shown in Table 1, the maximum rainfall on one day at the different stations has high values; sometimes more than the average annual rainfall. This rain is obviously due to accidental cloudbursts and not to a wide-spread phenomenon. Most of the years are rainless, particularly at stations south of Cairo latitude. Such accidents will leave their effect on the plants and their habitats. The wadis and water runnels will suddenly be transformed into torrential streams sweeping in their way the floors and probably uprooting many of the plants. These reservoir of ephemeral streams may also replenish the underground/water which receive but very little of the normal rainfall.

In the Mediterranean coastal zone, exceptionally heavy rainfall form floods or "Seyl" which runs down the valleys to the sea carrying with them large quanti-ties of soil, this causes serious erosion to parts which otherwise would be with more stable and naturally developing substrates. Erosion by these floods is un-doubtedly more accentuated through the absence or poverty of the vegetation cover. Some of this water accumulates in depressions where it infiltrates to form a fresh water table floating over the saline water table and constitutes the main source of underground water in the area.

EDAPHIC ARIDITY

As a consequence of severe climatic aridity, the soil moisture supply to the plants is very austere and variable. In the southern and western practically rainless deserts, there is no available moisture in the soil that would support natural vegetation. The desert soil (surface deposits) is almost air dry all the year round except for few days in winter and spring. Subsurface layers of deep soils may comprise a permanently wet layer. This represents a permanent source of moisture to deeply penetrating roots of perennials.

K.H. Batanouny

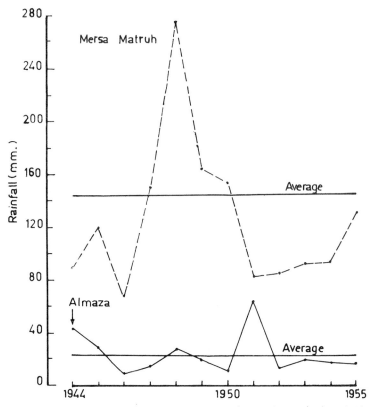

Fig.2 – Annual rainfall (mm) at Mersa Matruh (coastal station) and Almaza
(inland station near Cairo) for the period 1944–1955.

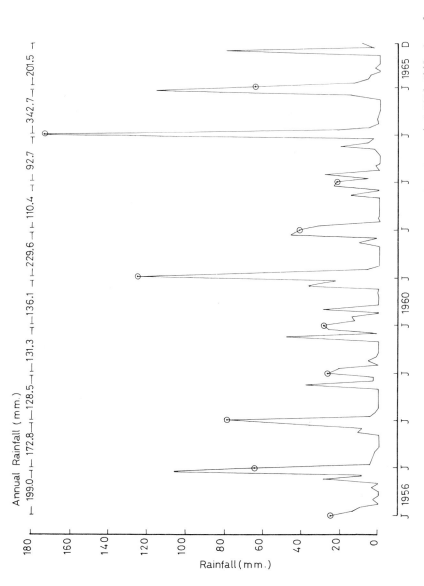

Fig. 3 – Monthly rainfall (mm) at Sidi Barrani, along the Mediterranean coast, for the period 1956–1965. Annual rainfall in the different years is indicated at the top of the figure.

Perhaps the physical properties of soil, including depth, penetrability, permeability and texture are the most important factors affecting the plant life in the desert. The importance of these physical attributes of soil is related to their influence on the water resources. Usually, the modification of the plant cover proceeds in coincidence with the modification of the soil thickness (Batanouny and Sheikh, 1972; Batanouny and Hilli, 1973; Batanouny and Zaki, 1974). Soil may be deep, but not easily penetrable to roots (physical resistance) or not permeable to water and does not allow good infiltration of water to deep layers. Penetrability and permeability are major factors affecting the soil moisture regime and consequently the plant distribution and growth. When two habitats have soils with almost the same depth, the texture (and structure) is an effective factor involved in the plant life.

Batanouny and Abdel Wahab (1973) found that the amount of the available moisture in the soil volume exploited by the root system of a small Leptadenia pyrotechnica bush amounts to 23000 kg. The root penetrates to a depth of 11.5 m and has a lateral extension of 10 m; the whole root system occupies 850 m^3 soil. The annual water output of this bush, which is 160 cm high, has been estimated to be 5700 kg. This means that the available water in the soil occupied by the root system is sufficient to supply the plant with its needs of water for a period of about 4 years without replenishment by rainfall. The plant can survive under the adverse moisture conditions in its habitat.

Desert plants may make use of the water vapour movement in the soil along a vapour pressure gradient, as the movement of film water under the conditions of low moisture content in the desert must be very low. As a result of differences in temperature and humidity at the various soil strata, water may be condensed in layers adjacent to the roots, which are depleted from their moisture content. This is evinced by the existence of desert plants in a green state under the adverse moisture conditions not sufficient for rapid movement of water by surface forces.

Dew plays a role in the plant life, particularly in the Mediterranean coastal zone, where the climatic conditions are in some seasons favourable for water vapour condensation, such as considerable temperature gradients between different soil strata and overlying air, high relative humidity and still wind. The gain in moisture content due to water vapour condensation in a locality in the Mediterranean coastal zone was estimated by Abdel Rahman, Ayyad and El-Monayari (1966) as ranging between 0.38 and 1.35%. In the same area, Arvidson and Hellström (1955) collected amounts of dew in funnels with surface areas of 1 m^2 each, ranging between 0.64 and 1.10 ml/night. The number of nights in which dewfall was recorded ranged between 72 and 82 per year.

Usually, the plants inhabiting the coastal dunes, where there is considerable dewfall, produce long fibrous roots running parallel to the soil surface at shallow depths not exceeding 10 cm. These superficial roots may benefit from the condensation in the uppermost layer.

THE WATER OUTPUT OF THE DESERT VEGETATION

Under arid conditions with extremely low rainfall, evaluation of water consumption is of paramount importance in the water economy. Limitations exist in applying a purely physical formula in the determination of water loss from a sample of desert vegetation. In the desert, water loss from deep layers is mainly restricted to root absorption and transpiration, whereas evaporation from the soil ceases due to the presence of the dry upper layers acting as a protective layer. The loss is proportional to the density of the plant cover. The water output from a sample of desert vegetation has been found to depend mainly on the fresh weight of plants, their density, the climatic factors, the floristic composition, and the availability of soil moisture, and these factors may interact with each other.

Using the data of the daily mean transpiration rate and the total fresh weight of the shoots of each species, the water output from a unit area in different micro-habitats of a desert wadi has been calculated (Abdel Rahman and Batanouny, 1965a). In spring, the water output values in the different microhabitats amount to : 44.8, 45.9, 114.2 and 8.3 kg/100 m^2.day in the plateau, shaded microhabitat, first wadi terrace and second terrace, respectively. A slight increase was observed in summer in most microhabitats due to the rise in the transpiration rate of plants in that part of the year. Abdel Rahman and El-Hadidy (1958) recorded water output values of 16.0 kg/100 m^2.day for a sample of desert vegetation along the Cairo-Suez Road. This low figure is due to the sparseness of vegetation in the desert area studied, where the total fresh weight of the perennials in February reach 3.21 kg/100 m^2. Fresh weight values range from 6.15 kg to 47.4 kg/100 m^2 in the different microhabitats of a desert wadi in the wet season, and from 5.5 kg to 44.3 kg/100 m^2 in the dry season.

The average annual water output in the various microhabitats in mms are about : 175, 175, 427 and 30 in the plateau, shaded microhabitat, first terrace and second terrace, respectively. It is notable that the average annual rainfall is 25.4 mm in the study area, namely Wadi Hof near Helwan. The widely different water output values reveals the mosaic pattern of the water regime in the different parts of the same locality as mainly affected by topographic irregularities. These microhabitats are few metres apart, but with different microenvironmental condi-tions (Batanouny, 1973).

LANDFORM AND WATER RESOURCES

Topography, geological structure, lithological features of parent rock, geomorphological patterns and features, characteristics of surface deposits, etc. are factors affecting not only the plant life and animal life, but also the whole complex of ecological relationships. Through its direct and/or indirect effects on the water revenue of the habitat, the landform affects the desert vegetation. A slight fall in the ground surface, a rock fissure, a stone block may create a new and special environmental set-up and produce habitats for a characteristic type of vegetation.

In the Egyptian desert, runoff is of paramount importance to the plant life, particularly in wadis which are common in the Eastern Desert lying between the Nile and the Red Sea. Topographic irregularities in this desert are the most ob-vious factors affecting the distribution and growth of plants. Many microhabitats can be distinguished, each of them varies widely from the other regards the water resources, soil properties, microclimatic conditions and consequently the plant cover (Abdel Rahman and Batanouny, 1965b, 1966; Batanouny, 1973). The growth of plants is mainly restricted to depressions and low parts regards the local topo-graphy receiving runoff and water-borne material.

The vegetation of the coastal plain west of Hurghada along the Red Sea coastal zone indicates conditions of extremely arid climate; but the vegetation types of the high mountains (over 1500 m), the runnels that dissect their slopes and the wadis that collect the drainage at their feet indicate less arid condi-tions (Kassas and Zahran, 1965, 1971). It is persumed that peaks of high mountains intercept some of the cloud moisture in the form of orographic rains or condensa-tion. In the wadis running at the feet of the mountains, there are several shallow wells of fresh water. On the slopes or cliffs of mountains there are cracks of fissures that oozes a continuous trickle of water. These form the habitat of ferns and hygrophilous plants. The courses of runnels dissecting the slopes of the moun-tains may contain potholes that are periodically filled with water.

WATER RESOURCES AND TYPES OF VEGETATION

The decisive factor responsible for the wide variation of plant cover in
the different parts of the desert is the water regime of each habitat. The amount
of water available to plants during the rainy season differes considerably in different localities of the same terrain. Three types of vegetation are recognizable
according to the water regime of the habitat, namely : (a) accidental (Kassas,
1966) in the rainless parts where rainfall is not an annually recurring incident
as in the Lybian (Western) and Nubian Deserts of Egypt; (b) restricted type
(Walter, 1963) or mode contracte (Monod, 1954), in arid areas where rainfall though
low and variable, is an annually recurring phenomenon, vegetation is confined to
rather restricted areas (Depressions, runnels and wadis) with relatively adequate
water supply, as in the Eastern Desert of Egypt ; and (c) diffuse type in less arid
areas, that is a vegetation more or less evenly distributed, as in less arid parts
of the Mediterranean zone in Egypt. Usually, the accidental type of vegetation is
composed of ephemerals or perennials which aquire an ephemeral growth form.

WATER RESOURCES IN THE MEDITERRANEAN ZONE IN EGYPT

Rainfall represents the main source of water supplies to this zone. Variation in its amount and distribution (both in time and space) may preclude dry farming. A summary of barley experiments in 1946-1953 at Burg El Arab, reported by
Kassas (1972) is given in Table 2. It is clear that the crop varies between a
level of famine to a level of plenty. Kassas (1972) states that this is a serious
disadvantage of depending on an annual crop in an area with notable variation in
annual rainfall.

Groundwater Supplies

1. Shallow native wells : These are hand-dug wells, less than 5 m deep with their
   bottom higher than the sea level, and are restricted to a narrow coastal strip;
   200 m to 1 km away from the shoreline. Their water, usually raised by "Shadouf"
   is mainly for civic uses, partly for irrigation of some vegetables grown on a
   very small scale to the south of the coastal dune belt. In some parts (between
   Garawla and Mersa Matruh) these wells are located inland in the perched water
   tables of the wadis.
2. Deep native wells : These are also hand-dug, the depth of which seldom exceeds
   50 m, and they are concentrated along the coastal strip within/10 km from the
   shore.
3. Boreholes : Few boreholes, drilled for geological rather than hydrological purposes, are in operation at Fuka and Hatwa areas. They are less than 80 m deep
   and generally end at 6 inches diametre.
4. Coastal dune galleries : These galleries are constructed either as covered
   trenches or underground tunnels, 16 to 2250 m long and 0.5 to 2.0 m broad.
   An average of 656 m^3/day is pumped from all the galleries along the coast
   (Paver and Pretorius, 1954$_a$).

The water table of the coastal dunes is recharged through : (a) infiltration from precipitation; (b) lateral seepage of accumulated surface runoff behind
the dunes in areas of favourable inland drainage; and (c) subsurface seepage from
the main water table when it is higher than that in the dunes. Discharge of water
from the dunes occur through : (a) subsurface seepage to the sea and the lagoonal
areas inland where the water level in the dunes is relatively high; (b) absorption
and transpiration by plants; and (c) collecting galleries and wells.

Fluctuations in the water levels, which are relevant to the season of the
year, lead to variations in the quantity and quality of water raised from the galleries. Marked lowering of water levels and increase in salinity are obvious in
summer due to excessive water use.

Surface Water Supplies

The supply of surface water to the zone is derived from different sources. The pipe-line and the rail-borne water represent a limited supply of drinking water to the main settléments and towns till Mersa Matruh. In Sallum, to the far west, one distillation plant is operating and condenses approximately 36 m³/week of potable water from sea water.

Exogenous water supplies for irrigation of the West Nubaryia Project in the eastern part of the zone are available from Nubaryia canal. This canal brings the mixed Nile and drainage water (1:6.32), with a salinity in the mixture of 600 ppm, to the newly reclaimed land. All the water needed for irrigation is pumped to higher elevations by electrical pumping stations connected by open transport canals. The introduction of irrigated agriculture on the newly reclaimed land created a series of problems. Amongst the most severe problems are : the steady rise in water table (average rise of 4 m/year), accompanied by the formation of level groundwater mounds and reversals of groundwater flow direction, and the outflow of saline groundwater into the principal irrigation canals (Schulze and Ridder, 1974).

Underground storage cisterns

The number of cisterns in the zone is estimated to range from 2000 to 3000 (Shafei, 1952; Paver and Pretorius, 1954$_a$; Murray, 1955), with total storage capacity of 400 000 m³. Ball (1935) describes cisterns as large underground chambers excavated in the limestone ridges in Roman times and serve as covered-in rain water reservoirs. The chamber is plastered inside to prevent leakage. The site of a cistern is carefully chosen so as to collect runoff from considerable areas, small drainage channels conduct water to an orifice leading to the underground chambre. The average capacity of the cistern ranges from 200 to 500 m³, some in Sallum have a storage capacity of 2000 m³. Water stored in these cisterns is usually fresh with salinities ranging from 30 to 100 ppm in terms of NaCl (Paver and Pretorius, 1954$_a$). Most of the cisterns became filled with sediments, but those that have recently been cleared and restored to their original function fill with water in rainy seasons. Kassas (1972) reports that this may be taken to indicate that climate (rainfall) has not substantially changed since these cisterns were excavated.

Runoff

In the eastern sector of the zone, till about 100 km west of Alexandria, the topographic features of the region comprises a series of limestone ridges that run parallel to the shore line and extend from east to west for different distances. These ridges are effective means of natural redistribution of rain water; farms are usually located at the feet of these ridges where runoff water accumulates.

In the part west of Fuka till Sallum, there is a distinct hydrographic network of about 218 wadis. The ramified ravines of these wadis and the rocky nature of the upstreams render these wadis sensible to the rainfall. The wadis collect surface runoff and dilate in some parts, especially in their downstreams. Fresh deposits, which vary in thickness and depth according to the meandering of the main channel and its width, are found in terraces bordering the sides of the wadi. These deposits are thick and broad on the inner curve of the meander, rendering possible the cultivation of olives and other fruit trees. In the deltas of some wadis, there are wells or cisterns yielding good quality water. Unfortunately, the major part of water collected by some wadis is lost to the sea passing through the lower points between the dunes. Moreover, suspended material are lost.

Ball (1935) conducted investigations in wadi El Kharruba area 10 km south west of Mersa Matruh, and concluded that in given good rainfall years, a dam 17 m high could have a reservoir capacity capable of supplying 700 m³ of water per day. According to his experiments in that wadi, Ball (1935) found that showers of less

than 10 mm/day do not create a considerable quantity of runoff. Showers of more
than 10 mm/day result to a runoff the quantity of which amounts to 3/4 of the fal-
len water, after a substraction of 8 mm which represents the water vaporated and
retained by the soil. If the shower of more than 10 mm/day is followed the next
day or days by a shower of 5 mm or more, this rainfall is added to the first shower before substracting the said 8 mm. The conclusion of Ball can be expressed by
the formula :

$$V R \ = \ 0.75 \ (h' - 8) \ S \ X \ 1000$$

where

    VR = quantity of runoff in m^3.
    h' = shower more than 10 mm in mm.
    S   = catchment area in km^2.

        Based on the rainfall data in Mersa Matruh and Ball's formula, Economides
and Harhash (1967) calculated the quantity of runoff per year in the period 1951-
1965 in wadi Magid west of Matruh. It has been found to range from 53 000 m^3 in
1962 (total rainfall 72.5 mm) to 2 950 000 m^3 in 1965 (207.4 mm rainfall).

GROUNDWATER SUPPLIES IN THE WESTERN DESERT

        The Western (Lybian) Desert of Egypt stretches westward from the Nile val-
ley to the borders of Lybia and embraces an area of more than two thirds of the
whole area of the country. It is one of the most arid regions in the world, the
water resources within it being in many places hundreds of kilometres apart. These
are the oases, which owe their existence to the combined and interrelated effects
of topographical, geological and hydrological factors. The habitable oases are :
Siwa, Baharyia, Farafra, Dakhla and Kharga.

        The source of the artesian waters of the oases is a matter of discussion.
Some hydrologists believe that this water is derived from the rain that falls in
the Sudan and flows underground in the permeable beds of the Nubian sandstone.
Others believe that it is merely Nile waters which have penetrated into the adjoining deserts. Ball (1927) believes that under the large area of the Lybian desert, there is a continuous sheet of subterranean water from which all the desert
supplies are derived.

        The report of Paver and Pretorius (1954$_b$) on hydrological investigations
in Kharga and Dakhla oases was followed by many studies on the hydrology of the
oases in response to requests by the Government. The many data collected are summarized in a booklet published in Arabic by the Excutive Agency for Desert Projects,
A.R.E.(1973). The data given here are extracted from this booklet.

        The present cultivated area in the main oases, above mentioned, is about
41 940 feddans (one feddan is about 0.420 hectares), while the area suitable for
cultivation is estimated to be 1 433 000 feddans. The groundwater potentialities
and their economic exploitation are the main factors controlling the development
of land in the oases. Groundwater studies show that the amount of stored water in
the groundwater reservoir of the Western Desert ranges between 23.4 X 10^4 billion
cubic metres to 21 X 10^9 billion cubic metres. The daily recharge along the Lybian
and Sudanese fronts amounts to 3 057 300 m^3/day, an amount enough to irrigate
153 000 feddans with a water requirement of 20 m^3/day. At present, the cultivated
area of 41 940 feddans and the water used nearly amounts to 829 800 m^3/day.

        For a long-term planning for the exploitation of groundwater hydrological
conditions of the groundwater reservoir of the Western Desert were simulated in
the form of resistor-capacitor Analog Model. The results indicated the possibility
of reclaiming 110 000 feddans in Dakhla and Kharga. The average expected draw-down

in Kharga and Dakhla will be 60 to 40 m, respectively, after 50 years of continuous production. Pumps become necessary to lift water to the surface after gradual decreasing of the artesian pressure due to continuous exploitation.

Losses in irrigation water reach 70% including losses beside the wells (30%), conveyance losses from the canal system (15%) and field losses (25%). Drainage and salinization of the land represent major problems in the newly reclaimed land in the oases.

SUMMARY AND CONCLUSIONS

1. Desert conditions prevail throughout the whole country. Scanty, variable and irregular rainfall as well as high evaporation are aspects of the climatic aridity. The rainfall decreases as one proceeds inland from the coast, it does not exceed 10 mm/annum in most parts of the country, particularly south of Cairo latitude.

2. As a consequence of climatic aridity, the moisture supply to the plants is very austere and variable. Desert soil (surface deposits) is almost air dry all the year round except for few days in the wet season. Subsurface layers of deep soils may comprise a permanent wet layer, representing the source of moisture to perennial plants. The physical soil attributes have a great influence on the plant life in the desert through their effect on the soil-moisture relations. Water vapour movement and dewfall play a role in the plant life under desert conditions.

3. The water output values from a sample of the desert vegetation show wide variations in the different habitats depending on many factors. The average water output in different microhabitats (few metres apart) in a desert wadi ranges from 8.3 to 114.2 kg/100 m^2.day in the wet season.

4. The landform has a direct and indirect effects on the water resources of the different habitats. Topographic irregularities, through their effect on the water resources, have a marked influence on the distribution and growth of plants. Peaks of high mountains in the Red Sea zone intercept some of the cloud moisture in the form of orographic rain or precipitation. This has a paramount effect on the distribution of plants in this zone.

5. Three types of vegetation are recognizable according to the water regime of the habitat, namely : accidental, restricted and diffuse types of vegetation.

6. The water resources in the Mediterranean coastal zone in Egypt comprise (a) Groundwater supplies, including water obtained from shallow and deep native wells, boreholes and coastal dune galleries; and(b) Surface water supplies, including : exogenous supplies, underground storage cisterns collecting runoff water. Water resources in this zone are relatively higher than in the inland desert.

7. Groundwater supplies in the western desert are represented by the artesian water of the oases. The origin of these supplies is still a matter of discussion. The groundwater potentialities and their economic use are the main factors controlling land development in the oases. Great losses in irrigation water (about 70%) are due to losses beside the wells, conveyance losses from canal system and field losses.

8. From the foregoing points, it appears that a great part of the water bestowed by nature is allowed to go waste. There must be a rational use of the available water resources in the arid and semi-arid zones. In some parts, with relatively good supply of ground or exogenous water, there is an extravagant use of water. This creates a series of problems, including the rising of water table, salinization of the soil etc., all these result in the diminution of the land

productivity. The concepts of agriculture development under conditions of limited water resources should not be the same as those followed in areas with considerable water supply, e.g. in the Nile valley and delta.

9. For proper utilisation of the water resources in arid and semi-arid zones, there is a great need for numerous studies, which vary according to the source of water and the suitability of the land.

In areas with good supply of ground or exogenous water, there is a great need for the determination of the most economic use of irrigation water. This can be achieved by : (a) study of the effectiveness of the different methods of irrigation; (b) determination of the consumptive use of various crops and droungh-resistant trees; and (c) work on the crops and cropping patterns in relation to the economic use of water. These studies must take the cost of water into consideration.

In rain-fed (runoff-fed) areas, studies should be carried out on the water resources and the factors influencing them.

Study of the factors pertaining to suitability of the land in arid and semi-arid zones is indispensable. The anthropogenic factors must be involved in the evaluation of the land.

In areas with meagre water resources (low, irregular rainfall and limited groundwater supply), where water deficiency preclude dry farming, endeavour becomes essential to store the water in cisterns. These represent water points for the drinking of nomads wandering with their herds.

REFERENCES

ABDEL RAHMAN, A.A., AYYAD, M.A. and EL-MONAYARI, M.M., Hydro-ecology of the sand
      dunes habitat at Burg El Arab. Bull.Fac.Sci., Cairo Univ. 40 : 29-54, 1966.
ABDEL RAHMAN, A.A. and BATANOUNY, K.H., The water output of the desert vegetation
      in the different microhabitats of wadi Hoff. J.Ecol. 53 : 139-145, 1965.
ABDEL RAHMAN, A.A. and BATANOUNY, K.H., Microclimatic conditions in wadi Hof.
      Bull.Soc.Géog.d'Egypte 39 : 137-153, 1966.
ABDEL RAHMAN, A.A. and EL HADIDY, M.N., Observations on water output of the desert
      vegetation along Suez road. Egypt.J.Bot. 1 : 19-38, 1958.
ANONYMOUS, The New Valley (El Wadi El-Gedid), in Arabic, 107 pp. Excutive Agency
      for Desert Projects. Government Press, Cairo, 1973.
ARVIDSON,I. and HELLSTRÖM, B., A note on dew in Egypt. Bull.Inst.Hydraul., Stockh.
      48 : 416-426, 1955.
AYYAD, M.A., Vegetation and environment of the Western Mediterranean coastal land
      of Egypt. I-The habitat of sand dunes. J.Ecol. 61 : 509-523, 1973.
BALL, J., Problems of the Lybian Desert. Geog.J. 70, 1927.
BALL, J., The Water supply of Mersa Matruh. Survey and Mines Dept. Paper No.43,
      Cairo-Egypt, 1935.
BATANOUNY, K.H., Soil properties as affected by topography in desert wadis. Acta
      Bot.Acad.Sci.Hung. 19 : 13-21, 1973.
BATANOUNY, K.H. and ABDEL WAHAB, A.M., Eco-physiological studies on desert plants.
      VIII-Root penetration of Leptadenia pyrotechnica (Forsk.) Decne. in rela-
      tion to its water balance. Oecologia (Berl.) 11 : 151-161, 1973.
BATANOUNY, K.H. and HILLI, M.R., Phytosociological study of Ghurfa desert, central
      Iraq. Phytocoenologia 1 : 223-249, 1973.
BATANOUNY, K.H. and SHEIKH, M.Y., Ecological observations along Baghdad-Huseiba
      road, Western Desert, Iraq. Feddes Repertorium 83 : 245-263, 1972.
BATANOUNY, K.H. and ZAKI, M.A.F., Edaphic factors and the distribution of plant
      associations in a sector in the coastal Mediterranean zone in Egypt.
      Phyton (Austria) 15, 1974.
ECONOMIDES, P. and HARHASH, I., Surface water management technical report. Wadi
      Magid Exp.Dev.Project.Pre-investment survey of the North Western coastal

region of the U.A.R. 30 pp., 1967.

KASSAS, M., Plant life in deserts, in Arid Lands, E.S.Hills,Ed. 145-180. Methuen, London, UNESCO, 1966.

KASSAS, M., A brief history of land-use in Mareotis region, Egypt. Minerva Biologica 1 : 167-174, 1972.

KASSAS, M. and IMAM, M., Climate and microclimate in the Cairo desert. Bull.Soc. Géog.d'Egypte 30 : 25-52, 1957.

KASSAS,M. and ZAHRAN, M., Studies on the ecology of the Red Sea coastal land. II-The district from El-Galala El-Qiblyia to Hurghada. Bull.Soc.Géog. d'Egypte 38 : 155-193, 1965.

KASSAS, M. and ZAHRAN, M., Plant life on the coastal mountains of the Red Sea, Egypt. J.Indian Bot.Soc. 50A : 571-589, 1971.

MONOD, Th.,Modes contracté et diffus de la végétation saharienne, in Biology of Deserts, J.L. Cloudsley-Thompson, Ed. 35-44, Institute of Biology, London, 1954.

MURRAY, G.W., Water from the desert : some ancient Egyptian achievements, The Geog. J. 121 : 171, 1955.

PAVER, G.L. and PRETORIUS, D.A., Report on reconnaissance hydrological investigations in the Western Desert coastal zone, Publs.Inst.Désert d'Egypte No.5, 145 pp., 1954ᵃ.

PAVER, G.L. and PRETORIUS, D.A., Report on the hydrological investigations in Kharga and Dakhla oases, Publs.Inst.Désert d'Egypte No.4, 108 pp., 1954ᵦ.

SCHULZE, F.E. and DE RIDDER, N.A., The rising water table in the west Nubaryia area of Egypt, Nature and Resources 10 : 12-18, 1974.

SHAFEI, A., Lake Mareotis, its past history and its future development. Bull.Inst. Desert d'Egypte. 2 : 71-101, 1952.

THORNTHWAITE, C.W., MATHER, J.R. and CARTER, D.B., Three water balance maps of southwest Asia. Publs.Clim.Lab.Climatology. Centerton, New Jersey 11 : 57pp. 1958.

TUSSUN, Omar., Mémoire sur les anciannes branches du Nil : Epoque Arabe. Mémoire Inst.d'Egypte 4 : 65-213, 1922.

WALTER, H., The water supply of desert plants, in The Water Relations of Plants, A.J. Rutter and F.H. Whitehead, Eds. 199-205, British Ecological Society, 1963.

Table 2 : Barley crop at Burg El Arab experimental farm

Year	Rainfall (mm)	Area (feddan)	Crop (ardab)
1946	205.0	200	513
1947	52.5	160	5
1948	206.0	180	357
1949	280.0	200	600
1950	242.0	100	140
1951	57.5	100	0
1952	156.0	140	117
1953	85.0	100	0

Feddan = about one acre (0.420 hectare).

Ardab = 198 litres (5.44 bushels).

Table 1-Rainfall data and mean annual evaporation at different stations in Egypt
(Data obtained from Climatological Normals, U.A.R., 1960)

Station	Lat.°,N	Log.°,E	J	F	M	A	M	J	J	A	S	O	N	D	Total	No.of rainy days 1 mm	Max.rainfall one day (mm)	Date	Annual mean of evaporation (mm/day)
A-Coastal Stations																			
Sallum	31 33	25 11	15.6	7.1	13.6	0.6	4.3	Tr	Tr	0.0	0.9	17.5	39.7	20.4	119.7	12.9	120.8	22.11.1947	8.7
Sidi Barrani	31 38	25 58	30.5	7.4	11.4	1.3	5.2	Tr	Tr	0.4	0.1	19.0	23.2	40.0	136.5	25.8	37.3	27.11.1953	6.5
Mersa Matruh	31 20	27 13	27.1	16.4	13.7	2.3	3.2	Tr	0.0	0.0	0.6	15.4	26.7	38.7	144.1	24.1	75.5	22.11.1947	8.3
Alexandria	31 12	29 57	48.3	28.4	14.0	2.7	1.5	Tr	Tr	0.5	0.4	7.9	32.2	56.2	192.1	31.3	47.9	10.1.1957	5.2
El-Arish	31 07	33 45	14.5	16.0	12.9	4.3	3.7	Tr	0.0	0.3	0.7	5.3	18.3	20.8	96.8	16.1	59.0	12. 5.1950	4.3
B-Lower Egypt																			
Mansoura	31 03	31 23	12.1	9.9	7.6	3.3	3.1	0.0	Tr	Tr	0.2	3.4	6.0	9.2	54.8	13.0	46.8	13. 6.1933	4.7
Tanta	30 47	31 00	9.0	7.5	4.2	1.9	4.2	Tr	Tr	0.0	0.2	4.2	4.6	9.7	45.5	11.4	39.0	27.10.1937	4.5
Zagazig	30 35	31 30	5.1	5.1	4.0	1.8	1.3	Tr	0.0	0.0	Tr	1.9	4.4	5.7	29.3	7.9	24.0	5.11.1932	4.1
Cairo (Ezbekia)	30 03	31 15	4.5	3.9	3.7	1.7	2.0	0.3	0.0	Tr	Tr	1.7	2.0	6.3	26.1	5.9	43.2	17. 1.1919	5.0
C-Upper Egypt																			
Giza	30 02	31 13	2.9	4.2	2.3	0.7	1.6	0.0	0.0	Tr	0.0	3.5	2.3	5.9	23.6	5.2	53.2	27.10.1937	6.1
Fayoum	29 18	30 51	0.9	1.9	1.6	0.7	1.2	0.0	0.0	0.0	Tr	1.0	0.7	5.7	13.7	3.3	44.0	30.12.1944	6.9
Bei Suef	29 04	31 06	0.8	2.0	1.1	0.8	Tr	0.0	0.0	0.0	Tr	0.1	0.1	3.6	8.5	2.1	16.6	21.12.1949	6.2
Asyut	27 11	31 06	Tr	0.4	Tr	Tr	Tr	0.0	0.0	0.0	0.0	Tr	0.0	Tr	0.4	0.2	2.5	2. 2.1952	5.0
Qena	26 10	32 43	0.2	1.0	0.1	Tr	0.3	Tr	0.0	0.0	0.0	0.6	2.2	0.9	5.3	0.6	55.3	22.11.1943	8.0
Aswan	24 02	32 53	0.1	Tr	0.1	0.3	0.6	Tr	0.0	0.0	Tr	0.2	0.1	Tr	1.4	0.3	5.5	10. 5.1935	15.4
D-Red Sea Coast																			
Suez	29 56	32 33	2.5	4.8	2.0	0.9	1.5	Tr	0.0	0.0	0.1	2.8	4.1	4.9	23.6	5.1	32.3	9.11.1939	9.4
El-Tor	28 14	33 37	1.3	1.3	1.3	0.2	0.2	Tr	0.0	0.0	0.0	1.1	0.8	3.2	9.4	1.4	22.0	7.12.1955	10.2
Hurghada	27 17	33 46	Tr	Tr	0.5	Tr	0.5	0.0	0.0	0.0	0.0	Tr	0.2	2.8	4.0	1.0	24.7	19.12.1954	13.4
Quseir	26 08	34 18	Tr	Tr	0.3	0.1	Tr	0.0	0.0	0.0	0.0	0.6	2.2	0.2	3.4	0.3	34.0	6.11.1934	11.8
E-Oases																			
Siwa	29 12	25 19	0.7	2.7	0.3	1.1	2.1	0.0	0.0	0.0	0.1	0.4	0.2	2.4	9.9	2.0	23.0	15. 5.1945	10.3
Baharyia	28 20	28 54	Tr	1.2	0.0	0.6	0.1	0.2	0.0	0.0	0.0	0.2	0.7	1.3	4.3	0.8	16.0	18. 4.1948	9.6
Dakhla	25 29	29 00	Tr	0.4	Tr	Tr	0.2	Tr	0.0	0.0	0.0	Tr	Tr	0.1	0.7	0.1	8.0	15. 2.1942	16.4
Kharga	25 26	30 34	0.1	0.4	Tr	Tr	0.3	0.0	0.0	0.0	Tr	0.6	0.1	0.4	1.3	0.4	7.5	22.12.1943	14.9

PART THREE

WATER QUALITY MODELS

Modeling and Simulation of Water Resources Systems, G.C. VANSTEENKISTE, (Ed.)
North-Holland Publishing Company (1975)

TRANSIENT ANALYSIS OF WATER QUALITY IN THE
DELAWARE ESTUARY SYSTEM VIA ONE-DIMENSIONAL,
INTRA-TIDAL, TIME-VARYING MODELS WITH APPLI-
CATION TO THE IDENTIFICATION OF THE TIDAL
DISPERSION COEFFICIENT USING DISCRETE-SPACE
CONTINUOUS-TIME OCEAN SALINITY DATA

B. Davidson, Y. S. Shieh*, and S. M. Yih
Department of Chemical and Biochemical Engineering
Rutgers University-The State University of New Jersey
New Brunswick, New Jersey 08903, U.S.A.

ABSTRACT**

Water quality in the Upper Delaware River Estuary System was analyzed
using an intra-tidal, time-varying, deterministic, one-dimensional,
non-isothermal, multi-state variable model. The model was calibrated
with actual field data and applied to several system analysis problems. The unique features of the model are associated with its time
and space scales which are of the order of 30 minutes and one mile,
respectively, and its state equation format which included an ad hoc
intra-tidal velocity equation and conservation balances on dissolved
oxygen, biochemical oxygen demand, and thermal energy. Numerical
routines on an IBM 360 computer using central differences for the
space derivatives provided stable and accurate results for the integration of the system equations. The capabilities of the proposed model were demonstrated by comparing the stationary-state, tidal-
averaged simulated results with corresponding field data. Parameter
sensitivity analysis and shock-loading studies were made in addition
to obtaining stationary-state results associated with simulated treatment plant, regionalization plans.

For relatively large estuarial systems, of which the Upper Delaware
River Estuary is one, where dye studies become impractical, it was
found that under certain situations ocean salinity data can be utilized in a distributed parameter identification scheme to obtain
estimates of the longitudinal dispersion coefficient. This was demonstrated using an ad hoc, intra-tidal, velocity equation in
conjunction with a salinity mass balance. Continuous recordings of
ocean salinity at four locations in the estuary were used as input
data. The data was selected under conditions where the freshwater
inflows were low and the salinity concentrations and gradients were
correspondingly large. The integrations of the partial differential
equations were performed using the discrete-space, continuous-time
method of lines. An algorithm for the identification procedure was
developed based on a modified Marquardt's method. Because of limited
data, a linear polynomial expression for the dispersion coefficient
in terms of longitudinal distance was used.

* Presently with the New Jersey State Department of Environmental
Protection, Bureau of Water Pollution Control, Trenton, New Jersey, U.S.A.

** Work sponsored by the Office of Water Resources Research, U.S. Dept.
of the Interior, U.S.A. (Grants B-045, B-049, A-036, and A-045 N.J.)

INTRODUCTION

Water quality management personnel have traditionally made use of mathematical models as simulation tools in their decision making processes. These models have been related to mathematical descriptions of water quality variables and their functional interdependencies. Water quality analysis and available environmental control procedures involve examination of various water use patterns, prevailing water quality criteria, and order of magnitude of waste inputs.

The estuarial system is without a doubt one of the most complex environmental systems with which water resources analysts must deal. Not only is the system irregular in geometry and unsteady in its hydrodynamic and hydrologic behavior, but it is often the focal point of intense human activity that can drastically alter the system's behavior.

The general tone of the mathematical developments and prototype applications in this work is in the sense of enlarging the scope of state-of-the-art modeling and simulation methods with respect to tidal velocity, temperature, DO, and BOD which are all inter-related variables. That is, the aim is to more fully exploit the undeveloped and underdeveloped application potentials of one-dimensional, intra-tidal, time-varying (i.e., real-time-varying) models for estuarial systems which incorporate all of these variables together. These models are found to have use in the determination of location and time phasing of best BOD waste and thermal discharge patterns to attain a specified DO standard, shock loading effects, and other such impacts. Not withstanding is the problem of parameter identification in the distributed models using, as input data, noise corrupted field measurements. The Upper Delaware River Estuary between Trenton and Reedy Island is particularly well suited for exploration of these ideas because of its high degree of pollution in which DO and ocean salinity intrusion play significant roles. Therefore, the Upper Delaware River Estuary has been selected for case study examples throughout the work of this investigation.

Space available in this communication does not permit a complete expose on the subject matter. Basic mathematical equations and samples of typical results will be presented with the understanding that the theses by Shieh (1974) and Yih (1974) should be consulted for detailed developments.

MATHEMATICAL MODEL FOR THE SIMULATION STUDIES

The physical system chosen for the simulation part of the study was the estuarial waterbody between Trenton and Wilmington, a distance of 64.7 miles. The momentum and continuity equations were satisfactorily replaced by an ad hoc, intra-tidal velocity expression which was calibrated using prototype data in conjunction with the Vicksburg hydraulic model. The expression developed by Shieh (1974) was given by

$$u(x,t) = u_f(x) + u_t(x) \sin \left[\frac{2\pi}{T_d}t - F(x) \right] \tag{1}$$

where $u(x,t)$ = tidal velocity as a function of time and distance, mile/day

$u_f(x)$ = freshwater velocity as a function of distance, mile/day

$u_t(x)$ = maximum tidal velocity as a function of distance, mile/day

T_d = tidal period, 0.518 day (12 hours-25 minutes)

t = time, day

$F(x)$ = phase lag as a function of distance, dimensionless

The next feature of the model was the formulation of an intra-tidal-time water quality model for temperature, carbonaceous and nitrogenous BOD, and dissolved oxygen. Using the techniques of turbulence time-smoothing and sectional averaging to the one-dimensional form, the following partial differential equations were derived:

Thermal Energy:

$$\frac{\partial T}{\partial t} + u \frac{\partial T}{\partial x} = \frac{1}{A} \frac{\partial}{\partial x} \left(E_T A \frac{\partial T}{\partial x} \right) - \frac{K_e(T - T_e)}{\rho C_p d \cdot} + \sum_{j=1}^{m} \frac{q_j}{A} (T_j - T) \tag{2}$$

Carbonaceous BOD:

$$\frac{\partial L}{\partial t} + u \frac{\partial L}{\partial x} = \frac{1}{A} \frac{\partial}{\partial x} \left(AE_C \frac{\partial L}{\partial x} \right) - K_r L + \sum_{k=1}^{p} W_{L_k} \tag{3}$$

Nitrogenous BOD:

$$\frac{\partial N}{\partial t} + u \frac{\partial N}{\partial x} = \frac{1}{A} \frac{\partial}{\partial x} \left(AE_N \frac{\partial N}{\partial x} \right) - K_n N + \sum_{\ell=1}^{q} W_{N_\ell} \tag{4}$$

Dissolved Oxygen:

$$\frac{\partial C}{\partial t} + u \frac{\partial C}{\partial x} = \frac{1}{A} \frac{\partial}{\partial x} \left(AE_{DO} \frac{\partial C}{\partial x} \right) + K_a(C_s - C) - K_r L - K_n N + \sum_{m=1}^{n} W_{DO_m} \tag{5}$$

The following terms are defined:

T = temperature

t = intra-tidal-time, $\Delta t = 30$ min.

u = tidal velocity, defined by equation (1)

x = longitudinal channel dimension, $\Delta x = 1$ mile

A = cross-sectional area of channel

K_e = effective heat-exchange coefficient

T_e = effective equilibrium temperature

ρ = density

C = dissolved oxygen concentration

C_p = mean heat capacity

d = mean depth

q_j = lateral discharge

L = carbonaceous BOD

K_r = carbonaceous BOD removal coefficient

N = nitrogenous BOD

K_n = nitrogenous BOD removal coefficient

K_a = atmospheric reaeration coefficient

C_s = dissolved oxygen concentration at saturation

E_T, E_C, E_N, E_{DO} = effective, overall, real-time, longitudinal tidal dispersion coefficients for temperature, carbonaceous and nitrogenous BOD, and dissolved oxygen, respectively

W_L, W_N, W_{DO} = lateral inputs of BOD and DO, respectively

The state-of-the-art in modeling the various dispersion coefficients on an intra-tidal-time basis was given in the works of Harleman et al at M.I.T. (i.e. Lee, 1970 and Thatcher, 1972). The formulations due to Harleman for the dispersion coefficient were adopted for use in the simulation part of this study. It was modified, however, by equating E_T, E_C, E_N, and E_{DO} to each other. Thus,

$$E_T = E_C = E_N = E_{DO} = E(x,t) = E_0(x) + 230n(x)u(x,t)[R_h(x,t)]^{5/6} \qquad (6)$$

where $E_0(x)$ = apparent longitudinal dispersion coefficient for salinity intrusion

$n(x)$ = Manning's roughness factor

u = tidal velocity

R_h = hydraulic radius

The atmospheric reaeration coefficient, K_a, in equation (5) was formulated using a modified O'Connor-type expression written in terms of actual time-varying parameters, thus:

$$K_a(x,t) = \frac{[D_L u(x,t)]^{1/2} 1.024^{(T-20)}}{[H(x,t)]^{3/2}} \qquad (7)$$

where $K_a(x,t)$ = intra-tidal-time-varying atmospheric reaeration coefficient

D_L = molecular diffusivity of O_2 in water at 20°C

$u(x,t)$ = average tidal velocity at a cross-section

T = temperature, °C

$H(x,t)$ = average tidal height at a cross-section

The remaining parameters of equations (2)-(5) were chosen in a conventional way (i.e., K_e and T_e were derived from the works of Edinger and K_r and K_n were estimated using DRBC data).

NUMERICAL INTEGRATION ROUTINE

The system of equations (1)-(5) constitute a set of non-linear, partial differential equations which were solved numerically on a digital computer using a discrete space, continuous-time method of lines (MOL). Spatial derivatives were discretized using central differences and the time derivatives were solved by a standard fourth-order, Runge-Kutta routine. Detailed information on the problem related or physical criteria which were used to quantify in this work numerical stability and accuracy associated with the MOL simulation can be found in a summary paper by Vichnevetsky (1974). The following, however, do represent some of the more important conclusions drawn using the MOL:

(i) The left-hand sides of equations (2)-(5) contain the property of conservation.

(ii) Periodic fluctuations which are represented numerically with the MOL approximation deviate from the analytic solution. A qualitative way to analyze these deviations was developed based on the notions of dissipative, diffusive, and dispersive effects which were scrutinized using sinusoidal solutions of a given spatial frequency, ω.

(iii) If sinusoidal solutions of different frequency do not travel at the same velocity, non-sinusoidal solutions will lose their shape as they propagate. This is the dispersive effect of the MOL approximation. It was found that the central difference approximation introduced a spurious dispersive effect.

(iv) If sinusoidal solutions decay in amplitude with the assigned frequency, then the effect is termed diffusive. It was found that when $(\omega\Delta x) \leq 1$, spurious diffusion does not occur. Outside of this range, diffusion will, in fact, generally develop. The effect is described by a second-order, spatial derivative term.

(v) If sinusoidal solutions decay in amplitude with ω as described by a term that is proportional to the state variable, then the effect is designated as dissipative. No spurious dissipative effect can be present in the MOL, since this would contradict the conservation property previously found in (i) when (iv) is obeyed.

(vi) In the numerical simulation of periodic fluctuations of wavelength, λ, the ratio, $N_\lambda = (\lambda/\Delta x)$, must always be equal to or larger than 2π, and preferably larger than 4π. Spurious diffusion is introduced by numerical approximations when $N_\lambda \leqslant 2\pi$ or $(\Omega \cdot \Delta x/u) > 1$, where $N_\lambda = 2\pi / \frac{\Omega \cdot \Delta x}{u}$.

(vii) If fluctuations are created by periodic imposed boundary conditions of frequency, Ω, then Ω must be constrained upwards by $(\Omega \cdot \Delta x/u) \leqslant 1$, and preferably less than 0.5.

(viii) Use of the above physical criteria in the model resulted in the selection of finite difference increments of one mile and 30 minutes for the spatial and temporal variables, respectively.

SAMPLED SIMULATION RESULTS

Representative results for simulation cases involving man-made, shock loads are shown in Figures 1, 2, and 3. After the stationary-state condition is reached and maintained, the responses of DO to an assumed thermal shock load of 5×10^9 Btu/hr, released at 30 miles from Trenton uniformly over two tidal cycles, are studied and shown in Figure 1. As indicated on curve 3 of this figure, DO concentrations reach minimum values of 3 mgO_2/ℓ. DO levels then start to increase finally arriving back at their previously unperturbed states within a period of time, approximately 30 tidal cycles. Effects on DO from thermal shock loads occur in the region of mile points 18 to 62. The maximum transient effect is found from M.P. 35 to M.P. 45 at a DO difference of 0.5 mg/ℓ. Minimum DO is observed at M.P. 50. The solid lines below the curves represent existing DRBC DO standards.

At stationary-state, assumed loads of 2.5×10^5 lbs/day of CBOD and 1.5×10^5 lbs/day of NBOD are discharged at M.P. 30 over two tidal cycles. The transient responses on DO due to these shock loads are calculated and presented in Figure 2. After 10 tidal cycles, minimum DO is observed at the point where the shock load is released and has the difference of 1.2 mgO_2/ℓ. A large DO improvement at M.P. 30 is indicated on curve 2 after 20 tidal cycles. The DO will go back to the initial unperturbed state (curve 1) after a period of time, approximately 30 tidal cycles.

Transient effects on DO resulting from locating a new plant with assumed loads of 1.0×10^5 lbs/day of CBOD and 0.4×10^5 lbs/day of NBOD at M.P. 30 are represented in Figure 3. The DO profile is affected by the new loads in the region from M.P. 15 to M.P. 60. Transient responses of 5, 10, 25, and 50 tidal cycles are shown on curves 2, 3, 4, and 5, respectively. After 25 tidal cycles, a nearly

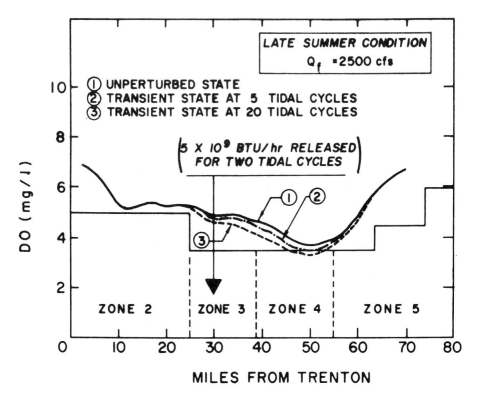

FIG. I   Transient DO response from a simulated thermal
shock load released at M.P. = 30   in the
Delaware Estuary.

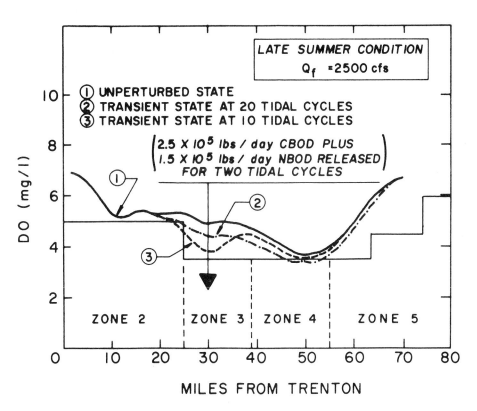

MILES FROM TRENTON

FIG. 2 Transient DO response from a simulated waste shock load released at M.P. = 30 in the Delaware Estuary

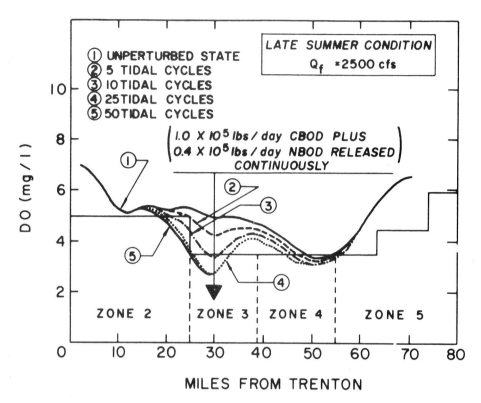

FIG. 3 Transient approach to a new stationary-state DO
distribution resulting from a simulated continuous
waste discharge at M.P.=30 in the Delaware Estuary.

new pseudo-stationary-state is observed. At the point where the new plant is located, the DO drops from 5 mgO_2/ℓ for the unperturbed state to 2.7 mgO_2/ℓ for the
new pseudo-stationary-state.

Figure 4 shows the effect of various assumed values of E on the tidal flushing times for a slug of conservative pollutant released at M.P. 40 at Philadelphia.
The material is released uniformly for two tidal cycles and its magnitude is 5×10^5
lbs/day. For the case where equation (6) is used, it takes 135 tidal cycles to
flush out 98% of the material past Wilmington. Discernable amounts (o.2 mg/ℓ) of
the material first reached Wilmington (M.P. 64) in 19 tidal cycles.

Figure 5 represents a comparison between a temporal and a steady-state wastewater dumping policy. In this case, double amounts (compared to uniform dumping
in time at the values shown in Fig. 5) of BOD are discharged when the tide moves
seaward, and the wastes are stored when the tide flushes landward. The DO concentration using the temporal policy improves by a maximum value of 0.3 mg/ℓ. Considering the size of the estuarial reach and the cost of waste treatment, this is
not an insignificant result.

The doctoral thesis by Shieh (1974) should be consulted for detailed information concerning other simulations using equations (2)-(5) as well as results of
the model calibration studies.

IDENTIFICATION OF PARAMETERS USING PROTOTYPE DATA

Introduction--As an alternative to the semi-empirical formulation developed by
Lee (1970) and Thatcher (1972) for E(x,t) given by equation (6), a rigorously
applied distributed parameter identification scheme is developed instead which
utilizes, directly, noise corrupted prototype salinity data. Details of the
methodology can be found in the thesis by Yih (1974). In order to justify use of
the method, conditions in the estuary must be such that background salinity levels
do not significantly dominate the magnitude of the measured input signals. The
drought period in September, 1965, was found to be ideally suited for this purpose. Monitored salinity data collected on September 15, 22, and 29 at Pier 11
North, Chester, Wilmington, and Reedy Island were used as the prototype input data.
This 46-mile long section of the Delaware Estuary for September 1965 is essentially
in the salinity zone where a significant salinity gradient exists and the background salinity noise (from Industrial, Municipal, and Urban Runoff sources) is
relatively small. The intra-tidal dispersion coefficient is adequately represented in this section by E(x) = a + bx as studied by Yih (1974); but a higher
ordered polynomial can be used if more than four monitoring stations are available. The monitoring stations at Pier 11 North and Reedy Island are used as
boundary conditions, whereas the two stations in between (i.e. Chester and
Wilmington) are used for identification of the two parameters "a" and "b".

The Distributed Parameter Model--Equation (1) for the 46-mile long test section
was developed by Yih (1974) and is given by

$$u(x,t) = u_f(x) + u_t(x) \sin \left[\frac{2\pi}{T_d}t - F(x)\right] \tag{8}$$

where $\quad u_t = 2.65 + x/150 \quad ; \quad x = 0$ at Pier 11 North
$\qquad F(x) = \pi \left[1 + 1/24T_d + 5.25 \times 10^{-3} (x - 58)/T_d\right]$

Values of the freshwater velocity, $u_f(x)$, were obtained from A(x,t) values and the
total freshwater inflow data at Trenton, the major tributaries, plus the estimated
contribution from the drainage area below Trenton. The total estimated freshwater
inflows for the three test days are as follows (Yih, 1974): September 15 ($Q_f =$
2824 cfs); September 22 ($Q_f = 2645$ cfs); and September 29 ($Q_f = 3644$ cfs). The
distributed parameter model for salinity which incorporated $u(x,t)$, the continuity

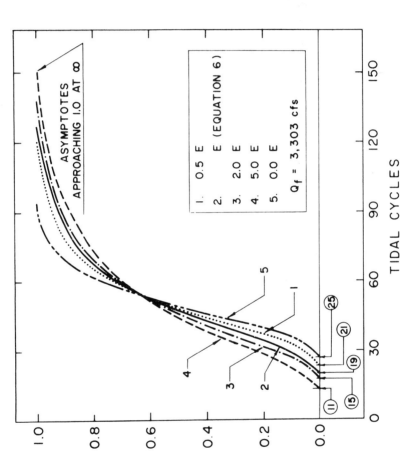

FIG. 4 Flushing time analyses for various dispersion coefficients under simulated conditions.

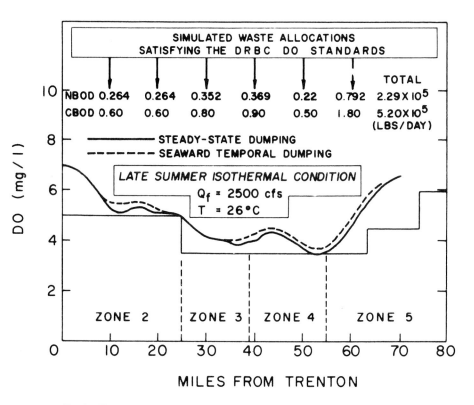

FIG. 5 Incremental increases in DO resulting from a
a seaward temporal waste discharge policy.

balance, and the $E(x)$ coefficient is given by

$$\frac{\partial s}{\partial t} = -u\frac{\partial s}{\partial x} - \frac{s}{A} \sum_{i=1}^{n} q_i + \frac{1}{A} [E(x) \frac{\partial s}{\partial x} \frac{\partial A}{\partial x} + H(x) \frac{\partial s}{\partial x} + E(x) \frac{\partial^2 s}{\partial x^2}]$$ (9)

where q_i = the i-th lateral freshwater inflow per unit length along the test
              section

      $H(x)= b + 2cx$

      $E(x)= a + bx$

Boundary and initial conditions are fully described elsewhere (Yih, 1974).

Identification Procedure--Consider equation (9) with $u(x,t)$ and q_i as specified inputs, then the objective is: from a given number of salinity monitoring stations over a prescribed distance and time period, with salinity data, $s^*_{\ell m}$, taken at discrete locations x_ℓ, $\ell = 1, \ldots L$, and discrete times t_m, m = 1, ... M, find the best values of "a" and "b" in $E(x) = a + bx$ which minimizes a least squares error criterion for equally spaced Δx and Δt. Thus,

$$\text{Min } J = \sum_{\ell=1}^{L} \sum_{m=1}^{M} \{s(x_\ell,t_m) - s^*(x_\ell,t_m)\} \Delta t \Delta x$$ (10)

The constants "a" and "b" are to be selected according to a suitable gradient method. Yih (1974) investigated the relative efficiencies of the first-order gradient, conjugate gradient, and Marquardt's method using the MOL to integrate equation (9) or its variational form. It was concluded after considerable simulation research that the Marquardt's method was the most efficient one for the purpose of finding Min J in equation (10). The results are shown graphically in Figure 6 where it is shown that Marquardt's method is the best of the three tested in terms of Min J and convergence rate.

Sample Results--The results of the prototype studies using Marquardt's method with the MOL integration routine (Δx = 1 mile and Δt = 1/2 hour) are plotted in Figure 7 for the three test days in September 1965. The intercepts and slopes for each of the identification cases are very close in magnitude to each other. The corresponding dispersion coefficients do not show any discernable variation between September 15 and September 29, 1965 in the test section between Reedy Island and Pier 11 North. The boundary salinities at Pier 11 North and Reedy Island are plotted in Figure 8. A comparison between prototype data and calculated data from the identification at the Chester and Wilmington locations is shown in Figure 9. The agreement between observed and calculated salinity values is close showing that the identification method indeed gives a rapid and rather accurate estimation of the intra-tidal-time, longitudinal dispersion coefficient. Also plotted in Figure 7 are the results of Lee (1970) and Thatcher (1972) which are superimposed for comparison with the results of the identification procedure. The results of the identification represent a fair extrapolation of the results of Lee (1970) and Thatcher (1972) to regions where the total freshwater inflows are considerably lower.

ACKNOWLEDGMENTS

This work was sponsored by the U.S. Dept. of the Interior, Office of Water Resources Research (grants B-045, B-049, A-036, and A-045 N.J.). R. C. Ahlert and R. Vichnevetsky are acknowledged with thanks for their assistances in physical and numerical modeling, respectively.

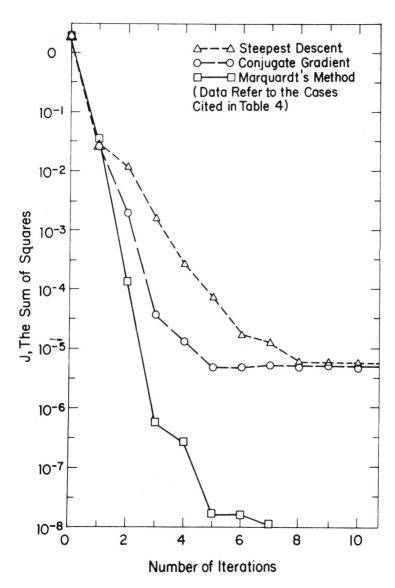

Fig. 6 Comparison on rate of convergence for the 3 algorithms

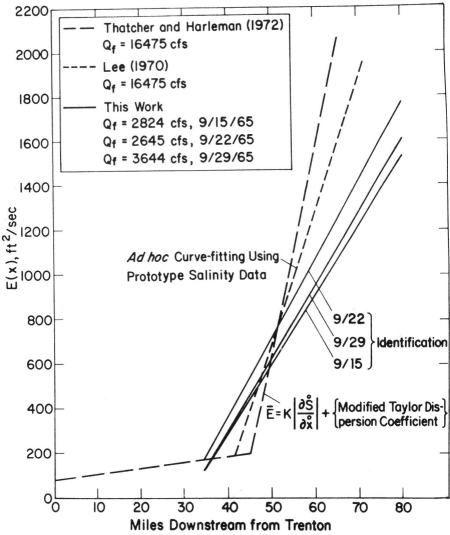

Fig. 7   The longitudinal dispersion coefficient as a
function of distance in the salinity region of the
Delaware River Estuary as determined by identification using prototype input data.

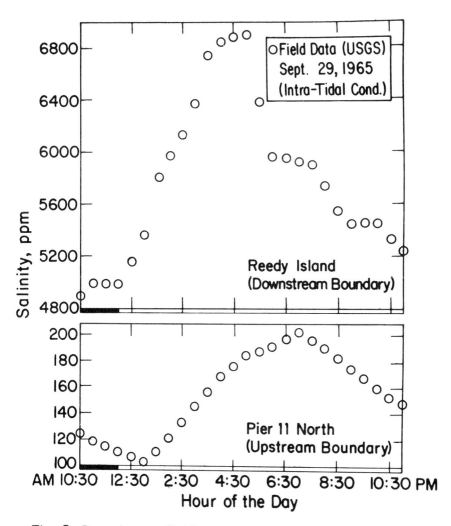

Fig. 8 Boundary salinities at Pier 11 North and Reedy Island

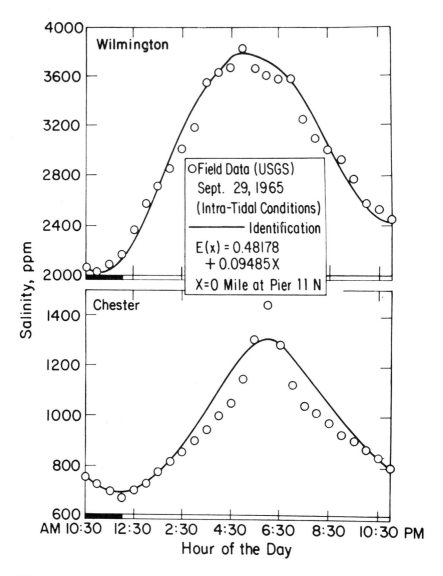

Fig. 9 Prototype and calculated salinity profiles (Sept. 29, 1965)

REFERENCES

Shieh, Y.S. (1974). "Intra-Tidal, Time Varying Analysis of Water Quality in the
Upper Delaware River Estuary System", Ph.D. dissertation, Rutgers University,
New Brunswick, New Jersey 08903, U.S.A.
Lee, C.H. (1970). "One-Dimensional, Real-Time Model for Estuarine Water Quality
Prediction", Ph.D. dissertation, Rutgers University, New Brunswick, New
Jersey 08903, U.S.A.
Thatcher, M.L. (1972). "A Mathematical Model for the Prediction of Unsteady Salini-
ty Intrusion in Estuaries", Ph.D. dissertation, M.I.T., Cambridge, Mass. 02139,
U.S.A.
Vichnevetsky, R. (1974). A.I.C.A., Vol. XVI, No. 1, 1.
Yih, S.M. (1974). "Identification in Nonlinear, Distributed-Parameter, Water Quali-
ty Models", M.S. thesis, Rutgers University, New Brunswick, New Jersey 08903,
U.S.A.

DISCUSSION

Did you actually find out then what the results were ? (BALAKRISHNAN)

Yes, we found the first coefficient, at appropriate distance, for three
days in 1965. (DAVIDSON)

*What about the model you built to predict   what would happen when you
built this water treatment plant.* (BALAKRISHNAN)

That was in the first plant on the slide, where you saw the depression of
DO over several patterns. (DAVIDSON)

Did that include some decision making ? (BALAKRISHNAN)

Yes. (DAVIDSON)

*May I ask a question on diffusivity : basically the concept is established
in a situation with well behaving boundary conditions. In the use of the detailed
equation with periodic data conditions you end up with an apparent diffusivity
which is complex and is a function of frequency.* (PHILIP)

In the region I am working in, the permanent disturbing phenomena is almost
negligible in comparison with the longitudinal dispersion coefficient. It's only
in the transport part where the river is about 1000 feet accross that this does not
happen. (DAVIDSON)

Current research field of author : *Analysis of water quality in the Delaware river
Estuary system using one-dimensional, intra-tidal, time-varying models - Distributed
parameter identification of the tidal dispersion coefficient using discrete-space,
continuous time salinity data.*

Modeling and Simulation of Water Resources Systems, G.C. VANSTEENKISTE, (Ed.)
North-Holland Publishing Company (1975)

A DYNAMIC-STOCHASTIC MODEL FOR WATER QUALITY
IN PART OF THE BEDFORD-OUSE RIVER SYSTEM

P. Whitehead and P. Young [*]
Control and Systems Division
University of Cambridge, ENGLAND

ABSTRACT

A number of methodologies are presented for the development of dynamic stochastic models of water quality in a river system; models that describe the
day to day variations in water quality and account for the inevitable uncertainties encountered in a system of this type. A deterministic streamflow model is enhanced by a "black box" stochastic rainfall-runoff model,
estimated using the Instrumental Variable Approximate Maximum Liklihood
(IV-AML) method of time series analysis. Water quality models for BOD-DO
(biochemical oxygen demand-dissolved oxygen) are then combined with the flow
model and identified and estimated using the extended Kalman filter and a
multivariable version of the IV-AML technique, respectively. This overall
approach to identification and estimation has been applied to a 55 km
stretch of the Bedford Ouse River System in Eastern England.

INTRODUCTION

In his 1962 monograph on water pollution[9], the eminent Water Research Economist, Allen Kneese, suggested that one of the major research needs in the area of
water quality control was the development of "a methodology for keeping track of
quality changes and quickly computing the concentration of pollutants (and significant associated variables such as dissolved oxygen) at all relevant points of use,
as a function of a variety of conditioning factors (including) waste loads at particular outfalls, biological, chemical and physical conditions, and volume of stream
flow".

In many ways, this could be considered as the "<u>raison d'être</u>" of a recent
research study aimed at assessing the feasibility of constructing a simple but
rugged dynamic-stochastic model of a 55 km stretch of the Bedford Ouse River System
in Central-Eastern England. For while it is true that, in the intervening period
since Kneese's book was published, there has been a great deal of research carried
out on water quality modelling, it is also undeniable that there are comparatively
few, if any, examples of true dynamic water quality models of long stretches of

[*] Peter Young is a Fellow of Clare Hall. Paul Whitehead is a member of Wolfson college

river that have been satisfactorily validated against practical field data.

The dynamic modelling studies on the Bedford Ouse are part of a larger systems analysis study of the whole Bedford Ouse River System; a study initiated in September 1972 by the Great Ouse River Division of the Anglian Water Authority and the Department of the Environment, in association with the Control Division of the Engineering Department, University of Cambridge. The study is mainly concerned with the present utilisation and future potential of the Ouse as a source of potable supply and recreation: this includes all facets of the problem, from short term water quality management and control, to long term planning of investment in water and effluent treatment facilities associated with the river system.

But it is the short term problems with which we, in the Control Division at Cambridge, are principally concerned. It is now generally admitted that day to day water quality mangement must involve some appreciation of the dynamic aspects of river pollution since it is the transient violations of water quality standards that cause most problems in the short term. In this paper, we will describe the current status of the dynamic modelling study and show how dynamic-stochastic models for biochemical oxygen demand (BOD) and dissolved oxygen (DO) have been identified and validated by reference to practical field data collected over extended periods of time during the past two years. In line with Kneese's requirements, these models, which are now being extended to other water quality states such as chloride and nitrates, account for the effect of conditioning factors such as biological, chemical and physical conditions and utilise a combination of deterministic and stochastic time-series models to introduce the effects of changes in river flow.

1. RIVER SYSTEM DESCRIPTION

The stretch of the Bedford Ouse of particular interest to the dynamic modelling part of the Bedford Ouse study is between the proposed discharge point of Milton Keynes effluent at Tickford Abbey and the Bedford Water Board abstraction point, 55 kms downstream at Clapham. The principal features of the area such as major tributaries, weirs, and towns, which discharge localised effluent, are shown in Figure 1. The flow gauging stations at Newport Pagnell and Bedford define the upstream and downstream boundaries of the system.

2. A STREAMFLOW FORECASTING MODEL FOR THE BEDFORD OUSE

Before embarking on any systems analysis of a river system, it is essential to consider the objectives of such a study, the types of model that can fulfill those objectives, and the availability of suitable data. The primary purpose of the dynamic model of the Bedford Ouse is to study the effects of Milton Keynes effluent discharge on the water quality 55 kilometres downstream at Bedford Water-

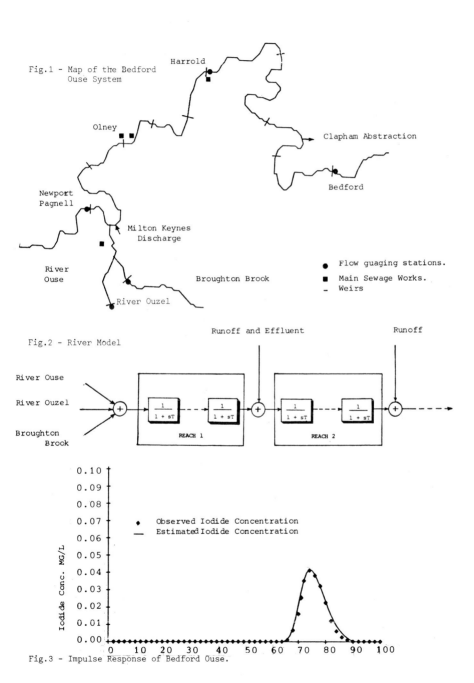

Fig.1 - Map of the Bedford Ouse System

Harrold

Olney

Clapham Abstraction

Newport Pagnell

Bedford

Milton Keynes Discharge

River Ouse

Broughton Brook

River Ouzel

● Flow guaging stations.
■ Main Sewage Works.
− Weirs

Fig.2 - River Model

Runoff and Effluent   Runoff

River Ouse

River Ouzel

Broughton Brook

$\frac{1}{1 + sT}$ $\frac{1}{1 + sT}$ REACH 1 $\frac{1}{1 + sT}$ $\frac{1}{1 + sT}$ REACH 2

◆ Observed Iodide Concentration
— Estimated Iodide Concentration

Iodide Conc. MG/L

Fig.3 - Impulse Response of Bedford Ouse.

board Clapham abstraction plant. Essentially this problem is one of forecasting;
and since water quality is highly dependent on flow, an important requirement is a
satisfactory streamflow model which is able to explain flow variations in a computationally efficient manner.

But most streamflow forecasting tends to be based upon compartmental hydrological models; models that are, of necessity, fairly large and so difficult to
justify in the context of the present study. For this reason a new approach has
been utilised here: a simple deterministic model which is used to relate flow
variations at different points in the river system to input variations at the system boundary, is enhanced by stochastic time-series models that are used to represent the residual flow variations due to rainfall and runoff effects; in other
words, having accounted for the major part of the flow variations by the deterministic model, the residual between this deterministic model output and the observed flow is modelled using stochastic methods of time-series analysis[*]. In this
manner, the best aspects of deterministic and stochastic systems analysis are combined to yield a relatively small but, in the event, an accurate model of flow
behaviour; a model that is particularly well suited to the Bedford Ouse Study,
where the primary aim is to model behaviour at selected points on the river system
between Newport Pagnell and Bedford.

2.1.   DETERMINISTIC MODEL

Flow gauging stations at Newport Pagnell and Bedford define the upstream and
downstream boundaries of the system as shown in Figure 1, and a gauging station at
Harrold provides an additional source of flow data with which to validate the model.
Spatial characteristics are incorporated into the model structure by the decomposition of the river into sixteen reaches. The reach boundaries are based on the location of weirs (which control the river level to some extent), effluent discharges
and tributaries; the reach length depending to a large extent on the intensity of
phenomena affecting quality or flow[4]

The temporal variation in flow at each reach is modelled by a set of first
order differential equations or exponential lags, as shown in Figure 2, a combination which accounts for the basic mass balance effects, while at the same time
reproducing dispersion characteristics similar to those observed in a river system.
This is demonstrated in Figure 3, which compares the impulse response of the model
with the impulse response obtained using iodide tracer experiments: the steep
leading edge and long tail effects are clearly visible and are a direct consequence
of the multiple lag structure of the model. Similar effects could have been obtained with a high order partial differential equation (distributed parameter) model but this would have meant adding complexity and considerable computational diff-

---

[*] This is somewhat similar in concept to the approach suggested by Jamieson and
Wilkinson[7], although they modelled the residual of a full compartmental model in
stochastic terms.

iculties. It is interesting to note, however, that a first order partial differential equation, so often quoted in the literature, would not have been satisfactory since it can only produce a symmetrical impulse response and is clearly not
able to simulate the observed behaviour. This kind of deterministic model has been
used to simulate flow in the river at Harrold over a one year period using input
data collected at the upstream flow gauging stations. The residual error between
the observed and estimated downstream flows, shown in Figure 4, exhibits a definite
long term seasonal variation with short term effects clearly related to rainfall.
Since no information on small streams and distributed effects is incorporated into
the deterministic model, it is clear that this error series may be considered as
an indication of runoff flow into the river.

2.2. STOCHASTIC RAINFALL RUNOFF MODELS

Conventionally, the hydrological modeller simulates catchment behaviour by
compartmental models such as the Stanford Watershed Model IV considered by Ibbitt.[6]
These are quite complex and completely deterministic models which exclude explicit
evaluation of the stochastic aspects of system behaviour. The model parameters are
adjusted until the flows correspond closely with a sequence of observed streamflows.

In contrast to these compartmental models, which are designed to mirror the
detailed flow behaviour, the time-series representation is based on input-output
analysis of the system and there is no attempt to include any information on the
internal structure or behaviour. Rainfall runoff are inferred directly from the
observed data and an empirical input-output (black box) model is obtained by methods
of statistical inference.[14]

The form of this model is the discrete time-series or pulse (z) transform
transfer function representation of a linear stochastic dynamic system, as shown
schematically in Figure 5. Here, the runoff is considered as the output of a discrete dynamic system which has two inputs: the first a deterministic rainfall input, which is assumed to be the cause of most of the runoff flow variations; and
the second a stochastic input which is included to account for unavoidable uncertainties in the relationship, such as those arising from additional disturbances and
measurement noise.

From Figure 5 we see that the observed flow at the kth instant, y_k, is given
as the sum of the deterministic and stochastic components at the same instant, x_k
and ξ_k respectively.

i.e. $y_k = x_k + \xi_k$

where x_k, is obtained from the following autoregressive moving average (ARMA) discrete time model.[5]

$$A\left[z^{-1}\right]x_k = B\left[z^{-1}\right]u_k \tag{1}$$

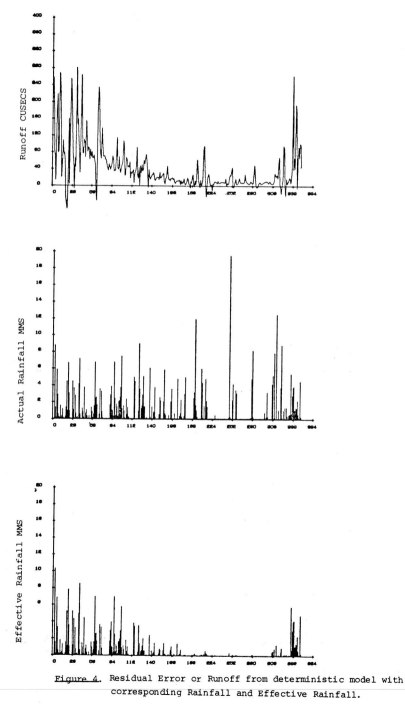

<u>Figure 4</u>. Residual Error or Runoff from deterministic model with corresponding Rainfall and Effective Rainfall.

where z^{-1} is the backward shift operator, ie. $z^{-1} x_k = x_{k-1}$

while $A\left[z^{-1}\right] = 1 + a_1 z^{-1} + a_2 z^{-2} + \ldots\ldots + a_n z^{-n}$

and $B\left[z^{-1}\right] = b_o + b_1 z^{-1} + \ldots\ldots\ldots + b_n z^{-n}$

are polynomials in z^{-1}. Written as a difference equation, this model is of the form

$$x_k = -a_1 x_{k-1} - a_2 x_{k-2} - \ldots - a_n x_{k-n} + b_o u_k + \ldots + b_n u_{k-n}$$

ξ_k is also generated by an ARMA model   this time of the form

$$C\left[z^{-1}\right] \xi_k = D\left[z^{-1}\right] e_k \tag{2}$$

where

$$C\left[z^{-1}\right] = 1 + c_1 z^{-1} + \ldots\ldots\ldots + c_n z^{-n}$$

and $\quad D\left[z^{-1}\right] = 1 + d_1 z^{-1} + \ldots\ldots\ldots + d_n z^{-n}$

where e_k is a serially uncorrelated sequence of random variables with variance σ^2.

In this way, the x_k variable is assumed to depend upon the past x_k variables, as well as the present and past rainfall data, while ξ_k is generated in a similar manner, but from some hypothetical "white noise" (ie. serially uncorrelated) input e_k.

Constructing models such as that shown in Figure 5 and described by equations (1) and (2) is referred to as time-series analysis and involves the use of computer aided methods such as those available in the Control Division at Cambridge.[17] It will suffice here merely to say that they are based on sophisticated but computationally quite simple recursive methods of parameter estimation in which the estimates are obtained by passing through the data sample by sample, rather than analysing the complete block of data and obtaining a single set of estimates based on this data block. The programs for this analysis utilise the instrumental variable approximate maximum liklihood (IV AML) method of time-series analysis and because of the recursive nature of the algorithm where the estimates are updated at each sampling instant, it is quite straightforward to identify and estimate possible parameter variations. This facility is particularly useful during the model identification stage where the structure of the model is being assessed prior to parameter estimation. A particular example of this approach to identification is discussed in the next section.

2.3.   IDENTIFICATION OF THE RAINFALL-RUNOFF MODEL

In order to identify the structure of the rainfall-runoff model a preliminary analysis of the data is required using methods similar to that described by Box-Jenkins[2]: the rainfall "input" series is numerically filtered in a special manner

to transform it into a series which is serially uncorrelated ; this "prewhitened"
series is then cross-correlated with the similarly filtered residual flow "output"
and the cross correlation function provides a rough estimate of the "impulse response" between rainfall and residual flow. In the present case, the rainfall was
found to be significantly correlated up to lag 3 (3 days) and a possible prewhiten-
ing filter would be of third order autoregressive form. Having prewhitened the
data, the cross correlation function is considered and a high correlation was obtained between rainfall and runoff for two lags. [*]

The approximate impulse response suggests a time-series model for the rainfall-runoff process of a second order autoregressive, second order moving average,
single time delay form; in other words

$$Y_k = \frac{b_1 z^{-1} + b_2 z^{-2}}{1 + a_1 z^{-1} + a_2 z^{-2}} U_k + \xi_k$$

This model contains no implicit adjustment to account for the seasonal variations in runoff and a secondary identification stage was considered whereby time
variable parameter estimation was utilised to study seasonal variations. The moving average parameters b_1 and b_2, shown in Figure 6a, are estimated in this way and
these reflect the long term seasonal variations as well as some shorter time period
fluctuations; in particular the evaporation effects appear to generate an overall
seasonal pattern while the soil moisture deficit effects appear due to long periods of dry weather during summer months and becomes apparent when summer storms
occur. This soil moisture dificit effect is illustrated, for example, on day 250
where the parameter estimate falls from 1000 to 120 following the end of a dry period ; the parameter is inaccurately estimated during this period and only when the
system is excited by a storm is sufficient information available to update the estimate.

This exercise in time variable parameter estimation is a valuable one in understanding the nature of the system; indeed the time varying estimates provide a
means of judging the efficacy of seasonal adjustment terms: different empirical
rainfall adjustment procedures can be evaluated and the one chosen which best transforms the resulting time-series model into stationary (time invariant) parameter
form.

In order to obtain a seasonally adjusted rainfall series of this type, evaporation and soil moisture deficit effects are removed from the daily rainfall data

---

[*] It is interesting to note that the effects of the headwaters would have produced
a high correlation at greater lags had these not been simulated using the deterministic model; the cross correlation functions tends to verify, therefore, the lumped
parameter model which redistributes the flow down the river system

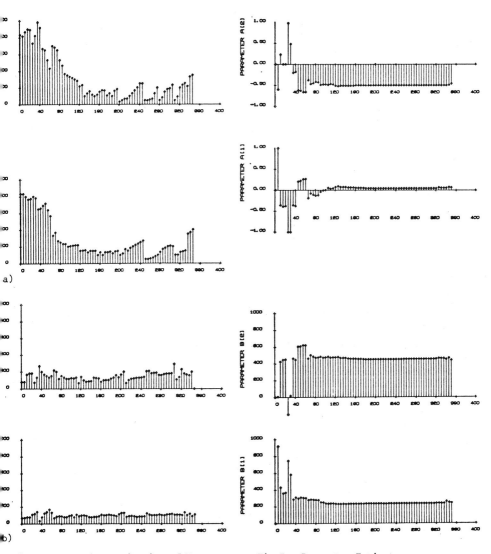

Fig.6 - Recursive Estimation of Parameters
(a) Using acutal rainfall - runoff data
(b) Using effective rainfall - runoff data

Fig.7 - Parameter Estimates over one year.

using the following relationships.

$$R_k^* = R_k \cdot \frac{(T-Tm)}{C}$$

$$S_k = S_{k-1} + \frac{1}{Ts} (R_k^* - S_{k-1})$$

$$U_k = R_k^* \cdot S_k$$

Here R_k represents rainfall and R_k^* is the effective rainfall accounting for evaporation, which is a function of the monthly mean temperature, Tm and two constants T and C. For the soil moisture deficit effect an exponentially weighted moving average of R_k^* , S_k, is determined such that after a long dry spell S_k is small and the final effective rainfall series U_k is significantly reduced. The time variable parameter estimating capability is used to check the efficacy of the rainfall adjustment procedure; for where the time variable algorithm is applied to the analysis of the adjusted data it should reveal no tendency for parameter variations. This is seen in Figure 6b which gives the recursive estimates of b_1 and b_2 obtained in this manner, which can be contrasted with the results obtained with the raw data given in Figure 6a. The methodology of using the recursive algorithm to develop essentially heuristic adjustment procedures is suggested as being a highly practical approach for identifying water resource systems.

The final adjusted or effective rainfall series is plotted in Figure 4, where the pattern of the seasonal modifications is clearly apparent.

2.4. PARAMETER ESTIMATION FOR THE TIME SERIES MODEL

The "effective" rainfall-runoff data may now be used to estimate the time-invariant model paramters a_1, a_2, b_1, b_2. These are initially estimated using a recursive least squares IVAML algorithm and the parameter estimates over one iteration are shown in Figure 7. The final values were then set up as the initial conditions for an iterative version of the IVAML procedure. After nine iterations through the data a convergent set of parameters were identified where,

$$a_1 = -0.09$$
$$a_2 = -0.36$$
$$b_1 = 275$$
$$b_2 = 383$$

Thus the final black box model is of the form

$$y_k = \frac{275 \ z^{-1} + 383 \ z^{-2}}{1 - 0.09 \ z^{-1} - 0.36 \ z^{-2}} \ u_k + \xi_k$$

From the autocorrelation and partial autocorrelation function the residual noise series ξ_k appears as a serially uncorrelated white noise sequence, thus eliminating the necessity for a more complicated ARMA noise model.

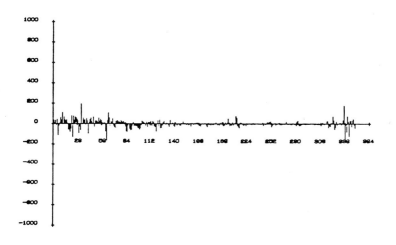

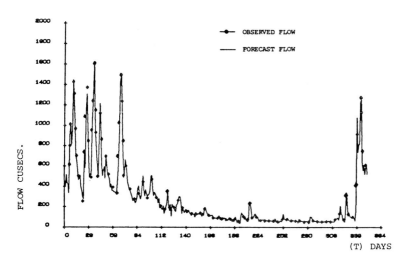

Figure 8   Final Flow Estimates with Residual Error.

TIME-SERIES MODEL USED FOR FLOW MODELLING

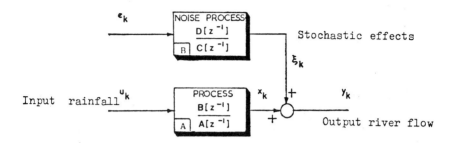

Where z^{-1} is the backward shift operator, i.e. $z^{-1}x_k = x_{k-1}$

Figure 5. Time Series Model used for Flow Modelling.

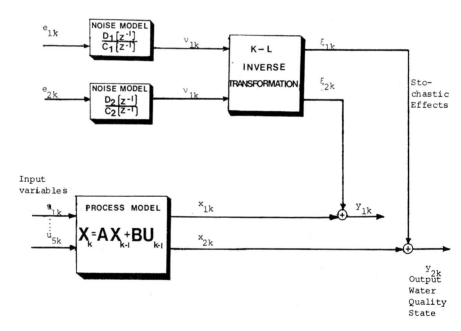

where B^{-1} is the backward shift operator ie $B^{-1}X_k = X_{k-1}$

Figure 9 Multivariable Process and Noise Model

Having identified the model, the runoff flows were forecast using the effective rainfall data. Summing the estimated deterministic flow and the estimated runoff then produced an estimate of the river flow at Harrold, as shown in Figure 8: this shows the estimated river flow superimposed on the observed flows together with a plot of the residual error. The mean percentage error of 8.6% is within the accuracy of the flow gauging station estimated at 10% by the Great Ouse River Authority. In addition, the model explains 99% of the variance of the original flow series and the errors are within 10% of the observed flows for 70% of the time.

3. WATER QUALITY MODELS

One possible method for maintaining the DO in a river at some prescribed "satisfactory" level is to control the level of BOD in the effluent discharges from sewage works adjacent to the river system. Since most methods of control system synthesis currently available to the control engineer require parametric models of the dynamic system under consideration, it is clear that such an approach necessitates the construction of a dynamic model for the in-stream interaction of DO and BOD. And if this model is to be useful for short term water qaulity studies or operational control purposes it is desirable that it should possess the following properties:

1. It should be a truly dynamic model, being capable of accepting time varying input functions of DO and BOD and operating upon them to give time varying output response *.

2. It should be as simple as possible consistent with the ability to adequately characterise the important dynamic and steady state aspects of the system behaviour.

3. If possible, it should provide a reasonable mathematical approximation of the physico-chemical changes occurring in the river system and should be verified against real data collected from the river over an extended period of time.
This section of the paper discusses briefly the choice of a suitable DO-BOD model in the light of various models that have been proposed in the published literature and in view of the available field data against which the model can be verified.

3.1. THE BOD-DO MODEL

Research on the modelling of DO-BOD interaction in a river system has been dominated by the classical model of Streeter and Phelps[10] ,which first appeared in a seminal paper published in 1925, and which has been improved in various ways by other investigators such as Dobbins[5] and Camp[3]. Theoretically, the quantity of fluid mixing in the stream provides a convenient parameter by which to distinguish

---

* This may seem a rather obvious requirement to the control engineer but it needs to be emphasised in the present context since there is a certain amount of confusion in the literature on the subject as to what constitutes a "dynamic" model (see Young and Beck)[13].

between the presently available physico-chemical models:

(i) **Partial Mixing**; a second order partial differential equation represented by

$$\frac{\partial \underline{c}(z,t)}{\partial t} = \underline{f}_1 \left[\frac{\partial^2 \underline{c}(z,t)}{\partial z^2} , \quad \frac{\partial \underline{c}(z,t)}{\partial z} , \quad \underline{c}(z,t) \right]$$

$$z_0 \leq z \leq z_1; \ t_0 \leq t \leq t_f$$

(ii) **No mixing**; a first order partial differential equation model represented by

$$\frac{\partial \underline{c}(z,t)}{\partial t} = \underline{f}_2 \left[\frac{\partial \underline{c}(z,t)}{\partial z} , \ \underline{c}(z,t) \right]$$

$$z_0 \leq z \leq z_1; \ t_0 \leq t \leq t_f$$

(iii) **Intimate mixing**: a first order ordinary differential equation with associated transportation delay T_d to allow for distributed effects between spatial points z_0 and z_1

$$\frac{d\underline{c}(z_1,t)}{dt} = \underline{f}_3 \left[\underline{c}(z_1,t) , \ \underline{c}(z_0,t-T_d) \right]$$

$$t_0 \leq t \leq t_f$$

In these equations, t is the independent variable of time, z is the independent variable of distance, $\underline{c}$ is a vector of dependent concentration variables and $\underline{f}_1$, $\underline{f}_2$, $\underline{f}_3$ are vector functions in the variables, as shown. z_0 and z_1 represent the spatial boundaries of the system while t_0 and t_f indicate the operational time interval.

From the theoretical point of view, model (i) would appear to represent the system dynamics most accurately, but for control and practical dynamic investigations the lumped parameter model (iii) seems the most attractive. Recent research in this area (see Beck[1]) has shown that a simple model based on (iii) can describe most of the observed temporal variations of DO and BOD in a single stretch or "reach" of a typical non-tidal river system. The particular form of the model (iii) used as the starting point for this study is the following:

(3) D.O. $\dfrac{dx_1}{dt}(t) = -(k_1 + \dfrac{Q}{V_m})\ x_1(t) - k_2 x_2(t) + \dfrac{Q}{V_m} c(t) + k_1 c_s + D_B$

(4) B.O.D. $\dfrac{dx_2}{dt}(t) = -(k_2 + \dfrac{Q}{V_m})x_2(t) + \dfrac{Q}{V_m} L(t) + L_A$

where

x_1 is the output (i.e. downstream) DO in mg/litre.

x_2 is the output BOD in mg/litre.

L is the input (i.e. upstream) BOD in mg/litre.

C is the input DO in mg/litre.

C_s is the saturation concentration of DO in mg/litre.

Q is the volumetric flow rate in metres^3/day.

V_m is the mean volume of water held in the reach in metres^3.

k_1 is the reaeration rate constant days^{-1}.

k_2 is the BOD decay rate constant days^{-1}.

L_A is the mean rate of addition of BOD to the reach by local runoff in mg/litre

per day.

D_B is the net rate of addition of DO from the reach by the combined effects of

photosynthesis, respiration and mud deposits in mg/litres/day.

3.2. IDENTIFICATION OF THE BOD-DO MODEL

In order to assess the suitability of the model given in equations (3) and
(4), data were collected continuously for a seventy day period during the summer of
1973 over two reaches of the Bedford Ouse. During the early stages of the river
system modelling exercises both for the River Ouse and for a similar study on the
River Cam[13], the extended Kalman filter (EKF) has proved to be a flexible tool with
which to identify suitable dynamic water quality model structures. An initial
model is formulated based on some heuristic feeling or physico-chemical understanding of the system, and the EKF then used to test the efficacy of these models
and, where necessary, to supplement the basic model with additional terms to account
for disturbances[11].

For example by considering the bias terms as random variables, it was possible
to obtain recursive estimates of their variation over the sample period. These estimates showed most variation during periods of prolonged sunlight and, as a result,
it was concluded that the discrepencies between the model response and the observed
data were most probably due to photosynthesis effects such as this.

Further investigations revealed that in the case of the River Cam, the release of oxygen by photosynthetic activity on algae populations and the BOD load
exerted by the mass deaths of algae were both suitably accounted for in terms of a
pseudo-empirical relationship dependent upon temperature and sunlight conditions.

In order to estimate the effect of photosynthetic activity in the Ouse,
chlorophyll A data were recorded in addition to temperature and sunlight and an
oxygen production equation developed originally by the Water Pollution Research
Laboratory[12], was used to define D_B in the following manner

$$D_B = k_3 (0.95 + 31.7 \ C_A) \ (I-ITHRESH)$$

where k_3 is the gain constant to be estimated.

C_A is the chlorophyll A in mg/L.

I is the sunlight hours.

ITHRESH is the sunlight hours threshold level below which there is no net addition by photosynthesis.

A complete statistical analysis of the model using a continuous-discrete version of the EKF is described elsewhere[1] but the application of the EKF to develop a photosynthetic term illustrates the utility of the technique during the identification stage.

3.3. ESTIMATION OF THE BOD-DO MODEL

Unfortunately there are certain limitations of the EKF as a tool for final parameter estimation; in particular, the EKF does not provide a very systematic approach to parameter estimation in those situations where large quantities of data are available for several reaches of the river. In these situations, there is a need for a more rigid estimation procedure where the model structure is assumed known a priori and where it is desirable to have some form of repeated iteration through the data in order to "refine" the estimates of the parameters and so obtain better statistical efficiency (lower variance estimates).

Such a technique is available in the iterative instrumental variable approximate maximum liklihood (IVAML)[17] approach utilised already during the rainfall-runoff time series model. The extension of this technique to the multivariable situation in which the model is composed of a coupled set of dynamic equations has been restricted to the following discrete-time state equations.[16]

$$\underline{x}_k = A\underline{x}_{k-1} + B\underline{u}_{k-1}$$

where $\underline{x}$ and $\underline{u}$ represent the states (eg. BOD and DO) and the inputs (eg. sunlight etc) respectively, while A and B represent coefficient matrices which include unknown parameters to be estimated by reference to the available data.

However, transforming the differential equation model for BOD and DO into the discrete-time form tends to destroy some of the simplicity of the model. This simplicity may be retained, however, by writing the model directly in discrete form while retaining all the salient features identified in the previous EKF studies. The discrete equations for BOD and DO obtained in this manner take the following form.

$$(5) \quad \underline{x}_k = \begin{bmatrix} k_1 & 0 \\ k_4 & k_5 \end{bmatrix} \underline{x}_{k-1} + \begin{bmatrix} k_2 & 0 \\ 0 & k_6 \end{bmatrix} \begin{bmatrix} L_{k-1} \\ C_{k-1} \end{bmatrix} + \begin{bmatrix} k_3 \\ k_7 \end{bmatrix} S_{k-1} + \begin{bmatrix} 0 \\ k_8 \end{bmatrix} C_{S_{k-1}} + \begin{bmatrix} 0 \\ k_9 \end{bmatrix} W_{k-1}$$

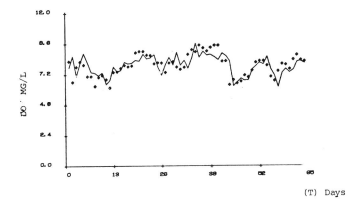

(T) Days

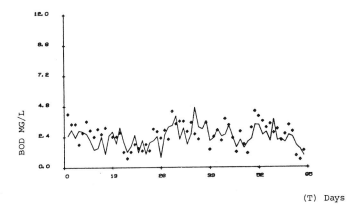

(T) Days

<u>Figure 10</u> BOD and DO simulation - Reach 2 Bedford Ouse.

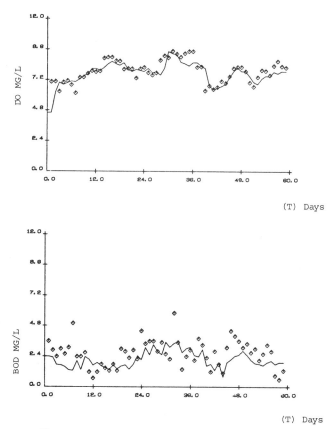

Figure 11 BOD and DO simulation -River Ouse

where $\underline{x}$ represents the states at the downstream point

L is the upstream BOD mg/l

C is the upstream DO mg/l

S is the sunlight and algae term mg/l

C_s is the DO saturation level mg/l

W is the DO input at weirs or from runoff during periods of high flow.

At first sight, this discrete-time model differs from the differential equation model by the absence of the time varying flow effects i.e. the Q/V_m terms (where Q is the volumetric flow rate and V_m is the mean reach volume). This problem is overcome by the simple device of allowing the parameters k_1 and k_5 in (5) to vary such that

$$k_1 = \frac{V_m}{Q_{k-1}} \, k_1^* \quad \text{and} \quad k_5 = \frac{V_m}{Q_{k-1}} \, k_5^*$$

In this way, the time variation is treated deterministically via the varying flow rate, Q_{k-1}, and k_1^* and k_5^* are then estimated as slowly variable or constant parameters.

The parameters defined in the discrete-time model are estimated simultaneously using the multivariable IVAML method (MIVAML), a detailed description of which is given in reference (16). In addition to the basic process model estimation, a noise model for the residual error series is also formulated in which the coupled BOD and DO error series are first transformed using a Karhunen-Loeve expansion[8] to a vector of instantaneously uncorrelated random variables. After this, the approximate maximum liklihood techniques of time series analysis are applied to determine time series models for each of the resulting time - series. Figure 9 shows schematically the combined noise model, the transformation and the state space process model.

During the BOD-DO simulation based on these types of model the orthogonal series are used to forecast the noise at the next recursion. The noise estimates are then transformed by the inverse transformation to their "natural" correlated state and added to the deterministic output of the process model.

The systematic estimation procedure was applied initially to the River Cam data which is of particular interest to the Bedford Ouse Study because of the effluent effects from Cambridge Sewage works. Beck initially used the EKF to identify a continuous-time BOD-DO model for the Cam[1] but, as previously mentioned, the parameters were estimated over one cycle of the data and little statistical refinement of the parameters was possible. With the MIVAML technique however the discrete-time model parameters were estimated over twelve iterations of the data and the results are presented in reference (16)

Applying the same MIVAML technique to the River Ouse data gave substantially different parameters to those of the Cam, although there was considerable agreement between the two reaches on the Ouse as shown in Table 1. This disagreement is not

	REACH 1	REACH 2
k_1	0.32	0.36
k_2	0.57	0.60
k_3	0.05	0.03
k_4	−0.17	−0.21
k_5	0.14	0.15
k_6	0.53	0.53
k_7	0.06	0.04
k_8	0.31	0.31
k_9	0	0.74
K-L Transformation Matrix u (see reference 16)	$\begin{bmatrix} 0.95 & 0.16 \\ -0.16 & 0.95 \end{bmatrix}$	$\begin{bmatrix} 0.99 & 0.07 \\ -0.07 & 0.99 \end{bmatrix}$
BOD Noise Model	$\xi_k = \dfrac{1}{(1-0.48z^{-1}+0.32z^{-2})} e_k$	$\xi_k = \dfrac{1}{(1-0.17z^{-1}+0.13z^{-2} -0.25z^{-3})} e_k$
DO Noise Model	$\xi_k = \dfrac{1}{(1-0.09z^{-1}-0.1z^{-2})} e_k$	$\xi_k = \dfrac{1}{(1-0.27z^{-1}-0.14z^{-2})} e_k$

TABLE 1 – COMPARISON OF REACH MODELS FOR BEDFORD OUSE

surprising since it probably reflects the differing character of the two rivers.

The final simulation of the second reach is shown in Figure 10 and, as with the Cam data, the ·DO result is entirely satisfactory. On the other hand, the BOD tends to vary in a rather random manner and the model characterisation does not appear so good. At the low levels of BOD observed in the Ouse, however, this result is only to be expected since not only is the BOD model hardly being activated, but also the measurement error is likely to be rather large.

4. COMBINED FLOW AND QUALITY SIMULATION

The reach models described above allow for the simulation of the entire stretch from Tickford Abbey, the approximate discharge point for Milton Keynes effluent, to the Bedford Waterboard Abstraction point 55 km downstream at Clapham. In addition the flow model discussed in Section (2) provides information on the Q_{k-1}/V_m term in each reach so that the flow model can therefore be superimposed on the quality model.

The predicted water quality at Clapham based on the input information at Tickford Abbey is shown in Figure 11 : considering the stochastic nature of the aquatic environment and the noise associated with the measurement of the variables (particularly BOD) the simulation seems quite satisfactory. The DO, in particular, compares well with the observed values and, while the BOD comparison is not so good, this is only to be expected remembering the considerable incertainty on the BOD measurements. In this connection, the results in the Cam data may be of more signification due to the higher level of effluent activation [13].

5. CONCLUSIONS

In this paper we have outlined the major aspects of an on-going study of short term water quality variations in a non-tidal river system. At this point in time, we have been able to develop a complete dynamic-stochastic model for flow BOD-DO in a 55 km stretch of the Bedford Ouse River System between the site of the New City of Milton Keynes and the Bedford Waterboard Abstraction Plant at Clapham, near Bedford. We believe that this model is one of the first examples of a dynamic-stochastic water quality model for a long stretch of river to be satisfactorily identified and statistically validated by reference to practical field data.

The research carried out so far has demonstrated the initial feasibility of constructing realistic dynamic water quality models for non-tidal river systems : in particular the models described in this paper seem to provide a potentially useful and computationally efficient characterisation of the flow-BOD-DO phenomena in the river system; a characterisation which explains the dynamic behaviour of these water quality states and so provides a firm foundation on which to base the investigation of other water quality states, such as chlorides and nitrates; investigations which will form the major part of subsequent research on the dynamic aspects of water quality in the Bedford Ouse River System.

In developing realistic dynamic-stochastic models of water quality, we also feel that we have been able to demonstrate the particular utility of recursive methods of time-series analysis both for the identification and estimation of water resource system models. The recursive Instrumental Variable-Approximate Maximum Liklihood (IV-AML) method, both in the single variable and multivariable (state-space) forms, has proved to be invaluable for obtaining relatively efficient estimates of the various model parameters in a straightforward and simple manner. And when used in conjunction with the Box-Jenkins and Extended Kalman Filter (EKF) methods of model identification, it provides a powerful general method of data processing, well suited to the sort of modeling problems encountered by water quality and resource engineers.

In this latter sense, we feel that the recursive methods of analysis provide the basis for the kind of methodology specified by Allen Kneese in the quotation at the beginning of this paper. And to echo his thoughts once more, we hope that this methodology will, in future, be useful "in the identification of critical problem areas, especially when predictions are tested in actual streams". For model evaluation is only the first step in systems analysis; and a model is only useful if it provides a general improvement in our understanding of the real system which in its turn, both leads to the identification of potential problems and aids in their solution.

REFERENCES

(1) Beck, M.B. (1973) PhD Thesis, Cambridge University.

(2) Box Jenkins. (1974) Time series analysis forecasting and control. Holden Day.

(3) Camp, T.R. (1965) Field Estimates of oxygen balance parameters, A.S.C.E. J. Sanit. Eng. Div., Vol. 91, No. SA5, Oct. 1965.

(4) Dixon, N. and Hendricks, D.W. (1969) Simulation of spatial and temporal changes in water quality within a hydrological unit. 5th Annual Am. Water Resources Ass. Conference, October, 1969.

(5) Dobbins, W.E. (1964) BOD and oxygen relationships in streams, A.S.C.E., J. Sanit. Eng. Div., Vol. 90, No. SA3, June, 1964.

(6) Ibbitt, R.P. (1970) Systematic parameter fitting for conceptual models of catchment hydrology. PhD Thesis, Dept. of Civil Eng., Imperial College, London.

(7) Jamieson, D.G., Wilkinson, J.C., Ibbitt, R.P. (1971) Hydrologic Forecasting with sequential deterministic and stochastic stages. International Symposium on Uncertainties in Hydrologic and Water Resource Systems.

(8) Kittler, J. and Young, P.C. (1973) A New approach to feature selection based on the Karhunen Loeve expansion. Pattern Recognition, 1973 Vol.5.

(9) Kneese, A.V. (1964) The Economics of Regional Water Quality Management. John Hopkins Press, Baltimore, 1964.

(10) Streeter, H.W. and Phelps, E.B. (1925) A study of the pollution and natural purification of the Ohio River. Bulletin No. 146, U.S. Publish Health Service.

(11) Whitehead, P.G. and YOUNG, P.C. (1974) The Bedford Ouse Study dynamic model. 2nd Semi-annual report to the Steering Group of the Great Ouse associated committee, 1974. Control Group Internal Note CN/74/1, University of Cambridge.

(12) W.P.R.L. Annual Report, Water Pollution Research, 1968, Section 3.2.

(13) Young, P.C. and Beck, M.B. (1974) The modeling and control of pollution in a river system. Automatica. (to appear in September 1974)

(14) Young, P.C. and Shellswell, S.H., and Neethling, C.G. (1971) A recursive approach to time-series analysis. Rpt. No. CUED/B-Control TR16, Cambridge University Eng. Dept.

(15) Young, P.C., Whitehead, P.G., and Beck, M.B. (1973) The Bedford Ouse Study Dynamic model. 1st Semi-annual report to the Steering Group of the Great Ouse associated committee. Control Group Internal Note. CN/73/4, University of Cambridge.

(16) Young, P.C. and Whitehead, P.G. (1974) A recursive approach to time-series analysis for multivariable systems. IFIP Working conference on Modeling and Simulation of Water Resources systems.

(17) Young, P.C. (1974) Recursive approaches to time-series analysis. Bulletin of Inst. Maths. and its Application. Vol. 10, Nos. 5 and 6, pp. 209-224.

Modeling and Simulation of Water Resources Systems, G.C. VANSTEENKISTE, (Ed.)
North-Holland Publishing Company (1975)

PRACTICAL EXPERIENCES IN FORMULATING A WATER QUALITY MODEL FOR
THE RIVER NECKAR

Hermann H. Hahn and Rainer W. Abendt
University of Karlsruhe
F . R. Germany

ABSTRACT

The river Neckar is central and vital to the densely populated area of Mittel-
württemberg. The area is furthermore heavily industrialized. Thus, the river
serves many purposes. Above all wastewater from domestic and industrial sources,
including thermal wastes, accentuate the difficulties of the multipurpose use.
Immediate amelioration of the water quality in the river along with long range
planning becomes mandatory.

The discussion presented here deals in a first chapter with the practical goals
of water quality modeling. Realistically, they are not only to be seen in the
formulation of an optimization model. This constitutes the last phase of any
water quality modeling. The first benefits derive from its use in the phase of
information gathering, information compaction and screening and testing of additional information. Still in the initial phases of the modeling activities, it
will become apparent that such way of exploiting information leads to a more
intensive use of available data, that information transfer is simplified and
that in a sort of trial-and-error method all kinds of alternative solutions may
be tested or conceived. Only after the collection and exploitation of much
information does it become meaningful to use simulation and optimization as
preparation or aid for decision making.

INTRODUCTION

Attempts to describe water quality of a river and its possible changes date back quite
far. In part, such formulations are used to predict changes in water quality due to natural or
man-made changes in the river system (compare Summary Report (1)). Contrary to the situation
in the field of water quantity arichment, it is not possible to use laboratory models or other physical replicas. Consequently, descriptive and also predictive water-quality models for rivers are
usually mathematical models.

The properties describing river water with respect to water supply and wastewater disposal were in the past mainly the biochemical oxygen demands (BOD) and dissolved oxygen. In
many instances it is still useful to employ these descriptive parameters today. However, with increased disposal of organic substances that are not easily bio-degraded, and also of waste heat
one has to resort to additional parameters in order to describe water quality of such rivers.

Almost all water quality models used today to describe the characteristics of a river
and to possibly predict changes in these characteristics are formulated on the basis of extensive
observations of the river. In first approximation these models could be called data-reproducing
or also data-extrapolating models. There are only very few attempts to explain and describe in
a very basic and detailed manner, all possible processes in this system. Therefore, these models
are constructed with relatively few and simple mathematical terms describing on one hand hydrodynamic processes like mixing phenomena and transport phenomena and on the other hand, chemical and biological processes of decay, storage, or re-introduction of certain water constituents.

TABLE (1): Water Quality Parameters and their Possible Simulation in Mathematical Models

PARAMETER describing water properties	Possibilities for mathematical modelling	Relationships between parameters	Availability of data material
Chlorides / Conductivity	Dilution, transport	Characteristic for all conservative water constituents	Conductivity data partly available
Temperature	Cooling according to first-order equation	–	For a few points of sampling
Turbidity / Filter residue	Reduction through aggregation and sedimentation – first or second order	–	Very few data
Suspended organic matter	Decomposition and sedimentation – first or second order model	cf. Turbidity and BOD	Very few data
BOD / COD	Decomposition first order model	cf. TOC DOC	Sufficient data, however not consistent
TOC / DOC	Possibly slow first order decay	cf. BOD	Very few data
Organic Nitrogen	Decomposition first order model	cf. BOD	Very few data
Nitrite / Nitrate	Production according to a first order model	cf. organic nitrogen	Next to no data
Oxygen	Consumption acc. to first order model and production acc. to first order model	cf. BOD	Sufficient data, however not consistent
Carbon dioxide	Production and loss to atmosphere, both acc. to first order model	cf. Oxygen	Very few data

All these formulations for the different water constituents that are simulated in such water quality models are comparable (see Table 1). Difficulties in formulating such water quality models for rivers arise therefore on one hand from the lack of statistically satisfactory data for the formulation of a simulation model, and on the other hand from conceptual problems in combining various different water-quality parameters into one water-quality index for a certain type of water use.

Water quality models are not only used for the description and extrapolation of characteristics of a river system but are also the basis for developing amelioration schemes for polluted rivers. In addition to the mere description of properties of the aqueous system it becomes necessary to set water quality standards and limits with respect to certain constituents (thus for instance an upper limit for biochemical oxygen demands and a lower limit for dissolved oxygen in the river water). These standards must be such in agreement with insight from natural sciences (such as certain requirements that a specific species of fish shows), or they are formulated on the basis of economic considerations.

Some of these aspects shall be discussed in detail on the basis of the experience gathered in formulating a water quality model for the river Neckar.

I. THE DIFFERENT LEVELS OF ACCOMPLISHMENT IN FORMULATING WATER QUALITY MODELS

Not all attempts of formulating a water quality model must lead to a definite strategy of amelioration in the form of decision-aiding solution or actual decisions. Rather a number of different accomplishments can be envisioned in the formulation of a water quality model and its stepwise improvement. These accomplishments are in many instances quite different from the final goal, the optimization model. In subsequent paragraphs, some of these possible applications are to be shown. Necessarily this discussion cannot be exhaustive in all parts.

I.1 The Use of Water Quality Models in Collecting Information, in Condensing Information, and in Controlling the Quality of Additional Information

Already in first attempts to develop a water quality model on the basis of existing data material, it is found frequently that very important parameters have not been determined, or that complete series of data are lacking. Very often, one will also find that a number of observations, gathered by different agencies, are very little comparable with each other. Furthermore, these different agencies frequently use different methods in taking samples and exploiting the information. In order to illustrate these statements, the determination of the dissolved oxygen on one hand according to a wet analytical method and, on the other hand, by means of a dissolved oxygen electrode is mentioned. With great likelihood these measurements will lead to different results if no intercalibration has taken place between the various laboratories.

In other instances one finds that a large number of observations have been made and that these are documented very carefully. But the availability of these data or, more specifically, the control over the ever-growing material has decreased over time. In such instances, mathematical models will help to condense data material and to make it manageable and readily available. A simple mathematical model like the Streeter-Phelps-Model existing of two reaction steps can ideally condense a whole set of data into two reaction parameters.

If a descriptive and possibly predictive model has been formulated and tested, on one hand for conservative water constituents (like chloride ions) and also for non-conservative substances (such as biochemical oxygen demands), it is much simpler to check the quality and consistency of subsequently gathered information. If any of the newly gathered data differ significantly from the existing and condensed observation, then either these new data are wrong or the river has experienced some drastic changes. In both instances certain measures will have to be taken for which a basis is now existing.

1.2 Water quality models allow a more intensive use of existing information, facilitate information transfer, and enhance understanding of the river system.

By means of a mathematical water quality model conceived on the basis of existing information,
it is possible in so-called sensitivity analyses (whether they are of a more formal nature or performed in a more simulative manner) to determine the most important parameters of the system.
Furthermore, one can test the sensitivity of the system due to changes in various input parameters.
In summary one can use the model as if additional information would be available or could easily
be collected. Thus, in actual modeling it is possible in certain instances to combine various
small tributaries if they are close together, or also to combine various wastewater outlets if the
quantity of wastewater introduced is small and these outlets are not too far from each other.
Such simplifications, however, can only be made if the model is fully formulated and available
for sensitivity analyses.

As mentioned in the previous paragraphs, it is possible by means of model calculations, to condense very extensive data material. At the same time this can be used to make this data material
more accessible even to non-specialists. Here, graphical representations (Figure 1) are of great
use. The example given in Figure 1 contains results of various simulation runs on changes in dissolved oxygen content in the river Neckar. Even a layman to this field can recognize in these
representations what the effects of certain measures taken on the river are. It becomes, for instance, apparent how increased temperature does accentuate difficult situations in the dissolved
oxygen concentration of the river water. Or similarly, the effect of dilution water is recognized
as ameliorating conditions in one place and causing a deterioration of conditions in other places
further down the river.

At the same time such simulations as shown in Figure 1 may be used to study quantitatively the
effect of various events or envisioned measures on the river system. By moving wastewater inlets
up- or downstream the river access, it becomes possible to find the optimum location for such inlets. Similarly the effects of dilution water may be quantitatively compared to the effects of river re-aeration by mechanical devices. With such experiments it is frequently possible to define
adequate means for cleaning up polluted rivers.

1.3 Water quality modeling in the form of simulation or optimization can help or prepare
decision-making.

The very simple and condensed representation of all important data describing a river in conjunction with the effects of certain measures upon the river characteristics is in itself already an aid
in decision-making. Simulation may either be used as a first attempt to describe quantitatively,
the effects of alternative clean-up strategies upon water quality, or they may be employed after
such clean-up strategy has been decided on in order to explore the long-range effects of such decisions. Various aspects of such application of water quality models in water resources planning
have been discussed elsewhere ((2), (3), and (4)). It has also been shown how at least on a conceptual basis, costs of various alternatives can be calculated and how a departure from a conceptual optimum (minimum of costs or maximum of benefits or similar criteria) can be quantitatively
determined.

Finally it is impossible to, at least in a conceptual way, prepare or indicate decisions. For this
purpose, the mathematical water quality model has to be changed such that one of the available
optimization methods can be used. Furthermore, all cost and benefit factors have to be known
and must be quantifiable. Only if so-called non-quantifiable or intangible factors can be neglected relative to all quantifiable factors, and if these latter ones can all be combined in one or
more objective functions it is possible to identify one optimal solution for the system described by
the pertinent constraints. The previously discussed water quality model is a necessary input for
the formulation of constraints. This latter application of water quality modeling, frequently the
ultimate goal of all such attempts, is only rarely attained in practice. And even then it is fre -
quently debated. All other applications, however, as they have been sketched in the previous

FIGURE 1   Results from various Simulation Runs (2)

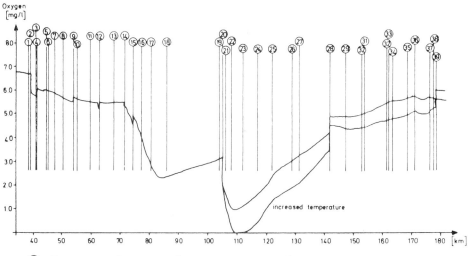

(a) Change in Dissolved Oxygen along the River Neckar
for the Year 1971 (NNQ$_7$)

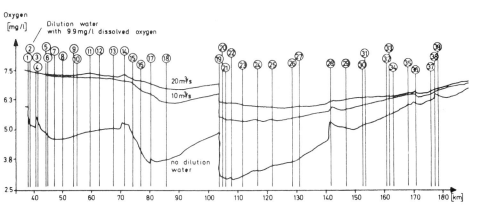

(b) Change in Dissolved Oxygen along the River Neckar
for the Year 2000 (NNQ$_7$)

paragraphs, are more frequently encountered.

II.   A BRIEF CHARACTERIZATION OF THE WATER QUALITY MODEL USED IN THIS EXAMPLE

When selecting a specific type of water quality, one has to decide whether one wants to formulate a data-reproducing model or whether by means of this model physical, chemical and biological phenomena should be investigated in detail (see F (5)). The most crucial question for a non-specific data-reproducing model is the following one: "How many parameters are necessary in order to describe in a satisfactory manner given data material?" On the other hand, this typical question for a specific or more scientific model must be formulated as follows: "Which are the basic reaction steps and reaction types in a system that may explain all observations, and how can all these basic processes be described in the most concise way?"

Existing models cannot easily be classified according to these two opposite criteria. In most instances, however, one deals in first approximation with a data-reproducing model which was developed on the basis of a certain understanding provided by natural sciences. In this connection it has to be stated that such non-specific models are not very satisfactory in view of the ever-increasing knowledge about aqueous systems and rivers in particular. Therefore, frequently a large number of correction factors are added in order to make the original model more realistic. One does overlook, however, that such a basically data-reproducing or non-specific model can not be transformed into a specific model that is more acceptable from the point of view of natural sciences by adding additional pseudo-reaction steps by the adjustable parameters.

Oxygen is a water constituent which on one hand is consumed due to physical, chemical and biological reactions and on the other hand produced or imported due to another group of physical, chemical, or even biological processes (see Figure 2). The model, therefore, contains only two overall reaction steps:

a.   oxygen-consuming processes as for example respiration of biomass oxydation of organic water constituents in suspension, or oxygen demand of the benthos etc.

b.   oxygen-producing processes like physical re-aeration from the atmosphere, photosynthetic oxygen production, apparent reduction in oxygen demand due to sedimentation etc.

All these different reactions are grouped together in two counteractive processes described by two parameters (analogous to the proposal of Streeter and Phelps (6)). The parameter describing these overall provesses are no longer true reaction-rate constants as they are known from chemistry. They are global parameters and therefore functions with respect to time and location.

In addition to these two physical, chemical, and biological constants one needs parameters that describe hydraulic conditions in the river:

c.   immediate mixing at the point of inflow (flow rates in the river and in the wastewater outlets as well as total freights of the substance under consideration)

d.   convective mass transport (assuming that transport due to dispersive processes can be neglected relative to other reactions)

Now the river is divided into a number of segments. Since this is only a one-dimensional model, segmentation is done only in longitudinal direction. The cuts are performed such that the ensuing segments represent river stretches with close to homogeneous characteristics: the global parameters describing oxygen-consuming and oxygen-producing reactions are constant in first approximation as well as the pertinent hydraulic parameters (flow rate, flow velocity, etc.). Segments are thus determined partly on the basis of physical, chemical, and biological criteria. They are, however, also necessary wherever water abductions or water introductions, tributaries, weirs, and other discontinuities exist. Figure 3 illustrates this fact, showing the variation in the overall coefficient of oxygen consumption along the river axis. What has been said earlier about the variation of these global coefficients with respect to time and location is demonstrated once again in this picture. Furthermore, Fig. 3 suggests the extent of segmentation in order to deal

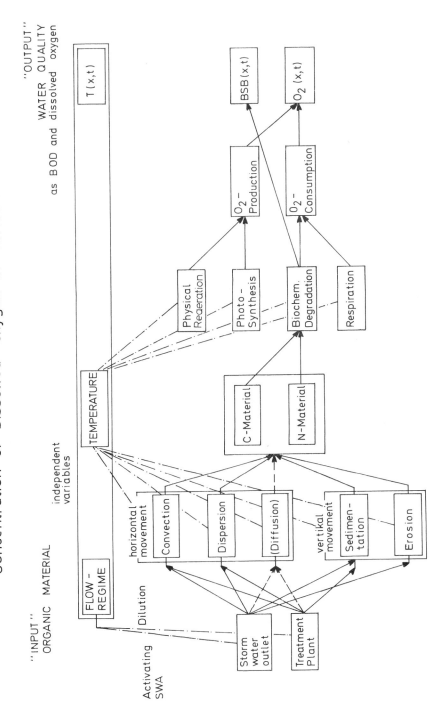

FIGURE 2 Schematic Representation of different Reaction Steps Affecting the Concentration of Dissolved Oxygen in Rivers .

with pseudo-homogeneous river segments.

II.2 Additional aspects in determining the number of adjustable parameters in the water quality model.

If a data-reproducing model has been chosen for description and possibly prediction of water quality, then it is necessary to choose the degree of complexity of the model such that initially available information is sufficient to determine all parameters. Furthermore, in improving models and extending information gathering, an optimum has to be found between the cost of further information-gathering and additional benefits from improved model output. In using a tested and calibrated water quality model in conjunction with an ongoing monitoring program, it must be kept in mind that costs for additional information-gathering might increase exponentially while benefits from increased information density might grow logarithmically. Thus, there is definitely a point where further improvement of the model in order to attain a higher degree of precision leads to lower returns.

III. CALIBRATION OF THE MODEL - USING AVAILABLE DATA MATERIAL FOR THE DETERMINATION OF MODEL PARAMETERS

For the water quality model as used for the river Neckar, containing convective transport, oxygen consumption, and oxygen production as reaction steps, the following input parameters have to be known: flow rates, flow velocities, total amounts of biochemical oxygen demands, respectively dissolved oxygen transported in the river or introduced in the river, parameter describing oxygen introduction.

In a first step in the calibration procedure, the Neckar is according to topographical, hydrographical, and biochemical characteristics, divided into some one-hundred and seventy segments along the river axis. The next step is the determination of the flow velocity in each segment either from direct observation or by recalculation from flow rates and cross section. Usually, any discussion of clean-up strategies is based on the assumption of a critical low flow in the river. Thus all flow velocities determined for the various river segments correspond to a certain conceptual flow rate. The third step is a calculation of all loads of biochemical oxygen demand, respectively dissolved oxygen, introduced into the river and transported in the river. Frequently these loads are to be calculated from concentration values. The fourth step is the calculation of the rates of oxygen impletion in the river in each segment due to the comparison of oxygen demand values for various points in this segment. In this particular instance, so-called half-life for biochemical oxygen demand has been determined for each segment. When the parameter describing oxygen consumption has been determined for each segment, then in a fifth step the parameter of oxygen production can be determined from measured dissolved oxygen values in each segment through nonlinear regression between observed values and values predicted by the model. This latter parameter can also be determined from empirical equations on the basis of flow velocity, flow depth, water temperature, and other characteristics of the system.

III.1 Actual situation with respect to available data material

The river Neckar is an intensively and manifold used river. It is essential and vital to a densely populated and heavily industrialized area. Above all wastewater from domestic and industrial sources, including thermo-waste, accentuate the difficulties of the multipurpose use. The necessity of a monitor and control program and possibly a cleaning up of the river have been noticed since quite some time as official reports and publications portray.

A first inspection of all the data material found shows that fourteen different agencies or institutions collected and documented these data. In some instances, different institutions have measured different parameters, while in other instances, different time series of one parameter have been collected and documented in different places. In addition, one can find measurements of one parameter done parallel by various agencies.

III.2 Characterization of the available data material

In the present situation, sufficient hydrologic information on flow rates etc. was available for a first modeling. On the other hand, there was no continuing or consistent time series describing physico-chemical and biological reactions in the river. Almost all observations on water quality stem from the bi-annual inspection of the river (until the intensified monitoring program in 1971 began). These measurements made during inspection trips on the river were performed at different flow rates at different meteorological conditions such that the usefulness of these data for today's modeling activities is relatively small. In addition, these data were gathered and exploited by different agencies as has been noted before. Thus, they are not reported in uniform manner, which complicates their usage.

For illustration's sake, some more obvious difficulties in using the data material shall be mentioned. Continuous recordings of dissolved oxygen concentration over a whole day, for instance in order to define the effect of biorganic re-aeration, or continuous recordings over a whole week in order to determine fluctuations resulting from changing wastewater loads are lacking. Similarly one would need recordings over a whole season in order to evaluate reliably influences of temperature etc.. All these observations should not only be available for each river segment or for each type of river segment, but also for different time periods. They must be available in such a number that statistical tests and statistical exploitation can be performed. On the contrary, actual sampling has been done at ever changing intervals with respect to time and location. Most water quality observations result from inspection trips on the river while field data were collected at stationary sampling points.

In addition to this lack in agreements in sampling methodology, sampling time intervals, and sampling points, one will notice that some parameters have not been observed at all in various river segments or are completely missing. There is no continuous recording of overall loads of biochemical oxygen demand or dissolved oxygen introduced at every single wastewater outlet. All water quality parameters beyond biochemical oxygen demand and dissolved oxygen such as nitrogenous compounds for instance, have not been observed prior to the intensive monitoring program which was begun in 1971. Therefore, the first water quality model had to be restricted physical, chemical, and biological reactions in the river that were supported by observations on biochemical oxygen demand and dissolved oxygen.

IV. IMPROVEMENT OF THE WATER QUALITY MODEL

The first results of all modeling activities have been an intensification and improvement of the monitoring system for the river. With that, the amount and quality of collected information increased. The inspection of first modeling results along with some site inspections on the river identified where additional information was lacking, or where the situation was so complex that for instance continuous monitoring had to be set up. Furthermore, the first model calculation also showed where due to a consistency of modeling results and observed data, the frequency of data collection could be reduced. Finally, carefully designed sensitivity analyses indicated with what frequency and with what precision the various parameters had to be observed.

These and other findings can not be condensed in the form of general recommendations for monitoring and control programs in all instances. Water quality control and measures for the prediction of rivers will change from river to river in agreement with the characteristics of the individual rivers. Nevertheless, one can try to summarize by formulating questions which contain most of these deliberations:

a. which parameters can be measured continuously and also should be measured continuously (costs of such programs, correlation of continuously measured parameters with other non-continuously measured parameters, etc.)?

b. What is the optimal frequency for the measurement of parameters that cannot be determined by continuous measurements if on one hand, correlation with continuously measured parameters exists, or if on the other hand these parameters have no relation to any continuously measured parameter (In this instance, statistical derivations will help to decide sampling frequency etc.)?

c.   In which locations should continuously measuring devices be installed, where should continuously sampling devices be installed, and in what points will samples be taken to be analyzed by laboratory means?

d.   What are the costs and possibly the benefits of additional information leading to increased precision of river quality description and prediction?

e.   How will the envisioned storage and retreatal of the data and the future use of all these observations affect data collection?

On the basis of more extensive data material that is also more reliable from a statistical viewpoint, the existing water quality model will be extended to include the following phenomena: biorganic re-aeration (where the parameters have been determined from continuous oxygen measurements in an intensively supervised river segment); effect of sedimentation and erosion upon the oxygen content of the aqueous system; oxygen consumption of the benthos. Besides these additional physico-chemical and biological reaction steps that are to be included in the standard model, dispersion due to turbulent river flow will be considered as an additional transport step.

Parallel to the improvement of the dissolved oxygen model, it becomes possible now to set up material balances as well as dynamic models for other water constituents. With the availability of reliable data material, for instance on heavy metals, or on the total sum of non-biodegradable organic material if measured by ultraviolet light extinction, reaction parameters needed to describe decay or disappearance of these materials can be determined in a calibration step.

Both types of models describing dissolved oxygen as an indicator of water quality, and describing a number of other water constituents that are of particular interest for certain uses, will be exploited in simulation runs on a daily basis, taking actually changing flow rates and changing temperatures into account. Thus it becomes possible to simulate in a simplified manner, the dynamic changes in river characteristics occurring over time. The results of such simulation runs may allow statistically useful output if the input data, in particular with respect to hydrographic and temperature information, are statistically meaningful.

V.   SAMPLE CALCULATION FOR THREE RIVER SEGMENTS AS AN ILLUSTRATION

The well-known equation describing the change in biochemical oxygen demand with time and the related change in dissolved oxygen were re-written for computer simulation in the following manner:

$$BOD_i = \frac{L_{i-1} \cdot \bar{v}_{i-1} \cdot \frac{1}{\bar{I}_{i-1}} - k_{i-1} \cdot L_{i-1} + L_i^{\ast}}{\bar{v}_i \cdot \frac{1}{\bar{I}_i}} \cdot \frac{\bar{v}_i}{Q_i \cdot I_i}$$

and:

$$DO_i = \frac{C_{i-1} \cdot \bar{v}_{i-1} \cdot \frac{1}{\bar{I}_{i-1}} + r_{i-1} (CS_{i-1} - C_{i-1}) - k_{i-1} \cdot L_{i-1} + C_i^{\ast}}{\bar{v}_i \cdot \frac{1}{\bar{I}_i}} \cdot \frac{\bar{v}_i}{Q_i \cdot I_i} \cdot$$

where: BOD_i - BOD concentration in each segment $i=1, \ldots.n$ ppm
          L_i - BOD load in each segment $i = 1, \ldots. n$ kg
          $L_i^{\ast}$ - BOD load introduced into segment   kg/d
          $\bar{v}_i$ - average flow velocity in segment i m/s

l_j — length of segment j   m
k_j — parameter describing oxygen consumption in segment j   1/d
r_j — parameter describing oxygen introduction into segment j   1/d
Q_j — flow rate in segment j m^3/s
DO_j — dissolved oxygen concentration in segment j   ppm
C_j — dissolved oxygen load in segment j   kg
$C_j^{\times}$ — dissolved oxygen load introduced into segment j   kg/d
CS_j — dissolved oxygen load at the saturation point in segment j   kg

     — conversion factors

Sample calculation for the following situation:

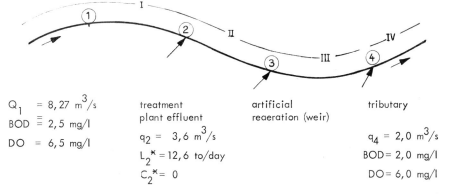

Q_1 = 8,27 m^3/s treatment   artificial   tributary
BOD $\bar{\bar{=}}$ 2,5 mg/l   plant effluent   reaeration (weir)
DO = 6,5 mg/l q_2 = 3,6 m^3/s q_4 = 2,0 m^3/s
                       $L_2^{\times}$ = 12,6 to/day   BOD = 2,0 mg/l
                       $C_2^{\times}$ = 0   DO = 6,0 mg/l

The following specifications apply to the individual segments (conditions resemble the actual situation in a certain reach of the Neckar). Water temperature is uniformly 15°C.

Segment number	Flow velocity	Flow rate	Oxygen Consumption parameter	Oxygen introduction param.
I	0.10 m / s	8.27 m^3 / s	0.25 days^{-1}	0.30 days^{-1}
II	0.09 m / s	11.87 m^3 / s	0.93 days^{-1}	0.30 days^{-1}
III	0.06 m / s	11.87 m^3 / s	0.74 days^{-1}	0.82 days^{-1}
IV		13.87 m^3 / s		

NOTE: All segments are of the same length, with L_j = const = 500 m .

Course of the calculation:

   a.   Segment II

$$L_I = \frac{2.5 \cdot 8.27 \cdot 500}{0.1 \cdot 10^3} = 103.4 \text{ kg BOD in segment}_I$$

$$C_I = \frac{6.5 \cdot 8.27 \cdot 500}{0.1 \cdot 10^3} = 268.8 \text{ kg dissolved oxygen in segment}_I$$

$$CS_I = \frac{10.0 \cdot 8.27 \cdot 500}{0.1 \cdot 10^3} = 413.5 \text{ kg dissolved oxygen at } 15^\circ C \text{ in segment}_I$$

$$BOD_{II_b} = \frac{103.4 \cdot 0.1 \frac{86\,400}{500} - 0.25 \cdot 103.4}{0.1 \cdot \frac{86\,400}{500}} \cdot \frac{0.1}{8.27 \cdot 500} \cdot 10^3 = 2.46 \text{ mg/l}$$

(i.e. at beginning of segment II, before wastewater inflow)

$$BOD_{II_a} = \frac{103.4 \cdot 0.1 \frac{86\,400}{500} - 0.25 \cdot 103.4 + 12\,600}{0.1 \cdot \frac{86\,400}{500}} \cdot \frac{0.1}{11.87 \cdot 500} \cdot 10^3 = 14.0 \text{ mg/l}$$

(i.e. at beginning of segment II after wastewater inflow)

$$DO_{II_b} = \frac{268.8 \cdot 0.1 \cdot \frac{86\,400}{500} + 0.3\,(413.5 - 268.8) - 0.25 \cdot 103.4}{0.1 \cdot \frac{86\,400}{500}} \cdot \frac{0.1}{8.27 \cdot 500} \cdot 10^3 = 6.53 \text{ mg/l}$$

$$DO_{II_a} = \frac{268.8 \cdot 0.1 \frac{86\,400}{500} + 0.3\,(413.5 - 268.8) - 0.25 \cdot 103.4 + 0}{0.8 \cdot \frac{86\,400}{500}} \cdot \frac{0.1}{11.87 \cdot 500} \cdot 10^3 = 4.55 \text{ mg/l}$$

    b.   Segment III

$$L_{II} = \frac{14.0 \cdot 11.87 \cdot 500}{0.09 \cdot 10^3} = 923.2 \text{ kg (with } BOD_{II} = 14.0 \text{ mg/l)}$$

$$C_{II} = \frac{4.55 \cdot 11.87 \cdot 500}{0.09 \cdot 10^3} = 300 \text{ kg} \quad \text{(with } DO_{II} = 4.55 \text{ mg/l)}$$

$$CS_{II} = \frac{10.0 \cdot 11.87 \cdot 500}{0.09 \cdot 10^3} = 639.4 \text{ kg}$$

$$BOD_{III} = \frac{923.2 \cdot 0.09 \frac{86\,400}{500} - 0.99 \cdot 929.2}{0.09 \cdot \frac{86\,400}{500}} \cdot \frac{0.09}{11.87 \cdot 500} \cdot 10^3 = 13.16 \text{ mg/l}$$

$$DO_{III} = \frac{300 \cdot 0.09 \cdot \frac{86400}{500} + 0.90\,(659.4 - 300) - 0.99 \cdot 929.2 + 0}{0.09 \cdot \frac{86\,400}{500}} \cdot \frac{0.09}{11.87 \cdot 500} \cdot 10^3 = 3.82 \text{ mg/l}$$

(Since there is no abduction or introduction of water, these values are valid for the whole segment)

    c.   Summary of all calculations for segments I to IV: (compare Figure 4)

It can be seen from these sample calculations that the computation follows the "flowing wave" (it follows so-to-speak a control buoy that is carried down the river with the flow velocity). Thus, it is possible to compute nonstationary conditions if this is desirable and if necessary input data for such situations are available. Furthermore, this type of formulation allows the computation or description of all kinds of fluctuation, trends, periodicities, etc..

FIGURE 3   Variation of the Parameter describing all
Oxygen Consuming Processes. (2)

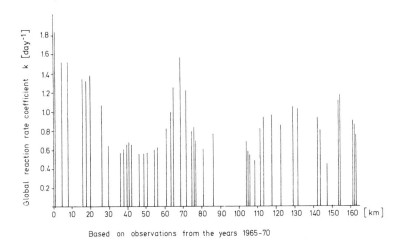

Based on observations from the years 1965-70

FIGURE 4   Graphical Representation of Results
of Simple Calculation

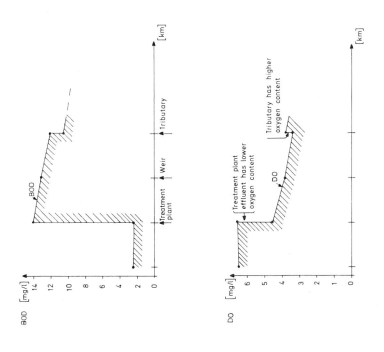

SEGMENT I		SEGMENT II		SEGMENT III		SEGMENT IV	
Load parameters kg	Concentrations mg/l	Load kg	Concentr. mg/l	Load kg	Concentr. mg/l	Load kg	Concentr. mg/l
$L_I = 103.4$			$BOD_{II_b} = 2.46$				$BOD_{IV_b} = 12.2$
$C_I = 268.8$	(not needed	$L_{II} = 923.2$		$L_{III} = 1301.7$		(not needed	
	for		$BOD_{II_a} = 14.0$		$BOD_{III} = 13.16$	for	$BOD_{IV_a} = 16.7$
$CS_I = 413.5$	cal- cul-	$C_{II} = 300$		$C_{III} = 377.9$		cal- cul-	
	ation)		$DO_{II_b} = 6.53$		$DO_{III} = 3.82$	ation)	$DO_{IV_b} = 3.37$
		$CS_{II} = 659.4$		$CS_{III} = 989.2$			
			$DO_{II_a} = 4.55$				$DO_{IV_a} = 3.75$

References

1. Kühner, J., Hahn, H. (1971) "Mathematische Modelle und Methoden in der Wasser-gütewirtschaft". Wasserkalender 1971, S. 22 - 41.

2. Hahn, H. (1972) "Die Sanierung des Neckars im mittelwürttembergischen Raum". 4. Fortbildungslehrgang für Hydrologie, Karlsruhe.

3. Hahn, H., Abend, R. (1971) "Gewässerschutz als reale Planungsaufgabe mit system-analytischen Hilfsmitteln". Symposium für wirtschaftliche und rechtliche Fragen des Umweltschutzes - Verlag Huber, Frauenfeld/Schweiz.

4. Hahn, H., Abend, R. (1973) "Beispiel einer Flußsanierung mit systemanalytischen Hilfsmitteln". Österr. Ingenieur- und Architektenzeitschrift 16, S. 1 - 9.

5. Hahn, H. (1972) "Sinn und Grenzen der Modellrechnung" - Unveröffentlichtes Manu-skript eines Vortrages im Wassertechnischen Kolloquium Universität Karlsruhe.

6. Streeter, H.W., Phelps, E.B. (1925) "A Study of the Pollution and Natural Purifi-cation of the Ohio River". US Public Health Bulletin 146, pp. 127 - 149.

7. WAQUAMA II - Technischer Zwischenbericht zur Sanierung des Neckar - Institut für Siedlungswasserwirtschaft, Universität Karlsruhe (1971).

Current research field of author : *Regional aspects of water supply, of wastewater disposal, of solid waste disposal, of water pollution control.*

A WASTE CONTROL PROGRAM FOR A RIVER WITH HIGHLY VARIABLE CONCENTRATION
OF CONSERVATIVE SUBSTANCE

V. Hrazdil
Hydraulic Research Institute
Brno, CZECHOSLOVAKIA

ABSTRACT

The water quality in streams seems to be highly affected by wastewater discharges. In this paper the problem of mathematical modeling of variable
stream pollution by conservative pollutants (non decaying substances) is
solved. Partial differential equation describing water quality changes in
time and space in a stream represents a parabolic type with one space variable. Using the DSCT-method known for hybrid computer programming the
partial differential equation was adapted to an equation system. The problem was solved on a digital computer by aid of a sub-routine based on a
Runge-Kutta-formula.

A practical example involves a variable sulphate-concentration caused by
highly mineralized mine water discharges.

The mathematical model of conservative pollutants based on the optimaliza-
tion of parameters enabled to perform the analysis of measuring the water
quality in streams. The calculation of the longitudinal dispersion coefficient was described. The solution was based on the Newton-Raphson iterative
technique.

INTRODUCTION

Mathematical modeling of water quality changes on computers seems to be
the most effective in the proposal of the optimal water quality control in river
basins. Using well-known laws of water quality changes, it is possible to design
a simulation of natural processes taking place in streams.

Bella and Dobbins (1968) explored the mathematical solution of deterministic models of water quality changes. Krenkel et al. (1968) tried to determine the
parameters of mathematical quality models.

The pollution of a stream can be either conservative or non-conservative
(Novotný 1967). As non-conservative pollutants, the BOD, COD, O_2, coliform bacteria
etc., may be taken into account and in this case, the solution of the mass balance
seems to be more difficult than that of conservative pollutants (e.g. for VSS,
chlorides, sulphates, etc.).

BASIC EQUATIONS OF THE MODEL

With the following general relation the concentration changes of contamination substances in a stream can be described :

$$\frac{\partial Y}{\partial t} = D_x \frac{\partial^2 Y}{\partial x^2} - U \frac{\partial Y}{\partial x} - KY \tag{1}$$

where x   = axis of the flow direction
      Y   = concentration of the substance
      t   = time
      D_x = longitudinal mixing coefficient
      U   = mean velocity of flow in x-direction
      K   = decay coefficient.

In our case where the concentration of conservative substances is being modeled,
the last term on the right side of the equation should be left out. (K=0).

MODELING WATER QUALITY ON A DIGITAL COMPUTER

Using the method of the first approximation the equation (1) can be rearranged. For to calculate the time variations of the quality in the i-element the
following differential equation can be used :

$$\frac{dY_i}{dt} = (\frac{D_x}{(\Delta x)^2} - \frac{U}{2\Delta x}) \ Y_{i+1} - 2 \ \frac{D_x}{(\Delta x)^2} \ Y_i + (\frac{D_x}{(\Delta x)^2} + \frac{U}{2\Delta x}) \ Y_{i-1} \qquad (2)$$

In the last element the following relation is valid for the calculation of
the quality temporal variations :

$$\frac{dY_n}{dt} = (\frac{D_x}{(\Delta x)^2} + \frac{U}{\Delta x}) \ Y_{n-1} - (\frac{D_x}{(\Delta x)^2} + \frac{U}{\Delta x}) \ Y_n \qquad (3)$$

The concentration of the traced substance on the begin of the stream section represents a boundary condition (for x = 0, t = < 0,T >). The initial conditions (for t=0) in the stream elements are given.

The numerical solution of the equation system (2), (3) uses a sub-routine.
The second-order Runge-Kutta-formula with variable step-length depending on the
precision of the solution represents the numerical basis of this method. The precision control was made by checking the solution with a double step of integration
(Runge's principle of inaccuracy estimate).

The model was then controlled and the stream section with the average
long-trend flow rate of 0.43 m3/sec., where variable sulfate contamination occurs
involved by discharging strongly mineralized mine waters was selected. The sulphate concentration was traced in three points : at the begin and the end of the
model course of 13.77 km long stream and in a point spaced 4.86 km from the begin
of the course. Fig. 1 shows the scheme.

For the computation purposes the river course was divided into elements
of 0.81 km. On fig. 2 the measured sulphate concentrations and the model outputs
in elements 6 and 17 are compared.

AUTOMATIC METHOD OF COMPUTING THE DIFFERENTIAL EQUATION PARAMETER

The task consists in the determination of longitudinal dispersion coefficient D_x in the equations (2), (3) by optimizing the model fault compared to the
original system. The determination of the fault is made by comparing the measured
sulphate concentrations with the model outputs in the i-element. The method based
on the Newton-Raphson iteration technique can be used. The correction of D_x in the
k+1-step of the repeated calculation can be determined as follows :

$$\Delta D_x^{(k)} = \frac{\int_{t_o}^{t_o+T} \sum_{i=1}^{n} \varepsilon_i^{(k)}(t) \cdot \frac{\partial \varepsilon_i^{(k)}(t)}{\partial D_x^{(k)}} \, dt}{\int_{t_o}^{t_o+T} \sum_{i=1}^{n} \left(\frac{\partial \varepsilon_i^{(k)}(t)}{\partial D_x^{(k)}} \right)^2 \, dt} \tag{4}$$

The derivation of the fault functions according to D_x can be calculated using the sensitivity equations, where

$\frac{\partial \varepsilon_i}{\partial D_x}$ is designed as v_i.

The equation for the control element of the model section shall be written as :

$$\dot{v}_i = \frac{1}{(\Delta x)^2} (Y_{i+1} + Y_{i-1}) + \left(\frac{D_x}{(\Delta x)^2} - \frac{U}{2\Delta x} \right) v_{i+1} -$$

$$- \frac{2}{(\Delta x)^2} Y_i - \frac{2D_x}{(\Delta x)^2} v_i + \left(\frac{D_x}{(\Delta x)^2} + \frac{U}{2\Delta x} \right) v_{i-1} \tag{5}$$

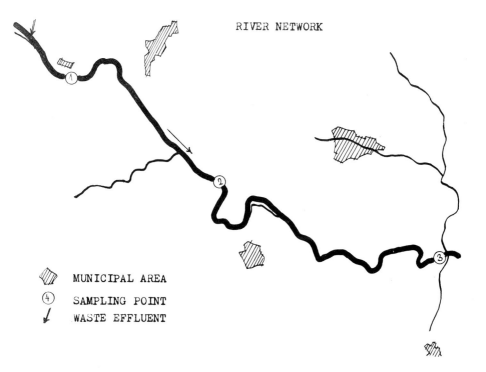

RIVER NETWORK

MUNICIPAL AREA

SAMPLING POINT

WASTE EFFLUENT

Fig. 1 - Scheme of the disposition of the control profiles

For the last element the following equation is written :

$$\dot{v}_n = \frac{1}{(\Delta x)^2} (Y_{n-1} - Y_n) + (\frac{D_x}{(\Delta x)^2} + \frac{U}{\Delta x}) v_i + (\frac{D_x}{(\Delta x)^2} \frac{U}{\Delta x}) v_{i-1} \qquad (6)$$

In case of simulating measured curves of the sulfate concentration described in the graph No.2 the formula (4) could be modified to :

$$\Delta D_x^{(k)} = \frac{\int_{t_o}^{t_o+T} [\varepsilon_6^{(k)}(t) \, v_6^{(k)}(t) + \varepsilon_{17}^{(k)}(t).v_{17}^{(k)}(t)] \, dt}{\int_{t_o}^{t_o+T} [(v_6^{(k)}(t))^2 + (v_{17}^{(k)}(t))^2] \, dt} \qquad (7)$$

When the value of the coefficient $D^{(k+1)}$ for the k-step is a negative number, the value of $D_x^{(k+1)}$ shall be zero according to the algorithm made.

The computation is finished when $\Delta D_x^{(k)}$ is smaller than the given minimal correction.

REFERENCES

BELLA, D.A., DOBBINS, W.E., Difference Modeling of Stream Pollution, Journal of the
      San. Eng. Div., Proc. ASCE, 94, SA 5, 885, 1968.
HRAZDIL, V., Numerical solution of water quality changes in streams for water management shown on an example of Ohře-river basin, Report VÚV Brno, 1974.
KRENKEL, P.A., HAYS, J.R., THACKSTON, E.L., Least Square Estimation of Mixing
      coefficients, Journal of the San. Eng. Div., Proc. ASCE, 93, SA 3,47,1967.
NOVOTNÝ, V., Numerical solution of water quality changes in streams in water management, Study, VÚV Brno, 1967.

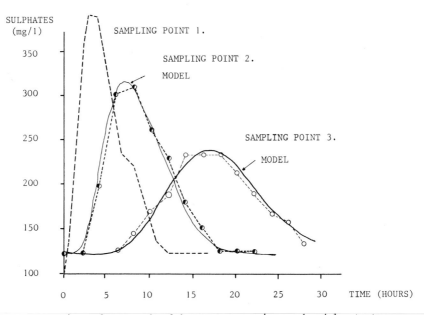

Fig. 2 - Comparison of measured sulphate concentrations and model outputs

Modeling and Simulation of Water Resources Systems, G.C. VANSTEENKISTE, (Ed.)
North-Holland Publishing Company (1975)

DYNAMIC MODELS AND COMPUTER SIMULATION OF WASTEWATER TREATMENT SYSTEMS

John F. Andrews
Environmental Systems Engineering
Clemson University
Clemson, South Carolina
U.S.A.

ABSTRACT

Dynamic models and computer simulations are tools of substantial
value for describing the behavior of wastewater treatment systems.
Specific examples of dynamic models and computer simulations are
presented for two biological processes used in wastewater treatment. The anaerobic digestion process is potentially unstable and
simulation is of value in exploring process stability and control
strategies for the prevention of process failure. Simulations of
the step feed activated sludge process indicate that variation of
the point(s) at which wastewater is added along the length of the
aeration basin offers a valuable control action when poorly settling sludge is encountered.

INTRODUCTION

The need for consideration of dynamic behavior in both the design and operation of wastewater treatment plants is frequently greater than that for industrial plants because of the large temporal variations which occur in wastewater
composition, concentration, and flow rate. However, our understanding of this
dynamic behavior and how it may be modified through the application of modern
control systems is in it's infancy. Gross process failures are all too frequent
and even when these are avoided, it is not unusual to find significant variations
in plant efficiency, not only from one plant to another but also from day to day
and hour to hour in the same plant.

One of the major reasons why the dynamic behavior of wastewater treatment
plants has not been qualitatively considered in past years is that only recently
have the tools necessary to predict the dynamic behavior of such complex systems
become available. Being practical people, most environmental engineers have said
"Why develop a dynamic mathematical model when it is not possible to obtain a
solution?" However, computer simulation has largely eliminated this bottleneck
and the current problem is not so much one of being able to obtain a solution as
it is to insure that the model adequately describes the dynamic behavior of the
process being simulated.

When the dynamic behavior of a plant has been defined, the environmental
engineer then should become interested in modifying this behavior so that it will
conform to some desired behavior. This can be accomplished either by redesign of
the process or incorporation of a control system. However, the design of a control system is substantially different from process design in that it is primarily
involved with the handling of information. Environmental engineers are familiar
with the theory and technology involved in the collection, transportation, processing, and distribution of materials and energy. However, they are not as
accustomed to thinking of information in the same terms even though this is of
equal or greater importance. One reason for this may be that only in recent years
has an adequate aid to information processing, the digital computer, become

available.   Greater familiarity with the quantitative handling of information
should result in improved performance of wastewater treatment plants.

The author is a relatively new user of systems engineering techniques and
makes no claim of being an expert in any of the techniques illustrated in this
paper.   His emphasis has always been, and will remain, on improvement of the system which in this case is a wastewater treatment plant.   However, he has been de-
lighted with the knowledge gained about the system by the use of these techniques
and looks forward with confidence to obtaining considerable improvement in plant
performance by the further application of these techniques.

ANAEROBIC DIGESTION

Anaerobic digestion was the first wastewater treatment process to be
studied by the author using dynamic modeling and computer simulation.   The relationship of this process to the other components of a wastewater treatment plant
is portrayed in Figure 1.   The process is widely used in municipal wastewater
treatment for the treatment of organic sludges and has several significant advantages over other treatment methods.   Among these are the formation of useful by-
products such as methane gas and a humus like slurry well suited for land reclamation.   Unfortunately, even with these advantages the process has in general not
enjoyed a good reputation because of its poor record with respect to process stability as indicated through the years by the many reports of "sour" or failing di-
gesters.   At the present time, operating practice consists only of sets of empirical rules and there is a significant need for a more rational control strategy to
put process operation on a quantitative basis.   Dynamic modeling and computer simulation can be of considerable value in evaluating the effectiveness of such control
strategies and would also assist in improving process design by allowing selection
of design parameters which contribute to improved process stability.

The dynamic model proposed for the process, which is summarized in Figure
2, was developed from material balances on several components in the biological,
liquid and gas phases of a continuous flow, complete mixing reactor.   There are
strong interactions between the phases as well as internal to each phase.   These
interactions must be considered in the model for prediction of the dynamic response
of the five variables most commonly used for evaluating process performance.   These
variables are; (1) volatile acids concentration (S), (2) alkalinity (HCO_3^-), (3) pH,
(4) gas flow rate (Q), and (5) gas composition (% CO_2).   Several relationships such
as Henry's law, equilibrium and kinetic expressions, and charge balances were used
to express these interactions on a quantitative basis.

Digital computer simulations have provided qualitative evidence for the
validity of the model by predicting results which are commonly observed in the
field.   Among the results predicted by the model are; (1) under steady state conditions, the numerical values of the state variables approximate those observed in
the field, (2) process failure can be caused by hydraulic, organic, and toxic material overloading, (3) the simulation of manual control techniques commonly used
in the field will result in process recovery, and (4) the course of failure, as
evidenced by the behavior of the five variables most commonly used for evaluating
process performance, is qualitatively the same as that observed in the field.
This last point is illustrated in Figure 3 which shows a simulated process failure

Hybrid computer simulations were used to analyze process stability by simulating digester overload and observing what changes in design and operational
parameters provided the best buffer against process failure.   The analysis procedure involved making a change in a parameter, such as the residence time, followed
by simulating larger and larger step increases in digester loading until failure
occured.   By plotting the locus of points of critical loading vs. the parameter of
interest, it was possible to obtain a semiquantitative measure of digester stability.

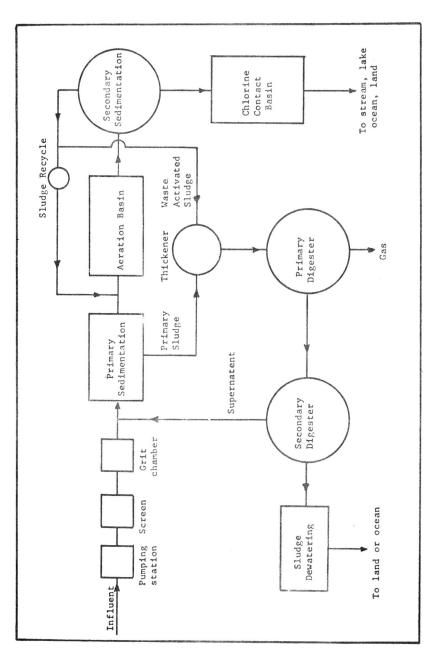

FIGURE 1. A CONVENTIONAL WASTEWATER TREATMENT PLANT

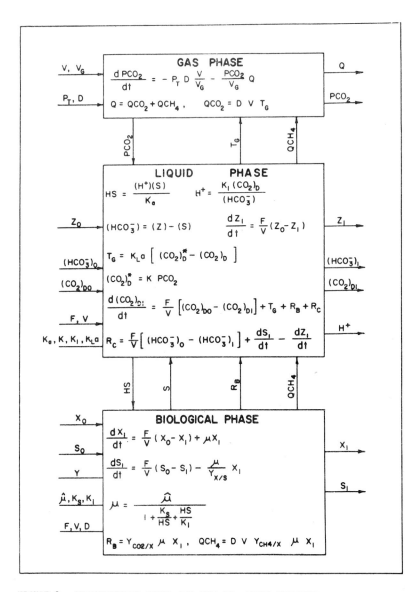

FIGURE 2.   MATHEMATICAL MODEL FOR THE ANAEROBIC DIGESTER

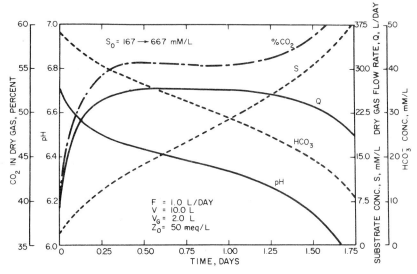

FIGURE 3. SIMULATED FAILURE OF THE ANAEROBIC DIGESTER BY A STEP CHANGE IN ORGANIC LOADING

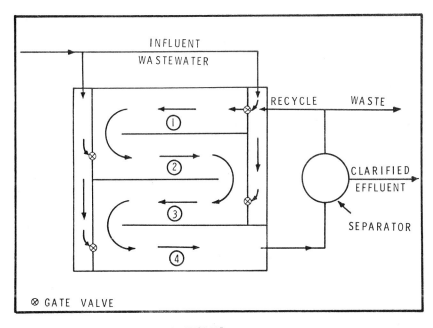

FIGURE 4. THE STEP FEED ACTIVATED SLUDGE PROCESS

A variety of control signals, controller modes, and control actions are available for use in developing control strategies for the anaerobic digester and several combinations of these were explored using the hybrid computer. From these studies two new control strategies, one using a new control action and the other a new signal, were shown to have sufficient promise to warrent future field investigations. The new control action is the recycle of digester gas from which carbon dioxide has been scrubbed and the new signal is the rate of methane production.

The dynamic model and computer simulations discussed herein have evolved over the past ten years and are discussed in more detail in the publications of Andrews (1968,1969), Andrews and Graef (1971), and Graef and Andrews (1974a, 1974b). They are by no means complete and still require considerable field verification. However, they should be of semiquantitative value for digester design and operation as well as serving as a guide for field experimentation and a valuable framework for future modifications of the model.

ACTIVATED SLUDGE PROCESS

The activated sludge process is the most commonly used process for the treatment of wastewaters and consists of two units, an aeration basin and a sedimentation basin, as illustrated in Figure 1. The three major inputs to the aeration basin are the wastewater, concentrated activated sludge from the sedimentation basin, and air. The microorganisms in the activated sludge react with the organic pollutants in the wastewater and oxygen in the air to produce more activated sludge, carbon dioxide, and water. The effluent from the aeration basin flows to the sedimentation basin where the activated sludge is separated from the liquid phase. The process effluent consists of the clarified overflow from the sedimentation basin. This basin also serves to concentrate the solids which settle to the bottom of the tank for recycle to the aeration basin.

The recycle of concentrated sludge from the sedimentation basin to the aeration basin is an essential feature of the process. Recycle serves the purpose of both increasing the concentration of microorganisms in the aerator and maintaining the organisms in a physiological condition such that they will readily flocculate. However, recycle has also resulted in difficulties in understanding and modeling the process since it creates a feedback loop thereby causing a strong interaction between the aerator and settler.

Over the years, several distinct versions of the process have been developed and the one which has been of most interest to this investigator is the step feed activated sludge process as illustrated in Figure 4. In this version of the process, the wastewater can be admitted at several discrete points along the length of the aeration basin. The basin is usually constructed in a "folded" fashion (Fig. 4) for economy of construction. This ability to regulate the point(s) at which wastewater is added along the length of the reactor provides an additional control action which gives this version of the process much more operational flexibility than other versions. This control action is especially effective for poorly settling or bulking sludge which can lead to process failure by loss of the activated sludge in the overflow from the sedimentation basin. Andrews and Lee (1972) have illustrated the value of step feed as a control action by computer simulation using a simplified dynamic model. Figure 5 shows the transient effect of suddenly shifting from an operational mode where all of the wastewater is admitted to stage one (see Fig. 4) to an operational mode where all of the wastewater is equally divided between stages two and three. The sludge in the settler is rapidly transferred to the aerator and there is also a rapid decrease in the solids flux to the settler. Both of these responses would have the short term effect (hours) of decreasing the mass of solids carried over in the effluent from the settler. These predictions are qualitatively verified through the field studies reported by Torpey (1948) in his work on the step feed process at the Bowery Bay plant in

New York City. Torpey has also demonstrated that there is a long term (days) improvement in the settling characteristics by application of this control action.

The simulations presented in Figure 5 are based on a simplified model since their purpose was to prove the qualitative validity of regulating the point of addition of wastewater as a control action. The investigation of more detailed control strategies requires a more sophisticated model. Bryant (1972) has improved the model by adding a dynamic model of the secondary sedimentation basin which can predict changes in sludge blanket height and underflow solids concentration. Busby and Andrews (1973) have improved the model for the aeration basin by considering the sludge mass to be structured into three components. Structuring of the sludge mass provides a rational basis for time lags and makes the model more general so that it can be used to simulate the behavior of a wide spectrum of versions of the activated sludge process. Busby and Andrews (1973) also studied, using hybrid computer simulations, a wide variety of control strategies for the process.

WASTEWATER TREATMENT PLANTS

The author's current research is oriented toward combining dynamic models for the individual processes into an overall dynamic model for a wastewater treatment plant with subsequent use of the model to explore computer compatible control strategies for the plant. This will be the author's third attempt toward developing such a model. Previous attempts with Bryant (1972) and Busby (1973) were reduced to an investigation of the activated sludge process when it became obvious that much additional research was needed to develop an adequate dynamic model for this process. However, preliminary models for both the primary sedimentation basin and the chlorine contact basin were developed and have since been improved. Current efforts are being devoted to the development of an improved objective function for the plant and an exploration of the interactions between the individual processes. The next step will be the exploration of control strategies for the entire plant.

In connection with the computer control of wastewater treatment plants, it should be noted that at least 40 plants throughout the world have either installed or placed process control computers on order. As an example of the current interest in this topic, the author was program chairman for an IAWPR Workshop on Instrumentation, Automation and Control of Wastewater Treatment Systems which was held in London during September of 1973. Of the 75 papers presented at this workshop, more than 25 were concerned with some aspect of computer control.

REFERENCES

Andrews, J.F. (1968). Biotech. & Bioengr, 10, 707.
Andrews, J.F. (1969). J. Sanit. Engr. Div., Amer. Soc. Civil Engrs., 95, 95.
Andrews, J.F., and Graef, S.P. (1971). Anaerobic Biological Treatment Processes,
    Advances in Chemistry Series No. 105. (Amer. Chem. Soc., Washington), 126.
Andrews, J.F., and Lee, C.R. (1972). Proc. IVth Inter. Ferment. Symp. (Soc.
    Ferment. Tech., Osaka, Japan), 35.
Bryant, J.O. (1972). Ph.D. Dissertation, Clemson Univ., Clemson, S.C.
Busby, J.B. (1973). Ph.D. Dissertation, Clemson Univ., Clemson, S.C.
Busby, J.B. and Andrews, J.F. (submitted for publication, preprint available).
Graef, S.P. and J.F. Andrews. (1974a). AIChE Symp. Series, 70, No. 136, 101.
Graef, S.P. and J.F. Andrews. (1974b). J. Water Poll. Cont. Fed., 46, 666.
Torpey, W.N. (1948). Sewage & Ind. Wastes, 27, 121

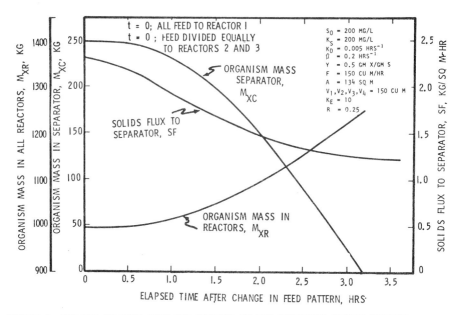

FIGURE 5. THE USE OF STEP FEED FOR CONTROL OF THE ACTIVATED SLUDGE PROCESS

DISCUSSION

I was a little bit startled by your proposal to go back bulking by intro-ducing sewage at an other point. It seems to me that this approaches the proposal which has recently appeared in the literature by Chudoba, a Czechoslovakian author. May be you have seen it. They proposed the actual reason why bulking occurs and the actual way to combat it is not to feed in a particular concentration but to feed in a gradient of concentrations. They have also a biochemical basis to really sup-port that proposal. In your method do you have a lot of actual data in the field that it really works and do you think it relates to that Chudoba proposal. (VERSTRAETE)

It does not relate to the Chudoba proposal because that is at a steady state design. I am talking about an operation strategy. The data I have to go on comes from 1948 from a paper by a person who was the former chief operations en-gineer of New York city. He curved the strategy on a qualitative basis. It does work in that sense. (ANDREWS)

It is interesting to us to know how much flexibility there might be in the future in activated sludge treatment plants. Do you foresee a reasonable amount of flexibility in control over the actual discharge. (YOUNG)

I think so. Some engineering professions are accustomed to not giving the operational engineer any flexibility. By the way that is a good strategy for a small plant, where you obviously will not have good operations, but in a large plant it is different. We had some success. I was mentioning to Burton Davidson how we can solve the problem in Philadelphia. It is amazing to me that an idea that was first used in 1948 is not going to be accepted. But it is because I think, in most instances in design, we worked in a steady state domain and not the time domain. Unfortunately they don't really operate that way. (ANDREWS)

Were these plants that much more difficult to operate presently ? (BIGGAR)

Not in my opinion. We are talking about very large plants sometimes which are very expensive. When we are talking about the Chicago plant, is treats a little over one billion 45 gallons of waste water/day and the cost of that plant is 1/2 billion dollars so these are very expensive structures. (ANDREWS)

Is it true that capital investments far outweigh what you may have on running costs ? Is it possible to make a case that introducing control saves running cost ? (BECK)

Oh yes, to big city managers, the word automation in the true sense, is important, to eliminate operating personnel. (ANDREWS)

What about having poisoning through these plants ? (DAVIDSON)

Obviously you do have toxic materials coming in and in the model there is built in a depth for this purpose and here part of our models are empirical. We simply say that's a toxic material, we don't know what it is, but to be valid the model must fail with toxic material. There is one material balance for depth. (ANDREWS)

In the activated sludge cycle of the sewage plant, there is a possibility of recycling toxic material, and never getting an accumulation of material that is toxic to the micro-organisms.

As can be seen in the treatment plant schemes that would be one advantage of this as a control strategy. In the case of New York, there is left in some reserved capacity and the organism is actually stored in case something like this happened, the toxic material is never used. This is one way one could handle it. The quality of your product would of course suffer under this, but at least you would not have to go to start up the thing again, which should take a couple of weeks. (ANDREWS)

Could you give any idea of the percentage of capital investment you gained by dynamic modeling.

No I could not, we have a research named "workshop" ruled by the US Environmental Protection Agency in September, which will be a national workshop. The purpose is to answer the question you just asked. I can make some relative statements though.   Control versus capital investment in the plant is like 1 %. Petrochemical industries in the US would run as high as 14 to 15 %. An occasional water treatment plant might well run into 40 %. That gives you a rough indication.   (ANDREWS)

In the chemical process industry the justification for on line digital computer control in the large refinery lies not in the control but in the other uses of that computer. They are tied in to the stock market, to book keeping and other data acquisition not related to the plant. In that case it can be justified. (DAVIDSON)

Have you any idea how long it would take to have reliable instrumentation quantities like the microorganism concentration in activated sludge. (BECK)

In my work at Philadelphia, those are covered reactors using high purified oxygen. I don't want to get on to details of the process, but in a sense you have an on-line material balance of oxygen consumption at any point of time and that is a direct measure of the activity of the microorganism. As we go frequently, we need these measurements. No one really knows if that is going to take a rather firm dynamic analysis of the process, perhaps in some cases daily analysis or weekly analysis whereas in other instances seconds. (ANDREWS)

Have you had any experience using large retention ages to damp out these large fluctuations in quality and quantity of effluent.

They are not used too much in large municipalities but they are widely used in industry and to me it would be an effective technique for damping. (ANDREWS)

Current research field of author : *Dynamic modeling and control strategies for biological processes used in wastewater treatment plants − Computer control of wastewater treatment plants − Management information systems for monitoring treatment plant performance by regulatory agencies.*

Modeling and Simulation of Water Resources Systems, G.C. VANSTEENKISTE, (Ed.)
North-Holland Publishing Company (1975)

SIMULATION AIDED MODELING
OF THE DYNAMIC BEHAVIOUR FOR SOME ELEMENTS OF
A SURFACE WATER TREATMENT PLANT

M. Klinck
Philips Forschungslaboratorium Hamburg GmbH,
2 Hamburg 54, Germany

ABSTRACT

For the instrumentation and control of a complex water
treatment plant it will undoubtedly be necessary to get
in a first step the knowledge about the dynamic behaviour
of the incoperated elements as e.g. sand filters, storage
reservoirs, pumping stations etc. Based on the physics of
such elements the dynamic behaviour can be investigated
by means of simulation languages and hybrid computer systems. The results of such investigations up to the control
of a complete plant will be presented.

INTRODUCTION

In an anonymous paper (1969) it was supposed that the
growth rate for the delivery of drinking water will be in the range
of 30 to 50 percent within the next decade. Therefore a sufficient
number of water treatment plants must be constructed. We suppose
that in most of these future plants a high degree of automation will
be realized by means of electronic control equipment and process
computers.

For projecting the automatic control loops a sufficient
knowledge of the dynamic behaviour of the plant elements is necessary. Simulation by means of continuous systems simulation languages or hybrid computer systems is a good tool for the necessary
investigations. The corresponding results are also very important
for overcoming or avoiding difficulties during the set-up phase
of the system.

Some results of investigations concerned with the input
station of a surface water treatment plant will be presented by
Klinck (1974) in autumn of this year.

In this paper the results of the investigations concerned
with the dynamic behaviour of controlled elements and of the complete system for the final station of a complex surface water
treatment plant are presented.

The simulations were done by means of the continuous systems simulation language COSILA on a Philips P1400 computer system.
COSILA has a source deck similar to that of CSMP.

SURFACE WATER TREATMENT PLANT

This paper deals with the structure of the final station
of a surface water treatment process, which is constructed for

an hourly effluent of about 5000 cubicmeters. A global overview of
the plant is given in Fig. 1. A pumping station pumps the pre-
filtered water from an input station through a pipeline into a

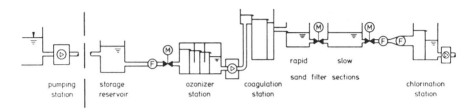

Fig. 1: Surface water treatment plant

storage reservoir with a large surface area. The effluent through
a few parallel pipes is measured and can be controlled by means
of motor driven butterfly valves. Out of an ozonizer station the
water is pumped into a coagulation station, where most of the
chemical content of the water is removed. From this station the
water is fed to a rapid sand filter section, the effluent of each
can also be controlled by motor driven butterfly valves. By means
of the incorporated sand beds most of the turbidity is filtered out.
In the following section with slow sand filters and incorporated
thin layers of living particles the bacterial content is removed
out of the water. In each output pipe of these filters a motor
driven butterfly valve and a flowmeter are installed. A common pipe
with an extra flowmeter feeds the water to a chlorination station.
Out of this station the drinking water is transported to a distribution network.

        The aim of the project this paper deals with is to automate
this water treatment plant by means of electronic measurement and
control equipment and a process computer in order to get a satisfactory behaviour with as few as possible manual operations. The
main setpoint for the plant effluent is given by a central control
station of a municipal distribution facility. The process computer
shall be used mainly for datalogging and alarm purposes and for
some control functions. The different control loops for the elements of the plant and the main control loop shall be completely
equipped with electronic controllers.

LEVEL CONTROLLED STORAGE RESERVOIR

        The storage reservoir at the input of this plant is
connected via a pipe with the pumping station of the input plant
some distance away. This storage reservoir has a stand by function.
In normal operation only a fraction of the influent flows through
the reservoir for refreshing purposes, the remainder is directly
fed to the ozonizer station. But in case of faults in the influent path the water for the plant is completely taken out of this
reservoir. To secure the necessary contents for this reservoir a
level control loop is provided. Furthermore this control loop
guarantees a continuous system flow, because in the steady state
the influent equals the effluent. The loop consists of the pumping
station as an actuator, the pipe and the reservoir besides the
level meter and the controller.

The behaviour of the pumping station is described in a paper by Klinck (1974). This station consists of three centrifugal pumps which are driven with constant speed. The effluent can be controlled by varying the position of the blades by means of switching a constant speed dc-motor on and off. The number of operating pumps is determined by the demanded effluent with a switching network. In case of switching a new pump on or off there are large spikes in the effluent because of the minimal effluent for the low position of the blades. For each pump there is a flow control loop equipped with a three position stepping motor in order to determine the effluent due to an incoming setpoint value.

The dynamic behaviour of the pipe is that of a delay element with a delay time which is determined by the pipe length and the sonic velocity in water. The value of this delay time is small therefore the pipe behaviour is not taken into account for this loop.

The storage reservoir itself can be described by the water level as a function of the inverse value of the surface area multiplied with the integral of the difference between the influent and the effluent. This is a pure integral behaviour.

After some simulation runs a satisfactory result for this control loop was obtained which is shown in Fig. 2. There is a test function for the effluent QROUT. The level HWR shows nearly no reaction, but the influent QRIN follows satisfactorily the effluent. The influent spikes are due to pump switchings and the control behaviour of the three position stepping controllers for the pumps can be seen. This behaviour is achieved by a feedforward control concept. The main part of the pumping station setpoint value is determined by an internal plant setpoint and only a fraction by the output signal of the continuous PI controller for the water level in the reservoir.

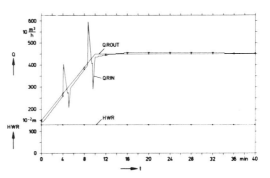

Fig. 2: Storage reservoir, test function response

FLOW CONTROLLED OZONIZER STATION INPUT

The effluent out of the storage reservoir is established by a set of flow control loops for each parallel pipe. These control loops are fed with the internal plant setpoint value divided by the number of parallel loops in order to get equal flows in the pipes. The loops are equipped with three position stepping controllers which actuate the dc-motor driven butterfly valves. The behaviour can be described by a constant slope response with saturation where the response time is proportional to the setpoint step and the saturation value is proportional to the setpoint itself.

LEVEL CONTROLLED OZONIZER STATION OUTPUT

In the ozonizer station an amount of ozone proportional to the water flow is introduced. For the dynamic behaviour of the ozonizer station itself see the chapter on the coagulation station.

From the output stage of this station the water is pumped to the coagulation station by means of speed controlled pumps. The number of operating pumps depends of the demanded flow. A level control loop is introduced in the output stage in order to secure a continuous system flow. The loop consists of the speed controlled pumps and the output reservoir besides a level meter and a continuous PI-controller.

The dynamic behaviour of this reservoir is also a pure integral one. The difference to the storage reservoir is the very small value of the surface area, thus there is a larger sensitivity of this system due to flow changes. This must be taken into account in the tuning procedure for the controller.

The speed controlled pumps can approximately be described by a first order lag system with fixed values for the time constant and the transfer gain. Since there is no flow measurement in the output section the flow signal from the input can be used for the pump switchings.

In Fig. 3 a test function response is shown for this control loop. The effluent QOUT follows satisfactorily the influent QOIN. The level HO shows the expected sensitivity, but is within the boundaries of the demands for this loop. Especially in the case of pump switching there are quick variations of the water level in this basin.

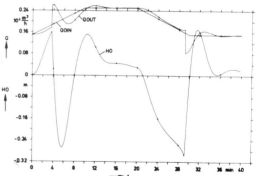

Fig. 3: Ozonizer station output, test function response

COAGULATION STATION

In the coagulation station no selfcontained control loop is necessary because the effluent equals the influent due to gravity forces under steady state conditions.

The dynamic behaviour is nonlinear. This is due to the formula for an overflow height at a weir. But some simulation runs show that it can be approximated by a first order lag with a small value for the time constant.

LEVEL CONTROLLED RAPID SAND FILTER

The rapid sandfilter section has the effluent out of the coagulation station as the influent at an upper weir. With the

assumption that all filters operate in parallel it is sufficient to describe the dynamic behaviour of one filter. In a paper of Hilder (1973) the behaviour of an uncontrolled filter bank is presented due to a periodic cleaning procedure. In the papers of Klinck (1973) the dynamic behaviour of a level controlled rapid sand filter is presented. So at this point only the result of a simulation run with the specific parameters for the filters in this section is shown in Fig. 4. In this figure the step responses of the water level HRF, the effluent QRF and the valve disc position PHR are presented. In the behaviour of the effluent QRF the influence of the three position stepping controller can be easily recognized. The overall behaviour of this nonlinear system can be approximated by a second order system.

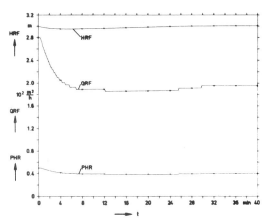

Fig. 4: Rapid sand filter, step
response

FLOW CONTROLLED SLOW SAND FILTER OUTPUT

The slow sand filters are fed by a ring pipe below the surface. For each filter there is a flow control loop. There are two reasons for these loops. The first one is to ensure an equal effluent out of each filter whereas the second one is due to one of the main system demands that is to secure that a fixed value for the alteration velocity of the filtration rate in these filters will not be exceeded.

After investigating the static behaviour of such a filter, i.e. the effluent as a function of the valve disc position with the water level remaining constant, a full travel time for the dc-motor driven butterfly valve can be determined to ensure this demand. Because the valves are standard ones with small full travel times a special device VZ (Fig. 1) must be provided.

The output pipes of the filters are connected with a common pipe. In this pipe a main flowmeter is installed and a further flow controller is provided for controlling the plant effluent due to the central set point. For this purpose a continuous PI-controller is introduced in this main loop whereas for the filter outputs three position stepping controllers are provided for these minor loops.

The step responses due to a central setpoint step are shown in Fig. 5. It can be seen that the effluent QSF has during some time a constant slope corresponding to the full travel time of the valve. The same can be seen from the valve disc position

PHS. The signal WSF is the
output signal of the main
flow controller. This
signal is divided by the
number of operating filters
and fed to the minor loop
controllers to ensure
equal effluents out of
the filters.

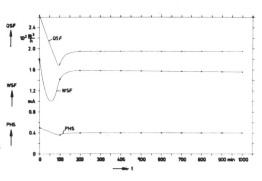

MAIN SYSTEM CONTROL LOOP

        The controlled flow
out of the slow sand filters
due to the central setpoint
acts as a disturbance to
the level balance. In case
of an increasing effluent
the level can only be kept
constant if the flow in

Fig. 5: Slow sand filter, step
       response

the backward system elements will also be increased. Therefore the
level of the slow sand filter is established as the main controlled
variable. A continuous PI-controller is provided for this loop.

        Two alternatives for this system control loop are in-
vestigated. In the first one the output signal fully represents
the internal plant setpoint which mainly determines the actuating
signal for the pumping station in the storage reservoir control
loop. Furthermore the internal plant setpoint is fed to the flow
control loops at the input stage of the ozonizer station after
deviding it by the number of parallel pipes. A schematic representation of the water treatment plant with the element control loops
and the system control loop is shown in Fig. 6. The dashed line
for the introduction of the central setpoint W_{ges} is true for this
direct control concept.

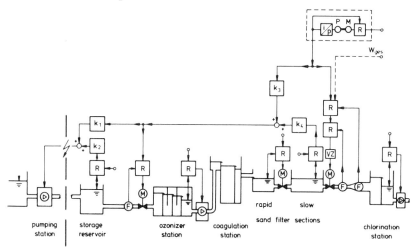

Fig. 6: Surface water treatment plant, control concept

A second possibility for the system control loop was also investigated. In this alternative a feedforward control concept is realized in the system control loop and a smoothing circuit is introduced into the central setpoint path. This is represented by the continuous lines for the central setpoint W_{ges} in Fig. 6. The internal plant setpoint is determined by a main fraction of the smoothed central setpoint and a smaller fraction of the output signal of the level controller for the slow sand filters. The smoothing circuit for the central setpoint transforms an input step to a constant speed signal with saturation. The speed is chosen equal to the full travel time of the actuators in the output pipes of the slow sand filters. The response time until reaching the saturation level is proportional to the introduced step whereas the saturation level itself is proportional to the central setpoint value.

The results of the investigations for these two system control concepts are shown in Fig. 7 for some flows and in Fig. 8 for some niveaus in the system corresponding with a central setpoint step.

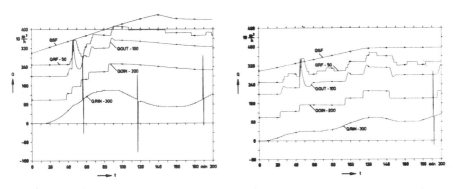

a) direct control concept   b) feedforward control concept
                                             with setpoint smoothing

Fig. 7: System flow step responses

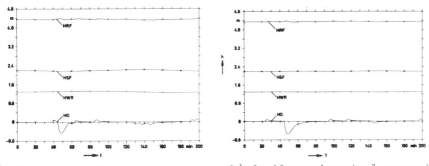

a) direct control concept   b) feedforward control concept
                                             with setpoint smoothing

Fig. 8: System niveau step responses

In Fig. 7 the different element flows are displaced for a better survey. QSF is the slow sand filter effluent, QRF the rapid sandfilter effluent, QOUT the ozonizer station effluent, QOIN the ozonizer station influent and QRIN the storage reservoir influent. It can be seen from Fig. 7a and b that the introduction of the feedforward control concept with a setpoint smoothing circuit results in a more smoothed step response for the several flows. This is especially true for the pumping station flow QRIN in the storage reservoir loop. There is now only one pump switching operation in the same time. The pump switching operation in the ozonizer output flow QOUT acts as a disturbance in the fast sand filter effluent QRF but cannot be discovered in the slow sand filter effluent QSF. In the QRF and QOIN graphs the three position stepping controller actions can be recognized.

In Fig. 8 the true water levels of some different system elements are shown. HRF is the rapid sand filter level, HSF the slow sandfilter level, HWR the storage reservoir level and HO the water level in the output stage of the ozonizer station. It can be seen that with the direct control concept in Fig. 8a the different water levels are more disturbed than with the feedforward control concept and setpoint smoothing. The large amplitude of the unsteady level breakdown in the output stage of the ozonizer station (HO) corresponds with the switch-on operation for the second pump.

The results of the investigations in the dynamic behaviour of the system with feedforward control concept and a smoothed central setpoint are in good agreement with the demands. In applying such feedforward control concepts some care must be taken if system faults occur. If e.g. the output pipes of the storage reservoir must be closed for some reasons with the direct control concept the appropriate control signal is generated to slow down the pumping station. With the feedforward control concept only a fraction of the pumping station setpoint is due to the control action, the remainder remains constant and the corresponding effluent can give an overflow in the storage reservoir. For such cases special alarm messages must be given to the operating people in the central operating room.

CHLORINATION STATION

Before the water leaves the plant as drinking water some chlorine is introduced in the chlorination station. In this station only a level control loop is necessary to ensure that the effluent equals the influent. There are no special problems with this control loop.

CONCLUSION

The simulation tool was chosen for the investigation of the dynamic behaviour of some elements of a surface water treatment plant. In a first step the models of the elements as e.g. rapid sandfilters, reservoirs etc. are derived with the corresponding physics as a background. To these element models the appropriate controller models were added and the results of the investigations in the dynamic behaviour were shown. Finally the behaviour of the complete system was demonstrated for two different control concepts.

One of the major problems in using simulation techniques is to check the validity of the results before the realization of the project is finished. In some cases a comparison with similar systems is possible by input/output measurements. But in most cases one must rely on the physical credibility of the results as done for these investigations. In all cases great care should be taken to ensure the sufficient accuracy, e.g. in chosing the appropriate integration routine of the simulation language.

The results throughout this paper demonstrated that the simulation tool is very good suited for modeling and designing automatic control loops in the water treatment field. All the simulations were done by means of a continuous system simulation language.

ACKNOWLEDGEMENT

Thanks are going to Mr. Ir. van Zutphen, Mr. Ir. Prinsen Geerligs and their coworkers of Gemeente Waterleidingen Amsterdam and Mr. Ir. Verharen of Philips Eindhoven for the detailed information about the system.

REFERENCES

Anonymous (1969). "Het waterbeleid in Belgie", $H_2O(2)$, Nr. 8, pp. 185-189.
Hilder, D.W. (1973). "The computer simulation of the operation of a bank of rapid gravity filters", Proceedings of the Conference "Computer Uses in Water Systems", Reading, UK, Sept. 25-27, 1973.
Klinck, M. (1973). "The input/output behaviour of a level-controlled rapid sand filter", Proceedings of the IFAC Symposium on "Control of Water Resource Systems", Haifa, Israel, Sept. 17-21, 1973.
Klinck, M. (1973): "The start-up model of a rapid sand filter", Proceedings of the Conference "Computer Uses in Water Systems", Reading, UK, Sept. 25-27, 1973.
Klinck, M. (1974). "Simulation aided design of the automatic control concept for a water treatment plant", to be presented at the AICA Symposium on "Hybrid Computation in Dynamic Systems Design", Rome, Italy, Nov. 11-14, 1974.

Current research field of author : *Simulation of industrial processes by means of simulation languages and a hybrid computer system : Investigation of the dynamic behaviour and design of the control concepts for a surface water treatment plant - Hardware and software of minicomputer systems for industrial instrumentation and control - Set-up of a hybrid computer system.*

Modeling and Simulation of Water Resources Systems, G.C. VANSTEENKISTE, (Ed.)
North-Holland Publishing Company (1975)

SIMULATION AND OPTIMISATION OF A BIOLOGICAL WATER TREATMENT PLANT

P. E. Erni
Swiss Federal Institute for Water Resources
and Water Pollution Control (EAWAG)
at the Federal Institute of Technology   (ETH)
Duebendorf, Switzerland

ABSTRACT

Several basic conditions for the adaptiv control of an activated sludge unit were established. The mathematical model is
similar to that of Monod, but in contrast does not produce
conflicting results when used for simulation with low yield
coefficients. Laboratory experiments were carried out to obtain data for the verification of the model and the identification of its parameters. Due to reciprocal dependency among
the constants, only 3 of the 4 constants could be identified.
For the optimisation only a closed loop regulation of the ac-
tevated sludge unit could be considered, due to the expected
fluctuations in the input variables.

INTRODUCTION AND PROBLEM FORMULATION

For the treatment of waste water exists a large selection of
mechanical, biological and chemical treatment methods which can be
applied singly or in combination. Widely used are water treatment
plants in which a part of the treatment is carried out with the aid
of an activated sludge unit. In this work the optimal control of the
biological part (activated sludge tank) of a waste water treatment
plant was examined with the aid of the amount of sludge pumped back
into the activated sludge tank from the settling tank. A sewage treatment plant can only be adaptively controlled since the biophysical
processes are 1) extremely complex, therefore making a mathematical
approach very difficult, and 2) subjected to uncontrollable changes
in external disturbances (quality, quantity and concentration of in-
flowing waste water, rain, pH, temperature, etc.).

THE NEW MATHEMATICAL MODEL

Using adaptive control the mathematical model can be quite
simple; for the model parameters are constantly adjusted to the changing status of the waste water by means of an identification process.
For this reason the dependence of the biological constants on the
physical (temperature, pH-value, etc.) and hydraulic variables as
mathematically formulated by other authors (for example [1]) may be
neglected. Nevertheless the mathematical model contains the parameters which describe the biological process (specific growth rate u,
yield coefficient Y, specific decay rate of the microorganisms k_d).
With the Michaelis-Menten term [2]:

$$\mu = \hat{\mu} \cdot \frac{s_1}{s_1 + K_s} \tag{1}$$

$\hat{\mu}$ = maximal growth rate
s_1 = substrate concentration in the aeration tank
K_s = positive constant

the experimentally observed non-linear decrease in the specific growth rate by decreasing substrate concentration can be essentially reproduced. The complete model is represented as follows:

$$\dot{s}_1 = \frac{F_I \cdot s_I}{V} + \frac{F_R \cdot s_R}{V} - \frac{F_I \cdot s_1}{V} - \frac{F_R \cdot s_1}{V} - \hat{\mu} \cdot \frac{s_1}{s_1 + K_s} \cdot x_1 \tag{2a}$$
$$+ k_d \cdot x_1$$

$$\dot{x}_1 = \frac{F_R \cdot x_R}{V} - \frac{F_I \cdot x_1}{V} - \frac{F_R \cdot x_1}{V} + \hat{\mu} Y \cdot \frac{s_1}{s_1 + K_s} \cdot x_1 - k_d \cdot x_1 \tag{2b}$$

x_1 = microorganism concentration in the aeration tank
x_R = microorganism concentration in the feedback stream
s_I = substrate concentration in the incoming waste water
s_R = substrate concentration in the feedback stream
F_I = hydraulic feed rate
F_R = flow rate of the feedback stream (controlled by the return sludge pump)

The new model differs from the similar model of Monod [3] in that it does not produce conflicting results for small values of the yield coefficient Y. The resulting improvement of the new model means that no numerical difficulties can occur in the calculation of the model parameters, in case the yield coefficient would momentarily approach zero during the identification process. The fact that this new model is capable of describing enzyme reactions (with Y=0) also shows that it has a wider range of application than the one of Monod.

LABORATORY MEASUREMENT

        The verification of the matematical model and the identification of the parameters were carried out on the basis of experimental data. Since values in the literature were unusable for several reasons, the data were obtained from experiments on a large laboratory sewage treatment unit (40 liter activated sludge tank, 30 liter settling tank). The biological variables (substrate and microorganism concentration) were determined with the aid of chemical oxygen demand (COD) [4] measurements. The COD measurement of filtered samples yielded the substrate concentration; the concentration of microorganisms was obtained indirectly by subtracting substrate concentration from the COD measurement of the unfiltered samples. The determination of COD, especially for an adaptive control, is not without disadvantages (lengthy (2 hr) measurement, measures both live and dead cells) however it is taken to be sufficient for this study.

IDENTIFICATION OF THE PARAMETERS IN THE MATHEMATICAL MODEL

The mathematically determined constants given in the literature have been obtained by "curve-fitting" methods using steady state
values of the state variables. Only Chiu et al. [5] have determined
the constants on the basis of good experimental data obtained from a
biological reactor which functions in a transient state. It was
attempted in this work to identify the biological constants on the
basis of experimental data which were characterised by relatively
strong fluctuations.

The identification of the parameters was carried out with a
Davidon algorithm, which is based on that of Fletcher+Powell [6]. An
important point of non-linear identification algorithms is their reliable convergence behavior. On the basis of the introduction of sensitivity coefficients in the performance index the convergence behavior of the Davidon algorithm could be considerably improved. The
performance index is represented as follows:

$$Z = \int_0^T \{s_s \cdot (s_1 - s_{1B})^2 + \lambda \cdot s_x \cdot (x_1 - x_{1B})^2\} \cdot dt \qquad (3)$$

s_{1B} = measured substrate concentration

x_{1B} = measured microorganism concentration

s_s, s_x = sensitivity coefficient

λ = weighting factor   (λ=0.01)

with

$$s_s = \left|\frac{\partial s_1}{\partial \hat{\mu}}\right| + \left|\frac{\partial s_1}{\partial Y}\right| + \left|\frac{\partial s_1}{\partial K_s}\right| + \left|\frac{\partial s_1}{\partial k_d}\right| \qquad (4a)$$

$$s_x = \left|\frac{\partial x_1}{\partial \hat{\mu}}\right| + \left|\frac{\partial x_1}{\partial Y}\right| + \left|\frac{\partial x_1}{\partial K_s}\right| + \left|\frac{\partial x_1}{\partial k_d}\right| \qquad (4b)$$

for the identification of the parameters $\hat{\mu}$, Y, K_s and k_d. If
less parameters are to be identified equations (4) are re-
duced by the corresponding terms.

Due to the strong fluctuations of the experimental data and
the apparent interdependency of the parameters, only 3 of the 4 parameters could be identified, in spite of the introduction of the sensitivity coefficients in the performance index. For this reason, an
unequivocable characterisation of the convergence behavior cannot be
made. However, it can be assumed that with better data, measured in
short time intervals, this difficulties could be overcome. In spite
of the somewhat poor experimental data, the convergence behavior of
the method was very good in the identification of 2 parameters ($\hat{\mu}$, Y:
5-7 iterations); for 3 parameters it was slower ($\hat{\mu}$, Y, k_d: 10-20 iterations) but still reliable. The parameter values obtained (for
K_s=50 mgO$_2$/l) in the identification of 3 constants lie in the following ranges for the various experimental series:

$$0.260 - 1.673 \ [h^{-1}] \ \text{for} \ \hat{U}$$
$$0.385 - 0.882 \ [-_{1}] \ \text{for} \ Y$$
$$0.034 - 0.879 \ [h^{-1}] \ \text{for} \ k_d$$

The values obtained for these constants are in good agreement with the values given by other authors.

OPTIMISATION

In contrast to other studies (for example [7]) where the main emphasis was on the optimal control of biological reactors with constant input variables, this work examined the optimum control of a treatment plant with transient input variables.

Having no adequately automated reactor at ones disposal, the control could only be simulated, whereby it was assumed that $s_R = s_1$ and x_R was constant at 4000 mgO_2/l (see model equations 2). By selecting the control variable (flow rate of the return sludge pump) and two alternative performance indices (equations 5 and 6), special consideration was given to realistic demands and technical realisation. In the first performance index

$$Z = \int_0^T (s_1{}^2 + a.F_R{}^2).dt \tag{5}$$

a = weighting factor

it is required that in spite of a very small flow rate of the pump (corresponding to low costs) as small a substrate concentration s_1 as possible in the outflow of the activated sludge tank should be accomplished (corresponding to best possible treatment of water). In the second performance index

$$Z = \int_0^T \{s_1{}^2 + a.F_R{}^2 + b.(x_1 - x_s)^2\}.dt \tag{6}$$

a, b = weighting factor
x_s = specific value of the microorganism concentration

the third requirement is placed on the system, that the microorganism concentration in the activated sludge tank should reach a specified value x_s.

Due to continuous changes in the input variables, as occur in practice, only a closed loop regulation of a sewage treatment unit can be considered. The optimisation problem was solved by the linearisation of the system about the operating point, followed by calculation of the control variable with the degenerated matrix Riccati equation for a short time interval. This optimisation method functions reliably, although large and sudden changes in the input substrate concentration s_I cannot be completely compensated. The gain from the optimisation, 5-10%, is not very high, nevertheless no definite conclusions concerning the gain due to optimisation could be made on the basis of these simulations.

One disadvantage of the chosen optimisation method is that restrictions in the control variable can only be allowed for after the optimisation. The flow rate of the pump is however restricted due to technical reasons to a range of $0 \leqslant F_R \leqslant F_{R_{max}}$. In order to find a criterium for the efficiency of the somewhat restricted closed loop control, the (quasilinearised) system was optimally controled with the help of the method of "convex feedback" [8] for <u>constant</u> input variables. This study has shown that the performance index of the optimally controlled system, in comparison to the regulated (closed loop) system, is 6-12% smaller when the control variable is restricted to a certain range.

CONCLUSIONS

The work has shown that an adaptive control of a sewage treatment plant is possible and leads to an improvement of the efficiency of such a plant. However, before a practical realisation is possible, the problem of the fast and automated determination of the biological variables must be solved. This can be obtained either through improvement of measuring equipment or through the estimation of biological variables through other parameters which are more readily determined. Only then can one reasonably examine the economic feasabiliy of an adaptively controlled plant.

REFERENCES

[1] T.B. Young, H.R. Bungay: Dynamic Analysis of a Microbial Process A Systems Engineering Approach, Biotechnol. Bioeng., <u>15</u>, 377 (1973)

[2] L. Michaelis, M.L. Menten: Die Kinetic der Invertinwirkung, Biochem. Z., <u>49</u>, 333 (1913)

[3] J. Monod: Recherches sur la croissance des cultures bactériennes, Hermann et Cie, Paris, 1942

[4] Standard Methods for the Examination of Water and Waste Water, 12th ed., American Public Health Association Inc., 1965

[5] S.Y. Chiu, L.T. Fan, I.C. Kao, L.E. Erickson: Kinetic Behavior of Mixed Populations of Activated Sludge, Biotechnol. Bioeng., <u>14</u>, 179 (1972)

[6] R. Fletcher, M.J.D. Powell: A Rapidly Convergent Descent Method for Minimization, Computer J., <u>6</u>, 163 (1963)

[7] G. D'Ans, P. Kokotović, D. Gottlieb: Time Optimal Control for a Model of Bacterial Growth, J. Optim. Theroy Applic., <u>7</u>, 61 (1971)

[8] H.A. Nour Eldin: Optimierung linearer Regelsysteme mit quadratischer Zielfunktion, Lecture Notes in Operations Research and Math. Systems, Springer Verlag, Berlin, 1971

DISCUSSION

You have not got an integral action in your control law so you will drift due to any error in the assumption of the model who will cause errors in the output between set point levels and so any drift in the system would not be handled. This is the common problem in optimum control when using his sort of cost. (YOUNG)

Modeling and Simulation of Water Resources Systems, G.C. VANSTEENKISTE, (Ed.)
North-Holland Publishing Company (1975)

THE IDENTIFICATION OF ALGAL POPULATION DYNAMICS IN A FRESHWATER STREAM

M.B. Beck [*]
Lund Institute of Technology, Division of Automatic Control
P.O. Box 725, Lund 7, SWEDEN

ABSTRACT

The results presented in this paper describe the application of Maximum
Likelihood (ML) parameter estimation to the analysis of dynamic models for
the prediction of biochemical oxygen demand (BOD) and dissolved oxygen (DO)
in a freshwater stream. Significantly, the characterisation of algal
population growth and decay is achieved through a combination of both
"black box" and so-called mechanistic modelling and identification
techniques. Thus, using arguments parallel to those for the description of
micro-organism cultures in activated-sludge and anaerobic digestion process
dynamics, a composite model for DO-BOD-algae interaction is postulated.
Sunlight conditions are taken to be the growth-rate limiting factor for
algae in a Monod-type function and it is required that component mass
balances be considered for living and dead populations; validation of the
dynamic model is inferred by the comparison of deterministic simulation
responses with observed DO and BOD data from the River Cam in England.

1. Introduction

The plentiful supply of nutrients for the growth of micro-organisms in a reach of
non-tidal river produces an aquatic environment in which so-called "blooms" of
algae can be readily precipitated under favourable conditions. In general nutrients
enter the stream in effluents or from agricultural land drainage and surface runoff. It has been observed that during periods of prolonged, dry, sunny weather
significant algal populations are established which not only increase the amplitude
of diurnal oscillations and mean daily levels of dissolved oxygen (DO) but also
increase the biochemical oxygen demand (BOD) in the river. Subsequently, with the
onset of dull, cloudy weather the DO falls rapidly to low values, partly due to the
cessation of photosynthetic production and partly a result of the oxygen demand
created by mass algal deaths. Ultimately, if it desired that the DO be maintained
at suitably high levels the presence of excess nutrients and the stimulation of
algal blooms constitute a control problem in water quality [6],[24].

The current discussion is an extension of studies on the identification and modelling of the dynamics of BOD-DO interaction [5]. The previous work included the
collection of field data over an 80-day period during the summer of 1972 from a
4.7km stretch of the River Cam in eastern England. An initial deterministic simulation led to the approximate validation of a dynamic model for DO and BOD with the
introduction of pseudo-empirical terms to account for the effects of algae [8];
this involved the discrete low-pass filtering of data on the hours of sunlight
incident on the system each day for the quantitative prediction of the algal population. However, considering the presence of random disturbances of the system and
hence errors of measurement a more complete statistical analysis of the model
using a continuous-discrete version of the extended Kalman filter (see e.g.
Jazwinski [16]) confirmed the preliminary identification of the model structure and
allowed a more precise estimation of the parameters [8].

In this paper two other methods of identification are applied to the field data
from the River Cam. The first is a black box maximum likelihood technique [2], for
which it is assumed that the prediction of BOD and DO at the downstream end (i.e.
output) of the reach of river are independent of each other and can be considered,

---

Visiting research fellow under the European Science Exchange Programme.

therefore, as two multiple input-single output systems. The time-series models obtained in this manner agree with the a priori knowledge of the system and further indicate important features in the DO and BOD data which had hitherto remained ill-defined; it is found that the effects of the sunlight conditions (and hence, indirectly, the algal population) on the DO and BOD are asynchronous. Thus, assuming complete knowledge of all other interactions between BOD and DO a maximum likelihood method applied to stochastic differential equations with discrete-time observations enables the exploitation of the black box identification results in order to derive a more complete physical picture of the disturbances caused by algae.

Now, while it is possible to extend the original pseudo-empirical expression, what is really required is a more fundamental growth and decay model for algae. Bearing in mind the type of mathematical description used by Chen [9] in ecological modelling and the dynamics of micro-organism species in the activated-sludge and anaerobic digestion processs (see e.g. Andrews [1]), a Monod function [17] is hypothesised for algal population growth in which the sunlight conditions are assumed to be the rate-limiting factor. Consequently, a combined DO-BOD-algae model is proposed, where the living and dead populations are described as separate state variables; except for the interaction of algae the DO-BOD model remains unaltered. Unfortunately, due to data restrictions[+] the algal model can only be verified in a largely qualitative manner through the observed disturbances of the DO and BOD levels. The parameters are accordingly not uniquely identifiable without such necessary observations and, moreover, in view of the nonlinearities deterministic simulation is of merit in a verification study for the time-being.

It is worth mentioning that the paper describes a study in which both physical reasoning and black box modelling are valid approaches to the mathematical representation of a system's dynamics. And if it is required that we define our objectives for the overall modelling procedure, let us state that the complexity and level of biochemical, biological detail included is a balance between that which satisfies theoretical completeness and that which can be adequately tested against field observations.

2. The a priori model for algal population dynamics

The starting point for the present analysis is the model identified using the extended Kalman filter which is given by the set of lumped-parameter differential-difference equations [8],

DO: $\dot{x}_1(t) = -(K_1+Q(t)/V)x_1(t)-K_2x_2(t)+(Q(t)/V)u_1(t)+K_1C_s(t)+K_3(I(t_k)-\bar{I})+D_B$ (i)

BOD: $\dot{x}_2(t) = -(K_2+Q(t)/V)x_2(t)+(Q(t)/V)u_2(t)+K_4(I(t_k)-\bar{I})+L_A$ (ii)

$$I(t_k) = I(t_{k-1})+\frac{1}{\tau}\left[u_3(t_k)(T(t_k)-\bar{T})/\bar{T}-I(t_{k-1})\right]$$ (iii)

$(I(t_k)-\bar{I}) = 0$ for $I(t_k)<\bar{I}$ (iv)

$\left.\begin{array}{c}\\\\\\\\\end{array}\right\}$ I

(the dot notation denotes differentiation with respect to time t (in days))
Here, x_1=concn. of DO at the downstream end (output) of the reach (mg/1)
$\quad\quad x_2$=concn. of BOD at the downstream end (output) of the reach (mg/1)
$\quad\quad u_1$=concn. of DO at the upstream end (input) of the reach (mg/1)
$\quad\quad u_2$=concn. of BOD at the upstream end (input) of the reach (mg/1)
$\quad\quad T$=river water temperature (°C)
$\quad\quad u_3(t_k)$=sunlight incident on the system during day t_k (hrs/day)

[+] i.e. the absence of observations on variables more directly related to the quantity of algae (e.g. chlorophyll-A, algal counts) and the absence of measurements of nitrogen- and phosphorus-bearing materials, which could also be growth-rate limiti‐

$I(t_k)=$"sustained sunlight effect" at day t_k [+]
$\bar{I}$ = a threshold level for the sunlight effect [+]
$\bar{T}$ = a mean river water temperature ($^\circ$C)
K_1= reaeration rate constant for DO (day^{-1})
K_2= BOD decay rate constant (day^{-1})
K_3= coefficient for the sunlight effect in the DO equation [+]
K_4= coefficient for the sunlight effect in the BOD equation [+]
Q = volumetric flow-rate in the reach (cuft/day)
V = mean volumetric hold-up in the reach (cuft)
C_s= saturation concentration of DO in the reach (mg/1)
τ = time constant of the discrete low-pass filter for the sunlight effect
D_B= rate of addition of DO to the reach by decomposition of bottom mud deposits ((mg/1)/day),i.e. typically $D_B<0$ as described by eqn I(i))
L_A= rate of addition of BOD to reach by local surface runoff ((mg/1)/day).
The model of eqn I applies to a reach of river as defined in figure 1.

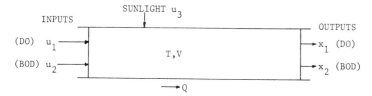

Figure 1   Schematic representation of a reach of river (all variables as
defined for eqn I)

The experimental field data from the River Cam and the derivation and identification of model I are presented in detail elsewhere [5],[8]; however, it is pertinent to discuss the features of the sustained sunlight effect and its interaction with the DO and BOD equations. Firstly, the low-pass filter mechanism of eqn I(iii), albeit a heuristic data manipulation, has a structure which would appear intuitively to agree with the true dynamics of an algal population. The time constant, τ, chosen to be 4 (days) in previous work, implies that a prolonged period of persistent sunny weather is necessary for a population to establish itself and produce observable disturbances of the DO and BOD; in other words, the choice of τ permits a certain degree of discrimination between the effects of isolated sunny days and sequences of consecutively bright days. However, low-pass filtering the sunlight data gives $I(t_k)>0$ for all t_k and thus the constraint of eqn I(iv) is introduced so that the effects of algae are only discernible in the DO and BOD when $I(t_k)$ is greater than an estimated threshold level $\bar{I}$.

The temperature coefficient $(T(t_k)-\bar{T})/\bar{T}$ in eqn I(iii) is included for completeness, since the deterministic simulation responses of model I, given in figure 2 and with the parameter values of table 1, are based on this version of the model. However, omission of such a coefficient has almost negligible effect on the responses over the "critical" periods $t_{36} \rightarrow t_{48}$ and from t_{60} onwards (approximately), where algal effects are significant.

Table 1 Parameter values for model I (from [8])					
K_1	0.17	K_4 0.32	V 5.4(10^6)		$\begin{cases} -2.7 \text{ for } 0 \leqslant t \leqslant t_{19} \\ -0.4 \text{ for } t > t_{19} \end{cases}$
K_2	0.32	$\bar{I}$ 6.0	τ 4	D_B	
K_3	0.31	$\bar{T}$ 8.0	L_A 0.0		

[+]No specific units are assigned to these quantities owing to the dimensional anomoly of eqn I(iii).

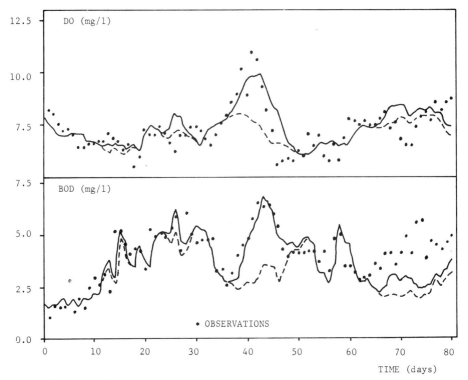

Figure 2   Simulation responses for model I; dashed line represents responses
           with no algal effects included.

Clearly, the sustained sunlight effect only describes those factors which were
observed in the DO and BOD data and it does not quantify explicitly the dynamics
of an algal population. Nevertheless, in addition to the River Cam experiment more
recent work with a seventy-day period of observations from the Bedford Ouse has
further validated this type of model for DO-BOD interaction [22],[23]. With more
data on other variables available in the latter study it has been possible to
improve the prediction of photosynthetic production of oxygen from algae by a
term which utilises measurements of the chlorophyll-A content in the river water.

The usefulness of such a pseudo-empirical relationship as eqn I(iii) is not in
doubt if the objective is to model only the DO-BOD dynamics of a reach of river.
Yet it would be more satisfying to clarify in mathematical terms the simplified
pictographic relationships between BOD,DO and algae in figure 3 and to have some
kind of quantitative view over the bloom conditions in an algal population. The
following, therefore, is an initial step in such a direction; the key to the
extended model is the observation that, unlike the single time constant τ of eqn
I(iii), the interaction of the sustained sunlight effect with the BOD and DO is
asynchronous.

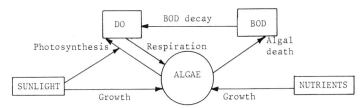

Figure 3   Some DO-BOD-algae inter-relationships

3. Model identification

The identification of a DO-BOD model has been tackled previously with the recursive scheme of the extended Kalman filter [8],[25]. Here the problem is approached with an off-line maximum likelihood technique applied to two different types of model for the system:

(i) if the system's fundamental mechanisms are unknown or too complex to be described in tractable mathematical form, a black box approach may be used, whereby no assumptions are made about the physical nature of the system's cause-effect relationships other than that the inputs should observably disturb the output;

(ii) alternatively, a mathematical model based on physico-chemical or biological principles is defined, and here the parameters involved will have strict physical interpretations related to the real system.

A detailed presentation of such techniques is beyond the scope of this paper; we merely indicate that good reviews of identification methods are given in [3],[13]. A more complete discussion of the statistical aspects and parameter estimation results of this particular application are presented in [7].

3.1. Black box modelling: the asynchronous disturbance of the DO and BOD dynamics by an algal population

The black box analysis of the BOD and DO data was executed on a PDP-15 computer using a suite of programs specifically designed for this type of maximum likelihood estimation [2],[14],[15]. Our primary concern is to identify the general time-dependency of the noisy observed outputs, DO and BOD, defined by figure 1 and

$$\text{DO: } y_1(t_k) = x_1(t_k) + e_1(t_k) \\ \text{BOD: } y_2(t_k) = x_2(t_k) + e_2(t_k) \Bigg\} \quad k=1,2,\ldots,N \qquad (1)$$

upon the input sunlight conditions u_3; e_1 and e_2 are, loosely speaking, random errors of measurement. Since we do not yet know precisely how u_3 acts so as to disturb the DO and BOD in a mechanistic sense, this part of the identification phase enables us to establish those causal relationships between the inputs and outputs which are statistically significant. In view of such limited objectives the necessary assumption that the DO and BOD dynamics can be decoupled is not particularly restrictive and each process can be considered independently as a multiple input-single output system[+].

Of course, a certain degree of caution should be exercised in drawing physical interpretations from black box models but in the current study it is just such that leads to the final form of the explicit description for algal population dynamics. Expressed as a functional relationship, it is found that

---

[+]Note that, quite apart from our present purposes, a model for DO prediction on this basis possesses desirable characteristics for control application since it is not dependent upon the inconvenience of measuring BOD (see [24]).

$$DO: \quad y_1(t_k) = f_1\left\{y_1(t_{k-1}), u_1(t_{k-1}), u_3(t_k), u_3(t_{k-1})\right\}$$

$$BOD: \quad y_2(t_k) = f_2\left\{y_2(t_{k-1}), u_2(t_{k-1}), u_3(t_{k-2}), u_3(t_{k-4})\right\} \tag{2}$$

and we can deduce that the dependence of DO and BOD on the sunlight input, u_3, is asynchronous and not simultaneous as implicitly assumed by model I. In other words it appears that the production of DO in the reach at time t_k is a function of the incident sunlight during that day and the previous day (t_{k-1}); in contrast, a BOD production results from longer delayed effects of approximately 2 to 4 days behind the current time. Clearly, these interpretations agree with the observed dynamics of the field data shown in figure 4.

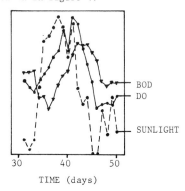

TIME (days)

Figure 4   Observed data during the period of significant algal growth

3.2.   State space model parameter estimation: an extension of the pseudo-empirical relationships of model I

The black box modelling results provide us with a good basis for re-examination of a state space model for DO-BOD interaction with algal disturbances. This section discusses an extension of the pseudo-empirical sustained sunlight effect of the a priori model, eqn I, such that the asynchronous responses of DO and BOD to an algal population can be identified and their dynamics quantified.

For the maximum likelihood scheme used here (see [4],[11]) a linear, continuous-time model is preferable and the discrete low-pass filter mechanism of eqn I(iii) should be represented in the equivalent form, say,

$$\frac{dI(t)}{dt} = (-1/\tau_1)I(t) + (g_1/\tau_1)u_3(t) \tag{3}$$

where τ_1 is a time constant (in days) and g_1 is a gain coefficient. Additionally, from the observed dynamics of figure 4 it seems reasonable to suggest that while DO is related to $I(t)$, the BOD could be dependent upon the output $I'(t)$ of a second filter "in series" with eqn (3), i.e.

$$\frac{dI'(t)}{dt} = (-1/\tau_2)I'(t) + (1/\tau_2)I(t) \tag{4}$$

in which τ_2 is a time constant (in days). Thus, defining two further state variables,

$$x_3(t) = I(t) \; ; \; x_4(t) = I'(t)$$

it is possible to represent DO-BOD interaction as the following set of differential equations (from eqns I(i),I(ii),(3) and (4)):

$$\dot{x}_1(t) = -(K_1+Q(t)/V)x_1(t)-K_2x_2(t)+K_3(x_3(t)-\bar{I}_D)+(Q(t)/V)u_1(t)$$
$$+K_1C_s(t)+D_B \qquad \text{(i)}$$

$$\dot{x}_2(t) = -(K_2+Q(t)/V)x_2(t)+K_4(x_4(t)-\bar{I}_B)+(Q(t)/V)u_2(t)+L_A \qquad \text{(ii)}$$

$$\dot{x}_3(t) = -(1/\tau_1)x_3(t)+(g_1/\tau_1)u_3(t) \qquad \text{(iii)}$$

$$\dot{x}_4(t) = -(1/\tau_2)x_4(t)+(1/\tau_2)x_3(t) \qquad \text{(iv)}$$

II

Here $\bar{I}_D$ and $\bar{I}_B$ are threshold levels[+] referring to the individual effects of x_3 on the DO and x_4 on the BOD, respectively.

The formulation of the estimation problem is partly a function of necessity and partly a matter of intention; it is not possible to estimate some of the coeff- icients of eqn II in an off-line scheme since they are time-varying, but, on the other hand, it is reasonable to assume that the DO and BOD dynamics are well- known apart from their relationships with the algal effects. Hence, the objective of the identification is to estimate the dynamic components τ_1 and τ_2 and allow the "gains" $g_1, K_3,$ and K_4 to adjust so that the system responses are consistent with the observations given by eqn (1).

Accordingly, assuming the values for the parameters of table 1, with $\bar{I}_D=\bar{I}_B=\bar{I}$ for simplicity, we obtain the estimates

$$\tau_1=1.95(\text{days}) \text{ and } \tau_2=1.42(\text{days}),$$

which give the deterministic simulation responses of figure 5. These results tend to confirm the inferences drawn from the black box model identification and it is also possible to observe that the shape of the predicted peaking effect in the DO between t_{35} and t_{46} is an improvement on that shown in figure 2 for the a priori model.

4. A model for algal population dynamics

The final step in the synthesis of a combined DO-BOD-algae model is the trans- lation of the structure of eqn II into a more meaningful physical terminology. Essentially, parts of the state space model identified in the previous section still have a pseudo-empirical appearance; but what is important is that the dynamical features of the model agree well with the experimental observations of the real system. The task, therefore, is to retain the structure of the model and hypothesise variables and parameters which are plausible descriptions of the manner in which an algal population might interact with the DO and BOD concentr- ations of a reach of river.

Firstly, in general it can be stated that photosynthetic production of DO is dependent upon living algae, while dead algae in due course exert a BOD. Bearing this in mind, inspection of eqn II shows that the pseudo-empirical variables x_3 and x_4 operate similarly in the description of DO-BOD interaction; indeed, we shall make the following redefinitions,

x_3 = concentration of living algae at the output of the reach (in mg/l say)
x_4 = concentration of dead algae at the output of the reach (in mg/l say).
Thus, it is required that a mathematical representation be postulated for the growth and decay of algae, together with terms accounting for photosynthetic/ respiratory activity and subsequent production of a BOD. Many of the ideas behind the model originate in parallel modelling and control problems in waste-water treatment (see e.g. Olsson et al [18]) and reference will be made to such material in support of the argument.

[+]Note that no nonlinear constraint of the form eqn I(iv) can be suitably accomod- ated in the structure of the linear model given by eqn II.

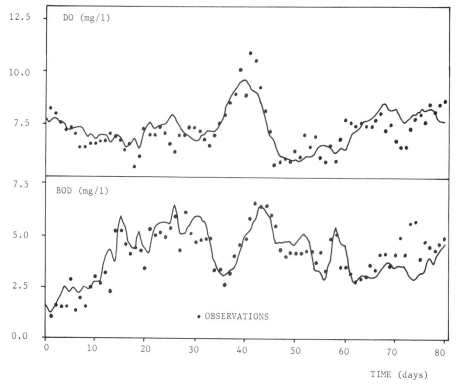

TIME (days)

Figure 5   Simulation responses for model II

The growth of algae in a river can be likened to the continuous culture of auto-trophic micro-organism species in the activated-sludge and anaerobic digestion processes (see e.g. Curds [10], Andrews [1]). In fact, the well-known Monod [17] development of the Michaelis-Menten equation for enzyme-substrate interaction has already been used for the study of algal growth kinetics [9],[20]. However, for the purposes of the present model the Monod function is employed in a slightly different manner so that, together with a specific decay rate for the algae [1], [19], the following is proposed:

Net production rate of living algae, x_3 (in (mg/l)/day)

$$= \hat{\mu} \left[\frac{u_3(t)}{K_s + u_3(t)} \right] - K_D x_3(t) \qquad (5)$$

where $\hat{\mu}$ is the maximum specific growth rate of algae ((mg/l)/day), K_s is a satur-ation coefficient for the limiting nutrient u_3 (hrs sunlight/day) and K_D is the specific decay rate constant for algae (in days^{-1}). The important features of the above expression are that sunlight is taken to be the rate-limiting "nutrient" or substrate[+] and, since the growth rate is independent of x_3, it is implied that algae are not autotrophic organisms. It is not intended that biological theory be

---

[+]The field data would suggest that this is so and, in any case, no observations are available for other possible rate-limiting nutrients such as nitrate, phosphate or carbon dioxide etc.

contradicted, but for a mathematical description the following two mitigating circumstances should be considered. Firstly, preliminary simulation showed that if the specific growth rate is assumed to be dependent on x_3 the dynamics of an algal population do not correspond at all with their observed interaction with the DO and BOD. Secondly, in view of the fact that the river is a flowing system it seems unreasonable to propose that the output concentration of algae is a factor governing the growth rate of algae in the reach. Suffice it to say that with the convenient lumped-parameter structure [5] of the overall model it is not possible to transfer directly all the characteristics of micro-organism culture in waste-water treatment to the prediction of algal growth in a river.

In some studies of activated-sludge and anaerobic digestion units the significance of dead organisms is assumed to be negligible. Nevertheless, for the algal population under consideration here the omission of a separate dynamic description of dead algae seems to be inadmissible if the observed BOD variations are to be simulated correctly. Thus, making deductions from the parallel investigations of Westberg and co-workers [12],[21] the following is postulated:

Net production rate of dead algae, x_4 (in (mg/l)/day)

$$= K_D x_3(t) - K_R x_4(t) - R_s \qquad (6)$$

in which K_R is a rate constant for the redissolution of dead algae (day^{-1}), and R_s is the rate of sedimentation of undissolved dead algal material ((mg/l)/day). In fact Westberg proposes more complex expressions for the decay rate of organisms in (5) and (6) and for the redissolution of dead material in (6), which strictly speaking may not be applicable here. The reasons for the inclusion of R_s are perhaps tenuous, but the model fitted the data better in this form and there is evidence that such a process could be of significance in the real system [9],[20].

Having defined eqns (5) and (6) we are now in a position to make component mass balances across the reach of river (see figure 1) in order to derive the differential equations for x_3 and x_4. Adjoining these equations to those for the DO and BOD and proposing new terms for the interaction of x_3 and x_4 with the state variables x_1 and x_2, we obtain,

$$\dot{x}_1 = -(K_1 + Q(t)/V)x_1 - K_2 x_2 + \gamma_1 x_3 (u_3)^s - \gamma_2 x_3 + (Q(t)/V)u_1 + K_1 C_s(t) + D_B \qquad \text{(i)}$$

$$\dot{x}_2 = -(K_2 + Q(t)/V)x_2 + \gamma_3 K_R x_4 + (Q(t)/V)u_2 + L_A \qquad \text{(ii)}$$

$$\dot{x}_3 = -(K_D + Q(t)/V)x_3 + \hat{\mu}\left[\frac{u_3(t-T_d)}{(K_s + u_3(t-T_d))}\right] \qquad \text{(iii)}$$

$$\dot{x}_4 = -(K_R + Q(t)/V)x_4 + \gamma_4 K_D x_3 - R_s \qquad \text{(iv)}$$

III

where s is the exponential power for the dependence of algal photosynthetic production of oxygen on sunlight conditions, $T_d = (t_k - t_{k-1})$ is a pure time delay of one day (i.e. the sampling interval of the data)[dagger], and $\gamma_i, i=1,2,3,4$, are proportionality constants so that the model can be fitted to the data. All other variables are as previously defined and the argument t has been omitted from the inputs u and the state variables x for notational convenience; no living or dead algae are assumed to be present in the material influx across the upstream boundary of the experimental reach of river.

Remarkably enough, the model of eqn III contains all the features of the system which have hitherto been identified:

[dagger]This small data manipulation allows more accurate prediction of the DO conditions over the observational period $t_{35} \to t_{46}$; indeed, such delayed effects could be due to the presence of a stored mass of algal population.

(i) Eqn III(i) shows that the photosynthetic production of oxygen at time t is dependent upon the living algae and the sunlight conditions at time t (c.f. section 3.1); also respiration occurs at a rate proportional to the concentration of living algae.

(ii) Eqn III(ii) expresses the concept that a BOD is exerted by dead algal material which has redissolved; note that our implicit definition of BOD refers to soluble substances and is therefore not related to particulate matter which has been sedimented (e.g. R_s in eqn III(iv)).

(iii) And, finally, if $Q(t)/V$ is taken to be the dominant factor in the dynamics of x_3 and x_4, it turns out that the associated time constants when algal effects are significant are approximately 1.5(days) (c.f. τ_1 and τ_2 in section 3.2); thus, it has been possible to retain the important dynamical structure of the pseudo-empirical model given by eqn II.

Unfortunately, with such a nonlinear model it is only possible to make a verification by comparison of the deterministic simulation responses of x_1 and x_2 with the DO and BOD field data. The eventual quantification of the many additional parameter values in table 2 is not unique, but the model responses shown in figure 6 are very satisfactory; all other relevant parameter values are as previously given.

Table 2 Estimated parameter values for eqn III				
K_D 0.35	$\hat{\mu}$ 2.1	R_s -0.11	γ_1 1.45	γ_3 16.0
K_R 0.25	K_s 20.0	s 0.55	γ_2 2.0	γ_4 3.0

Perhaps the significant feature of the final model is the more adequate prediction it gives over $t_{60} \rightarrow t_{80}$, whose effects the a priori model, eqn I, does not describe at all well; this suggests that the disturbances caused by algae are sensitive to the low flow-rate through the reach of river during this period.

5. Summary and conclusions

A dynamic model for the characterisation of DO-BOD-algae interaction in a freshwater stream has been synthesised and verified against field data on the DO and BOD. The structure of the model depends essentially on the separation of algal dynamics into the consideration of both a live and a dead population; it is evident that the effects of the algal population are sensitive to the flow-rate and residence time conditions in the reach.

The biochemical and biological principles governing the growth and decay of microorganisms are complex and the proposals of this paper are doubtless a considerable simplification of the true dynamics. The model is developed from a combination of heuristic reasoning, a cross-breeding of ideas from studies on the modelling of waste-water treatment processes, and systematic identification of empirical observations. Indeed, the value of real data and the treatment of such with several different methods of identification cannot be emphasised too strongly. But the results remain tentative solutions to the problem in the sense that we have been forced to hypothesise a model for living and dead algae in the absence of any observations relating directly to such quantities. In particular, the manner in which decomposing algal material exerts a BOD remains unclear and it is quite possible that the BOD test itself could obscure the identification of this process.

Naturally, the model presented here could be criticised as a control engineer's view of ecology and biology; nevertheless, it seems to be a step in the right direction. If nothing else it may stimulate a contraction of the lamentable gap in communications between biologists and control engineers.

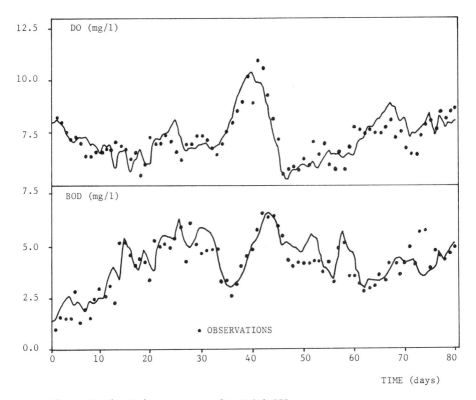

Figure 6   Simulation responses for Model III

References

1. ANDREWS J.F.,"Kinetics of biological processes used for wastewater treatment", Workshop on Research Problems in Air and Water Pollution, University of Colorado, Boulder, Colorado, Aug 1970.
2. ÅSTRÖM K.J. and BOHLIN T.,"Numerical identification of linear dynamic systems from normal operating records",Proc. IFAC Symposium on the Theory of Self-Adaptive Control Systems,Teddington,England, 1965.
3. ÅSTRÖM K.J. and EYKHOFF P.,"System identification-A survey", Automatica,Vol.7, No.2, Mar 1971.
4. ÅSTRÖM K.J. and KÄLLSTRÖM C.G.,"Application of system identification techniques to the determination of ship dynamics", Proc.IFAC Symp. on Identification and System Parameter Estimation, The Hague, The Netherlands, Jun 1973.
5. BECK M.B., Ph.D. thesis, Engineering Dept., University of Cambridge, Dec 1973.
6. BECK M.B.,"Water quality maintenance and control theory", Lund Inst. of Techn., Divn. of Automatic Control, Sweden, Feb 1974.
7. BECK M.B., in preparation.
8. BECK M.B. and YOUNG P.C., in preparation.
9. CHEN C.W.,"Concepts and utilities of ecologic model", Proc. ASCE, J.Sanit.Eng. Div.,Vol.96,No.SA5, Oct 1970.
10.CURDS C.R.,"A theoretical study of factors influencing the microbial population dynamics of the activated-sludge process-I", Water Research, Vol.7,pp.1269-1284, 1973.

11. EKLUND K. and GUSTAVSSON I.,"Identification of drum boiler dynamics", Proc.IFAC Symp. on Identification and System Parameter Estimation, The Hague, The Netherlands, Jun 1973.
12. ERICSSON B. GUSTAFSSON B. and WESTBERG N.,"En studie av aktivslamprocessens kinetik-III", Vatten, pp.146-153,(in Swedish),1969.
13. EYKHOFF P.,"System Identification-Parameter and State Estimation", John Wiley and Sons, London, 1974.
14. GUSTAVSSON I.,"Parametric identification of multiple input, single output linear dynamic systems", Lund Inst. of Techn.,Divn. of Automatic Control, Sweden, 1969.
15. GUSTAVSSON I.,SELANDER S. and WIESLANDER J.,"IDPAC-User's guide", Lund Inst. of Techn., Divn. of Automatic Control, Sweden, 1973.
16. JAZWINSKI A.H.,"Stochastic Processes and Filtering Theory", Academic Press, New York, 1970.
17. MONOD J.,"Recherces sur la croissances des cultures bacteriennes", Hermann et Cie, Paris, 1942.
18. OLSSON G.,DAHLQVIST K.I.,EKLUND K. and ULMGREN L.,"Control problems in waste-water treatment", Technical report, The Axel Johnson Institute for Industrial Research, Nynäshamn, Sweden, 1973.
19. OTT C.R. and BOGAN R.H.,"Theoretical analysis of activated-sludge dynamics", Proc. ASCE, J.Sanit.Eng.Div.,Vol.97,No.SA1, Feb 1971.
20. RICH L.G.,ANDREWS J.F. and KEINATH T.M.,"Diurnal pH patterns as predictors of carbon limitation in algal growth", Water and Sewage Works, pp.126-130, May 1972.
21. WESTBERG N.,"A study of the activated-sludge process as a bacterial growth process", Water Research, Vol.1,pp.795-804, 1967.
22. WHITEHEAD P.G. and YOUNG P.C.,"A dynamic stochastic model for water quality in part of the Bedford-Ouse river system", Proc. IFIP Working Conference on Modelling and Simulation of Water Resources Systems, Ghent, 1974.
23. YOUNG P.C. and WHITEHEAD P.G.,"A recursive approach to time-series analysis for multivariable systems", Proc. IFIP Working Conference on Modelling and Simulation of Water Resources Systems, Ghent, 1974.
24. YOUNG P.C. and BECK M.B.,"The modelling and control of water quality in a river system", Automatica (in press, to appear Sep 1974).
25. YOUNG P.C.,"A recursive approach to time-series analysis", Bull.Inst. of Math. and its Appl.(IMA), Vol.10, Nos.5/6,pp.209-224, 1974.

DISCUSSION

I don't remember many instances of sampled data of sunlight on the Cam. You think this might be worthwhile trying to model sunshine in that area ? I am wondering if a laboratory experiment on algae is worth doing. (SHAH)

With a laboratory experiment you always have the situation that it is not in situ which is the river itself. You change the whole environment by taking it away from the river back into the laboratory. (BECK)

When you express the sunshine what are you doing ? (VAN KEULEN)

It is just so many hours of sunshine per day, just very crude measurements. I did not have any measurements, on light intensity. (BECK)

For me that's the first reason why you have discrepancies because the light intensity is the first strong nonlinear function. So light intensity would be much better than sunshine hours. Secondly, in Wageningen, there has been done quite some work on fotosynthesis and respiration of algae partly on the biochemical level. So if you are interested in the biology of algae, this would be worthwhile looking at. Also the discrepancies when after a sudden growth of the algae, you get increased respiration, because the algae consists mainly of very young material and the respiration rate of young algae is of course much higher than of the older ones, which don't have such quick turnover of proteïnes, etc. (VAN KEULEN)

I thought with such little amount of data, we are going in such complexity and say this is what's happening. (BECK)

I agree, but what I would propose in such a situation is that again you try to establish some kind of cooperation. You don't have to use the exact algae growth model in a model which predicts BOD in a big river. But you can lay the model on a biochemical level of algae growth and from there on get an output as an input for a model of BOD production where you can have light intensity or the respiration rate as a function of the amount of algae. (VAN KEULEN)

In Sweden we did have some contacts with biological people. (BECK)

There has been quite a lot of work done in Japan that would be of interest to you, there was a symposium in 1966 on the dynamics of microbial cultures. There was a second one in last spring in Minneapolis. They are beginning to work pretty actively in this area. (ANDREWS)

And did you have very great experience to try to translate this information yourself into dynamic models. (BECK)

One thing that might break the time lag that you exhibited might be something on the beginning of the sequence of growth instead of the end. You have death. You can also have storage of mass which makes your differential equations not simultaneous in a sense. This so called structurized model was first used in the biochemical engineering field by Frederickson and Tuchi in Minnesota. You have two terms you have structured the so called mass into dead mass and life mass. You need a third mass a stored mass. That comes out, in actuating such analysis but earlier came out in the microbiological literature and biochemical engineering literature. (ANDREWS)

It seems to me that this is a good example again of what we have been talking about previously in the week. You see, you start up with a model and you increase the sophistication and it's the function of the model which is important, for instance it is unlikely that you will need to go to depth that Bruce Beck was talking about if you want this model for control purposes. (YOUNG)

Have you tried to model or notice any correlation in the residual between your observations and your model.

In the last model not yet. (BECK)

Is there any immediate prospect of using the model if derived on a very short basis on a longer list of records to get more confidence to see if it would apply for a longer period.

I want to rely an Whitehead's study. He has more data on his type of river. (BECK)

You feel a bit uncomfortable with half a dozen coefficients based on 18 points. (NEUMAN)

Exactly. All that I am saying is that this could possibly happen, that it reasonably fits the data ; can you try to say whether the biochemistry of the system is reasonable ?   (BECK)

Is it plausible, and so.   (NEUMAN)

Yes, it can be discussed.   (BECK)

*Should a hungry man refuse dinner just because he just does not fully under-
stand the process of digestion. Another thing, cloud cover is something that is recorded by weather statement. Cloud cover might be a very important parameter. We
found it very successfull in predicting water temperature. Fotosynthesis even goes
on at moonlight ! You don't have to have sun to have fotosynthesis !   (DAVIDSON)*

Modeling and Simulation of Water Resources Systems, G.C. VANSTEENKISTE, (Ed.)
North-Holland Publishing Company (1975)

DESCRIPTION OF AN INTENDED PROJECT ON WATER QUALITY ESTIMATION

J. Wetzel
Swiss Federal Institute for Water Resources
and Water Pollution Control (EAWAG)
at the Federal Institute of Technology (ETH)
Duebendorf, Switzerland

ABSTRACT

The definition of a user dependent water quality function
is proposed. To evaluate this function, water quality
parameters must be known, which cannot be measured on-line.
To overcome this difficulty, a model of the polluted river
is established and estimation techniques will be applied
to calculate approximate values for the unknown parameters.
Finally a short description of the layout of practical
experiments is given.

STATEMENT OF THE PROBLEM

River water is used in many processes as a rawmaterial. Cities
treat it to have drinking water, industries may use it for cooling
or agriculture needs it for irrigation, to cite but a few examples.
Every one of these water consumers has to set certain standards,
concerning the properties of the water to be used. If the river
water meets these standards at a specific time, he can accept it,
if it does not, he cannot use it anymore. Therefore we propose
the following definition of a water quality function:

$$(1) \quad Q(p) = \begin{cases} \text{acceptable} \Leftrightarrow p \in P_a \\ \\ \text{non-acceptable} \Leftrightarrow p \notin P_a \end{cases}$$

$$P_a = \left\{ p_i \mid p_i \text{ within standards} \right\}$$

where
Q : Water Quality Function
p : State of the Water (Vector of all water
parameters, that are important for a
specific user), time dependent
P_a : Set of all states, that meet the user's
standards.

This water quality function is a time dependent logical function.
It depends on the actual values of the water quality parameters,
which form a vector p. This vector may be called the actual state
of the water. The elements of this vector are time dependent too.
If this vector is element of the set of all states that are
acceptable for a specific user, the water quality function is
given the value "acceptable".

To give a simple example, we may consider a river water treatment
plant. To run the plant efficiently, the river water has to meet
specifications with respect to
       - dissolved organic carbon, DOC
       - suspended biomass, SB.

These two parameters form the vector of the state of the water.
The concentration of DOC and SB must not exceed certain values
(standards), which are given by the layout of the plant and the
properties of the water filters and other installations.

For this case P_a would be the set of all vectors with elements
smaller then the specified standards. Hence the water quality
function assumes the value "acceptable", when both the actual DOC
and SB are less then the given standards, else the value is set
to "non-acceptable".

To determine the value of the water quality function, we need
to know at every time the actual values of the water quality
parameters (DOC and SB). The continuous measurement of these
parameters is not yet well established. It is our thesis, that
with a suitable estimation algorithm, reliable estimates of their
actual value can be derived from continuous measurements of other
parameters.

ESTIMATION OF DOC AND SB

On-line measurements of DOC and SB are not available, for the
determination of these parameters is tedious and needs a considerable amount of time. The resulting time lag prevents immediate
control measures to be taken.

However there are several parameters, which can be measured continuously and without a significant time delay. Such parameters are:

       - dissolved oxygen, for which reliable electrodes exist,

       - water temperature,

       - light intensity,

       - meteorological data.

These parameters either form part of the physical system (diss.
oxygen, temperature) or are driving forces to it (light int.,
meteorol. data).

A system of partial differential equations may be written to describe the concentration of d_ssolved oxygen in river water. To formulate the equations, the following processes must be considered:

- aeration and deaeration from and to the athmosphere,

- oxygen production by photosynthetic microorganisms,

- oxygen consumption by microbial respiration, which is dependent on the size and composition of the microbial population and in many cases on the supply of DOC (organic substrate) in the river.

These relations are expressed by partial differential equations of the following form:

$$(2a) \qquad \frac{\partial c_O}{\partial t} = -u \frac{\partial c_O}{\partial x} \quad + \quad \sum S_O(x,t)$$

$$(2b) \qquad \frac{\partial c_D}{\partial t} = -u \frac{\partial c_D}{\partial x} \quad + \quad \sum S_D(x,t)$$

where
c_O : Concentration of dissolved oxygen

c_D : Concentration of dissolved organic carbon

u : Flow velocity of the river

S_O : Sources and Sinks of dissolved oxygen

S_D : Sources and Sinks of DOC

O'Connor [1] describes this sort of equation, which is used in various other papers (Koivo,Koivo [2], Koivo,Phillips [3],[4]).

The terms $S_O(x,t)$ and $S_D(x,t)$ are short notations of several functions. Each function describes one specific process, e.g. photosynthesis, microbial respiration, reaeration among others. These source-sink terms interconnect equations (2a) and (2b).

The task to be solved in this project is, to develop suitable estimation algorithms for the unknown part of this system. There is one unknown state variable, the dissolved oxygen concentration c_D, and several unknown parameters, e.g. photosynthetic activity and other coefficients. Modern estimation techniques (deterministic or stochastic) can be adapted to partial differential equations (cf. Eykhoff [5]). The decision, wether stochastic methods have to be used, will be made after a close examination of the errors involved in the measurements.

The estimates are used to form the vector p, which is needed to
determine the value of the water quality function Q(p).
(See equation (1)).

DATA COLLECTION

To test the models and estimation algorithms, data will be used,
which are collected on an artificial shallow channel. This channel
is fed with subsoil water. Oxygen content and water temperature
are continuously recorded at distances of 5m, 60m and 90m from
the start of the channel. Furthermore flow velocity and light
intensity are recorded. In addition samples of the dissolved
organic carbon are taken at certain intervals.

On occasions DOC is added in the form of sewage or some defined
organic substance.

REFERENCES

[1] Donald O'Connor: The temporal and Spatial Distribution of
     Dissolved Oxygen in Rivers, Water Resources Research, Vol.3,
     No.1 (1967), S. 65-79.

[2] H.N. Koivo, A.J. Koivo: Optimal Estimation of Polluted Stream
     Variables, 3rd IFAC Symposium on Identification and System
     Parameter Estimation 1973, North-Holland/American Elsevier.

[3] A.J. Koivo, G.R. Phillips: Identification of Mathematical
     Models for DO and BOD Concentrations in Polluted Streams
     from Nois Corrupted Measurements, Water Resources Research,
     Vol.7, No.4,(1971), S.853-862.

[4] A.J. Koivo, G.R. Phillips: On Determination of BOD and Para-
     meters in Polluted Stream Models from DO Measurements Only,
     Water Resources Research, Vol.8, No.2,(1972), S.478-486.

[5] P. Eykhoff: System Identification, Wiley 1973.

Current research field of author : *Systemsanalysis in the field of water resources,
namely : Estimation of water quality parameters.*

DISCUSSION

You attempt to measure the dissolved organic carbon. (BIGGAR)

We take samples of this and analyse it in the laboratory just to compare the response of the model against these DOC values in the real channel. (WETZEL)

Would it be difficult to determine the total energy in the carbon ? (BIGGAR)

Yes, we must determine the amount of substrate for the living biomass in the channel. (WETZEL)

You mentioned in the beginning that you were looking at the acceptable or non acceptable relationship. Have you found people who are prepared to give a yes/ no answer ? That's a problem for system-analysts as decision makers to decide what you really want.

Not yet, we think on simpler models. (WETZEL)

I would be very interested to have comment from some experts of the audience. Even if you succeeded in getting out what you wish in this experimental way, what real impact would it have on actual field data. (BALAKRISHNAN)

I am not the expert yet. (WETZEL)

On the expert of data collection have you thought as to the accuracy of data, say in oxygenmeters. (SHAH)

No, not yet. The manufacturers of the meters state that the measures are within 5 %. (WETZEL)

The experimental channels observed have been there for perhaps 15 years or so, and have been used for many other purposes. (ANDREWS)

Certain standards have already been set up not necessarily based on what people would accept but based on what certain experts think are required. They are studying standards for all the rivers, therefore discharges will be based on what discharges will do to a changing of quality of the rivers, in the negative way. (BIGGAR)

Are these absolute standards ? (YOUNG)

It's under a lot of heated discussion. (BIGGAR)

We have two kind of standards : string standards and effort standards. The latter specific concentrations or mass loading rates in industrial plants or municipal plants. (ANDREWS)

Modeling and Simulation of Water Resources Systems, G.C. VANSTEENKISTE, (Ed.)
North-Holland Publishing Company (1975)

SIMULATION OF BIOMASS PRODUCTION BY CHORELLA PYRENOIDASA AND NITROGEN AND PHOSPHORUS DEPLETION IN A CARBON LIMITING MEDIUM

J.W. Biggar and Ming C. Yaug
Department of Water Sciences and Engineering
University of California, Davis, U.S.A.

INTRODUCTION

Assimilation of carbon, nitrogen and phosphorus by algae continues to be an area of great interest, especially because it relates to environmental problems. While mathematical models of these phenomena in the complex environment are sought by several investigations, the present paper describes an attempt to model the growth of Chorella pyrenoidasa in a carbon limiting medium in laboratory chemostats.

It has been found in the experimental phase of work repeated here and to be published by the authors in more detail elsewhere, that a simple relationship exists between the total inorganic carbon in the ambient medium of the algae and the algal cell carbon. It must be understood that the only source of carbon is that supplied through aeration of the medium.

The following equation is which C_T is the total inorganic carbon and (AC) the algal cell carbon was found to hold for algal biomass grown in carbon limiting medium both for batch and continuous medium flow chemostat studies when the aeration rates ranged between 51.0 $\pm$ .05 and 0.0 liters per hour.

$$C_T = (4.0 \pm 0.5) + (0.10 \pm .04)\ (AC) \tag{1}$$

Fig. 1 shows a plot of several experiments conducted to establish this relationship where the line was determined by regression analysis.

FREE CO_2 POOL

The experiments of Osterlind (1949, 1950a, 1951a) demonstrated that Chorella was capable of utilizing only free CO_2 in its environment. It therefore seemed evident that the algal biomass production could be simulated if the free CO_2 pool could be calculated and other growth functions taken into account.

To calculate the free CO_2 it is necessary to know the pH of the ambient medium. A model to simulate the pH change of the algal culture is in the initial stages of development so that for purpose of simulation in this paper the pH data of several cultures of both batch and continuous medium flow experiments were utilized in the model instead. The relation between pH and time is presented in fig. 2 for six rates of aeration. Curve six is a culture in which the aeration rate was 51 liters per hour and curve one for a culture in which there was no aeration. The other curves are for intermediate rates. Data corresponding to the time intervals of the simulation model were obtained from the curves and utilized in the computer program.

These same pH data were utilized in conjunction with basic carbonate equilibrium equations as follows to calculate the free CO_2 pool from which the algae

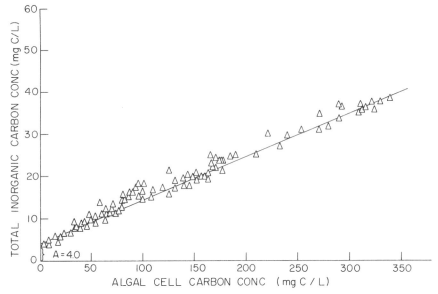

Fig.1 - Total inorganic carbon accumulation as a function of algal cell organic
carbon for both batch and continuous medium flow growth experiments.

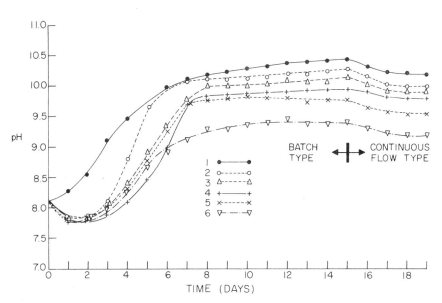

Fig.2 - The pH patterns in culture chambers under different aeration rates.
Aeration rates in liters.hr⁻¹ were as follows; 1 - no aeration, chamber E;
2 - 3.3 ; 3 - 5.5 chamber C ; 4 - 12.4 ; 6 - 51 chamber A.

obtained their carbon. (Park 1965, 1969 ; Stumm and Margan 1970)

$$[H_2CO_3]^* = \frac{[H^+]^2}{[H^+]^2 + [H^+] K_1' + K_1' K_2'} \cdot C_T \tag{2}$$

$$[H_2CO_3]^* = [CO_2]_{ag} + H_2CO_3 \tag{3}$$

$$[HCO_3^-] = \frac{[H^+] K_1'}{[H^+]^2 + [H^+] K_1' + K_1' + K_2'} \cdot C_T \tag{4}$$

$$[CO_3^=] = \frac{K_1' K_2'}{[H^+]^2 + [H^+] K_1' + K_1' K_2'} \cdot C_T \tag{5}$$

where C_T is the total inorganic carbon and K_1', K_2' are the first and second apparent dissociation constants of carbonic acid, respectively.

BIOMASS PRODUCTION

For simulation purposes each culture chamber was considered a "single stage stirred reaction". The equation describing the change in biomass for such a system may be assumed as follows.

$$\frac{dN}{dt} = \gamma N - SN - \frac{F}{V} N \tag{6}$$

N is the algal cell concentration (mg. liters^{-1}), V the volume of the culture, (liters), F the flow rate of the medium, (ml.hr^{-1}), S the rate constant for algal respiration and excretion (day^{-1}) and γ the specific growth rate constant (day^{-1}). For batch type cultures, where F = 0, the third term on the rhs of equation six is zero.

The rate constant S was estimated in the present investigations for steady state growth conditions by measuring the dissolved organic carbon which is presumed to result from the end products of algal respiration and excretion. Reported respiration rates are of the order 0.05 - 0.10 day^{-1} of the growth rate (Ditoro, 1971). In these studies a value of S = 0.03 day^{-1} was found by experiment and used in the model.

SPECIFIC GROWTH RATE

As an initial step for modeling purposes, the assumption was made that the specific growth rate of the algae may be calculated from the widely accepted Michaelis-Menten equation

$$\gamma = \gamma_{max} \left(\frac{S_L}{K_S + S_L}\right) = \frac{1}{N} \frac{dN}{dt} \tag{7}$$

where S_L is the growth limiting substrate concentration, K_S the limiting substrate concentration at $\gamma_{max}/2$ and γ_{max} the maximum specific growth rate.

Growth limiting factors considered in the present model and related experiments lead to an equation of the form for the specific growth rate constant

$$\gamma = \gamma_{max} \left(\frac{C_{CO_2}}{K_{mCO_2} + C_{CO_2}}\right) \left(\frac{I_L}{K_{IL} + I_L}\right) \left(\frac{T_{OX}}{K_{mT} + T_{OX}}\right) \tag{8}$$

C_{CO_2} is the concentration of free CO_2 in solution, I is the light intensity and
T_{ox} is the concentration of algal excreted toxic substances.
The constants K_{mCO_2} , K_{IL} and K_{mT} are Michaelis-Menton constants for free CO_2,
light intensity and toxic substances respectively.

In pure cultures, the amount of extracellular carbon increases as cultures
age and proportions are as high as 12-15 percent, have been observed in old cultures. The role of these excretions in affecting the growth rate is not clear at
this time. In the simulation model they were assumed of neglisible importance and
the third term on the rhs, of equation 8 was deleted.

The effect of the second term on the other hand is very real. When the
cell density in the culturing chamber increases, the "mutual shading" effect modifies the growth rate. The two major peaks for absorption of light by chloropyll
a, the most abundant pigment present in algae, occur in the red region at 665 nm
and the blue region at 430 nm (Fogg, 1953). Because light in the blue wave length
region enhances the efficiency of absorption of red light (Brock, 1970), and because of the lower penetrating characteristics of the blue light, this wave length
was considered the key factor in limiting algal growth when the culture becomes
dense. The reduction in light intensity when it passes through the algal culture
can be described by Beer's law. The M.M coefficient K_{mI}, equation 8, obtained from
experiments of optical density versus algal cell carbon (cell density) and plotted
as such for blue light (4300 Å) was 0.00705 and this value was used in the model.
The maximum specific growth rate, γ_{max}, is attained when the number of cells in
the culture chamber are few and no factors are limiting growth. Experimentally
γ_{max} can be ascertained by means of a series of culturing chambers in a continuous
medium flow mode where the medium dilution rate is increased and at a constant
aeration rate. When the dilution rate is increased to the rate at which the "wash
out" of cells is slightly less than the maximum rate of biomass production, the
condition for maximum growth has been obtained. The dilution rate should then
equal γ_{max}. Fig. 3 shows the results of experiments in continuous medium flow culture chambers where γ_{max} is 0.97. The value of K_{mCO_2} is the limiting CO_2 concentration when the specific growth rate is 0.5 of the maximum value.

NITROGEN AND PHOSPHORUS SIMULATION

Although not previously mentioned, nitrogen and phosphorus were supplied
in concentrations well above threshold. It was concluded however that simulation
of the uptake of these two nutrients could be achieved by assuming their assimilation proportional to the uptake of carbon based on the stochiometry of algal
protoplasm, (Stumm and Margan 1970), as $C_{106}H_{263}O_{110}N_{16}P_1$. A $\Delta P/\Delta C$ value of
0.02435 was used for calculation of phosphorus uptake in the simulation model ba-
sed on this equation. On the other hand it was found the ratio of $\Delta N/\Delta C$ provided
a poorer simulation of the experimental data. Upon review of the elemental analysis of Chlorella pyrenoidasa it was found that Hanck (1949) reported an analysis
of $C_{5.1}H_{9.8}O_{2.3}N_{1.0}$. Using this expression the $\Delta N/\Delta C$ value used in the simulation
model was 0.205 which provided a better simulation of the experimental results.

SIMULATION OF ALGAL BIOMASS

The simulation of the algal biomass production, and nitrogen and phosphorus assimilation was accomplished on a Burrough 6700 computer using "Dynamo" simulation language, (Forrester 1968). The program is available, on request from the
authors.

Utilizing the changes in pH (fig. 2) and equation one, the available free
CO_2 was calculated according to equations 2, 3, 4, 5 for each time step. For each
time step there is a specific growth rate according to equation 8.

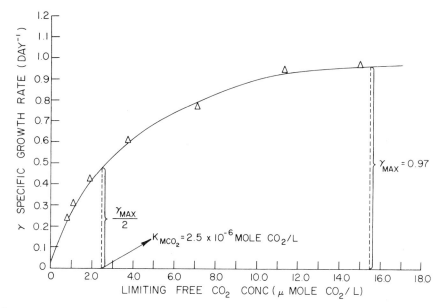

Fig.3 - The specific growth rate, γ, for the determination of the maximum specific
growth rate γ_{max}. The half saturation rate constant K_{MCO_2} occurs at 0.5 γ_{max}

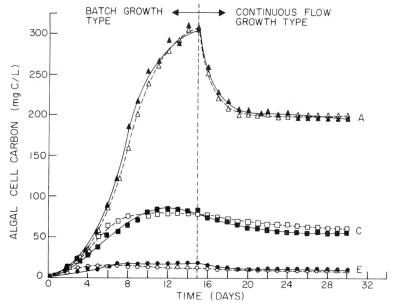

Fig.4 - The simulated and experimental results of biomass growth (algal cell carbon)
for batch and continuous medium flow at aeration rates given in fig.2 .
~~The solid line represents experimental results.~~

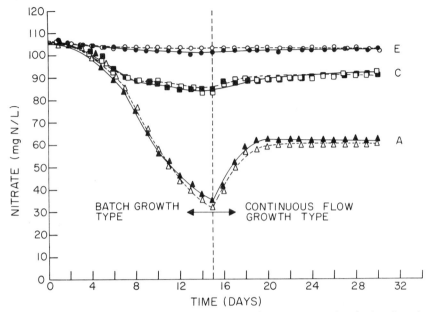

Fig.5 – Simulated and experimental results of nitrate depression in batch and
continuous medium flow culture at aeration rates given in fig.2 .

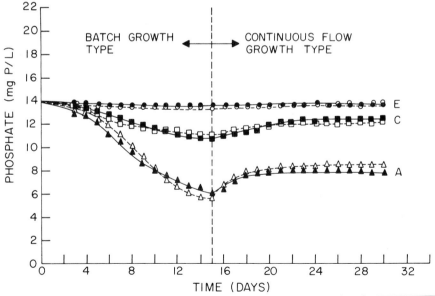

Fig.6 – Simulated and experimental results of phosphate depression in batch
and continuous flow cultures at aeration rates given in fig.2 .

The biomass in each culture chamber identified according to aeration rate for each time step was obtained by integrating the growth equation (6).

The computer simulation for biomass in compared with experimental results (solid lines) in fig. 4 for three aeration rates, namely (A) 51.0 $1.hr^{-1}$, (C) 5.5 $1.hr^{-1}$ and (E) 0.0 $1.hr^{-1}$. Both batch growth (no medium flow) and continuous flow. Where as the biomass increased sharply at the high aeration rate (A), the carbon supply was depleted so quickly in chamber (E), no aeration, that very little biomass was produced. The assumption of neglecting a toxic factor and using the blue light intensity as the limiting wavelength appear to be reasonable in view of the agreement with the experimental data.

The reduction in algal carbon when the continuous flow growth phase was begun on day 15, results from introducing a no carbon medium which diluted the free CO_2 pool.

Fig. 5 and 6 present the comparison of simulated nitrate and phophate uptake with experimental data for the aeration rates as described previously for algal carbon, respectively. The depression of the nitrogen and phosphorus concentration is quite significant and the simulated results correspond well with the experimental data.

It is concluded that the simulation model can be used to explore the effect of other factors such as toxic elements that might be purposely or accidentally introduced into the algal environment.

REFERENCES

BROCK, T.D., Biology of Microorganism, Prentice-Hall, Inc., New Jersey, 737 p., 1970.
DI TORO, et al., A dynamic model of the phytoplanton population in the Sacramento-San Joaquin Delta, in Nonequilibrium System in Natural Water Chemistry, Adv. in Chem. Series 106, Am. Chemical Soc., Washington, D.C., pp. 131-180, 1971.
FOGG, G.E., The Metabolism of Algae, John Wiley and Sons, Inc. New York, 149 p., 1953.
FORRESTER, J.W., Principles of Systems, Wright-Allen Press, Inc. Cambridge, Massachusetts, 1968.
FRANCK, J. and W.E. LOOMIS, Photosynthesis in Plants, The Iowa State College Press, Ames, Iowa, 499 p., 1949.
OSTERLIND, S., Growth conditions of the alga Scenedesmus quadricauda with special reference to inorganic carbon sources, Symb. Bot. Upsal., 10, No.3, 1949.
OSTERLIND, S., Inorganic carbon sources of green algae I, Growth experiments with Scenedesmus quadricauda and Chlorella pyrenoidasa, Physiologia Pl., 3 : 353-360, 1950a.
OSTERLIND, S., Inorganic carbon sources of green algae III, Measurement of photosynthesis in Scenedesmus quadricauda and Chlorella pyrenoidasa, Physiologia Pl., 4 : 242-254, 1951a.
PARK, K., Total carbon dioxide in sea water, J. Oceanog. Soc. Japan, 21 : 54-59, 1965.
PARK, P.K., Oceanic CO_2 system : An evaluation of ten methods of investigation, Limnol. and Oceanog., 14 : 179, 1969.
STUMM, W. and J.J. MORGAN, Aquatic Chemistry, John Wiley and Sons, Inc., New York, 583 p., 1970.

DISCUSSION

I have a question on the curve that you just have showed in the inoraanic cu
and in the medium versus growth. That's a straight line. I suggest, perhaps that's
not applicable in the field, since your straight line went up to about $3\frac{1}{2}$ millimals
of carbon which corresponds to an occuminity of about 175 mgrams/l. In many surface
waters you have a very soft or low buffered capacity of water and the amount of in-
organic carbon you can hold would be dependent upon the experiments and so you might
never get that high in soft surface water. (ANDREWS)

These were cultures in the laboratory and I am not saying that we can extrapolate these correctly to fields. However one of the things that has been observed
is that we only found that data gathered in the field would follow exactly the
same kind of linear relationship. (BIGGAR)

Perhaps that was in a hard water region where the water was low buffered
in California where water is coming from snow belt, ours is not from snow but it
is very soft. You will have quantities of 15 of 20 mgrams/liter which results in
drastic pH fluctuation over a period of a day. Your laboratory medium was probably
loaded with buffered capacity. I am sure most algae medium is. (ANDREWS)

The pH changed quite a bit there. Even in the bigger surdrawing situations,
where you expect the calculated amount of free CO_2 that would be available   far
below what the so called limiting quantity is to be.
In those cases the pH went up quite high. We have many waters in California that
are not soft. (BIGGAR)

Modeling and Simulation of Water Resources Systems, G.C. VANSTEENKISTE, (Ed.)
North-Holland Publishing Company (1975)

MATHEMATICAL MODEL OF THE INFLUENCE OF BACTERIAL ACTIVITY ON
WATER COMPOSITION AND ITS IMPLEMENTATION ON A HYBRID COMPUTER

G. Billen
Laboratoire de Chimie Industrielle, ULB and
Laboratorium voor Ekologie en Systematiek, VUB, BELGIUM

F. Nero
European Computation Center, E.A.I., Brussels, BELGIUM

J. Smitz
Institut de Mathématique, Université de Liège, BELGIUM

ABSTRACT

This paper defines an oxydation-reduction model of the influence of bacterial activity on water composition in the last 120 Km of the Scheldt river.
The bacterial activity, a result of the polluting organisms is the cause
of the deterioration of biological properties of natural water.

Five different oxydants are considered in this model. This leads to five
transport diffusion equations describing the correspondant concentrations
in time and space dimension.

These five equations are solved on a hybrid computer using the so called
CSDT Continuous-Space-Descrite-Time method i.e. continuous integration in
space on the analog computer and discretisation of the time matching process organized by the digital computer.

To insure stability of the discretised equation a decomposition method is
applied to the second order equations to reduce them into several first
order equations integrated in different directions.

In this type of problem, the hybrid computer insures fast and parallel integration of the five equations on the analog computer and all the flexibility needed to organize the time matchingprocess on the digital computer.

INTRODUCTION

The deterioration of chemical and biological properties of natural waters
by domestic pollution is not the direct consequence of the presence of an organic
load in the water, but is rather the result of heterotrophic bacterial activity
which modifies oxidation-reduction characteristics of the water while degrading
this charge. Basically the same phenomena occurs in natural water systems sustain-
ing an intense heterotrophic activity, such as bottom water of stratified basins :
(Richards, 1965) or interstitial water of sediments (Thorstenson, 1970); In all
these situations, because other oxidants than oxygen can be used by anaerobic res-
pirations, a complete oxidation-reduction balance is necessary to describe correctly the evolution of the chemical composition of the water under bacterial influence.
This work present an oxidation-reduction model of the influence of bacterial activity on water composition, applied to the case of the Scheldt estuary.

The Scheldt Estuary is heavily polluted upwards Antwerp by important a-
mounts of organic matter. Owing to the intense bacterial activity, the redox potential decreases from Dendermonde (Km 120) to about Antwerp (Km 80). Oxygen is
rapidly entirely depleted, and others oxidants are used by anaerobic metabolisms.
Then, near Km 70, owing to increasing salinity, floculation and precipitation of

the suspended organic matter occur (Wollast, 1973), bacterial activity falls down and a phase of recuperation begins, accelerated by mixing with unpolluted sea water. During this stage, reaeration not only restores the oxygen concentration but also regenerates the previously used oxidizing agents.

Typical longitudinal profiles of concentration of several oxidation-reduction compounds are shown in Fig. 1 for a winter and a summer situation. Note abrupt transitions between zones where a given substance is reduced or oxidized. The order in which the different oxidants are successively reduced in the upwards zone is O_2, Mn^{IV}, NO_3^-, Fe^{III}, SO_4^{2-}. In the downwards recuperation zone, the oxidants are regenerated in the opposite order. This is conform with the predictions of thermodynamic equilibrium models such as the models theoretically developed by Stumm (1966). In the winter, when bacterial activity is low, the reductive stage proceeds less far than in the summer : for instance, reduced iron does not appear in the winter.

All these phenomena will be simulated by a model in which measured values of bacterial activity are introduced as a command parameter modifying the composition of the water without disturbing the thermodynamic internal equilibrium between all the involved oxidation-reduction couples.

PHYSICAL PRINCIPLES OF THE MODEL

The variations in the concentration of the considered chemical compounds are the result of advection, turbulent diffusion or consumption by oxidation-reduction processes :

$$(\frac{\partial x_i}{\partial t})_s = - u(s,t) (\frac{\partial x_i}{\partial s})_t + D (s) (\frac{\partial^2 x_i}{\partial s^2})_t - C_i(s,t)$$

where x_i is the concentration of the ith species,
  u is the residual velocity of the water,
  D is the turbulent diffusion coefficient,
  C_i is the rate of oxidation-reduction consumption.

For oxygen, an additional aeration term occur. It was taken as proportional to the oxygen saturation deficit, with a proportionality coefficient K about 6 $10^{-3} h^{-1}$ by Wollast (1973).

The residual velocity of the water has been calculated as the quotient of the residual outflow (the seasonal variation of which is given by the measurements published by the Antwerpse Zeediensten (1966) to the wet section area (reported by Wollast (1973) to fit a logarithmic function of the distance to the mouth).

For the turbulent diffustion coefficient, integrating the effects of the tide, we used values calculated by Beckers (personnal communication) from a salinity profile of May 1973 according to the method described by Wollast (1973).

The oxidation reduction processes, represented by the term C_i, are controlled by heterotrophic bacterial activity in the water. Heterotrophic activity has been experimentally evaluated along longitudinal profiles of the river at several seasons by the method of dare 14_C bicarbonate incorporation (Billen, 1974a and b). Bicarbonate incorporation has been assumed to represent about % of total heterotrophic carbon utilisation. The relation of heterotrophic activity with temperature of the water ($t°$) and the river discharge (d) has been empirically established as follows :

mean heterotrophic activity : $\frac{1}{d} \cdot 10^{t°/10}$

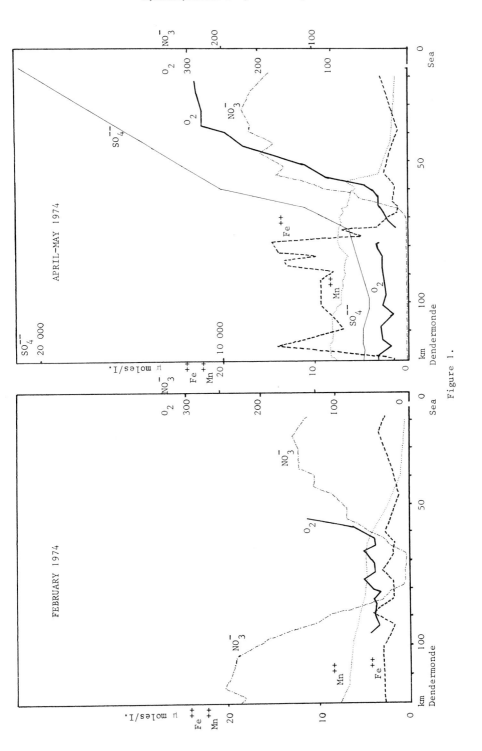

Figure 1.

This bacterial activity can be viewed as an electron flux imposed to the water system, according to the reaction :

$$CH_2O + H_2O \xrightarrow{\quad bact. \quad} CO_2 + 4H^+ + 4e^-$$

By writing this equation, we assumed that, from an overall point of view, fermentations play no important role, i.e. that no accumulation of uncompletely oxidized organic compounds (acids, cetones or alcohols) occurs. This electron flux $H(s,t)$, provocates one or several of the following reactions to go on :

$$4e^- + O_2 + 4H^+ \rightleftharpoons 2H_2O \tag{1}$$

$$8e^- + NO_3^- + 10H^+ \rightleftharpoons NH_4^+ + 3H_2O \tag{2}$$

$$2e^- + MnO_2 + 4H^+ \rightleftharpoons Mn^{++} + 2H_2O \tag{3}$$

$$1e^- + Fe(OH)_3 + 3H^+ \rightleftharpoons Fe^{++} + 3H_2O \tag{4}$$

$$Fe^{++} + HCO_3^- \rightleftharpoons Fe\,CO_3 + H^+ \tag{4'}$$

$$14e^- + 2SO_4^{--} + Fe^{++} + 16H^+ \rightleftharpoons FeS_2 + 8H_2O \tag{5}$$

so that $H(s,t) = \sum_i \nu_i \, C_i(s,t)$

Some of these reactions are biologically mediated and the presence of the responsible organisms has been demonstrated in the Scheldt (oxygen consumption, denitrification, nitrification, sulfato-reduction), other occur spontaneously although direct biological mediation can occur in certain circumstances (Iron oxidation and reduction, Manganese oxidation and reduction). However, this distinction in the reaction mechanisms is not essential for the overall balance we are doing.

It is assumed that an internal thermodynamic equilibrium is achieved in the system for the reactions (1) to (5), so that the following relations hold :

$$Eh = 1.26 - 0.59 \, pH + 0.015 \, \log O_2 \tag{1'}$$

$$Eh = 0.882 - 0.074 \, pH + 0.007 \, \log NO_3^-/NH_4^+ \tag{2'}$$

$$Eh = 1.229 - 0.118 \, pH - 0.029 \, \log Mn^{++} \tag{3'}$$

$$Eh = 1.057 - 0.177 \, pH - 0.059 \, \log Fe^{++} \tag{4'}$$

$$\log Fe^{++} - \log HCO_3^- + pH = -0.286 \text{ for } -0.215 \; Eh \; 0.053 \tag{4''}$$

$$Eh = 0.354 + 0.008 \, \log SO_4^{--} - 0.067 \, pH + 0.004 \, \log Fe^{++} \tag{5'}$$

This is equivalent to saying that the bacteria only use thermodynamically favorable half reactions in their energy yielding metabolism. The validity of this assumption as a usefull schematisation has been discussed by Stumm (1966), Thorstenson (1970) and by Billen (1974c) for the special case of nitrification in the Scheldt estuary.

Together with the relations (1) to (5) the following mass conservation relations form a system of equations which determinates the chemical composition of the water system at any stage of the bacterial action, i.e. at any value of Eh.

$$\overline{X}(NO_3^- + NH_4^+) = 0 \tag{6}$$

$$\overline{X}(MnO_2 + Mn^{++}) = 0 \tag{7}$$

$$\underline{X}(Fe(OH)_3 + Fe^{++} + FeCO_3 + FeS_2) = 0 \tag{8}$$

$$\underline{X}(SO_4^{--} + 2\ FeS_2) = 0 \tag{9}$$

where $\underline{X}$ is written for $(\frac{\partial}{\partial t})_s + u(s,t)\ (\frac{\partial}{\partial s})_t - D(s)\ (\frac{\partial^2}{\partial s^2})_t$

The chemical composition in function of Eh is diagramatically represented in Fig.2 for the gross chemical composition of the water at Dendermonde (upwards limit of our model).

Given a set of limit conditions (composition of the water at Dendermonde and at the sea), the knowledge of the bacterial activity allows to calculate the complete evolution of the water composition along a longitudinal profile of the estuary. Note that by introducing directly bacterial activity as a command para-meter of the system, we take implicitely into account a lot of phenomena that it would be difficult to consider explicitely, such as lateral imports of organic matter, sedimentation of organic matter, modification of the bacterial population with salinity... etc.

SOLUTION SCHEME

The final mathematical model used to calculate the concentrations of the considered oxydants will comprise five transport diffusion equations : partial dif-ferential equations with time and one space dimension as independent variables.

Four equations based on mass conservation describe the concentration of the specie Z_i ($i = 1,...4$) are of the form :

$$\frac{\partial Z_i}{\partial t} + u(s,t)\ \frac{\partial Z_i}{\partial s} - D\ (s)\ \frac{\partial^2 Z_i}{\partial s^2} = 0$$

Z_i is the total mass of one oxydo-reduction couple as explained in equations (6) to (9), for example in equation (6)

$$Z_i = NO_3^- + NH_4^+$$

The fifth equation based on the overall mass conservation describes the weighted sum of the five oxydants including oxygen.

$$\frac{\partial F}{\partial t} + u(s,t)\ \frac{\partial F}{\partial s} - D(s)\ \frac{\partial^2 F}{\partial s^2} = P(x_5) - H(s,t)$$

$F(s,t) = \sum\limits_i v_i\ X_i$ weighted sum where v_i are known constants.

X_5 (s) : concentration of oxygen along the river.

$P(X_5)$: oxygen production term due mainly to reaeration.

$H(s,t)$: is the consumption term. This term representing the heterotrophic bacte-rial activity has been experimentally evaluated.

The logarithmic relations (1') to (5') enable to express the concentration of oxy-dants as a function of the redox potential Eh. The minimum considered concentra-tion is 10^{-6} moles/litre. The maximum is of course the total mass of the oxydo-reduction couple Z_i.
This devides the redox potential range into three domains for every oxydant :

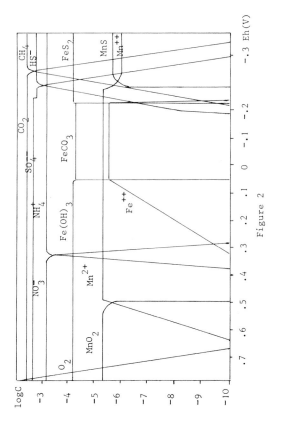

Figure 2

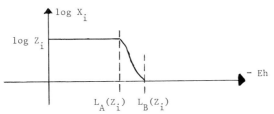

If $Eh > L_A$: $X_i = Z_i$

If $L_B < Eh < L_A$: X_i : follows one of the logarithmic laws (1') to (5')

If $Eh < L_B$: $X_i = 0$

The method of solving the model on the hybrid computer implies a time discretization. For one time interval the solution scheme is the following :

First step — Solution of the four equations in Z_i which give the concentration of the oxydo-reduction couples along the river : $Z_i(s)$.

Second step — Calculation of the limits $L_A(Z_i)$ and $L_B(Z_i)$ for every oxydants in the Eh domain.

Third step — Solution of the fifth equation, in F, giving the weighted sum of oxydants along the river : $F(s)$.

Fourth step — Solution of an implicit relation :

$$F(s) \equiv \sum_i \nu_i \, X_i = \sum_i \nu_i \, f \, (Eh, L_A(Z_i), L_B(Z_i))$$

This relation allows to calculate the redox potential versus s, $Eh(s)$, from which the concentration of the oxydants can be derived via the logarithmic relations (1') to (5').

As the fifth equation is implicit for the oxygen, the expression $P(X_5)$ is calculated with one time interval delay.

IMPLEMENTATION OF THE SOLUTION ON A HYBRID COMPUTER

As the five equations are similar and are solved by using the same method the implementation of one equation only is described.

The equation to be solved is the following :

$$\frac{\partial Z}{\partial t} + u(s,t) \, \frac{\partial Z}{\partial s} - D(s) \, \frac{\partial^2 Z}{\partial s^2} = P - H \tag{10}$$

The method used is detailed in the Electronic Associates, Inc. - SCD-72/5 (cfr Ref.)

The classical hybrid CSDT (continuous-space-discrete-time) method of discretization is applied to make the equations suitable for the hybrid computer.
It consists in expressing the solution along equi-distant lines parallel to the s axis in the(s,t) plane, i.e. the time is devided into time intervals and for every interval the equations are integrated continuously by means of the analog computer along the space dimensions.

After time discretization the equation becomes an ordinary differential equation of the second order (for the $\bar{\gamma}$ the time step) :

$$L \, Z^{\gamma} = R^{\gamma-1}$$
(11)

L is a second order operator :

$$L = D \frac{d^2}{ds^2} - u \frac{d}{ds} - (\frac{1}{\theta \Delta t} + \frac{dv}{ds} + H)$$

and

$$R^{\gamma-1} = - \frac{Z^{\gamma-1}}{\theta \Delta t} - D^{\gamma}$$

$Z^{\gamma-1}$ represents the interaction of the previous time step and is calculated by the recurrence relation.

$$Z^{\gamma-1} = Z^{\gamma-1} + \frac{1}{0} (Z^{\gamma} - Z^{\gamma-1})$$

The second order operator has unstable error propagation properties in either direction of integration. The method of decomposition alleviates this difficulty. L is decomposed into two first order operators L_B and L_F which yield stable integration respectively in the backward and forward direction.

$$L \equiv L_B . \, L_F \equiv (\frac{d}{ds} - \lambda_B(s)) \, (D \frac{d}{ds} - \lambda_F(s)) \, Z^{\gamma} = R^{\gamma-1}$$
(12)

$$\lambda_B \geqslant 0 \; ; \; \lambda_F \leqslant 0$$

The solution of (11) is obtained by the following sequence of integrations :

$$L_B \, Z_1 = R^{\gamma-1} \text{ and}$$

$$L_F \, Z^{\gamma} = Z_1$$

By identification of (12) with (11) equation (13) is obtained which yields λ_F.

$$\frac{d\lambda_F}{ds} = - \frac{\lambda_F^2}{D} + \frac{M\lambda_F}{D} + [\frac{1}{\theta \Delta t} + \frac{dV}{dX} + H]$$
(13)

The flow diagram for the solution of one equation is shown on the next page. The hybrid implementation of this problem was undertaken at the E.A.I. European Computation Center Brussels on a Hybrid PACER 600 system.

CONCLUSIONS

The use of the hybrid computer in solving this type of problems brings three advantages :
1. Due to the parallel working feature of the analog computer all the equations can be solved at the same time (i.e. in parallel).
2. A high speed analog integration along the space dimension is insured by the analog integrator.
3. The time working process requiring a lot of logic operation is done on the digital computer which multiplexes the analog computer along the time axis.

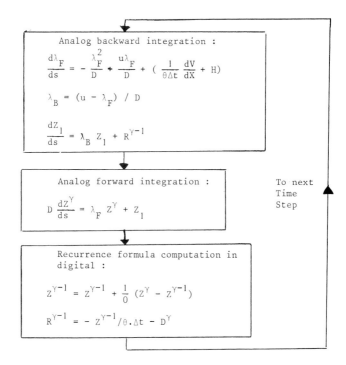

REFERENCES

Antwerpse Zeediensten, Stormvloeden op de Schelde, Ministerie van Openbare werken, bestuur der waterwegen, 1966.

BILLEN, Tentative d'estimation de l'activité hétérotrophe dans l'Estuaire de l'Escaut par incorporation de bicarbonate marqué à l'obscurité, Technical report CIPS, SCHELDT/01.1974, 1974.

BILLEN, G. and JOIRIS, C., Estimation de l'activité bactérienne hétérotrophe, Intercalibration de différentes méthodes, Technical report CIPS - in preparation, 1974.

BILLEN, G., Nitrification in the Scheldt Estuary (Belgium and the Netherlands Submitted for publication to Estuarine and marine Coastal Science, 1974.

RICHARDS, F.A., Anoxic basins and Fjords, In chemical oceanography, Eds. Riley, S.P. and Skirrow, G. Academic Press, New York, Vol. 1 pp. 611-645, 1965.

SNYDER, BISHOP, VICHNEVETSKY, (EAI SCD report N°72-5 : Mathematical models and hybrid computer simulation of water quality in rivers and estuaries.

STUMM, W., Redox potential as an environmental parameter : conceptual significance and operational limitation, Proc. Int. Water Pollution Res. Conf. (3rd, München) 1, 283-308, 1966.

THORSTENSON, D.C., Equilibrium distribution of small organic molecules in natural waters, Geochim. Cosmochin. Acta, 34, 745-770, 1970.

WOLLAST, R., Origine et mécanismes de l'envasement de l'Estuaire de l'Escaut, Rapport de synthèse, Recherche effectuée dans le cadre de l'étude de l'envasement de l'Escaut dirigée par le laboratoire de recherches hydrauliques, Borgerhout, Ministère des Travaux Publics, 1973.

WOLLAST, R., Circulation, accumulation et bilan de masse dans l'Estuaire de l'Escaut, In modèle mathématique de la pollution en mer du Nord, Rapport de Synthèse 1972, Commission interministérielle de la politique scientifique (Belgium), 1973.

Modeling and Simulation of Water Resources Systems, G.C. VANSTEENKISTE, (Ed.)
North-Holland Publishing Company (1975)

MATHEMATICAL MODELING OF BIODEGRADATION PROCESSES IN WATERS AND SOILS

W. Verstraete and R. Vanloocke
Laboratorium voor Algemene
en Industriële Microbiologie
Rijksuniversiteit Gent, BELGIUM

J. Mercy
Seminarie voor Toegepaste Wiskunde
en Biometrie
Rijksuniversiteit Gent, BELGIUM

ABSTRACT

Kinetics of aerobic microbal biodegradation processes in waters and soils
were mathematically simulated. Physiologically adapted and ecological
divers microbial communities most generally degrade organic matter
according to first order kinetics, although at high velocities, the
latter kinetics approach the second order. The metabolism of non-adapted
communities occurs quite often according to asymmetric sigmoidal curves
which can be simulated by logistic or by consecutive first order reaction
models. Composite biodegradation curves, resulting either from the lack of
physiological versatility or from the lack of ecological diversity of the
microbial community involved, can be simulated by simultaneous or subsequent combination of the non-composite conventional models. Methods
to calculate the fit of the different models and the corresponding kinetic
parameters of these models are discussed. Numerical examples are presented.

INTRODUCTION

The cycling of anorganic and organic matter in nature is intimately linked
to microbial biotransformation processes. A variety of these processes as e.g.
solubilisation, mineralisation, immobilisation, oxidation, reduction, isotope
fractionation etc... have been unraveled in the last decades. Particularly the
qualitative aspects of these processes have been examined and most studies have
focused either upon microbial metabolism as a function of physico-chemical parameters as e.g. pH, temperature and redox-potential, or upon microbial metabolism
as a function of the physico-chemical nature of the substrates. A third and more
recent type of qualitative approach to microbial biotransformations is aimed at
the assessment of biotransformations in relation to the composition of the
metabolising microbial community.

In order to evaluate the overall impact of microbial metabolism in relation
to the cycling of elements in nature and with regard to the equilibrium of natural
ecosystems in particular, the need has arisen to complement the qualitative studies
with kinetic studies which integrate the various component processes. Initial
attempts in this direction most often were restricted to the measurement of the
timecourses of substrate removal, or to the estimation of the rate of biotransformation on the basis the classical Michaelis-Menten model for enzymatic reactions
(Wright and Hobbie 1966). However, few biotransformation in natural ecosystems are
that simple that they can be adequatly interpreted by means of such straight forward approaches. Indeed, biotransformations in soils, waste treatment systems and
aquatic biotopes relate to not a single substrate but to mixtures of intrinsically
different compounds. Furthermore, the actual processes in nature are not brought
about by an assemblage of genetically and physiologically identical organisms, that
is by one species population, but they are brought about by a mixture of species
populations in which each species population has its own substrate affinity and
reaction kinetics.

Finally, the biotransformations do not occur in a constant environment since most environmental factors in an ecosystem fluctuate, either as a result of climatic changes or as a result of the biotransformation processes themselves.

In view of this, the task of the environmental microbiologist is to develop integrated models which characterise the biotransformation of a complex array of substrates by a complex assemblage of species populations in a hetero-geneous and continuously changing environment. This paper is an attempt in that direction. However, the models described pertain only to aerobic transformations in ecosystems or samples thereof, which are devoid of external physico-chemical fluctuations.

EXPERIMENTAL

1. First order kinetics

The biodegradation rate is directly proportional to the amount of available organic matter

$$\frac{dy}{dt} = k \ (L - y)$$

or $\quad y = L \ (1 - e^{-kt})$
$\qquad = L \ (1 - 10^{-k't})$

y : oxygen uptake, $mg\,l^{-1}$ or $mg\ kg^{-1}$

t : time

L : initial substrate concentration expressed as $mg\,l^{-1}$ or $mg\ kg^{-1}$ potential oxygen uptake

k, k': biodegradation constant, $time^{-1}$

In biology, several methods for hand computation of k and L have been develLopped. Some of the best known are the Fair log difference method (1937), the Fujimoto difference method (1964), the Thomas slope method (1937), the method of Moments (Moor et al. 1950) and the method of Reed and Theriault (1931). All these methods have in common that they allow in a relatively rapid and simple way to approximate by means of a handcalculator the best fitting values for k and L from a given set of y-t values. If a computer is available, the parameters can most elegantly be determined by the sum of squares surface method. This method has been discussed in detail by Marske and Polkowski (1972). The least squares estimates $\hat{k}$ and $\hat{L}$, of k and L will be those that make the sum of the squared discrepancies between the observed values and the calculated values a minimum. The computer is pro-grammed to determine the sum of squares for a series of k-L pairs. The program was based on Marquardt's algorithm for least squares estimation of nonlinear para-meters. The values obtained are presented in a x-y plot as shown in Fig. 1. The equal values within the plot define a contour which shape indicates the precision of the estimates. Indeed, flat curvature at the minimum indicates that several values of k and L, almost as good as $\hat{k}$ and $\hat{L}$, occur over wide ranges and that there are large errors in the estimates of the parameters. A sharp curvature at the minimum indicates the opposite. In addition, the contours corresponding to a particular degree of confidence, relate to the minimal sum of squares (S_{min}) according to :

$$S_c = S_{min} \left[1 + \frac{p}{n - p} \ F\alpha \ , \ (p, \ n-p) \right]$$

where $\quad S_c$: sum of squares of a contour with confidence degree α
$\qquad p$: number of parameters estimated
$\qquad n$: number of (y-t) observations used to compute $\hat{k}$ and $\hat{L}$

Table 1 summarizes the results of the calculation of the biodegradation constant and of the initial substrate concentration by means of the various methods. To evaluate the methods, the degrees of confidence of the respective k'-L values were compared with the 95 %-contoures of confidence for the different jobs.

Table 1 : Comparison of the calculation of k' and L for first order biodegradation kinetics by means of several methods

Job nr.	Fair log difference		Method of moments		Fujimoto		Reed and Theriault		Thomas slope		Sum of Squares Surface	
	k'	L	k'	L	k'	L	k'	L	k'	L	k'	L
1	0.14	2.2	0.090	2.5	0.09	2.4	0.090	2.5	0.095	2.6	0.09	2.49
2	0.165	740	0.10	920	0.11	849	0.11	900	0.09	1 000	0.11	889
3	0.040	44	0.15	25	0.30	21	0.14	25	0.14	25	0.14	25
4	0.158	14.0	0.172	14.0	0.17	13.8	0.172	14	0.155	14.5	0.17	13.8
5	0.12	24	0.19	20	0.19	20.1	0.19	20	0.17	21	0.20	19.6
6	0.11	260	0.22	220	0.26	213.3	0.22	220	0.18	245	0.23	218
7	0.11	24	0.23	19	0.29	18.2	0.23	19	0.20	21	0.23	19.0
8	0.21	11 500	0.25	10 500	0.25	10 538	0.25	10 500	0.24	11 000	0.24	10 530

_____ : not within 95 % contour of confidence with regard to the least sum of squares surface.

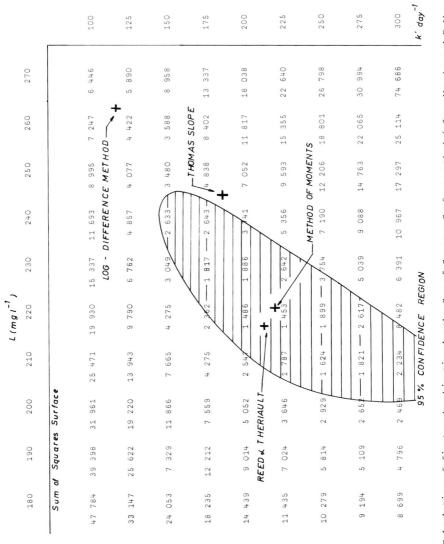

Fig. 1 – Calculation of first order kinetics by the Sum of Squares Surface method (after Marske and Polkowski 1972).

The results indicate that the method of Moments and the method of Reed and Theriault compare in all cases well with the method of the Sum of Squares Surface. The method of Moments outranks by far the method of Reed and Theriault in terms of ease of computation and is therefore best fit for calculation of $\hat{k}$ and $\hat{L}$ without computer.
The methods of Thomas, Fujimoto and particularly the Fair log difference method turn out to be unreliable and inaccurate.

2. Second order kinetics

In this case, the rate of oxygen uptake is proportional to the second power of the organic matter remaining available for bio-oxidation.

$$\frac{dy}{dt} = k (L - y)^2$$

or

$$y = \frac{t}{(\frac{1}{L})t + \frac{1}{kL} 2}$$

For the calculation of k and L from a given set of y-t values, the Sum of Squares Surface method has to be applied.

From the shape of the y-t curve, it is not always evident for the biologist if a process follows a first rather than a second order rate. In table 2, some biotransformation processes in water and soil were examined by the method of the Sum of Squares Surface. Apparently, in soils as well as in aquatic biotopes, certain biodegradation processes respond best to first order kinetics while others are better represented by second order models. According to Marske and Polkowski (1972), biodegradation kinetics generally fit better to second order models if the first order rate constant k' is greater than 0.20. These results show that, as a rule of thumb, the postulation of the latter authors is only partially valid. Indeed, the k'value for the jobs 4,9 and 13 is smaller than 0.20 but these processes are better represented by second than by first order kinetics. The results also indicate that second order estimates of the L-values surpass first order ones by factors ranging up to 2.0. This illustrates the absolute necessity of selecting the best fitting model, particularly if precise estimates of the L-values are required.

3. Sigmoidal kinetics

   3.1. Logistic models

The bio-oxidation rate is proportional to the amount of available substrate and to the amount of oxidised substrate as well.

$$\frac{dy}{dt} = k (L - y) \quad y$$

or

$$y = \frac{L}{1 + e^{B - (k^L)t}} = \frac{L}{1 + e^{B - Ct}}$$

with B : integration constant
     C : logistic rate constant

Biologists quite often calculate by hand the B and C values. Hereto, the integral is transformed to $\ln \frac{\hat{L}-y}{y}$ = B-Ct. The ultimate oxygen uptake is then taken as $\hat{L}$.

When a computer is available, all three parameters can be approximated by means of the least Sum of Squares Surface method.

Table 2 : Comparison of the fitness of first and second order kinetics for representation of bio-oxidation processes in water and soil

	First order				Second order			
	k'	L	*SSS	**ID	k	L	SSS	ID
Aquatic biotopes								
Job 1	0.09	2.49	0.029	0.9950	0.044	3.56	0.037	0.9936
2	0.11	889	3501	0.9927	0.00013	1347.7	4882	0.9898
3	0.14	25	17.07	0.9621	0.0074	35.4	18.18	0.9596
4	0.17	13.8	0.931	0.9936	0.0184	18.68	0.887	0.9939
5	0.20	19.6	0.388	0.9987	0.0161	25.82	0.315	0.9990
6	0.23	218	1384	0.9695	0.0023	259	588.23	0.9870
7	0.23	19	0.265	0.9992	0.0214	24.31	0.271	0.9992
8	0.24	10 530	68 501	0.9988	0.0000326	14 535	10 701	0.9998
Soils								
Job 9	0.0459	26.24	5.89	0.9927	0.00180	40.65	4.57	0.9943
10	0.0364	27.06	4.12	0.9944	0.00118	44.64	4.14	0.9943
11	0.0171	39.51	4.17	0.9920	0.00029	72.99	4.84	0.9918
12	0.0082	31.47	11.30	0.9170	0.00014	66.23	11.32	0.9168
13	0.0413	25.49	9.06	0.9873	0.00151	40.98	9.03	0.9873

* : Sum of Squares Surface ; ** : Index of Determination $= 1 - \dfrac{\Sigma (y_i - \hat{y}_i)^2}{\Sigma (y_i - \bar{y})^2}$

In addition, the parameters can also be computed for the differential adjusted for going through the origin :

$$\frac{dy}{dt} = k \ (L-y) \ (y+E)$$

or

$$y = \frac{A}{1 + e^{B-Ct}} - \frac{A}{1 + e^{B}}$$

In order to take into account a certain asymmetry in the S-curve, which quite often occurs, a further modification is proposed :

$$\frac{d}{dt} \ (y^{1/D}) = k \ (L-y^{1/D}) \ (y^{1/D} + E)$$

or

$$y = \left[\frac{A}{1 + e^{B-Ct}} - \frac{A}{1 + e^{B}} \right]^{D}$$

with D : coefficient of asymmetry

Generally, the shape of the y-t curve leaves no doubt if either a symmetric or a asymmetric model should be applied. In table 3, a number of bio-oxidation processes as they occur in soils have been calculated for symmetric and asymmetric logistic kinetics. Although for all jobs, a quite satisfying fit is obtained by the symmetric S-curve, the asymmetric model gives a quite better fit for the jobs 14, 16, 17 and 19. Hence, it seems advisable to simulate the S-shaped biodegradation curves by the asymmetric model.

3.2. Consecutieve first order reaction model

A handsome method, in which S-curves are treated as consecutive first order irrevesible reactions, has recently been proposed by Baily et al (1974). In this model a single nonlineair regression program is used to estimate values of the reaction constants for any chain length. The number of reactions is treated as a parameter, which can also be estimated. The mean transit time (Θ) through the system of reactions is equal to the sum of the reciprocals of the reaction constants or :

$$C_1 \xrightarrow{k_1} C_2 \ \xrightarrow{k_2} C_3 \xrightarrow{k_3} \xrightarrow{kn-1} Cn \xrightarrow{kn} Cn + 1$$

$$\text{with} \ \Theta = \overset{\leqslant}{} \frac{1}{k_i}$$

The consecutive first order reaction model has been applied to the jobs 14 to 19.

Assuming that initially all organic substances are constraint within the first compartment, one gets :

for n = 1 (single first order reaction y $\xrightarrow{k_1}$ y$_2$)

$$y_2 = y_1 \ (0) \ |1 - e^{-k \ t} \ |$$

Table 3 : Logistic kinetics of bio-oxidation processes in soil

| Job n° | Symmetric | | | | | Asymmetric | | | | | |
	A^{+}	B	C	SSS[*]	ID[**]	A^{++}	B	C	D	SSS[*]	ID[**]
14	41.1	- 0.024	0.33	8.2	0.9910	91.4	- 2.19	0.31	1.36	6.17	0.9932
15	140.3	2.26	0.38	75.8	0.9978	165	2.40	0.40	0.96	75.67	0.9979
16	147.5	2.92	0.59	109.3	0.9982	39.2	1.89	0.50	1.41	91.52	0.9985
17	45.2	1.88	0.79	72.1	0.9839	20.9	- 1.45	0.617	2.66	40.80	0.9909
18	110.7	3.30	0.59	62.6	0.9982	76.0	3.03	0.57	1.09	61.7	0.9982
19	108.8	3.15	0.64	118.5	0.9966	35.0	2.25	0.53	1.34	110.5	0.9969

[*] : SSS = Sum of Squares Surface ;   [**] : ID = Index of determination

$$^{+} L = A - \frac{A}{1+C^{B}} = \frac{A}{1+C^{-B}}$$

$$^{++} L = \left| A - \frac{A}{1+C^{B}} \right|^{D} = \left(\frac{A}{1+C^{-B}} \right)^{D}$$

for $n = 2$ (two consecutive first order reactions $y_1 \xrightarrow{k_1} y_2 \xrightarrow{k_2} y_3$

$$y_3 = y_1 (o) \left| 1 - k_2 \frac{e^{-k_1 t}}{k_2 - k_1} - k_1 \frac{e^{-k_2 t}}{k_1 - k_2} \right|$$

for $n = 3$ $(y_1 \xrightarrow{k_1} y_2 \xrightarrow{k_2} y_3 \xrightarrow{k_3} y_4)$

$$y_4 = y_1(0) \left| 1 - \frac{k_2 k_3 \, e^{-k_1 t}}{(k_2 - k_1)(k_3 - k_1)} - \frac{k_1 k_3 \, e^{-k_1 t}}{(k_1 - k_2)(k_3 - k_2)} - \frac{k_1 k_2 \, e^{-k_3 t}}{(k_1 - k_3)(k_2 - k_3)} \right|$$

To estimate the number of compartments needed, a preliminary calculation using a simplified equation solved for the case when all k-values are equal, is run and indicates that to the jobs 15,16,18 and 19 a minimum number of 3 compartments and to job 17, a minimum number of 4 compartments. The corresponding y(o), k and SSS-values are tabulated in table 4.

When these results are compared with those of the simulations using the logistic model (Table 3), it appears that for the jobs 14 and 17, reaction kinetics are equally well and even slightly better represented by the consecutive first order reaction model. The jobs 16,18 and 19 can possibly be simulated better by increasing the number of compartments but this is not the case for job 15 for which a minimum SSS-value is obtained for n=3. A final remark : consecutive first order models fit more closely S-shaped biodegradation curves for low substrate values than do the logistic models.

3.3. A variety of other approaches can be used to simulate S-shaped biodegradation curves. Fletcher(1974) has developped, as an extension of the logistic law of growth, a new deterministic law, called the quadric law of damped exponential growth. It is resolved from the general nonlinear defining relation :

$$y' + ay^2 + by' + gy^2 + hyy' = 0$$

$$y' = dy/dt \; ; \; a,b,g,h = \text{constants}$$

However, since in this law y is not defined explicitly, the Marquardt's algorithm for least squars estimation cannot be applied which restricts, from a computational point of view, the applicability of this model.

4. Composite curves

4.1. Sequential biotransformations

Quite often, the oxidation of mixtures of substrates does not proceed in a straightforward continuous way but occurs in steps. Each of these steps can be simulated by one of the models discussed above. The overall process corresponds then to a composite model as shown in fig. 2.

4.2. Simultaneous oxidation of several products at different rates

When the decomposition rate of the different components of a mixture of substrates varies considerably, then the pattern of total oxygen uptake corresponds to the sum of these individual oxidations. Such a composite curve, representing the decomposition of organic matter in forest litter has been calculated for the data found by Minderman (1968) and is given in fig. 3. The actual degradation curve was also simulated by the first order and the second order models

W. Verstraete, R. Vanloocke and J. Mercy

Table 4 : Simulation of S-curves by a consecutive first order reaction model

Job	Number of compartments (n)	Corresponding values				SSS	ID
		$y(0)$	k_1	k_2	k_3		
14	2	22.45	0.187	–	–	10.1	0.9889
	3	20.94	0.246	2.24	–	4.43	0.9951
15	3	163.9	0.216	0.212	–	118.5	0.9966
	4	160.0	0.208	0.236	9.82	124.6	0.9964
16	3	177.0	0.280	0.266	–	514.5	0.9915
	4	151.5	0.517	0.506	0.500	148.8	0.9975
17	4	40.29	0.485	1.681	1.821	35.4	0.9921
18	3	160.2	0.203	0.217	–	403.4	0.9884
	4	124.6	0.418	0.427	0.434	164.1	0.9953
19	3	134.1	0.274	0.276	–	356.2	0.9898
	4	114.9	0.508	0.510	0.511	190.5	0.9945

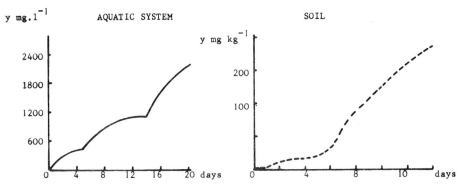

Fig. 2. Simulation of sequential bio-oxidation phases

Aquatic system

$$y = 550 [1 - e^{-0.46t}] + 550 [1 - e^{-0.33(t-5)}] U(t-6) + 1400 [1 - e^{-0.20(t-13)}] U(t-14)$$

with $U(t-to) = o$ for $t < to$
$ = 1$ for $t \geqslant to$ (after Mc Ghee et al. 1973)

Soil

$$y = \left| \frac{108.2}{1 + e^{0.70-0.37t}} - \frac{108.2}{1 + e^{0.70}} \right|^{0.49} + \left| \frac{25.3}{1 + e^{-1.05-0.37(t-3)}} - \frac{25.3}{1 + e^{-1.05}} \right|^{2.75} U(t-4)$$

with $U(t-to) = o$ for $t < to$
$ 1$ for $t \geqslant to$

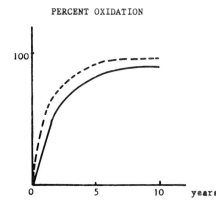

PERCENT OXIDATION

$$y = p_1 L(1-10^{-k_1't}) + p_2 L(1-10^{-k_2't}) + \ldots$$

p_1 : percentage of compound with k_1' in L; etc.

Composition of litter

	p	k'
Phenols	0,05	0,07
Waxes	0,05	0,13
Lignin	0,40	0,30
Cellulose	0,20	0,63
Hemicellulose	0,15	1,00
Sugars	0,15	2,00

Fig. 3. Simulation of simultaneous first order biodegradation processes (after Minderman 1968). _____ actual biodegradation ; _____ simultaneous first order model.

discussed above. The following comparative values were found :

Parameters	Sum of partial first orders	Single first order	Second order
SSS	1174	14.9	115
k	-	0.682	0.00702
L	100	91.8	109.2

Apparently, the composite curve approximates not so well the actual degradation curve as e.g. the single first order model. An attempt was made to obtain a better fit with the composite curve by computing the set of k'-values which gave for the actual set of p-values, a minimal SSS. The following equation was obtained.

$$y = 5(1-10^{-0.07t}) + 5(1-10^{-0.13t}) + 40(1-10^{-0.30t}) + 20(1-10^{-0.87t})$$

$$+ 15(1-10^{-0.87t}) + 15(1-10^{-0.87t})$$

The minimal SSS thus obtained still amounted to 24.2, however. These results suggest that the simultaneous biodegradation of a complex array of substrates in soils, although logically corresponding to a summation of individual biodegradation processes, can be sometimes conveniently represented by an overall first order model.

DISCUSSION   AND   CONCLUSIONS

The goal of these preliminary modeling studies is to simulate biological degradation phenomena occuring in waters and soils. These models must allow the biologist to identify and quantity the kinetic parameters governing the biotransformation processes, thus allowing him to interprete more precisely the fundamental biological phenomena involved. Ultimately, the biologist should be able to predict by means of these models, the fate of a given set of substrates in a given ecosystem

Of the non-composite models which have been examined, the first order model and the logistic S-curve, can be explained quite logically in biological terms. The first order model reflects the exponential growth of a physiologically adapted microbial community as a funtion of the metabolism of the available substrate. As to the logistic S-curve, the initial lag phase corresponds to a gradual enzymatic and/or ecological adaptation of the microbial community to the substrate and to the environmental conditions. The succeeding positive and negative acceleration phases are then a function, both of the remaining substrate and of the amount of biomass formed from the substrate oxidised. The consecutive first order reaction model can also quite easely be translated in biological terms since a variety of biodegradation processes actually consist of consecutive metabolic steps, each of them governed by first order kinetics.

Of the composite curves, the sequential oxidation type is quite frequently encountered. It results either from the subsequent enzymatic adaptation of the microbial community towards more and more recalcitrant components of the available substrate or from subsequent shifts of microbial populations within the microbial community as a result of environmental changes during the biodegradation process. Typically, these type of changes seem to occur in communities with a low to medium species diversity.

Job Listing

Jobs nr	1	2	3	4	5	6	7	8	9	10	11	12
Days	0.47	0.74	1.17	1.42	1.60	1.75	1.84	1.95	2.19	2.18	2.17	
1	168	336	468	570	660	708	696					
2	9	9	16	20	21	21.5	22					
3	4.3	8.2	9.5	10.35	12.1	12.6	13.1					
4	6.8	12.7	14.8	15.4	17	18	19.9					
5	109	149	149	180	191	205	213	220	223	224		
6	8.2	10.2	19	16	15.6	18	19.8					
7	4710	7080	8460	9580								
8												
9	3.2	5.4	7.8	9.4	10.6	12	13.2	14.8	15.7	17	18	19
10	1.7	4.5	6.3	7.5	9.7	11	11	13.6	14.6	15	16.4	17.5
11	1.2	2.4	3.8	5	7.4	8.8	10	11.2	12	12.6	13.7	15
12	0	0.2	1.4	2	2.5	3.5	3.9	5.2	5.8	6	6.4	5
13	3	5	6	7.2	10	11	12	15	15	15	15.8	17.4
14	2	7	10	12	14	15	17	18	18	19	20	
15	3	12	26	35	44	57	72	86	97	105	110	
16	3	12	31	45	67	92	108	117.5	126	132.5	138	
17	3	12	25	30	33	35	36	39	40	40	40	
18	6	9	15	25	42	61	75	85	92	99	104	
19	4	12	19	32	55	72	83	89	95	100	105	

LITERATURE

Bailey, R.C., G.S. Eadic, and F.H. Schmidt (1974). Estimation procedures for
    consecutive first order irrevesible reactions. Biometrics 30 : 67-75.
Fair, G.M. (1937). The log-difference method for estimating ʰe constants of the
    first-stage biochemical oxygen demand curve. Sewage ..orks Journal 9 (3) :
    430.
Fletcher, R.I. (1974). The quadric law of damped exponential growth. Biometrics
    30 : 111-124.
Fujimoto, Y. (1964). Graphical use of first-stage BOD equation. J. Water Pollut.
    Contr. Fed. 36 : 69.
Mc Ghee, T.J., R.L. Torrens, and R.J. Smaus (1973). Aerobic treatment of feedlot
    runoff. J. Water Pollut. Cont. Fed. 45 (9) : 1865-1873.
Marske,D.M., and L.B.Polkowski (1972). Evaluation of methods for estimating
    biochemical oxygen demand parameters. J. Water Pollut. Contr. Fed. 44 (10):
    1987-2000.
Marquadt, D.W. (1965). An algorithm for least squares estimation of nonlinear
    parameters. J. Soc. Indust. Appl. Math. 11 : 431-441.
Minderman, G. (1968). Addition, decomposition and accumulation of organic matter
    in forests. J. Ecol. 56 (2) : 355-362.
Moore, E.W., H.A. Thomas, and W.B. Snow (1950). Simplified method for analysis of
    BOD data. Sewage and Industrial Wastes 22 (10) : 1343.
Reed, L.J., and E.J. Theriault. (1931). The statistical treatment of reaction-ve-
    locity data. II. Least-Squares treatment of the unimolecular expression
    $Y = L (1 - e^{-kt})$. J. Phys. Chem. 35 : 950-971.
Thomas, H.A. Jr. (1937). The slope method of evaluating the constants of the
    first-stage biochemical oxygen demand curve. Sewage Works Journal 9 (3) :
    425.
Wright, R.T. and J.E. Hobbie. (1966). Use of glucose and acetate by bacteria and
    algae in aquatic ecosystems. Ecology 47 (3) : 447-464.

DISCUSSION

*What do you call the difference between a logistic model and a sigmoidal
model ? (BALAKRISHNAN)*

I called sigmoidal the S shape type of curve and we approached it on the
classical logistic mathematics. (VERSTRAETE)

*I heard the term logistic used when you are creating basic models before
you try to verify your actual data. Is that correct ? (BALAKRISHNAN)*

I agree with that. (VERSTRAETE)

Modeling and Simulation of Water Resources Systems, G.C. VANSTEENKISTE, (Ed.)
North-Holland Publishing Company (1975)

THE INFLUENCE OF THE QUALITY OF WATER ON ECOLOGICAL SYSTEMS

D.M. Dubois [*]
Institute of Mathematics
Université de Liège, BELGIUM

ABSTRACT

Recently, a general model was proposed to explain the
fluctuations and the spatial structuration in plankton
populations in the sea. An index of fluctuations,
directly connected to the diversity and the stability
of ecological systems was given (Dubois 1973) :

$$D_o = \sum_{i=1}^{S} (p_i \ln p_i/\bar{p}_i + \bar{p}_i - p_i)$$

The spatial structuration of interacting populations
(Dubois 1974 ab) is well explained by our model. A
critical wavelength λ_c is a basic characteristic of
this structuration :

$$\lambda_c = 2 \pi (2D/\omega)^{1/2}$$

The purpose of this working-paper is to exhibit the
great influence of the quality of water on ecological
systems. The quality of water can be characterized not
only by suitable values of such properties as temperature, salinity, dissolved oxygen and dissolved nutrients,
but also by such mechanical properties as movement of
water and turbulent diffusion.

Several cases were simulated on computers and it is
shown that populations exhibit fluctuations and a
spatial inhomogeneity with a rather long lifetime.

[*] ————————

From 15th January to 20th March 1975 : Fisheries and
Marine Service, Marine Ecology Laboratory, Bedford
Institute of Oceanography, Dartmouth, N.S. B29 4A2 ,
Canada.

From 21st March to 15th June 1975 : University of
Florida, Dept. of Environmental Engineering Sciences,
A.P. Black Hall, Gainesville, Florida 32611, U.S.A.

INTRODUCTION

Plankton populations such as phytoplankton and herbivorous copepods can be considered as living in some sea-water mass characterized by suitable values of such properties as temperature, salinity, dissolved oxygen and dissolved nutrients.

Moreover, in the sea, plankton populations are almost entirely at the mercy of water movement and yet display considerable spatial inhomogeneity, i.e. patchiness.

In view of studying the influence of the quality of water on plankton populations, let us consider the one-dimensional problem of a long and narrow mass of sea-water limited on the two sides by natural boundaries. We assume further that, outside this region of length L, the diffusivity becomes large or that the water is physiologically unsuitable for the organisms. Either condition requires that the concentrations of organisms drop to zero at the two sides. As the transverse cross-section is small, compared to the length L , we can neglect transverse diffusion and consider the populations N_1 and N_2 to be a function of the longitudinal position only :

$$N_1 = N_1(x,t) \tag{1-a}$$

$$N_2 = N_2(x,t) \tag{1-b}$$

Let one side be at $x = 0$ and the other at $x = L$. The boundary conditions will be

$$N_1(0,t) = N_2(0,t) = N_1(L,t) = N_2(L,t) = 0 \tag{2}$$

Plankton can be considered as small organisms of identical size embedded in a turbulent flow and their number is sufficiently large so that a deterministic continuous model can be used.

THE MATHEMATICAL MODEL

Let $\underline{v}(\underline{r},t)$ and $C_1(\underline{r},t)$ be the velocity and concentration of the phytoplankton at position $\underline{r}$ and time t , respectively. The instantaneous equation for organisms is given by (Dubois 1974 b)

$$\partial C_1/\partial t + \nabla \cdot (\underline{V} \, C_1) = k_1 C_1 - k_2 C_1 C_2 + D_{1m} \nabla^2 C_1 \tag{3-a}$$

where D_{1m} is a diffusion coefficient due to Brownian motion of organisms, k_1 is the rate of growth of the phytoplankton and k_2 is the rate of interactions between phytoplankton and herbivorous copepods, the concentration of which is given by $C_2(\underline{r},t)$. In general the diffusion term D_{1m} can be neglected except for microorganisms.

Similar equation can be written for C_2

$$\partial C_2/\partial t + \nabla \cdot (\underline{V} \, C_2) = - k_3 C_2 + k_4 C_1 C_2 + D_{2m} \nabla^2 C_2 \tag{3-b}$$

As only statistical properties of C_1 and C_2 can possibly be studied, let us divide the random quantities into the mean i.e. an ensemble average and a fluctuation from this mean.

$$\underline{V} = \underline{U} + \underline{w} \tag{4-a}$$

$$C_1 = N_1 + c_1 \tag{4-b}$$

$$C_2 = N_2 + c_2 \tag{4-c}$$

with $\langle \underline{w} \rangle = 0$, $\langle c_1 \rangle = 0$ and $\langle c_2 \rangle = 0$, where brackets are ensemble averages.

Substitution of eqs. 4-abc into eq. 3-a and averaging leads to

$$\partial N_1 / \partial t + \underline{U} \cdot \nabla N_1 + \nabla \cdot \langle \underline{w} \, c_1 \rangle = k_1 N_1 - k_2 N_1 N_2 -$$
$$- k_2 \langle c_1 c_2 \rangle + D_{1m} \nabla^2 N_1 \tag{5}$$

The dominant form of motion in the open sea is turbulent lateral diffusion. Using the gradient-type diffusion assumption, the turbulent flux term for organisms-concentration flux is expressed as

$$\langle \underline{w} \, c_1 \rangle = - \kappa_1 \nabla N_1 \tag{6}$$

where κ_1 represents the turbulent diffusion.

With eq. 6 , eq. 5 is written

$$\partial N_1 / \partial t + \underline{U} \cdot \nabla N_1 = k_1 N_1 - k_2 N_1 N_2 + \nabla \cdot (D_1 \nabla N_1) -$$
$$- k_2 \langle c_1 c_2 \rangle \tag{7-a}$$

where $D_1 = D_{1m} + \kappa_1$.

Similarly, eq. 3-b is written

$$\partial N_2 / \partial t + \underline{U} \cdot \nabla N_2 = - k_3 N_2 + k_4 N_1 N_2 + \nabla \cdot (D_2 \nabla N_2) +$$
$$+ k_4 \langle c_1 c_2 \rangle \tag{7-b}$$

where
$$D_2 = D_{2m} + \kappa_2 \quad .$$

It may be pointed out that eqs. 7-ab are formally identical to the original ones, i.e. eqs. 3-ab except a term representing the average of the product of the fluctuations of the two populations. In this work, $\langle c_1 c_2 \rangle$ is neglected. A full discussion about this term is given elsewhere (Dubois 1974-b).

The coefficients of turbulent diffusion are taken identical for the two populations and we assume that there are constant, i.e. $D_1 = D_2 = D =$ constant.

If we assume that the mean current $\underline{U}$ is constant, terms like $\underline{U} \cdot \nabla$ can be dropped with this appropriate change, $\partial / \partial t = \partial / \partial t' - \underline{U} . \nabla$

With all these assumptions, eqs. 7-ab become

$$\partial N_1 / \partial t = k_1 N_1 - k_2 N_1 N_2 + D \nabla^2 N_1 \tag{8-a}$$
$$\partial N_2 / \partial t = - k_3 N_2 + k_4 N_1 N_2 + D \nabla^2 N_2 \quad . \tag{8-b}$$

The non-zero stationary solution uniformly distributed in space, i.e. N_{10} and N_{20} are given by

$$N_{10} = k_3 / k_4 \tag{9-a}$$

$$N_{20} = k_1/k_2 \tag{9-b}$$

In view of studying the behaviour of the populations, let us consider solutions having the following form

$$N_j(x,t) = N_{jo} + n_j \exp(\Omega t + i\, 2\, \pi\, k\, x) \quad j = 1,2 \tag{10}$$

where n_j , Ω and k are constants. Any solution of eqs. 8-ab can be developped in Fourier series with terms similar to eq. 10. The dispersion relation for the linearized equations 8-ab is (Dubois 1974 a):

$$\Omega = - D\ (2\ \pi\ k)^2 + (-k_1 k_3)^{1/2} \tag{11}$$

A critical wave-number k_c is obtained when $\Omega = 0$, i.e.

$$2\ \pi\ k_c = \pm\ \left((-\ k_1 k_3)^{1/2}\ /D\right)^{1/2} \tag{12-a}$$

or

$$k_c = \pm\ (1 + i)/\lambda_c \tag{12-b}$$

where

$$\lambda_c = \pm\ 2\ \pi (2\ D/\omega)^{1/2} \text{ with } \omega = (k_1 k_3)^{1/2}$$

With eqs. 12-b , eq. 10 is written

$$N_j(x,t) = N_{jo} + n_j \exp(\pm\ i\ 2\ \pi\ x/\lambda_c \mp 2\ \pi\ x/\lambda_c) \tag{13}$$

From eq. 13 we see that populations should exhibit a spatial inhomogeneity characterized by the critical wavelength λ_c .

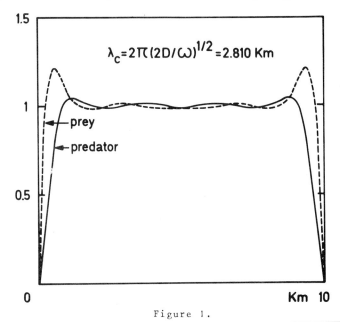

Figure 1.

In figure 1, we give the spatial behaviour of the two populations described by the functions $f_1(x)$ and $f_2(x)$ (symmetric around $L/2$).

$$f_1(x) = N_{10}(1 - \exp(-2\pi x/\lambda_c)(\cos 2\pi x/\lambda_c - \sin 2\pi x/\lambda_c) \quad (14\text{-}a)$$

$$f_2(x) = N_{20}(1 - \exp(-2\pi x/\lambda_c)(\cos 2\pi x/\lambda_c + \sin 2\pi x/\lambda_c) \quad (14\text{-}b)$$

for $x \in (0, L/2)$ and

$$f_1(x) = N_{10}\left[1-\exp\left(2\pi(x-L)/\lambda_c\right)\right]\left(\cos 2\pi(X-L)/\lambda_c - \sin 2\pi(x-L)/\lambda_c\right)$$
$$(14\text{-}c)$$

$$f_2(x) = N_{20}\left[1-\exp\left(2\pi(x-L)/\lambda_c\right)\right]\left(\cos 2\pi(X-L)/\lambda_c + \sin 2\pi(x-L)/\lambda_c\right)$$
$$(14\text{-}d)$$

for $x \in (L/2, L)$.

The values of the parameters are $L = 10$ km , $D = 10^5$ m^2 day^{-1} and $N_{10} = N_{20} = 1$. By comparison with the exact result, eqs.14-abcd represent a very good approximation of the steady state solution of eqs. 8-ab.

Now, let us give simulations of the space time behaviour of the two populations described by eqs. 8-ab. for initial conditions far from the steady state solution.

SIMULATION OF SPACE-TIME DEPENDENT POPULATIONS BEHAVIOUR

In view of studying the space-time dependent behaviour of the

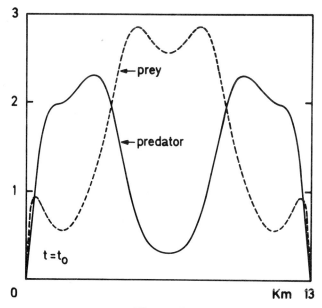

Figure 2-a.

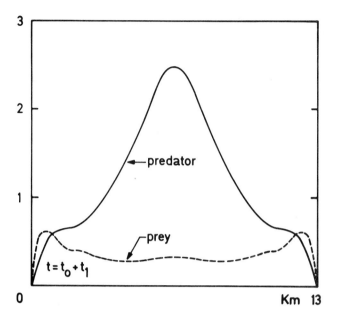

Figure 2-b.

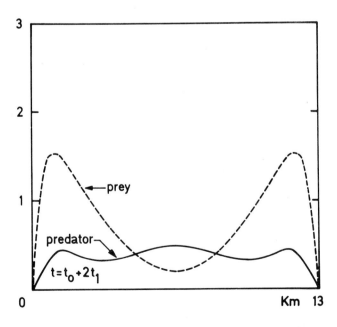

Figure 2-c.

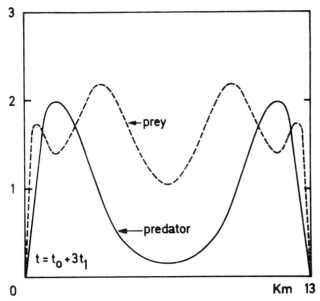

Figure 2-d.

two populations described by eqs. 8-ab, let us take the following
initial conditions $N_1(x,0) = f_1(x)$ and $N_2(x,0) = f_2(x)$. The values
of the parameters are : $N_{10} = 0.1$, $N_{20} = 1$, $L = 13$ km, $D = 10^5 m^2 day^{-1}$
$k_1 = k_2 = k_3 = k_4 = 1$ day^{-1} (then, $\omega = 1$ day^{-1}).

     Figures 2-abcd show the spatial behaviour of the two popula-
tions at four times (a) at $t = t_0 = 43$ days, (b) at $t = t_0 + t_1 =$
45 days ($t_1 = 2$ days), (c) $t = t_0 + 2t_1 = 47$ days and $t = t_0 + 3t_1 =$
49 days. This period of 6 days corresponds approximately to the
period T associated to the frequency ω , i.e. $T = 2 \pi/\omega = 2\pi = 6.28$
days. **Moreover ,**   the same spatial behaviours appear periodically with a period equal to T .

     From the inspection of figures 2-abcd, we remark that the
populations exhibit very important inhomogeneity. Moreover, the
maximum number of maxima for the population N_1 , i.e. the prey, is
four (see figure 2-d).

     If, instead of taking a lengh $L = 13$ km, we take a length
$L = 8$ km , the maximum number of maxima is only three. Indeed, this
can be seen by inspection of figure 3 (the time $t = 49$ days as in
figure 2-d).

     Finally, it must be noted that the time necessary to the two
populations to reach a steady state is large, compared to the period
T associated to the cyclic phenomena. This relaxation time is of the
order of $\tau_c = L^2/(m^2\pi^2D) = 171$ days, for $L = 13$ km, $D = 10^5 m^2 day^{-1}$
and $m = 1$ (m corresponds to the number of modes considered in the
Fourier transform of the solution).

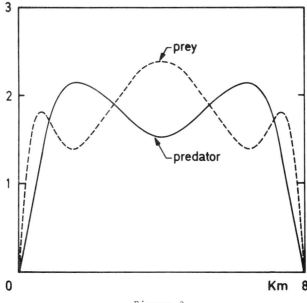

Figure 3.

ACKNOWLEDGEMENTS

We want to thank J.P. Foguenne for the programming of the
Mathematical model and Miss F. Hanesse for the typewriting of the
manuscript.

REFERENCES

DUBOIS, D.M. (1973a) "An index of fluctuations, D_0, connected with
diversity and stability of ecosystems : applications in the
Lotka-Volterra model and in an experimental distribution of
species" Rapport de Synthèse III, Programme National sur
l'Environnement Physique et Biologique, Projet Mer,
Commission Interministérielle de la Politique Scientifique,
étabétyp (Liège).

(1973b) "Aspect mathématique de l'invariant en
cybernétique : applications en écologie et en biologie",
Cybernetica, vol. XVI, N°3.

(1974a) "Learning, adaptation and evolution of the
environment - ecosystem couple" Advances in Cybernetics and
Systems Research, Proceedings of the European Meeting,
Vienna, 1974, Transcripta Books, London.

(1974b) "Comments on stability of ecosystems : fluctuations and structuration of plankton populations" Proceedings
of the Sixth Liège Colloquium on Ocean Hydrodynamics, Mem.
Soc. Roy. Sc, Liège.

DISCUSSION

There has been a lot of interest at our university in these equations also.
The details apart, the most interesting to us would be : has there be any attempt
to verify the optimum result in terms of observations. *(BALAKRISHNAN)*

Yes, many tests on the results have been done in the ocean (Northsea).
Another effect has to be added to these experimental data : namely a spectrum of
patchiness effect in the ocean which is the same as turbulent spectrum. (DUBOIS)

What is the reason for choosing a sinusoidal variation of the constants
k_1 *and* k_2 *which really lead you to the solution ? Very often we allow the constants*
k_1^1 *and* k_2^2 *to contain a random motion. Have you looked at that ?* *(BALAKRISHNAN)*

The variation of k_1 with a period of 1 day represented a variation of day
and night and that's the reason why it is periodic. (DUBOIS)

I have a few questions : - how did you integrate your equations ?
*   - is the model one dimensional steady state or*
*   two dimensional or three dimensional ?*
*   - is the turbulent diffusivity for the predata and*
*   the other equal, have you looked at unequal va-*
*   lues for the D's ?* *(DAVIDSON)*

I simulated one "two dimensional case". There was not much difference
(rectangular geometry). Now I am working in polar coordinates. (DUBOIS)

There is much discussion on modeling the stochastic version of these things
with D equal or not equal. How did you solve the equations on the computer ?
(BALAKRISHNAN)

With the finite element method. (DUBOIS)

How would you know the initial conditions for integration in a verification
scheme, how would you know where the integration starts. *(DAVIDSON)*

I have taken the distance x = 0 to L ; boundary conditions : L_1 and L_2
equals 0. I look on the behaviour starting from this initial configuration. The
structure is also a function of the initial conditions in other words. (DUBOIS)

Is it possible to arrive at a limit cycle with your model, because one of
the drawbacks of the Volterra model is that. It is conservative, which gives closed
curves in the phase plane. *(D'HOLLANDER)*

Yes, but not here, we have a diffusion term, function of time. But it is
included in the model to go eventually from one limit curve to another by changing
initial conditions. (DUBOIS)

Current research field of author : *Environmental systems and biological systems.*

PART FOUR

SYSTEM ENGINEERING IN
WATER RESOURCES
MANAGEMENT

Modeling and Simulation of Water Resources Systems, G.C. VANSTEENKISTE, (Ed.)
North-Holland Publishing Company (1975)

SIMULATION IN THE MANAGEMENT AND CONTROL OF DUTCH WATER RESOURCES

Ir. M.S. Elzas
Ass. Prof. Computer Science
Wageningen Agricultural University
Wageningen, NETHERLANDS

INTRODUCTION.

To the tourist Holland is not only famous for its wooden shoes and windmills, but also for its dykes.

In all national planning, since the beginning of written history in northwestern Europe, water always has had a predominant role in our country. Its influence was critical for the development of the Netherlands as a liveable landarea and as a country in the socio-political sense.

HISTORICAL BACKGROUND.

It seems appropriate to first state a few facts about the historical development of the Netherlands in relation to the water in the country and the water surrounding it, in order to understand the water resource problems that the country faces in our time.

The first intelligible charts of the Netherlands date back to the end of the Roman Empire. Figure 1 shows the structure of the country according to a map made between the 3rd. and the 8th. century a.c.. The map shows clearly that the country did not have the delta structure in the South Western part at that time, nor the string of islands ("wadden") in the northwest, and that the later Zuiderzee was only a relatively small inland fresh water lake, "the Flevomeer". Figure 2 shows the influence of the floods in the 9th. and 10th. century: the South Western delta comes into being, the North Western coast is invaded by water and a string of sand islands (the "wadden") start their existence. The inland sweet water lake gets connected to the sea and becomes salty, the country gets covered by a myriad of small, shallow, lakes. Flevomeer becomes Almere (meaning: great lake). The sea however keeps pounding on our coasts, severe floods follow, some islands in the southern delta disappear completely under sealevel taking into oblivion the cities built om them. In the north whole land-areas are washed away and so the 14th. century map illustrated in fig. 3 shows the Zuiderzee in its fullest expansion.

In the 17th. century the Dutch traders start to be concerned about safeguarding the profits they make, and so seafarers get converted into land-owners as the first large "polders" start to created as capital investment projects (//// area in fig. 4). The population also increases considerably, a.o. because of the protestants immigrating to our country from Belgium and France. During the next centuries the process of polder-building goes on, with the advent of mechanisation and the steamengine-driven pumps larger projects are taken on and in the 19th. century, the Haarlemmermeerpolder in the very heart of Holland is laid dry (\\\\ area in fig. 4).

At the beginning of the 20th. century, the need becomes apparent for the country to achieve, on short term, independence in the safeguarding of its basic agricultural resources, so as to cover the food supply for its population.

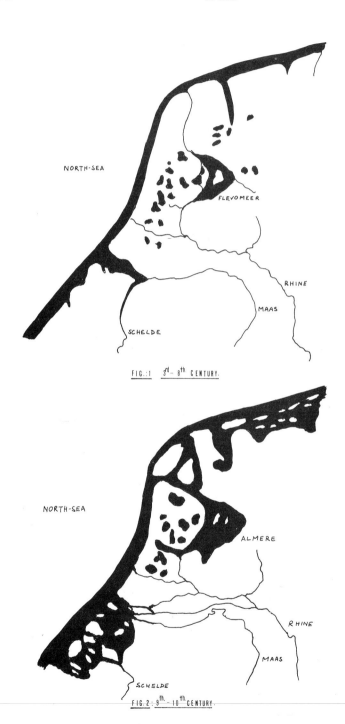

FIG.:1   3rd – 8th CENTURY.

FIG.2 : 9th – 10th CENTURY.

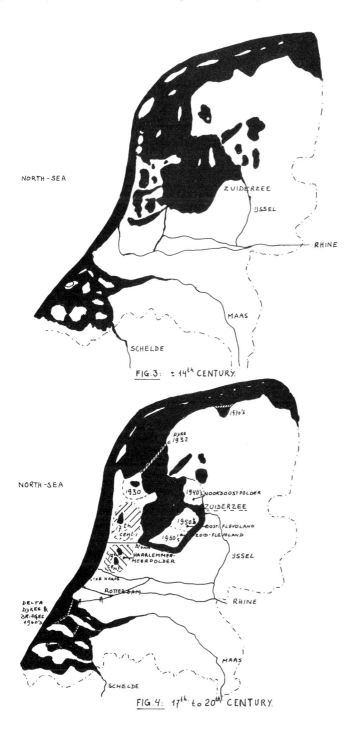

FIG. 3: ≈ 14th CENTURY.

FIG. 4: 17th to 20th CENTURY.

Specifically during the first world war, in which the Netherlands were a neutral country facing severe food shortage, the idea originated to increase the useful agricultural area of the country. A major flood in January 1916 - which caused the Zuiderzee dykes to break - engendered great public support for the ideas of a modern waterworks pioneer Ir. Lely, to close off the Zuiderzee from the sea by a large dyke and as a consequence provide for the construction of a quantity of safe polders. After elaborate·laboratory model studies, the project got on its way. In the first place the Wieringermeer-polder was laid dry in 1930, followed by the great Zuiderzee-dyke in 1932. The Noordoost-polder came into existence around 1940. Oost-Flevoland in the 1950's and Zuid-Flevoland is now being finished.

Another great flood occured in 1953, causing many dykes in the southwestern delta and surroundings to break. This caused the so called "Delta-Plan" to come into existence. In this plan most of the islands in the Delta are being connected by dykes, closing off the inland waters from the sea. The plan also caters for re-inforcing and heightening the dykes in the rest of the country.

Meanwhile the Dutch population has increased from about 8 million souls before the war to about 13 million people now, making the Netherlands the second country in average population density in the world. The western coastal region has known a revolutionary industrialisation, as a consequence the area between the sea and about 20 miles inland has one of the highest industrial densities in the world. Urbanisation problems abound as the old Dutch cities cannot cope anymore with the huge population increase and the modern urban demands.

In the past 20 years the rivers flowing into our country have become more and more polluted, by the population and the industry in the countries surrounding us.

Clearly, the Netherlands have no real control over what happens to its water resources before they penetrate the country.

The modern methods of agriculture allowing more intensive use of the available landarea, more space has become available in the newly built polders for the much needed additional recreative and urbanisation space.

The closing of many sea-arms face us now with the problems of large bodies of more or less polluted semi-stagnant water, from which the public water supply has to be partially provided.

Figure 5 tries to illustrate briefly the problems of Dutch water-management by means of a simplified sketch of the input/output situation.

EARLY COMPUTIONAL VENTURES:

Influenced by the 1953 catastrophy, which caused many leading Dutch mathematicans to study the nature of extreme tidal circumstances, influenced also by the advent of modern computing tools, computational projects were started to help in the design of a whole water defence network to protect the country against future disasters.

In 1956 a project was started to design and utilise electronic techniques for the study of the propagation of tidal waves from the sea into the Dutch waterways system. This system was designed to include also watershed data of the rivers entering our country from the surroundings, so that realistic data could be obtained. A choice was made for a direct analogy system, very similar to the analog computers developped later in the U.S.A.

Water currents (or hydraulic conductivity) should be represented by electrical currents, waterways wet cross-section should be represented by resistances, so that Ohm's law should provide user with flow-data:

$$V(t) = I(t) . R(t) \Rightarrow F(t) = C(t) . \quad S(t)$$
$$\text{Flow = current.section}$$

The waterways were represented in sections chosen in such a way that the main parameters were almost constant for any given section . Reservoir areas or lock sections were represented using integratordevices. The design of the system called "DELTAR" was finished by 1959, the system was operational by 1962 and could represent about 300 different sections. Paper tape input and output were provided by that time to input measurement data, or past time history data into the system. This aided the possibility to the system to work (slowly) iteratively and cover large areas with diverse parameters by recording the data from one run on papertape and use these data for the next run with new sections.

The hydraulic feasibility of the Delta dyke system and the design of stormlock locations was so achieved, in close agreement with the laboratory scale model studies.

In the mean time another large project was started to establish the consequences of extreme high water situations on the inland rivers. To illustrate the problem fig. 6 shows a typical Dutch river basin cross section. As in this case the cross sections vary considerably with the height of the waterlevel in the river basin, the choice was made to use a deterministic model and an early digital computer (Stantec Zebra). The resulting partial differential equations were solved by means of a method that could be considered as a simplified early forerunner of the finite element method. The program ran succesfully after 3 years of implementation effort and is still in use to this day.

Another group of people, interested in the hydrological aspects of drainage, was meanwhile solving the related P.D.E.'s by direct analogy methods using either the electrolitic tankmethod, the resistive paper method or R.C. networks.

These original schools of thought:
1) the pure mathematical-physical group, 2) the analog oriented group and 3) the deterministic numericists have influenced the actual simulation going on nowadays to a great deal.

I want however to stress at his moment that in many cases the methods used for simulation, are comparable in merit, while the main problem for the engineer and scientist is to get this project accepted and funded by the community, so that the presentation of the results becomes increasingly more important with respect to the simulation method used. It appears to be especially important that the people to which the results of our studies are presented get convinced that the results are realistic, and that we give them the opportunity to get a "feel" of the sensivity of the solution to the change of those parameters that are considered to be critical by the community.

PRESENT SITUATION:

Although efforts are spent in trying to co-ordinate all the simulations going on so as to be able to work as a team on the problem of the entire Dutch water system, like elsewhere in the world organisational and political forces work against this, while - on the other hand - it became apparent in this context that the pure "systems" people can provide a sound co-ordinating basis to all the separate efforts. It seems usefull to point out that all the techniques mentioned in the previous paragraph, still lead a prominent life in modern water resource-simulation in the Netherlands. It is apparent however that in many of the projects going on the "systems" approach has acquired a strong influence.

As it is impossible in this context to discuss all simulation projects active in our country, I have selected three of them, more or less at random, that cover different areas of the entire field.

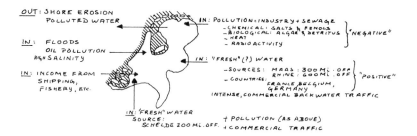

FIG. 5: INPUT/OUTPUT SYNTHESIS.

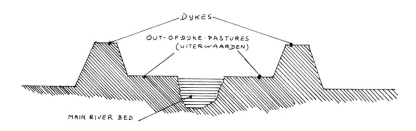

FIG. 6 : A TYPICAL DUTCH RIVER PROFILE

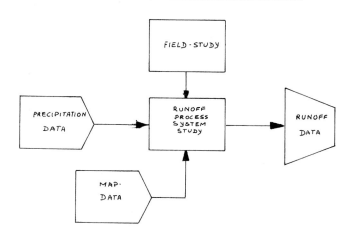

FIG. 7 : RUNOFF EXPERIMENT ORGANISATION.

A PRECIPITATION-RUNOFF MODEL.

At the hydrological laboratory of Wageningen Agricultural University, an electronic analog/hybrid model has been built to study and verify experimentally a simple
systems-approach to describe predipitation transport phenomena due to runoff
and infiltration (percolation).

The experimental areas were concentrated around a few small Dutch rivers,
while measurements were made in the winter when evapotranspiration phenomena
play a negligible role in our country.

Fig. 7 shows the organisational set-up of the experiment.

The system analysis was based on the linearisation assumption resulting in
the following equation:

$$\frac{\partial y}{\partial t} = \frac{K.D}{U} \frac{\partial^2 y}{\partial x^2}$$

For the transient water table flow where

Y: is the local height of the groundwaterlevel above the adjacent water
   table level of the brook or canal
K: is the saturated hydraulic conductivity
D: is the average groundwaterlevel height above the impermeable layer
U: is the percentage of active volume of pores of the soil

System analysis prompted the idea that the precipitation transport phenomea,
could be split into two sections: a "fast" and a "slow" linear diffusion (or
dispersion) model. A physical reasoning can back-up this idea as this situation
can represent more or less the direct overland runoff and the indirect transportation by infiltration and precolation through the soil.

A schematic of the model set up is shown in fig. 8, where

α: is the direct runoff-infiltration distribution coefficient
η: represents the ratio of precipitation (after consumptive losses) causing
   the runoff

j_1 and j_2: represent diffusivity constants in the 2 diffusion models
   τ: represents a delay caused by waterpropagation time between precipitation
   and measurement points (o.a. dependent on shape of waterchannel) and
   the influence of the unsaturated soil area.

The system was finally built up to optimise α, η, j_1 and j_2 and τ so as to
obtain the best fit.

For this purpose the set up in fig. 9 was used. Precipitation and resulting
watertransportation data for a long period of time (200 to 300 measurement intervals) are stored in the function generator, and the parameters are adjusted until
c.w. (the criterium) is minimal.

Until now this optimisation was handcontrolled, but recently the whole system
was implemented on a random search, steepest descent, technique.

An illustration of the quality of the obtained results is to be found in
fig. 10.

A GENERALISED WATERQUANTITY AND WATERQUALITY MODEL.

In the last few years interdisciplinary contacts were laid in the Netherlands for
the purpose of coming to management and control of the entire Dutch watersystem.

The ground concept of the management and control of our water is schematically indicated in fig. 11.

It is quite clear that such an ambitious project cannot be carried out in
one team and through one model. The different water areas under consideration moreover are too diverse in parameters to have one uniform set of equations apply
to the whole system.

M. Elzas

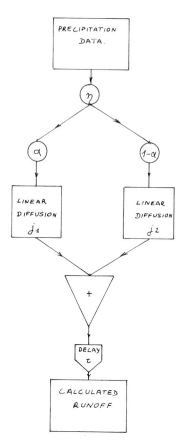

FIG. 8 :   MODEL SET UP. (FOR RUNOFF ANALYSIS)

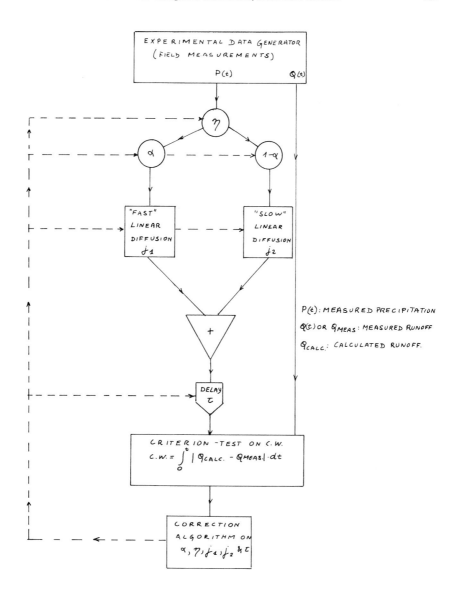

P(t): MEASURED PRECIPITATION

Q(t) OR Q$_{MEAS}$: MEASURED RUNOFF

Q$_{CALC}$: CALCULATED RUNOFF.

FIG. 9: MODEL OPTIMISATION SET-UP.

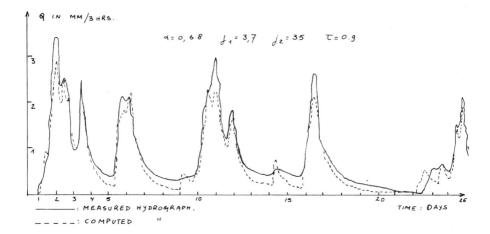

Q IN MM/3 HRS.

$d = 0,68$ $d_1 = 3,7$ $d_2 = 35$ $\tau = 0.9$

————— : MEASURED HYDROGRAPH.   TIME : DAYS

— — — — — : COMPUTED   "

FIG. 10 : SAMPLE OF RESULTS.

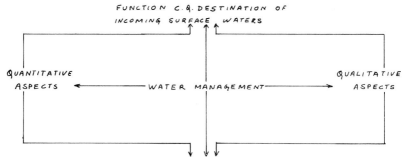

FUNCTION C.Q. DESTINATION OF
INCOMING SURFACE WATERS

QUANTITATIVE   QUALITATIVE
ASPECTS   ←——— WATER MANAGEMENT ———→   ASPECTS

CONTROLING MEASURES & ACTIONS:

• TREATMENT OF LOCAL WASTEWATER LOAD
• WATER HOUSEKEEPING CONTROL
• OPERATIONAL COUNTERMEASURES FOR THE
  CONSEQUENCES OF CALAMITIES
• INTENSIVATION OF SELF-CLEANING PROCESSES
• FLEXIBLE " FLUSHING " SYSTEM

FIG. 11 : CONCEPT OF WATER MANAGEMENT & CONTROL.

At this point the systems analysts in the team came up with the idea to unify the structure of the models needed and modularize the simulation in such a way that entire modules can be replaced from one simulation problem to the next, without disturbing the overall structure.

That means that only those modules that really should be different from one water area to the next are replaced.

The modules themselves are intended to be "free" in their internal structure. So, while the inputs and outputs of the models, linking an individual module to the rest of the system are strictly defined, the internal operation of the module can be formulated in a deterministic - (P.D.E. or similar) way, a stochastic - (e.g. time series) way, or some form of continuous / discrete simulation technique (systems-approach).

In this way each subteam designing a module for the whole system has the freedom to choose the modeling form that is most appropriate for the subject (or which fits best with the background of the team), while the form of the overall system stays unchanged and remains clear and comprehensive.

The model consists of 4 basic sections, to be expanded with 2 more sections at a later date.

Every basic section, and its relation to the other sections, has been constructed on a basis of system techniques such as:
- input-output analysis
- feedback (and feedforward) loop analysis
- isolation of control functions
- physical, chemical and biological process descriptions
- study of possible measurement-data and -techniques
- compartment-analysis

Mathematically this approach seems very straightforward and simple, it is its application to the widely differing waterareas in the country cause the (future) complication, a.o. by the inclusion of the interactions between the different water-systems that will be connected after having been modelled separately.

In the initial fase described here only those balances are represented that define the "rough" behaviour of the system. Sophistication will only be added when its necessity is proven. In the transfer of information from one section (or any one module) to another, a certaion sequence can be established. Under the assumption of certain simplifications the water-balance can be computed, from these results the energy- and chloride balance can be derived, then the oxygen-balance, where again some assumptions are needed about the biomass and so on. Then, when one "iteration" has come to its end, the assumptions are corrected (giving rise to a "feedback" mechanism") and a next run through the model is started, etc.

The 4 basic sections are the waterbalance, the chloride balance, the heat-balance and the oxygenbalance. To be added later are sections including non-conservative materials (floating, solved, fixed, sunk- and suspended materials) and the ecological loop of organic components (detritus, dead, organic material, excrements, aerobic bacteria etc.).

Each of the balances consists of larger sections, which on their turn are split into modules. There is naturally a large amount of interaction between the balances that have been mentioned, so the inputs and outputs of the modules are common to different balance-systems.

As it will take us too far to descri-be the entire system on a module by module basis, the balances will be described through their mainsections only. More details are to be found in litt. 1.

The waterbalance consists of the following main sections:

. Biomass influences
. Geometrical data generation
. Input/output data generation
. Residence time data generation
. Watersinks descriptions
. Watersources description
. Transportation to - and from associated surface waters ("natural")
. Artificial watersources,(higher grounds, polders, used cooling water, sewage etc.)
. Artificial watersinks (public watersystem, polders, cooling water, industrial water etc.)
. Precipitation and evaporation
. Seepage-in and seepage-out

The chloride balance consists of the following main sections:

.Cl^- total mass and concentration
.Cl^- sources and sinks
.Effective Cl^- transportation
.Advective Cl^- transportation
.Molecular diffusion of Cl in stagnant groundwater

The heat balance consists of the following main sections:

. Watertemperature data generation
. Heatcapacity data, heatsinks and -sources.
. Advective heat transportation
. Effective heat diffusion
. Molecular heat conduction in bottom
. Nett global shortwave radiation
. Nett longwave atmosferic radiation
. Longwave water radiation losses
. Flow of latent evaporation heat
. Flow of "feeleable" heat

The oxygen balance consists of the following main sections:

. O_2 oxygen mass and concentration
. O_2 sources and sinks (including a.o. bacterial decomposition and chemical reactions)
. Advective O_2 transportation
. Effective diffusive O_2 transportation
. Molecular diffusion O_2 from groundwater
. Atmosferic interaction
. Photosynthesis and primary producing agents
. Respiration and secundary producing agents
. Oxygen use by aerobe bacteries (decomposites)

Although techniques that are common to dynamic system concepts as outlined by Forrester and Meadows have been used for notational purposes to define the system, it is not the intention of the group to use only the modeling approach predicated by this school of thought.

It should be mentioned, however, that such an approach can be helpful in the set-up of the first outlines of the modules concerned, and will be useful in that case for the purpose of providing an interdisciplinary language in the early stages of the teams' work.

A STUDY OF THE MANAGEMENT GOALS AND EVALUATION PROCEDURES IN REGIONAL WATER-SOURCE CONTROL (Gelderland province, Netherlands).

Litt. 2

The study considered in this context is socio/economic in its nature. The study intends to establish decision criteria for the waterresource managers and tries to evaluate the economic consequences of the use of surface waters for different purposes. The intention of the study is to find:
a) a descriptive, collective utility function for the waterresources
b) a way to maximize this function through comprehensive management techniques.

The "utility" criteria used are dependent on the concepts of "Welfare Economics".

These principles can be illustrated by the following figure (fig. 12), taking into account that the "utility" of commodities is dependent on income if the commodities are marketeable goods, and dependent on general scarcity if the commodities are of environmental nature.

The willingness to pay a more for more of a commodity creates a situation of marginal utility (e.g. relation of marketprice to need for goods).

A general utility function can be written as:
$U = f(L, K, F)$ where U is the utility function
L : is the amount of labour involved
Q : quantity of good(s) concerned
K : the amount capital involved and F : the amount natural resources utilisation involved
$\frac{\partial U}{\partial Q}$: is the marginal utility (function)

The intent and purpose of Welfare Economics is to maximize U.

In a situation, like in our country, where not only the natural resources but nature itself is a scarce commodity, and where time is of importance while the situation under study deteriorates progressively in time, the utility function could expanded to be written as:
$U = f(L, K, F, N, T)$, where N is the amount of nature degredation involved; and T is the maximum time involved to make control actions still useful.

The conditions for an optimum are found when:
$\frac{\partial U}{\partial Q}$ = constant, that is to say when the marginal utility of an unit quantity is equal for all its users (domestic, industrial and recreative).

$\frac{\partial K}{\partial Q}$ = constant, meaning that the marginal costs of all production forms of the unit quantity (of water) become equal.

As many data pertaining to the field of economical statistics are known for the province under study (a mixed industrial/agricultural/urban/recreational area) the studyteam wording on this matter expects to be able to describe the before-mentioned utility functions in sufficient detail for optimisation purposes.

Mostly above conditions for marginal utilities and marginal costs cannot be created for a sufficiently wide water quantity interval, while the marginal costs can be shown to increase for increased waterproduction, so the next best optimum is when $\frac{\partial U}{\partial Q} = \frac{\partial K}{\partial Q}$

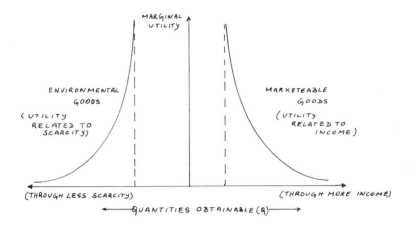

FIG.12 : ILLUSTRATION OF MARGINAL UTILITY FUNCTIONS $\left(\frac{\partial u}{\partial q}\right)$

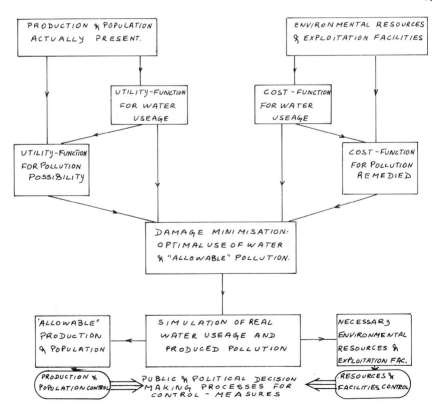

FIG.13 : LONG RANGE PLANNING & CONTROL PROCESS

The optimisation will in first instance be carried out only for two kinds
of water:
    a) water for consumptive use and b) water as a polluteable medium. Where b
is based on the assumption that some pollution is unavoidable and so has its
utility. The intent of the study is to optimize the utility function, taking
into account the schematic development shown in fig. 13, so as to obtain long-
range planning criteria for the economics and control of waterresources. It
should be noted that model sections of similar concept are a perequisite in
making the model described in the previous paragraph, usefull in a national
decision making process. It is hoped that the provincial model treated here will
provide a good initial study for a wider application on a national basis at
some later date.

FINAL REMARKS.

- It is already clear from the Dutch exaples that there are many ways in
  which to model water resource problems.
- The methods used depend on the locally available tools,
  the personal philosphy and -background of the people engaged in the
  modelling process and the nature of the problem area attacked.
- Even with extensive experience it seems to be increasingly difficult for
  the modeller to decide on pure rational grounds which modelling technique
  he should apply.
- The boundary conditions of the modelling efforts bring with them extra
  difficulties, such as:

a) funds for large simulation project financing are hard to find.
b) political decisions tend to be taken before the simulation studies
   have reached a conclusive stage: so time is always too short.
c) predictions are wanted under heavy odds of uncertainty .
d) the effective influence of the achieved results is almost totally
   dependent on the presentation of these to the "interested" parties.
e) the modelling groups are very often assembled from people from widely
   varying backgrounds, which do not understand each other too well in
   their technical discussions.
- It is my opinion that the situation will never be reached where
  conclusive proofs can be given that one modelling technique is better than
  another for any large class of problems.
- Therefore, it is the duty of mathematicans, computer scientists and
  systems people to provide the community with a wide variety of easily
  useable modelling tools.
  In the past the construction of these tools has been succesfully undertaken.
  The additional effort that we have to spend, and I am confident we will do so,
  is to provide concepts and techniques with the different modelling
  approaches can work together in a unified system on a module by module
  basis.

LITERATURE.

Litt. 1: Procesanalyse waterkwantiteit en -kwaliteit
         Ir. G.J.G. Kok, Rijkswaterstaat Deltadienst
         Afd. Milieu-onderzoek

      2: (Nota 768), Instituut voor Cultuurtechniek en
         Waterhuishouding, Wageningen
         Drs. L.J. Locht

DISCUSSION

*Who is giving you the coefficients of the cost function you have to minimize
I am a bit critical on this point. You usually get those coefficients from politicians.   (TODINI)*

One can establish those coefficients à priori in another way. If one records the production costs on one hand and the use of these brooks, which is done
in Holland by the European Center of Statistics, one can get the complete input
output matrix for a column in which its cost function is incorporated. There are
techniques to calculate this. (ELZAS)

*Yes, but you have social aspects to take into account and those are not
given by any matrix. (TODINI)*

The cost function does not have social aspects, the modular utility does ;
on the markable loops because they depend on the income, and on the nonmarkable
loops because they depend on the real need. I just had a discussion with some people
in how much water a person needs ; the number differs by a factor of ten ! (ELZAS)

On what time base did you develop that model ?

The first model was a device built from electronics, so it took about two
years to do that. The second model is still being built. The concept of   building together   models and how they work together is the only thing we worked out
up to now. **(ELZAS)**

*Could you make a few comments on the use of CSMP from the computer scien-
tist point of view ?*

On the use of CSMP for water resource problems : it is one of the simulation languages. People who don't know differential equations, can solve them, it's
an easy language, moreover it's readable. If you have a system approach you can
readily write it down. In the simulation languages field, there are little revo-
lutions going on. New languages will appear combining the systems approach and the
stochastic approach. When we are that far then it's very useful. (ELZAS)

*Could you elaborate on the way that you are determining the utility func-
tions and how sensitive is your result to the way that you determine these functions ? (NEUMAN)*

We are in the process of establishing this sensitivity. As far as the utility
functions is concerned : if I throw that back to people in economics, some people
say exponential function, others logarithmic function, others hyperbolic. Very often
it is only a series of Fourier polynomials. It is very difficult to judge which is
best because while setting up a function, you can only test it by simulating decisions. The purpose is to get tools with which the decision making people can play
to implement as many as possible utility functions with reasons for it. (ELZAS)

*Didn't you mention that together with this delta model, there was also run
a physical model ? (BRUTSAERT)*

We trusted, in the beginning at least, this model and most of the decisions
are based on this model although there was strong interaction between the two models
(ELZAS)

*With respect to your runoff model, did it apply to a whole watershed, tak
ing Holland as a whole ? (DE BOODT)*

Certainly not, it was one small brook. The model was original run only in the rainy periods in winter. There was no evaporation. You really have the runoff problem without other terms which were not simulated. You measure the runoff for a whole area, everywhere where water cames out. It is very heavily instrumented. It is continuously measuring the whole year. (ELZAS)

You mentioned that the political decisions were made before the results of the measurements became available and that the implementation could only succeed if the engineers and physicists could sell the system. Now in a socio-economic project of this type, it is always the case, one has to take into account the effectiveness of impact of implementation. What efforts are you making ? (SHAH)

The real scientist, the man who is serious about his job, takes his time to make his model. This time is in practice simply longer that the time that the politician want to have for his decisions. On the other hand the presentation problem we cannot solve, because we have with modern equipment all means of making more dimensional pictures, depicting what will happen, giving the results in a way that the decision maker is used to seeing results. I think this is something which is important to make the results of our ideas clear to others.(ELZAS)

Modeling and Simulation of Water Resources Systems, G.C. VANSTEENKISTE, (Ed.)
North-Holland Publishing Company (1975)

SYSTEMS ENGINEERING APPROACH TO AGRICULTURAL AND RURAL DEVELOPMENT SYSTEMS

M.M. Shah
Department of Electrical Engineering
University of Nairobi, KENYA

ABSTRACT

During the last two decades the rapid progress in the areas of
systems engineering and computers has played a major role in increasing
the living standards of many nations. Paradoxically, the developed nations
of the world have been the ones that have benefited the most from the
advancement in these areas, to such an extent, in fact, that in many cases
the gap between them and the developing countries has increased. This
aspect has been repeatedly voiced by many of the major donor aid agencies,
e.g. The World Bank, and a host of internationalists working in the field
of development and planning.

The economics and development strategies of the majority of developing
countries are based on Agricultural and Rural Development Systems which are
the backbone of the overall economy. In order for these countries to
develop and "catch up" with the advanced nations, the developing countries
need to take urgent measures to find out how their Agricultural and Rural
Development Systems are functioning, managed and planned in the context of
their overall socio-economic development.

In this paper I consider the scope of Systems Engineering Approach to Agricultural and Rural Development Systems. These systems are very complex,
large dimensional and stochastic in nature. Also predictably reliable
causal explanations of its socio-economic aspects are not available.
Systems Engineering Approach offers an ideal tool for structuring and
analysis (in the presence of uncertainties) of these systems from the point
of planning and evaluation of alternative strategies for development. In
the past traditional planning in these areas has not been very successful
since an integrated approach to the overall problem has generally not been
carried out.

In recent times many developing countries have plunged into the application
of systems engineering approach to their development and planning problems.
The paper describes some of the more interesting studies in Kenya, Nigeria,
Venezuela, Mexico, Argentina and Thailand. This aspect has shown that the
systems engineering approach needs considerable care and modification to
adapt it to the type of administration, technical manpower, scarcity of
resources, data availability etc. which are all very different in a developing country as compared with a developed country. Also note that each
developing country has its own particular problems based on the unique
social, economical, historical and technical assets. The problem of training suitable technical manpower is discussed in some detail as this is one
of the more acute difficulties faced by many of the developing countries.

This paper describes the systems application studies in Kenya. A conceptual hierachical model of the Agricultural and Rural Development Systems
as well as the present work on the construction of a normative model of
peasant agricultural and an overall macro-economic model of Kanya are
briefly described.

INTRODUCTION

Agricultural and Rural Development Systems in the Developing Countries

More then two thirds of the people of the developing countries live off the
soil. The majority of these people are small farmers and they are the so called
'absolute poor' of the world, McNamara /1/. If the quality and standard of life
of these people are to be improved then the developing countries need to take some
urgent measures for the short and long term future of their people. At the present
time the developing countries import millions of pounds worth of food and F.A.O.
estimates that to provide a decent level of nutrition for the worlds people the
production of food will have to be doubled by 1980 and trebled by the year 2000.
Not only time is running out but also the patience of these poorest people may be
exhausted. This will result in numerous breakdowns of society and peace on earth.
If development in the developing countries is to have any meaning then it is the
agricultural and rural development sectors that must get priority in the overall
plan for economic and social development. The term 'rural development' signifies
a comprehensive and an integrated approach to the various sectoral programmes e.g.
rural communications, rural education, rural health, rural nutrition, etc.

It is only in recent times that developing countries have realized that
agriculture makes an important contribution to social and economic development.
Agriculture forms not only a major part of the economy but it is also the sector in
which the majority of new entrants to the labour force have to find their livlihood.
Present day agriculture is a labyrinth of shifting patterns and forms. Economic
and social growth usually occurs in a series of small related sequences, each
determing the possibilities for the next. Clearly different approaches and strategies need to be emphasized as each sequence is reached, as others begin. The
need for an integrated systems engineering approach stems from the fact that
obstacle to, or constraints on, rural development are numerous and often independent, and thus demand a broad based approach.

Systems Engineering Approach

A systems engineering approach to the problem of development of a country,
is a systematic analysis and design of the numerous choices and options that are
open to the planners, economists, policy and decision makers in that country. A
system is defined as a set of resources of personnel, material, facilities and
information which are recognized to perform designated functions in order to
achieve desired results. With the world population explosion and dwindling earths
resources, it is increasingly being recognized that we need to review all aspects
of how our resources are being used and how the efficiency and output of this
usuage can be maximized. This aspect has prompted a review of resource allocation
and optimization in industrial concerns /2/, /3/, national governments /4/ and
also on the world scale, Forrester /5/.

The last decade has seen rapid progress in the theory, Mesarovic /6/ and
practical aspects, Wismer /7/, of the systems engineering approach. In the developed countries it has been widely and successfully applied in such diverse fields
as industrial processes, corporate business and management systems, urban, regional
and transport planning systems, economic and social planning. Examples of these
are Mitter and Dy-Liacco /8/, Rakic /9/, Wismer and Lasdon /10/, David /11/,
Pearce /12/ and Ellis /13/. The success of these various systems application
studies have no doubt contributed to the rising prosperity and better standards and
quality of life in the developed countries. The situation in the developing countries is very different. Most of these countries have embarked on ambitions 5 or
10 year development plans and the experiences of the last two decades show that in
the majority of cases it has been difficult to achieve any real measure of develop-

ment targets and ambitions. One of the reasons for this failure is that although
elegant plans for development have been produced, practical difficulties have been
encountered in the implementation stage and this aspect has resulted in the disturbingly low level of success in the developing countries.

Systems Engineering Approach offers an ideal tool for the design, dynamic
analysis and evaluation of alternative development strategies in agricultural and
rural development systems. In the developing countries there has been a lot of
criticism and prejudice on the part of planners, economists and sociologists in
that a systems engineering approach may be suitable for studying the 'nice' compact
industrial process or business firm but when it comes to socio-economic problems in
developing countries these are not only difficult but often defeating because of
the lack of data, trained personnel, scarcity of resources and the unique social,
economic, historical and technical assests in each developing country.

Agricultural and Rural Development Systems

These systems are complex in the sense that they are multi-dimensional,
highly interacting and stochastic in nature. Also in many of the socio-economic
aspects of these systems, reliable causal explanations of their behaviour may not
be available or even understood. However, the importance of these systems
in the overall economic development can be recognized from their three main
functions. Traditionally in the majority of developing countries these systems
have to supply the majority of the food for the population of the rural and urban
areas and also through the export of food to earna significant part of the foreign
exchange earnings. Furhtermore, it is the agricultural and the rural development
sectors which have to find new job opportunities for the ever increasing new ent-
trants in the labour forces. This aspect has been repeatedly stressed by many
donor agencies and quoting from the Pearson Commission on International Development,
/14/,

> "The main burden of absorbing the increase in the labour force falls
> inevitably on agriculture...... Only a fraction of the new workers
> can find employment in non-agricultural sectors even if these expand
> very rapidly. A strategy for agricultural development which increases
> employment opportunities rapidly without depressing incomes must
> focus on labour using and capital saving ways of improving agricultural
> productivity".

If the above three functions of Agricultural and Rural Development Systems
are to be achieved then the developing countries have to evaluate why the traditional planning approaches have failed or have had limited success and also how
this elements of failure or limit can be eliminated.

Traditionally planning of Agricultural and Rural Development in the develop-
countries has been a paper excercise to produce elegant and ambitious plans. Often
the plan formulation stage has been completely divorced from the plan implementation stage. A result of this has been that since Agriculture and Rural development
systems are highly dynamic and interacting new situations and crises in these
sectors have not only resulted in outdated plans but in many cases more harm then
good has been done in continuing to implement the outdated plans in a changed environment in these sectors.

A systems engineering approach offers the possibility of not only plan and
target formulation for these systems but also a dynamic facility for continuous
evaluation and replanning to encounter new situations and changing patterns of
resources, weather, product markets and social changes. The stress here is on the
fact the plan formulation and implementation form one integrated excercise and not
separate entities as has been the case in the past.

Procedures for a Systems Engineering Approach

The main steps in the application of a systems engineering approach are:

1. Problem Formulation
2. Mathematical and Heuristic Modelling
3. Simulation Studies on the Model
4. Model Implementation and Application to the problem solution.

1.   Problem Formulation

In the developing countries the planning of agricultural and rural development systems is as much a political effort as it is a socio-economic one. Some of the main constraints are the scarcity of resources in an uncertain natural and human environment of complex interactions among physical, social, economic and political forces. A system engineering approach is in itself a valuable excercise because it obliges us to define the problem accurately. In the problem formulation stage it is important that there is close cooperation and dialogue between decision makers, planners, administrators, economists, rural experts, systems engineers, technologists, social scientists and other specialists. This creative interaction between specialists and decision makers is required for effective problem formulation and definition. For example the key factors for discussion are,

A.   Problem formulation and definition of Needs and Goals.
B.   System and its interaction with the environment.
C.   Effects of socio-techno-economic criteria.

Once the basic problem has been formulated then the next step is to consider the construction of a mathematical model and this requires an inter-disciplinary effort from the technical specialists such as agricultural and rural experts, economists, systems engineers and the technologists.

2.   Mathematical and Heuristic Modelling

In modelling the agricultural and rural development system the configuration of the overall system is not self-evident. Hence the first aim should be to consider specifications regarding the structure of the system and the way the different parts of the system are interconnected. Many possible configurations of the system are possible, and the problem is to design the one most appropriate for the particular requirements. Selection of a poor system configuration may obscure the workings of the system, may prevent its smooth operation and may also make future extensions and alterations of the system model very difficult.

Since the system is very large dimensional and complex the first step should be the construction of an analytical model. The theory of multilevel and hierarchial systems, Mesarovic /6 /, Wismer /7/ and Lasdon /15/, provide a natural conceptual structure for the system as it exists in practice. A benefit of this formulation is that it not only provides an insight into the dynamics of the system but it also enables critical path analysis of information collection and processing activities.

The next stage of the mathematical model building excercise is to consider which subsystems of the conceptual model can be quantified and which subsystems cannot be quantified. For example subsystems representing socio-political, psychological, institutional and administrative issues are often difficult to analyse and quantify. However, it is important that these subsystems are accounted for in some manner because in practice these particular subsystem effects determine the project impact and effectiveness. At the present time this problem of quantitative descriptions of socio-economic system is receiving research attention. An interesting approach to modelling of such systems has been presented by Gabus and

Figueiredo /16/ utilizing traditional quantitative models linked with "event generators" which take care of the more unpredictable parts of the socio-economic systems.

Once an approximate mathematical model has been obtained then this requires considerable testing and refinement to enable simulation studies. Some of the model analysis to be carried out are: evaluation of the internal consistency of model, model response to exogenous shocks and disturbances, parameter sensitivity studies etc. This type of analysis will lead to specifications and programs for necessary data collection, field tests, empirical research and socio-economic experiments so that this information can be used to correct and improve the approximate model. This continuous process of learning and model updating has to be carried out until a model suitable for simulation studies has been obtained. Together with this construction of a simulation model, specification regarding the performance objectives have also to be considered. In an Agricultural and Rural development system the performance criterion will include levels and rates of Gross Domestic Product, Employment, total and per capita income, nutrition, tax revenue, income distribution, trade balances, investments, social aspects etc. Hence the performance function will essentially be a multi-dimensional multi-objective function. It is not always easy to consider these complex performance functions for a system which itself is very large dimensional; however in an actual practical example compromise, approximation and ingenuity will be required to choose the appropriate mathematical programming methods. Examples of suitable programming methods are linear and non linear programming, dynamic programming, program evaluation and review techniques (PERT) etc.

In the modelling of socio-economic systems the modelling excercise could last for ever if the aim is to obtain a perfect model. However, Newtonian uncertainty and determinism are not essential in socio-economic system since even in the presence of uncertainties much can be achieved from the analysis and simulation of approximate mathematical models.

3.   Simulation Studies on the Model

The urgency of the Agricultural and Rural Development problems in the developing countries demands that even an approximate model can be used to simulate and 'predict' the results of alternative development strategies. In any case the simulation model is not to provide exact answers but rather it is a tool to make available the necessary information so that policy and decision makers can use this to make their decisions. However, it is important that as more information on data, parameter values, empirical relationships etc.become available then this should be used to improve and update the model. This aspect is particularly true in the developing countries since there is a general lack of data and statistical information from the past. This is another area where programmes and procedures have to be set up to collect relevant and essential data. Our experiences in Kenya, Belshaw, Bjorlo and Shah /17/, have shown that a systems formulation of the Agricultural and Rural Development systems is in itself useful in enabling decisions as to how and what data needs to be collected and processed.

The aim of the simulation studies on the model is also to show and test for model validity so that decision makers are aware of the scope and limits of the model. The decision makers, for example, expect that the results of a simulation study are 'reasonable' and valid. This reasoning may be ba sed on data and experiences from the past or even on intuition.

Since the simulation models of Agricultural and Rural Development Systems tend to be very large dimensional and complex, it is conceivable that computational difficulties will be encountered in carrying out simulation runs on a computer. If a large enough computer is available then this will not be a serious problem but in many of the developing countries only small computers are available. In this case it will be essential to use efficient and computer-saving methods for simulation studies, Aoki /18/.

In carrying out simulation studies of socio-economic systems some of the important aspects to be fulfilled are:

    A. Physical and financial feasibility.
    B. Economic and Social worthiness.

Based on the fulfillment of these aspects, simulation of alternative development strategies can be carried out and the results on the consequences of a particular development strategy made available to the decision makers.

4.   Model Implementation and Application to Problem Solution

Once the simulation of the model to evaluate the results of alternative development strategies has been carried out the next important step is to enable this information to be used by the decision and policy makers. This can occur if the decision makers have confidence and this is built if the decision makers have been in close contact throughout the modelling and systems effort to analyse the Agricultural and Rural Development System.

Experience shows that many an economic and policy evaluation studies of these systems in the developing countries have been carried out by "experts". However often these experts are working on a particular project for a limited period of time e.g. 2 years. Their study often tends to be done in isolation not only from the administrators but also local participation such as research students. In such cases an elegant report is produced at the end of the project and this is often left on the library shelves perhaps to be used by future students and not by the decision and policy makers for whose benefit the whole excercise was carried out. This consequence is not entirely the fault of the expert or the decision maker. The latter has little time to indulge in 'report and thesis reading'. In order to ensure some degree of success it is absolutely essential that there is a close contact between decision makers on the one hand and the experts and local specialists on the other. The local specialists may be students under-going training and their presence is crucial in that they may be able to carry on with the project even after the experts leave. As is often the case in these types of socio-economic studies, by the time the project is completed and the model available, the situations and assumptions within the system as well as the country may have changed. Some of these "new" situations and constraints may be accounted for by updating the model but others will lead to new problems and difficulties in the implementation stage. This may be a result of physical changes e.g. scarcity of materials and services or even social changes e.g. change of governments and politics. In this context it is important that the administrative structures and channels within the Government and the country are considered during the modelling study to minimize the possibility of major structural problems in the implementation stage.

The final result as to whether the decision makers base their decisions on the model evaluations is of course in the hands of the decision makers. However, there is a good chance that if the modelling excercise was carried out by a coherent and compatible team of specialists and decision makers then model implementation and application should have good prospects for success.

Systems Engineering Approach Experiences in Developing Countries

The success of the systems engineering approach in the developed countries has not automatically meant that success will to achieved in the developing countries. This is visible from the disturbingly low number of successful projects as compared to the total number of projects that have been underway in the developing countries. The main reason for this state of affairs has been the scarcity of material and human resources. Many of the developed countries and donor aid

gencies have made available considerable funds and "expert" personnel to help with
various development project in the developing countries. Each developing country
has to give the highest priority to plan its own development strategies because of
the unique social, economic, historical and technical assests. In these countries
the social scientists, economists, politicians and international "experts" as well
as the technologists have to come together and study the situation as it exists and
decide on goals and needs of their own country. The so called "experts" have to
have a strong background of the country in which they are working if they are
to   contribute to the success of the project. It would be more suitable and efficient if the "expert" and technologists were 'home' grown. Over the
last decade a large number of students from the developing countries have been
studying system engineering in the developed countries. However it is noticeable
that only a small proportion of these return to their countries to participate and
contribute to their development goals. Why does such a situation arise? There are
a number of varied reasons for this situation. Often these students study systems
engineering methods in the context of problems as they exist in the developed
countries. The problems in their own country are very different and so they feel a
certain amount of detachment and uncertainty as to whether the knowledge they have
acquired will be useful at home. Also they have got used to a higher standard of
living in the developed country and are a little hesitant to give up this for the
difficulties and frustrations they might encounter at home. Furthermore, in the
developing countries very little effort and long term planning is put into making
it possible for their returning graduates to apply their acquired knowledge and
contribute to the country's development. A cry often heard from these graduates is
that they are completely frustrated and not given a chance at all by the policy
makers and people in authority who may not be 'qualified' since they did not have
a chance to learn the new methods and techniques that the returning technologists
have had. The developing countries as well as the developed countries have to
review how the former can best help the latter with "expert" manpower training
as well as executing development projects to the final implementation stage.

In addition to this problem of trained manpower requirements, another major
difficulty in the developing countries is the lack of data from the past as well as
proper machinery for the collection and processing of data. Data on all socio-
economic aspects of the Agricultural and Rural Development Systems is essential
and hence it is important that proper channels for relevant data collection and
processing be set up. We use the word 'relevant' because of late many government
offices in the developing countries have become 'data-hungry'. A lot of unnessary
and unrelated data is collected at the expense of considerable man-hour efforts.
Before any data collection programmes are started it is important to answer questions such as, what the data is required for and how it will be processed and used?
What is the necessary format and to what accuracy is the data to be collected? etc.
A systems formulation is useful in this context in that it helps in answering some
of the above basic questions.

Inspite of the above two difficulties of the lack of specialized manpower
and data, a number of promising development aid projects have been carried out in a
number of developing countries. Here some of the more interesting and successful
development projects in Argentina, Venezuela, Nigeria, Mexico, and Thailand are
briefly described.

The Argentina - M.I.T. Project, Major /19/

This joint project had two main objectives, namely, to apply modern investment criteria and mathematical modelling techniques for water resource planning in
the Rio Colorado basin and in this process to train Argentine professionals in the
use of these techniques. The requirement was to develop alternative management and
development plans for irrigation and power systems. The study lasted a period of
two years, 1970-1972, and in this time a mathematical programming model in tandem
with a hydrological simulation model of the river basin was developed. The design

and formulation of this simulation model was conducted in such a manner that the Argentine professionals were able to simulate these models on computers available in the Argentine. This is one of the few success stories of a development project where a problem in a developing country was solved and at the same time a systems capability was created in the developing country.

Venezuela - Oregon State University, Halter and Miller, /20/.

This project was to consider the application of simulation modelling techniques to the Venezuelan Cattle Industry. This industry forms an important component of the overall economy of Venezula. The project was carried out from 1971 to 1973 and the central aim was to modernize the traditional cattle industry characterized by poor performance in the sense of low extraction and calving rates, high death rates, lack of dry season nutrition, low milk production per cow, general overstocking of range lands and rising input costs. A valid simulation model of the cattle industry was obtained to predict and analyse the results of alternative development strategies. To some extent the results of this project have been utilized by the Venezuelan Government Agencies in the decision making process. Perhaps the participation of Venezuelan professionals, along the lines of the Argentine - MIT project, would have led to a continued effort in the model application and implementation.

Nigeria - Michigan State University, Manetsch et.al, /21/.

This project is concerned with the application of general simulation modelling techniques to the development policy formulation in Nigeria. The MSU team have developed an extensive planning-oriented simulation model of the Nigerian Agricultural economy. The model consists of three basic systems representing the Northern regional agricultural model, the Southern regional agricultral model and the non-agricultural national accounts model. This applications study considers a very comprehensive adaptation of mathematical programming and simulation modelling techniques in the presence of multiobjective social and economic criterion. This project represents a valuable and a welcome effort of the analysis and evaluation of social and economic development strategies. However it appears that local participation of professionals in Nigeria should have been utilized to ensure a continued use of the model in the decision making process.

Mexico/World Bank Project, Goreaux and Manne, /22/

This work represents a pioneer effort to apply mathematical modelling and simulation studies for the analysis and evaluation of   multilevel planning and development strategies in Mexico. This study was conducted jointly by Mexican professionals and specialists seconded from the World Bank. Throughout the project, policy and decision makers were kept in close touch with and also participation in the model building exercise.

A large multilevel simulation model, CHAC, was constructed and the simulation studies are enabling the policy and decision makers on their choice of pricing policies, trade policies, employment programs and investment allocation. It also enables investigation on the relationships between sector policies and economy-wide development strategies. At the present time this model is fulfilling two important functions in that it is a tool for the Mexican Government in their evaluation of Agricultural sectoral policies and also it serves the World Bank's interest in the methodology of project appraisal techniques and in general policy planning models.

Thailand - Asian Institute of Technology, Bangkok, Frankel, /23/

This project considers a systems analysis approach to evaluate the effectiveness of the National Portable Water Project in Thailand. The aim was to determine the role of resource constraints and complementary inputs in the development of the rural water supply systems. In addition to the economic aspects the social and public health aspects of rural water supply systems have been accounted for in the formulation of the objectives of the program. These latter aspects are particularly important in a developing country since it is these factors which determine project impact and effectiveness. A very intensive and careful effort was put into the collection of relevant social and economic data from the rural environment. The results show that the success of the National Potable Water Project depends on whether the technical design of the system is compatible to local environmental conditions and whether the administrative procedures adopted are adequate for the local conditions to ensure operator efficiency. This project has shown that a systems approach has much to offer in the planning, development and execution of effective rural water systems projects.

System Engineering Approach Experiences in Kenya

As a first step in the application of the systems Engineering Approach to Rural development in Kenya a conceptual hierarchical model of this system was developed and is described in Belshaw, Bjorlo and Shah /17/. Fig. 1 shows this basic rural development planning and control system as a multilevel optimization problem. This formulation has enabled planners to appreciate the relationships between the system inputs at all levels of the hierarchy and performances at the levels of all the subsystems as well as the performance of the overall rural system. The crucial information channels, data collection and processing for efficient decision making suggested by this hierarchical model has shown that these types of management planning and control strategies have proved to be an extremely useful tool for the coordination, control, implementation and planning of rural development systems. Since 1973 work has been in progress to simulate this hierarchical model of the Agricultural and Rural Development System. A number of problems and areas for further research have resulted in trying to construct a simulation model. For example in Fig. 1, we need to consider how the "National Political Process" and the "Social Control" elements can be quantized and modelled.

In trying to construct a simulation model we have realized that in a majority of developing countries the private sector, Fig. 1., is a major part of agricultural and rural development systems. This sector represents the small scale farmers. It appears from the literature that very little work has been done in a systematic study of the small scale peasant farmers in the developing countries. For example the significant questions we would like to answer are:

1. why do peasant farmers behave the way they do?
2. what are the economic, technical and social factors that constrain their expansion of production?
3. what new inputs-methods, tools, systems, services, institutions-can best break the most difficult bottlenecks and motivate farmers to adopt better, more productive ways of working the land?

In trying to answer these questions we have embarked on a systematic study of the decision making process in the context of a small scale peasant farmer. A first conceptual model, Belshaw and Shah /24/, shown in Fig. 2   is presently being constructed as a simulation model. It is hoped that this study will answer the above questions and will also result in a model of a private sector process which can be incorporated in the overall simulation model of Rural Development Process in Kenya. This interdisciplinary project has been underway since 1971 and we hope that our systems approach will lead to the planning and simulation models for design and evaluation of alternative policies and programmes in the Agriculture sector. Lately, it has also become apparent that our Agricultural sectoral simulation model will be complementary and can be used in tandem with a macro-economic model of Kenya, Slater and Walsham / 25/.

CONCLUSIONS

The use of analytical and simulation models of Agricultural and Rural

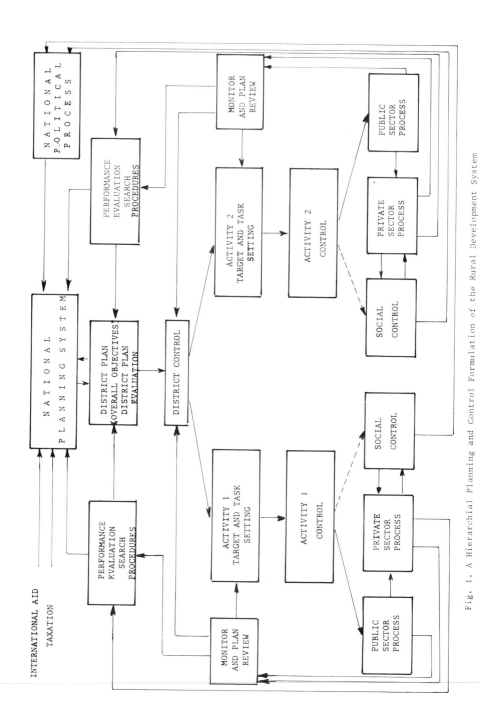

Fig. 1. A Hierarchial Planning and Control Formulation of the Rural Development System

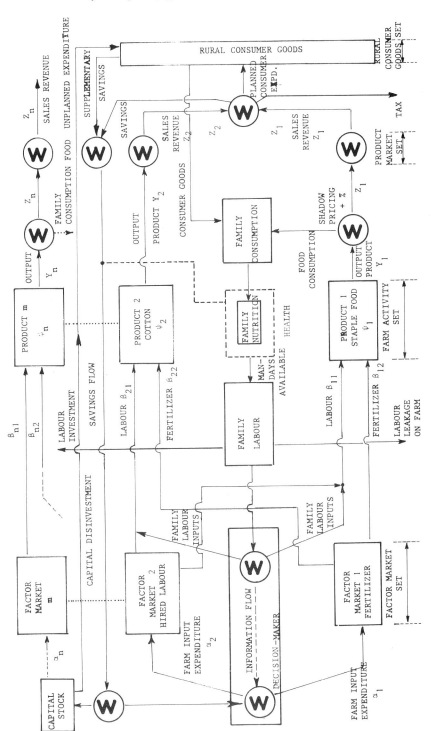

Fig. 2. Normative Model of peasant agriculture

Development Systems have much to contribute to the decision-making process in the developing countries. In these countries the modeling excercise is made particular ly difficult since the economical, social and political structures are fragile, there are often acute regional disparities as well as serious communication and coordination problems and there is a general nonavailability or lack of data and skilled manpower. International donor aid agencies and developed countries are making a considerable effort to assist the developing countries. However, in many instances this effort has not been very successful since there has been a lack of local participation in the design and evaluation of development projects. There are many socio-economic aspects which need to be researched into and this will be fruitful only if the 'experts' work in close cooperation with local pro-ressionals.

The interdisciplinary problem of applying a systems Engineering Approach to develop an integrated development plan for Agricultural and Rural Development Systems is a socio-techno-economic challenge to the experts and professional in the developing countries.

ACKNOWLEDGEMENT

The author would like to appreciate the contribution of Deryke Belshaw of the University of East Anglia, U.K. in the development of the systems project in Kenya.

REFERENCES

/1/   McNamara R., President of the World Bank's Address to the Board of Governors 1973 meeting, Nairobi, September 1973.
/2/   Ullicny, J.,"Model of a three-level hierarchic system of optimal resource distribution in the production process", Paper No. 26.2, pp 1-10, Part 3, 5th World Congress of IFAC, Paris, June 1972
/3/   Akhmetzianov, A.V., "Hierarchical Resource Allocation Systems in the Oil and Gas Industry", pp 371-377, Systems Approaches to Developing Countries, IFAC-IFORS Conference, Algiers, May 1973.
/4/   deHaen, Hartwig and Jeung Han Lee, "Dynamic Models of Farm Resource Alloca-tion for Agricultural Planning in Korea: Application of Recursive Program-ming within a General System Simulation Approach," Agricultural Sector simulation Working Paper, Michigan State University, East Lansing, October 1972.
/5/   Forrester Jay,"World Dynamics", Cambridge, MIT Press,1971
/6/   Mesarovic, M.D. et al, "Theory of Hierarchical, Multilevel Systems", Mathematics in Science and Engineering, Vol.68, New York, Academic Press, 1970.
/7/   Wismer, D.A. (Editor),"Optimization Methods for Large Scale Systems with Applications", McGraw-Hill, New York,1971.
/8/   Mitter, S.K. and Dy-Liacco,T.E., "Multi-level Approach to the Control of Interconnected Power Systems", IFAC Conference on Computer Control, Menton, France,1967.
/9/   Rakic,M.V.,"A Multi-level Approach to Steady State Control of a Multi-product, Multi-factor firm, "Session on Industrial Management Systems, 5th World Congress of IFAC, Paris, June 1972.
/10/   Wismer, D.A. and Lasdon, R.E., "A Hierarchical Systems Formulation for Urban Systems Engineering,"Session on National, Regional and Urban Systems. ibid.
/11/   David, Y., "Present Situation and Prospects of Automation in Transportation, "Survey Session, 5th World Congress of IFAC, Paris, June 1972.
/12/   Pearce, I.F.,"The Southampton Econometric Model of the U.K. and Trading Partners", "The Econometric Study of the United Kingdom, (Hilton and Heathfield, Eds.), MacMillan, 1970.
/13/   Ellis, J.R., "Outdoor Recreation Planning in Michigan by a Systems Analysis Approach", Technical Report No. 1, State Resources Planning Program, Michigan Department of Commerce, May 1966.

/14/   Pearson, L.B., "Partners in Development", Report on the Commission on
       International Development", pp 59-60, Praeger, 1970.
/15/   Lasdon, L., "Optimization Methods for Large Scale Systems", New York, McGraw-
       Hill, 1971.
/16/   Gabus, A. and Figueiredo, J.B., "Why and how to introduce the event dimen-
       sion into the simulation of development policies", pp. 33-37, Systems Ap-
       proaches to Developing Countries, IFAC-IFORS Conference, May 1973.
/17/   Belshaw, D.G.R., Bjorlo, T., and Shah, M.M., "A Hierarchical Systems Formu-
       lation of the Rural Development Process in Developing Countries", pp. 125-
       137, ibid.
/18/   Aoki, M., "Some Iterative Schemes for Decentralized Dynamic Systems Control",
       Session No. 30.2, pp 1-6, 5th World Congress of IFAC, Paris, June 1972.
/19/   Major, D.C., "Investment Criteria and Mathematical Modelling Techniques
       for Water Resources Planning in Argentina : The MIT-Argentina Project",
       pp. 235-241, Systems Approaches to developing countries, IFAC-IFORS Confe-
       rence, Algiers, May 1973.
/20/   Halter, A.N., and Miller, S.F., "Simulation in a practical policy-making
       setting : The Venezuelan Cattle Industry", pp. 109-117, ibid.
/21/   Manetsch, T.J. et al., "A Generalized Simulation Approach to Agricultural
       Sector Analysis with Special Reference to Nigeria", Michigan State Univer-
       sity East Lansing, Nov. 1971.
/22/   Goreux, L.G. and Manne, A. (Editors), "Multi-level Planning : Case Studies
       in Mexico", North-Holland, 1973.
/23/   Frankel, R.J., "A Systems Approach to Assessement of Rural Water Supply
       Program Effectiveness", pp. 241-247, Systems Approaches to Developing Coun-
       tries, IFAC-IFORS Conference, May 1973.
/24/   Belshaw, D.G.R. and Shah, M.M., "Systems Analysis Approach to a Normative
       Decision Model for Peasant Agriculture", Manuscript in preparation.
/25/   Slater, C.C. and Walsham, G., "A General Systems Simulation of the Kenyan
       Economy", Institute of Development Studies, Working Paper No. 174, Nairobi,
       July 1974.

DISCUSSION

*I wonder how are you keeping a monitoring action on the agricultural pro-
duction looking to the investment. You cannot hold that view in a periodical meeting.
Do you introduce forms to the farmers, are you making sampling experiments.   (SIKKA)*

The first point : we are fortunate that the decisionmakers listen to us.
This asks patience. The first thing I said when I went back to Nairobi was : I am
a systems engineer and I will solve all your problems. It is quite true that the
system engineering was a perfect tool to solve all these problems : the decision
maker, the economist, all these chaps. Over 2 years I just managed to change this
sentence : system engineering may be useful, it might be nice to use it, let's see
what happens. I think this kind of approach with decision makers is always useful;
try to talk   their own language and remember that you are under them. If I would
be as good as them, I would not be a system engineer. The second point : trying to
keep track of agricultural output.This is a difficult measure. It is not only the
gross national product of the gross capital income which is important. We have to
look at the social aspects. In order to account for this our plans were reviewed
at a period of a month and at a period of a year. At the end of the year all the
reports have come in and then we had a series of meetings on a period of 3 months
to find out what has happened, how did the plan go, what changes do we need to
make. You cannot implement this in the 2nd year but you can have an influence
the third year.   (SHAH)

I think that what you said is very true. Building a model in order to under-
stand the interrelationships that are going on is fine. It is an ethical problem.
I think when you start to say to decision makers, this is what the modeler predicted
when you know in your own mind that that model is not capable of that sort of pre-
diction. What do you think on the basis of having analyzed the system. (YOUNG)

We did not have a model in the sense that we are able to say this is what
our model says. What we have done is to use systems-analysis as a tool. First to
understand what is the problem. You don't have to go to the extent of making an
actual model to make decisions. Because the problem is so complex that you can,
by a systematic analysis, try to build up a situation which can be used. There are
of course microproblems within this overall system : for instance on water resources : where do you put your dams, in what position, etc. (SHAH)

Yes, but you did say one thing when you spoke about the economic model.
I am sure, for it has not worked anywhere else in the world that you have got an
economic model that you statistically validate against data and which will give
you reasonable forecast. It is something much less than that. The danger seems to
be in telling the customer that it is something more than that. To say this is a
model and this gives such a forecast. I think this is an actual problem. If you
say it is a computermodel, he might believe it more than when in actual fact it
is much less than that. When it fails the computer would be blamed not you. (YOUNG)

This has two aspects: for instance this rural migration problem which was
predicted by the model that it can happen by 1978. But if the present trend continues, we could not have made this decision on intuition, because there are so
many projects implemented, so many people involved. You need some kind of systematic
analysis to show this and the simulation model of the economy has shown this.
(SHAH)

I have a question on some of the things you said about present trend con-
tinuing. Surely the model must be more sophisticated than that. Take the operational
reservoir. When it starts looking like it's going to fail, things like water ra-
tioning comes in. There are self correcting devices which surely are not built into
a socio economic model. (HELY-HUTCHINSON)

When I talk about present trends I mean : the government expects so much
money to come in ; our investment plans in industry, in all other facilities for
the next five years, are so much , internationally, which has already been assigned
for the next five years, is so much. Based on aggregation of all these sources,
the educational trends the states of the country, based on this, our output would
not be able to meet what is the situation in 5 years. (SHAH)

I would ask if you could give some accuracy on the data of your model, be-
cause I heard something about the Club of Rome discussed by Tinbergen from the
Netherlands. He said that with the variation of the parameters within the model,
you could write easily your name. (D'HOLLANDER)

The first model, the simulation of the economy was completed just before
I came. I have a paper which gives some of these results. We have at this stage
not done any sensitivity analyses. We just fitted the data we had from 1971. Predicted what happens in 1972 and based on what we predicted to 1978. You will say
it is not enough to predict from 1971 data. That is true but it is better than
nothing. I don't say that our decisionmakers accepted it yet. We have to be very
careful in telling the politicians. That's a system problem in itself. You tell
them only so much, if you tell them too much you are out of the job ; if you tell
them too little they take no action. (SHAH)

Modeling and Simulation of Water Resources Systems, G.C. VANSTEENKISTE, (Ed.)
North-Holland Publishing Company (1975)

DYNAMIC MODEL FOR LONG-TERM DEVELOPMENT OF WATER RESOURCES MANAGEMENT[x]

dr. László Dávid, National Water Authority, Budapest, Hungary
dr. Ferenc Szidarovszky, University of Economics, Budapest, Hungary
dr. Lucien Duckstein, University of Arizona, Tucson, USA

ABSTRACT

The purpose of this paper is to develop a dynamic model to compare alternative water resources development strategies under limited resources /economic, manpower, natural/. At each yearly stage t the following variables and functions are defined: state variables and constraints, input variables, state transition functions and output functions.

A realistic example based on a case in a region of Eastern Hungary is presented with a 50-year horizon. Seven alternative strategies are examined under several different hypothesis for resources availability which yields 44 alternative cases of development. The computational algorithm is coded in ICL FORTRAN language: the total run time was 10 minutes on an ODRA 1304 computer for the example considered.

INTRODUCTION

The purpose of this paper is to develop a dual objective dynamic model which enables one to compare alternative sequential water resources development schemes when economic, manpower and natural resources are limited. The methodology is illustrated by an example based on an Eastern Hungary case.

There are two objectives because a sole economic case objective such as minimize cost in unsufficient to account for social goals. A second objective has thus been chosen to represent social factors under the form of a proxy variable namely, the number of individuals that have to be restrained from living in the region considered because of insufficient water. In a sence, the model developed here may be considered as a subproblem extracted from a study made according to the proposed standards of the US Water Resources Council /1971, 1973/ and the subsequent discussion of Cicchetti et al /1973/ concerning the potential encouregement of unefficient projects. Also, the model may be viewed as the continuation of a collective utility model developed earlier /Duckstein and Kisiel, 1971/ after the theory of Lesourne /1964/ and as the continuation of the dynamic planning model of Dávid and Szidarovszky /1974/. While many systems analysis models have been proposed in the literature, an excellent review of the potential use of multi-objective decision making models in water resources has been given by Cohon /1973/.

In the next section, the elements of the model are defined. Presentation of the example follows; then, results and extension of the model are discussed.

---

[x] The model was prepared within the framework of the cooperative research project between NWA Water Resources Centre, Budapest and University of Arizona, Tucson.

DYNAMIC MODEL

     As written earlier, the model is designed to compare alternative water resources development schemes: thus, it is not an optimization model, but a discrete-time continuous state machine - in system   theoretic terms /Wymore, 1967/. Elements of the model to be described in detail below include: /1/ the state variables and parameters, /2/ the input variables and function, /3/ the state transition function including constraints, and /4/ the output or objective functions.

State variables and parameters describe the system during every time period t, chosen as one year is this model. State parameters are constants built into the system, as described below. Given the geographic area, the state variables are divided into three groups as shown in Fig. 1.

     a/ Three fundamental variables: regional income $T/t/$, population $L/t/$, fresh water demand $I/t/$.

     b/ Ten dependent variables: consumptive water demand $H/t/$ as a pro-portion of $I/t/$, volume of effluent discharge $SZ/t/$, volume of treated effluent discharge $KT/t/$, percentage of runoff control $X/t/$, capacity of water produc-tion and supply $KK/t/$, controlled natural water supply available $KH/t/$, dam-age situation j, which, as discussed later, it essentially depends upon which activity is constrained, total capital avaible for socio-economic development $P/t/$, professional manpower available $SA/t/$, power available $E/t/$.

     Each of the last there variables is in turn decomposed into three ele-ments corresponding, respectively to the following three components of water management activities: /i/ runoff and flow regulation, /ii/ water produced and supplied by the system, /iii/ wastewater disposal, especially treatment.

     c/ Built-in parameters: three state parameters $U/t/$, $V/t/$, and $W/t/$, which determine the dependent variables $P/t/$, $SA/t/$, $E/t/$ as a function of the two fundamental variables $T/t/$ and $I/t/$; the initial state $T/o/$, $L/o/$, $I/o/$ of the system, which is given; the sequence of state variable values that would be obtained without resource constraint /"ideal" development values/.

Input variables. A distinction may be made between two types of input variables /Fig. 1./:

     a/ Three feedback variables, which are output /or state/ variables computed at time t, then used as inputs at time t+δ, when δ is a delay or lag. They are respectively: the annual percentage growth coefficient $p/t/$ of region-al income $T/t/$, whose delay time is denoted by δ /p,j/ where j is the damage situation /see later/; the annual percentage growth coefficient $q/t/$ of popula-tion $L/t/$, whose delay time is denoted by δ /q,j/; the annual percentage growth coefficient $r/t/$ of fresh water demand $I/t/$, which is assumed to be a given function of $p/t/$ and $q/t/$.

     b/ Six decision variables: these variables are given as a 3 x 3 non-negative matrix $[A/t/]$ whose rows sum up to unity. We thus have nine varia-bles or percentage coefficients with three relations between them, which yields six independent decision variables. The nine variables correspond to a decision to allocate the three resources to three goals as shown in Table 1, where, for example, $C/t/$ is the proportion of total manpower allocated to water quality goal at time t.

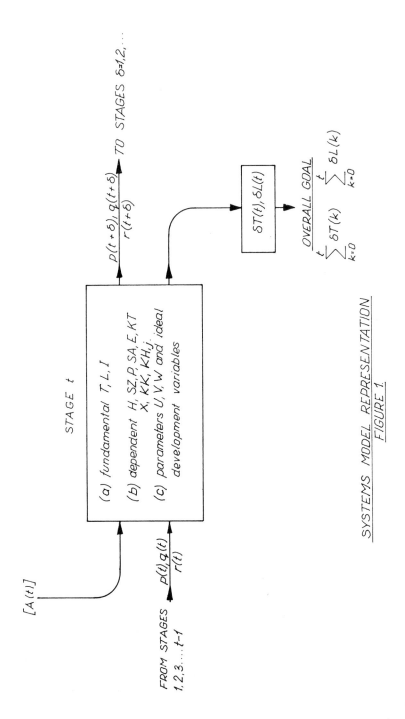

SYSTEMS MODEL REPRESENTATION
FIGURE 1.

Decision matrix $\underline{\underline{A/t}}$ Table 1

GOALS RESOURCES	Flow Regulation and Control	Water production and supply	Water quality
Money, $P/t/$	$a/t/$	$b/t/$	$c/t/$
Technical manpower,$SA/t/$	$A/t/$	$B/t/$	$C/t/$
Energy, $E/t/$	$\alpha/t/$	$\beta/t/$	$\gamma/t/$

Note: $\left[\underline{\underline{A/t}}\right] \geqslant 0$, and the rows of $\left[\underline{\underline{A/t}}\right]$ add to unity

State transition function computes the state at time t given the state at time t-1 and the input at time t, as follows

$$T/t/ = T/t\text{-}1/ \ /1 + \frac{P/t/}{100}/ \qquad\qquad /1/$$

In a similar fashion, $L/t/$ and $I/t/$ can be determined using respectively $q/t/$ and $r/t/$. /Eqs. 2 and 3/.

A time independent relationship computes r as a function of p and q:

$$r/t/ = r\left[p/t/, q/t/\right] \qquad\qquad /4/$$

Using Eqs. 1,2,3, the dependent state variables can be computed as follows:

$$H/t/ = u/t/ \ I/t/ \qquad\qquad\qquad /5/$$
$$SZ/t/ = I/t/ - H/t/ \quad \text{with} \quad KT/t/ \leqslant SZ/t/ \qquad\qquad /6/ - /7/$$
$$P/t/ = U/t/\frac{T/t/}{100}; \quad SA/t/ = V/t/\frac{I/t/}{100}; \quad E/t/ = W/t/\frac{I/t/}{100}. \qquad /8/-/10/$$

Constraints are, strictly speaking, part of the state transition function; the conditions described in Table 1 for the elements of the decision matrix A are one set of contraints. If s is the coefficient of regulation losses and $y/t/$ is the ratio of unusable water to the total untreated effluent discharge, another constraint giving the potential amount of water available at stage t $KPR/t/$ as a function of the total potential water available KP is:

$$KPR/t/ = KP - \frac{SZ/t/ - KT/t/}{y/t/} - s \cdot X/t/ \cdot KP \qquad\qquad /11/$$

Eq. 11 is in turn used to calculate the available water supply $KH/t/$, as

$$KH/t/ = KMIN + X/t/ \ KPR/t/ - KMIN \qquad\qquad /12/$$

where KMIN is the minimum natural water supply.

The remaining state variables $X/t/$ and $KH/t/$ are determined by straighforward methods desribed in detail in David and Szidarovszky /1974/.

State variable j is determined by considering the magnitude of the shortage relatively to "ideal" development variables which are denoted by a star. Five situations $j=1,\ldots,5$ can be distinguished.

Situation $j=1$: $KH/t/ > I^x/t/ = KK/t/ > H^x/t/ = H/t/$ /13/

The demand for fresh water is equal to the water production supply capacity; since the available water supply is larger, corresponds to zero damage in situation $j=1$.

Situation j=2: $KH/t/ > I^x/t/ > KK/t/ > H^x/t/ > H/t/$ $\qquad$ /14/

Although the available water supplies are not utilized to their full extent, some slight damage may still occur, since the ideal freshwater demand is greater than the actual water producing capacity. The effect on socio-economic evolution is perceptible with a long delay only; thus, the growth rates $p/t/$ and $q/t/$ are slightly reduced with a long delay.

Situation J=3: $I^x/t/ \gg KH/t/ > KK/t/ > H^x/t/ > H/t/$ $\qquad$ /15/

a damage of medium size and perceptible with an eaverage delay may be is anticipated, since neither the water producing-supplying capacity, nor the available water supplies are sufficient for meeting the ideal fresh water demand.

Situation j=4: $I^x/t/ > KK/t/ > H^x/t/ \gg KH/t/ > H/t/$ $\qquad$ /16/

The available supplies are smaller than the actual freshwater demand characterized by the actual water production-supply capacity, or smaller than the ideal water consumption. For this reason little delay and heavy damages are likely to occur, i.e., both $p/t/$ and $q/t/$ are greatly and promptly reduced.

Situation j=5: $I^x/t/ \quad KK/t/ \quad H^x/t/ \quad H/t/ \quad KH/t/$ $\qquad$ /17/

here the damage is very heavy, since the available supplies are insufficient to cover even the actual water consumption. A considerable reduction in $p/t/$ and $q/t/$ occurs virtually without delay.

In estimating the damage situations, the delay and the reduction in the rate of socio-economic evolution play roles of paramount importance. The value of $\delta/p,j/$ indicates the number of years elapsed after the occurrence of the damage situation j before the reduction in the growth rate of regional income becomes perceptible. Simirlarly quantities $d/p,j/$ and $d/q,j/$ may be defined where, for example, $d/p,j/$ indicates the percentage reduction in the growth rate of regional income following situation j.

Output functions. As shown in Fig.1, there are two classes of outputs:

a/ the growth coefficients $p/t+\delta/$, $q/t+\delta/$ and $r/t+\delta/$;

b/ two criteria measuring the dual goal attainments, namely, the amount of regional economic efficiency loss $\Delta T/t/ = T^x/t/ - T/t/$ and that of population growth hindered $\Delta L/t/ = L^x/t/ - L/t/$ because of water resource curtailment; over the entire horizon, the total loss in income δT and the total loss in population δL are, respectively

$$\delta T = \sum_{t=1}^{N} \left[T^x/t/ - T/t/ \right] \quad \text{and} \quad \delta L = \sum_{t=1}^{N} \left[L^x/t/ - L/t/ \right] \frac{1}{m} \qquad /18/-/19/$$

where m is the average life expectancy.

Eqs. 18 represents the economic objective while Eqs.19 corresponds to the social objective. Given among a number of alternative development strategies in the same socio-economic environment, preference should be given to the one for which the values δT and δL are smallest. Since there are two objective functions, it is necessary to specify a trade-off criteria for selecting an optimal strategy. The alternative strategies considered may be arranged separately according to both δT and δL in sequences of growing magnitude. In this way two "order numbers" are obtained for each strategy. The optimal strategy will be chosen such that some function of the two order numbers is smallest.

The above relations yield the computational algorithm shown in Fig.2. The method has been programmed in ICL FORTRAN language and tested successfully on an ODRA 1304 using an example based on a water development

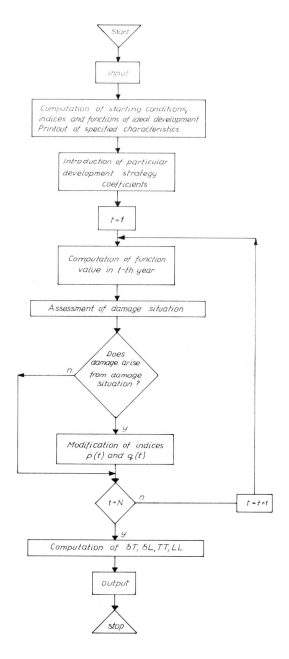

FLOW CHART OF COMPUTATION FOR A POTENTIAL
DEVELOPMENT STRATEGY
FIGURE 2.

planning case of Eastern Hungary /a part of the Tisza River Basin/.

EXAMPLE AND DISCUSSION

The basic data of this example are tabulated in Dávid and Szidarovszky /1974/. Six alternative resource allocation schemes /arabic numbers/ defined by matrices $[A/t/]$, were combined with seven development strategy alternatives /roman numbers/ defined by vectors of coefficients$[U/t/, V/t/, W/t/]$ to yield 42 development plans; in addition, two more combinations were tested, to obtain a total of 44 runs. An examination of the ranking of alternatives listed in Table 2 shows that in long-term development planning, the choice of development strategy is of utmost importance.

In other words, even in systems with highly limited resources, a proper choice of water management development strategy may, over the full development period, yield better results then systems with substantially more resources, but developed with a poor strategy. Thus, alternative VII-7, involving the smallest decline in income, though using ample resources, yields only slightly better results than the optimal alternative I-1. Also, alternative I, involving the smallest amount of resources, proved to be optimal, since it was combined with an efficient strategy 1. At the same time, alternative V, involving ample resources, but combined with a poor strategy 2 yielded the poorest results. Next, alternative VI, involving perhaps the greatest amount of resources, combined with development strategy 1 proved third best, while it dropped to 43rd place if coupled with strategy 2.

The impact of the development strategy on the state and output variables is illustrated in Fig.3. in which the optimal and poorest alternatives are compared. In development strategy 1, resources are mostly utilized for runoff control and effluent treatment over the full development period. As a consequence for optimal alternative I-1, the available supplies exceed almost all the time the actual freshwater demand, which is appreciably smaller than the ideal freshwater demand. Thus, only moderate damage situations occur: during 85 % of the period, damage situations 2 and 3 prevail.

In contrast with strategy 1 the resources in strategy 2 are highly concentrated on water production- and supply, and effluent treatment, allocating only a small share to runoff control. Consequently, in the poorest alternative V-2, the supplies which could be made available for utilization hardly increase and although the capacity for meeting the freshwater demand is virtually identical to the ideal freshwater demand throughout the latter cannot be met over 70 % of the period /damage situation 4/.

The variation of the fundamental water management activities in response to the diverse development strategies have been analysed in Fig.4. The resources pattern VI has been adopted for the analysis, since it contains alternatives midway between the worst and best development alternatives. Moreover, in the case of alternatives VI-4, VI-5 and VI-6, which are rather poor ones, situation 1 prevails for 10 to 15 years, i.e., identically with the ideal development case. As seen from Fig.4, strategies 1,3,7 and 5 are favorable for developing the supplies available for use, whereas strategies 2 and 4 are not. The highest extent of runoff control /80.5 %/ is attained with strategy 1. Concerning water production and supply, the situation is essentially a reversed one. The highest level is attained with strategy 4. Concerning effluent treatment, strategy 6 is most successful, since resources are concentrated on this activity, especially towards the end of the period. Alternatives 5, 6 and 7 reflect the effect of change is strategy during the development period. In strategy 5, for instance, the growth rate of available supplies and of effluent treatment is accelerated at the same time as the growth of capacity for meeting water demand is decreased.

L. David, F. Szidarovszky and L. Duckstein

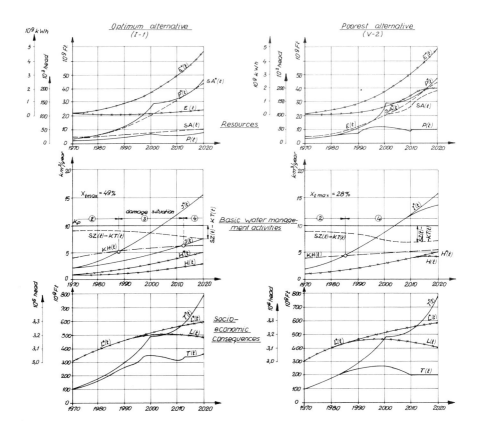

COMPARISON OF OPTIMUM AND POOREST DEVELOPMENT ALTERNATIVES

FIGURE 3.

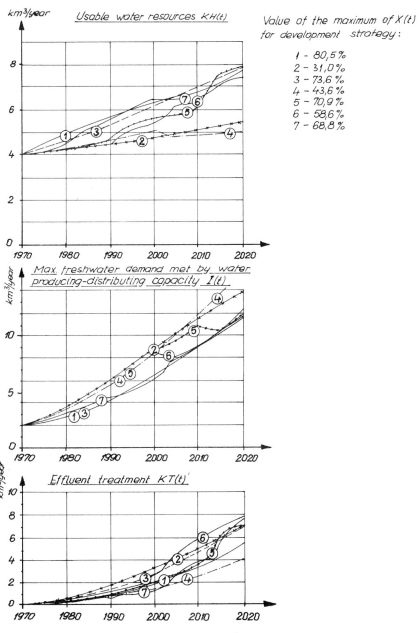

Value of the maximum of $X(t)$
for development strategy:

1 - 80,5 %
2 - 31,0 %
3 - 73,6 %
4 - 43,6 %
5 - 70,9 %
6 - 58,6 %
7 - 68,8 %

BASIC WATER MANAGEMENT ACTIVITIES AS A
FUNCTION OF DEVELOPMENT STRATEGIES FOR RESOURCES PATTERN VI.
FIGURE 4.

Table 2

Arrangement of development alternatives

Se-quence	Loss of income			Loss of population			Combined aspect	
	Symbol of alterna-tive	δ_T 10^9 Ft	TT %	Symbol of alterna-tive	δ_L head	LL %	Symbol of alterna-tive	Sequence number
1	VII-7	5740	29,8	VI-1	16600	0,73	I-1	5
2	I-1	5940	30,8	II-1	16900	0,75	II-1	5
3	II-1	6050	31,5	I-1	17000	0,75	VI-1	7
4	I-7	6070	31,6	VI-7	17100	0,76	I-7	9
5	I-3	6100	31,7	I-7	17700	0,78	VI-7	11
6	VI-1	6110	31,7	III-7	17800	0,79	II-7	15
7	VI-7	6140	32,0	II-7	17900	0,79	III-7	16
...38	I-4	8330	43,4	IV-4	38800	1,72	IV-2	74
39	IV-2	8500	44,3	V-5	39100	1,74	V-4	76
40	II-2	8580	44,6	III-2	40700	1,79	II-2	76
41	II-4	8640	44,9	V-4	40800	1,80	IV-4	80
42	IV-4	8660	45,2	II-4	40800	1,80	II-4	83
43	VI-2	8770	45,6	VI-2	41500	1,83	VI-2	86
44	V-2	8850	46,2	V-2	41600	1,84	V-2	88

It must be remembered that results shown apply only to the date /albait realistic/ chosen for example. The choice of a development strategy, including runoff control for the entire development period however, may convey implications extending beyond the example.

SUMMARY AND CONCLUSIONS

The main interest of this model is that the water management viewpoint is expressed through out: in other words, water resources are placed in to the proper perspective of economic growth and use of other irreplaceable resources /professional manpower and energy in this case/.

Further features of the model are:
- the presence of two objectives, corresponding to an economic efficiency measure and a social criterion;
- a continuous state discrete time system representation, which should enable optimization by dynamic programming. However, special care should be taken because of the feedback variables;
- the possibility to introduce uncertainty by proper assumptions on the stochastic nature of one or more input variables or transition function elements.

The model may be used as is to find the best alternative development among a large number of feasible ones by generating synthetically matrices $\left[A/t/\right]$ and vectors $/U/t/$, $V/t/$, $W/t/$, then performing the same type of analysis as has been done in this paper for 44 alternatives.

It is granted that many assumptions have been used to develop the dynamic model; however, it is hoped that insight may be developed for a better utilization of natural resources in general and water resources in particular.

ACKNOWLEDGEMENT

Part of the research reported in this paper was supported by funds provided by the National Water Authority in Budapest and a US National Science Foundation Grant no. GF-38183. The administrative support of the Hungarian Institute for Cultural Relations and the University of Arizona, which makes this US-Hungarian Co-operative research possible, is also gratefully acknowledged.

REFERENCES

Cicchetti, C.J., Davis, R.K., Hanke, S.H., and Haveman, R.H. /1973/. Evaluating federal water projects: a critique of proposed standards, Science, Vol. 181. 723-738.

Dávid, L., Szidarovszky, F. /1974/. Long-range planning of water management development with dynamic model, /in Hungarian, with English summary/, Hidrológiai Közlöny, Budapest, No. 1974/6.

Duckstein, L., and Kisiel, C.C. /1971/. Collective Utility: a systems approach to water pricing policy /application to Tucson area/, Proceedings, International Symposium on Mathematical Models in Hydrology, Warsaw Poland.

Lesourne, J. /1964/. Le Calcul Economique, Paris: Dunod.

Water Resources Council, /1971/. Principles and standards for planning water and related land resources, Federal Register, Vol. 36, No. 256, 24143-24194.

Water Resources Council, /1973/. Water and related land resources: establishment of principles and standards for planning, Federal Register, Vol. 38, No. 174, 24778-24869.

DISCUSSION

What is the action taken in the area for this study, does it involve the whole country ? (SIKKA)

It is the Tisza river basin essentially a fairly large, international river in East Hungary. They have some dams built, they plan to irrigate quite a bit. They have a flying water table because they are over exploiting the groundwater. What they are trying to do, is a multipurpose project. They develop water for agricultural and municipal use. This was for me a particular project in a specified area. (FOGEL)

I am still a bit critical on those models ; is that a linear programming model you are using ? (TODINI)

No, if you are using a linear programming model this gives you a fixed picture of the situation now. This is dynamic. It looks at the sequences.

Modeling and Simulation of Water Resources Systems, G.C. VANSTEENKISTE, (Ed.)
North-Holland Publishing Company (1975)

NEW TECHNIQUES IN PLANNING A WATER MANAGEMENT SYSTEM:
A CASE STUDY OF COOPERATIVE RESEARCH BETWEEN HUNGARY
AND THE USA

Dr.Martin Fogel, University of Arizona, Tucson, USA
Dr.István Bogárdi, Water Resources Center, Budapest, Hungary
Dr.Donald Davis, University of Arizona, Tucson, USA

ABSTRACT

Decision-making under uncertainty is the main theme of a cooperative
water resources research project between the Hungarian National
Water Authority and the University of Arizona, USA. Several categories of uncertainties have been distinguished and efforts are being
made to quantify them by the application of existing techniques or the
development of new ones. Within the cost-effectiveness framework,
the techniques of interactive computer programming, Bayesian decision theory and the Hungarian-developed induced safety algorithm are
being applied at various levels of the decision-making process. For
situations where agricultural water requirements are to be met the
cooperative research is investigating the use of inventory control
theory for scheduling irrigation water. Event-based stochastic precipitation models are being developed to describe natural uncertainty
which, for example, can be used in determining the hydrologic effects
of land modifications.

INTRODUCTION

The cooperative research described in this paper concerns engineers and
scientists at the National Water Authority, Budapest, Hungary and at the University of Arizona, Tucson, USA. Started informally in May 1972 and formalized
one year later, the research involves work on problems of joint interest in the
area of decision-making in water resources systems. Of primary importance is
the definition and solution of practical problems which may require the application of existing techniques or the development of new ones to solve these problems.

The research recognizes the multi-objective nature of water resources development which generally includes at least one economic objective / satisfy expected demand at minimum cost/ and one social objective /distribute income or
improve some non-economic measures of quality of life/. To satisfy one or more
objectives, multi-purpose structures such as dams may be built in an effort to
manage water for augmenting food supplies, for energy production, for flood
control and for transport. In the cooperative research, the multi-objective and
multi-purpose aspects of planning and design are seen as involving, but not limited to, the four elements described below:

1. Decision-making under uncertainty. Decisions about sizing and operating the
chosen system are subject to many uncertainties /Kisiel and Duckstein, 1972/
discussed in the next section.

2. Forecasting water requirement. Water resources systems are sized according to the needs of the various sectors, e.g. agricultural, industrial, domestic
etc., which has to be forecast on the basic of historical data or a theoretical
model. Such forecasting involves quantification or at least assessment of all the
uncertainties listed above.

3. Stochastic inputs to simulation models. The development of such models is aimed at describing natural uncertainty and circumventing sample uncertainty by attempting to reconstitute a stochastic process of nature such as precipitation.

DECISION MAKING UNDER UNCERTAINTY

In recent years new approaches for making engineering decisions in the face of uncertainty have been under development in the water resources field.

Uncertainty in water management stems from natural phenomena /called natural uncertainty/, insufficient information /sample uncertainty/ and the limited understanding of natural, technical and economic processes /model uncertainty/. Decision analysis tackles these uncertainties in three steps: 1. distinguishing the various sources of uncertainties, 2. characterizing them in a quantitative way and 3. embodying them into the decision-making in order to reach optimal solution under uncertainties /Bogárdi, 1974 a/. The effective use of decision theory often requires a systems approach to the decision problem at hand /Duckstein et.al. 1974 a/. Cooperative research efforts are developing prescriptive models for decision making under uncertainty; some of these models will be outlined.

Natural uncertainty is an objective category which has a common property of randomness in nature, economy, policy and social life. An optimal release policy for a large and shallow lake subject to the double natural uncertainty of average monthly hydrologic input and instantaneous wind-induced rise has been calculated /Bogárdi et.al. 1973 a, 1973 b/. A stochastic dynamic programming formulation yields the optimal release policy for the case of lake Balaton, Hungary.

There are hydraulic structures where both the load and the resistance should be taken as variable. In that line Duckstein et.al. /1973 a/ have analyzed the reliability of a levee reach. The probability of failure is a complex natural uncertainty; failure may be caused by overtopping, boiling or subsoil failure, slope failure or by wind waves. The probability of failure of the reach as a system is a joint function of the load and the resistance to each mode of failure. Use of this model gives a more realistic information on the existing safety of a levee reach and enables decisions to be made concerning an economic reinforcement.

The input to a levee system may also be a complex natural uncertainty. Szidarovszky et.al. /1974/ have analyzed the uncertain backwater effect above the confluence of a tributary with a main river. The probability model developed depends on the joint distribution of the flow of the two rivers and the backwater curves associated with these flows.

The optimal design and operation of a hydrologic forecasting system requires the consideration of natural uncertainty inherent in hydrologic forecasting methods. A decision theoretic evaluation of short-term flood forecast has been developed /Sniedovich et.al. 1974/ which is deemed advantageous because: 1/ a systems approach rather than a purely statistical one has been used, 2/ measures of effectiveness have been expressed in economic and social terms, 3/ the hydrologic and non-hydrologic uncertainties have been considered and 4/ many forecasting and response policies may be considered.

Sample uncertainty originates from the limited number of observation data. Natural uncertainty could be perfectly described if we had an infinite number of observation data or samples. The effect of sample uncertainty to the optimal solution can be analysed by Bayes Decision Theory /BDT/. The studies of sample uncertainty usually give us sample distributions or confidence intervals, given knowledge of the parameters in the model. However, the design engineer would like knowledge of the distribution of possible parameters, given the sample data. The engineer is certain about sample values; the parameters of the model from which the sample was generated are the uncertain quantity. Davis et.al. /1972/ showed the use of BDT in the optimum design of a levee. The uncertainty in the knowledge of the parameters of the log-normal model describes the annual peak flows in a distribution /the normal-gamma/ obtained by use of Bayes' Theorem in conjunction with the sample statistics for the mean and the variance.

An alternative method of BDT to give optimal solution under natural and sample uncertainties has been developed by Bogárdi and Szidarovszky /1974 b/ and called Induced Safety Algorithm /ISA/.

BDT and ISA methods that account for the uncertainty due to limited record length have been compared using a case study /Duckstein et.al. 1974 b/. Both methods are applicable to the design of any hydraulic structure and ISA is a mathematical approximation of the BDT. Consequently ISA is easy to use and is recommended for cases where a relatively long record is available while BDT, which involves more computation than ISA, should nevertheless be chosen when the record is short.

Since models of nature, economy, social and political life are never able to simulate "real life", the difference between the observed "real life" output and model output is regarded as model uncertainty. Among the numerous kinds of model uncertainties the effect of economic uncertainty is mentioned. Economic calculations as a cost-benefit optimization are generally performed under the assumptions that the values of benefits, losses and costs can be determined without any model error. In reality this assumption is not satisfied, since the "true" model of economic analysis is generally unknown. The Economic Uncertainty Programming /ECUP/ method uses simulation to compute for each development alternative a probability that the alternative is the "true" optimal solution /Bogárdi et.al. 1974 c/. These probabilities are influenced by the possible errors committed in benefit and loss cost estimations.

FORECASTING WATER REQUIREMENT

Forecasting is a risky endeavor which planners are forced to undertake for practically all major water resources systems. Forecasts of population, water demand, rate of development and economic factors influence the ultimate success of the project. Methods have been investigated for determining safety factors in sizing control structures which provides a hedge against the uncertainties of the future.

The Hungarian have expended considerable effort in forecasting future water requirement /Csermák and Domokos, 1970; Csermák, 1972/. They conclude that because of the difficulties and inevitable uncertainties in forecasting water requirements, several methods or alternatives should be applied simultaneously. Another conclusion states that for extendedrange forecasting, the demand function cannot be other than stochastic. In this connection, the cooperative research is exploring the use of inventory control models for scheduling irrigation /Fogel et.al. 1974, Dávid, 1973./.

The object of this effort is to adapt currently available inventory models for determining the optimal irrigation policy, as for example, the timing and amount of water application that results in the minimum irrigation cost to the farmer. Under the assumption that all other production costs remain constant, this optimal policy can be considered as one which maximizes net benefits.

It has been shown that by considering the soil water reservoir as a store-house of goods that are consumed at varying rates and that must be replenished periodically, an analogy exists between the irrigation farmer who stores water in the soil and the business man who stores goods in a warehouse. Both must make decision on the timing and quantity of goods to be ordered so that a sufficient supply is on hand to meet an expected demand. Both require a balance between overstocking and understocking. An overstock would require a greater capital outlay per unit time but less frequent occurrence of water shortages and number of irrigations. On the other hand, an understock would require less capital per unit time but would increase the frequency of irrigations and may run the risk of water shortage in a sensitive growth stage. Neither extreme will generally be the optimum case. Decisions regarding the quantity and timing of irrigations are based on the minimization of an appropriate loss function which balances total costs resulting from overirrigation and underirrigation.

With the inclusion of a stochastic model of rainfall during the growing season and the probability distribution of a parameter that is indicative of potential evapotranspiration, it becomes possible to obtain a simulation model of irrigation water requirements.

STOCHASTIC INPUTS TO SIMULATION MODELS

In situation where hydrologic data are available in sufficient quantity, it may be possible to optimize parameters of a simulation model for generating synthetic streamflow records to produce reliable results of future conditions. One of the first models that simulated catchment hydrology is the deterministic Stanford Watershed Model /Crawford and Linsley, 1966/. Like most other models of this type, it requires several years of continuous output /streamflow/ data to obtain optimal values for various watershed characteristics. Historical inputs /precipitation and other climatic data/ are normally used to obtain a sequence of events that hopefully will be some indication of what will happen in the future.

Where the availability of streamflow data is limited such as in many of the developing nations of the world, it is still possible to generate sequences of streamflows by coupling a stochastic precipitation model with a deterministic hydrologic model in which watershed characteristics have been previously determined.

The University of Arizona has pioneered in the development and use of an event based stochastic precipitation model that has been validated for a variety of conditions /Fogel et.al. 1971, Duckstein et.al. 1973 b/. While the initial focus has been on the intense, short-duration convective storm that occurs during summer months subsequent efforts have centered on winter precipitation /Kao et.al. 1971, Cary et.al. 1974/.

Essentially the precipitation model requires the estimation of parameters for two frequency distributions, e.g., the amount of precipitation per event and the number of events per time interval. The events are defined in a way that makes use of readily available data while still maintaining the characteristics of the type of storm under consideration. For example in the case of winter storm involving snowfall, a storm is defined as a continuous sequence of days each one receiving more than a certain value of snow water equivalent. Storms are separated in time by one or more dry days.

The random variables in question, then would be the number of storms in a given time period generally determined to be a Poisson variate and the total amount of precipitation for storm or event.

As shown by Duckstein et. al. /1972/, the above two probability distributions can be combined to derive the maximal distribution for determining the return period for an event of given magnitude. In addition, compounding the Poisson number of events with the distribution of precipitation amount per storm, generally found to be a gamma, results in a distribution of the total amount of precipitation in a given time interval during which a random number of storms occurred. Using classical combinational analysis techniques and Monte Carlo simulation, a synthetic rainfall set can be generated. In conjunction with deterministic rainfall-runoff relations the simulated rainfall set can be transformed into a simular sets of water and sediment yields.

HYDROLOGIC EFFECTS OF LAND MODIFICATIONS

The control and utilization of streamflow is a function of both land use within the drainage basin and hydraulic control structures built on the stream. Changes in land use on the watershed will affect substantially the streamflow regime, the movement of sediments and will have a direct influence on the effectiveness of control structures. Land use changes will effect every event in which precipitation is eventually transformed into the measurable products of a watershed, namely, vegatation, water and sediment. Thus, future watershed modifications may become a technological uncertainty in that they alter the probability distributions of floods, the rate of erosion, the long-term build up of sediments in reservoirs, and the basin water yield.

Hydrologic variables that may be used for determining the effects of modification include volume of flow, peak flow rates, chemical and bacteriological water quality parameters. A problem may arise when attempting to evaluate the relative merits of more than one consequence of manipulating the land.

There is a distinct possibility that a given course of action may result in both beneficial and harmful changes. The question arises, for example, what is the tradeoff between the desired increased water and the undesired poorer water quality? That is a problem of the decision maker.

Predicting the effects of a proposed action that in some way modifies the land implies that the hydrologic variables can be estimated under a variety of rainfall and watershed characteristics. Since outside of the major river systems most of the worlds basins are either ungaged or have limited hydrologic data, an added constraint is placed on a useable procedure. In the United States, the application of the synthetic unit hydrograph is the most common procedure for determining the hydrologic input in the design of water control structures.

The design of structures for preventing floodwater, erosion and sediment damage is generally based on a methodology developed by the U.S. Department of Agriculture /Soil Conservation Service, 1972/. The method relates runoff to rainfall using a combined parameter expressing soil and land treatment characteristics. Information for estimating this parameter has been compiled for many areas of the United States. A synthetic hydrograph is obtained from storm runoff using a rainfall parameter and another basin parameter. The procedure for evaluating the hydrologic effects of changes in land use simply uses this method in a probablistic formulation and the previously mentioned event based stochastic precipitation model /Fogel et. al. 1973/. In this manner, the technological uncertainties of the hydrologic effects caused by land use changes are quantified by obtaining a probability distribution function of these effects.

REFERENCES

Bogárdi, I., Duckstein, L. and Kisiel, C.C. /1973 a/. Distribution of Dynamic
    Water Level in a Shallow Lake. Bulletin of the IAHS, 12.
Bogárdi, I., Duckstein, L. and Metler, W. /1973 b/. Release Control Policy
    for a Large Subject to Wind Waves. Proceedings, IFAC Symp. on Control
    of Water Resources Systems, Haifa, Israel.
Bogárdi, I. /1974 a/. Uncertainty in Water Resources Decision Making. Paper
    prepared for the U.N. Interregional Seminar on River Basin and Inter-
    Basin Development.
Bogárdi, I. and Szidarovszky, F. /1974 b/. Induced Safety Algorithm for
    Hydrologic Design Under Uncertainty Water Res. Research, Vol. 10.
    No. 2
Bogárdi, I., Szidarovszky, F., Duckstein, L. and Davis, D.R. /1974 c/.
    Economic Uncertainties in Environmental Protection. to be published.
Cary, L.E., Gupta, V.K. and Fogel, M.M. /1974/. A Stochastic Model of
    Snow Accumulation and Ablation. AGU 55th Annual Meeting, Washington,
    D.C.
Crawford, N.H. and Linsley, R.K. /1966/. Digital Simulation in Hydrology:
    Stanford Watershed Model IV. Stanford Univ. Civ. Eng. Dept. Tech.
    Report 39. 210 p.
Csermák, B. /1972/. Methods for Water Requirements Forecasting. U.N. Ad
    Hoc Group of Experts.
Davis, D.R., Kisiel, C.C. and Duckstein, L. /1972/. Bayesian Decision
    Theory Applied to Design in Hydrology. Water Res. Research, Vol. 8.,
    No. 1.
Domokos, M. /1974/. Theory of Water Restriction and Water Deficiency
    Tolerance. VITUKI, Publ. in Foreign Languages, 9. Budapest.
Duckstein, L., Fogel, M.M. and Kisiel, C.C. /1972/. A Stochastic Model of
    Runoff-Producing Rainfall for Summer Type Storms. Water Res. Res.
    Vol. 8. p. 410-421.
Duckstein, L., Bogárdi, I., Szidarovszky, F. and Kisiel,C.C. /1973 a/.
    Reliability of a Levee Reach. Submitted for publication, Journal of
    Hydraulic Division. ASCE.
Duckstein, L., Fogel, M.M. and Thames, J.L. /1973 b/. Elevation Effects on
    Rainfall: A Stochastic Model. J. of Hydrology, Vol. 18. p. 21-35.
Duckstein, L., Davis, D.R. and Bogárdi, I. /1974 a/. Applications of Decision
    Theory to   Hydraulic Engineering. ASCE Specialty Conf., Prob.
    Methods in Eng., Stanford Univ., Stanford, USA.
Duckstein, L., Bogárdi, I., Szidarovszky, F. and Davis, D.R. /1974 b/.
    Sample Uncertainty in Flood Levee Design: Bayesian Versus Non-
    Bayesian Methods. Submitted for publication, Water Resources Bulletin.
Fogel, M.M., Duckstein, L. and Kisiel, C.C. /1973/. Predicting the
    Hydrologic Effects of Land Modification. ASAE Annual Meeting,
    Lexington, Kentucky, USA.
Fogel, M.M., Duckstein, L. and Kisiel, C.C. /1974/. Optimal Timing of Irri-
    gation Water Application. Accepted for publication in Automatica.
Kao, S.E., Duckstein, L. and Fogel, M.M. /1971/. A Probabilistic Model
    of Winter Rainfall. AGU. Fall Annual Meeting, San Francisco.
Kisiel, C.C. and Duckstein, L., Editors /1972/. Proc. Int. Syp. on Un-
    certainties in Hydrology and Water Resources. Tucson, Arizona, USA,
    Vol. 1, 2 and 3.
Soil Conservation Service. /1972/. Hydrology. Sec. 4. National Engineering
    Harnbook. USDA.
Dávid, L. /1973/. Characterization of Water Demand in Irrigation Systems.
    ICID Ninth Europ. Conf., R:2.2/17, Budapest.

DISCUSSION

This is an adaptive control model by keeping record of where you are at a certain time. What we hope to do is to be able to determine how many irrigations are necessary to maintain a level. (FOGEL)

I would like to use such thing but I have difficulties, because plant roots are not distributed uniformly through the soil and the typical pattern of plant water uptake between one irrigation and the next starts from the top zone ; as it depletes gradually the region of maximum uptake migrates downwards. I have great difficulty to determine where to localize the entire root zone as you have here. (HILLEL)

We recognize the problem, it is a big problem. (FOGEL)

What was the average size of farm lands, holdings in Hungary as compared to Arizona. (SIKKA)

State farms are larger in Hungary than in Arizona. (FOGEL)

Current research field of author : *Stochastic precipitation models – Mathematical simulation of watershed hydrology – Decision making techniques for the management of natural resources.*

Modeling and Simulation of Water Resources Systems, G.C. VANSTEENKISTE, (Ed.)
North-Holland Publishing Company (1975)

PLANNING MODEL FOR SIMULATING DISTRIBUTION AND COST
IN A REGIONAL WATER SUPPLY SYSTEM

R.C. Steiner
Central Water Planning Unit
Reading, ENGLAND

ABSTRACT

The resource allocation and costing model is specified by drawing a map
showing the potential sources, notional demand centres and interconnecting
links. The fundamental data needed to run the model consists of source
yields, demand centre deficiencies, link characteristics and unit costs.
Allocation is based on the financial ranking of water transhipment along
all feasible source to demand routes. Staged construction of system
constituents is specified and may be varied as desired. Results produced
by the model include annual real and discounted capital and running costs
of the system, yields of sources, flows in links and satisfied and
unsatisfied demands (if any).

INTRODUCTION

The planning of long term water resources development lends itself well to
simulation modelling techniques. In this particular study the operation of a
large number of potential sources, demands and interconnecting links was examined
over a planning period of 26 years. The model was run many times in order to
compare different source configurations, deficiencies, discount rates, and other
measures of sensitivity. By thus simulating the development of water resources in
a region, it was possible to experiment with many different plans for the future
and to support a recommended plan by comparison with alternatives.

SPECIFICATION OF THE RESOURCE SYSTEM

The system is specified by first drawing a diagrammatic map showing all
potential and actual sources, notional demand centres and feasible links. Many
types of strategic sources are considered in order to give maximum flexibility of
resource development in the simulation exercises; they are run-of-the-river and
off-channel pumped storage surface reservoirs, bunded reservoirs in estuaries,
direct river abstraction, large groundwater development areas (in some cases
combined with recharge), desalination, and the enlargement or redeployment of
existing reservoirs. Additionally, the conjunctive use of several sources and the
re-use of effluents are also considered as sources where appropriate. In total

there are 72 sources specified from which the model chooses the water required to meet demands.

For the purpose of demand specification, the planning area (most of England and Wales) is considered to be supplied at 40 centres. Some of these are notional to the extent that the transmission link terminates at the geographical centre of gravity of several existing or potential distribution reservoirs. The links are routed on Ordnance Survey maps along feasible paths, and in some cases are already in existence and available for strategic redeployment.

Thus the framework of the system is formed by sources and demand centres with pipelines linking them. As the system develops, pumping stations, treatment works, etc. are added to the map.

DATA SELECTION

The data consists of source information, demand centre deficiencies, link characteristics, source to demand link routes, operational variables and unit costs. Associated with each source is an annual potential yield, capital and running costs (if applicable) and estimated construction period. These figures are derived from individual studies of the specific sites to determine optimum storage potential of the sources. To each demand centre is assigned an annual deficiency made up from public water supply and direct industrial demand. Two methods of forecasting the public water supply portion of the demand are adopted and tested:- reliance upon the estimates of statutory water undertakings, and projection of per capita consumption multiplied by future population estimates. Substantial effluent returns to rivers are taken into account and assessment of demand is made above this gain to dry weather flows.

Each link or pipeline route has a specified static head, length, "run cost" factor[1], bankside storage factor, construction period, existing spare capacity and diameter (if any) and assigned tunnel costs (if applicable). In the system each link has a pump, and water may flow in either direction: one way under a pumping head and the other way by gravity. The link sequences along all feasible source-demand routes and unit capital and running costs for the various other constituents are specified for the system. Operational variables are also required to set the rate for interest and discounting, the number of years for the planning period, numbers of potential sources, demands, links, load factors and type of run.

---

[1] A numeral assigned to each link which determines the type of flow and cost computations required.

All the above comprises a broad base from which a particular strategy is developed. All that is required is to specify which sources are required and when they should be introduced in a strategy --- (a very simple hand exercise) --- in order for the model to run. A preliminary computer program selects from the data base only that which is associated with the stated sources. This procedure effectively reduces the storage necessary when running the allocation and costing programs of the model.

DISTRIBUTION OF SOURCE YIELDS

The allocation procedure is based on the financial ranking of water transhipment along all feasible source-demand routes. An assumed annual average flow (unique to each source-demand combination) is first costed over each route. These costings are then ranked and form the basis of the allocation routine which proceeds from one year to the next satisfying the deficiencies by drawing upon the lowest ranked source first. The programs making up the model are sufficiently robust to accept a wide range of specifications in the data, computing constraints and output formats. The allocation program will proceed to completion even though a small number of deficiencies may not be met. After any unsatisfied demands have been computed, the allocation results may be adjusted by hand, allowing the model to proceed to costing.

STAGING OF SYSTEM COMPONENTS

Constructional considerations in the staging of system components influence the specifications of the model. Source works are staged as determined in preliminary studies; treatment works and terminal storage reservoirs are staged according to the volume of water put into supply. Transmission works, however, have a more specific sequencing procedure: pipes are staged at intervals of not less than six years, with a maximum of two stages in the planning period. More frequent staging is considered to cause too much physical disturbance. The size and staging of the pipes along a route are optimised by a short routine such that the minimum capital and running costs are incurred over the period and to perpetuity. Pumps are staged at four year intervals in such a way that the total installation at the beginning of the interval is of sufficient capacity to transmit the maximum flow during the ensuing four years. Finally, pumphouses are staged in conjunction with pipe laying.

COSTING PROCEDURES

The links are sized and costed separately for the actual flows computed, and for each one is given:- the years of staging, costs of pumps, pipes, pumphouses and intakes, total capital costs and running costs discounted back to a present value datum, and the present value[2] of the total costs.

In a summary of annual costs the following information is output:- real and present value source and link costs, service reservoir and water treatment capital costs and total capital costs. Running costs including power, groundwater pumping, administration and primary water treatment as well as their total present value are also given; as are grand total real and present value costs. Additionally, there is a facility within the model for taking into account engineering supervision, contingencies, maintenance and capital replacement.

PRESENTATION OF RESULTS

The output from the model is formatted as tables with titles and column and row headings. Given in tabular form are source yields, unsatisfied demands (if any), satisfied demands, flows in each link and individual source to demand allocations. The foot of each relevant page of printout is labelled with the title of the computer run, number and title of development strategy, interest rate and date of computation. A subsequent program outputs results in graphical form and a visual display unit is used for rapid access to results.

ACKNOWLEDGEMENT

The author thanks the Director of the Central Water Planning Unit for permission to publish this paper.

REFERENCES

Armstrong, R. B. and Clarke, K. F. (1972) Journ. I.W.E. vol. 26, p.11,
    Water Resources Planning in Southeast England.

Water Resources Board, (1973). Water Resources in England and Wales;
    WRB Publication No. 23, (Her Majesty's Stationery Office, London).

Current research field of author : *Simulation of allocation and costing of national long-term water resources development strategies - Simulation of regulated river-basin systems as a planning aid to inter-river transfers.*

---

2 Discounted cost over the planning period with running and replacement costs to perpetuity.

Modeling and Simulation of Water Resources Systems, G.C. VANSTEENKISTE, (Ed.)
North-Holland Publishing Company (1975)

INTEGRATED SURVEYS OF LAND AND WATER RESOURCES FOR DEVELOPMENT PURPOSES

W. H. de Man
ITC-Unesco Centre
for Integrated Surveys
Enschede, The Netherlands

ABSTRACT

The main objective of this paper is to attempt to indicate in
what way concepts such as modeling, simulation, etc. can be
applied to integrated surveys of land and water resources for
development purposes.

INTRODUCTION

One of the objectives of integrated surveys is the identification and analysis
of the (complex) problems that cause stagnation of development in a particular
area. A general difficulty in integrated surveys is the necessity to present the
collected data about different items as well as the analysis of the above-mentioned
problems in one overall framework. Although this difficulty is recognized, in
many practical executions of "integrated surveys" it can be shown that this has not
been solved fully. An explicit application of concepts as models, simulation,
etc. (more general: a systems approach), may contribute to the solution of the
problem: bringing different items together in one overall framework. On the other
hand, serious troubles can be created when applying sophisticated mathematical methods and procedures to integrated surveys for development purposes because of the
scarcity of sufficient and reliable quantitative data.

This leads to the question: in what way should concepts such as modeling,
simulation, etc. be applied to integrated surveys?
This paper attempts to answer this question in very general terms.

INTEGRATED SURVEYS

Introduction

The number and complexity of surveys for natural resources development has
increased considerably during the last twenty years. Economic and social investigations have become an essential part in pre-investment and feasibility studies for
resources development. The intricate complex of parameters on which the proposals
for development have to be based urges for a coordinated and integrated study of
the natural and human factors.

The importance of integration in the study of natural resources for potential
development was extensively treated during the Unesco Conference ("on principles
and methods of integrating aerial survey studies of natural resources for potential
development") in Toulouse, France in 1964. Immediately after this conference
Unesco requested the I.T.C. in The Netherlands to study and promote methods and
techniques and to develop study and teaching programmes on integrated surveys for
resources development. The ITC-Unesco Centre for Integrated Surveys commenced its
activities in 1965.

Although many different definitions of the term "integrated surveys" are available, within the scope of this paper, "integrated surveys" includes:
1) all activities related to the formulation of the survey objectives, survey tasks, and survey activities, and
2) the subsequent collection, analysis, and interpretation of all kinds of relevant information needed for the (re)formulation of concrete action programmes (or their alternatives) for development purposes.
The objective of integrated surveys is to ensure that the interrelated (monodisciplinary) survey activities are in accordance with the common survey goals.

Phasing of the Survey

Integrated surveys is a problem-oriented process in which a certain phasing can be arranged with, of course, the possibility of a reappraisal of objectives of the survey on the basis of findings during the preceding phase. The phasing can be arranged according to two criteria:
1) from general into detailed;
2) the most important data will be collected first.

In an integrated survey for land and water resources, the phases arranged according to the above-mentioned criteria, are:
1) pre-survey;
2) reconnaissance survey;
3) semi-detailed survey;
4) detailed survey.

The main objectives of the pre-survey are to investigate whether the survey fits into the country-wide development pattern, to investigate whether the survey to be undertaken is worthwhile and to formulate both the goals of the development and the objectives of the reconnaissance survey. The main objectives of the reconnaissance survey are to identify the areas of high potential for development. The main objectives of the semi-detailed survey are to compare the projects selected on the basis of the survey results of the previous phase, to determine both their technical feasibility and economic justification and to recommend priorities with respect to them. Finally, the main objectives of the detailed survey are to investigate the economic justification of the projects as a preparation for their financing and to collect all relevant technical information that is needed for the execution of the project.

The Different Steps in Each Phase

An integrated survey should be strictly oriented towards one or more definable goals. It is quite common that in the early phase (or stage) of the survey, these goals are only roughly defined. From the goals of the particular development the objectives of the survey are derived. Both the design and the execution of the survey should be guided by these pre-formulated objectives. This holds for each phase of the survey and so, in each phase, the following steps may be recognized:
1) (re)definition of the development goals;
2) definition of the objectives of the survey;
3) design of the survey;
4) monitoring of the survey under execution;
5) presentation of the survey results.

During the monitoring step it may appear to be necessary to reconsider the definition of the objectives or the design of the survey. The process of an integrated survey, in one specific phase, can be explained by scheme no.1.

Related to each phase of an integrated survey, a certain model should exist describing both the existing situation and the expected and/or desired direction

Scheme   nr. 1.

The process of an integrated survey
(for explanation see text.)

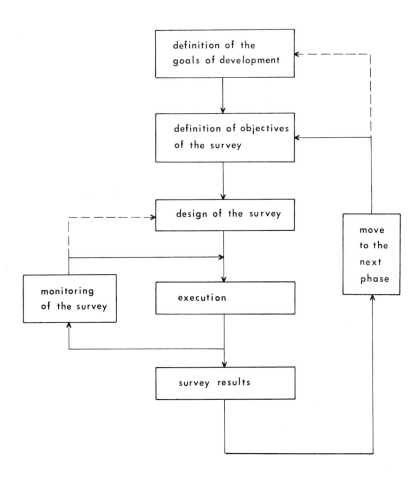

frequent relation   _ _ _ _   exeptional

Scheme   nr. 2.

The process of development

(for explanation see text.)

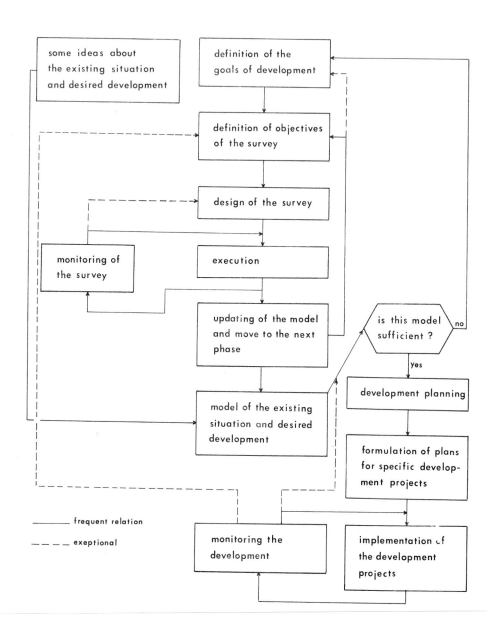

of development.   In the successive phases of the survey this model becomes more
and more specific.

Three different sub-systems should be distinguished within the development:
(1) surveys, (2) planning, and (3) implementation of the plans.   The relation
between them can be explained by scheme no.2.   In this scheme the model of the
existing situation and the desired development is the central element.   The development is planned on the basis of this model.   The model itself becomes more
specific by updating the model after each phase of the survey.

THE EXPLICIT APPLICATION OF MODELING AND SIMULATION TO INTEGRATED SURVEYS

From the foregoing, it is clear that the concept of integrated surveys can be
regarded as an application of the concept of a systems approach.   When this is
done explicitly, remarks of both support and warning can be made:
- The explicit application of a systems approach to integrated surveys can help in
  recognizing and describing the interrelation between various phenomena.
- Many methods of modeling, simulation, optimization, etc. make use of sophisticated procedures which can hardly be applied in situations where sufficient and
  reliable quantitative data are lacking.

To what extent modeling-, simulation-, optimization methods can be applied
depends on the specific situation.   More precisely: it depends on the availability
of quantitative data of good quality. Where several procedures seem to be too sophisticated to be applied to integrated surveys for development purposes, these
procedures should be adapted.

When the method of simulation, for example, is applied for optimization and
the targets and the criteria for the system cannot – or only with difficulties –
be made explicit in mathematical terms, only then should the physical process be
described in quantified terms.   In the mathematical model itself, no considerations should be implemented for an optimal use of the existing system.   The physical consequences of this system can be studied under preset conditions and pre-
defined decision rules with the help of the method of simulation.   By defining
the decision rules differently for each simulation run, different <u>alternative</u>
trends can be simulated and these alternative trends can be compared.   Among the
various alternatives, the one can be chosen that meets the preset aims the best.
This alternative may be regarded as the optimal one.

<u>Such an approach guarantees that the choice of an optimal alternative will be
guided, not only by quantified targets and criteria but also by targets and criteria which cannot be described in a mathematical way</u>.   This choice can be made,
for instance, by a panel in which not only the technical specialists who formulated the model are represented, but also the local population.   In this way, the
applied methods can be kept rather simple and remain therefore, understandable for
a broader group of concerned people.

CONCLUSION

An <u>explicit</u> application of concepts like modeling, simulation, etc. to integrated surveys has great advantages.   However, the lack of reliable quantified
data causes troubles when existing sophisticated methods and procedures are applied.

There is a need for adapted, relatively simple methods and procedures in
order to apply concepts of modeling, simulation, etc. fruitfully to integrated
surveys.   Although working along these lines does not have a great scientific
appeal, it is valuable enough to be undertaken.

Cases where a systems approach is realized successfully by means of such adapted procedures, should be reported with more emphasis. With respect to development, they can contribute to the solution of urgent problems much more than the exceptional cases do, where highly sophisticated methods and procedures were applied fruitfully.
In the example following, such an almost trivial case is described.

An Example -

In April 1974, a team of the ITC-Unesco Centre for Integrated Surveys undertook field investigations in one of the Gouvernorats of Northern Tunisia. The team consisted of staffmembers of the Centre as well as participants of the Standard Course.

The region is one of the most important agricultural areas of the country. Tourism has developed rapidly over the past five years and continues to expand. The demand for water is anticipated to exceed the locally available water resources representing eventually, a major constraint upon development.

The purpose of this reconnaissance survey was to supply basic qualitative and quantitative data for the formulation of development alternatives with emphasis on the optimization of water utilization in the context of a regional development plan. The survey included:
1) Evaluation of present agricultural practices and scope for future development of rainfed and irrigated agriculture, livestock, forestry and fisheries, in view of physical, technical and socio-economic constraints.
2) Evaluation of the present situation and scope for further development of tourism in view of physical, technical and socio-economic constraints and its impact on urbanization.
3) Evaluation of present and future surface and groundwater resources, the possibility of maintaining the present level of development, and the scope for further development eventually in conjunction with other sources of water supply.

From the beginning it was clear that no sophisticated mathematical procedure could be applied in order to define the optimal water use within the gouvernorat. At least at this phase of the survey, no objective function could be expressed in mathematical terms and essential data were missing.

However, several policy measures open to the decision makers for implementation can be fairly accurately described in a quantitative way. For instance, the area of certain types of soils under cultivation of specific crops. At the present stage of the survey, the consequences of such policies are described in terms of employment.

Through a comparison with the projected development of the labour supply and taking into account the labour requirements in tourism and in services, indications can be obtained concerning the relevance of certain alternative policies of agricultural development. As a project year, 1986 was agreed upon. For the analysis and interpretation of the collected data, the gouvernorat was subdivided into four regions. For the sake of convenience in this paper only, the entire gouvernorat will be considered.

Summary of the Available Data

With respect to agriculture, three different types of resources are relevant in this phase of the survey: land, water, and human resources.
a) Land resources
The soils of the area were subdivided into a number of classes according to their agricultural capabilities. The total acreage per soil capability

```
class was measured:
    irrigable for all crops              54,200 hectares
    irrigable for all crops except        9,400    "
        for orchards
    rainfed for all crops                29,500    "
    rainfed, moderate                    43,400    "
    pasture                              33,200    "
    forestry                             90,700    "
    total agriculture                   260,400    "
```

b) Water resources

The amount of available surface water per year is 18 million m^3. The amount of available groundwater is not exactly known. Estimates in different studies vary from 63 million m^3 (lowest) to 92 million m^3 (highest) annually. For the year 1986 a domestic use of 11 million m^3 is anticipated. So, for agriculture in 1986 there is available:

    a low estimate of 70 million m^3
    a high estimate of 99 million m^3.

c) Human resources

In the year 1986 the total labour force is estimated at 135,000 workers. In that year, the employment in tourism is estimated to be within the range of 19,200 to 24,000 workers. Accepting the rate of unemployment at 10% of the total labour force in 1986, the residual to be employed in agriculture, services, transport and communications, industries and mines, will be within the range of 97,500 to 102,300 workers. (In 1966 the employment figure in services other than tourism was 19,000).

Besides the information on the available resources, some characteristics of cultuvated crops are known. For example, the required labour and irrigation water inputs per hectare, per year, and to what soil class the crop is restricted.

Based on the above-mentioned data, the consequences of some policies are calculated. In the table below some extreme policy goals are summarized with their respective consequences on employment, described in thousands of man-years (1 man-year is assumed to be equivalent to 200 man-days).

policy goal	employment (1,000 man-years)
1) maximum employment in agriculture	56 – 61
2) maximum citrus cultivation	48 – 50
3a) minimum water use with maximum employment in rainfed agriculture	43
3b) minimum water use with maximum vineyards	41

These calculated figures have to be compared with the projected residual to be employed in sectors other than tourism, being in the range of 97,500 to 102,300 workers.

It is far beyond the scope of this paper to draw conclusions on these calculated figures. However, it will be clear that in this relatively simple way some conclusions could be drawn concerning the relevance of certain alternative policies of agricultural development. Moreover, the direction which further, more detailed, calculations and investigations should be given, may be concluded. And finally, to a certain extent, the aimed benefit of further detailed investigations may result in a more exact estimate of available groundwater resources. This figure lies somewhere between the low and high estimate (viz. 63-92 million m^3).

Subject to the detailed survey, therefore, is an amount of 29 million m^3 groundwater or, at maximum, 5,000 man-years (viz. the difference between 56 and 61 thousand man-years from the table above).

RECOMMENDATION made by W.H. DE MAN and M.M. SHAH

This working conference has shown that there are numerous situations where sufficient and reliable data are not available. The methodology and concepts of systems
analysis, modeling and model validation, simulation, etc., need to be developed and
adopted for these types of situations.
There is an urgent need for reporting case studies and examples on this aspect.

DISCUSSION

*I think what the group in ITC is doing is very interesting because in try-
ing to develop an area, the first aspect is the area survey or the possibilities
for development and since that is so complex, if a systematic start is made at the
outset then there is chance that to the final point there is some systematic procedure all the way through. I think such a study is of tremendous importance especially in developing areas. (SHAH)*

*We have similar problems in Mexico where bigger areas were not yet surveyed
and they want for planning purposes critical data. So a very good tool was the area
survey which totally examined every area. In the same time we came to very interesting conclusions. If area photos are made by infrared pictures, practically with co-
lour screening you can get all kind of information from this area, because you can
identify the different area problems with known areas where similar discolouration
occurs. And in this respect the Mexican government was quite efficient and also in
the U.S. we followed the same lines - based on earth satellite infrared area photos,
we tried to put together databanks where not only the vegetation-, flood- and surface water information but also the geologic information are very valuable, especially in these areas where we are working at the detailed survey. (HALASI-KUN)*

Current research field of author : *attempt to apply more explicit concepts as models,
etc., to the current practices of integrated surveys for development purposes.*

Modeling and Simulation of Water Resources Systems, G.C. VANSTEENKISTE, (Ed.)
North-Holland Publishing Company (1975)

KEY NOTES AND IMPACTS OF SIMULATION AND MODELING TECHNIQUES
FOR DECISION MAKING WATER RESOURCES PROJECTS IN DEVELOPING AREAS

D.R.Sikka,
Chief Engineer,
Mahanadi Bodhghat Hasdeo
Major Multipurpose Projects,
Madhya Pradesh Government,
RAIPUR(M.P.) INDIA

ABSTRACT

One of the foremost requirements for modeling and simulation of water resources systems is to understand the objectives and the alternatives to be
worked out for taking final decision by those responsible for making release of large scale public investments on these projects like construction
of dams and canal across the rivers for providing irrigation hydro power
industrial and domestic water supply and flood control etc. for the welfare
of mankind in the river basin/region concerned. Not only the input data
based on the economical and technical factors are to be sound but also the
impact of political legal, social and environmental parameters have to be
correlated in right perspective. Planning with a particular objective so
as to fit in the predetermined water related socio economic programmes requires not only adequate finance competent men and appropriate material
resources to harnus for useful investment and cost benefits, but also techniques of data collection and assessment to match with changing needs. The
best could be achieved if the efficient criteria gained in other projects
in similar circumstances were applied and made use of, with corrective
coefficients. Besides parameters for the various systems, as defined for
optimization efforts, physical, biological changing agricultural patterns
most of which at times have non quantitative dimensions, it would be necessary to apply the hierarchical approach in some cases particularly in
urban watersheds and environmental control. Concept of equivalent rural
watersheds has been suggested. Classification of projects in the system
for development of new parameters and corrective coefficients has been emphasized to keep stochastic modeling to minimum. New concepts for University water resources syllabus with realistic parameters have been suggested.
To ensure an integrated and comprehensive water developing areas for example for single irrigation to intensive irrigation with single or multiple
cropping patterns, or hydro power releases, it is necessary first to know
for the model as to what should be the size and the system of action plan
in a large country like India. It will equally apply to a large river
basin in more than one State in the same country or in number of countries.
Larger the areas and lesser the development with single or multipurpose
objectives with implementation time as the key strategy would mean entirely new set of parameters for the model. The administrator, project manager,
public and modeller have to be in time with a systems approach. Perhaps
in developing areas as "requirement approach" may have to be phased into
the various model operations both for short term and long term plans keeping in view the increase in population and increase in use of water, as in
case of California State Water Plan in USA. In case of Mahanadi Hasdeo Optimization for benefits by undertaking time bound stage construction programmes in large projects involving heavy investments has been suggested
at minimum investment rate.

METHODOLOGY FOR INVESTIGATIONS - NEW PARAMETERS

In the field of decision making therefore, an individual water resource project or a group where single or multipurpose may have to be considered from the point of view of getting maximum benefits like providing irrigation water in the large culturable areas in order to maximise food production as in most of the regions in India where economy of agricultural operations is to get rid of the variations in rainfalls and runoff, will have different parameters. The method of investigation and project formulation has to be such so that within a frame work of say a five year plan systems approach with latest modeling and simulation techniques may have to be adopted in a manner, we will have to bifurcate the survey investigation and simulation operations as first chapter in our planning, and the second chapter the construction and implementation programme. What should be the methodology for such programme and what should be the period normally made available between first and second chapter is very important matter. In the concept of total water management, the coefficients and parameters for the systematic analytic planning should be defined and stochastic modeling kept to minimum. Concept of total water resources management and vis-visa rural development as a key note for recommending norms and criteria for undertaking simulation techniques by pre-determining area action plans for developed as well as developing regions is suggested. Simulation effort has to avoid purely non deterministic mechanism to take the role of evaluators so that the statistical data for econometric model is focussed as a pivot for the various linear programmes. An outline for an effective design system for the above applications has been discussed for planning and implementation where hydrological data required is also available for a considerable period. It is proposed to classify water resources systems and corresponding items with adequate as well as inadequate data, in order to make river basin planning for total water management for optimum harvesting as a key strategy in the overall development of country, as in the ultimate analysis water alone would be in short supply.

SYSTEMS APPROACH AND MODELING WATER RESOURCES SYALLABUS FOR
DEVELOPING AREAS

In India we have number of projects already constructed on the various rivers systems where hydrologic irrigation and agriculture pattern, soil and climate groups, economic, studies have been done of course under requirement approach, there should be first supplemented for mathematic modeling and results compared with those actually available. Such research projects would be very useful. Latest upsets are due to price escalation. It would therefore be necessary to introduce a chapter for such studies not only in the engineering courses in the University syallabus but also in the departmental manuals of the administration in case modeling and simulation techniques for water resources system have to be effective from practical applications. We should therefore finalize a syallabus for such a course it should be based on experience and interactions of development in developing and developed countries for highly industrialized urban, rural and developing urban areas i.e. for classified zones. Whether the projects are to be completely commercial quasi-commercial or socio objective oriented will have to be decided. Whether the results in the model have to be on direct benefits or indirect benefit for example due to increased food production increased storage and transport and market complex growth in an irrigated area, have all relevance in the overall economics of the area rather than applying input for water rates alone.

CLASSIFICATION PROJECTS - DETERMINATION COEFFICIENTS

Experience in completion and construction of such projects with multiple objective system as different from multipurpose system are fare.

Investment policies priorities under Governmental
actions public reactions go on changing looking to the developed under developed
and the size of the region, State or the country. Present inflationary tendencies
are also upsetting direct benefits cost relationships. Subject to above analysis
made in the earlier paragraph, a major irrigation on multipurpose project in India
is one which costs more than Rs. 5 crores, a medium Rs. 25 lakhs to 5 crores, a
minor less than Rs. 25 lakhs (1 lakh = 1 million, 1 crore = 10 million). Whether
we can straightway go in for this classification which will have large number of
variable or to go in for large major, very large major, super major and so on or
to classify on the basis of areas to be irrigated from each project or the size
on hydro power development from each project or for example for 20,000 acres to
10 lakhs acres irrigated area with steps rising rate of 10,000 acres and in respect of hydro power from micro to incidental to firm power from 5 MW onwards using
at rate of 5 MW for the rural areas and 50 MW onwards for urban areas. Unless these
parameters are defined it would create problem even in case of analog computers.

MODELING EQUIVALENT RURAL WATERSHEDS IN URBAN AREAS

Impact of development efforts in upstream areas for optimization reservoir
life, as well as of those required in the downstream areas including the operation
and releases from the created resources are relevant. In the systems analysis
hierarchical formulation of water development programmes in the developing areas
may have to be attempts. Some of the exercises made in the commanded areas of these
project, for example newly irrigable areas one sees that the rate of development
does not match with the commissioning of the water resource unless and until an
integrated action on the project engineering and non-engineering sectors is taken
up simultaneously with large scale public participation. Action plans for land-
shaping, levelling availability of inputs for intensive agriculture operations
etc. termed as ayacut development measures will have to be recognized. The behaviour of water changes from rural to urban areas and under such circumstances even
a dynamic model would meant lot of indeterminate variables. The problem would be
further complicated where the rural lands are getting converted into urban lands
with different parameters in the upstream watershed area and the downstream irrigated area (unless and until the entire valley is irrigated). The run-off from
a urban watershed is quite different from the rural watershed and will have,there-
fore, to adopt methods for applying equivalent rural watersheds being more uniform so that the output would be same in respect of both methods. Effects of interception, infiltration depression, storages in pervious and impervious areas will
have to be considered seriously while fixing computer programme for urban watersheds established or those growing under a developing economy.

MAHANADI-HASDEO PROJECTS OPTIMIZATION OF BENEFITS BY TIME
BOUND STAGE CONSTRUCTION/MINIMUM INVESTMENT RATE

Under the Mahanadi/Hasdeo river regions where four multipurpose projects
have been taken it is proposed to study impact of constructing one project on the
same river in the earlier stages and the second or supplementary at later stage
for computer based analytical programme for working out minimum cost alternative
for future development. What is intended is to evolve man-computer interactions
and wherever possible to sponsor computer aided programme for maintenance of sophisticated equipments in the regions. This could be appreciated from the fact
that in case of river Hasdeo valley, Hasdeo Barrage was constructed at place near
Korba in 1967 with catchment area of 3,000 sq.miles and with the projection of
an upstream Hasdeo Dam with catchment area 2602 sq.miles for supplementing the
storage and releasing water to this Barrage for irrigating about 8 million acres
of land and generate 50 MW hydro-power and giving water for the industrial complex at Korba. Looking to the short term immediate gain, Right Bank Canal project
has been taken up from the Barrage for irrigating a 4 million acres as a pilot

project to become an integral part of the overall area of irrigation preparation after the completion of upper Hasdeo Dam. A system analysis proposed on latest modeling and simulation techniques could work out the various alternatives by making use of existing data of the project as well as similar number of projects in the district, for working out a phased programme of construction of the remaining canal system so that investment starts flowing along with the stage construction of the upper dam. Optimization for benefits will need a matching construction programme of the dam and the canal system. We will have to follow an entirely different approach in most of our water planning systems. The method of construction looking to the results of above study and techniques of men material, plant and equipment applied and funds released every year would have to be coordinated in the two work systems of the dam and the canal. Similarly in case of Mahanadi Reservoir Project, at present under construction at Rudri in Raipur District upstream of the existing about 50 year old Rudri weir, whether for increasing the present irrigation of 3.5 lakh acres. Construction programme of phase II canal works will have to be tuned along with construction of main dam already started, such that large investments, could be kept to minimum while benefits could flow under a time bound programme. Unnecessary blocking of scarce capital is to be avoided.

ENVIRONMENTAL QUALITY-HIERARCHICAL SYSTEM

The latest emphasis in USA on environmental quality has impact on decision making. This aspect is being given priority now all over the world, although objectives and priorities in industrially developed countries and agriculturally developed/developing areas are bound to be different. Statutory and administrative requirements must be satisfied. National regional and local interests must be considered. Short and long term goals along with efficiency economy and safety have to be assured, which require alternatives in planning design and construction. One of the measures considered desirable is to introduce multi-disciplinary teams in project planning.

In USA, another system for evaluating environmental impact of alternative project plans has been developed by Batelle-Columbus for the Bureau of Reclamation. It incorporates a highly structured hierarchical system containing 78 parameters making up 18 environmental components such as species and population, environmental pollution, land esthetics, and human cultures.

Methods of measuring the environmental parameters are developed which result in commensurate units that can be totaled to give an environmental impact for each alternative plan. The system has been tested. The major weakness is the inability to measure many of the parameters with a high degree of confidence.

We have seen that the emphasis on environmental quality results in new tools for the decision maker, such as multi-objective planning interdisciplinary team efforts, and modified design and construction practices. The decision itself however, must remain for the foreseeable future a matter of judgment. In making that judgment, the decision maker will find no solution for development of a resource which completely satisfies the objectives of national economic development regional development, and environmental quality, and the included social factors. He should, however, explore all reasonable alternatives. He should keep basic values and objectives in mind. He should also seek out qualified opinions, preferably differing opinions, so that good and bad points can be discovered. From this effort, the decision maker should find an alternative which will optimize the positive benefits and minimize the negative impacts of a water resource project.

Environmental quality, then, is one of several objectives which are based upon basic national values. Those objectives and the ways of attaining them often conflict. This is particularly true in situations such as water resources development where the many demands of economic development and environmental quality rely upon the same resource for satisfaction. It is the function of the decision maker to select an alternative which will provide an optimum satisfaction of all those demands.

To do this, the decision maker should consider alternatives, as well defined as practicable, which are the result of interdisciplinary team efforts.

But in case we emphasize the above approach towards maximization alone, for example in India where water resource development has an immediate and direct interest in developing irrigation projects involving consumptive use, many of the plans would be delayed which we can not afford. A middle path under the circumstances depending upon intensity of irrigated area, water utilization coefficients, whether rivers are showed or otherwise, whether conjunctive surface and underground water developments programmes are coordinated, etc. may have to be adopted. An electric transmission tower and network or a man made impoundment in one region may cause environmental pollution. While in the other may be necessary for survival these two extremes have to be reconciled.

Practical application of systems analysis in the water resources system based on the above guidelines, is of such an importance that in respect of siting and sizing of reservoir in preliminary planning and dam development, the subject has been proposed for discussion as one of the four questions proposed to be discussed at the XII International Congress on Large Dams going to be held in Mexico during 1976.

REFERENCES

SIKKA D.R., Paper on Guidelines systems Planning in Developing area, ISA-USA, Proceedings of Systems Approach to Developing Countries.
ARMSTRONG E.L., Consideration of Alternatives in Decision making, ASCE, Engineering Issue, April 1974.

Modeling and Simulation of Water Resources Systems, G.C. VANSTEENKISTE, (Ed.)
North-Holland Publishing Company (1975)

THE DEVELOPMENT OF MODELLING AND SIMULATION TECHNIQUES APPLIED TO A COMPUTER-BASED TELECONTROL WATER SUPPLY SYSTEM

F. Fallside, P.F. Perry
   Cambridge University
     ENGLAND

R.H. Burch, K.C. Marlow
East Worcestershire Waterworks Company
       ENGLAND

1. INTRODUCTION

Developments in modern control theory and its applications are increasingly concerned with the overall control of complex plant, containing many control variables and inputs. It is often appropriate to use an optimal control in which the control inputs are calculated to minimise a performance index subject to certain constraints imposed by the plant. This is particularly true for distribution systems such as water supply networks, since the operating cost is well defined and can be included in the performance index, and thus successful implementation of an optimal control leads to operation of the network at minimum cost.

The technical problems in implementing such a control are several. Considerably more variables have to be measured and made available centrally than in more conventional non-optimal control schemes and thus a centralised computer for data collection and system control is essential. Since optimisation implies the minimisation of a performance index over a period of time, e.g. one day's or week's operation, it is necessary to predict the behaviour of some variables, such as the water consumption of the network, over that period of time. The computer algorithms used for optimisation and other calculations must be economical to run, capable of dealing with systems of high dimensionality and computationally robust – in particular they must be relatively insensitive to failures and noise in on-line data measurement. In implementing an optimal control a balance must be struck between the computer power needed for data measurement and system control and that needed for the more complex optimisation calculations. One solution is the use of linked computers for these separate tasks and this in turn leads to a hierarchical viewpoint[1] in which the system and its computers are separated into levels of control functions of ascending complexity.

Considerable progress has been made in solving these technical problems, for example in the electricity supply industry[2], and it is believed that optimal control methods can be applied successfully in the water supply industry. It is also believed that they will become increasingly significant with the reorganisation of the industry into a regional basis with larger networks and more centralised operation.

The authors are working on a collaborative project on the introduction of an optimal on-line control for the East Worcestershire Waterworks Company water supply network, together with Kent Automation Systems. The East Worcestershire network, which has been described elsewhere[3], is well suited to such a control scheme because of its existing computer-controlled operation, with extensive on-line centralised data collection and monitoring. In control terms the complete system can be described by approximately 21 states, 27 control inputs and 6 disturbances, related by non-linear differential equations. The project divides into several parts – the development of suitable prediction[4], analysis, simulation and optimisation[5] algorithms, and programs which are being studied off-line at present using data logged from the system and then their implementation as an integrated program for the on-line control of the system. In this paper attention is concentrated on the data gathering, modelling and simulation aspects of the project. Some aspects of the work are already well known in classical water network analysis form, our intention has been to give a unified treatment of analysis, modelling and simulation from a viewpoint of modern control theory.

2. GENERALIZED MODEL FOR WATER SUPPLY NETWORK

Although much progress has been made in recent years towards developing automatic equipment and sensors for data gathering, remote control and supervision for water supply networks, much research must still be done to determine the best

method of utilizing this equipment for making real time operational control
decisions. While computers are at present used for a variety of tasks from data
logging to automatic sequencing of plant, their full potential has not been
realized owing to the lack of suitable control guidelines, logic and mathematical
methods for utilizing the generally limited amount of telemetered data either to
reconstruct conditions in the entire network or to adequately represent the system.
        The major objective of this section is to develop a generalized mathemati-
cal model which is suitable for steady state analysis, dynamic simulation and real
time control techniques for a typical water distribution system. Basic data for
the proposed model include a physical description of the water distribution system
including pipe length, diameters, friction coefficients, pumping stations, storage
tanks and reservoirs, loop definitions, as well as the variables affecting network
operation, such as nodal consumptions, tank levels and head-flow curves for
various pumping combinations or speeds. The model is presented in a general
purpose form and may easily be applied to a wide class of distribution systems.

2.1 <u>Network Synthesis</u>: A water distribution system consists essentially of a
number of interconnected hydraulic elements each with a characteristic relationship between the variables chosen to describe its operation. These characteristic
relationships are obtained from laboratory or field tests of the elements using
parameters which adequately describe their operation and are readily available for
measurement. The two variables which are usually used for describing the
operation of these elements are the water head and flow, both of which are
physically meaningful and measureable quantities. Given the variables describing
the elements it is necessary to choose a principle for assembling the network from
its constituent components. This is provided by the property of an hydraulically
balanced system that the head loss between two points in the network is independent
of the path taken between them, which suggests a convenient method of synthesizing
a network of elements interconnected at specific nodes for which the above law
holds.

2.2 <u>Network Variables</u>: The following three types of **variables** may be used to
describe almost every possible operating condition in a supply network.

2.2.1 <u>Heads</u>: The water head at node is a measure of the energy per unit weight
of water at that point and may be determined by measuring the level to which water
rises in a stand pipe connected to the network at that node. The unit used is
feet (or meters) of water although in some cases it is convenient to convert this
to a pure pressure by applying an appropriate conversion factor. The system nodal
pressures are usually monitored only at a small number of important internal nodes,
and it is normal to have to supply continuous sensing equipment at about 15% of
the nodes chosen for modelling purposes. Such continuous records allow the
validity of a proposed model to be checked under a variety of loading conditions.

2.2.2 <u>Consumptions</u>: The consumption at a network node is simply defined as the
rate at which water is demanded by the consumer. Ideally it would be desirable to
have all nodal consumers metered, so that the total demand in an area is known
even if the proportion of it at a number of synthetic nodes cannot be determined
exactly. In practice, however, it frequently happens that only industrial
consumers are metered and that domestic consumption must be estimated.

2.2.3 <u>Flows</u>: The flows in a supply network depend on the head difference across
the elements and their characteristic relationships. In some network models the
flows are considered to be dependent variables and the unknowns of the network are
the nodal heads. In other formulations, the flows are unknown and are directly
manipulated to arrive at a network solution.

2.3 <u>Types of Hydraulic Element and their Physical Laws</u>: A very wide variety of
elements are encountered on distribution systems and it is hardly possible or even
desirable to have a model flexible enough to handle such a large number of
components. The accepted practice is to restrict the model to an analysis of the
most important of these elements, whose model parameters are chosen in such a way
that they may be easily adjusted to simulate most practical systems. For example,

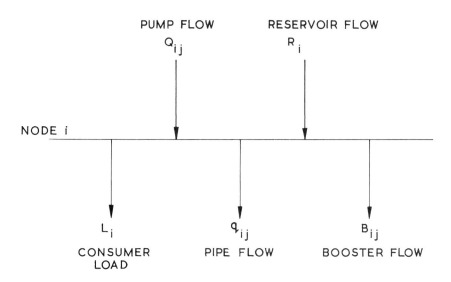

FIG. I (a) GENERAL MATHEMATICAL REPRESENTATION
OF A NODE.

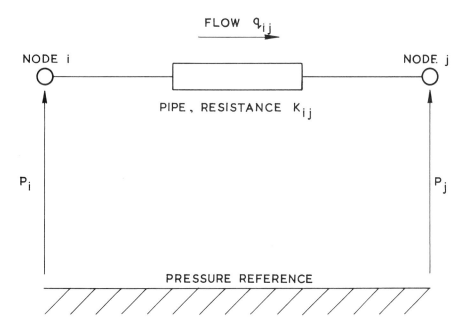

FIG. I (b) GENERAL MATHEMATICAL REPRESENTATION
OF A PIPE.

the simple model of a straight pipe may be conveniently used to simulate a curve in the line simply by increasing its resistance parameter, or to simulate a cut-off valve by setting its resistance to a very large value. This approach of concentrating on deriving flexible models for the major hydraulic elements is found to be successful in practice, at least in the present state of the art.

The following is a description of four elements encountered on most systems and which can be used to describe a wide class of supply networks.

2.3.1 <u>Pipes</u>: These are, of course, the most commonly occurring elements in a network and several empirical laws have been developed to describe their operation. A convenient representation is shown in Figure 1(b) and a characteristic relationship may be determined by laboratory experiment for the range of pressures and velocities usually encountered under normal operating conditions on a network. In particular, the widely used Hazen-Williams equation is valid for the range of velocities which normally exist on practical systems and which justify the neglect of kinetic energy in the determination of the total head at a node. The basic form is as follows:

$$q_{ij} = K_{ij} \, \text{sgn}(H_i - H_j) \, |H_i - H_j|^n \tag{1}$$

where
$$q_{ij} = \text{flow rate between nodes } i \text{ and } j$$
$$H_i = \text{water head at node } i$$
$$K_{ij} = \beta \frac{C_{ij} D_{ij}^{2.63}}{L_{ij}^{0.54}} \tag{2}$$

where C_{ij}, D_{ij} are respectively the Hazen-Williams roughness coefficient, the diameter and length of the pipe joining node i to node j, and β a constant for the system of units being used. The value of the parameter n is usually 0.54 .

2.3.2 <u>Pumps</u>: From the control viewpoint the most important energy consuming items on the system are the pumps. For supply purposes these fall into two categories: borehole pumps, which deliver the water from underground boreholes into surface contact tanks, and high lift pumps, which deliver the water to different points on the system. Both sets may be either fixed or variable speed, this latter type allowing an additional degree of control action.

The simplest hydraulic representation of the pump is obtained from the characteristic curves relating head, flow and efficiency for various speeds or combinations of parallel pumps. The first of these relations relates head increase across the pump to pump flow for various operating conditions, i.e. for different speeds or various combinations of parallel pumps. The relationship may be expressed mathematically as

$$\Delta H_i = a_{ij1} + a_{ij2} Q_i^{1.85} \quad ; \quad j \in N_c(i) \tag{3}$$

where
$$\Delta H_i = \text{head increase for } j^{th} \text{ operating condition}$$
$$i = \text{pump station number}$$
$$Q_i = \text{station flow for } j^{th} \text{ operating condition}$$
$$a_{ijk} = \text{array of station constants}$$
$$N_c(i) = \text{set of combination numbers}$$

The second of these relationships relates efficiency of pumping to the flow at each operating condition in a pumping station. This may be written

$$\eta_i = \sum_{k=1}^{m} b_{ijk} Q_i^{k-1} \quad ; \quad j \in N_c(i) \tag{4}$$

where
$$\eta_i = \text{efficiency of pumping station } i \text{ for } j^{th} \text{ operating condition}$$
$$m = \text{order of polynomial fit}$$

This relationship must be determined accurately since it appears explicitly in the expression for total pump energy consumed.

A third equation relates suction head at each station to pump flow and total demand. This may be written as

$$S_i = C_{i1} + C_{i2} L_i^{1.85} + C_{i3} Q_i^{1.85} \tag{5}$$

where $\qquad$ S_i = suction head at station i

$\qquad\qquad$ L_i = demand at station i

$\qquad\qquad$ C_{ik} = station constants

and is, of course, the same functional relationship for each pumping combination. Clearly, then, the delivery head H_i^d is given by

$$H_i^d = S_i + \Delta H_i \tag{6}$$

In each of the equations (3) to (6) the expressions are valid for each node having a pump or booster attached to it and the index i merely refers to the pump in question, varying from 1 up to the maximum number of pumps on the system.

Another useful relationship is given by the equation for head drop from source to reservoir, expressed as follows: assume there are M_p separate pumps delivering water independently to a service reservoir, then the head drop from the ith pump to the tank is given by

$$\Delta H_i^t = d_{i1} + d_{i2} L_i^{1.85} + \sum_{j=1}^{M_p} d_{i(j+2)} Q_j^{1.85} \tag{7}$$

where the constants d_{ij} are found by regression analysis on actual plant data.

The energy consumed by the pumps in their various operating configurations is the time integral of the power input. The power output is simply the product of the head increase across the pump and the rate of flow output from it, but the input power required for the motors exceeds that imparted to the water by an efficiency factor. Thus the energy input for the ith pump is simply

$$E_i = \int_{t_o}^{t_f} \frac{Q_i \, \Delta H_i^*}{\eta_i(Q_i)} \, dt. \tag{8}$$

for the interval of operation $[t_o, t_f]$, where the pump head increase ΔH_i^* is related to the station head increase ΔH_i by the equation

$$\Delta H_i^* = \Delta H_i + r_i Q_i^{1.85} \tag{9}$$

The determination of the constants in equations (3) to (7) may be achieved by fitting data from actual flow and pressure measurements on the system. Since manufacturer's curves may frequently be inaccurate or represent average values it is very desirable to use actual measurements from the network for this purpose.

2.3.3 <u>Reservoirs</u>: The simplest model of a reservoir relates the time derivative of its <u>water height</u> to the net inflow to the storage element according to the relationship

$$\alpha_i \frac{dx_i}{dt} = R_i(t)$$

$$x_i = x_i^o + h_i \tag{10}$$

where $\qquad$ x_i = reservoir level above a datum

$\qquad\qquad$ x_i^o = base elevation

$\qquad\qquad$ h_i = water depth

$\qquad\qquad$ i = reservoir no.

$\qquad\qquad$ $R_i(t)$ = reservoir flow rate

$\qquad\qquad$ α_i = proportionality factor

The proportionality factor α_i is a function of the geometry of the reservoir and is independent of height for vertical walled elements. Even in cases where the taper is significant the value of α_i may sometimes be assumed approximately constant for a range of operating heights.

In some cases, for particularly large reservoirs, a convenient approximation is to assume that $\dot{x}_i = 0$ or that changes of reservoir level in time are relatively insignificant. This leads to a number of constant pressure nodes in the network and reduces the state dimensionality of the control problem given in ref.(2). In general, however, it is necessary to consider the time variation of all system reservoirs.

2.3.4 <u>Valves</u>: A number of different types of valves are encountered in distribution studies including throttling valves, designed to increase the head difference between 2 nodes, and one-way valves, which are designed to allow flow in one direction only. In general, the pressure reducing valve is designed to produce a constant outlet pressure for a range of high inlet pressures up to a certain limit. Consider such a valve connected into the line between nodes i and j; assuming the flow is from i to j, the valve can be considered to be adjacent to node i, and if H_r is the constant reduced pressure, the flow is

$$q_{ij} = K_{ij} (H_r - H_j)^{0.54} \tag{11}$$

where

$$H_j \leqslant H_r \leqslant H_i \tag{12}$$

and if ever H_r becomes greater than H_i then it can be set equal to H_i and the presence of the valve has no effect on the normal flow between nodes i and j. Alternatively, if $H_r < H_j$ then H_r can be set equal to H_j to give zero return flow. Such a model is clearly ideally suited to digital simulation.

2.4 <u>Describing Equations of the Network</u>: The mathematical model of the process is essentially the set of equations describing the flow conditions encountered in the network under normal loading conditions. In general there are two dynamic scales relevant to the study. Firstly, there are short-term dynamic effects caused, for example, by pump start up or failure, which are characterized by short time constants of the order of a few seconds. In general, disturbed parameters will settle down to a steady value quickly. But there are also longer term variations in parameters, such as the cycle of reservoir height over the day, whose time constants are much longer than those previously mentioned. These alone are significant for control purposes and are the only effects considered in this present study.

There are in general two types of describing equation, the so-called nodal and loop expressions, both of which have a characteristic method of solution. A short description of both formulations is now given.

2.4.1 <u>Nodal Equation Formulation</u>: This description of the network is based on the approach which relates the variables describing the individual elements by a set of mass balance equations at each of the nodes, analogous to the continuity of flow in electrical networks. Referring to Figure 1(a), which is a schematic representation of a general node, it can be seen that associated with each junction i are some or all of the following variables:

(i)   Source pumps, with a flow rate Q_i
(ii)   Booster pumps, with a flow rate B_i
(iii)   Reservoirs, with a flow rate R_i
(iv)   Pipelines, with a flow rate q_{ij}
(v)   Water consumption, at a rate L_i

These individual time varying parameters are inter-related by the following set of nodal mass balance equations

$$Q_i + R_i - \sum_j q_{ij} - B_i - L_i = 0 \quad ; \quad i = 1,2,\ldots,p \tag{13}$$

where Q_i, R_i, B_i and L_i are the ith elements of p-vectors having zeros everywhere except, respectively, where a pump, reservoir, booster or consumer appears. The summation is taken over all the nodes connected to node i, up to a maximum of m_t, and there are p such equations for a p-node system.

The substitution of the equations of section 2.3 into this set of flow equations gives a set of p non-linear equations in the system nodal heads. For a system of n storage nodes there are, in general, n non-linear differential equations and (p-n) algebraic equations describing the operation of the system. In this way the nodal formulation yields a set of equations whose efficient solution is an essential part of any dynamic control scheme.

It is convenient for the purpose of writing these equations in standard control notation to combine the pump station and booster flow rates into a vector of controls $\underline{u}$, and to call the consumer demand rates a vector set of disturbances $\underline{c}$. The p-vector of system nodal heads may be partitioned into an n-vector of storage nodal heads, which is the state $\underline{x}$ of the system, and into a (p-n)-vector of non-storage nodal pressures $\underline{y}$.

Using this notation the p equations describing the nodal mass balance may be represented by, firstly, the system differential equations

$$\underline{\dot{x}} = \underline{g}(\underline{x}, \underline{u}, \underline{c}, \underline{y}, t) \tag{14}$$

where

$$\dim \underline{x} = n$$
$$\dim \underline{u} = m_Q + m_B$$
$$\dim \underline{c} = m_L$$

where m_Q, m_B and m_L are respectively the numbers of pumps, boosters and consumers on the network, and secondly, by the algebraic flow equations associated with non-storage nodes

$$h_i(\underline{x}, \underline{u}, \underline{c}, \underline{y}, t) = 0 \quad ; \quad i = 1,2,\ldots,m \tag{15}$$

or

$$\underline{h}(\underline{x}, \underline{u}, \underline{c}, \underline{y}, t) = \underline{0} \tag{16}$$

where m = (p-n) and $\underline{h}$ is an m-vector functional.

The equations (14) and (16) together represent the dynamics and equality constraints of a classical optimal control system driven by a disturbance $\underline{c}$ which, in general, may or may not be deterministic. The solution to the control problem is obtained when a control is found which extremizes some index of performance for the system over a given time period, subject to the above dynamic and equality constraints as well as inequality constraints described later. This is in general a very difficult problem to solve and it has been examined in detail elsewhere[5].

A much simpler problem to solve is the steady state analysis problem which arises when examining the network variables for a single static condition, such as the average operating level over a given period. Setting $\underline{\dot{x}} = \underline{0}$ yields, from equations (14) and (16), a set of p non-linear algebraic equations which can be solved for at most p-variables. This problem and the associated static optimization scheme are examined elsewhere[6,7].

2.4.2 Loop Equation Formulation: This description of the network is based on the approach which relates the describing variables by a set of energy conservation equations. This is done by defining a series of loops encompassing all the network elements and writing equations for each of these continuous loops. It is normal practice to define two types of loop, closed loops which start and end on the same node, and open loops, which start and end on nodes of known pressure. For the former case, a typical set of describing equations is

$$f_i = \sum_{k \in L_p(i)} \Delta_k = 0 \quad ; \quad i = 1,2,\ldots,n_L \tag{17}$$

where $L_p(i)$ is the set of pipe numbers in loop i , n_L is the total number of loops, and Δ_k is the head drop across the kth pipe in loop i . Pumps and tanks may be defined as nodes of known pressure, which may be determined from the characteristic curves or reservoir constants, given the flows associated with each element. Thus, to incorporate these elements into the describing equations it is necessary to define an appropriate number of open loops such that each pump or tank node is associated at least once with a terminal node of such a loop.

In general, for a system described by n_L^c closed-loops and n_L^o open-loops the describing equations may be written

$$f_i = \sum_{k \, \varepsilon \, L_p(i)} \Delta_k = 0 \quad ; \quad i = 1, 2, \ldots, n_L^c \tag{18}$$

and

$$f_i = \sum_{k \, \varepsilon \, L_p(i)} \Delta_k = H_{\alpha_i} - H_{\beta_i} \quad ; \quad i = n_L^c + 1, \ldots, n_L \tag{19}$$

where

$$n_L = n_L^c + n_L^o \tag{20}$$

is the total number of loops and $H_{\alpha_i}, H_{\beta_i}$ are the known heads at the terminal nodes α_i and β_i. The head loss Δ_k is related to the system flows by eqn.(1), and substitution in eqns.(18) and (19) leads to a set of n_L equations in the system variables.

These describing relations contain as many dynamic equations as there are storage nodes and the rest of the equations are purely algebraic in nature, as in the case of the nodal formulation. The loop formulation, however, is not as amenable to state space description as is the nodal approach, since the definition of loops is essentially an arbitrary task. In certain analysis studies it is found that, although there exists a minimum number of loops necessary to completely specify a given network, the use of mathematically redundant loops frequently enhances the convergence characteristics of network solutions. For this, and other reasons, the nodal approach is easier to describe in modern control terminology.

2.5 Operational Constraints on Variables: A significant feature of any process control model is the number and complexity of the constraints on the describing variables. In the water supply case any practical system contains a very large number of such constraints and their inclusion in an iterative optimum scheduling scheme poses a large computational problem due to the fact that the feasibility of the control solution must be checked at each iteration until convergence to the optimum is obtained. For this reason the nature of the system constraints must be examined in some detail.

It is usual to distinguish between two possible types of constraints, equality constraints which are typically balance equations in the network, and inequality constraints which represent the upper and lower bounds on system variables and thus define a permissible range for them. The various methods of including these in control algorithms are described elsewhere. Attention is focused here on their mathematical form and physical meaning.

As has been mentioned, the equality constraints are essentially the flow or energy conservation equations as obtained from the nodal or loop formulations. Normally these separate into the plant dynamic equations and an algebraic set whose solution is essentially analogous to the load flow problem in electric power networks. Efficient solution methods are available and are examined in detail elsewhere[7]. The general form of these equations is

$$\underline{h} \, (\underline{x}, \, \underline{u}, \, \underline{c}, \, \underline{y}, \, t) = \underline{0} \tag{21}$$

where

$$\dim \underline{h} = m$$

and the solution for any m variables obtained by some iterative technique.

The inequality constraints, on the other hand, take on the much simpler form of upper and lower bounds on the plant and network parameters. The reservoir heights are physically constrained by the size of the plant

$$\underline{x}^m \leqslant \underline{x} \leqslant \underline{x}^M \tag{22}$$

where m and M superscripts refer, respectively, to minimum and maximum values. The upper limit is near the top of the reservoir, but the lower limit is not necessarily the base of the element, since in some cases it is desirable to keep a certain volume of water in store at all times for fire fighting contingencies, pump failure or burst mains. The size of this reserve obviously depends on the location and importance of the reservoir in question and may be estimated from practical experience. A further constraint on the reservoir flow may be included

$$\underline{R}^m \leq \underline{R} \leq \underline{R}^M \qquad (23)$$

where R_i is related to x_i by equation (10), and is effectively a constraint on the rate of change of the ith reservoir height with time.

The non-storage nodal pressures $\underline{y}$ are also constrained

$$\underline{y}^m \leq \underline{y} \leq \underline{y}^M \qquad (24)$$

where the maximum values are determined by the maximum design pressure, although these are usually well above the operating pressures which can be achieved in the network under normal conditions. The lower limits are determined by the minimum desirable consumer pressure, which may be the equivalent of about 100 feet of water. Although both of these limits are physically well defined, in practice they may be considered soft as opposed to hard constraints in the sense that their violation by a small amount is not critical. This is an important characteristic which allows the use of penalty functions and other simplifications for handling these constraints in an overall control scheme.

A further set of constraints applies to source station parameters

$$\underline{u}^m \leq \underline{u} \leq \underline{u}^M \qquad (25)$$

which specify maximum and minimum values for booster and pump station flows. The maximum values are typically the maximum output the plant can physically produce and the minimum limits may be set to zero. In practice, however, a narrower band of operation may be specified in which the operating efficiencies vary only a few per cent from the optimum value. For example, in the case of base load plant, it may be desirable to have a pump operating at a fixed output flow at the maximum efficiency, and to allow other pumps and reservoirs to take up the diurnal fluctuation in water demand. Such a condition may be achieved by setting the upper and lower bounds equal to the desired level of output.

2.6 Performance Indices: One of the most important items in the mathematical description of a control problem is the definition of an adequate index of performance for the system. An appropriate criterion for the operation of a water control scheme might be, for example, the delivery of a given quantity of water to the consumer with the minimum expenditure of electrical energy; or it might be desirable to minimize maximum demand charges, or total operating costs, or line transmission losses. System operators will, in general, strive to minimize as many of these as possible within the overall constraint of maintaining supply to the consumer at all times. On the other hand, in the design problem it is required to minimize some index of the total cost of piping that has to be laid to meet future long term estimates of the water demand, in which case an adequate description of design costs is required. Since this study is primarily concerned with the short term minimum cost operation most attention will be focused on costs relevant to this time scale.

A general index of performance for a system subjected to continuous loading over a time interval $[t_o, t_f]$ may be written as

$$J = F(\underline{x}(t_f)) + \int_{t_o}^{t_f} f(\underline{x}, \underline{u}, \underline{c}, \underline{y}, t) \, dt \qquad (26)$$

where $F(\underline{x}(t_f))$ is a terminal cost depending only on the final state of the system. The discrete time form of this is obtained by sub-dividing the time interval into K increments and approximating the integral by a summation

$$J = F(\underline{x}(K)) + \sum_{k=0}^{K-1} f_k(\underline{x}(k), \underline{u}(k), \underline{c}(k), \underline{y}(k), k) \qquad (27)$$

which gives the total cost under, in general, K loading conditions. The time scale here may vary from several hours to several years for, respectively, short term operational and long term design problems.

Consider the case of short term (e.g. 24 hour) minimum energy control. In this case, referring to equation (8), the total pump energy is given by

$$J = \sum_{i=1}^{m_Q + m_B} \int_{t_o}^{t_f} \frac{Q_i \ \Delta H_i^*}{\eta_i(Q_i)} \ dt \tag{28}$$

where the summation is taken over all the source station and booster pumps. In control terminology the flow at the ith pump is simply the ith control, and the efficiency η_i is related to it by equation (4). It is a relatively simple matter to relate ΔH_i^*, the head drop across the ith pump, to the height x_j of the jth reservoir which receives water from this source. From equations (6) and (9),

$$\Delta H_i^* = H_i^d - S_i + r_i \ Q_i^{1.85} \tag{29}$$

where H_i^d is the delivery head at the ith pump. Using equation (7) relating head drop from source i to tank j

$$H_i^d - x_j = d_{i1} + d_{i2} \ L_i^{1.85} + \sum_{k=1}^{m_p} d_{i(k+2)} \ Q_k^{1.85} \tag{30}$$

and

$$S_i = C_{i1} + C_{i2} \ L_i^{1.85} + C_{i3} \ Q_i^{1.85} \tag{31}$$

and substituting for H_i^d and S_i in equation (29) it is possible to obtain an analytic expression for ΔH_i^*, and hence for the total energy J, in terms of source flows, reservoir heights and system demands.

In this way an analytical expression for total energy in terms of the system states, controls and disturbances may be obtained. The final expression is, of course, rather complex to evaluate and minimize, and poses large computational problems when incorporated into an optimal control scheme.

The electricity tariff structure normally encountered, however, is usually concerned both with the maximum demand charges during the interval and with the unit energy cost of pumping. The simplest method of approaching the problem of minimizing the maximum electricity demand is to discretize the time interval into increments appropriate to the existing tariff structure. Thus, if the tariff is levied on the basis of the maximum demand at half-hourly intervals it would be sensible to discretize a daily interval into 48 stages, and to use the expression for the energy consumed during a half-hourly interval.

Maximum demand charges are frequently levied on the basis of the maximum energy consumption in a pumping station, containing perhaps several units, rather than on the individual pumps on the system. For this reason the suitable quantity to be minimized is a function of the maximum total energy consumed in a pumping station during the control interval,

$$\max_{k} \sum_{i=1}^{n_s} \frac{Q_i(k) \ \Delta H_i^*(k)}{\eta_i(Q_i)}$$

where the summation is taken over the number of sets n_s in that station, including both highlift and borehole elements. Calling this quantity the maximum demand (MD), the control problem is to determine the optimum pump schedule consistent with a minimum of MD charges.

In general, it is a very difficult task to incorporate such complex performance indices into an on-line optimal controller. Such controllers frequently require the cost function to assume a certain mathematically convenient form, such as a linear or quadratic function of the variables[1], if on-line computation is to be achieved. The role of the more complex expression is, firstly, to determine the best set of constants to be used in a simpler representation of total costs and, secondly, to provide an accurate, true cost controller for off-line computation.

3. EAST WORCESTERSHIRE TELECONTROL SYSTEM

3.1 Introduction: Following the description of a general purpose mathematical model in the previous section, attention is focused here on a description of the

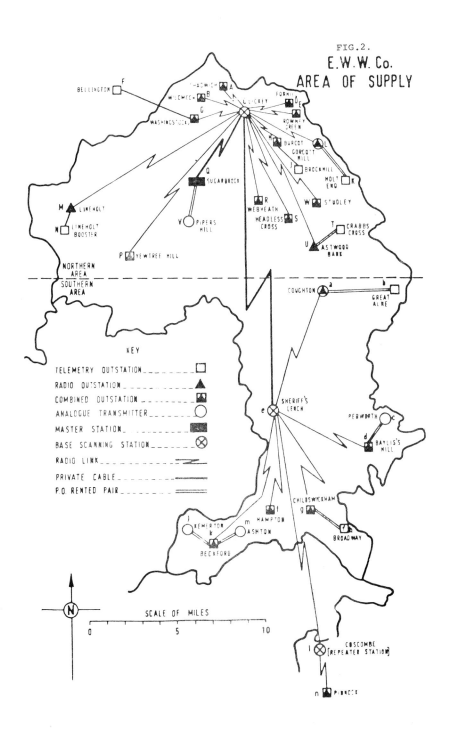

FIG.2.
E.W.W. Co.
AREA OF SUPPLY

actual network to which it has been applied, the East Worcestershire Waterworks Company. Being one of the most advanced networks of its kind it is ideally suited to the application of modern control methods and provides an excellent pilot study for automation in the industry. This section concentrates on a description of that system incorporating advanced telemetry and set point control schemes to allow the development of a mathematical model and the subsequent implementation of simulation and control methods.

3.2 Description of Network: The East Worcestershire Waterworks Company supplies water to a population of 200,000 over an area of 300 square miles in the county of Worcestershire, England (Figure 2). Existing supplies are derived from boreholes in the Bunter and Keuper Sandstone with a small quantity being abstracted from springs in the Cotswold Hills situated in the extreme south of the district. The creation of a New Town and expansion of existing towns will increase the population to about 300,000 by 1980 with a water demand of 85 Ml/day. This growth in daily demand will be met by the development of a further six boreholes source stations and a river abstraction scheme. The existing and future borehole stations will provide over 86 Ml/day and the river abstraction station an additional quantity varying from 23 Ml/day to 145 Ml/day in four equal stages of development between 1980 and 2010.

The Company, which has been in existence for 97 years, embarked on a scheme of modernisation of source works some 14 years ago following a detailed cost analysis of methods of water production.

Existing diesel stations were converted to electrical operation and automatic control equipment was installed at all pumping stations. This allowed a reduction from 3-shift to single shift manning, resulting in a considerable saving in manpower. This system of largely unattended plant operation necessitated a reliable form of local alarm detection and plant protection, combining local automatic control loops with inherent fail-safe facilities, so that stations could run unattended for comparatively lengthy periods. It was decided to switch the alarms from the pumping stations to the site staff houses during out-of-works hours and, in order that a duty rota could be operated, pumping stations were paired and connected to staff houses. The communication links were effected by a combination of Post Office lines and multicore cables laid by the Company.

It therefore became increasingly apparent that, as the Company expanded, some form of centralised monitoring and control system would be necessary as a logical progression in the evolution of the Company's policy of unattended operation of plant. The decision to embark upon a system of telecontrol was therefore taken, particularly in view of the number, complexity and widely scattered location of the sources and other works, together with rising labour costs and the difficulty in obtaining staff in a predominantly industrial area.

3.3 The Telecontrol System: The system as installed uses time-division multiplexing techniques with a central master station scanning sequentially remote outstations. Each input and output on the system has its own unique address enabling data to be requested by transmitting a binary coded function-address word which is broadcast to all outstations but only the outstation recognising its own address will respond.

Whilst outstations are scanned sequentially for information, priority is given to control functions and any controls initiated from the centre interrupt the scan and are transmitted immediately.

For actual data transmission, frequency shift keying (F.S.K.) techniques are employed using a carrier frequency of 1500 Hz and a frequency shift of 100 Hz. This information is transmitted at a rate of 200 Bauds giving a total scan time for the whole system of 64 seconds.

Communication is in most cases over the U.H.F. system previously described, with the master radio scanner operating continuously, but with outstation radios keyed only when information is required or controls are to be effected. At some locations it has been necessary to install the radio transmitter remotely from the telecontrol outstation cabinet. In these instances, the radio transmitter is keyed by a 1.98 kHz tone superimposed on the line carrying the F.S.K. data and also in some cases an analogue signal.

FIG. 3a AUTOMATIC CONTROL SCHEME 1.

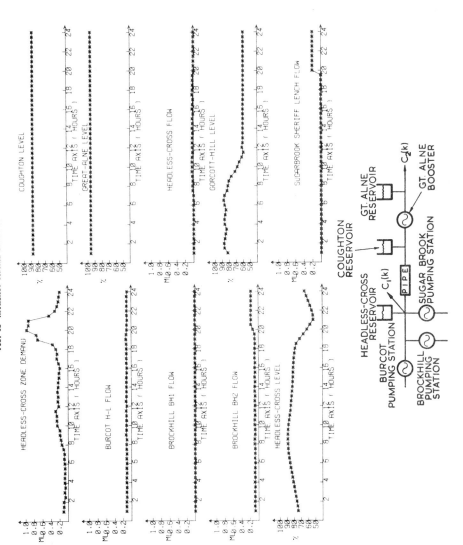

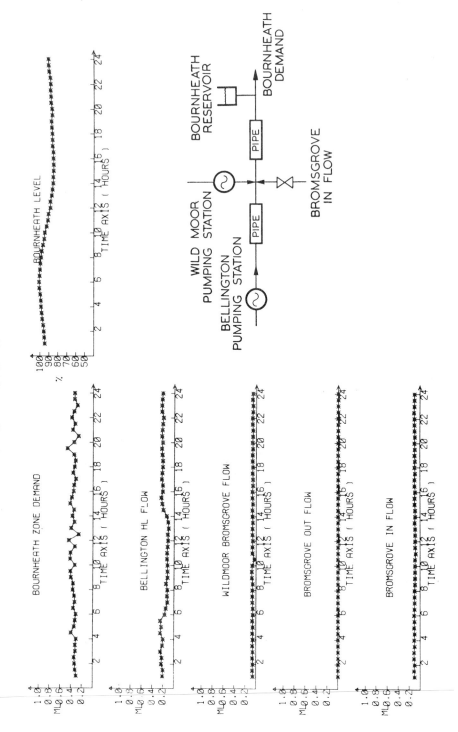

FIG. 3b AUTOMATIC CONTROL SCHEME 2.

The basic word length of 12 bits is used to give compatibility with the digital computer and adequate capacity for addressing with sufficient resolution for digitised analogue values. Each message is preceded by a single start bit to give synchronisation and four parity bits are generated after each word for checking purposes. Any parity discrepancy or start bits of inadequate length cause the resultant corrupted message to be rejected and the address reinterrogated. In the request word, three of the 12 available bits are used to indicate the function code and six bits to indicate the group address; the remaining three bits indicate the point address.

Under normal circumstances the master station is controlled by a minicomputer with 16K words of 12 bit core store with a 32K back-up disk. The computer is linked to two teletypewriters, two"golf-ball" typewriters, an alphanumeric C.R.T. display, a high-speed punched tape device and a microfilm reader/printer.

The telecontrol master unit is normally directed by the computer, but is able to carry on scanning inputs should the computer fail or be taken off-line, thus giving complete information access and control availability in this event.

The master station controls the outstation operation by the transmission of function/address words, these words being normally generated by a programme in the computer and transferred to the telecontrol master unit via the processor interface. In the standby mode, however, scanning is controlled by a function address generator using a patch panel with a pre-set scanning sequence.

Control Panels : Both the operator's control panel and the standby panel are situated side by side on the control desk which also houses the visual display unit, radio control unit with link changeover switches, and telephone. These two operator's panels are provided with push-buttons for the selection of addresses, for the display of analogue and digital information and for performing control functions. The main operator's panel has two digital indicators for the display of selected parameters in real engineering units.

C.R.T. Visual Display : The C.R.T. visual display can be used to display the following formats :
(1) Total dynamic information at any source works.
(2) Display of state of water storage in the Company's reservoirs and towers.
(3) Summary of parameters at all booster outstations.

This display is up-dated at the rate of 1200 Bauds from the computer memory database.

3.4 Source Works Equipment :
Automatic Control : The types of pumping control systems adopted by the Company at the various source works are as follows :
Scheme 1 Variable speed borehole pumps deliver into a contact tank and their output is controlled by level measuring equipment installed in the contact tank. The output of the high lift pumps is governed by a combined flow/level control signal, with the level signal being taken from an associated service reservoir. If the rate of flow is assessed correctly, then the reservoir is replenished by the pump during the off-peak periods. Should the reservoir level fall below the control band setting, then the level control-overrides the desired value setting on the flow control and increases pump output. A similar control sequence effects a decrease in pump speed should the level rise outside the control band limit (Figure 3a).
Scheme 2 Up to a maximum of four borehole pumps are operated in sequence to deliver into a contact tank. Level control equipment is used to vary the speed of the high lift pumps, thus maintaining contact tank level within a predetermined band (Figure 3b).

Diesel alternator plant at all the main source stations have been fitted with automatic control equipment and extensive protection devices and alarms.

Local automatic control systems were also designed for treatment processes: chlorination taking the usual form of a controlled residual with alarms and protection designed to shut down the station in the event of abnormal conditions and fluoridation using a similar process but in this case out-of-limit conditions merely inhibiting the treatment process.

Plant : All high lift pumps are driven by variable speed A.C. commutator motors
with speed control effected by induction regulators, the limits of speed variation
in respect of the Company's plant being 800-1800 r.p.m.
        Three types of borehole pump are employed throughout the Company's area,
these being :
(1) Shaft driven pumps coupled to variable speed A.C. commutator motors.
(2) Shaft driven pumps coupled to induction motors with limited speed adjustment
    by means of rotor resistance.
(3) Fixed speed submersible pumps.
        Standby diesel alternators capable of supplying all the station load have
been installed at each source works; these units being of the high speed type fitted with anti-vibration mountings and supplied with battery starting equipment.

Treatment : A very high standard of purity obtains in respect of the raw water abstracted from the Bunter/Keuper Sandstone, but in view of the unattended operation
of source stations, it was considered necessary to incorporate super chlorination
procedures.
        Fluoridation, carried out on behalf of the Public Health Authority, employs
two methods of dosing - sodium silico fluoride in powder form and dilute hydro-
fluosilicic acid.

3.5 Diesel Alternator Load-Shedding : In addition to data acquisition and remote
manual controls, the computer is used to effect a peak-lopping programme whereby
the diesel alternators take over from the grid supply at six major source works
from 08.00-16.00 hours during five months of the winter. The following sequence
is carried out twice daily :
                    Shut down high lift pumps
                    Shut down borehole pumps
                    Switch off grid supply
                    Start alternator
                    Switch in alternator breaker
                    Start borehole pumps
                    Start high ligt pumps
This procedure must be followed to a strict timetable to avoid heavy electricity
tariff penalties and the reserve procedure followed at night. This somewhat complicated changeover was made necessary since the local electricity supply authority would not at the time of system design allow the parallelling of the diesel
alternator and grid supplies. During the time that these operations are proceeding,
the station being operated is displayed on the C.R.T.
        This load-shedding operation effects a considerable saving in operating
costs.

4. DYNAMIC SIMULATION
4.1 Introduction : A network simulator is essentially a computer program which
may be used to analyse the behaviour of the system over a variety of loading conditions. The basic purpose of the calculation is to examine the behaviour of the
parameters as loading conditions vary, or to provide a means of testing different
pumping policies to meet a given water demand at minimum cost. The main purpose
of this section is to describe a program used for this purpose on the East Worcestershire system and to illustrate briefly some typical results.

4.2 Description of Programs : The program divide essentially into two classes.
Firstly there are those which are used for analysing and preparing the input data,
and secondly, those for carrying out the actual time simulation, given a correct
network description.
        The preparation programs basically take the input data directly from a
prepared network diagram. The input includes the following parameters :
1. Number of zones, nodes and pipes.
2. Diameter, length and roughness coefficient of each pipe.
3. Definition of pipe interconnections.
4. Definition of pump and reservoir nodal positions.
5. Elevation, average demand and zone for each node.
The program checks the validity of the defined network, calculates pipe resistances

FIG.4. DATA PREPARATION PROGRAM FLOWCHART.

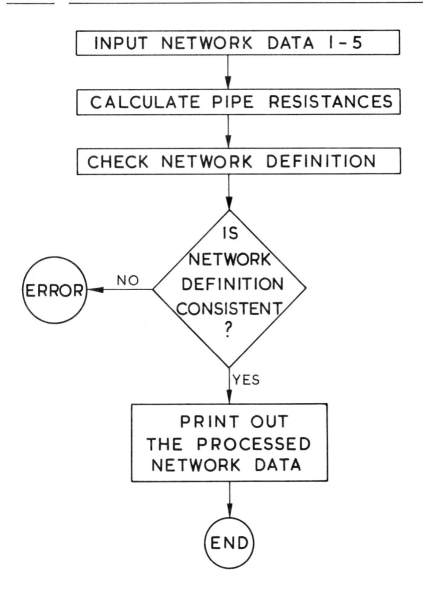

FIG. 5. DYNAMIC SIMULATION PROGRAM.

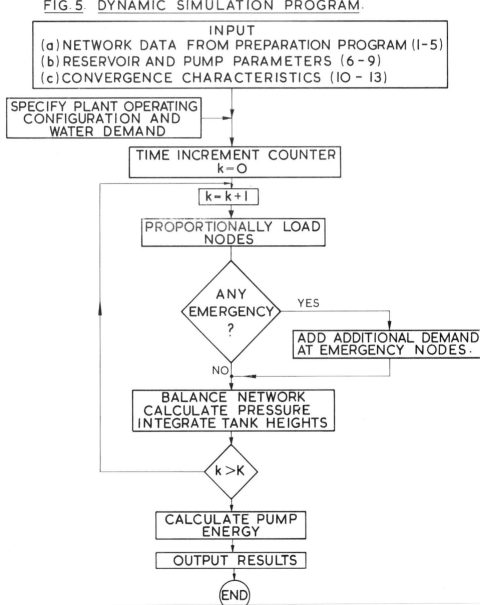

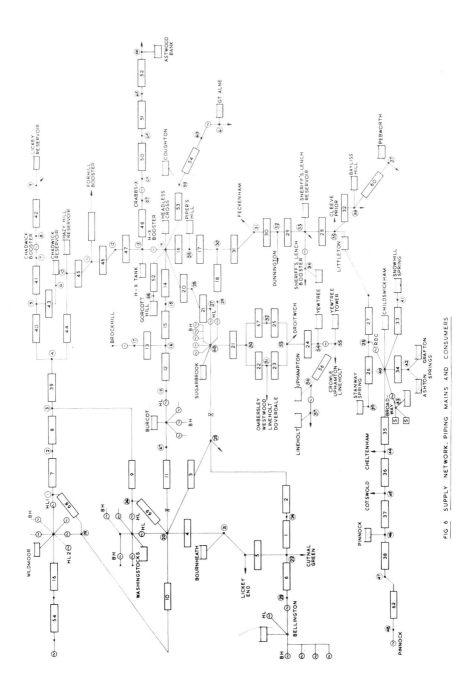

FIG 6 SUPPLY NETWORK. PIPING MAINS AND CONSUMERS

Fig. 7.   FIRST OPERATING CONDITION.

DYNAMIC SYSTEM SIMULATION, TIME = 8 HOURS

TOTAL SYSTEM WATER DEMAND = 14.298 MGD

PUMPS		RESERVOIRS				RESERVOIRS		
	FLOW MGD		FLOW MGD	HEIGHT FT			FLOW MGD	HEIGHT FT
WILDMOOR HL1	1.069	CHADWICK RES	0.041	7.002	BROADWAY RES		-.162	7.032
WILDMOOR HL2	1.494	LICKEY RES	-.149	6.896	LINEHOLT RES		-.236	6.438
WASHINGSTOCKS 1	2.078	HAZYHILL RES	-.079	7.016	UPHAMPTON RES		0.026	6.208
WASHINGSTOCKS 2	1.881	ASTWOOD BANK	0.186	7.684	YEWTREE RES		-.026	7.012
BROCKHILL BH	1.307	GURCOTT HILL	0.189	8.491	YEWTREE TOWER		-.061	6.919
BURCOT HL	0.061	HEADLESS-X TANK	-.189	6.552	SHER-LENCH RES		0.146	7.025
SUGARBROOK H-X	3.083	COUGHTON RES	-.412	6.800	SHER LENCH TANK		-.300	6.664
SUGARBROOK S-L	1.695	GREAT ALNE	0.504	8.389	BAYLISS HILL		0.266	7.375
BELLINGTON	2.336	PIPER'S HILL	0.445	7.841	PEBWORTH TANK		-.243	6.390
PINNOCK HL	0.498	PINNOCK RES	-.011	6.812	LITTLETON TANK		0.406	7.098
		STANWAY SPRING	-.003	7.010	HEADLESS-X RES		-.504	6.955
		CHILDSWICKHAM R	0.011	7.007	BOURNHEATH RES		0.741	6.963
		SNOWSHILL SPRING	-.183	6.855	BURCOT C-TANK		0.495	7.274
		GRAFTON SPRING	-.058	6.939	SUGARBROOK C-TK		0.365	7.028

PUMPING STATION COST SUMMARY

ENERGY CONSUMED (KWH)

TIME (HOURS)	W/MOOR 1	W/MOOR 2	W/STOCK 1	W/STOCK 2	B/HILL	BURCOT	S/BRK H-X	S/BRK S-L	BELLING	PINNOCK
2	0.0	21.739	636.893	404.721	0.0	80.452	168.612	153.940	0.0	51.251
4	0.0	22.071	674.402	406.302	0.0	99.537	188.952	157.776	0.0	52.046
6	0.0	25.085	756.320	288.152	0.0	43.967	221.830	165.071	188.444	53.530
8	149.859	28.703	382.111	327.245	162.323	35.774	272.592	200.881	274.697	62.471
10	151.799	28.201	392.287	357.104	162.328	39.962	275.221	202.359	347.622	62.846
12	149.909	27.237	381.879	389.038	162.315	35.506	272.391	200.585	442.778	62.405
14	124.657	24.483	274.269	361.963	259.089	0.0	294.046	186.142	359.153	56.615
16	133.585	24.664	307.065	401.297	260.392	0.0	346.336	195.683	482.133	59.164
18	144.506	24.064	354.889	478.276	262.133	0.0	581.012	207.570	793.808	62.244
20	142.147	23.392	343.770	501.440	261.745	0.0	491.753	204.972	977.438	61.654
22	139.903	22.888	333.590	518.187	261.368	0.0	433.401	202.456	1174.575	60.993
24	0.0	21.959	910.703	469.246	259.722	0.0	320.258	188.823	723.934	56.838

TOTAL ELECTRICITY DEMAND   =   28267.906   KWH

Fig. 8.   SECOND OPERATING CONDITION.

DYNAMIC SYSTEM SIMULATION, TIME =   8 HOURS

TOTAL SYSTEM WATER DEMAND =   14.298 MGD

PUMPS		RESERVOIRS				RESERVOIRS	
	FLOW MGD		FLOW MGD	HEIGHT FT		FLOW MGD	HEIGHT FT
WILDMOOR HL1	1.076	CHADWICK RES	0.042	7.003	BROADWAY RES	-.116	7.106
WILDMOOR HL2	1.458	LICKEY RES	-.145	6.897	LINEHOLT RES	-.236	6.438
WASHINGSTOCKS 1	2.089	HAZYHILL RES	-.071	7.019	UPHAMPTON RES	0.026	6.208
WASHINGSTOCKS 2	1.967	ASTWOOD BANK	0.174	7.619	YEWTREE RES	-.026	7.012
BROCKHILL BH	1.309	GORCOTT HILL	0.184	8.419	YEWTREE TOWER	-.061	6.919
BURCOT HL	0.129	HEADLESS-X TANK	-.184	6.574	SHER-LENCH RES	-.345	6.842
SUGARBROOK H-X	3.606	COUGHTON RES	0.067	7.119	SHER LENCH TANK	-.290	6.649
SUGARBROOK S-L	1.031	GREAT ALNE	0.285	7.929	BAYLISS HILL	0.278	7.493
BELLINGTON	1.367	PIPER'S HILL	0.420	8.065	PEBWORTH TANK	-.227	6.080
PINNOCK HL	0.555	PINNOCK RES	0.046	7.031	LITTLETON TANK	0.351	7.047
		STANWAY SPRING	-.001	7.025	HEADLESS-X RES	-.285	6.970
		CHILDSWICKHAM R	-.046	6.999	BOURNHEATH RES	-.182	6.883
		SNOWSHILL SPRING	-.181	6.863	BURCOT C-TANK	0.511	7.305
		GRAFTON SPRING	-.053	6.963	SUGARBROOK C-TK	0.353	7.025

PUMPING STATION COST SUMMARY

ENERGY CONSUMED (KWH)

TIME (HOURS)	W/MOOR 1	W/MOOR 2	W/STOCK 1	W/STOCK 2	B/HILL	BURCOT	S/BRK H-X	S/BRK S-L	BELLING	PINNOCK
2	0.0	19.534	642.315	523.475	0.0	40.403	124.252	32.929	0.0	56.838
4	0.0	19.885	680.280	522.982	0.0	67.187	128.258	53.368	0.0	57.643
6	0.0	20.520	788.181	525.896	260.173	0.0	137.399	52.091	0.0	59.378
8	150.522	28.281	385.581	349.493	162.401	48.020	139.792	58.638	158.211	67.673
10	152.479	27.959	395.909	371.961	162.417	50.039	139.560	59.096	182.528	67.997
12	150.535	27.159	385.284	397.456	162.390	47.935	139.805	58.562	208.336	67.474
14	125.862	24.316	278.492	374.167	260.460	0.0	137.249	54.342	185.147	61.417
16	134.732	24.679	311.813	405.748	261.834	0.0	135.210	57.330	216.659	63.958
18	145.847	24.367	361.648	470.350	263.717	0.0	134.230	60.648	270.423	67.208
20	143.462	23.637	349.992	493.604	263.282	0.0	134.206	57.987	293.857	66.534
22	141.138	23.102	339.230	510.684	262.880	0.0	134.328	59.285	314.214	65.840
24	0.0	22.102	924.289	469.141	261.303	0.0	135.665	54.905	267.409	61.477

TOTAL ELECTRICITY DEMAND   =   21138.016   KWH

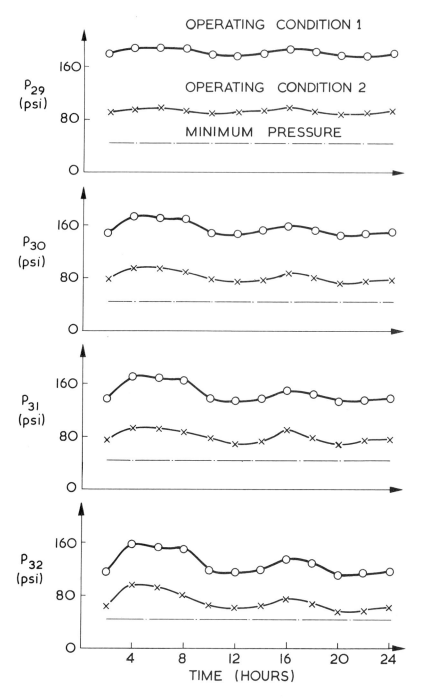

FIG. 9   DYNAMIC PRESSURE RESPONSE

and generally manipulates the data to a form suitable for setting up the network equations easily in the simulation program. A simple flowchart illustrating this sequence is shown in Figure 4.

The dynamic simulation program receives as input data the following plant parameters in addition to the network definition already mentioned :

6. Reservoir conversion factors.
7. Tank depth at start of simulation interval.
8. Head-flow constants and efficiency-flow constants for a range of pump speeds and operating configurations.
9. Source pump resistances.

Since the simulation involves a network analysis at each time increment a number of convergence factors must be specified :

10. Initial guess for unknown parameters.
11. Maximum number of iterations beyond which it may be assumed the solution will not converge.
12. Tolerance or convergence criterion.
13. Acceleration factors for convergence.

Given the above information the program will simulate the behaviour of the network under a specified operating configuration for a given system demand. The sequence of operations involved in the calculation is shown in Figure 5.

4.3 Simulation Results : The set of programs described in the previous section have been used extensively in the simulation of daily loading conditions on the East Worcestershire network. The usefulness of this approach is its ability to provide the system operators with suitable guidelines for operating the network in an open loop manner, i.e, given a forecast of the demand the operator obtains the total cost of operation under a specified pump configuration. Several operating modes may be examined and the "best" solution adopted. Clearly there are several criteria which may be used to define the "best" solution and the simulation simply gives a print out of a large number of network variables to facilitate this definition.

A sample print out of source station conditions at one increment is shown in Figure 7. When the program has repeated this calculation, including a full print out of system pressures at each time increment throughout the demand period, it generates a full cost summary together with the total cost of that operating policy. An example of this cost information is shown in Figure 7 also. The same print out is shown in Figure 8 for a different source station pump configuration. Referring to Figures 6 and 9, it was found that under the first operating condition, excessive pressures were being generated at nodes 29-32 in the Sheriffs Lench zone, as well as at the nodes intermediate between the Bellington source station and associated Bournheath service reservoir. Consequently, the program was re-run under a second operating mode which involved reducing speed at both of these stations. Examples of the reduction in pressure are shown in Figure 9.

The development of an accurate model and simulation program is essential to the problem of obtaining a computationally efficient on-line optimum controller. It is a relatively simple matter to introduce feedback action into the program shown in Figure 5 by evaluating some general cost function and its gradient and iterating to find the optimum set of pump controls minimizing this function and satisfying the network constraints. In practice, however, this poses a large computational problem. A simpler approach is to develop a controller which only takes account of the most important system variables but whose structure is chosen, after extensive off-line simulations, to closely resemble the more complex model. Such an approach to on-line control is at present being actively pursued.

5. CONCLUSIONS

A necessary preliminary to the establishment of a control scheme for a complex system is the setting up of an accurate mathematical model of the system. This allows the thorough testing of various control schemes - for the best choice of performance index, for the most suitable choice of control algorithm with a balance between optimality in the control sense and ease of implementation in an on-line form.

In the paper we have attempted to gather together the significant features

of water network analysis to establish a unified model for large water supply networks from a control viewpoint. A simulation program has been established to allow
the off-line investigation of control schemes for a particular network and a number of results have been given for it.

   While the application is to a specific system the methods presented are
general and we hope will be of interest to others concerned with the analysis and
control of water supply networks.

6. REFERENCES

1. Fallside, F. and Perry, P.F. : "A decentralized controller for high dimensional
   water control problems", Cambridge University Technical Report.

2. Brewer, C. et alia : The performance of a predictive automatic load dispatching
   system, IEE Colloquium on "The CEGB automatic system control experiment in the
   South-Western region", May 1968.

3. East Worcestershire Waterworks Company : "The Company's works and development
   programme", New Road, Bromsgrove.

4. Fallside, F., Perry, P.F. and Rice, P.D. : "On-line prediction of consumption
   for water supply network control", submitted to 6th IFAC Congress, Boston, 1975.

5. Fallside, F. and Perry, P.F. : "Optimal control of a water supply network by a
   decomposition technique", submitted to IEE.

6. Shamir, U. and Howard, C.D.D. : "Water distribution systems analysis", Proc.
   ASCE, Hydrology Div., Vol.94, No.HYl, Jan. 1968.

7. Dommel, H.W. and Tinney, W.F. : "Optimal power flow solutions", IEEE Trans.
   on Power Apparatus and Systems, Oct. 1968.

DISCUSSION

In what unity are measured D and L ?   (TODINI)

   D is measured in inches and L in feet. This explains the exponent.   (PERRY)

   This morning we had a bit of a discussion between physical and black box
models and we said at various times there was in practice no conflict between them.
On a river this might bring up this a little bit by looking at figure 1 which shows
various levels of control applied to a real system. If one looks for example at the
lowest level, the regulator function, that is designed on basically a combination
of physical approach using the laws of system actuators etc. plus an input output
calculation. The next level, the optimizing level has been done using physical laws
again for a reduced system, but it is checked out by using a least squares input
output method. The third level the adaptive function which has been described again,
is based on physical laws, but it is turned up by a hill climbing method which is
certainly not particularly physical and again the fourth level, the self organizing function is concerned with things like prediction etc., which used totally non-
physical ruling but the structure adopted is formed by physical rules. Finally the
whole diagram is a mathematical concept of decomposition which you might say is
not physical, but on the other hand if you look carefully of what a good planning
member of any operating company does, he roughly thinks in a number of levels possibly four. So I just wanted to make this point to indicate that there is no real
contradiction between a physical approach and a deterministic or black box approach
when you are faced with a natural large scale problem so that you in fact use what
is most useful and best.   (FALLSIDE)

Modeling and Simulation of Water Resources Systems, G.C. VANSTEENKISTE, (Ed.)
North-Holland Publishing Company (1975)

WATER RESOURCES DATA BANK IN NEW JERSEY AND COMPUTATIONS OF EXTREME FLOWS

George J. Halasi-Kun
Columbia University Seminars
on Pollution and Water Resources, New York*

ABSTRACT

The conditions of New Jersey, USA are described from the viewpoint of
interdisciplinary data gathering concentrated in water interaction on the
natural environment including its quantity and quality.

Surface-water data collecting for drainage basins of an area less than
250 km² presents inadequate information for peak or lowest flow computation in planning because the data are collected generally only for a
shorter period and at random. Since the various empirical formulas,
unit hydrographs, flood frequency methods are computations based on
probability, the constructed flow curves furnish rather trustworthy
average flow diagrams than forecast reliable extreme values of peak
(100-year flow) or lowest flows for practical planning purposes.

Despite the shortcomings of the data collecting, it can be efficiently
evaluated and utilized with the help of local geologic survey and meteorologic conditions establishing correlation and similarities between permeability of the geologic subsurface and extreme values of the meteorologic records on one side and the extreme flows from smaller watersheds
on the other side. As a by-product of this method, the ground water
capacity of the various hydrogeologic regions can be also established.

This approach utilizes the statistical data of over 90,000 well records
and 101 selected stream gaging stations gathered in the period 1945-1974
for the wells and 1882-1974 for the streams. In an area of 20,295 km²
this statistical information gives adequate values to develop peak and
lowest flow formula for smaller watersheds where data for planning are
almost nonexistent. The formulas were developed with help of the gathered
data not only from New Jersey, USA but also from Central Europe, Soviet
Union and other sources.

Finally, a partial but detailed description is given about the Data Bank.
The advantages and disadvantages of storing data by computer, microfilm
and magnetic tape/selectric typewriter's (MT/ST) method is also discussed.

INTRODUCTION

In choosing New Jersey, USA, for developing an environmental oriented
data bank system and for evaluating extreme surface flows in smaller areas, there
were several considerations. It was felt that efficient environmental resources
planning needs interdisciplinary data gathering concentrated in water interaction
on the natural environment. To succeed in developing a model for a water resources data bank, a region with a variety such as New Jersey seemed to be appropriate.

New Jersey is a state of contrasts in many respects. It is not only one
of the most densely populated regions of the world (400 persons per km² with an
area of 20,295 km²) sandwiched between two overpopulated metropolitan areas of
the world (New York City and Philadelphia) but also 45% of its territory is still

---

*Mailing address: 31 Knowles Avenue, Pennington, New Jersey 08534 USA

forest. The highly urbanized area has only two cities with a population over
100,000 inhabitants and accounts for 19% of the land. 27% of the region is agricultural with a highest per hectare dollar value for crops produced in the U. S.
The transportation network, both highway and railroad, has the greatest traffic
density in America. The chemical industry of New Jersey is one of the most
developed in the U. S. but its largest industry is still the recreation, related
to the Atlantic Coast bathing beaches. The mineral industry, especially in
dollar value of minerals produced per km^2 of the area, is within the top 16% of
the U. S. Artificial and natural lakes, including swamps, are occupying 9% of
its surface and the territory of the state is bordered by fresh or salt water
except in the north.

        Geologically, 60% of the region is underlain by Cretaceous or later sedi-
ments, which are primarily unconsolidated sands and gravels including the area
of the famous Pine Barrens Natural Park. 20% of the state, the most densely
populated part (over 10,000 persons per km^2) consists of Triassic shale and sandstone with diabase flows or basalt intrusions, which over considerable areas,
are in the recreational park systems but in others are actively quarried to make
the state one of the leading producers of diabase-type "trap rock". The remaining 20% of the region is underlain by Precambrian crystallines and early or middle
Paleozoic limestones and shales, Widmer (1964).

        The climate of the area is moderate with an average rainfall of 1200
mm/year. Periodically, severe droughts occur such as in the years 1961-1966
with an average rainfall of 800 mm/year. The extreme point rainfall intensity
for 24 hours reaches 250 mm value in many parts of the state with a 2-5 years
frequency. The northern half is characteristic for moderately high mountains
(up to 600 m). On the other hand, the southern half is flat with less than 70 m
above sea level. The whole area can be characterized as one of smaller rivers
with a watershed less than 300 km^2 (except Delaware, Passaic and Raritan rivers)
and with many natural and artificial lakes. The evapo-transpiration and interception average 450-550 mm from the annual precipitation. The ground water
availability indicator has a value from 0 to 450 mm yearly, depending on the
permeability and storage capacity of the geological formations in accordance
with the yearly precipitation, Halasi-Kun (1971).

        Finally, the last but never the least reason in selecting the area for
developing the data bank was the fine cooperation of the N. J. Bureau of Geology
and Topography with the Columbia University Seminars on Water Resources by making
available the collected over 90,000 well records and other valuable land-use,
demographic, geologic and surface-flow data, and by supporting materially the
whole project. Furthermore, N. J. Department of Community Affairs helped also
to develop the program as it will be described as "The Technique of the Data Bank".

BASIC PHILOSOPHY IN DATA COLLECTING

        The environmental data collecting reflects the interaction of the water
on the natural environment. The inventory of the natural resources is gathered
from the viewpoint of its utilization by man. Since water and its quantity and
quality is utmost important to our life, the data bank is water resources oriented. It should give basic information about its quantity and quality in connection with surface streams including extreme values, ground water storage
capacity based on permeability of the geologic subsurface. Climatic description
of the area as primary source for water is also needed. Inasmuch as land-use
development is the source of demand for water, both for consumption and for
treatment, it is necessary to identify current water distribution, sewage systems,
treatment and polluting activities (point and area pollution). As additional
information, other natural resources inventory including geologic survey, geographic description together with areas utilized for transportation, historic
sites and public spaces is essential.

Man being the center in evaluation of the environment, updated demographic data is also an important part of the data bank. The demographic information is based on the latest census giving area density and concentration of the population within each community including its boundary.

Finally, the data collecting and its importance is governed not only by demographic and water resources information but also by the real estate values in land-use. The taxation is an excellent indicator in defining the grade of importance of the area in question. Therefore, data from tax maps and information maintained locally after being evaluated and computerized, should also be an incorporated part of the data bank. The tax considerations are leading to the conclusion that the smallest unit of the data bank in land-use may cover 3 hectares in the settlements and 12 hectares outside the community.

The itemized information of the data bank may be stored by computer, map, magnetic tape-selectric typewriter's method whichever fits better the character of the gathered data. The advantages and disadvantages in the case of the New Jersey data bank will be discussed later.

AVAILABLE WATER AND EXTREME SURFACE FLOW VALUES

The most important part of an environmental oriented data bank is the water resources inventory and the computation of the available water with its average and extreme values, including the ground water capacity of the area.

The various sophisticated methods such as those of unit hydrographs, flood frequency, log Pearson Type III curves etc., give excellent values for larger areas. Generally it is accepted that the available data can be interpreted with a workable accuracy only for a time no longer than twice the period of observation. This means that for computation of 100-year extreme flow it is necessary to have at least 50-year observations which is, or may be, available for larger rivers in many regions but almost non-existent for smaller streams. The need for data on peak and lowest flow occurs at random and in emergency conditions; therefore, there are no collected data nor is there time to collect data for longer periods, Halasi-Kun (1972). Since these methods are based on probability, the curves at their lowest and peak value are less reliable. Extending the curves and forecast extreme values for periods twice as long as the observation, can give already ±20-30% error. Further extension of any forecast makes the computations highly unreliable and even for an estimate in regional planning not workable. On the other hand -- regardless of the size of the watershed --, these methods give excellent average flow values even for streams with shorter observation periods or with no data where conditions are similar to the known and recorded watersheds. Analogous difficulties can occur with surface flow formulas using too many parameters. In general, they are based on probability computations and so the errors and deviations accumulate.

Despite these shortcomings, it can be efficiently evaluated and utilized with the help of local geologic survey and meteorologic conditions establishing correlation and similarities between permeability of the geologic subsurface and extreme values of the meteorologic records on one side, and the extreme flows from smaller watersheds with an area of less than 300 km^2 on the other side. At watersheds over 300 km^2 of area, the geologic and meteorologic conditions are less affecting the extreme flows except in regions where greater uniformity for these factors prevails such as certain areas of Australia, Midwestern United States, Soviet Union, etc., Halasi-Kun (1973).

Research conducted in Czechoslovakia, West Germany and New Jersey confirmed the principle that in rural areas the 100-year peak runoff of smaller watersheds has up to a 90-95% dependence on the permeability of the geologic subsurface of the watershed and, in addition, on point rainfall intensity and configuration of the terrain. The vegetative cover and the form (concentration) of the watershed are additional parameters. This approach in New Jersey utilized the statistical data of over 90,000 well records and 101 selected stream gaging stations gathered in the period 1945-1974 for the wells and 1882-1974 for the streams. Furthermore, historical flood data and point rainfall intensity observation for the period 1825-1882 was also taken into consideration.

The developed formula of peak runoff has the following pattern, Halasi-Kun (1974):

$$Q = C \cdot A^{-e}$$
$$\text{or} \quad Q = (P_1 \cdot P_2) \cdot (i_1 \cdot i_2) \cdot A^{-e} \cdot (C_v \cdot C_e)$$

where

Q = peak runoff in $m^3/sec.\ km^2$
C = coefficient which varies from 0.5 to 147 according to geologic and climatologic conditions (coefficients for vegetative cover and concentration of the watershed not included)
A = area of watershed in km^2
e = configuration of terrain (geographic region and slope characteristic): 0.32 for plains up to 0.5 for Alpine type mountains
P_1= permeability factor of the soil and of the geologic subsurface with a value from 1.0 to 18.5
P_2= urbanization factor, from 1.0 to 14.0, in accordance with the impervious land-use and permeability of the geologic subsurface
i_1= 24 hrs. point rainfall intensity, from 0.5 to 2.0 (0.5 for 35 mm/day; 1.0 for 125 mm/day; 2.0 for 250 mm/day)
i_2= storm characteristics, from 1.0 to 4.1 (depending on the size and pattern of the extreme storms and on the wind velocity)
C_v= coefficient of vegetative cover, from 0.95 to 1.05 (from 40% to 70% watershed area covered by forest)
C_c= concentration coefficient, from 0.90 to 1.05 (0.90 for elongated shape or at least 1.5; 0.95 for horseshoe-shaped and 1.05 for fan-shaped watersheds)

For lowest runoff (50 years?) a similar formula was developed based on the 1961-1966 drought in New Jersey and it is as follows; Halasi-Kun (in press):

$$Q = C \cdot A^{-e}$$

where

Q = lowest runoff (50 years?) value in $l/sec.\ km^2$
C = coefficient depending on the geological subsurface from 0 to 5.75
e = 0.065

The validity of this formula was confirmed by observation for watersheds up to 100 km^2 area. If the catch basins have over 100 km^2 area, this computation method is not recommended because of complexity of factors influencing the lowest flow, Vladimirov and Chebotarev (1973).

Based on the above formulas and principles, the surface runoff extreme values were computed and the results organized by the hydrogeologic regions were put in the data bank. As a by-product of this method, the ground water capacity of the various hydrogeologic areas was also established.

TECHNIQUE OF THE DATA BANK

Based on the outlined principles, the Bureau of the Statewide Planning,
N. J. Department of Community Affairs, Bureau of Geology and Topography, N. J.
Department of Environmental Protection, with the help of the Columbia University
Seminars on Pollution and Water Resources, developed a data bank system in two
general parts and the data were recorded from many sources and files.

The Information System was originally conceived for the purpose of developing a system capable of continuous revision which would permit the quick assembly
of data relative to land-use planning. With the cooperation and assistance of
the Department of Community Affairs and the Bureau of Geology and Topography,
there has been developed a system of land-use, regional geologic, geographic, and
environmental maps and fact sheets covering the entire State of New Jersey. The
aspects of the system consist of four group items:

The first part:

   1) Computerized Land-Use Data, based on real estate values

The second part:

   2) Atlas Sheet Descriptions - Bulletin #74, Geologic and Geographic
      Factors and References - N. J. Information System

   3) Block Descriptions - An MTST (magnetic tape/selectric typewriter)
      printout of 16 environmental factors specifically identified
      with the above maps

   4) Block Maps - A series of maps covering about 88 km^2
      (34 square miles) each or 6' latitude and longitude based on
      the rectangular coordinates in use by many agencies for filing
      purposes since 1890

Real estate values, detailed land use and similar data are assembled from
tax maps and information maintained locally and by the appropriate County Board
of Taxation assisted by the Bureau of Local Property Tax, Department of Treasury.
This information is computerized by the Bureau of Statewide Planning, Department
of Community Affairs which uses the State Plane Coordinate System for the location
of the centroid of properties. The Plane Coordinate System is a legally accepted
system for designating property corners with x and y values in feet. The origin
is a point ESE of Cape May at $74°$ 40 min. West Longitude and $38°$ 50 min. North
Latitude with x = 1,000,000 and y = 0. This coordinate system is shown on the
Federal U.S.G.S. 7.5 min. Quadrangle Maps. Origin was selected for easy handling
and to always have positive values.

The part of the system covering physical parameters of the environment such
as geology, topography, drainage basins, water and other resources together with
the specific types of land-use such as historic sites or sanitary landfills, is
based on the long-standing Rectangular Coordinate System. The (17) State Atlas
Sheets are the base for the system with the map number being the first two digits
of a seven-digit number. There is a uniform rectangular grid for each Atlas Sheet
consisting of (25) blocks, most of which are 6 min. of latitude by 6 min. of longitude. Each full block (designated by the third and fourth digits) covers an area
of approximately 34 square miles and only 228 maps, based on the block, are required to cover the entire state. Each block is divided into (9) rectangles of
2 min. of latitude and longitude (the fifth digit) which can then be again divided
in a similar manner into (9) squares (6th digit); and finally into (9) units each
of which is 30 acres or 0.12 km^2 (7th digit).

A computer program, which was experimented with and successfully developed, will permit the regional data of the Rectangular Coordinate System to be further subdivided by using additional digits into a unit of approximately 0.013 km^2 (3.3 acres), or by further subdivision to 0.0014 km^2 (0.36 acres). Community Affairs found it most convenient when using tax data to determine the x and y coordinates of the centroid of the tax units for use in a computer program. Conversion from x and y coordinates to the appropriate block number under the Rectangular Coordinate System, or vice versa, is easily done on the computer. Thus the two systems of data presentation are compatible.

Furthermore, there have been prepared so-called "Quickmaps" of land-use from the tax data base with a 7-acre unit. This is the smallest area that can be shown with a distinct symbol under the present program developed for Passaic Township which covers 32.4 km^2 (12.5 sq. mi.) and has some 6,000 tax parcels. Identification of locations using the Plane Coordinate System is, of course easy, because it is a Cartesian Coordinate System which is referenced on the U.S.G.S. Maps of New Jersey. The development of larger grids is easily accomplished.

The Rectangular Coordinate System, used for the State Atlas Sheets is confusing at first, but as indicated above, can be used to locate a specific area by extending the normal 7-digit reference number to the 8th and 9th digits. For the purpose of the data bank, however, only 4 digits are required to produce maps covering the 88 km^2 (34-square-mile) area of the block. To assist in converting to other coordinate systems, each block map has the latitude and longitude and the x and y coordinates given for the lower left-hand corner of the block. Since the New Jersey State Atlas Sheets are based on a scale of 1 mile to the inch (1:63360) a mechanic's rule can be used to measure distances in feet to within about 61 m (200 feet) of the actual location on the ground. The finest line on the map represents approximately a width of 38 m (125 feet) on the ground.

The data bank, based on the State Atlas Sheets, has developed into three parts:

(a) general information about the Atlas Sheet area given as a descriptive tabulation with a uniform format

(b) block descriptive material including some of the specific items from the Atlas Sheet summary, but giving data which applies specifically to the 88 km^2 (34-square-mile) area of the block

(c) block maps (at present the series, which is to be expanded to between ten and twenty multi-parameter maps as data becomes available, consists of four maps: population, water resources, drainage basins and geology)

The system is supplemented by base maps and Atlas Sheet Overlays, however, it is possible to revise or enlarge the amount of material provided for the Atlas Sheet or blocks by transferring the existing tape information and the additions or corrections to a new tape. Map changes for each block can readily be accomplished by changing the microfilm in the appropriate Atlas Sheet microfilm jacket. Given the 4-digit reference of the system, maps and descriptions can normally be recovered within minutes.

There were many changes as the work progressed from the initial concept. The general information about the Atlas Sheets was originally planned for issuance through the MTST (magnetic tape/selectric typewriter) as needed. The information contained on these Atlas Sheet descriptive summaries has proved to be of such general interest that it is now proposed to print a source book of environmental parameters which will include the Atlas Sheet descriptions for all 17 sheets with key maps to show counties and municipalities within the Atlas described and the block references needed for more detailed information.

There was much discussion as to whether the block maps should show only a single environmental factor. Experimentation suggests that it would be desirable to go ahead with the four basic maps with multiple parameters on some and complete the coverage in these four areas for the entire state before going on to other equally desirable block maps.

The population map at present shows only the municipal boundaries, the average population density for the municipality, and the percentage of the municipality in the block being considered. It is proposed to rectify this at a later date to show where the people are in the municipality. It has not yet been determined whether this will be done with respect to a generalized land-use symbol or whether it will be by showing major highways and market centers.

The water resources map shows service areas for water and sewage, or areas served by both. Also indicated are the major trunk sewers and water supply lines, the location of sewage treatment plants and their capacities, and sanitary landfills as fast as the certifications are issued. It remains to be determined as to whether dumps that are no longer used will be retained as part of the system. At a later date, surface water intake points will probably be added. Because of clutter on this map, the major water wells have been placed on the geologic map.

The drainage basin maps show the actual streams as shown on the Atlas Sheets or the so-called County Stream Maps. The drainage divides, as shown on the Drainage Basin Map of New Jersey Overlay, are also indicated. Floodplain delineation, stream flow information, points of diversion, and points of potential pollution may be indicated on these maps in the future.

The geologic map has been assembled from the most recent data and may, from time to time, be modified to give additional information. The characteristic industrial public supply and other wells from 90,000 well records assembled in 1945-1974, are shown which may have logs from which geologic cross-sections may be constructed.

The State Archaeological Society is ready for the preparation of maps showing archaeological and historical sites, including for the former, sites which have not yet been published. A method of flagging the block map so that such an unpublished archaeological site will not be endangered by construction, has been developed. It may be that this map will include other items connected with the general interest in our heritage and history.

A land-use block map has been investigated and samples prepared. Other areas would include transportation routes, public utilities, airport locations, and federal, state, county and municipally owned lands for recreation or other purposes. A map series prepared for any particular activity will require only 228 block maps. Where there are only a limited number of blocks needed to show sites for a particular activity, reference to the appropriate special block maps could be included within the Atlas Sheet descriptive material or prepared as a special listing.

It is believed that the work completed so far indicates that the data bank is compatible with other land-use or water resources data systems, makes the maximum use of available files in various state agencies, is flexible enough to permit retrieval from many different points of view, and is capable of quick and easy expansion whenever the need arises. The material prepared for the data bank is a necessary first step for any computer program which may be developed for this type of information especially when it includes a larger than 20,000 sq. mi. (or 50,000 km^2) area. Similar considerations must be given in case that a wealth of point-type information is available.

DESCRIPTION OF THE WATER RESOURCES AND LAND ORIENTED DATA BANK IN NEW JERSEY
(LOIS-Land Oriented Information System and LORD-Land Oriented Reference Data)

The material presented here is mainly part of the Water Resources and Land Oriented Information System which is based on the New Jersey Bureau of Geology and Topography Topographic Atlas Sheet Rectangular Coordinated System. A diagram showing the use of the system is included. The maps and narrative data are filed by the Atlas Sheet and block number, or the first four digits of the Rectangular Coordinate (the first two steps in the diagram). The total area of an Atlas Sheet is about 800 square miles (2072 km^2); of the reference block about 34 square miles (88 km^2); of a unit (7th digit designation) about 1/4 x 3/16 of a mile or about 30 acres (0.12 km^2). Each full block covers six minutes of latitude and longitude as compared to the 7.5 minute U.S.G.S. Topographic Quadrangle Map. For convenience the two minute wide strip, the right edge of each Atlas Sheet (05, 15, etc.) is included with the blocks immediately to the left (04, 14, etc.).

As of June 1974 there are four available maps for blocks of sheets 21 through 37 microfilm printouts.

The four maps provided are Geology, Drainage, Water Resources, and Population. On the Geologic Map the location of major industrial water wells is indicated. On the lower right of the Drainage Maps you will find the name of the 7.5 minute U.S.G.S. Quadrangle map or maps which cover the area of the block. The Water Resource Map shows drainage for orientation, the service area for water supply and/or sewerage, the sewerage treatment plants with their capacities, major water distribution mains, reservoirs, and sanitary landfills. The Population Map shows the average population density of the municipality and the percent of municipality shown within the block.

Narrative data on the MTST (magnetic tape/selectric typewriter) printouts is provided: (a) for items which pertain to or explain conditions within the entire Atlas Sheet, and (b) information about items which are found on a particular rectangular coordinate block.

A legend sheet indicating the symbols and significance of terms used on the four maps is available. For the Geologic Map, depending on the complexity of the geology of the area, there are one or two pages of legend explaining the geologic symbols and rock formation designation letters.

BRIEF ANALYSIS OF THE USERS

The request profiles of the users of the data bank are expected to result from user query categories as follows:

1) Point information: information sought by a citizen or corporation such as prospective owner or builder who is interested in a point or limited area, where he needs all information which can influence his future construction or planned use of his property.

2) Area information: information sought by a planner from the local, county, state or federal level who needs all information which can affect the planning decisions.

3) Vertical, group information: specified governmental or research agencies or corporations interested in special group information only, such as Bureau of Water Pollution Control.

4) Horizontal, point or areal information, prevent or avoid: looking for information concerning a point or an area, possibly only of a certain type, due to some legal or financial problem.

Any one of these user categories may involve request matching or cross-correlation of information.

STORING DATA BY TAPE, FILM AND COMPUTER - INCLUDING ITS EVALUATION

Studies were conducted as to methods of storage and retrieval at lowest cost and highest efficiency. The gathered data were classified as follows:

1) areal or map type information

2) descriptive type data including references

3) point type information or data pertaining to smaller standard size area, especially in land-use, streamflow records, water quality gaging stations, etc.

The available methods could be summarized into

a) computerized data systems

b) map type information service based on

(1) maps and

(2) microfilms

c) descriptive magnetic tape/selectric typewriter's methods

It was determined that all or most of the information in the program would have been compiled in a descriptive or map-type form before the data could be put into a computer program. In seeking information on the data required and method of storage and recovery, discussions were held with experts in computer science dealing with various computer programs including data bank. As a result of these discussions and from preliminary estimates of what would be required for New Jersey, it was found that once maps were prepared for use with a Micro Fiche reader/printer, recovery would be quicker (about 30 seconds) than by using computer plotting devices. Furthermore, the survey revealed that regions of less than 50,000 km^2 in size could not use efficiently a computerized system except that they are part of and tied into a larger system. On the other hand, any other method such as microfilms, tape recording, etc. cannot compete with a computerized one if they embrace larger areas or have a wealth of itemized point type information.

Therefore, it was decided to have a data bank with a combined method using:

a) Micro Fiche films and printer/reader for map-type information,

b) Magnetic Tape/Selectric Typewriter's tapes for general descriptive and reference material and,

c) Computerized system (Fortran or similar) for land-use, streamflow record, water quality control, etc.

This combined method has the advantage to cut the cost considerably in establishing the data bank by 94% (from an estimated $1,000,000 in 1972 to a real $60,000 in 1973/74) and the efficiency of information service for such size of area as New Jersey is better than any other non-combined system including the computerized one since it needs the least time for recovery. The disadvantage of the method is its apparent complexity. But, even with such diversity in training the necessary personnel and in purchasing the needed equipment, there could be no comparison in price including budget for continuous service and maintenance of equipment because of the still high cost of the computer at present. Further disadvantage of the combined system is having a limitation in capacity. Therefore,

the whole data bank must be prepared in such a form that it can be converted
easily into a fully computerized system. The itemized information should fit
without any difficulties for computer feeding, storage and recovery in the future.

REFERENCES

Halasi-Kun, G.J. (1971). Aspects hydrologiques de la pollution et des ressources
    en eau, dans les domaines urbains et industriels in Actes du Congres:
    Sciences et Techniques An 2000. (Societee des Civil Enginieurs de France,
    Paris).
Halasi-Kun, G.J. (1972). Data Collecting on Water Resources and Computations of
    Maximum Flood for Smaller Watershed in International Symposium on Water
    Resources Planning, Vol. I. (Secretaria de Recursos Hidraulicos, Mexico,
    D.F.).
Halasi-Kun, G.J. (1973). Improvement of Runoff Records in Smaller Watersheds
    Based on Permeability of the Geological Subsurface in Symposium on the
    Design of Water Resources Projects with Inadequate Data, Vol. I.
    (UNESCO-WMO-IAHS, Madrid).
Halasi-Kun, G.J. (1974). Ground Water Computations in New Jersey, USA
    (Nordic Hydrology, 5).
Halasi-Kun, G.J. (in press). Ground Water Capacity and Extreme Surface Flow
    Values of Smaller Watersheds in Proceedings of Columbia University Seminars
    on Pollution and Water Resources, Vol. V. (Columbia University-State of
    New Jersey).
Widmer, K. (1964). The Geology and Geography of New Jersey. (Van Nostrand,
    Princeton).
Enviro Control, Inc. (1972). The Development of a Procedure for Acquiring and
    Disseminating Information on Water Use, Vol. I-II. (Washington, D.C.).

DISCUSSION

*Do you have any detailed report about the structure of your data-bank.
The access time to the information is related to that. (VAN DER BEKEN)*

We can perhaps discuss that afterwards. (HALASI-KUN)

*You mentioned this procedure for identification of your educational system,
your traffic system, etc. Do you have any experience of identifying the interacting
structures between these systems ? (SHAH)*

We tried with this data-bank just the basic information because we don't
know what kind of information we are asking. This is just to have a picture at this
moment for each customer : about 4 types of map information, about 25 types of district information. Besides that it can have in the same scale area photos, set of
maps. The area photos are revised every 2 years, the other data are revised every
half year. In a country where you expect 30 % growth in 15 years we gave up the
area mapping because we could not follow. For this reason we switched the area
maps. We are updating every two years. I would stress the infrared area photos.
At present it might be expensive, but you can get 7 000 km^2 in about the size of
this small table for 100 $.

Modeling and Simulation of Water Resources Systems, G.C. VANSTEENKISTE, (Ed.)
North-Holland Publishing Company (1975)

WATERLO, A DATA BANK AND
COMPUTERSYSTEM FOR RIVER CHANNEL NETWORKS AND
RIVER BASINS IN BELGIUM

T. D'Hondt and A. Van der Beken
Hydrology Section
Institute of Environmental Sciences
Vrije Universiteit Brussel
BELGIUM

ABSTRACT

The main objective of the paper is to present a logical
extension, relative to time-dependent data, of the data-
bank and computersystem for river channels and basins.
The system has been denoted WATERLO and details about
its concept and development have been published elsewhere.
The aim is to develop a comprehensive system which maximizes availability of data collected by diverse admini-
strations, institutions and agencies. The data are identified by the point location method. The index used in
the WATERLO-system identifies precisely and without ambiguity any location on a river in Belgium. The master-
file possesses a sequential structure which is strictly
determined by the natural hierarchy of the river basins.
The extension we are proposing is on the level of the
data-records with the lowest possible significance in the
hierarchical structure of the main-file. One more level,
containing data of a dynamical nature such as water levels
and water quality measurements, enables us to introduce
an "indexed sequential" structure.

INTRODUCTION

The large amount of water-related data can become a nightmare
for the user in charge of water management, unless these data are collected and handled in a systematic and efficient way. The efficiency
may be obtained by means of the computer facilities, which will be
discussed in the next paragraph. These features are common to all
types of data-banks and therefore are well-known by information specialists.

The systematic approach, however, implies a fair knowledge of
the specific problems related to water management. This includes a
basic hydrologic and hydraulic background and an understanding of different measurement techniques. Moreover, one should know what type of
data are relevant and how they can be processed for further mathematical handling. Administrative requests form also a very important part
of the information-system.

The objective of the paper is to discuss these requirements
and to explain how WATERLO is built up to fulfill them. Earlier reports on the system can be found in the references given at the end
of the paper.

COMPUTER CONFIGURATIONS

The present paragraph is concerned with the physical background of the notion of a data-bank in general. The main issue is to give the less-informed reader a review of current-day computer facilities.

Most latter-day computer systems with some degree of sophistication comprise the following hardware entities :

- a high-speed computing device commonly known as central processor which is intended to perform the actual calculations;

- a more or less extensive core memory used for the storage of the programmed instructions as well as those data which have a marked degree of relevance;

- a set of peripheral processors connecting the central processor/ memory with the slower-moving input, output and storage devices;

- the peripherical material such as card-reader, line-printer, tape and disk units etc.

A very steep cost/efficiency ratio inhibits the use of very extensive core-memories; hence the bulk of the data-bank will always reside on one of the peripherical devices. We will not consider papertape or punched cards, except as media for the initial introduction of the data, seen their inherent lack of maniability. We will therefore have to take recourse to magnetic devices such as tapes and disks.

We now come upon the notion of teleprocessing. By this term we denote the interactive communication between a general user and the data-bank, using the computer as intermediary. In practice, this means that a user, with the aid of a remote terminal, asks a set of questions which are quasi-instantly answered by the computer. This implies a very fast type of interaction between the computer and the data-bank. It is therefore advised to use direct-access storage media for the data-bank.

On the other hand, both the type of data and the recording mode, impose a sequential structure on the data-bank. Consequently, it is interesting to have the data-bank reside on a device which enables a sequential type of throughput. This is doubly so if batch-jobs are envisaged intended to treat the data in a statistical way. In the latter case, whole series of (physically) seperate data-records have to be ordered one behind the other in order to maximise efficiency of the system.

Recent times have seen the development of a system of storage which encompasses these two types of data-arrangement. This system, commonly denoted by the term "indexed sequential", enables us to construct any file in a sequential way while keeping the relative addresses of each record in an index-block located at the end of the file. Using this file in an ordinary way, we obtain a sequential procedure, while the use of the index-block implies that direct access methods can be applied to the file. Therefore we propose an indexed sequential structure for the data-bank in question.

DATA COLLECTION

Data on rivers may be digitized from maps of different origin. E.g. maps of the non-navigable rivers in Belgium are collected in an atlas containing plans on a scale of 1:2500. Their classification is on the base of the municipality for which an identification code of five digits already exists. The maps are supplemented by tables describing the cross-sections and structures on the river.

In many cases, additional information of greater precision on cross-sections and structures may be obtained when channel improvement projects have been executed or have been prepared. The databank provides then a central repository for this information which is consequently protected against loss or obsolescence. Hydraulic and hydrologic computations may be planned if these basic information on cross-sections and structures is supplemented by characterization of the river network and the hydrologic features of the watershed.

Today river measurements of many kinds are made. They are principally 1° water level measurements and corresponding stage-discharge determinations;
2° water quality measurements with corresponding analyses of different chemical and biological parameters.

The first kind of measurements can be represented in a 3-dimensional graph, the second kind needs a 4-dimensional representation (Fig. 1). Hence, data-retrieval may be performed in different ways.

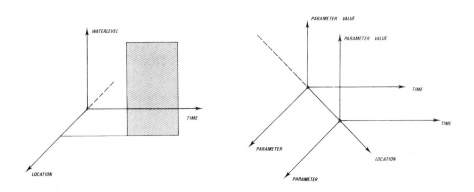

Fig. 1.   Three- and four-dimensional representation
of river measurements.

It is not necessary to bring all data from already existing systems (such as the hydrometeorological data-bank processing water level measurements) into one and the same data-bank i.e. WATERLO. However, data of different data-banks should be made exchangeable, in an advanced stage possibly by telecommunication. In order to reach this goal, WATERLO uses a point location method which identifies precisely any location on a river in Belgium. Therefore, data related to a given point may be located and retrieved without ambiguity. Full identification of measurement points along a given river, including all details about type, frequency and period of measurements, may be considered as an important feature of the system.

Related to the water quality is the very important information on outlets from municipal sewage, industrial waste water and water treatment facilities. Unfortunately, the geographic information of these data is non-existant, although urgently needed. Another kind of data which may be collected for special applications is the characterization of the fauna and flora of the river. Landscape information related to rivers is also a potential type of data to be incorporated into the system.

For practical and operational reasons, all these data of different kind and origins are represented by several subsystems (symbol S) of WATERLO. Collection, handling and analyses are performed on the basis of these subsystems. Hence, user's computerprograms are divided according to them as will be explained in the next paragraph. Table 1 lists the proposed subsystems and their data content. The references give more details about the present stage of development of each of these subsystems.

Table 1   Subsystems of WATERLO

N°	Subsystem	Data-content
01	ADIN	administrative data and classification
02	KAPER	cadastral parcels and roads along the river
03	PROBET	cross-sections and structures (descriptive tables)
04	PROKON	cross-sections and structures (actual and designed)
05	MEWAT	measurement and sampling stations on the river
06	LOZING	sewage outlets, water inlets, water treatment facilities
07	HYDROL	hydraulic and hydrologic data
08	BIOL	biological and landscape data
09	BURBA	land use, urbanisation and industrialisation

STRUCTURE OF THE DATA-BANK

The initial version of the data-bank resides on punched cards. These cards represent the combined output of a digitizer and the accompanied actions of the operator. The latter serve to introduce additional comments intended to divide the data into suitable blocks. Moreover, essential details not mentioned on the maps such as identification codes are recorded in this way.

In paragraph 2 sufficient reasons were given to have the data-bank reside on magnetic direct-access devices, the result being a file with an inherently indexed sequential structure. It is therefore clear that we will have to transform the initial data with the aid of a suitable computer program into a well-adapted form. Moreover, this form will have to fit the type of data in an optimal way.

We will make special use of the inherently hierarchical structure of the data. Indeed, the graph of a natural drainage basin gives rise to a non-ambiguous identification system, as was explained in the earlier reports.

Let us initially proceed with the description of the present established structure. The master-file, which is the essential part of the data-bank, is composed of variable-level and variable-length data-records. The data-records (g) with the lowest possible importance in the hierarchical structure of the master-file are attributed level four. They contain the output of the digitizer in an optimally coded form recorded between two predetermined points on one bank of a certain watercourse (w). In the actual development, these predetermined points are two successive municipal borders. An example of these so-called global-recordings is introduced in the schematical representation of the data-bank in Fig. 2 for the municipality Welden located on the river Zwalm, a tributary of the Upper-Scheldt.

All data-records pertaining to the same watercourse (w) are then sequentially ordered. First come all odd-numbered records representing data recorded on the left bank of the watercourse, followed by the even-numbered records which represent data concerning the right bank. These records are preceeded by a level-three record containing essential information about the watercourse in question. In Fig. 2 this is again illustrated for the river Zwalm. The information contained within level-three records concerns the name, administrative denomination and identification code of the watercourse as well as the number of records of level four following the present record.

We will now merge all data concerning a minor basin (m). All record groups pertaining to a watercourse located in a given basin are sequentially ordered within the master-file. In order to ease computer manipulation of the data, these record groups are sorted on an ascending key relative to the identification code of each watercourse.

All records containing data relative to one minor basin (m) are then again headed by a data-record, this time of level two. This data record contains information concerning the name of the minor basin (m), number of watercourses within this minor basin, origin of the data, status of the data, etc. Moreover, an identification code is given for the minor basin.

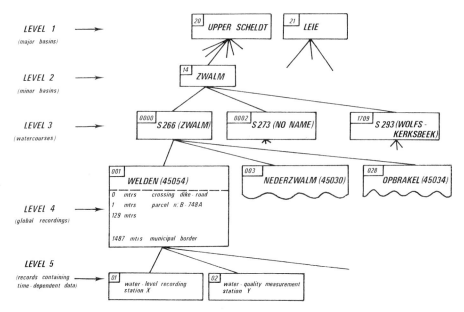

Fig. 2.   Graphical representation of the content of the master-file.

All data relative to a given major basin (M) are merged and headed by a record of level one. The latter contains information on the name and identification code of the major basin as well as the number of minor basins contained within this major basin.

It can easily be seen that the proposed identification procedure uniquely defines all data. Indeed, the statement of the identification codes of major and minor basin (M) and (m), watercourse (w) and global recording (g) together with the distance measured along the watercourse starting from the beginning of the global recording, defines every point-location on any given watercourse without ambiguity. Fig. 3 illustrates this procedure for parcel n° B-748A located in Welden on the Zwalm.

It is well-known that apart from a master-file, a data-bank requires a set of maintenance or "bookkeeping" programs. These serve to maintain the master-file in an up-to-date condition so as to represent a real situation. We will not treat these update programs at length, as they were discussed in sufficient detail in previous publications. Suffice it to say that a procedure which is the strict inverse of the one given in Fig. 3, is used.

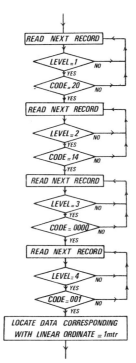

Fig. 3.   Sequential procedure for the retrieval of
data located in the municipality Welden on
the river Zwalm.

PROPOSED EXTENSION

We will now present a suitable structure for an additional
record-level purporting to data of a dynamical nature. There are
several ways of doing so.

We propose the following method : all data records containing
water-quality recordings, water-level recordings etc. will be denoted
by level 5. Moreover, all level 5-records relative to the same global recording will be systematically ordered immediately following
this global record. The content of the records of level 5 is not yet
rigorously established. Suffice is to say that within these records
the data will be chronologically ordered.

An important aspect of this structure is immediately apparent.
Indeed, it is often not possible to associate a precise point-location with a temporary water quality sampling point. Sometimes only
the name of the municipality in question is given in order to define
the location. The proposal to arrange all data records relative to
the same global recording can be seen to suit this practical situation in an optimal way.

Let us presently compare the proposed structure with an already operational one : the water-quality data-bank of the Belgian

Ministry of Public Health. A typical output-form of this data-bank
is given in Table 2.

Table 2.   Output of water quality data

Serial number	Munici-pality	Industrial or munici-pal waste outlet	Description of outlet or measurement point	Date	Hour	Physical and chemical parameter values

The entries are chronologically ordered within the data-bank, greatly
facilitating the updating process. Unfortunately, this structure inhibits the flexibility of the system. Indeed, it is apparently difficult or impossible to rearrange the data in other configurations than
chronological ones. This is not the case with the system proposed in
the present paper. By making use of a simple retrieve-and-sort routine, it is foreseeable to reconstruct an output giving parameter-
values at a given moment in upstream or downstream direction along
the whole river.

CONCLUSION

        The foregoing paragraphs report only in a very concise way
about the structure and advantages of the WATERLO-system. The reader
should keep in mind that the system is in his very early stage of development. The computer installation (i.e. the Brussels Free University Control Data 6500) used, does not offer teleprocessing facilities
as yet. Hence, this aspect of the data-bank remains to be initiated.
On the other hand, a number of batch jobs were constructed so as to
test the quality of the data-bank. In Fig. 4 the concept of the extant user's programs is described with the aid of a block-diagram.

        A large diversity and flexibility of these user's programs
are a measure for the usefulness of the data-bank.

REFERENCES

Van der Beken, A., D'Hondt, T. and Geelen, J. (1974).
        Een data-bank en computersysteem voor de waterlopen en stroom-
        gebieden (A data-bank and computersystem for rivers and basins).
        Vrije Universiteit Brussel, Hydrology Section, March 1974, 53 pp.

Van der Beken, A. and D'Hondt, T. (1974). Concept and development of
        a data-bank and computersystem for river channel networks and
        river basins using the data easily available in Belgium. Inter-
        national Conference "Data Processing and Environment", 20-22 May,
        1974, Arlon, Belgium.

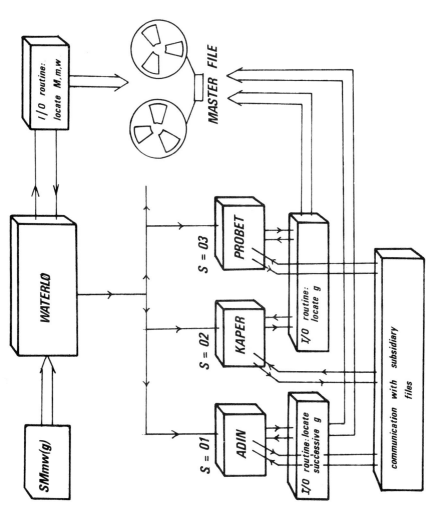

Fig. 4. Diagram of the extant user's program configuration

DISCUSSION

I think the approach we mentioned is valuable for Belgium I don't know if the same approach could be applied for another country, because we use the administrative classification very intensively. (VAN DER BEKEN)

Would you like to compare some of your procedures with those of dr. Kun.
                                                                    (SIKKA)

I cannot see what is common for the moment since I don't know the structure of dr. Kun's system. (VAN DER BEKEN)

Can you ask river levels be printed out in a certain fashion of hydrographs within the system itself.

This would be the subsystem HYDRO, for the moment it is not developed, it is planned. The system is in its very early stage of development. (VAN DER BEKEN)

Did you put some moisture data in your bank ? (NEUMAN)

It could be in the same structure for band use, urbanization and also for soil classification, then we have to introduce some soil moisture data. I am wondering if it is worthwhile to do so, since the system is for waterpollution agencies, they are not directly interested in soil moisture data. (VAN DER BEKEN)

Current research field of author : *Simulation of river flow using daily measurements of precipitation and temperature – Development of a data-bank and computersystem for riverchannel systems and drainage basins – Movement of moisture and pollutants in unsaturated zone.*

Modeling and Simulation of Water Resources Systems, G.C. VANSTEENKISTE, (Ed.)
North-Holland Publishing Company (1975)

STATIC AND DYNAMIC SIMULATION
OF WATER TRANSPORT IN
A COMPLEX NETWORK SYSTEM

L. Lijklema and G. van Straten
Department of Chemical Engineering
Twente University of Technology
The Netherlands

ABSTRACT

Increasing cultural eutrophication is threatening the
unique ecosystem of the water basin of Vollenhove. For
management decisions a knowledge of the transport and
fate of phosphates would be required.

A study of the water transport is presented. Dynamic
simulations, based on a nodes and links model, show
that considerable oscillations in flows and water levels
occur, induced mainly by the intermittent operation of
the pumping station. The dynamic behaviour reflects the
natural frequencies of the system. The results were compared with those obtained from a static model. It was
concluded that static models tend to underestimate the
degree of mixing in the network.

INTRODUCTION

The object of this study is the water transport in the basin
of Vollenhove, a polder district in the north-west of the province
Overijssel in The Netherlands. (Figure 1).

The district comprises several small polders draining into
canals and ditches interconnecting lakes and marshes. The marshes
(shaded areas) originate from peat digging and consist of strips of
reed land and peat swamps alternating with shallow strips of water.

These beautiful marshes are an important bird sanctuary of
international interest and have a unique biological structure. The
whole district is a well-known resort area. The watermark in the region is kept at 0.7 m below sea level by a powerful pumping station
(Stroink) that discharges the net drainage into the IJsselmeer.

During the last decades cultural eutrophication has imposed
an increasing stress upon the ecosystem of the marshes. Especially
phosphate originating from households, cattle breeding etc. is considered to accelerate the deterioration of the water quality. At this
time a program is in development to pipe the sewage from several villages to the treatment plant at Steenwijk. After reconstruction and
extension of this biological treatment plant phosphate removal will
become a major alternative for water quality management. The goal of
the present study is:
   a) to trace the transport of phosphates from this and other
      point sources into the region;
   b) to study the sedimentation of phosphates by iron salts oc-

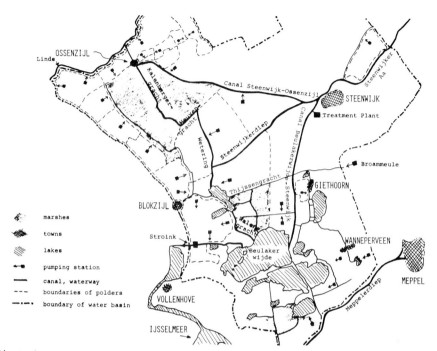

Fig.1 The waterbassin of Vollenhove

curring in the drainwater of several polders and to investigate the interaction with sediments;
c) to evaluate the significance of management alternatives
for the protection of the marshes (phosphate removal,
blocking of certain waterways etc.).

This report will focus on a description of the transport of
water.

STATIC VERSUS DYNAMIC MODELS

For management decisions a knowledge of the average transport
of phosphates during a season would be required and no information on
the hourly or daily variation in transport through canals. Hence a
static model for average inputs, outputs and flows for a period of
one or several months would serve the purpose. There were two reasons
however, that stimulated the construction of a dynamic model as well:

- the verification by comparison with field data is only
  possible for a dynamic model;
- the dynamic character of the flows in the canals induced
  by the intermittent pumping at Stroink might affect the
  mixing of phosphates.

It was decided to develop a dynamic model and to compare
simulations with results from an existing static model.

CONSTRUCTION OF A DYNAMIC MODEL

The approach in the construction of a dynamic model is a simplification of the procedure proposed by Orlob, Shubinski et al. (1). The canals and lakes are represented by a network of nodes (lakes and marshes), interconnected by links (canals).

Nodes are characterised by their surface area and the head (h). Nodes are also defined at the intersections of canals, the surface area of such a node being limited to half the sum of the surface areas of the connecting canals. The variables of velocity, flow, hydraulic radius, cross-sectional area, length and frictional resistance are related to the links.

The equation of motion used for description of the flow in links (constant cross-sectional area) is:

$$\frac{\delta u}{\delta t} = - g \frac{\delta h}{\delta x} - K \, |u| \, u \tag{I}$$

in which

> u = velocity
> h = water surface elevation
> $K = \dfrac{g}{c^2 . h}$ = frictional resistance coefficient
> C = Chezy's coefficient
> g = acceleration of gravity

In equation I the influences of wind stress, Coriolis forces and the Bernoulli acceleration $u \frac{\delta u}{\delta x}$ have been neglected.

The surface elevation in the nodes varies according to:

$$O \frac{\delta h}{\delta t} = \Sigma \, uA + \Sigma \, Q \tag{II}$$

where

> O = surface area
> A = wet cross-sectional area of connecting link
> ΣQ = the net effect of inputs and outputs except the flow through links

For a description of the major features of the region (Figure 1) 14 nodes were defined. Except inputs from outside the district at Steenwijk and occasionally near Ossenzijl and Broammeule, the main input is rain. The outputs are given by two pumping stations for water supply, by Stroink and by evaporation. Seepage is an important factor in the region between Ossenzijl and Vollenhove; exact field data are not yet available however.

The evaporation (per m^2) in polders and the areas draining by a natural slope in the water level is set at 70% of the open water evaporation as measured by a meteorological post. This is a normal reduction factor for grasslands.
The surplus water of polders is pumped into the appropriate node when the water level exceeds a fixed value that is considered to be desirable by the farmers. The corresponding "if" statement in the computer program thus simulates the daily decision of the local man in

charge whether to pump or not. The capacities of all these small
pumps are estimated at 0.25 mm per hour.

The run-off of the other areas is assumed to occur along
waterways with a comparatively high frictional resistance to allow
for the slowness of this process. Six nodes are used to define the
average water level in these areas.
The intermittent operation of Stroink (only during day time) is controlled by the water level in the lakes.

The simulation program was written in CSMP-III (2).
Equation I was discretised as:

$$\frac{u_{t+1} - u_t}{\Delta t} = - (g \frac{\Delta h}{\ell} + K |u_t| u_t) \tag{III}$$

in which ℓ is the length of the link involved and Δh the head difference between the nodes on either side.

THE STATIC MODEL

The static model used is an adaptation of an existing efficient model for computation of flows and pressures in a network for
the transport of compressible fluids e.g. natural gas (3). The distribution of flows through the network obeys Kirchhoff's laws. Starting with assumed initial flows satisfying the law of balancing flows
at each node, the actual distribution is approached by an iterative
procedure. The head losses around each circuit must sum to zero; correction factors for the flows are obtained by a Taylor series development of this law.
The network used is the same as the simplified scheme used for the
dynamic program.
In contrast with the dynamic program, however, a very detailed model
can be calculated in a relatively short time.
Inputs and outputs are averaged over the appropriate period.

RESULTS OF SIMULATIONS

Figure 2 represents the simulated flows in the "Wetering"
during a period of moderate rainfall. After an initial deviation between the calculated flows in the static and the dynamic program due
to the initial conditions, the "dynamic flow" can be seen to oscillate strongly around the average flow of the static model.

The average flow in the dynamic situation equals approximately the static flow. In situations with a great difference in storage
capacities of the surface waters on either side of a link, the
average flows do not match however. Figure 3 presents the flow from
Steenwijk to Ossenzijl during the same episode. The rapid lowering
of the waterhead near Steenwijk, due to the low buffering capacity at
this site, induces a reversal of the flow in the canal after about 3
hours of pumping at Stroink. Near the end of the daily pumping period
of 8 hours the flow resumes the original direction. This result demonstrates the general experience that intensive pumping highly affects the flow pattern and the mixing of pollutants in the region.

To test the reliability of the dynamic model field measurements of water velocities must be compared with results of simulations.
The velocities in the canals are generally low and small fluctuations
in wind stress cause relatively important variations. Current instru-

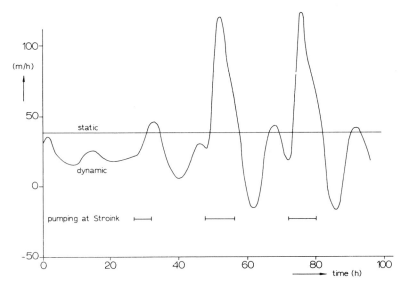

Fig.2 Simulated flow velocity in Wetering

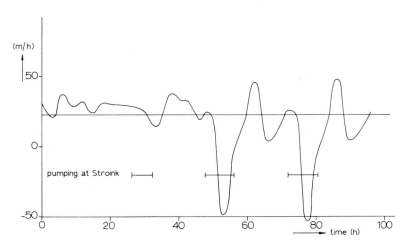

Fig.3 Simulated flow velocity in canal Steenwijk-Ossenzijl

ments for measurement of stream velocities become inaccurate below
150 m/hr (4 cm/sec).

For the model all inputs and outputs must be known, as well
as the intial conditions since events on previous days influence the
results due to the slowness of the system as a whole. As mentioned
before seepage is one of the factors studied insufficiently. The pro-
visional results of Figure 4, measured near the treatment plant at
Steenwijk, give a first indication of the reliability of the model.
Apart from the magnitude, the variation in stream velocity as
measured after stopping the pump is similar to the variation simulated for a wet period.

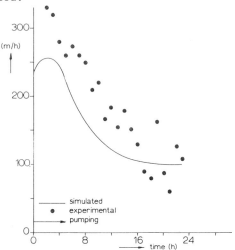

*Fig.4 Simulated and measured flow velocities
in canal Steenwijk-Beulakerwijde*

NATURAL FREQUENCIES

The results of most dynamic simulations clearly demonstrate
a certain periodicity in flows and water heads. Apparently the system
has its own characteristic frequencies. The oscillations observed in
the simulations are induced by sudden variations in inputs or outputs; this means that starting or stopping the pump at Stroink is the
main source of such oscillations. These oscillations are attenuated
by the frictional resistance of the system.
The influence of these oscillations is most pronounced in the lakes
and canals in close connection with Stroink. A periodicity of about
5 hours was observed in several simulations. To investigate the role
of the natural frequencies in the network a detailed study was made
of the part of the system nearest to Stroink: the nodes connected by
the links Walengracht, Thijssengracht and Canal Beulakerwijde-Steen-
wijk. For this three nodes - three links system equations I and II
were discretised and linearised, resulting in:

$$\frac{d(\delta u_{ij})}{dt} = - 2K_{ij} \; |\bar{u}_{ij}| \; \delta u_{ij} - \frac{g}{\ell_{ij}} \; (\delta h_j - \delta h_i) \qquad (IV)$$

and

$$O_i \ \frac{d(\delta h_i)}{dt} = \sum_j \pm A_{ij} \ \delta u_{ij} + \delta Q_i \tag{V}$$

for zero initial conditions.

Taking the Laplace transform of both equations and solving for the transformed δu_{ij} results in:

$$\delta H_i \left[sO_i + \sum_{j \neq i} \frac{A_{ij} \ g/\ell_{ij}}{s+2k_{ij}|\bar{u}_{ij}|} \right] - \sum_{j \neq i} \delta H_j \ \frac{A_{ij} \ g/\ell_{ij}}{s+2k_{ij}|\bar{u}_{ij}|} = \delta Q_i \tag{VI}$$

With

$$a_{ij} = \frac{A_{ij} \ g/\ell_{ij}}{s+2k_{ij}|\bar{u}_{ij}|}$$

this can be abbreviated yo:

$$\delta H_i \ (sO_i + \sum_{j \neq i} a_{ij}) - \sum_{j \neq i} \delta H_j \ a_{ij} = \delta Q_i \tag{VI-a}$$

For the system of three nodes (lakes) and three links (canals) this results in three (transformed) linear equations.

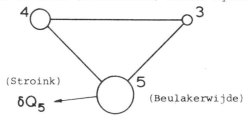

(Stroink)

δQ_5

(Beulakerwijde)

The corresponding equations in matrix form are:

δH_3	δH_4	δH_5	
$sO_3+a_{34}+a_{35}$	$-a_{34}$	$-a_{35}$	δQ_3
$-a_{43}$	$sO_4+a_{43}+a_{45}$	$-a_{45}$	δQ_4
$-a_{53}$	$-a_{54}$	$sO_5+a_{53}+a_{54}$	δQ_5

$$\tag{VII}$$

where $a_{ij} = a_{ji}$

Application of Cramer's rule yields: $\delta H_i / \delta Q_j = B_{ij}/A$

where A is the determinant of equation VII and B_{ij} is the same determinant with column i replaced by $0...Q_j...0$.

To estimate the effect of an input (output) at node 5 on the water level in node 4 the quotient $\delta H_4/\delta Q_5$ must be evaluated.

The B_{ij} determinant in this case is:

$$\begin{vmatrix} sO_3+a_{34}+a_{35} & 0 & -a_{35} \\ -a_{34} & 0 & -a_{45} \\ -a_{35} & 1 & sO_5+a_{35}+a_{45} \end{vmatrix}$$

Solutions for s obtained by equation A to zero give the natural frequencies of the system: when the denominator is zero in $\delta H_i/\delta Q_j$, the numerator δH_i must have a finite value representing the natural reactions of the system without external influences (Q = 0). The imaginary part in the solutions for s represent the frequencies, the real part the damping factor, e.g. for s = -4 + 6j, the solution will be

$$\delta H \simeq e^{-4t}\sin(6t + \phi).$$

When the numerator determinant yields a solution for s that is equal to (or close to) a solution obtained from the denominator, this means that this solution is not (or weakly) present in the final solution.

For the actual system of three lakes with interconnecting canals the natural response due to pumping at Stroink was evaluated along these lines with the frictions set to zero (K = 0). For this case the problem can be solved readily.
Solutions obtained were:

$$\frac{\delta H_5}{\delta Q_5} \simeq \frac{(s - 1.222j)(s + 1.222j)(s - 3.921j)(s + 3.921j)}{(s - 1.312j)(s + 1.312j)(s - 3.929j)(s + 3.929j)}$$

hence ω = 1.312 will be a possible natural frequency of node 5; the periodicity is $\pi 2/1.312$ = 4.8 hours.
Along the same lines for node 4 the same periodicity is found and for node 3 a periodicity of 1.6 and of 4.8 hours.
These calculations do not result in an estimation of the amplitude of the oscillations and since K was set to zero, the effect of frictional resistance on the periodicity was neglected. Therefore digital simulations for the same system were run and compared with the calculations.

Figure 5a,b presents the variations in water level of the three nodes, due to pumping at Stroink. The predicted periodicity is apparent though the magnitude of the 4.8 hours period in H_3 is not very pronounced. The comparatively low frictional resistance in the system has no apparent effect upon the frequencies. Node 5, a large lake, has a small amplitude. The damping factor is lower for a node with a small surface area.

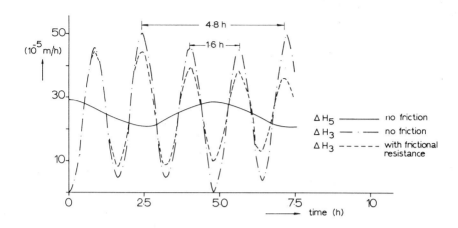

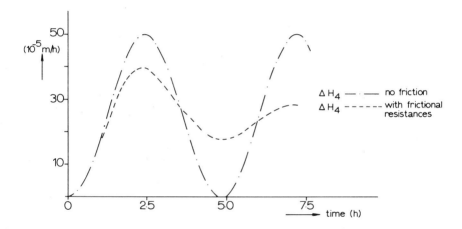

Fig. 5a,b *Simulation of* $\delta H_i/\delta Q_5$ *in a system of three lakes.*
ΔH *represents the time incremental part*
of the level decrease.

CONCLUSIONS

- The flow of water through the network of waterways interconnecting lakes is affected strongly by the dynamic character of inputs and outputs.

- The flow through the network under dynamic conditions reflects the natural frequencies of the system. Frictional resistance reduces the amplitude of the resulting oscillations, but has a negligible effect upon the frequencies.

- Static models tend to underestimate the degree of mixing in the network.

ACKNOWLEDGEMENT

The authors are grateful to Mr. J. Egberts for his field work and the cooperation in model building.
They thank Ir. J. Rijnsdorp for his valuable suggestions.

REFERENCES

1) G.T. Orlob - "Mathematical modeling of estuarial systems" International Symposium on mathematical modeling techniques in water resources systems. Ottawa, Canada 1972

2) Continuous System Modeling Program III (CSMP III) IBM - Manual SH 19-7001-2 (1972

3) H.J. Fontein - Twente University of Technology - The Netherlands. To be published.

Current research field of author : *Modeling of aquatic systems in water pollution control programs and water treatment processes - Estimation of field parameters - e.g. sediment-water interaction - iron-fosfate chemistry - dispersion etc.*

Modeling and Simulation of Water Resources Systems, G.C. VANSTEENKISTE, (Ed.)
North-Holland Publishing Company (1975)

OPTIMIZING A PRESSURIZED PIPE-LINE NETWORK USING A NEW METHOD

J. Wiggers and O. Groen
Ingenieursbureau
Dwars, Heederik en Verhey B.V.
Amersfoort - HOLLAND

INTRODUCTION

Centralized treatment of waste water has proved to be advantageous from an economic point of view. It is also known that the problems involved in centralization can be particularly well handled with the aid of systems analysis. The literature on this subject is already very extensive (see (1) and (2)).

However, when the ultimate plans for waste water pollution control in the Netherlands were drawn up no systems analysis was applied. Instead, as is common in sanitary engineering in our country, a general comparison was made of a number of alternative solutions. The main reason for this was that a large number of the plans had already been completed, and some had even been executed, before it was possible for the planners and designers who made them to have become familiar with methods from the fields of operational research and systems analysis.

Regrettably this means that the funds made available in the Netherlands to improve the quality of surface water are not being spent to the best advantage. Although there is still a possibility at this stage of analysing parts of the system to achieve optimal solutions, it is obvious that a number of optimal solutions for parts of the system do not imply the ultimate achievement of an optimal solution for the entire system.

The pressure line network is the part of the system for which it is worthwhile considering the execution of an analysis based on modern methods. In this contribution a new method is presented by which an optimal network can be designed in an efficient manner. A practical application of the method is also presented.

THE DUTCH POLLUTION CONTROL SYSTEM

The system is shown schematically in figure 1.

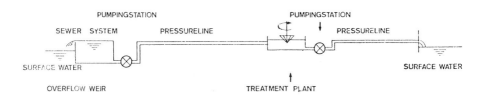

Fig.1 - POLLUTION CONTROL SYSTEM

The system contains the following parts in regard to its functioning :
- the sewer system (collection of waste water)
- the sewage pumping stations and pressure lines (transport)
- the sewage treatment plant (treatment)
- the effluent pumping station and the pressure main (disposal).

Sewer systems in the Netherlands are mainly of the mixed type. With a few exceptions they are located in very flat country. When heavy rainfall results in higher discharges than those for which the system is demensioned, the excess water is discharged into open water courses via stormwater weirs. The system is emptied by means of pumps. These transport waste water, both during rainfall and dry periods, to a following pumping station.
In its turn this pumping station pumps the water, together with that of the connected sewer system, to the next station. In this way the waste water finally reaches a waste water treatment plant.
In the flat regions of Holland the sewer system can be regarded as a storage tank in which both rainwater and sewage are collected. The tank is normally emptied by pumping, but when it is completely filled up part of the stored water discharges by overflow, via the stormwater weirs. This sewer system model is analogous with a model of a reservoir. If rainfall data are available for a long year period it is possible to determine both the average overflow frequency as a function of the storage and the necessary capacity of the pumps, in the same way as this can be done for reservoirs.

The Dutch authorities charged with safeguarding the quality of the surface water use the average overflow frequency as a measure of the pollution of the receiving waters on which overflows occur. (It would be outside the scope of this paper to discuss the effects of stormwater discharges on the quality of the surface water. It should be stated, however, that the average overflow frequency on its own cannot serve as an accurate measure for the degree of contamination ; other factors are also involved).

Figure 3 shows the overflow frequency, determined with the model already described, as a function of the storage in the system, and the capacity of the pumps. The authorities fix the permitted average overflow frequency for each individual case. With a known average overflow frequency the storage required decreases as are the capacity of the pumps increases.

In terms of capital investments for sewer systems this is to say that these decrease as the discharge capacity increases (see figure 4). The cost function is convex and downward.

Higher discharge capacities involve an increase in the capital investments and the costs of electric power and maintenance. The cost function is upward and also convex.

The costs arising from the equipment of the pumping stations are to a limited extent dependent on the discharge. The extra costs resulting from increased discharge manifest themselves chiefly in the greater number of pump running-hours. There is generally an increase in the storage required. (The constraint is the permitted engagement frequency of the pumps). The cost function is therefore upward and practically linear.

The costs arising from the treatment of waste water increase as the discharge increases. The resulting cost function however is concave.

Nevertheless, the total cost function is convex. Consequently there is a specific discharge at which the capital investments will be minimal. Of course the number of sewage treatment plants that should be included in the. network also plays a role in optimization. However, in the Dutch situation account seldom has to taken

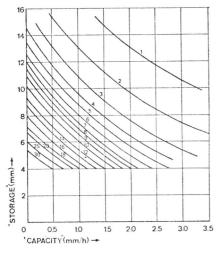

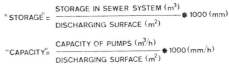

Fig.3 - STORAGE AS A FUNCTION OF PUMPING
CAPACITY FOR EQUAL OVERFLOW
FREQUENCIES

$$\text{"STORAGE"} = \frac{\text{STORAGE IN SEWER SYSTEM (m}^3)}{\text{DISCHARGING SURFACE (m}^2)} * 1000 \text{ (mm)}$$

$$\text{"CAPACITY"} = \frac{\text{CAPACITY OF PUMPS (m}^3/\text{h)}}{\text{DISCHARGING SURFACE (m}^2)} * 1000 \text{ (mm/h)}$$

Fig.4 - COSTFUNCTIONS

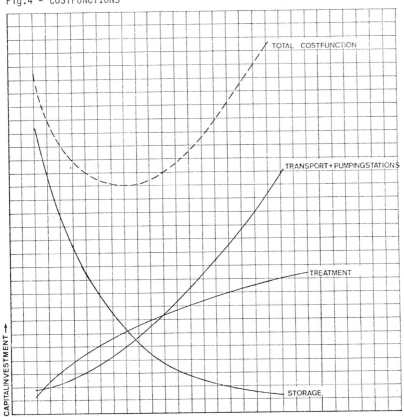

of this variable since the location and number of treatment plants have generally
already been decided upon.
The size of the area to be covered is formally also a variable. The dimensions of
such an area are often defined in the Netherlands by natural and (alas) administrative boundaries and therefore need not to be taken in account.

All Dutch towns and practically all villages have a sewer system. This means
that when establishing the optimal solution for a total waste water pollution control system the discharges from the existing sewer systems can be varied only within narrow limits. It is clear that in such cases the use of systems analysis can
only be considered for the treatment plant and the pressure line network.

The remainder of this contribution will deal with an efficient method of
optimizing a pressure line network.

OPTIMIZATION OF A NETWORK - A NEW METHOD

Figure 2 is a schematic sketch of a network. A characteristic of the system
is that each separate sewer system must be regarded both as a source and as a sink.
The distance between the sources is known, as is the amount of waste water to be
discharged as a function of time. The running hours of the pumps at dry weather flow
and during rainfall are known from observations made during a long year period.
The pump capacity required can now be calculated.

The cost function is as follows :

$$F = \sum_{j=1}^{n} l_j (a + b \, \phi_j^x + c \, \Phi_j^y + d \sum_{k=1}^{m} \frac{Q_k^3 \, T_k}{\phi_j^5}) \tag{1}$$

The prices and the economic value of the network are incorporated in the constants
a, b, c and d. The economic value is descounted by means of the method of present
value.

The first three terms of (1) concern the costs of laying the pumping mains.
The last term represents the electric power and other annual costs.
The construction cost of the pumping station and the cost of equipping it only affect the optimal solution to a limited extent, as has already been stated. These
costs are not included in (1).

The total costs are dependent only on the route chosen and the diameters.
Equation (1) shows that we are dealing with a non-linear and integer programming
problem. (The pipes are manufactured in fixed diameters only). The objective is
to select ϕ and the route in such a way that $F = F_{min}$. The minimization of (1) can
be done with the aid of well-known operational research techniques such as Branch
and Bound and dynamic programming. For an extensive network this will require a
large number of computations.

However the search for the cheapest route can be carried out quickly and
efficiently by means of an iterative process in which the total discharge is distributed over the total network step by step.
This technique is well-known in the traffic and transportation studies and has already been applied there for some time. Our firm has adapted the method for use
in optimizing pressure line networks. The adaptation is based on the work of Steel
(3) and Steenbrink (4).

Equation (1) can also be written as follows :

$$F = \sum_{j=1}^{n} F_j \, (Q_j, \, \phi_j) \tag{2}$$

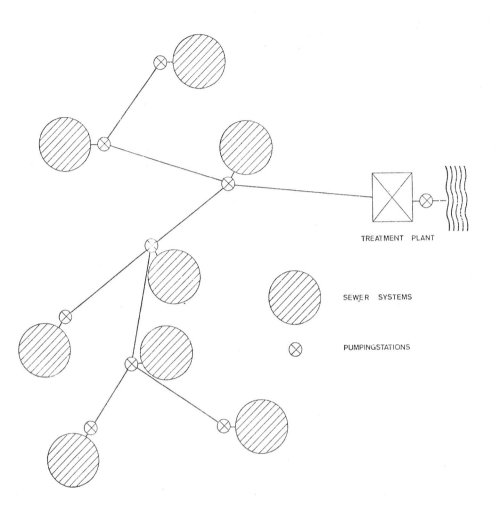

TREATMENT PLANT

SEWER SYSTEMS

PUMPINGSTATIONS

Fig.2 - NETWORK

The following constraints must be fullfilled :

$$v_{min} > v_1$$

$$v_{max} < v_2$$

$$h_{max} \leq h_o$$

In order to be able to minimize (2) the problem is subdivided into two problems : see Steenbrink (4). First the optimal diameter is determined per line :

$$F^* = \min_{\Phi_j} F_j (Q_j, \Phi_j)$$

Then the cheapest route to the central treatment plant is determined using a tree-builder algorithm. The total costs are derived from

$$F = \min_{Q_j} \sum F^*(Q_j)$$

F^* is always convex. According to Rockafellar (5) $F = F_{min}$ if the route is chosen for which

$$\sum_j \frac{dF^*}{dQ_j} \quad \text{is minimal (j belongs to the route)} \tag{3}$$

In the computation procedure applied the total trip matrix is loaded in stages. First a part a_1 of each connection is loaded. The criterion is :

$$\min_j \sum F_j (\Delta Q_j) \text{ for each connection}$$
$$\text{(j belongs to the route).}$$

In the second stage a part a_2 of each connection is loaded under the condition :

$$\text{Min} \sum_j (F_j (Q_j^{a_1} + \Delta Q_j) - F_j (Q_j^{a_1})) \tag{4}$$
$$\text{(j belongs to the route).}$$

for each connection.

The process is continued until $\sum_{p=1} a_p = 1$

It is clear that if (4) is divided by ΔQ_j it is identical to (3).

In the attempt to find the solution of the problem it is assumed in the first instance that a continuous series of pipe diameters is available. As soon as the iteration process is completed an available pipe diameter is selected for each line, taking care that the total costs per line are minimal. Of course a check is also made whether the constraints have been fulfilled.

Steenbrink (4) takes a fixed ΔQ_j. In some cases this resulted in physically impossible solutions. The ΔQ_j used here is drawn from a uniform distribution and is adapted to the iteration step (a_K). This eliminates impossible solutions.

More runs are required as a consequence of drawing ΔQ_j which raises the cost.
However there are the following compensatory advantages :

a. more solutions become available, all of which are near the optimum, so that the
   client can be provided with a number of good solutions.
   In view of the problems which may occur in legal, physical, environmental and
   other fields when the network is being implemented the availability of several
   "good" solutions has proved in practice to be very advantageous.
b. The trip matrix can be loaded in fewer stages by the application of drawing.

CONCLUSIONS

The method for finding the cheapest route for a pressure line network which
is presented in this paper requires more runs (each of which generates a possible
solution) than are necessary in other methods. This of course raises the cost to
some extent.
It has proved, however, to be advantageous to have several near optimal solutions
available.

The number of steps can be reduced to one or two by taking a random ΔQ_j.

APPENDIX

An application

The method described was used to determine the optimal pressure line network for the island of Walcheren. It has already been decided that the waste water
from the whole island would be treated at a central treatment plant.

The network contained 22 sources (see figure 5). Simultaneously with the
determination of the optimal network, a number of possible solutions were determined without making use of operational research techniques. Figure 5 shows both
the optimal solution and the solution obtained by traditional methods.
The solutions differ at a number of points (it should be noted that the part of the
network near the treatment plant had already been constructed).

The optimal solution was 8,6 % cheaper than the solution that was drawn up
mainly on the basis of experience. At a later stage of the design it appeared that
the optimal solution could not be implemented. Since other "best" solutions were
available a new choice could be made immediately.
The investment for this "next best" solution will be 6,7 % less than that which
would have been required for the "hand made" design.

Symbols

n	= total number of connections	—
m	= total number of installed pumps	—
k	= total number of running pumps	—
z	= total number of iteration steps	—
a	= constant	Dfl/m
b	= constant	Dfl/m^{x+1}
c	= constant	Dfl/m^{y+1}
x	= exponent of cost function	—
y	= exponent of cost function	—
d	= constant	$Dfl.s/m^4$

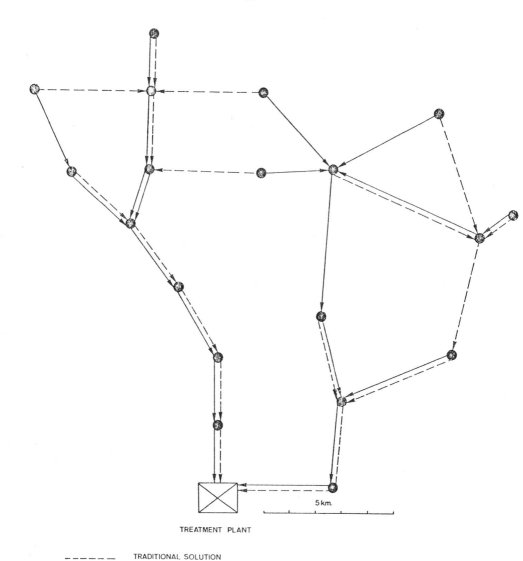

TREATMENT PLANT

------ TRADITIONAL SOLUTION
——— OPTIMAL SOLUTION

Fig.5 - NETWORK ISLE OF WALCHEREN

Q_k	= capacity for k pumps running	m^3/s
T_k	= running hours of k pumps	s
ϕ	= diameter of the pipeline	m
v	= average velocity	m/s
h	= pumping head	m
v_1	= allowable minimum velocity	m/s
v_2	= allowable maximum velocity	m/s
h_o	= allowable pumping head	m

LITERATURE

(1) DEININGER R.A., The Economics of Regional Pollution Control Systems Proc. 21st Industrial Waste Conf., Purdue University, Ext. ser. 121, 1966.
(2) HAHN H.H. et al., Regional Waste Water Management Systems, Paper presented at the NATO Advanced Study Institute on Systems Analysis for Environmental Pollution Control, 1972.
(3) STEEL M.A., Capacity Restraint - A new Technique, Traffic Engineering and Control, 1965.
(4) STEENBRINK P.A., Optimization of Transport Networks, John Wiley, 1974.
(5) ROCKAFELLAR R.T., Convex Programming and Systems of Elementary Monotonic Relations, Journal of Mathematics and Applications, 1967.

DISCUSSION

Was this nonlinear convex ? Yes. Why don't you use anti essex to control the problem ? (TODINI)

Yes, it is possible but we found that it has several bad solutions. By drawing the incremental flow rate in different runs, you have different possible roots. (WIGGERS)

This was a steady state optimization ? (ANDREWS)

No , it is allowed for heavy change in Q and t. All incremental flow can be put in. We have low pointers of sew-flow coming the treatment plant and we know more or less the relationship between more inhabitants and percent of use. All these figures can be put in the system. (WIGGERS)

Does it take into account storage on the system ? (ANDREWS)

Yes, this is only a part of the whole system, also the sewage system and the treatment plant have to be in it. (WIGGERS)

I have not looked into the optimization involved in the design of water distribution system. There are numerous programs on the market that have been used for many years. (ANDREWS)

We have looked in all of them. They are not very practical although very expensive. This algorithm has really some simplification in it. You don't find the exact optimal solution. But you don't need it, for the use it is sufficient. (WIGGERS)

As an exercise you said, you could do 2 % better than the experienced people without your program can do. Is that right ?   (BALAKRISHNAN)

9 % !   (WIGGERS)

Is that significantly higher because these are cases I think where the difference cannot be that distinctly made.   (BALAKRISHNAN)

The people are used to decide on those excessive networks. The people who are used to have mainly three or four sources of sews. You can do simple calculation and you find the best solutions.   (WIGGERS)

I know of at least three projects controlled on-line by computers.   (ANDREWS)

They are not too complicated when the person wants to pay so as done by the government. In this case, you better just generate several near optimal solutions. You go back and talk with the people. That's very important.   (WIGGERS)

Current research field of author : *Application of system analysis to environmental pollution control problems, optimization of sewer networks and pressure line networks, hydrology of urban areas, hydraulic design of purification plants.*

CONFERENCE PARTICIPANTS

ABENDT, R.W., Institut für Siedlungswasserwirtschaft der Universität Karlsruhe, Postfach 6380, 75 Karlsruhe 1, Deutschland.

ART, D., c/o E.A.I., Rue des Palais 116, 1030 Brussels, Belgium.

ANDREWS, J.F., Clemson University, College of Engineering, Environmental Systems Engineering, 501 Rhodes Research Center, Clemson, South Carolina 29631, U.S.A.

BATANOUNY, K.H., Cairo University, Faculty of Science, Botany Dept., Giza, Egypt.

BALAKRISHNAN, A.V., U.C.L.A., School of Engineering and Applied Science, System Science Dept., Los Angeles, California 90024, U.S.A.

BECK, M.B.c/o Prof. P.C. YOUNG, University of Cambridge, Dept. of Engineering, Control and Systems Division, Mill Lane, Cambridge, England.

BELMANS, C., Fakulteit der Landbouwwetenschappen, Afdeling Landelijke Genie, Kardinaal Mercierlaan 92, Heverlee, Belgium.

BIGGAR, J.W., University of California, Dept. of Water Science and Engineering, Davis, California 95616, U.S.A.

BOSMAN, R., Vrije Universiteit Brussel, Centrum voor Statistiek en Operationeel Onderzoek, Adolf Buyllaan 105, 1050 Brussels, Belgium.

BRUTSAERT, W.F., University of Maine, Dept. of Civil Engineering, 351 Aubert Hall Orono, Maine 04473, U.S.A.

DAVIDSON, B., Rutgers University, College of Engineering, Dept. of Chemical and Biochemical Engineering, New Brunswick, New Jersey 08903, U.S.A.

DE BACKER, L.W., Université Catholique de Louvain, Faculté des Sciences Agronomiques, Laboratoire du Génie Rural, Kardinaal Mercierlaan 92, 3030 Heverlee, BELGIUM.

DE BISSCHOP, F., State University of Ghent, Coupure Links 533, 9000 Ghent, Belgium.

DE BOODT, M., Professor, State University of Ghent, Coupure Links 533, 9000 Ghent, Belgium.

DE MAN, W.H., I.T.C., 144 Boulevard 1945, P.O. Box 6, Enschede, Nederland.

DE SCHUTTER, F., State University of Ghent, Coupure Links 533, 9000 Ghent, Belgium.

DE SMEDT, F., Vrije Universiteit Brussel, Instituut voor Wetenschappen van het Leefmilieu, Adolf Buyllaan 105, 1050 Brussels, Belgium.

D'HOLLANDER, E., State University of Ghent, Coupure Links 533, 9000 Ghent, Belgium.

DUBOIS, D.M., Université de Liège, Institut de Mathématique, 15 avenue des Tilleuls, 4000 Liège, Belgium.

ELZAS, M.S., Computer Centre "de Leeuwenborch", Hollandseweg 1, Wageningen, Nederland.

ERNI, P.E., EAWAG, Ueberlandstrasse 133, CH-8600 Dubendorf, Switzerland.

FALLSIDE, F., University of Cambridge, Dept. of Engineering, Trumpington Street, Cambridge CB2 1PZ, England.

FEDDES, R.A., Sleedoornplantsoen 10, Wageningen, Nederland.

FOGEL, M.M., University of Arizona, College of Agriculture, Dept. of Watershed Management, Tucson, Arizona 85721, U.S.A.

GABRIELS, D., State University of Ghent, Coupure Links 533, 9000 Ghent, Belgium.

GOREZ, R., Université Catholique de Louvain, Batiment S. Stevin, Place du Levant 2, 1348 Louvain-La-Neuve, Belgium.

HAVERKAMP, R., Université Scientifique et Médicale de Grenoble, Institut de Mécanique, Laboratoire associé au CNRS, B.P. 53, F-38041/Grenoble-Cedex, France.

HALASI-KUN, G.J., Columbia University, New York Institute of Technology and State of New Jersey, Dept. of Environmental Protection, 31 Knowles Avenue, Pennington, New Jersey 08534, U.S.A.

HELY-HUTCHINSON, J., Research Institute of the South African Council for Scientific and Industrial Research, National Electrical Engineering, Automation Division, P.O. Box 395, 0001 Pretoria, South Africa.

HILLEL, D., Hebrew University, Faculty of Agriculture, P.O. Box 12, Rehovot, Israël.

HIRSCH, Ch., Vrije Universiteit Brussel, Dienst Stromingsmechanica, Adolf Buyllaan 105, 1050 Brussels, Belgium.

HOFFMANN, J.A., former President of AICA, 496 avenue Molière, 1060 Brussels, Belgium.

ISERMANN, R., Universität Stuttgart, Keplerstrasse 17, Postfach 560, 7 Stuttgart 1, Deutschland.

KETTENIS, D.L., Computer Centre "de Leeuwenborch", Hollandseweg 1, Wageningen, Nederland.

KLINCK, M., Philips Forschungslaboratorium, Vogt-Kölln Strasse 30, Postfach 13545, 2000 Hamburg 54, Deutschland.

LAUDELOUT, H., Université Catholique de Louvain, 42 De Croylaan, 3030 Heverlee, Belgium.

LORENT, B., Fondation Universitaire Luxembourgeoise, Route de Villers-La-Ville 15, 6328 Sart-Dames-Avelines, Belgium.

NERO, c/o E.A.I., Rue des Palais 116, 1030 Brussels, Belgium.

NEUMAN, S.P., Institute of Soil and Water, Agricultural Research Organization, P.O. Box 6, Bet Dagan, Israël.

NIHOUL, J.C., Université Catholique de Louvain, Institut d'Astronomie et de Géophysique, Chemin du Cyclotron 2, 1348 Louvain-La-Neuve, Belgium.

NORTON, University of Cambridge, Control Engineering Group, Mill Lane, Cambridge CB1 2RX, England.

PANDOLFI, M., Politecnico di Iorino, **Istituto di Macchine**, Corso Duca degli Abruzzi 24, Torino 10129, Italy.

PERRY, P.F., University of Cambridge, Dept. of Engineering, Trumpington Street, Cambridge CB2 1PZ, England.

PHILIP, J.R., CSIRO - Division of Environmental Mechanics, P.O. Box 821, Canberra City A.C.T. 2601, Australia.

SCHAMP, N., Professor, State University of Ghent, Coupure Links 533, 9000 Ghent, Belgium.

SHAH, M.M., University of Nairobi, Electrical Engineering Dept., P.O. Box 30197, Nairobi, Kenya.

SIKKA, D.R., Irrigation-Major Multipurpose Projects, Madhya-Pradesh Govt., Raipur (M.P), India.

SMITH, D.K., University of Lancaster, Dept. of Operational Research, Cartmell College, Bailrigg, Lancaster LA1 4YL, England.

SMITZ, J., Université de Liège, Institut de Mathématique, 15 avenue des Tilleuls, 4000 Liège, Belgium.

STEINER, R.C., Central Water Planning Unit, Reading Bridge House, Reading RG1 8PS, Berkshire, England.

STROOSNIJDER, L., State Agricultural University, Dept. Soil Physics, De Dreyen 3, Wageningen, The Netherlands.

TODINI, E., Centro Scientifico IBM, Via S. Maria 67, 56100 Pisa, Italy.

TROISI, S., Water Research Institute, Via F. De Blasio 5, 70123 Bari, Italy.

TURRINI, E., c/o E.A.I., Rue des Palais 116, 1030 Brussels, Belgium.

VACHAUD, G., Université Scientifique et Médicale de Grenoble, Institut de Mécanique, Laboratoire associé au CNRS, B.P. 53, F-38041/Grenoble-Cedex, France.

VALADARES TAVARES, L., Portuguese Engineering Society, Rua Tristao Vaz - Nº37 - 2ºEsq., Lisbon-3, Portugal

VAN DER BEKEN, A., Vrije Universiteit Brussel, Instituut voor Wetenschappen van het Leefmilieu, Adolf Buyllaan 105, 1050 Brussels, Belgium.

VAN KEULEN, H., Landbouwhogeschool, Afdeling Theoretische Teeltkunde, De Dreyen 4, Wageningen, Nederland.

VANSTEENKISTE, G.C., Professor, State University of Ghent, Coupure Links 533, 9000 Ghent, Belgium.

VAN STRATEN, G., Twente University of Technology, Dept. of Chemical Engineering, P.O. Box 217, Enschede, Nederland.

VAUCLIN, M., Université Scientifique et Médicale de Grenoble, Institut de Mécanique, Laboratoire associé au CNRS, B.P. 53, F-38041/Grenoble-Cedex, France.

VOOGT, J., Rijkswaterstaat, Dienst Informatieverwerking, Boorlaan 8, Den Haag, Nederland.

WETZEL, J., EAWAG, Ueberlandstrasse 133, CH-8600 Dubendorf, Switzerland.

WHITEHEAD, P.G., University of Cambridge, Dept. of Engineering, Control Engineering Group, Mill Lane, Cambridge CB2 1RX, England.

WIGGERS, J.B., Ingenieursbureau Dwars, Heederik en Verhey, Laan 1914 nr. 35, Amersfoort, Holland.

WILKINSON, J.C., University of Lancaster, Dept. of Operational Research, Cartmell College, Bailrigg, Lancaster LA1 4YL, England.

WOOD, S.R., Anglian Water Authority, Water Resources, Grammar School Walk, Huntingdon PE18 6NZ, England.

YOUNG, P.C., University of Cambridge, Dept. of Engineering, Control and Systems Division, Mill Lane, Cambridge CB2 1RX, England.

ZANNETTI, L., Politecnico di Torino, Istituto di Macchine e Motori per Aeromobili, Corso Duca degli Abruzzi 24, Torino 10129, Italy.

AUTHOR INDEX